CM00798628

Model T Ford

The Car That Changed The World

By Bruce W.
McCalley

© 1994 by Bruce McCalley

All rights reserved. No portion of this publication may be reproduced or transmitted in any form
or by any means, electronic or mechanical, including photocopy, recording, or any
information storage and retrieval system, without permission in writing from the author,
except by a reviewer who may quote brief passages in a critical article or review
to be printed in a magazine or newspaper, or electonically transmitted on radio or television.

Published by

**krause
publications**

700 E. State Street • Iola, WI 54990-0001
Telephone: 715/445-2214

Library of Congress Catalog Number: 93-80697
ISBN: 0-87341-293-1
Printed in the United States of America

FOREWORD

This book has been researched and created in an effort to provide definitive and factual material at your fingertips. If you have a restoration in progress, this book will prove to be as valuable a tool as your wrenches and screwdrivers because it will provide an immediate reference for the specific parts indicated for your Model T. If you are in the process of researching a particular year Model T, you will find illimitable facts and figures.

Herein we define the evolution of the Model T Ford from its inception to its demise, and detail the changes in various components from year to year. For example, a reader can trace the changes in a carburetor or speedometer and determine which would be the proper one for a specified Model T. Engine serial numbers are listed by the day for all years except 1912 (records for 1912 are nonexistent to our knowledge).

Much of the information contained within this book is not obtainable from other sources unless the reader wishes to do intensive research. This study appears nowhere else except for portions which have appeared in *The Vintage Ford* magazine and in the author's *Model T Ford Encyclopedia*.

It is doubtful that there has been any invention which altered the lifestyle of humanity that can compare with the automobile. Among automobiles, the Model T Ford stands alone in this area. In its heyday, over half of the cars on the road, all over the world, were Model T Fords. It can truly be said that the Model T Ford changed the world.

Countless experts have studied the Model T. Old wives's tales abound in the lore of this car. "Any color so long as it's black," "all alike as in peas in a pod," are just two common quotes we hear; neither is fact. Sadly, most of the people who truly remember the Model T as the prominent car on the road have passed on, and the search for "facts" today is a difficult task.

Unfortunately for us, today, much of the written documentation from the Model T Ford era has been lost. Further, there were so many variations and changes in the car over its production years, as well as during the years that followed, that it is all but impossible to accurately define every detail. Opinions among the "experts" often conflict; none know all the "facts."

This book, then, defines the changes in the Model T Ford as they are seen from today's vantage point. It is next to impossible to describe every variation in the car. There were almost constant changes in detail, many being no more than the result of a different supplier of some component. Furthermore, Ford did not stop using one part and begin using another on any given date. New pieces were added and at the same time the old supply was being used up. There seems to have been considerable overlap in new versus old when a new style was introduced. Consequently, in our coverage of specific model years, there can be many variations.

The author has tried to be as accurate as possible. Information presented is based on information gathered from many sources, and where conflicts appear they are noted.

It is next to impossible to name all of those who have added their bits to this fund of knowledge. Any attempt to list these people would be a study in frustration since there were so many. It is to those unsung contributors who have donated their literature, information, and experience that this book is dedicated.

INTRODUCTION

When, in October 1908, The Ford Motor Company began production of its latest automobile, no one had any idea that the new Model T would endure for an incredible nineteen years and that over fifteen million would be produced. When the last car rolled out of the factory in 1927, no doubt everyone thought that the Model T was history.

Fortunately for us, the little four-cylinder basic transportation car would not go away. It seems that everyone from ditch-diggers to presidents had driven a Model T Ford at least once, and many knew of its idiosyncracies. By the late 1930's the hobby of restoring and driving antique automobiles was becoming popular, and by the early 1950's there were many clubs either catering to the general interest in antique cars or specializing in certain makes or models. It seems that among all of these cars, the Model T Ford was a prominent participant.

Because of the number of cars produced, and the numerous changes, modifications and revisions of the Model T, there seemed to be as many different versions as to what was "correct" for a particular year and model as there were cars. Misinformation was plentiful and it seemed that no one really knew for certain what was "right" and what was "wrong."

In 1966 the first issue of *The Vintage Ford*, a publication of *The Model T Ford Club of America*, appeared. According to that first issue, one of the main purposes of the new club and its magazine was to help ensure that Model T's all over the country could be restored to the same degree of authenticity. To this end, the first years of *The Vintage Ford* had many articles describing in detail the characteristics of the cars for the various years. These articles were eventually combined in the book considered to be the "bible" of Model T restoration, *From Here to Obscurity*. The two authors of the articles and book were Bruce McCalley and Ray Miller, both among the six founders of *The Model T Ford Club of America*.

When I bought my Model T in 1971, *From Here to Obscurity* was a godsend for me. I had never thought that such detailed information would be available. Since that time I have worked with Bruce on Club and other projects and have come to know him as a dedicated member of the Club and as a personal friend.

Bruce is the ideal person to compile this information. Besides being active in other Model T clubs prior to *The Model T Ford Club of America*, he

held the post of editor of *The Vintage Ford* from its inception until 1991. He also served as Office Manager for the club for many years, and was President of the national club in 1991. As if this were not enough service to the hobby, Bruce also held many offices in the local chapter of the club.

Unlike many knowledgeable people, Bruce is the type of person who is only interested in researching and disseminating the information. It matters little to him that he may be proved wrong on a point as long as the right information ultimately surfaces. For many years annual trips were made to the Ford Archives in Dearborn, Michigan, and other sources, to pore over their records. An interesting sidelight to his Dearborn trips is that the people at the Archives realized that Bruce knew more about the Model T than they did, and consequently referred inquirers about the car to him.

Over the years, Bruce continued his research, improving and updating his earlier work based on the information found in the Ford Archives, close examination of the Ford parts manuals, in minute inspections of Model T's in original condition, and from other persons with particular expertise. These efforts led him to realize, much to his chagrin, that *Obscurity* was anything but complete. Much new and enlightening information had been uncovered over the twenty-some years since the original material had been compiled.

Because the amount of new material collected was significant, Bruce authored *The Model T Ford Encyclopedia* which was published in 1989, and which detailed components of the Model T for each year, as well as listing accurate production figures and other information not previously published.

Now, this new volume combines the pictorial aspect of *From Here to Obscurity* with the detail in *The Model T Ford Encyclopedia* to produce a truly definitive text on this unique vehicle, the Model T Ford (if you can call a car with a production of fifteen million "unique"). This book is one which I have eagerly awaited, and I am sure it will surpass *Obscurity* as the standard reference for our hobby.

Donald L. Ball
President, 1985
Model T Ford Club of America

About the Author

Bruce McCalley is one of the six founders of the Model T Ford Club of America. He was the editor of the club's publication, *The Vintage Ford*, from its inception in 1966, until 1991.

Bruce is a relative newcomer to the Model T hobby, first acquiring a Model T in 1959. While always interested in automobiles, his profession was in the electronics field. Beginning as an electronics technician, he left that vocation and entered the wholesale branch of the field. He spent the next twenty years in a management position with a firm that has now grown to be one of the largest in the country. He left that firm in 1972 to devote his full time to researching the history of the Model T Ford, editing *The Vintage Ford*, and acting as business manager for the rapidly growing Model T Ford Club of America.

His other interests are in antique radios and associated literature. He has written a number of articles in that field, and was a member of the board of directors of one of the major antique radio clubs on the West Coast. He has also become involved in the computer field, having written a number of programs, including the comprehensive mailing program used by the Model T Ford club for its second class magazine mailings.

Bruce, in collaboration with another of the club's founders, Ray Miller, wrote the first definitive study of the Model T Ford, the book *From Here to Obscurity*, which was first published in 1971. Most of that book's model year coverage had appeared in earlier issues of *The Vintage Ford*.

During the past twenty-plus years the Model T Ford Club of America, through its magazine, has devoted most of its energies to the research and definition of the Model T Ford. The result of these efforts has been even more detailed and accurate studies of the car. These revised and expanded studies have been published in the club's magazine from time to time over the years, adding considerably to the original model year series which was the basis for *Obscurity*.

Bruce has been the author of most of these later studies but he did not write them without the assistance of many dedicated members of the club. Without this help, the task might well have been delayed for years, and the later detailed articles might never have appeared in print. These articles have been expanded and edited for inclusion in this book.

Dedication

It seems that almost every book, on any subject, has a page which dedicates the publication to someone. Can the author defy tradition?

I could dedicate the book to my parents, without whom it (and I) would have not been possible. I could dedicate it to my wife, Barbara, who has pushed and prodded me for several years to get the job done (in addition to a number of unrelated chores she finds necessary). And I could certainly dedicate it to the many people who have shared their knowledge, without which the project could not have been completed.

But I really want to dedicate this book to the thousands of Model T Ford enthusiasts who have supported our hobby by joining the Model T Ford Club of America over the years. To those people I have a great feeling of gratitude, and in this way I can perhaps express my appreciation.

CONTENTS

In the Beginning . . . . . .

Much has been written about the Ford Motor Company, and in particular about its establishment in 1903. A number of excellent books are available and are well worth reading by anyone interested in an in-depth study of the subject.[1]

Yet, in spite of the wealth of information, we find few Ford enthusiasts who are aware of the interesting beginnings of the manufacturer of their favorite car. Almost universally we hear "Henry Ford founded the company in 1903," or "it was Henry Ford's efforts alone that pushed the company ahead, in spite of the many obstacles in his path." There are many more similar "old-wive's tales" but the fact remains that very few have heard anything at all about the fascinating early history of the Ford Motor Company.

All that has been written has been the result of considerable research, plus a good deal of educated guessing by the many authors. The early days of the Ford Motor Company were no different than they were for the most of us when it comes to detailing the story of *our* lives. We all go about our daily business without writing things down as they occur. Given the opportunity of reminiscing, we all tend to add and subtracts bits of information as our minds attempt the recreation of a past event. The authors who produced the histories for today's readers have done the same; they have taken the facts they could find and added a bit of "this is probably what took place" to pull the facts together. In addition, some authors have a different viewpoint from others, and the written results reflect their particular views.

In the story presented here we have used bits and pieces of information from the listed sources, as well as a few more we have collected over the years. In no way do we suggest that "this is the true story" and that all others are suspect. Far from it; we will just add our conjecture to the collection. The story presented is believed to be as accurate as is possible — as seen from a vantage point of ninety years after the fact. Where this story might differ from another, it is just our interpretation of the data compared with that of someone else.

Let us first take a look at some of the commonly believed "facts":

Henry Ford formed the Ford Motor Company, with some help from others.

Ford pioneered with the first low-priced car for the masses.

Ford manufactured all of his cars in his own plant.

Ford alone designed his early cars.

It was Henry Ford who invested great sums of money to form the company.

There are many more but these will do for a start. Are these statements true? No, they are not.

Prior to 1903 Ford spent much time in developing cars of his own design. His first car, built in his home coal shed, and first driven on about June 1896 (there are conflicting dates on this event) marked the culmination of several years of experiments. During this period, Ford was employed by the Edison Illuminating Company in Detroit as Chief Engineer. He had other jobs as well, but the job with Edison was the most significant.

On August 15, 1899, he left Edison to join the Detroit Automobile Company, a newly-formed organization which had been set up to manufacture an automobile based on Henry Ford's designs. The accepted story is that Ford's inability to settle on a fixed design for his car caused the backers to lose interest; the operation disbanded. The company folded in late 1900 and formally ended its operations on February 1, 1901.[2]

With the demise of the Detroit Automobile Company, several of the backers, still having faith in Henry Ford's ideas, again supported him for the development of his car.[3] By this time Henry Ford had met another mechanically inclined enthusiast, a man named Childe Harold Wills. Wills apparently was not too fond of his first name, using either C. Harold, or C. H. Wills. Wills shared Ford's enthusiasm, and this pair, with the help of others, began to build a race car. Ford apparently had become convinced that the builder of a winning race car would have little trouble finding backers for future automobile manufacturing efforts.

The racer was built. It had two cylinders, horizontally opposed, of seven inches bore and stroke. This racer was entered in a race at Grosse Pointe, Michigan, against Alexander Winton on October 10, 1901. Ford won the race.

This success encouraged Ford's backers to establish the Henry Ford Company, filing the papers on November 30, 1901. There were six investors involved in this company. Henry Ford was one of the six but contributed no money. The other five[4] invested $30,500. While these five men may have had grand ideas of future riches, Henry Ford did not, apparently. Rather than getting on with the finalization of his proposed automobile, he continued working on race cars — the results of which (later) were the famed "999" and the "Arrow."

After just four months, the Henry Ford Company found its namesake had resigned, or had been forced out. Whatever — Ford left the firm on March 10, 1902. He took the rights to his name, as well as his tools and other items with him. The five

A scene at Alexander Malcomson's office. John Gray is at the left. Malcomson sits facing us, and James Couzens stands with a look of authority. The man at the extreme right is unidentified.

investors brought in Henry Leland (actually Leland had joined the company before Ford's departure), reorganized the operation, and the company became known as the Cadillac Automobile Company. (The same "Cadillac" that exists to this day.)

Henry Ford moved his material and tools to another location and resumed work on the 999 and Arrow racers. He, Wills, Ed "Spider" Huff, and Oliver Barthel, worked on the projects; no doubt there were others as well. Neither Henry Ford, nor any of the others, had any real money but they found a source of funds in a race driver named Tom Cooper. Cooper made them a deal; he would put up the cash but he would be the owner of one of the cars when they were completed.

The two cars were completed by summertime but neither Ford nor Cooper seemed interested in entering the cars in any races. They did run them in demonstrations against the clock but it was not until Cooper brought in Barney Oldfield that a real race was tried. The race was scheduled for October 15, 1902, almost a year after Ford's first race. Oldfield won by over a lap in the five mile event, setting a new American record. The race was for five miles on a one-third mile track. Oldfield's time was 5:28 for a new American record — just under sixty miles per hour average! He and Ford became relatively famous; certainly the name Barney Oldfield was to become the very symbol of speed for years to come.

It was at about this time that Ford and a man with the name of Alexander Malcomson joined forces. They had probably known each other for several years; Ford had purchased coal from

Malcomson's firm while he, Ford, was chief engineer at Edison, and had continued to do so for his home. Alexander Malcomson was one of the largest coal dealers in Detroit. Using the slogan, "Hotter than Sunshine," he had specialized in quick delivery, using many smaller horse-drawn wagons instead of a few large ones. He apparently had several branches and even owned, or had interest in, a coal field in West Virginia, and a plant in Toledo, Ohio.

Malcomson had become interested in the automobile, not as a mechanic, but as a new and additional business endeavor. He had become interested in Henry Ford's efforts and as a result the two formed a partnership. The partnership agreement was drawn up in the law offices of Horace H. Rackham and John W. Anderson, Malcomson's attorneys, on August 16, 1902, and signed on August 20. Malcomson agreed to invest $3,000 towards the development of Ford's car, and began with a payment of $500. The $3,000 grew to about $7,000 during the next six or more months; no doubt a good part of it going into the two race cars.

The success of the 999 in October apparently added fire to Malcomson's enthusiasm because he not only made money a bit more available to Ford but he and Ford also formed a business under the name of Ford and Malcomson Company, Ltd. The business was set up with a capital stock of $150,000, divided into 15,000 shares at $100 per share. The two partners took 6,900 shares for their efforts to date, and in addition agreed to invest an additional $3,500. The plan was to now sell the remaining shares to outsiders. The company's bank account

All photos from the Collections of Henry Ford Museum & Greenfield Village

was established in the name of James Couzens, Malcomson's business manager. Malcomson was already heavily in debt and apparently did not want his bankers to know of this new adventure.

People were not standing in line in those days with cash in hand to invest in automobiles or their manufacture. Many new firms started and failed in those early days, and investment was generally considered a bad idea. This must have been Malcomson's discovery when he begain trying to sell his company's stock.

Ford, of course, during this period was working on the two racers and on the proposed production car. Typical of Ford, though, the design never satisfied him and changes were being constantly made — at Malcomson's expense.

While Ford was working on the car, a number of other items needed attention. The new company would need a building in which the cars could be assembled, parts stored, and so forth. Outside suppliers for items such as bodies, tires, and most important, the running gear must be found.

In December of 1902, Malcomson had purchased a small coal business, on the property of which was a cabinet shop owned by Albert Strelow. Strelow was one of the larger building contractors in the city of Detroit at the time; the story being that he had the only equipment in the area necessary to build a building more than two stories high. Strelow, too, had met Ford earlier but the story goes that he was not impressed at the time. One item seems to come through, though; Albert Strelow was not particularly interested in automobiles, or their manufacture. In any event, the Strelow shop looked like an ideal spot for the new automobile plant. It was located on Mack Avenue next to a railroad line.

After a sales pitch and perhaps a little pressure, Strelow agreed to rent the building and to remodel it to make it more suitable for automobile assembly. Ford and Malcomson agreed to rent the place for $75 a month for three years. Ford moved into the new plant on April 1, 1903.

During this same period, the new company approached the two Dodge brothers, John F. and Horace E. The Dodges were quite successful machinists and among other things were producing engines and parts for Oldsmobile. The Dodges were quite impressed with Ford's design (Ford had developed a two-cylinder, horizontally-opposed engine while the Oldsmobile and most other cars in the price range were one-cylinder) and ultimately agreed to supply 650 complete chassis (less bodies, tires and wheels) at $250 each. An agreement was signed on February 28, 1903 in which Ford and Malcomson were to pay $5,000 on March 15 if the Dodges could show they had invested that much in tools and equipment for the Ford car. Another $5,000 was to be paid when the investment had reached $10,000, and so on. After deliveries had begun, payments were to be made twice a month.

C. Harold Wills

Almost Henry Ford's right arm during the early years, Wills was probably as much, if not more, responsible for the Ford automobiles as Ford himself. Rather than purchasing stock in the company, Wills had an agreement that he (Wills) would share in whatever profits Henry Ford made. Neither had any idea of Henry Ford's future income but it appears that Wills may have received as much as ten percent. As time passed, Henry Ford had misgivings about the deal, and in 1919 took action and finally caused Wills to resign. It was reported that Ford got out of the deal by mutual agreement, and gave Wills a settlement check for one million dollars. Wills went on to form his own company and produced the Wills Sainte Claire automobile during the 1920's.

The agreement also said that if the new company should fail, all tools and product would become the property of Dodge Brothers.

Around February 1903, a man named Charles H. Bennett came into town intent on buying a new Oldsmobile. Bennett was the president of the Plymouth Iron Windmill Company, whose principal product was now not windmills, but air rifles — Daisy air rifles! He had stopped in at his tailor's shop and during the conversations he mentioned his interest in a new car. In the shop at the same time was a cousin of Malcomson and on hearing parts of the conversation he suggested Bennett look into the new automobile to be produced by Ford. Ford was summoned and arrived with a working sample of his new car. Bennett was impressed enough to hold off his purchase of the Oldsmobile in favor of the new car.

In fact he was so impressed with the new car he became interested in joining the venture. While he did not have the kind of money it would take to begin manufacturing, the Plymouth Iron Windmill Company did have. Apparently his associates in the business were not so impressed, or perhaps other

Alexander Y. Malcomson

The real founder of the Ford Motor Company. He and Henry Ford each took 255 shares in June 1903 in exchange for their interest in the Ford and Malcomson Company. Neither contributed any cash to the Ford Motor Company. Malcomson took no active part in the management of the company. He was later forced out in 1906, and sold his 255 shares to Ford on July 12, 1906 for $175,000.

(We have no photo of Alexander Malcomson.)

John F. Dodge

The two Dodge brothers gave notes for $5,000 each, for fifty shares each. The notes were paid on January 28, 1904. The Dodges were the major suppliers of Ford chassis and parts (except for bodies, tires and wheels) until about 1913 when they brought out their own automobile. Ford purchased the Dodge Brothers stock in 1919 for twenty-five million dollars.

Albert Strelow

Strelow owned the building in which the Ford Motor Company began operations. Somewhat reluctant about the investment, he gave a note for $5,000 initially for fifty shares, and paid this note in full on July 11, 1903. He was the first to leave the company, selling out to Couzens in 1905 for $25,000. Strelow would seem to be the big loser in the affair. The story goes that he invested his money in a mine in British Columbia, and this investment failed. At the time of the formation of the Ford Motor Company, he was one of Detroit's largest building contractors, reputed to have had about 100 employees. He apparently lost everything in the mine investment, and was reported later as applying for a job as an assembler at the Ford plant.

Horace E. Dodge

interests in the windmill company had misgivings — or it is possible both were interested but the company couldn't afford it — whatever — the deal fell through. Bennett did not lose interest, though, and joined the venture himself. (In later years one writer suggested that had the deal worked out they might have given away a Daisy rifle with each Ford; and later, a Ford with each rifle.) (Or we could have been driving Model T Daisys today!)

Production had begun at the Dodge plant, and the Ford shop was ready for operations. Malcomson, no doubt with the aid of James Couzens, began looking for funds. The total number of persons and firms approached is unknown but the following did have enough interest to agree to invest in the venture.

John S. Gray

The man with the greatest financial investment in the Ford Motor Company. He purchased 105 shares for $10,500 in June 1903. Malcomson guaranteed Gray's money, assuring Gray that he would give him his $10,500 back in a year if he wanted out. Gray died on July 6, 1906. The Gray estate kept his stock until Ford purchased it in 1919 for $26,250,000.

The Ten New Stockholders

John S. Gray. Gray was the president of the German-American Bank in Detroit, and was Malcomson's uncle as well as his banker. Gray knew well just how involved Malcomson was financially with his coal business, and no doubt tried to discourage further indebtedness, but Malcomson could not be discouraged. Gray finally consented to invest $10,000, with the provision that Malcomson would not only guarantee the money but that he would buy Gray out after one year if he (Gray) was not happy with the deal.

Gray, in turn, discussed the investment with others and one, a Dr. Frederick E. Zumstein (also known as Dr. Jacob Zumstein in some sources), offered to buy five shares, and gave Gray $500 for this purpose.

Horace H. Rackham, Malcomson's attorney. Rackham had drawn up the Dodge agreement in February, and now agreed to invest $5,000.

John W. Anderson, Rackham's partner. Anderson borrowed $5,000 from his father, another doctor. The letter in which he asks for the loan is printed here and is well worth the reading.

Vernon C. Fry. Fry was Malcomson's cousin. He agreed to buy fifty shares, making a down payment of $3,000 on June 26, 1903.

Charles J. Woodall. Woodall was Malcomson's bookkeeper and under the apparent prodding of the boss he agreed to buy ten shares.

Horace H. Rackham

John Anderson's partner in the law office that handled Malcomson's affairs, as well as the legal affairs of the newly-formed Ford Motor Company. Rackham borrowed $5,000 on some property he owned and took fifty shares. He paid $3,500 on June 26, 1903, and gave a note for $1,500. He paid $800 on January 28, 1904; $200 on February 5; and the balance in July 1904. He sold out to Ford in 1919 for $12,500,000. He and Anderson each collected $4,935,700 in dividends during the sixteen years they held the stock.

John W. Anderson

Malcomson's attorney, and partner of Horace Rackham. Anderson borrowed $5,000 from his father (see accompanying letter) and paid this amount for fifty shares on June 26, 1903. Anderson sold out to Ford in 1919 for $12,500,000. It has been said that Anderson never owned a Ford automobile.

5

Vernon C. Fry

Fry was Malcomson's cousin. He paid $3,000 on June 26, 1903, and gave a note for another $2,000, for fifty shares. He paid $1,000 in December 1903 and another $1,000 in January 1904. He sold his stock to Ford on September 1, 1907, for an amount unknown to this writer.*

Charles J. Woodall

Woodall was Malcomson's bookkeeper at the coal office. He gave a note for $1,000 for ten shares, which he paid on September 17, 1903. Woodall sold to Ford in September 1906 for an unknown amount.*

Charles H. Bennett. While the Plymouth Iron Windmill Company would not or could not invest, he committed himself to fifty shares, using his own money. He made his first payment of $2,500 on March 24, 1904, apparently out of his dividends from the Ford Motor Company.

John and **Horace Dodge** each agreed to take fifty shares.

James Couzens. Malcomson's secretary, Couzens was perhaps the man most responsible for the success of the Ford Motor Company in its early years. Couzens had become quite enthusiastic about the new venture but had only been able to save $400 up to that time. In seeking additional funds he went to his sister, Rosetta, a school teacher, who consented to help with $100. Malcomson also had promised him a bonus and he received $500 from this — a total of $1,000.

Albert Strelow. Strelow was the owner of the Ford "factory" building. Apparently quite skeptical about the deal, he seemingly was pressured by

Charles H. Bennett

Bennett was president of the Plymouth Iron Windmill Company, Plymouth, Michigan, makers of the Daisy air rifle. He played it as safe as possible, giving a note for $5,000 for fifty shares. He made his first payment of $2,500 on March 24, 1904, and another of $2,500 on June 22, 1904, all of this apparently out of dividends from the Ford Motor Company. He sold out on September 1, 1907, selling thirty-five shares to Couzens and fifteen shares to Ford for an unknown amount.*

* Bennett, Fry, and Woodall were close friends of Alexander Malcomson, and probably left because of Malcomson's forced departure. One story is that Malcomson later tried to buy back into the Ford company by taking (buying) this trio's stock. The initial agreement among the founders was that none could sell without first offering his shares to another stockholder. Malcomson, of course, had sold his shares to Ford earlier and was no longer a member of the firm, so the purchase was illegal. The three then sold out as indicated to Ford and Couzens.

James Couzens

Initially purchased twenty-five shares, paying $1,000 (of which $100 was for his sister, Rosetta Couzens) on June 26, 1903, and the balance of $1,500 out of his profits on August 31, 1904. He later bought Strelow's fifty shares (in 1905) for $25,000, and thirty-five shares from Bennett in 1907 for $24,500. Couzens sold out to Ford in 1919 for thirty million dollars (approximately: other sources list this figure at $29,308,858, and also at $13,444 per share), the highest price per share of all the stockholders.

Malcomson into investing $5,000.

These ten men met with Malcomson and Ford on June 13, 1903 at Malcomson's office and agreed to form the new company, taking the name of the Ford Motor Company, apparently after Malcomson's suggestion. Gray offered his $10,000 and the $500 from Dr. Zumstein but the story goes that there was some superstition about thirteen stockholders and the doctor's offer was declined. Gray then raised his contribution to cover the $500, paying $10,500 for 105 shares.

Rackham agreed to pay $3,500 (and did so on the 26th of June), and gave a note for an additional $1,500. He paid the note in three installments: $800 on January 28, 1904; $200 on February 5, 1904; and $500 in July of the same year.

Anderson signed up for $5,000, which he paid on June 26, 1903.

Vernon Fry paid $3,000 on the 26th of June and gave a note for $2,000 which he paid in two installments: $1,000 in December 1903, and $1,000 in January 1904.

Albert Strelow, still apparently not too sure, gave his pledge but did not invest any money until July 11, at which time he paid $5,000.

Charles Bennett gave a note for $5,000. Playing it cool, he paid for his shares out of the profits; paying $2,500 on March 24, 1904, and $2,500 on June 22, 1904.

Couzens put in his $1,000, of which $100 was for his sister, Rosetta. He also gave a note for $1,500 and paid this out of his profits on July 31, 1904.

The two Dodges gave notes for $5,000 each. They, of course, had invested heavily in equipment and material and were the principal recipients of the company's money at the time. Their notes were paid on January 28, 1904.

Woodall gave a note for ten shares and paid this off on September 17, 1903.

Ford and Malcomson agreed to turn over the assets of the Ford and Malcomson Company in exchange for 255 shares each in the new company. Neither contributed any new money to the venture. Malcomson, of course, had supplied most of the cash to get the Ford automobile up to the production stage, including payments to the Dodge brothers under the terms of their contract. Some of this money he retrieved from the funds of the new company.

At this meeting they selected John S. Gray to be the president, Ford as vice-president, Malcomson as treasurer, and James Couzens as secretary.

The Ford Motor Company was officially established on June 16, 1903, with a capital stock of $100,000, at $100 per share. Of this, only $28,000 in cash was paid in initially.

It apparently had been Malcomson's intention to devote his full time to the Ford Motor Company, leaving Couzens in charge of the coal business. Perhaps Gray refused to go along with this because of his concern about Malcomson's debts to the bank, but in any event, Couzens made the move, becoming in effect the secretary-treasurer, and Malcomson went back to the coal business.

Gray, still president of the bank, went back to his profession, leaving Ford as the effective president of the Ford Motor Company. Of the twelve stockholders, only Ford and Couzens were to take an active part in the company. The Dodges, of course, would be working indirectly for the company — profiting not only from Ford, but also from their own business as supplier of Ford chassis.

Beginning with a fund of just $28,000, the roller coaster ride to riches began. It was rough at first. By July 11, 1903, the cash on hand had dropped to just $223.65. It was on that date that Albert Strelow made his first payment of $5,000, preventing perhaps the fastest bankruptcy of all time. On July 15, a Dr. E. Pfennig paid $850 cash for the first Ford automobile to be sold (but not the first one delivered to a customer). From here it was all uphill. By August 20 there was $23,060.67 in the Ford bank account.

In October Couzens issued a dividend of two

Henry Ford

Ford took 255 shares in the company in June of 1903, in exchange for his patents and expertise. He contributed no money. Ford purchased Malcomson's 255 shares on July 12, 1906, for $175,000. In September 1907 he took Woodall's ten shares for an unknown amount. On September 1, 1907, Ford purchased fifteen of Bennett's shares for $10,500 (Couzens took Bennett's thirty-five other shares), and Fry's fifty shares. The price of these shares is unknown to this writer. Ford now had controlling interest in the company, with a total of 585 shares. He bought out the remaining stockholders in 1919, paying $12,500 per share except to Couzens, who held out for and received some $13,000 per share (also see figures listed under Couzens' photo).

percent. In November, another ten percent. In January, 1904, still another dividend of twenty percent. On June 16, 1904, on the first anniversary of the Ford Motor Company, a dividend of sixty-eight percent was declared — a total of $100,000 in dividends in the first year!

The early Fords were not particularly good cars. They had a number of faults such as a tendency to overheat, even on level roads. Henry Ford was aware of the problems and apparently was not in favor of selling the cars until they were "perfected." Couzens, on the other hand, knew that the cars must be sold if the company was to survive. "Make the sale and fix them later" was his decision. Had it not been for James Couzens, Henry Ford might have pushed the company over the brink as he had apparently done twice before. Ford was the engineer, and Couzens was the sales manager; the sales manager, fortunately, prevailed.

In retrospect, the Ford cars were no worse than a number of others at the time. All automobiles in those days were expected to give trouble. Improvements were made all the time and within just a few years the Ford Motor Company was one of the largest in the country.

And profitable! For those who held on to their stock it was a bonanza. Couzens' sister, for example, received $95,000 in dividends and then sold her single share to Ford in 1919 for $260,000. Not bad

for an investment of just $100.

Thus we set the stage for the evolution of the Model T Ford. The Model T, of course, was not the first Ford automobile, but it was the most significant. The first Ford Motor Company product was the Model A (not to be confused with the Model A of 1928-31), followed by an alphabetical series during the first five years of the company's existence. There are a number of gaps in the alphabetical series; there seems to be no evidence of Models D, G, H, I, J, L, M, O, P, and Q. These designations may have represented experimental models but apparently there is no real evidence that any ever existed.

The following two pages are a reproduction of John Anderson's letter to his father, in which he outlines the structure of the newly-formed Ford Motor Company, and its proposed car. Dad was apparently convinced, and furnished the money.

NOTES

1. *Ford, The Times, The Man, The Company.* By Allan Nevins. *The Legend of Henry Ford.* By Keith Sward. *The Last Billionaire: Henry Ford.* By William C. Richards. *Young Henry Ford.* By Sidney Olson. *The Public Image of Henry Ford.* By David L. Lewis. *Independent Man, The life of Senator James Couzens.* By Harry Barnard

2. The Detroit Automobile Company was organized on July 24, 1899, capitalized at $150,000, with only $15,000 cash actually paid in. In the year that followed, the stockholders lost $86,000 in the operation, and gave up in late 1900. The stockholders were Frank R. Alderman, Clarence A. Black, Lem W. Bowen, Safford S. DeLano, Frank Woodman Eddy, Dexter Mason Ferry, Ellery I. Garfield, Mark Hopkins, Benjamin R. Hoyt, Everett A. Leonard, James, Hugh, and William C. McMillan, William C. Maybury, William Hubert Murphy, Frederick S. Osborne, Thomas Witherel Palmer, George Peck, and Albert E.F. White. All of these men were well known. Maybury, for example, was then Mayor of Detroit.

3. The five backers of the Henry Ford Company were Clarence Black, Lem Bowen, Mark Hopkins, William Murphy, and Albert White. It was this group that later brought in Henry Leland, and upon Ford's leaving, again reformed into the Cadillac Motor Car Company.

4. The five investors were Clarence Black, Lem Bowen, Mark Hopkins, William Murphy, and Albert White, who had also invested in the Detroit Automobile Co.

John W. Anderson's Letter to his Father

Detroit, June 4, 1903

Dear Father:

Horace and I have an opportunity to make an investment that is of such character that I cannot refrain from laying the details before you for consideration.

Mr. Ford of this city is recognized throughout the country as one of the best automobile mechanical experts in the U.S. From the very beginning he has been interested in their construction and development. Years ago he constructed a racing machine which was a wonder, and since then he has constructed others in which he has raced all over the country, East, and has won numerous contests on many tracks. I simply mention this to indicate his reputation as his name is widely known in automobile circles everywhere and consequently a very valuable and favorable asset to any automobile Co. Several years ago he designed, perfected and placed on the market a machine. A Co. was organized, but not long after, desiring to devote his attention to a new model entirely, he sold out his patents and interest, and retired. The machine is known as the "Cadillac" (you will see it advertised in all the magazines) and is now being manufactured here by a large Co. The only condition Ford exacted in selling was that the Co. should not use his name in the Co.

He then turned his attention to the designing and patenting of an entirely new machine. Mr. Malcomson, the coal man, backed him with money and the result is they have now perfected and are about to place on the market an automobile (gasoline) that is far and away ahead of anything that has yet come out. He has had applications taken out on every new point he has designed and has just received word of 17 of them have been allowed, everyone of which are incorporated in the machine and, of course, cannot be duplicated in any other.

Having perfected the machine in all its parts, and demonstrated to their complete satisfaction and to the satisfaction of automobile experts, and cycle journal representatives from all over the country who came here to inspect it that it was superior to anything that had been designed in the way of an automobile, and that it was a sure winner, the next problem was how to best and most economically place it on the market. After canvassing the matter thoroughly, instead of forming a company with big capital, erecting a factory and installing an expensive plant of machinery to manufacture it themselves, they determined to enter into contracts with various concerns to supply the different parts and simply do the assembling themselves.

So they entered into contract with the Dodge Bros. here to manufacture the automobile complete — less wheels and bodies — for $250 apiece, or $162,500.00 for the 650 machines, which were to be delivered at the rate of 10 per day, commencing July 1st if possible, and all by Oct. 1st. I drew the contract, so know all about it.

Now Dodge Bros. are the largest and best equipped machine plant in the city, They have a new factory, just completed and it is not excelled anywhere as an up-to-date and thoroughly equipped machine shop. Well, when this proposition was made them by Ford and Malcomson, they had under consideration offers from the Oldsmobile, and the Great Northern automobile Co. to manufacture their machines, but after going over Mr. Ford's machine very carefully, they threw over both offers and tied up with Mr. F. and Mr. M.

Now, in order to comply with this contract, which was made last Oct., Dodge Bros. had to decline all outside orders and devote the entire resources of their machine shop to the turning out of these automobiles. They were only paid $10,000 on account, and had to take all the rest of the risk themselves. They had to borrow $40,000, place orders for castings all over the country, pay their men from last October (they have a large force) and do everything necessary to manufacture all the machines before they could hope to get a cent back. I go into this fully, so that you may understand the faith that these experts and successful machinists have in the machine itself, in staking their whole business, practically, on the outcome, because under the contract if Mr. F. and Mr. M. did not pay for them, Dodge Bros. were to have the machines in lieu of the money — thus making the risk entirely theirs.

In addition to this, contracts for the remaining parts of the automobile — the bodies, seat cushions, wheels and tires — were made so that they are supplied as wanted. The bodies and cushions, by the C.R. Wilson carriage Co. at $52 apiece and $16 apiece respectively. The wheels by a Lansing, Mich. firm at $26. per set (4 wheels). The tires by the Hartford Rubber Co. at $46.00 per set (4 wheels).

They found a man from whom Mr. M. rents a coal yard on the belt-line R.R., with a spur track running into it. He agreed to erect a building, designed by Mr. Ford for their special use, for assembling purposes (which will cost between 3 & 4 thousand dollars) and rent it for three yrs. to Mr. F. and Mr. M. at $75. per month. This building has been all completed and is a dandy. I went through it today. It is large, light and airy, about 250 feet long by fifty ft. wide, fitted up with machinery necessary to be used incidental to assembling the parts, and all ready for business. To this assembling plant are shipped the bodies, wheels, tires, and the machine from Dodge Bros., and here the workmen, ten to a dozen boys at $1.50 a day, and a foreman fit the bodies on the machine, put the cushions in place, put the tires on the wheels, the wheels on the machine and paint it and test it to see that it runs "o.k.," and is all ready for delivery. Now this is all there is to the whole proposition.

Now, as to the investment feature. You will see there is absolutely no money, to speak of, tied up in a big factory. There is the $75 a month rent for 3 years, and the few machines necessary in the assembling factory. All the rest is done outside and supplied as ordered, and this of course is a big savings in capital outlay to start with.

The machines sell for $750., without a tonneau. With a tonneau, $850. This is the price for all medium priced machines and is standard. It is what the Cadillac and Great Northern sell for here, and what other machines elsewhere sell for. Now the cost, figured on the most liberal possible estimate, is as follows:

Machine	$250.00	Fixed by contract	
Body	50.00	"	"
Wheels	26.00	"	"
Upholstering	16.00	"	"
Tires	40.00	(all these fixed by contract)	
Cost of assembling	20.00	This includes wages, rent, insurance and all incidentals at factory	
Cost of selling	150.00	This includes advertising, all salaries, commissions, etc. 20% on each automobile. (It will be nearer 10 or 12.)	
Total cost	$554.00		
Cost of tonneau	50.00		
	$604.00		

Selling price, with tonneau		Without tonneau
	$850.00	$750.00
Cost price	604.00	554.00
	246.00	196.00
Throwing off $46	46.00	46.00
(For any possible extra contingency.)	$200.00	$150.00

On the seasons output of 650 machines it means a profit of $97,000, without a tonneau, and more in proportion to those sold with tonneau, and of course the latter is almost always bought, as it adds so much to the capacity of [the] vehicle.

Now, the demand of automobiles is a perfect craze. Every factory here, (there are 3, including the "Olds" — the largest in this country — and you know Detroit is the largest automobile in the U.S.) [sic] has its entire output sold and cannot begin to fill its orders. Mr. M. has already begun to be deluged with orders, although not a machine has been put on the market and will not until July 1st. Buyers have heard of it and go out to Dodge Bros. and inspect it, test it and give their orders. One dealer from Buffalo was here last week and ordered twenty-five; three were ordered today, and other orders have begun to come in every day, so there is not the slightest doubt as to the market or the demand. And it is all spot cash on delivery, and no guarantee or string attached of any kind.

Mr. Malcomson has instructed us to draw up articles of incorporation for a $100,000.00 limited liability company, of which he and Mr. Ford will take at least $51,000.00 (controlling interest) and the balance he is going to distribute among a few of his friends and business associates, and is anxious that Horace and myself go in with him. Mr. Couzens, whom Spencer met, is going to leave the coal business, for the present at least, and devote his entire time to the office end and management of the automobile business — and he is a crackerjack. He is going to invest, as he expresses it, "all the money he can beg, borrow or steal" in stock. Mr. Dodge, of Dodge Bros., is going to take 5 or 10 thousand, and two or three others, like amounts. Horace is going to put in all he can raise, and I want to do the same if I can, because I honestly believe it is a wonderful opportunity, and a chance not likely to occur again. Mr. M. is successful in everything he does, is such a good business man and hustler, and his ability in this direction, coupled with Mr. Ford's inventive and mechanical genius, and Mr. Couzens' office ability, together with fixed contracts which absolutely show what the cost will be, and orders already commencing to pour in, showing the demand that exists, makes it one of the very most promising and surest industrial investments that could be made. At a conservative estimate the profits will be 50%, with a good sinking fund in addition. The machines are turned into money as fast as delivered and indicate a return on the whole original investment practically by Winter, if nothing were turned into the surplus account. It is a well known fact that the Oldsmobile Works, with a capital of $500,000, cleared up a million dollars last year and are now preparing plans to double their capacity for next year, which indicates, as strong as anything can, what the demand is throughout the country.

I went over the Dodge Bros. plant and the assembling rooms today, and even into the room where the half dozen draughsmen are kept under lock and key, (all the plans, drawings and specifications are secret you know) making drawings and blue-prints of every part, even to the individual screws, and was amazed at what has been accomplished since last October. Not another Automobile Co. has started and got its product on the market inside of three years before this.

THE MODEL T

While there is positive proof at the Ford Archives that Model T Ford number one was made September 27, 1908, there is also much evidence to suggest that there were Model T's made before this date. No doubt these earlier cars were not numbered, and they were no doubt experimental, developmental models.

The following letter certainly indicates the Model T was well on the way in early 1908!

Detroit, Michigan, February 18, 1908

Mr. Henry Ford,
c/o L.C. Oliver,
Jacksonville, Florida.

My Dear Mr. Ford:

I got your telegram late yesterday afternoon saying: "Write c/o L.C. Oliver, Jacksonville," and I assumed that this was in response to my telegram to you on February 14th, c/o Hotel Cawthorne, Mobile, saying: "All fine here — where will a letter reach you?"

I was wondering why I did not get any reply to my telegram of the 14th, but assumed that you had migrated to some other sphere and as usual were keeping out of our way so was all the more pleased yesterday to get your telegram stating where I could write you.

I have been under the weather for several days, in fact, was very ill all yesterday afternoon and last night and did not get up until to-day noon, and, in fact, now should be home but I detest staying in bed.

We are calling all the Branch Managers in, one by one, so as to go over the selling situation in their territory. Just prior to calling in VanDerhoof of Philadelphia, he sent in his resignation but came in just the same as was here yesterday and practically admitted that he was a failure so he has gone and it is up to us to get our fourth man for the Philadelphia Branch.

Mr. Hay of Chicago is here to-day, Plantiff of New York to-morrow, and so on down the line.

Orders are coming in in good shape. In fact, we received orders for forty-eight from London this morning and have orders for about twenty-five from Paris, to say nothing of the orders for domestic shipments which are coming in quite rapidly. I must admit, however, that things don't look very bright for the new car getting out very early. In fact, yesterday afternoon, I guess one of the things that contributed to my illness more than anything was the pessimistic view taken by Mr. Flanders as to the outlook of producing Model T. In fact, he doesn't think he will get them out until May now, although he had expected April right along. I authorized him yesterday to go ahead and run night and day, to clean up the first twenty-five hundred S's before starting the T, at least, to clean up the machine work on them as he claimed it was not practical to put through both models at one time.

Mr. Wills tells me that he has got the magneto in fine shape and has fully advised you as to the success he has had. I am much encouraged on the outlook of this.

You certainly have missed a most rotten month as the weather has been something abominable and I was glad to note from Edsel's postal card that you were having good hot weather where you are, but was surprised to learn that you expected to go to Havana, but from your telegram I am not sure that you went but you look as though you were working North.

I hope that all the family are well and I will not at this time bore you with an unduely (sic) long letter for fear you don't give me an opportunity of writing you again.

With kind regards to Mrs. Ford, Edsel and yourself, beg to remain,

Yours very truly,
James Couzens

(Couzens was the number two man at Ford at the time.)

Another letter, from the Drafting Department, sheds a little light on the Model T's early development:

Dec. 24, 1908

Mr. C.H. Wills,
Office.

Dear Sir:

The following changes have been made on parts as follows:

T-1805: Transmission Cover (Right Hand Control). We have cut 1-3/8" slot on the Slow Speed Boss at point marked "A" on blue print; also shortened the boss at point marked "B," also located the oil pocket, T-1552 at point "C."

T-1820-F: Hand Brake Lever (Right Hand Control) — This lever has been changed at dimension "A," running the arm to one side, instead of having it directly in the center — also the location of the boss "B" has been changed.

T-873-BF: Hand Brake Lever (Left Hand Control) — This lever has been changed at dimension "A," running the arm to one side, instead of having it directly in the center — also the location of the boss "B" has been changed. These Levers (T-1820-F and T-875-BF) are both new designs.

T-867-B: Controller Shaft (Left Hand Control) — This shaft is a new design 1-3/16" shorter than the present shaft. The present shaft may be cut off 1-3/16" to conform with this new design.

T-1808: Controller Shaft (Right Hand Control) — This shaft is a new design 1-3/16" shorter than the present shaft. The present shaft may be cut off 1-3/16" to conform with this new design.

T-309-B: Controller Quadrant (Left Hand Control) — This is entirely new design — to be used after the first 500 cars.

T-1822: Controller Quadrant (Right Hand Control) — This is entirely new design.

T-311: Controller Shaft Bracket — There will be two required instead of one, after the first 500 cars.

T-314: Controller Bracket Felt — There will be two required instead of one, after the first 500 cars.

New Design Starting Crank

T-519-B: This crank is exactly the same as the old style, with the exception of location of holes, at point "A."

T-529-B: Crank Shaft Ratchet Pin — new design — to be used after first 500 cars.

T-527-B: Starting Crank Ratchet Pin — new design — to be used after first 500 cars.

T-523: Crank Shaft Ratchet Lock in — new design — to be used after first 500 cars.

T-525-B: Starting Crank Collar. This is made out of cold drawn seamless tubing, instead of a drop forging. To be used after the first 2500 cars.

T-1553: Notch and Pedals Pin — name changed from Reverse Lever & Pedals Pin. Number required changed from three to four, on Left Hand Control — to be used after first 500 cars.

T-1851: Clutch Lever Shaft (Right Hand Control) — length of shaft shortened.

T-1814: Slow Speed Shaft (Right Hand Control) — Length of shaft shortened.

The above changes were made by Mr. Joe Galamb.

P.S.

T-1525 Speed Lever Brazing Pin — size has been changed from 3/16" to 1/8" — also both ends have been made square, instead of one end round and one square.

December 29, 1908

Mr. C. H. Wills,
Office
Dear Sir:

Below herewith please find notations of changes on parts as listed:

T-302: Frame Side Member — The location of the Gasoline Tank Hole at point marked "A" on blue print has been changed, in order to enable us to have the Gasoline Tank set at right angles to the Frame.

T-300: Frame Assembly — The Gasoline Tank Hole has also been changed as per the above notation.

T-1803: First Floor Board (Right Hand Control) — Touring Car: The pedal slots have been changed from two slots to three slots — New design.

T-1802: Third Floor Board (Right Hand Control) — Touring Car: Entirely new design.

T-1404-B: Third Floor Board (Left Hand Control) — Touring Car: New design.

T-1098-B: First Floor Board (Left Hand Control) — Three pedal slots instead of two. New design.

T-1403-B: Fourth Floor Board (Right and Left Hand Control) — Touring Car: New design.

T-1402-B: Second Floor Board (Left Hand Control) — Touring Car: New design.

T-1801: Second Floor Board (Right Hand Control) — Touring Car: Three slots instead of two. New design.

T-1410-B: Running Board — Pressed Steel: New design.

T-1094-B: Side Lever Floor Board Plate — New design.

T-1921: Running Board Bracket Block
T-1920: Fender Block — Rear
T-1922: Fender Block — Front

Additional parts to go with the (new) Running Board

T-340-B: Running Board Bolt: New design.

T-1344-B: Running Board Fender Bolt: New design.

T-1095-B: Pedal Foot Board Plate (Clutch & Reverse) — New design.

T-1400-B: Pedal Foot Board Plate (On Top) — New design.

T-1094-A: Side Lever Floor Board Plate — obsolete after first 500 cars.

T-1094-1/2: Side Lever Floor Board Plate (Short) — obsolete after first 500 cars.

T-867-B: Controller Shaft — To be used after first 500 cars.

T-873-B: Hand Brake Lever (Left Hand Control) — To be used after first 500 cars.

T-701: Fly Wheel — The #12-24 Tap has been changed in depth from 3/4" to 9/16" at point "A."

T-541: Magnet Clamp Screw — Length of this screw has been changed from 2" to 1-3/4", at point "A."

T-311: Controller Shaft Bracket — Finish has been omitted on the sides of the bearing, at point "A."

T-61-F, T-92-F — Hub Brake Cam Shaft: The cam has been made from an oblong to an elipse, as per attached prints.

T-434: Pump Body — An additional boss has been put on the bottom of the Pump at point marked "A" on blue print, to receive 1/8" pet cock.

T-594: Pump Drain Cock — This will require three of this style pet cock per car, instead of two, which is the same as T-1515, Crank Case Overflow Pet Cock.

December 31, 1908

T-483-B: Cylinder Head Cap Screw — changed from 3/8"-24 threads to 7/16"-14 threads, U.S.S (Bastard size head).

T-550-B: Cylinder Head Outlet Connection Screw — same as T-483-B

T-402: Cylinder Head Gasket — It was necessary to change the bolting down holes in order to use the A and B Cylinder Heads. Note change at point "A" on blue print herewith.

T-445: Cylinder Head Outlet Connection Gasket — same notation as on T-402.

T-418-B: Piston — Oil grooves at point "A" have been removed.

T-49-B: Universal Joint Ring — We are drilling one hole each on the bosses at point "A," instead of two.

T-1407: Floor Board Plate Screw — Note at point "A" has been changed from 21 required for the first 2500 cars: 19 required thereafter, to 21 required for first 750 cars: 22 required thereafter.

Drafting Department

The changes noted above would seem to indicate that the three pedal design had been developed very early in Model T production. Just 308 cars were built between October 1908 and January 1909, yet these changes are specified during this era. Records vary; some noting that the three pedal design was used after the first 500 cars, and other after the first 800.

Note, too, that plans to replace the water pump engine were well under way, as noted in the "New Design Starting Crank." One might surmise that the first 2500 cars were produced primarily to "get something on the market" to satisfy the demand for the new Model T which had been created by earlier advertising.

1909

Body Type	Factory Price #	Shipping Weight Lbs.	Production Total *
Touring	$850	1200	7728
Runabout	825	—	2351
Town Car	1000	—	236
Landaulet	950	—	298
Coupe	950	—	47
Tourabout	850	—	**
Total			10660 ***

Note: 1200 pounds was the figure given for the Touring car "with others in proportion." The bare chassis weighed about 900 pounds.

\#   Prices effective October 1, 1908.
*   Fiscal year: October 1, 1908 to October 1, 1909.
**   Tourabout shown in Ford Times but not produced until July, and then called "1910" cars.
*** Ford News, Nov. 1, 1920, gives a figure of 10,607.

MODEL YEAR DATES. October 1908 to July 31, 1909. (Ford called the cars built after July 31 "1910.")

MAJOR MODEL YEAR FEATURES
Refer to component descriptions for details.

BODY TYPES. Touring, Tourabout,** Runabout, Coupe, Town Car and Laundaulet. Bodies supplied by several manufacturers. Most bodies were all wood but a good number of Pontiac bodies were built with aluminum panels over a wood frame.

EARLY 1909 (First 2500 cars)

COLORS. Touring: red or green. Runabout: gray. Town Car, Landaulet, and Coupe: green. Fenders, aprons, frame and running gear were painted body color.

UPHOLSTERY. Full leather in the open cars, in a diamond-tufted pattern. Closed cars used black leather seats with imitation leather trim on the door panels. The front seats in the Landaulet and Town Car were also leather.

FENDERS. Front: uniform-width top surface, with formed splash-apron area. No bill on front. Rear: similar in style to the front. Support irons were of the "butterfly" style which came out and up under the side the splash apron, not through holes in the apron as in the regular production. These irons were integral with the rear body support.

SPLASH APRON. Fairly uniform from front to rear. Cut back in a concave curve at the rear to clear the brake and radius rods.

RUNNING BOARDS. Linoleum (or "rubber") covered, with brass trim.

HOOD. Steel, with no louvers. Hinges were integral with the panels. Hold-down clamps had one "ear" and were of forged steel.

DASHBOARD (Firewall). Wood, with brass edge trim which did not overlap the wood. Added extension piece of several designs used when a windshield was supplied.

CHASSIS. Reinforcing plates riveted inside the side rails, unique to the early 1909 chassis. Rear body support integral with the rear fender iron forging. Painted body color.

STEERING COLUMN ASSEMBLY. Brass quadrant, brass-plated spark and throttle levers, with hard rubber knobs. Gear case was brass, riveted assembly. Wheel was 14-1/4" diameter, wood, and painted black. The wheel spider was brass and believed to have not been painted. Column was painted body color.

FRONT AXLE. "One-piece" spindles. Tie rod ran above the radius rod, had integral yoke/ball fitting on right end, and adjustable yoke, with the locking bolt in a horizontal plane (parallel to the road). Drag link threaded 20 t.p.i. at the column end. No oilers on most fittings. Radius rod fastened to the engine with studs and nuts.

REAR AXLE. "No-rivet" style. Inner axle and pinion bearings were babbitt bushings. No reinforcing plate in the driveshaft area. Very thin center flange with no reinforcing washers or plates. Axle shafts were non-tapered, with the hubs being secured with a key and a pin. Brake backing plates were relatively thin, with no reinforcing ribs on either side.

DRIVESHAFT HOUSING. No pinion bearing spool. Separate front housing for universal joint assembly.

REAR RADIUS AND BRAKE RODS. Had forged ends. Brake rod support brackets were unique in that the brake rods pass through a hole in them, instead of the "wrap-around" types used later on.

WHEELS. Used 30" by 3" tires in front; 30" by 3-1/2" in the rear. Original tires were an off-white color, with no tread. Hub flanges were 5-1/2 inches in diameter. Front wheels used ball bearings. Hub caps had "Ford" in block letters. Spokes were quite thin and somewhat oval in cross-section. Rear hub was quite long, looking much like the front hub.

SPRINGS. Tapered-leaf, front and rear. "Mae West" style shackles.

RADIATOR. Supplied by Brisco, Paris, and perhaps McCord. Construction varied, some having separate shells; others being integral assemblies. All used the "winged script" Ford on the top tank, and generally had a "Ford" brass name plate attached to the core near the center and in a horizontal manner (not on a bias as is often seen today).

ENGINE. Open-valve type with integral water pump and gear-driven fan assembly. Cylinder head was quite flat, with water outlet on the top surface. First 500 engines used 3/8" head bolts. After 500 engines, 7/16" bolts were used.

ENGINE PAN. One-piece type (no inspection door). Front bearing (support) was quite long, with rear rivet inside the engine area. Oil dam behind fourth cylinder area. No reinforcement at the rear flange.

OIL FILLER CAP. Long thin brass tube with a cup at the upper end, on left front side of the engine. Top of filler pipe was cup-shaped funnel with a screen covering. Later a small cap was used as a cover for the center tube, inside the top funnel.

ENGINE CRANK. Hard-rubber handle. Crank was held "up" when not in use by a ratchet arrangement.

ENGINE FAN. Gear-driven from the water pump. Steel blades riveted to the driving shaft flange.

FUEL TANK. Cylindrical, under the front seat. Mounting brackets riveted to the tank. Outlet was at the right end, outside the frame rail, and was riveted in place.

1909 (First 2500, continued)

MANIFOLDS. Exhaust was cast iron; pipe fits inside the threaded end and was packed with asbestos and held with a brass nut. Intake was aluminum, "doglegged" style.

CARBURETORS. Kingston "five ball" or Buffalo. Neither used a choke or a heating arrangement at the air intake.

CARBURETOR STOVE ASSEMBLY. None used.

MUFFLER. Cast-iron ends, mounted with pressed-metal brackets. Short, straight rear exhaust pipe extension. Wrapped with asbestos, secured with three steel straps.

COIL BOX ASSEMBLY. Heinze, with high-tension (spark plug) terminals on the underside, a continuation of the type used in the N-R-S Fords, was used on the earliest production, in addition to the Kingston 4200. Later production (before 2500) used the Kingston 4200, only, as on the later 1909 cars.

TRANSMISSION. The first 500 (approximately) cars used the two-pedal, two-lever system. One of the levers was the rear brake; the other operated the neutral and reverse gear. At about number 500 the three-pedal system began to be used on some production, and by number 800, three pedals became standard. Pedals were marked with "C," "R," and "B." Transmission cover was pressed steel in earliest production, then cast aluminum, with both types being used during early production. The inspection door was held with a single "bolt" which operated a latching lever on the underside.

LAMPS. Side and tail lamps were standard, made by either Edmond and Jones (E&J) or Atwood-Castle. Headlamps were optional, and supplied by the same firms. Prestolite tanks were often installed at the factory instead of the carbide generators.

HORN. Bulb type, double-twist, all-brass. Standard equipment on most cars.

WINDSHIELD. Optional equipment, but when supplied by the factory, most were either Rands or Mezger (Automatic). Other makes were also used in very limited quantities.

TOP. Open cars) Optional equipment. More than one supplier. Some had wool linings, generally in a dark-red color. Top color was black on the Touring, and either black or gray on the Runabout. Top sockets were oval in cross-section and fasten to a forged railing on the body. Top sockets curved outward from the body. Many tops had a roll-down windscreen which served as a windshield.

SPEEDOMETER. Optional. Stewart Models 11 and 12, National, and Jones were used by the factory.

1909 (After first 2500 cars)

BODY TYPES. Touring, Tourabout (after about June 1909), Runabout, Landaulet (very few, if any), Town Car, Coupe. Generally a continuation of the bodies used on the first 2500 cars. The Pontiac body with the aluminum panels was discontinued in September 1909.

COLORS. Touring: red, green, and a few gray. Runabout: gray. Town Car and Landaulet: green. Coupe: green. There were a few variations in the colors; i.e., some Runabouts came with green bodies, etc. **All cars were Brewster Green after June 1909.** Fenders, aprons, running board, chassis and running gear were painted body color.

UPHOLSTERY. Full leather in the open cars, in a diamond-tufted pattern. Closed cars used a cloth material with an ornate pattern. The front seats in the Landaulet and Town Car were leather.

FENDERS. Front: uniform-width top surface, with formed splash-apron area. Bill added on front. Rear: similar in style to the front. Support irons were of the "butterfly" style and now passed through holes in the fender apron.

SPLASH APRON. Fairly uniform from front to rear. Cut back in a concave curve at the rear to clear the brake and radius rods. (Later models may have had a straight cut at the rear.)

RUNNING BOARDS. Pressed-steel with embossed ribs running the length of the board.

HOOD. Steel, with no louvers. During the year the hood was changed to aluminum and the hinges were now separate from the panels, and riveted in place. Hold-down clamps had one "ear" and were of forged steel. The steel hood former still had the "notch" on both sides which was necessary to clear the earlier hood hinges.

DASHBOARD (Firewall). Wood, with brass edge trim which does not overlap the wood. Added extension piece of several designs used when a windshield was supplied.

CHASSIS. Rear body support integral with the rear fender iron forging. The riveted-in-place reinforcement inside the side rails was discontinued.

STEERING COLUMN ASSEMBLY. Brass quadrant, brass-plated spark and throttle levers, with hard-rubber knobs. Gear case was brass, riveted assembly. Wheel was 14-1/4" diameter, wood, and painted black. The wheel spider was brass and believed to have not been painted.

FRONT AXLE. "One-piece" spindles. Tie rod ran above the radius rod, had integral yoke/ball fitting on right end, and adjustable yoke, with the locking bolt in a horizontal plane (parallel to the road). Drag link threaded 20 t.p.i. at the column end. No oilers on most fittings. Radius rod fastened to the engine with cap screws.

REAR AXLE. "No-rivet" style. Inner axle and pinion bearings were babbitt bushings. No reinforcing plate in the driveshaft area. Thin center flange with reinforcing washers added in later production. Axle shafts were non-tapered, with the hubs being secured with a key and a pin. Driveshaft with removable pinion gear began at about number 7000 (July). Babbitt inner axle bearings changed to roller at about number 12,000 (October).

DRIVESHAFT HOUSING. No pinion bearing spool. Separate front housing for universal-joint assembly.

1909 (Continued)

REAR RADIUS AND BRAKE RODS. Had forged ends. Brake-rod support brackets now fold down along the side of the clamp, then out and wrap up around the brake rods.

WHEELS. Same as used in the earlier 1909 cars.

SPRINGS. Tapered-leaf, front and rear. "Mae West" style shackles.

RADIATOR. Supplied by Detroit, Briscoe, McCord, and Ford (beginning about October). All were integral assemblies. All were believed to have used the winged script "Ford" on the top tank (except, possibly, for the Ford-made radiators), and generally had a "Ford" brass name plate attached to the core near the center and in a horizontal manner (not on a bias as is often seen today).

ENGINE. Open-valve type, now with thermo-syphon cooling system. Water outlet was now on the front of the cylinder head. No babbitt in upper main bearing (cylinder) halves.

ENGINE PAN. One-piece type (no inspection door). Shorter front bearing, moving rear rivet outside the engine. No reinforcement at the rear flange. Had oil dam at rear of crank area.

OIL FILLER CAP. Thin brass tube with a screen at the upper end, on right side of the engine. Later, the mushroom-shaped cap, of brass, with six flutes and the Ford script appeared.

ENGINE CRANK. Hard-rubber handle. The ratchet arrangement used on the early cars was discontinued.

ENGINE FAN. Driven by a leather belt from a pulley at the front of the engine. The fan hub was brass (bronze), with the blades riveted in place. The fan blades had a much deeper embossed reinforcement than the 1911 and later types. Adjustment was by means of a spring between the fan arm and the engine front plate.

FUEL TANK. Cylindrical, under the front seat. Mounting brackets riveted to the tank. Outlet was at the right end, outside the frame rail, and was riveted in place.

MANIFOLDS. Exhaust was cast iron; pipe fitted inside the threaded end and was packed with asbestos and held with a brass nut. Intake was aluminum, "doglegged" style.

CARBURETORS. Kingston "five ball" or Buffalo. Neither used a choke or a heating arrangement at the air intake.

CARBURETOR STOVE ASSEMBLY. None used.

MUFFLER. Cast-iron ends, mounted with pressed-metal brackets. Short, straight rear exhaust pipe extension now integral with the rear cover plate. Wrapped with asbestos, secured with three steel straps.

COIL BOX ASSEMBLY. Kingston, with high tension (spark plug) terminals on the back side, passing through the firewall.

TRANSMISSION. Three-pedal standard design. The brake lever now operated the clutch as well as the rear brakes. Pedals were marked with "C," "R," and "B." Transmission cover was cast aluminum. The inspection door was held with four screws.

LAMPS. Side and tail lamps were standard, made by either Edmond and Jones (E&J), Atwood-Castle, or Brown (after about 10,000). Headlamps were optional, and supplied by the same firms. Prestolite tanks used on some production.

HORN. Bulb type, double-twist, all-brass. Standard equipment on most cars.

WINDSHIELD. Optional equipment, but when supplied by the factory, most were either Rands, Mezger (Automatic), and Troy (wood and brass frames). Other makes may have been used in very limited quantities.

TOP. (Open cars) Optional equipment. More than one supplier. Some had wool linings, generally in a dark-red color. Top color was black on the Touring, and either black or gray on the Runabout, until about June when all tops were then supplied in black. Top irons attach to a forged railing on the body. Top sockets were oval cross-section and curve outwards from the body. The front windscreen continued, and was often included even though the car came with the glass windshield.

SPEEDOMETER. Optional. Stewart Models 11, 12, and 24, National, and Jones Models 20 and 21 were used by the factory.

1910

Body Type	Factory Price #	Shipping Weight Lbs.	Production Total *	
Touring	$950	1200	16890	**
Tourabout	950	—		**
Runabout	900	—	1486	
Town Car	1200	—	377	
Landaulet	1100	—	2	
Coupe	1050	—	187	
Chassis	—	900	108	***
Total			19050	

Note: 1200 pounds was the figure given for the Touring car "with others in proportion." The bare chassis weighed about 900 pounds.

\# Prices effective October 1, 1909, include top, windshield, gas lamps and speedometer on all open cars. The Town Car, Landaulet and Coupe came with oil lamps, speedometer and horn only. Open cars could be had without this equipment (oil lamps, horn and speedometer only) for $75 less.

* Fiscal year, October 1, 1909 to September 30, 1910. Ford News, Nov. 1, 1920, gives a figure of 18,664.

** Tourings and Tourabouts grouped. 16,890 was the total of the two types.

*** Chassis not shown in the catalog.

MODEL YEAR DATES. August 1, 1909 to November 1910, approximately.

Note: Ford referred to the cars built after July 31, 1909 as "1910" cars but common usage is to call the cars built within calendar year 1909 "1909" models.

MAJOR MODEL YEAR FEATURES

Refer to component descriptions for details.

BODY TYPES. Touring, Tourabout, Runabout, Landaulet, Town Car, Coupe. Bodies supplied by several manufacturers. Wood panels over a wood framework. Basically unchanged from the 1909 styles except that the Coupe was slightly larger.

COLORS. All cars were painted Brewster Green, an all-but-black color. Fenders, aprons, running boards, chassis and running gear painted body color.

UPHOLSTERY. Full leather in the open cars, in a diamond-tufted pattern. The seats in the Coupe, Landaulet and Town Car were leather, with imitation-leather trim on the door panels.

FENDERS. Front: uniform-width top surface, with formed splash apron area. Bill on front. Rear: similar in style to the front. Support irons were of the "butterfly" style, the same as the later 1909 cars.

SPLASH APRON. Fairly uniform from front to rear. Cut back in a relatively straight pattern to clear the brake and radius rods.

RUNNING BOARDS. Pressed-steel with embossed ribs along the length of the board, but now broken up into a series of "dashes," beginning at about number 15,000.

HOOD. Aluminum, with no louvers. Hinges were now separate from the panels, and riveted in place. Hold-down clamps had one "ear" and were of forged steel. The steel hood former still had the "notch" on both sides which was necessary to clear the earlier integral hood hinges.

DASHBOARD (Firewall). Wood, with brass edge trim which does not overlap the wood. Added extension piece to support the now standard windshield.

CHASSIS. Rear body support integral with the rear fender iron forging. Painted body color.

STEERING COLUMN ASSEMBLY. Brass quadrant, brass-plated spark and throttle levers, with hard-rubber knobs. Gear case was brass, riveted assembly. Wheel was 14-1/4" diameter, wood, and painted black. The wheel spider was brass and believed to have not been painted. The column itself was painted body color.

FRONT AXLE. "One-piece" spindles. Tie rod ran above the radius rod, had integral yoke/ball fitting on right end, and adjustable yoke, with the locking bolt in a horizontal plane (parallel to the road). Drag link threaded 20 t.p.i. at the column end. No oilers on most fittings. Radius rod fastened to the engine with cap screws.

REAR AXLE. "Six-rivet" style. Inner axle and pinion bearings were now roller bearings. A reinforcing plate was added at the driveshaft area. Thicker center flange with reinforcing washers added or a reinforcing ring on one side, then on both sides of the flange. Axle shafts were non-tapered, with the hubs being secured with a key and a pin. Roller pinion bearing introduced in March, 1910.

DRIVESHAFT HOUSING. Pinion bearing spool was a casting and was held by studs and nuts, the studs being enclosed (not visible) in the housing. Separate front housing for universal-joint assembly.

REAR RADIUS AND BRAKE RODS. Had forged ends. Brake-rod support brackets now folded down along the side of the clamp, then out and wrap up around the brake rods.

WHEELS. Used 30" by 3" tires in front; 30" by 3-1/2" in the rear. Original tires were an off-white color, with no tread. Hub flanges were 5-1/2 inches in diameter. Front wheels used ball bearings. Hub caps had "Ford" in block letters. Continued in the style of the 1909 cars.

SPRINGS. Tapered-leaf, front and rear. "Mae West" style shackles.

RADIATOR. Supplied by Detroit, McCord, and Ford. Ford began making its own radiators about October 1909, and was the sole supplier after March or April 1910. All were integral assemblies. The winged script "Ford" on the top tank was to be replaced with the standard Ford script. (Possibly all Ford-made radiators used the standard script.) Radiators generally had a "Ford" brass name plate attached to the core near the center and in a horizontal manner (not on a bias as is often seen today).

ENGINE. Open-valve type, now with thermo-syphon cooling system. Water outlet was now on the front of the cylinder head.

ENGINE PAN. One-piece type (no inspection door). The internal oil dam was discontinued. A forged reinforcement was added at the rear flange during the year.

OIL FILLER CAP. The mushroom-shaped cap, of brass, with six flutes and the Ford script, appeared on all models.

ENGINE CRANK. Hard-rubber handle.

ENGINE FAN. Driven by a leather belt from a pulley at the front of the engine. The fan hub was brass (bronze), with the blades riveted in place. Adjustment was by means of a spring between the fan arm and the engine front plate.

FUEL TANK. Cylindrical, under the front seat. Mounting brackets riveted to the tank. Outlet was at the right end, outside the frame rail, and was riveted in place.

1910 (Continued)

MANIFOLDS. Exhaust was cast iron; pipe fit inside the threaded end and was packed with asbestos and held with a brass nut. Intake was aluminum, "doglegged" style.

CARBURETORS. Kingston "five ball," Holley, or a very few Buffalo. All used a choke and a heating arrangement at the air intake.

CARBURETOR STOVE ASSEMBLY. Generally a tube which ran upwards to the front of the exhaust manifold, and connected to a cast "stove" which fit against the manifold.

MUFFLER. Cast-iron ends, mounted with pressed-metal brackets. Short, straight rear exhaust pipe extension now integral with the rear cover plate. Wrapped with asbestos, secured with three steel straps.

COIL BOX ASSEMBLY. Kingston or Jacobson-Brandow.

TRANSMISSION. Three-pedal standard design. The brake lever now operated the clutch as well as the rear brakes. Pedals were marked with "C," "R," and "B." Transmission cover was cast aluminum. The inspection door was held with four screws.

LAMPS. All lamps were now standard except on the closed cars. Made by Edmond and Jones (E&J) or Brown.

HORN. Bulb type, double-twist, all-brass. Standard equipment on all cars.

WINDSHIELD. Standard equipment, were either Rands, Mezger (Automatic), or Troy.

TOP. (Open cars). Top color was black on all open cars. Support irons attach to a forged railing on the body.

SPEEDOMETER. Standard. Stewart Model 24.

18

The All New Ford Model T
The Fords for 1909 and 1910

INTRODUCTION

Past coverage of the first two years' production of the Model T has usually been broken down into three specific groups: the first 2500, the 1909, and the 1910 cars. Yet, the differences in these, aside from the radical change in engine design in the post-2500 cars, was evolutionary; with the first cars being quite similar to the last in most characteristics. One might gain a better insight to the evolution by looking at these cars as a single subject.

It is important to remember that changes were not all made at a specific date, but evolved over a period of time. For example, the first thermo-syphon (non-water pump) engine was not 2501 but 2448. Number 2455 was the second thermo-syphon, and 2456 was the third, and there were apparently some water pump engines built at the same time.

It is an absolute fact that Ford did not indicate any black cars in the first three years of production (after which there are no records known to exist), and that Ford did not even list a black final body paint even as late as 1914. Yet the great number of apparently original black cars which are still around might make one question the accuracy of the records. Black *was* used for the first coats of paint on the bodies and this could explain some of the "black" cars... but not all of them. Did Ford employees who filled out the shipping invoices look at black cars and call them green? Or blue? Ford's records indicate that all cars which came with tops were also supplied with side curtains, yet there seem to be original cars which never had the fasteners on the bows or bodies.

We could go on, but the list is seemingly endless. It is just these variances that make the Model T Ford so interesting. Always keep in mind that our descriptions of specific years are based on written and physical evidence; however, we have not seen *all* of the written material, nor have we seen *all* of the existing cars.

Ford number 220, restored by the late Ben Snyder of Riverside, California; then purchased by Harrah's Automobile Collection. The car is now owned by Kim Dobbins of Harbor City, California. No factory records exist for this car but it has been restored to be typical of cars of the era. Painted Carmine Red, with black striping, it has a black top with a front roll-down visor, and no windshield. This is one of the few true, two-lever, two-pedal cars known to exist; it had all of the original two-pedal components intact when it was found.

The all new Ford Model T was announced early in 1908 to the Ford dealers, with a description and specifications that created considerable excitement in the trade. Because of the new car's many advanced features, little publicity was given about this new model for fear that the then-current Models N and S would not sell. In the June 1908 issue of the *Ford Times*, pictures of the Model T Landaulet were shown. In the July issue, an article comparing the older Model A (1903) with the new Model T, including a picture of the Model T Touring, added excitement. Then in the September issue, an announcement appeared which stated, among other things, that the new Model T would be ready for delivery on October 1 but that no retail orders would be accepted until every dealer had a demonstrator. "By the middle of October we will have a Model T Coupe listing at $950," and "November 1 for the Town Car at $1000, and the Landaulet at $950." On the last page of the September issue of the *Ford Times*, there was a picture of the Model T Touring, printed in red.

Ford was a little ahead of time in its announcement. While a number of the new cars were assembled and tested during 1908, the first

1909 Ford demonstrator. The dealer was O. E. Houser of Chillicothe, Ohio, and the photo was supplied by Major Jim Barnhart, Wright Patterson AFB, Ohio.

This car was purchased from the dealer by Jim's grandfather, H. A. Barnhart in December 1909. It was serial number 8513 which had been assembled the previous August. Mr. Barnhart ordered it on December 4, giving a cash deposit of $100. He took delivery December 27, paying $875. Apparently the windshield had been added by the dealer and it was included in the purchase price. He also had the following accessories added: set of Weed chains, $7.60; a Reliable auto jack, $1.75; Model 26(!) Stewart speedometer, $20; a 30 by 3 innertube at $4.75 and a 30 by 3-1/2 innertube at $6.40; a pair of spring straps at $.75; and six gallons of gasoline at $.90; a total of $917.15.

Fords were known to give good service but by today's standards one might wonder. Mr. Barnhart saved invoices for service and parts for the next few years, and among them are statements for the following: four spark plugs ($3.00) on January 1, 1910; a valve job and carbon scraping at $1.70 labor on July 30, 1910; Another valve job ($2.00) on September 3, 1910 plus three front spring leaves ($1.50 plus 75 cents labor) on September 12, and then another front spring ($7.25) and a spark plug ($.75) on September 28. Grind valves and clean carbon again on October 5 ($1.50) plus repair brake rod ($.30) on November 1. A new rear tire on November 7 cost $22.00. Still another valve job on November 9. Then on November 28 the rear axle failed and the car had to be towed in. The bill: Hauling car five miles, $2.50; telephone and telegram, $.80; dismantling rear axle, $2.25; Express on new rear axle, $1.22; exchange on rear axle, $40.00; labor to install new rear axle, $3.00 and $.60 for six pounds of grease. It then cost him $2.03 more to reassemble the

old axle then crate and ship it back to the factory. January 9, 1911 the car needed a "sparker" repair at 10 cents. "Clean out engine" on January 14 for $1.50. One castellated nut ($.05) on the same day. A new rear spring leaf on January 17 at $1.65.

The list goes on but on April 29, 1911 Mr. Barnhart bought a set of valve grinding tools at $2.45! Enough of those high-priced auto mechanics!

Left: Mr. Barnhart in his dependable 1909 Model T Touring car. He kept it all his life and began to restore it in 1955, and had it together by 1961. Unfortunately by that time many items had been changed. It had a 1913 engine, a 1912 rear axle, and a later front axle, among other things. It has an aluminum Pontiac body.

production Model T engine was not built until September, and that car was not shipped until October 1.

The October 1908 issue of the *Ford Times* was filled with Model T specifications and prices. The extensive coverage noted that the new Model T engine block would cost $30; the same price as one cylinder-pair casting of the Models N-R-S. The price of the Touring was $850, without top, windshield or gas lamps. The price for the top was shown as $80

extra. With all the excitement, though, just 308 Model T's were produced in calendar 1908. Hardly enough to give one to every Ford dealer.

The Model T began a new era for American automobiles. Here was a quality car which looked good, ran well, and even more important, was priced low enough so that people in the middle income range could afford it. The phenomenal success of the earlier models N, R, and S had convinced the owners of the Ford Motor Company that great profits could be made in the low price field, and the new Model T was a giant step forward in capturing that market.

Not even Henry Ford seemed aware of just how successful this new car would be, even though it was destined to be his favorite model. (Note how new model designations were given to modest changes in his earlier cars; the Models A, C, and F were basically the same chassis, as were the Models N, R, and S. Yet in the years of evolution of the Model T, in spite of all-but-total redesigns, the car remained the Model T.) Twice during the period of 1908-1909 Ford was approached by William C. Durant, then president of General Motors, with an offer to buy the company. Ford agreed to sell both times but would only accept cash, rather than stock in General Motors. The deals fell through because the directors of GM did not feel that the Ford Motor Company was worth that much cash.

The Ford Motor Company had more or less specialized in lower-priced cars since its inception in 1903. The first Ford, the Model A, was a simple, two-cylinder car, and after a short run it was superseded with a similar but improved Model C, and still later a Model F.

Alex Malcomson, a major stockholder at the time, was a relatively wealthy man and a firm believer in the more luxurious car market. It was probably at his insistence that the Model B was produced in 1904. The Model B was a four-cylinder car, and proved to be a very poor seller.

The success of the Models A-C-F led to the development of a new low-priced car, the Model N. The Model N was an entirely new design. While the earlier models A, C, and F had been two-cylinder, chain-drive, automobiles, with the engine under the seat, the Model N had a four-cylinder engine under the hood, and shaft drive to the rear axle.

Not to be denied his "luxury car," Malcomson (perhaps) insisted on a new car to replace the Model

1910 Touring owned by John Montague of Uniontown, Pennsylvania. This is car number 24,627, assembled May 11, 1910. The original shipping invoice lists it as green, with a KH (Kelsey Hayes?) body, Rands windshield, Holley carburetor, Kingston coil box, Brown lamps, a Stewart 24 speedometer, and a Ford radiator.

B. This was the six-cylinder Model K which appeared in 1906 and floundered on through 1908.

The Model N was an instant success. To test the market for a more deluxe model, early in production it was dressed up in a slightly larger and fancier body, with full fenders, and called the Model R. The Model R sold well and resulted in the Model S which was somewhat of a compromise between the stark Model N and the fancy Model R. The Models N and S were the major Ford offerings between 1906 and the introduction of the Model T in late 1908. The "top of the line" Model K was another dismal failure, and was generally credited for Henry Ford's distaste for six cylinder automobiles.

The N-R-S cars were quite good by the standards of the day but they had a number of shortcomings. The planetary transmission was

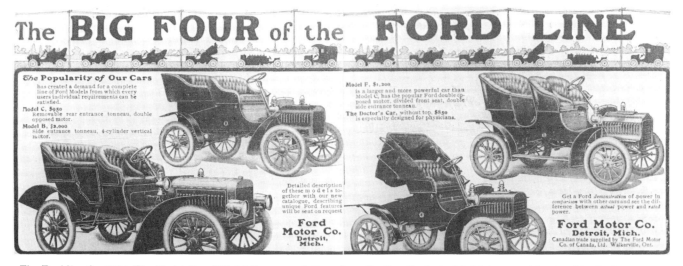

The Ford line for 1904. The Model C and Model F were evolutions from the first Ford, the Model A, now with a hood in the front and different bodies. The engines were a bit larger than that of the Model A but were of the same two cylinder design. The Model B, which had four cylinders, was the "top of the line" but did not sell well.

1909-1910

located at the rear of the engine, out in the open, protected only by a metal shroud, where dust and mud could get in, and lubrication could just as easily get out. The low gear was applied by pulling a hand lever on the right side of the car and this meant that the driver had to steer with one hand and hold the lever with the other on a hill or in the ever-present dirt and mud. The engine was of typical design for the era; castings of two cylinders each, bolted to an aluminum crankcase. Engine lubrication was by means of an external oiler, to which the owner had to constantly add oil. Ignition was by means of dry cells which had a relatively short life.

Some idea of some of the shortcomings of these models may be had from the following:

QUALITY CONTROL

The following letter was from Frederick H. Briggs, of Oliver L. Briggs & Son, Boston, Massachusetts. One could imagine the consequences of such quality in a new car today!

Boston, September 19, 1906

Mr. Henry Ford,
Detroit, Michigan
Dear Sir,

Last year I ran one of your Model C Runabouts some ten thousand miles and was extremely pleased with it. This year I bought a Model N which I ran perhaps five hundred miles and then disposed of it. During this time I discovered some points of which I think you as the designer of the car should be informed. I am now in the market to buy another car and prefer to use a Ford.

During my ownership of this Model N Runabout I found it almost impossible to keep sufficient oil in the crankcase. The oil would blow out through the breathe-hole and spatter all over the engine, deluging the wires and engine completely and reducing the level in the crank case to such an extent that the car would loose power, through the heating of the cranks and bearings. You can imagine my surprise on finding that this 4-cylinder car rated at 15 to 18-horse power would not climb hills equal to my 2-cylinder machine rated at 10-horse power. We tried in many ways to remedy the oil question but could not succeed. Stuffing up the breathe-hole with cotton waste so as to keep the oil in the crank case caused the

1906 Ford 6 Cylinder Touring Car
Price $2,500

6 cylinders—40 h. p. 4 to 50 miles per hour on high gear. *Perfected* magneto ignition—mechanical oiler, 114 inch wheel base, luxurious body for 5 passengers, weight 2000 pounds.

1906 Ford Runabout, as advanced as our touring car in design and even more surprising in price—will be fully illustrated and described in our next advertisement.

Both these Cars on exhibition at the New York Automobile Show.

Ford Motor Company
Detroit, Mich.

The large Model K of 1906, 1907 and 1908. It came in both Touring and Runabout bodies. While a better seller than the Model B, it came in a distant second when compared with the Models N, R, and S which were the major products of the Ford Motor Company. The Model K was the last "big" Ford car until Lincoln was acquired in the early 1920's.

compression in the case to increase to such an extent as to stop the flow from the oiler and necessitating every ten or fifteen miles refilling through the breathe-hole. I showed this to the man who purchased the car from me and he intended sending it to the Stevens-Duryea factory for a satisfactory system of lubrication where I suppose the car is now. He has promised to tell me what success he has.

I scarcely had the car more than a day or two before a bad short-circuit developed in the commutator wires necessitating new wires to the commutator. The commutator is so close to the transmission that it is extremely difficult to get at the points for rewiring. If a little more room could be given in that part it would

The catalog illustrations used in the earliest Model T brochures showed the two hand levers and three foot pedals, a configuration that never existed. The first 800 Model Ts had two levers and two pedals, then all had one lever and three pedals.

facilitate matters a great deal. I found the commutator wires soaked with oil, partially I imagine from the breathe-hole and partially I think from the transmission. Upon examination we found it necessary to remove every wire and had to make a special tool in order to screw up the screws to hold the wires on account of the extreme inaccessibility of the commutator.

While many parts of the car are extremely accessible there seem to be many that are inaccessible. For instance, my engine became loose from the frame after I had run it perhaps for two hundred miles. The bolts and nuts which bolted it down were in such a position as to make it extremely difficult to properly tighten without taking off the fly wheel. It was only by pounding the nut with a screw driver that the tightening could be affectually accomplished. In fact, many of the nuts on the car did not seem to hold. In my mud guards and step, and also the bolts which held engine down to the crank case loosened several times, and many other bolts and nuts throughout the car troubled me extremely by becoming loose and needing almost constant care. In fact, I lost some nuts that hold the frame to the springs before I knew that they were loose; they needing practically daily care to keep them tight. Many of the threads were not evenly cut, thereby making some inconvenience in starting them which was particularly annoying in some of the grease cups for instance. The hood also did not fit the space between the radiator and the dasher (sic).

The general idea of the car I liked and would quickly buy another if some of these details of construction could be successfully remedied. Another little thing which I noticed was that the mud guards on the front wheel were so placed that the mud would fly from the front wheel directly on to the upper side of the rear wheel mud guard. The emergency break (sic) seamed to be absolutely worthless. While the theory seemed good mine did not work at all satisfactorily. When I would finally get it set it would often be impossible to release it without getting out and lifting up the foot board. Moreover, sometimes it would set and in getting out of the car the motion would jar the foot board and throw it off. It got so that finally I never attempted to use it. If the clutches are a little tight and the emergency does not work, upon cranking the car will start, thereby making it inconvenient to get in, particularly if the grade is slightly down.

I have felt considerable dilicacy (sic) in writing you, but my father has strongly urged me to do so, saying that you ought to know the weak points which developed during my ownership of the car. Of course, the principal point is the lubrication. In this five hundred miles I used over ten gallons of cylinder oil, most of which was thrown over the engine and wires. At times the engine (would be) very bare of oil through the constant loss at the breathe-hole. The second point would be the lack of power in climbing hills as noticed in this car when compared with my last year's. The third point is the inaccessibility of the commutator. The fourth point the emergency break (sic). This fault could be obviated by a lever.

I have refrained from telling these facts to anyone, not wishing to do anything which might in any way tend to injure the sale of your cars. Moreover, your office in Boston has been most courteous and helpful, so much so that I intend to buy my next car of Mr. Fay. Now if you can make me one that is all right and without faults I should be very glad to have it and might do you some good in this locality, but I would not buy another like the last and with its faults under any consideration.

Trusting that you will take this in the friendly spirit in which it is intended, I remain,

Very truly yours,

F. H. Briggs

A new model began to take form almost as soon as the Model N appeared. This was to be the Model T. This new car was designed to eliminate many of the shortcomings of the automobiles of the day.

The Model T, upon introduction, offered at least seven major advances in automotive design. First was the en-bloc cylinder with a removable head. The majority of manufacturers at that time were casting cylinders in pairs, and these cylinders were of one piece. Valves were inserted through holes in the castings and covered with screw-in plugs. The Model T engine was a four-cylinder one-piece casting with a separate cylinder head which not only allowed a easier assembly but also easier servicing when required at a later date.

Second was the use of pressed steel engine, transmission, and rear axle housings. While experience would later prove this construction to have serious shortcomings, particularly in the rear axle and transmission cover, such deep and elaborate stampings had never been seen before in parts so large, and greatly lowered the cost of these components.

Third was the use of so-called "three-point" suspension. Previous Fords, and other cars, had employed some sections of the Model T suspension system but in the Model T the system was carried to its ultimate advantage. By mounting the engine, front, and rear axles in a triangular fashion, the twisting of the chassis caused by the poor roads of the day did not effect the operation of components. In the Model K, for example, a strain on the chassis caused by lifting one rear wheel would twist the engine mount so that a man could not crank the car. Not only did the three-point suspension prevent such stresses from effecting the engine, its very nature greatly reduced the twisting action itself since the front and rear axles could act independently of each other while imparting almost no distortion of the chassis.

Fourth, the entire mechanism was enclosed so that oil could stay in (remember, we are talking by 1909 standards!) and dirt could stay out. Additionally, self-lubrication was provided so that the owner didn't have to worry about filling oilers and oiling parts of the engine, transmission, or rear axle every few miles. The transmission was now sealed with the engine, making this new Ford a simple assembly of three major components (engine, front, and rear axles) to a light, yet strong chassis frame.

Fifth was the extended use of premium quality vanadium steel in stressed components. This steel had been used in the later Models N and S and not only made for a more rugged car, but it also allowed lighter weight assemblies. These in turn lessened the stress on the engine, axles, etc., giving the car a favorable power to weight ratio, which resulted in a "peppy" automobile.

Sixth was the introduction of left-hand drive in a major automobile, the advantages of which ultimately caused the entire American automotive industry to follow suit.

TOP: The Model N Ford as it appeared in the 1906 catalog.

LEFT: The Model N as it was shown in the 1908 catalog.

LEFT CENTER: The 1907 Model R, of which about 2500 were built. It was basically the same as the Model N except for a slightly larger body, larger fenders, and a running board.

LEFT LOWER: The Model S which used a body similar to the Model N but with full fenders and a running board.

The Model T's immediate predecessors, the Models N, R, and S. All used the same basic chassis but varied in bodies, fenders, etc. These models featured a four cylinder engine with the cylinders cast in pairs; the pairs being bolted to an aluminum crankcase. The flywheel was in the front and had cast-in fan blades so that it also acted as the cooling fan. The transmission was two speed and reverse, planetary, with the forward speeds controlled by the hand lever on the side (pull back for low, forward for high, neutral in between). The cars had three foot pedals: reverse, the transmission brake, and the rear wheel brakes. The front axle was suspended with a transverse spring as in the later Model T, but the rear springs were full eliptic, longitudinal. The rear axle also similar to the Model T in design, with the housings of cast iron in the pattern of the 1915 and later Fords.

The Model N was the basic car, with simple fenders and a step plate for entry. In 1907 Ford tooled up for 1000 of the Model R, apparently increased this to 2500, and found that sales exceeded expectations. Rather than retool for another run, they modified the Model N, using about the same body, but added full fenders and a running board, and called it the Model S. The Models N, S and the larger Model K were the Ford offerings for 1908.

The catalogs show only the Runabout bodies but apparently a limited number of Landaulets and, perhaps Tourings were produced. It is not known if these were available as standard models or were special custom cars.

Ford 4-cylinder—15-18 H. P. Runabout—Model "R"

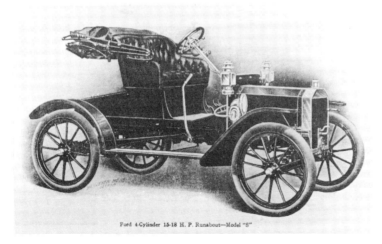

Ford 4-Cylinder 15-18 H. P. Runabout—Model "S"

COUPE

THERE are certain seasons of the year when an enclosed car affords the more acceptable method of travel. Not that the Ford Model T Coupe is necessarily only a cold weather car, it has enjoyed a large sale for all the year round use, more especially among physicians, but in the winter when an automobile is so much of a real necessity, this enclosed car affords the extra protection from the cold and wet which is so often wanted. In looks, this car compares more than favorably with any of its higher priced competitors. For service, the record of 15,000 Model T cars all built prior to January 1, 1910 and on this same chassis affords ample guarantee.

As all Model T bodies are interchangeable, a touring car or roadster body may be substituted for the coupe at the end of the winter season.

TOURABOUT

THE Ford Model T Tourabout is a four passenger car that is quickly converted into a runabout by removing the rear seat. The convenience of this will be quickly recognized by any one wanting a car which will ordinarily be used only by two persons but occasionally is required for four. As with the touring car and roadster, the price includes besides the magneto, an extension top, an automatic brass windshield, two 6-inch gas lamps and generator, a speedometer, three oil lamps, a horn and a kit of tools. This is the equipment that is usually figured at from $150.00 to $300.00 on other cars whose prices are already higher than the Ford price. The buyer of a Model T car has no extra equipment expense to consider.

THE FORD LINE FOR 1910. Basically the same as that from 1909. (Touring not shown here.) The Tourabout was added to the line in July 1909 and was shown as a "1910" model. The Touring and Runabout were much the same as in 1909 except that the windshields, tops and gas lamps were now standard equipment. The Landaulet was dropped in 1910. Total production of this style had been only 300, with most of these being built in 1909. (Production figures for 1910 show just two being built but the factory invoices show many more than this.) The Town Car continued unchanged other than the variations due to the body manufacturer. Both Wilson and Pontiac built Town Car bodies but Wilson was phased out during 1909. The later 1910 Coupes were a bit wider than the 1909 types. Both Wilson and Pontiac supplied the Coupe bodies in 1909, but just Pontiac in later 1909 and 1910. Strangely, the closed cars were not supplied with gas lamps as standard equipment.

ROADSTER

THE Ford Model T Roadster is a practical dignified and popular car. It is a man sized car, not a miniature, possesses speed, power and durability, and for all around use, business or pleasure, compares more than favorably with cars at considerably higher prices. The rear seat passenger has ample room instead of having to sit crowded into a space that was never designed to carry anything but a tool box. The running boards extend full length back affording easy access to this rear seat. It is in reality a three passenger touring car and, as the rear seat is detachable, all the conveniences of a runabout are at the disposal of the owner. As any Model T will turn in a 28 foot circle, this car finds considerable favor where streets are narrow or crowded.

TOWN CAR

THE Model T Town Car affords an excellent vehicle for those many requirements which necessitate or make more convenient the use of an enclosed car. It is provided with two small folding seats inside thereby accommodating two extra passengers. The cost of this car plus the wages of a driver for two years, plus the cost of maintenance for the same period, will total less than the purchase price of the usual type of limousine, while the Model T will answer equally well all the requirements of an enclosed car.

As a Taxicab this car offers an opportunity for its owner to realize a profit on his investment such as a higher initial and upkeep cost will not permit.

Actual practical every day service for over a year prior to our 1910 announcements, justifies the assertion that for 365 days in the year, the Model T car

Seventh was the ease of operation, particularly after the very early cars when the three-pedal system was standard. In 1909, most Americans had never driven a car, and here was a low-priced one that almost anyone could learn to drive in a very short time, and without worrying about clashing gears, grabbing clutches, and so on.

The ignition system was simple, with a built-in magneto. The magneto eliminated the worry of batteries or expensive magneto repairs, and while far from all new, it proved quite serviceable. It also created a vast market for entrepreneurs who offered millions of ways to improve upon it!

CHASSIS

The chassis (frame) of the Model T was the very essence of simplicity. Made of two long side members, and front and rear cross members, it was extremely light for its size. It could be easily twisted, but because of the three-point suspension, little twisting action reached it. That which did get through had no effect on the engine, since it, too, was mounted at three points.

The very early frames had riveted-in reinforcing plates on the inner side of the side members but these proved unnecessary and were eliminated early in production. Aside from modifications in the cross members, this simple design was to continue for the life span of the Model T.

An almost original 1909 Runabout, owned by Ramsey Araj of Oakland, California. The rear seat has been added to make it a "Tourabout" and the car has been repainted sometime in the past, but otherwise is all original except for the tires.

The car's second coat of paint has chipped away in many places, revealing the original color and striping which is almost the same as the second painting. The car is light gray, as are the top and top sockets. The body bracket, to which the top is mounted, and the top-supporting landau irons are black. Front and rear floor mats are off-white; typical for Fords of this era. The top has a red inner liner, a feature of many but not all earlier 1909 Fords, depending on the supplier.

A number of illustrations from this car are used in this coverage.

The assembly line in 1910. The rear axles all have the roller pinion bearing, introduced about March 1910, so these photos are March or later. None of the wheels are striped, and the engines appear to be unpainted. (Original cars which exist today indicate that apparently some engines were painted black and others were not painted at all.) Note that the brake backing plates are smooth-surfaced, unlike the later (1910?) designs. (Photos from the Collections of Henry Ford Museum and Greenfield Village.)

FRONT AXLE

The front axle was a vanadium-steel forging, as were the spindles for the front wheels. It was assembled to the frame by means of a transverse spring of seven leaves, with the outer ends secured to the axle, and the center of the spring clamped to the front cross member of the chassis. The axle position was established by a triangular "wishbone" that extended to the flywheel housing of the engine, and was held there with a ball-socket arrangement. Any twisting was absorbed by the springs, not by the chassis or engine.

The spindles on the 1909-1910 Fords were so-called "one-piece" in that the steering arm was integral with the spindle body, rather than the separate piece it later became. Ball bearings were used for the wheels, with an oil seal of felt to keep the dirt out.

The tie rod and steering link were both adjustable. The tie rod's adjustment was on the left side (until about 1918), and the steering link's was also on the left (at the steering arm). 1909-1910 cars used a steering rod with a fine (20 t.p.i.) thread for the adjusting yoke. No oilers were provided on the tie-rod bolts in early production; perhaps not until late in 1909.

The radius rod (wishbone) fastened to the spring perches on the axle at the front. The rear ball socket was held by studs and nuts in the very early 1909 cars, then by two cap screws, 3/8-inch by 20 t.p.i. No springs were used here as on the later (beginning about 1913) cars.

The front axle on the 1909, 1910 and early 1911 Fords used the so-called "one-piece" spindles. Whereas the later Model T used spindle assemblies with separate steering arms, the early cars had spindles with integral forged arms. The ends of the front axle fit rather close to the spindle body as can be seen in the photos. The steering tie rod was located above the radius rod (wishbone) instead of below as on the 1911 to 1918 cars. The toe-in adjustment was on the left end of the tie rod, and no provision was made for oilers on any part except for the spindles and spring shackles. Note that the tie-rod ends were attached to the spindle arms with slotted-head screws. The "drag link" which connects the steering shaft crank to the tie rod had an adjustment at the steering end, with a fine (20 t.p.i.) thread and a locking nut.

Front springs were taper-leaf and had seven leaves. The spring shackles were of the "Mae West" style, a figure-eight shape with one of the ends larger than the other. Brass oilers were fitted to the bearing end of each half, with the lower oiler being in front of the car, and the upper at the rear (it is reversed in the photo of the left spindle).

The upper leaves of the springs were often striped, as were the upper and/or front sides of the front axle. Striping does not seem to be "standard." Being a hand operation, each car varied according to the whims of the painter.

When equipped with a speedometer, a large and rather thin, steel drive gear was attached to the right front wheel hub. The photo shows one of these gears compared with the later types (which were cast iron instead of stamped steel).

REAR AXLE

The Model T rear axle was an example of simplicity carried almost to the extreme. The outer housings were drawn steel; one piece from the center seam to the brake flanges. These housings were the deepest drawing from one piece ever made to that date. The John R. Keim Mills, of Buffalo, New York, was the firm which developed the drawing process, and it was this company that initially made the axle housings, crankcases and transmission covers. Keim was purchased by Ford in 1911, and the Keim plant became Ford's Buffalo Assembly Plant.

At the time of its introduction, the rear axle used roller bearings at the wheels but babbitt bearings at the inner ends of the axles, and a babbitt pinion bearing. The axles were not tapered at the wheel end. The wheel was secured by a pin through the hub and axle, with this pin being held by the hub cap. A Woodruff key prevented the wheel from turning on the axle. The inner differential gear was held with a key and a riveted pin until sometime in 1910 when the pin was dropped in favor of collar, similar to the later T axles.

The driveshaft was also non-tapered, with the pinion gear riveted in place, and using a key to prevent the gear from turning. This type was used

on about the first 7,000 cars, at which time the shaft with the removable gear, held by a nut, appeared. This style continued until about number 18,000 when it was replaced with the tapered-end shaft which became the standard.

Initially, the brake flanges were stamped steel but these gave way to iron castings early in production. The first rear axles had the ring gear riveted to the differential carrier, rather than bolted in place as it was a bit later. The differential carrier was held together with studs and nuts, but no wires were used to keep the nuts from loosening. Rather, the nuts were made with a slot in the side, parallel to the top and bottom surfaces and near the upper or outer surface. When tightened in place they were hammered down on the slotted side and this prevented them from unscrewing. The ring gear rivets and these nuts made later service all but impossible, and the change to the castellated nuts with the retaining wire was soon adopted.

The design proved to be a poor one, however it was used with but minor changes until about car number 12,000 (October 1909) at which time the inner axle bearings were changed to roller. The inner bearing sleeves were held with an assembly which was riveted in place, creating the first "six rivet" rear axle. At about 18,000 (March 1910) the babbitt pinion bearing was also replaced with a roller bearing, a change which required extensive changes to the driveshaft assembly, and the addition of a reinforcing plate riveted and brazed to the center sections of the axle housings where the new driveshaft was fastened. (Rumors persist that there was a rear axle with the roller driveshaft bearing but without this reinforcement, but no such axle has "surfaced" to this writer's knowledge.)

The new driveshaft assembly, now using the shaft with the tapered end for the pinion gear, was held to the axle housings with 3/8" studs and nuts during the 1910 production. These studs were increased to 13/32" in 1911. The driveshaft housing had a separate universal-joint housing (the so-called "two-piece" type) and was generally similar to the housing used until mid-1913.

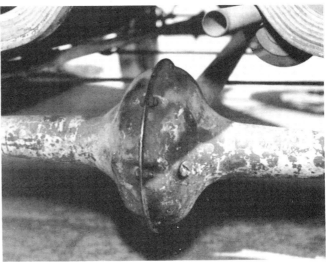

ABOVE: The rear axle shown here is from our featured 1909 Runabout. It is of the first "no-rivet" style, and is typical of the 1909 cars. The inner axle bearings, as well as the pinion bearing, are babbitt bushings. The driveshaft and axles are non-tapered and came in a number of variations (see text).

LEFT: At about 12,000 cars the inner axle bearings were changed to roller, and this modification required an inner bearing support which was secured with six rivets on each side; hence the first "six-rivet" housing. At about 18,000 the driveshaft pinion bearing was also changed to a roller type, and with this change came a forged reinforcement at the front where the driveshaft assembly is bolted.

BELOW: The photo of the 1910 rear axle is from Kim Dobbins' car and has the non-reinforced center (flange) section (see text). This basic axle design, with some improvements, was used until the summer of 1911, at which time the "1912" twelve-rivet axle replaced it.

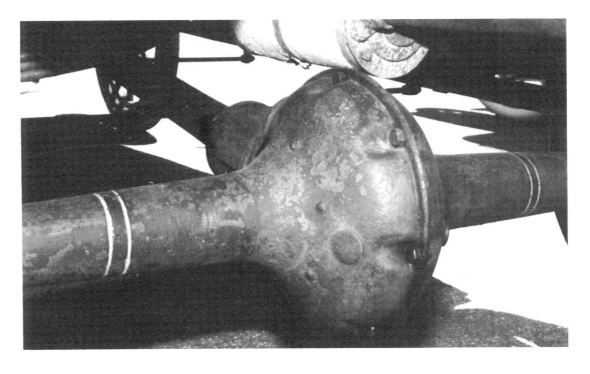

Other changes were made as well. The brake backing plates, initially (and after the first steel ones) were relatively smooth-surfaced on the outer (wheel) sides. These gave way to a stronger design with reinforcing webs. Early cars used bronze brake shoes but these were replaced with cast-iron shoes in early 1909.

Washers were added around the center bolt holes during 1910 (after the the change to the roller bearings), and still later a reinforcing ring was brazed in place, replacing the washers. The final design used two such rings, making the center flange considerably thicker. The dates of these changes are not certain but it is believed that the final "six-rivet" type (with the reinforced flanges) appeared in October 1910. Ford referred to this axle as the "1911 rear axle" on the shipping invoices.

During these early years, bronze bushings were used throughout the rear axle; for the differential gears, the differential gear housing, differential spider, etc.

ABOVE and BOTTOM: The rear axle shafts were not tapered for the wheel hub. They were straight, with a Woodruff key to prevent rotation. The hub was a snug fit when new, and it was held in place by a pin through the diameter of the hub and axle. The pin was held, in turn, by the hub cap. With minor variations, the non-tapered axle was used until the "1912" axle appeared in the summer of 1911. (It is not known if the tapered axle ever came as a part of the earlier axle assembly.)

Note the odd axle key used in the 1910 axle. Whether this is standard or some variation, or a later replacement is unknown. It may be original since the car is relatively low mileage, and the hub to axle fit is snug.

LEFT: The brake backing plates were smooth on both sides until late in 1910. The rear springs were eight-leaf, with tapered leaves. The spring shackles were similar to those used on the front axle except for having longer shafts. Striping appeared on the axle housing and on the upper spring leaves.

1909-1910

The Model T Differential showing the housing cut away exposing the drive and compensating gears

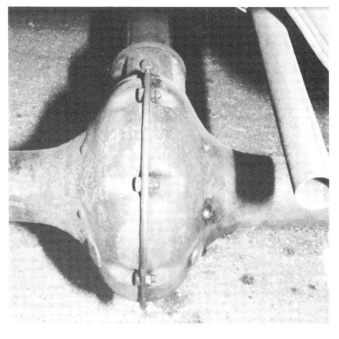

Some typical 1910 rear axle details. New was the addition of the driveshaft pinion roller bearing and the change to the inner axle roller bearings. The axle bearings required an internal support, held by the six rivets on each side as shown in the photo above. Note the typical "Mae West" spring shackles in the lower photos, which are typical of the shackles used from 1909 to 1912.

An original 1910 touring, owned by Kim Dobbins of Harbor City, California. This car is Brewster Green (body and fenders) and has never been repainted or otherwise changed. It might be considered a "typical" 1910, having been assembled on May 6, 1910.

The original factory shipping invoice indicates that the car came with a Rands windshield, Brown lamps, a Holley carburetor, a Stewart Model 24 speedometer and a Jacobson Brandow coil box (among other things) and that it was green. The car, today, is as described on the invoice.

The throttle and spark rods are brass-plated their entire visible length. The steering shaft is not plated. The steering column is black, as is the chassis and most other chassis parts, including the engine.

ENGINE

The initial Model T engine (the first 2500) was designed to have an integral water pump, driven from the timing gears at the front of the cylinder. The cylinder casting was made with no provision to cover the valve stems and lifters, which made it necessary for the owner to oil the valve stems from time to time. The cylinder head bolts were just 3/8" diameter in the first 500 engines, and then increased to 7/16" diameter. The first 500 cylinder heads had no identification cast into them, while the later early heads had "Ford Motor Company" cast on the top surface. These early engines were also unique in that they used connecting rods with oil dippers at the bottom end, and the rods had bronze bushings at the upper end for the piston pin. The piston pin was held in the piston by a screw so that it could not turn.

Because of the water pump drive gears, the crankshaft itself was unique in that it was shorter than the standard type used on all Model T's after the first 2500. The oil filler tube was located on the left front side of the crankcase, and had a large screen-covered cup at the top. The screen covering seems to have been a problem since every existing sample of these early engines has just the remnants of it left. Perhaps the early owners ripped it away to allow easier filling.

At approximately 2500, the water pump was discontinued. This required a new cylinder casting as well as a new cylinder head, plus many relatively minor modifications such as a different timing gear cover, etc. The piston and rod assemblies were changed to eliminate the oil dipper at the bottom end, and the rod now clamped to the piston pin which now rotated in bronze bushings in the piston. The crankshaft was made longer to accommodate a new crank ratchet. The oil filler was moved to its standard position in the right side of the engine, becoming part of the timing gear cover. The oil "cap" was just a tube with a screen at the upper end in early production, and then a brass cap was added with the "Ford" script embossed on its top.

The elimination of the water pump, with its attendant gear noise, was an improvement. The water pump engines had used a cooling fan driven from these gears, so a new belt-driven fan assembly became part of the new engine's design. Belt tension was by means of a spring between the timing cover and the fan end of the fan support arm. The cylinder

The early piston assemblies. Note the integral oil dippers on the rod caps, and the three piston rings all above the pin. Other early pistons can be seen with the lower ring below the pin, with two or three rings above, but all the Parts List pictures indicate the above-the-pin location as standard. Perhaps all these types were used. In any event, the assembly was redesigned to eliminate the dipper, and to clamp the piston pin in the rod and allow it to pivot in the piston early in 1909.

head was a bit larger for more water capacity and with the water outlet now on the front of the casting instead of on the top surface as it had been in the first engines. The head now was cast with "Ford" instead of "Ford Motor Co."

The crankcase was a drawn steel assembly even more complicated that the rear axle housings (though not as deep a drawing). The initial design had a rather long front-bearing casting, with rivets that extended into the crankcase area, and no reinforcing casting at the rear flange. An oil dam was provided behind the fourth rod to keep oil under the crankshaft. The crankcase underwent a number of modifications; the front bearing was made shorter, eliminating the rivets inside the engine area; a reinforcing casting was added at the rear to better support the driveshaft housing; the oil dam was ultimately eliminated; and reinforcing ribs were added to the stamping. None of the crankcases used in 1909 and 1910 had inspection covers to allow connecting rod adjustment. Such service required complete disassembly of the engine. This basic design continued into 1911.

LEFT: The water-pump engine block used on the first 2500 cars. Similar in design to the later blocks except for the front end. There was no water-jacket opening at the front, and the oil-filler tube was located on the left front side. As in all of the 1909 and 1910 engines, the upper main bearings in the cylinder were not babbitt-lined.

BELOW: An underside view of the early engine. Note the square-head screw which locks the piston pin, and the bronze bushing in the small end of the connecting rod. The lower end of the connecting rods had oil dippers but for some reason the ones in this photo have been ground off.

RIGHT: Two cylinder heads were used on the water pump engines. The first was held with 3/8-inch bolts, and has no "Ford" cast in its surface. The second used 7/16-inch bolts and and sports "Ford Motor Co." It is possible the earlier head had the logo, and that some of the later heads did not.

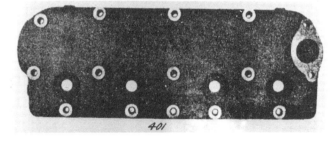

1909-1910

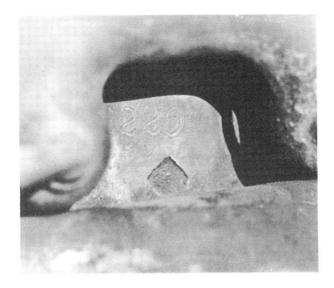

LEFT: The serial number of the earliest engines was stamped between the two center exhaust ports. The location was moved to a boss just behind the timing gear and remained in that location until 1912.

The water pump assembly of the first 2500 engines. Note the oil filler tube with its large cup-shaped funnel. Apparently there was a screen over the funnel originally, for remains of it can be found around the rims of most of the funnels seen. Perhaps it made filling difficult and it was therefore torn away.

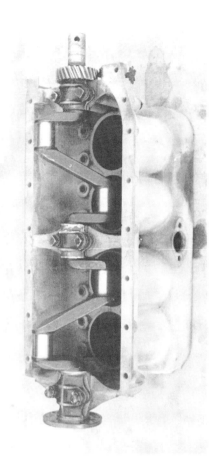

At about 2500 the cylinder was redesigned to eliminate the water pump. The water jacket was enlarged to extend ahead of the number one cylinder, and the cylinder head slightly enlarged to match. The oil filler was made a part of the timing gear cover and no longer had a large funnel. Its cover was a simple screen-top tube in the initial production but by 1910 the tube was given a brass top with the "Ford" script embossed on its top. The illustrated cylinder is serial number 6291 which originally went into a green Touring which was assembled July 6, 1909. This engine has bronze pushrod bushings and iron valve bushings, both removable. Early engines used bronze in both locations. All engines used pipe plugs for the water jacket seals (until 1913). Main bearings had babbitt only in the cap while the upper main bearing surface was just the cylinder metal. This engine continued into 1911, at which time the valve chamber was enclosed, and both halves of the main bearings were babbitted.

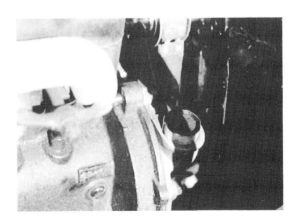

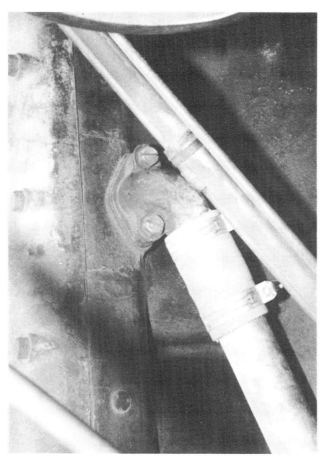

Opposite, top left (as viewed with the page rotated to a normal position): The water inlet fitting on this 1910 is held with slotted-head screws. The clearance in the casting is such that these may have been standard at the time but this is an open question.

Opposite, top right: Note the deep ribs in the fan blades, typical of 1909-1910 and perhaps even later. The fan hub is brass, and the belt tension is by means of a spring between the fan support arm and the timing gear cover (see lower right photo on this page). Note, too, the slotted-head screws used to hold the camshaft bearings; typical 1909 and 1910. The oil "cap" on this 1909 engine is a brass tube with a screen on the top, and with no cover as in the later engines.

Opposite, bottom left: "dogleg" aluminum intake manifold used from 1909 to 1911. The carburetor here is the "1910 Holley" with the hot-air tube directed to the front of the engine and with the hot air stove at the upper front of the exhaust manifold. Most 1910 engines had the hot air tube behind the carburetor, with the tube fitting to the rear of the exhaust manifold.

Opposite, bottom right: View of the fan tension spring. All hoses were red rubber and all clamps were of the style shown.

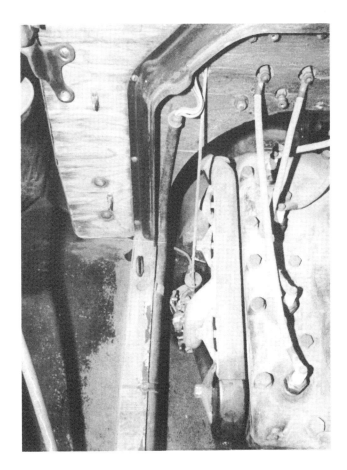

Right: Note the placement of the wiring loom, with its clamps and rubber end seal. The notch in the hood former is typical of the 1909 and 1910 Fords; a carry-over from the first models which used the steel hoods with the integral full-length hinge.

Right, center: The 1909-1910 hood former. In addition to the notch on the inner lip, there were two bulges above the side corners. These were needed to clear the upper steering post flange bolts, and were provided on both sides in order that the same former could be used in either right-hand or left-hand-drive cars.

Below: The timing gear cover used in 1909 (after 2500) and 1910. Variations in these are common; some don't have the indentations below the camshaft hole, as in the lower right photo of the 1911 cover. (The fan tension spring was replaced with a screw during 1911.)

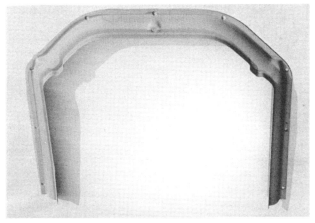

The front motor mount/spring clamp was quite different from later cars. Note its rather "square" construction with fairly pronounced 'ears.' The later units (perhaps beginning in 1911) were a bit stronger and more "filled in." (See reproduction of 1909 catalog page at the upper right, #3076, for a better view of the earlier design.)

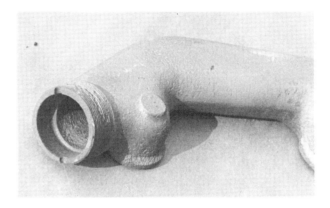

The intake and exhaust manifolds, typical of 1909 and 1910. Note the "doglegged" aluminum intake manifold (replaced in mid-1911) and that the exhaust manifold was counter-bored so that the exhaust pipe fitted into it rather than just butting up with a flange. The pack nut was much the same, but used asbestos packing to effect a seal. This type of construction lasted until about 1913.

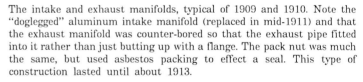

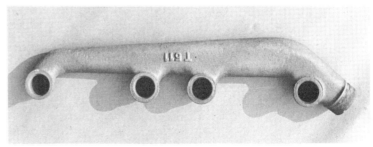

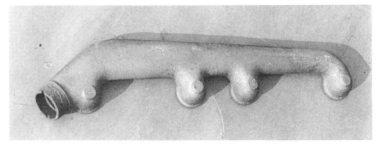

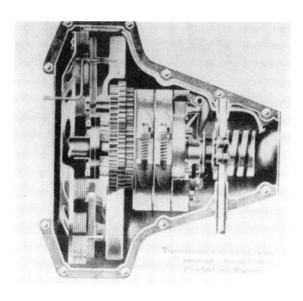

Catalog illustration of the Model T transmission. Note that it shows the early clutch arms with no adjustment screws. The adjusting screws were added during 1909.

TRANSMISSION

The Model T transmission was truly just an evolution from the planetary transmissions used in the earlier Fords but with one major difference; it was not exposed, and was immersed in oil. By reducing the size of its components, made possible in part by the use of vanadium-steel gears, it could now be enclosed within the engine assembly, and be lubricated by the engine's oil. As in the earlier models, it had a low gear, direct, neutral and reverse.

The Models N, R, and S used a hand lever to control the forward gears, and a pedal for reverse, which was not an uncommon practice at the time. The Model T started life with a different system; the lever now applied the reverse, and the forward gears were controlled by the left foot pedal. This greatly simplified the control of the car and allowed the driver to keep both hands on the wheel while going forward. While this design was an improvement, it was quickly superseded by the three-pedal system for which the Ford was to become so famous. The two-pedal system was factory installed on approximately the first 500 to 800 cars (various sources list both figures). The three-pedal system may have appeared earlier during a transition period, during which both types were used. Ford offered conversion "kits" to update the two-pedal system.

Internally, the transmission remained relatively unchanged during its nineteen year life span. The earliest transmissions did not have adjusting screws on the three clutch fingers but this oversight was quickly rectified early in 1909. There were bronze bushings on most components where wear might occur.

Transmission covers were another matter. Like the crankcases, they underwent numerous modifications over the years, and in particular, the first year. The initial design was pressed steel, with a "square" steel inspection plate for the band adjustments. This plate was held in place by a center "bolt" which revolved a lever which in turn engaged the insides of the cover. The second design was like the first but of a somewhat different shape. The third was cast aluminum but otherwise quite similar to the steel cover, using the same inspection plate arrangement. This aluminum casting was quite thin around the inspection hole, allowing the lever to engage the underside, and stops were cast in to prevent the lever from being turned too far. None of these covers, used on the first 800 cars, had an external low band adjustment. The three types may have been used simultaneously during this era.

The fourth change, made at the time of the change to the three-pedal system, was aluminum with the relatively minor changes needed for the reverse pedal but otherwise similar to the two-pedal aluminum cover. It now had the external low-band adjustment. The fifth type was still aluminum but the door was now a bit more rectangular in shape, and it was now secured with four screws. Initially it used the same inspection door as the previous design but without the bar latch arrangement, and with holes drilled for the screws. This door was superseded by a cast aluminum one, and even some steel ones have been seen (though these may have been "1911"). This cover continued until very late 1910, at which time it was made a bit wider to accommodate the larger magneto and to match the wider crankcase also introduced at that time.

Inside view of the typical 1909 and 1910 transmission cover. Note the oil scoop at the rear (bottom of the photo) which directed oil to the rear bearing. This scoop was held in place by the two rivets seen in the photos of the top side of the covers.

Top photos, and center right: the early pressed-steel cover.

The second pressed-steel cover

Transmission covers could be a study in themselves. At least six styles appeared during 1909 and 1910. The first types were pressed steel, similar to the pressed-steel crankcase. Two of this type are shown here. Note that one has somewhat of a "hump" at the rear of the inspection plate, while the other does not. The steel inspection plate has dimples in each corner and is secured by a rotating bar which engages the inner edge of the inspection hole. The third type was cast aluminum and used the same style of inspection door as the steel covers, but without the dimples. All three of these covers were used in the early two-pedal cars, and none had any provision for any external adjustments. (Photos courtesy of Donald Hess.)

The fourth type was similar to the third except that it was made for the three-pedal system. The low-speed adjustment is now external. The fifth type is like the fourth but now the inspection door is held with four screws. The doors for this type were initially the same as the earlier door except that the center hex head which turned the retaining lever was omitted and, of course, the holes drilled. This door was superseded by a cast-aluminum door with the Ford script.

A sixth type appeared in late 1910. This cover was similar in style to the fifth but was about an inch wider to match the "1911" transmission and crankcase, which were needed to accommodate the larger magneto.

The third two-lever cover, cast aluminum.

Fourth type

Fifth type

The 1910 (left) and "1911" (right) covers. Note that the "1911" was about an inch wider than the previous types.

1909-1910

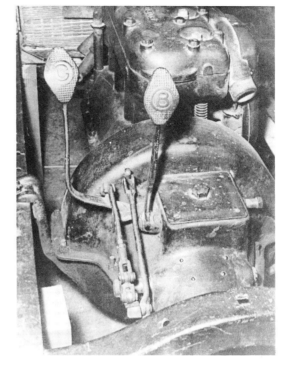

Views of the early (first 800) two-pedal, two-lever control system. Note the use of elaborate forgings and the roller in the reverse cam lever.

Above: The early 1909 flywheel assembly and magneto coils. Note that the magnet support was a bronze casting in the shape of a ring instead of the individual brass spools used in later 1909 and 1910 (below). The magnets were 1/2 inch thick and rather elaborate instead of the simple "V" shape used with the redesigned, larger, magneto introduced in late 1910.

ELECTRICAL SYSTEM

To eliminate the problems created by the use of dry cells for ignition, a built-in low voltage magneto was made a part of the engine assembly. It consisted of sixteen elaborately-shaped magnets, mounted on the front surface of the flywheel, which revolved past a fixed coil assembly attached to the rear of the cylinder casting (engine block).

As with other parts, the magneto also evolved. The first 2500 engines used 1/2 inch thick magnets with the outer ends supported by a bronze ring. After 2500, slightly different 1/2 inch magnets were used and the outer ends were now supported by bronze spools. At about 17,500 the magnets were increased to 9/16 inch thick, all of a similar shape. At about 20,500 they were increased to 5/8 inch, of the common "V" shape, which continued until late 1914.

The coils were wound on round bobbins, mounted on a pressed-steel frame during this period. Needless to say, the coils were modified when the magnet size changed.

The generated alternating current was supplied to four coils, one for each cylinder, which were selected by a commutator, at the front of the engine, which was driven by the camshaft to generate a spark at the proper time for each cylinder.

The coil boxes and coils were supplied by Kingston and Jacobson-Brandow during 1909 and

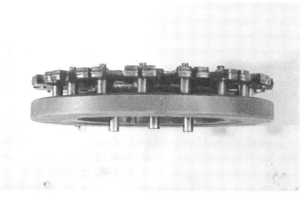

Car number 220 had this Heinze coil-box installed when found. This was a carryover unit from the previous N-R-S cars and was used only in the very early production. The Kingston coil box assembly was also used during the early production (car number 1 used a Kingston assembly) and was the standard unit until 1911. Note that the spark plug terminals are at the bottom on the Heinze coil box. The Kingston coil assemblies had the terminals on the rear, through the firewall, as did all later coils.

1910. Some very early cars used the Heinze coils used on the N and S cars, with the high-tension wires out the bottom, but early in 1909 the Heinze coils were discontinued. The Kingston (and J-B) coils had the terminals on the rear which extended through the firewall to the engine compartment.

This system was truly obsolete by 1909. Most manufacturers used a high-tension magneto or a distributor ignition. Nevertheless, Ford kept this system all through Model T production. Provision was made for the use of a battery (dry cells) in starting, since the magneto gave a relatively low output when the engine was cranked, especially in cold weather.

Except for some very early production, which used the Heinze coils left over from the Model N and S, coil boxes and coils were supplied by Kingston in 1909, and by Kingston and Jacobson-Brandow in 1910 cars. The Heinze coil boxes, often seen on 1909 and 1910 cars, were not factory-installed until 1911.

The Kingston coil box on the 1909 runabout. Kingston switches seem to have come in brass and in hard rubber.

The Jacobson-Brandow coil box on the 1910 Ford touring.

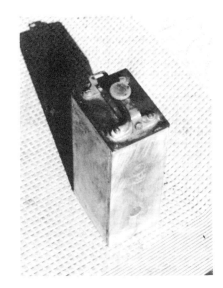

The Kingston coil box with the cover removed, and (right) one of the Kingston coils. Note the carburetor adjustment bracket. 1909 and 1910 models used a bracket with four screws to hold it to the firewall, while later cars used a similar bracket held with just two screws.

RIGHT: The 1909-10 "Two-piece" timer. The main housing was held in place by a flange on the rotor, which in turn was held to the camshaft with a nut. The brass cover was held to the housing with the two thumb nuts.

The Stewart Model 24 on the 1910 Ford touring is shown here.

Speedometers, when installed at the factory in 1909, were Jones Models 20 and 21, Stewart Models 11, 12, and 24, or National Model 50. Apparently just the Stewart Model 24 was used in 1910. Dealer-installed speedometers are another matter, with the Stewart Model 26, among others, being used.

CARBURETORS

The vast majority of 1909 Fords were equipped with Kingston 5-ball carburetors. These Kingstons did not have a choke valve, and the air intake was through an inlet at the bottom which made a right-angle turn upwards. A hot-air pipe fit this inlet and rose to the manifold at the rear of the carburetor. It is not certain if this hot-air pipe was used on all cars. During the early part of 1909, the factory shipping invoices also list a Buffalo carburetor. Buffalo had been a supplier of carburetors to Ford for the Model K, and perhaps others. The author has yet to see an actual sample of this Buffalo carburetor but it is believed to have been about the same shape as the Kingston. The Buffalo was not used after June 1909, until early 1910.

For 1910 the same Kingston continued for a time and then the air inlet fitting was modified to curve upward at about a 45 degree angle, and included a choke valve. This fitting faced toward the front of the engine, with the hot-air pipe running to a "stove" at the front corner of the exhaust manifold. Exactly when this change was made is unknown but it was believed to have been in late 1909 or early 1910.

In addition to the Kingston, a new Holley carburetor was used on a good number of cars. This was the Holley 4150 and it came in two types of the same design. One used a "pot metal" upper body while the other was a bronze casting. The air intake was similar to the later Kingston, with a choke valve and the same type of hot-air system.

Buffalo apparently convinced Ford they had something to offer because in the first three months of 1910 its name again appears on the shipping invoices. This Buffalo had the choke setup cast as a part of the lower housing. It was made of bronze, and was quite complex compared with the Kingston and Holley. In any event, it was last used about March, and Buffalo carburetors never again graced the manifold of a Model T Ford when it left the factory.

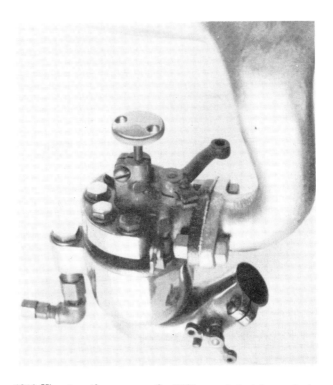

1910 Kingston, the same as the 1909 except that it now had a choke valve and the air intake faced to the front. The hot air tube now rose to the exhaust manifold heat stove at the front of the engine.

Six carburetors were used by Ford in 1909 and 1910: two Kingstons, both alike except for the air intake with the choke valve in 1910; two Holleys, identical except for the body castings, one of which was all bronze while the other was part bronze and part "pot metal"; and two Buffalos, the description of which is open to question (see caption regarding the pictured Buffalo carburetor).

The 1909 Kingston. The air intake was vertical (shown in the wrong position, it should point to the rear of the carburetor) and without a choke valve. It is possible that some early cars did not use a heat tube to the manifold but most had a tube that went up to the manifold from the rear of the carburetor. "Choking" was accomplished by flooding the carburetor by means of a lever just to the rear of the manifold fitting. This lever depressed the float, allowing the fuel level to rise.

The two "1910" Holley carburetors. They are identical except for one being all bronze while the other is part bronze and part "pot metal."

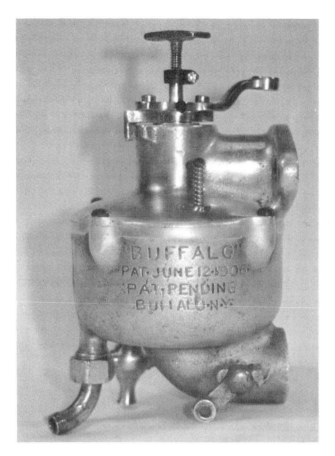

A Buffalo carburetor, believed to be the 1909 model, which appeared on a number of cars until about April 1909. Note that it had a choke valve in the air intake, an item not found on the Kingstons of that era. This photo was supplied by Russ Potter, of Bismarck, Illinois.

HORNS

Horns used in 1909 and 1910 were all similar. Made by Rubes or Non-Pareil, they were all brass and were "double twist." (These have been called "triple twist" but there are just two loops in the horn.) The flexible metal hose from the rear of the horn (where the reed assembly was located) ran unsupported to the bulb which was fastened on the left-side panel next to the driver on the wood-bodied cars, and on the front of the side panel wooden support on the Pontiac aluminum bodies.

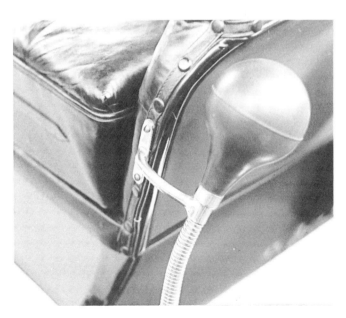

Horns were all brass and in several similar styles. Note how the shape of the loops varied. These variations seem to be in the same brand as well as from one brand to another.

LAMPS

Oil lamps were standard equipment on all cars. In 1909 they were supplied by Edmond and Jones (E&J), Atwood Castle, or Jno. Brown. The E&J lamps were marked "Pat. 1908," the Browns were model 60, and the Atwood Castles were model 204. (Tail and Side lamps.) The Atwood Castles were discontinued during 1909, leaving the E&J and Browns only in 1910 production.

Gas headlamps were options in 1909 but became standard late in the year on the open cars. They were always an option on the closed cars for some reason. The manufacturers which supplied the oil lamps also supplied the gas headlamps. The E&J's were model 466, the Browns were model 15, and the Atwood Castles (1909 only) were model 84. All lamps were all-brass.

The gas generators were also made by these firms. Generators were often replaced with Prestolite tanks at the factory, apparently as an option. The gas lamps were connected to the generator (or Prestolite tank) with metal tubing between the lamps and from the tank to the left-front lamp. Red rubber hoses were used as short couplings to the tank and lamps from the metal pipes.

WINDSHIELDS

During 1909, windshields were supplied by Rands, Troy (brass and wood), and Mezger. (Mezger was the manufacturer of the "Automatic" windshield.) In 1910, Troy was phased out, leaving Rands and Mezger as the suppliers. It is possible there were others but these are the brands listed on the shipping invoices of the period.

All (except for the wooden Troy) had brass frames, and all folded at the center. Dimensionally quite similar, the center hinges and other details varied according to the manufacturer's designs. Apparently not all windshields of the same manufacturer were exactly the same, for variations can be found from car to car.

E&J Model 466

1909 and 1910 cars came "stock" with a low firewall (called "dash") which barely extended above the hood former. The addition of a windshield required an additional wood section between the firewall and the bottom windshield frame. This wooden section varied a bit according to the windshield. The Automatic, for example, had mounting brackets which were bolted to the ends of this board, and the board was therefore about the same width as the original firewall, with relatively square ends. The Rands windshield, on the other hand, mounted to the top of the board, and the boards on these flared out towards the windshield-frame sides.

These add-on boards were bolted to the firewall using brass-plated steel brackets and brass-plated bolts and nuts. There was no brass trim other than the mounting brackets on the board.

All windshields were supported by brass (or brass-plated) rods which ran from the center hinge to the front of the chassis, fastening either to the radiator mounting bolt or to the forward fender bracket bolt.

(Continued on page 56)

Brown Model 15

It is sometimes difficult to define exactly what a lamp should look like. There are variations in various samples of the same brand, and from one lamp to another on the same car. For example, The Brown Model 60 is shown but Kim Dobbins' Brown Model 60 looks like the Atwood Castle 204. The bonnet on one Atwood Castle has four rivets on its top surface, while another sample has none. E&J top labels come in at least two variations, both marked 466. So, whatever it looks like, it's probably right. Or wrong!

Atwood Castle Model 84

Early E&J "Pat. 1908"

Variation in Atwood Castle 84 bonnet

Later E&J "Pat. 1908"

Atwood Castle 204 side lamp

Brown 60 side light

53

E&J "Pat. 1908" tail lamp

Brown 60 tail lamp

A variation in a Brown 60

Atwood Castle 204 tail lamp

A variation in the E&J 466

1910 Touring in Iowa. The driver is Peter J. Heiken, the lady is Louise Heiken, and the child is Maurice L. Keiken. The author cannot determine the source of this outstanding photo.

1909-1910

WINDSHIELDS
(Continued)

Windshields, which were optional equipment on the open cars, were supplied by three major manufacturers in the early part of 1909. Rands and Mezger (Automatic) were by far the most common and are shown here. Troy was the third and supplied both brass and wood-framed assemblies. By 1910 most, if not all, windshields were Rands and were now standard equipment.

The Rands and the Mezger were similar in general construction, differing mainly in the hinge arrangement. On both types, the top section could be folded to the rear.

The Mezger featured a hook-latch arrangement with an exposed spring as is shown. The hooks tend to hold the upper section in place when it is upright, while the springs aid in the support in either the upright or lowered position.

The Rands has a simple hinge with a telescoping upper tube with an internal spring. This tube is fully collapsed when the upper section is upright and because of the spring tension it holds the upper section in place. When folded to the rear, the two sections of the upper tube separate, then close again to hold the upper section firmly down.

All windshields required the installation of a spacer board between the firewall and the lower windshield frame. These add-on boards varied in shape, with some being the same width as the firewall, and others flaring out from the firewall to the windshield, being wider at the top.

ABOVE and BELOW: The Rands windshield and its spring-loaded hinge mechanism.

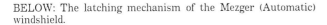

BELOW: The latching mechanism of the Mezger (Automatic) windshield.

OPEN CAR TOPS

Initially, and through most of 1909, tops were listed as optional equipment. Nevertheless, a good many Touring and Runabouts left the factory with tops, windshields, and gas lamps, so they could be considered more or less standard. The tops supplied on the Tourings were all black, with and without a red lining (in all samples the author has seen), and with and without the windshield curtain. The back panel on all could be rolled up.

Runabouts on the other hand came in both black and gray in the early part of 1909 (before the change to all green cars), and also with and without the lining, and with and without the roll-up windshield curtain. Later (green) Runabouts used only the black tops. The rear curtain on the Runabouts also rolled up.

Top sockets were painted body color on some, if not all, cars until about June 1909, at which time it is believed they were all the body color (Brewster Green) or black. The top sockets were all of the curved type, with an oval cross section. The sockets all were mounted on a separate forged "buggy rail" which in turn was bolted to the body. This rail was painted black on all cars and came as standard equipment.

The top was supported at the rear by leather straps which ran from the rear bow to the support rail in the rear, and from the front bow to a bracket at the radiator-mounting bolt in the front.

Interestingly, the roll-up front windshield curtain came with the top even though the car also came with a glass windshield. This arrangement continued well into 1910 when windshields were supplied on all cars. It is not known if all cars came with this windscreen.

Even though the open cars were not supplied with tops in some production in 1909, all were provided with the forged "buggy rail" to which the top was mounted. The top sockets on the touring cars had a gentle curve outward from the bottom, while the Runabout sockets were straight.

The tops were supported at the rear with leather straps which ran from the rear top bow to the support rail. Another leather strap ran from the front bow to a hook which in turn hooked to an eyelet at the radiator mounting stud. The eyelet came in at least three types, two of which are shown here. One was an eyelet with a round hole to which a snap-type hook mated. Another was a forged loop with an oblong hole, to which a plain hook fastened but the hook could only be inserted in the loop if it was turned sideways, thus preventing it from falling out in the normal position. The third type seen was a simple strap metal eyelet which used the snap-type hook.

Top sockets were painted body color when the top was supplied from the factory in early 1909, then all were believed to be either body color or black after about June 1909.

The tops themselves were mostly black leatherette, some with a red lining and some with no lining. Gray tops were also

used on some of the gray Runabouts built until June 1909, at which time green became the standard color for all bodies. All tops had a roll-up rear curtain, and many were supplied with a front curtain even though the car might have had a glass windshield.

BODIES AND PAINTING

Wheels on all 1909 and 1910 cars used 30 by 3 inch tires on the front, and 30 by 3-1/2 inch tires on the rear. None of the tires had any tread in those days; an advancement it took Ford (and others as well) some time to acquire. The wheel hubs all used flanges that were just 5-1/2 inches in diameter. Front and rear hubs appeared similar during the era of the non-tapered rear axle; the rear hub being the same general shape as the front. Wheels were painted body color (red, gray, or green) and were not all striped. When they were striped, the striping varied from car to car.

Bodies were offered in a number of styles, and were made by Pontiac or Wilson in 1909. In addition to the Touring car, a Runabout, Town Car, Landaulet, and a Coupe were offered. Touring bodies made by Pontiac came with wood or aluminum panels until about September 1909, at which time the aluminum was discontinued. All others had wood panels.

In late 1909 a Tourabout was added to the line. This style was similar to the Touring except that there were no doors in the rear compartment. Essentially the body consisted of two Runabout seat assemblies. Ford referred to it as a "1910" car, as they did for all cars built after about July 1909.

These styles continued through 1910 until the introduction of the "1911" cars in very late 1910. Wilson was dropped as a supplier in 1910, with Hayes being added. (The records are not clear as to the manufacturers. "KA," "KH," "Hayes," and "American" are shown on the shipping invoices and these may all be the same company. "KH" could be Kelsey Hayes; Hayes-American is believed to be the same company, etc. As in later 1909, all bodies had wood panels, so far as is known.

Bodies were offered in various colors until June 1909, at which time a very dark green, called Brewster Green, became standard for all cars. Records do not exist for cars built before 1,119, and colors were not listed until about 1,540, but at that time tourings came in either red or green, runabouts were gray, Town Cars were gray or green, and the Landaulets and Coupes were generally green. The records indicate an occasional variation such as a green Runabout or a gray Touring. There is no documented evidence of black cars even though some original cars which exist today appear to be black.

In early production the chassis and running gear were painted the body color but it is believed that this practice was discontinued by 1911, at which time such items became a uniform black.

Most, but not all, cars were striped throughout 1909-1910. The striping varied in style and placement. Some cars had body striping but none on the hood. Some wheels were striped and others were not. Striping on the axles, springs, etc. seems to have been quite common.

Fender design, typical of production 1909 and 1910.

Early 1909 front fender design with square front.

59

Robe rails were a common Ford-supplied accessory in the early years.

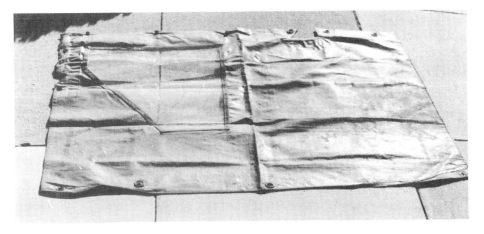

A side curtain supplied with the 1909 runabout.

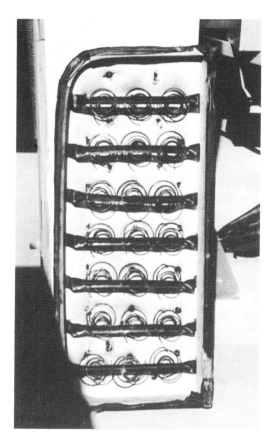

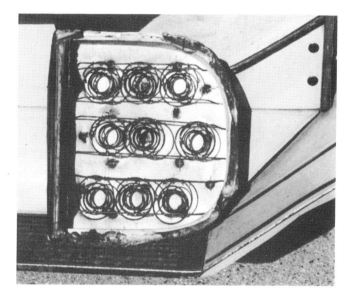

Views of the seat assemblies, typical of the period. Note the upholstery buttons had metal washers on the underside, with the "ears" bent over to hold the buttons in place.

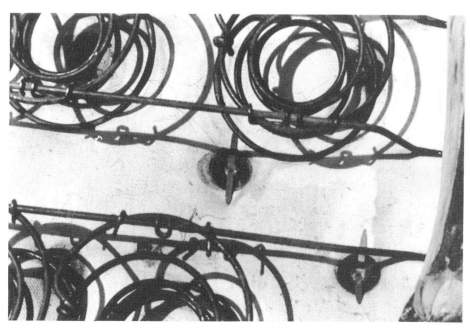

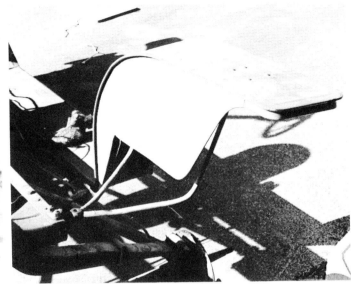

The fender design in 1909 and 1910 Fords was unique to that era. Note that the top surface was one piece, with parallel edges, and with the apron a separate piece which was molded to fit. Rear fenders were similar in pattern. Early front fenders were "square" at the front, with no bill. In early 1909 (date unknown, but apparently before May) a bill was added to a more rounded front.

Early rear fenders were supported by fender irons with were integral with the rear body brackets, and which came out and under the fender aprons. Early in 1909 these irons were modified, and the fender aprons pierced, so that the irons entered through the apron. This modification gave a slightly more rigid support.

MISCELLANEOUS

Little is known of the closed cars of 1909-1910. Our references are to the open models in most cases, but it is likely that where applicable, the closed cars would be similar.

Brass trim was common. Windshield brackets, side-lamp brackets, etc. were generally brass-plated steel. Pedal and brake trim plates were solid brass plates. The spark and throttle rods were brass-plated; just the upper parts in some cars, and their entire visible length in others. Nuts and bolts used to hold dashboard items were generally either brass or brass plated.

1909-1910

Fenders were of unique design for 1909 and 1910. In general, they were made of uniform-width top panels, with the aprons formed to fit. On the first cars, the front fenders were more or less "square" at the front, with no bill. The bulk of 1909-1910 production, though, had rounded fronts with relatively short bills.

Rear fenders were of a similar pattern. On the first cars the support irons, a part of the rear body support bracket, came out and under the apron of the fender. Early in 1909, though, the irons were modified in shape, and now entered through holes in the aprons, a slightly more substantial arrangement. Fenders were body color in all samples seen by the author.

Splash aprons were relatively smooth from front to rear, with a large gap between them and the rear fenders. The front edge of the apron matched the fender line, while the rear edge had a gentle concave curve on the early cars, and a slightly convex curve on the later production.

Running boards initially were linoleum (or "rubber") covered with brass trim but by early 1909 these gave way to all-metal boards with a series of parallel ribs running lengthwise. This style continued, apparently, through most of calendar 1909 and into early 1910. The parallel ribs were then broken up into a series of "dashes" and this later style continued until late 1910 when the 1911 styles appeared. As on the fenders, the aprons and running boards were painted body color.

Early 1909 linoleum-covered board with brass trim around the edges.

Typical 1909 and early 1910 with long ribs.

Hub caps were brass with a rather rounded end and with the "Ford" in block letters. Wheel-hub flanges were just 5-1/2 inches in diameter and the wheels had rather thin spokes of an oval cross section. Striping shown here is typical of production but not all wheels were striped, and there was considerable variation in the striping when it did appear. Wheels were body color (red, gray or green) in 1909 and 1910.

1910 board

The early 1909 steel hood. Note that the center and side hinges were integral with the panels rather than the riveted in place assembly of the production 1909 and later cars. The hinge rods extended the entire length of the hood, requiring the notch in the hood-former for clearance. The later riveted hinges were shorter, not extending to the edges of the hood, but the hood former notch remained through 1910. Hoods with the separate hinges were made of aluminum (until late 1915).

The engine hood was aluminum after the very early cars. (Initial production used a steel hood with integral hinges pressed from the hood material, but the aluminum hood appeared early in 1909.) The hood formers (on the firewall) of 1909 and 1910 cars were unique in that they had a "notch" pressed into them on the upper corners. It is believed that these notches were there to clear the hinge pins of the steel hood in the original design, and the dies that stamped the formers were not changed when the notch was no longer needed.

Hood clamps were iron, with just one ear to catch the hood. The hood clash strips were wooden, painted body color.

Difficult to photograph, but two styles of brake-rod supports were used in 1909 and 1910. The first, shown above, was a one-piece design which clamped over the radius rod and with a hole in the outer end through which the brake rod passed. During 1909 it was superseded with another type which clamped under the radius rod (clamp bolt was now on top) and with an arm which came out and rolled up and around the brake rod. This second type continued until about 1913. Brake rods and radius rods both had forged fork ends.

Above: The front-radius-rod clamp (on the engine pan) was held with screws, wired together to prevent their coming out. Note that there were no springs here. The dirt and grease are standard equipment on all Model Ts.

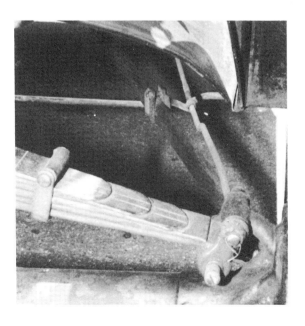

The fuel-tank sediment bulb (brass) and valves. Note the handles on both valves. The sediment bulb was on the right-hand end of the gasoline tank, outside the frame rail, which was more convenient than the usual near-center location used in later years. It is believed that the location was moved more to the center in later years to prevent fuel starvation when the fuel level was low and the car was on other than level ground.

On the Runabout the seats were split, making it easier to add fuel to the tank.

Radiators were supplied by several manufacturers. All were different, yet all of the same shape and therefore interchangeable. These companies were Briscoe, McCord, Detroit Radiator, and Ford Motor Co. Briscoe supplied radiators for the bulk of the first 2500 cars, but there are some factory invoices that list a "Paris" radiator, perhaps a fourth supplier. In any event, most of the early radiators were "one-piece" assemblies, with the Ford "Winged Script" on the top tank. Some of the earlier radiators were made with a separate outer shell which was soldered at the top, and some came without the script. Briscoe was dropped after 2500, and the major suppliers were McCord and Detroit until about October 1909 when Ford began making its own. By mid-1910 Ford appeared to have been making *all* its radiators. All were supplied with the brass "Ford" script on the radiator core.

Early cars had radiators with a relatively smooth design, as did this one found on car 220. Ramsey Araj's 1909 Ford has a seamed one, as does Kim Dobbins' 1910. One manufacturer's construction used a separate outer shell which was soldered at the top, rather than the integral top tank of most of the radiators. The filler necks were all machined brass and were soldered in place. The radiator caps were generally of the style with the rather sharp and high wings. A brass "Ford" script plate was used on the radiator core of 1909 and 1910 cars.

Radiators came in a number of styles, and were supplied by more than one manufacturer (see text). The 1909 and most of the 1910 Ford radiators did not have the heavy support bar across the bottom of the core, as did the later types. The "winged" script appeared on most of the 1909-1910 radiator cores (or core covers) until late 1910, perhaps when Ford began making its own radiators.

Steering wheels were just fourteen and a quarter inches outside diameter and were painted black. Unlike the wooden wheels found in later models, these were made in two halves of steam-bent wood sandwiched together (upper and lower surfaces) rather than the bent circle using one or more sections. The bronze spiders were not painted, nor were the retaining nuts.

The spark and throttle rods were brass-plated steel. Some samples have been seen where the plating extends the entire visible length down to the steering bearing, while others have been plated only on the parts visible above the top of the steering column. All had black hard-rubber knobs.

The steering gear housing and quadrant were also bronze, and not painted. The column itself was body color on most, if not all, cars in 1909 and 1910.

The lower steering bearing had no provision for an oiler in 1909 and 1910 cars.

The starting-crank handle on the first Model Ts used a wooden handle but this was changed early in 1909 to one of hard rubber.

1909-1910

The universal-joint housing was a part of the so-called "two-piece" driveshaft. This housing bolted to the driveshaft instead of being an integral part. Note the transmission dust pan. Engine side dust pans were supplied throughout Model T production but the transmission pans were discontinued during 1911, we believe.

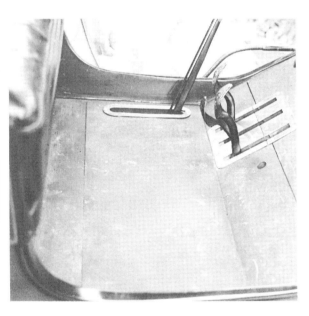

The striping shown here was typical of the style used on the wheels. Being a hand operation, done by more than one person, there was considerable variation from car to car, and even spoke to spoke. Apparently wheels were not striped on all cars. Note the typical valve stem cover, a brass cover over the brass stem. These covers were of varying design, depending on the supplier.

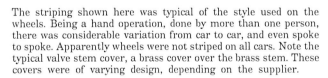

The front floor boards used on the 1909 Runabout, and typical of the touring. The trim plates were brass, or brass-plated steel. The floor mat was an off-white rubber.

1909-1910

68

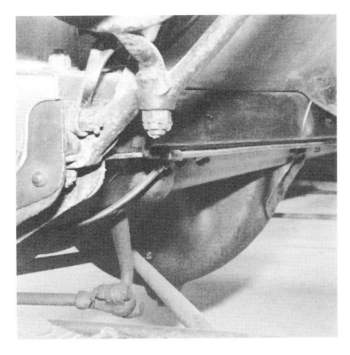

There were variations in the method of securing the windshield support rods at the front of the car. The featured 1909 runabout's support rod fastens to the radiator mounting bolt, along with the loop for the top-support strap. The 1910 touring had the windshield support attached to the front fender bracket rear bolt, and the top strap-loop to the front bolt. Others had the top-strap loop at the radiator mounting bolt with the windshield support rod at the fender iron rear bolt. Apparently the location depended on the brand of windshield used on the car.

A view of the right-front frame rail showing the routing of the gas-lamp hose. The front clamp shown here is a replacement. The hoses were all red rubber.

1909-1910

The chassis design evolved slightly during early production. The very early cars had a riveted-in-place reinforcing plate inside the frame rails (note the rivets in the photo). There were also variations in the shape of the heads on the rivets used to assemble the front and rear cross members to the side rails. Note that on this early car the gasoline tank has separate mounting straps (rather than the riveted-to-the-tank-type used in later models) to hold it in place, with wooden blocks between the tank and the frame rail. This may have been a modification made by some owner but this car (#220) seemed "original" when this picture was taken.

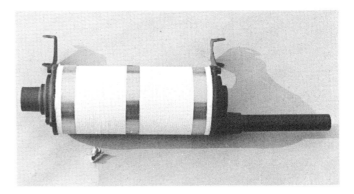

The muffler of the period. In the photo below the outer shell is missing but one can see the the straight, non-tapered extension pipe. The muffler was held to the frame by sheet metal brackets, front and rear. The outer shell was covered with an asbestos wrap which in turn was secured by steel bands of the type used on heating ducts used in buildings.

The rear doors on the Touring had a hook-latch arrangement which held the doors closed in spite of the twisting and bending of the body. A quarter turn of the handle retracted the hook but further turning was needed to retract the sliding bolt.

1910 Canadian-built Ford, similar to but not the same as the U.S. cars. Note the 30 by 3-1/2 tires front and rear, and the right hand drive made for some provinces of Canada and for export to other parts of the British Commonwealth. This photo was supplied by Bob Trevan, from Lismore, NSW, Australia.

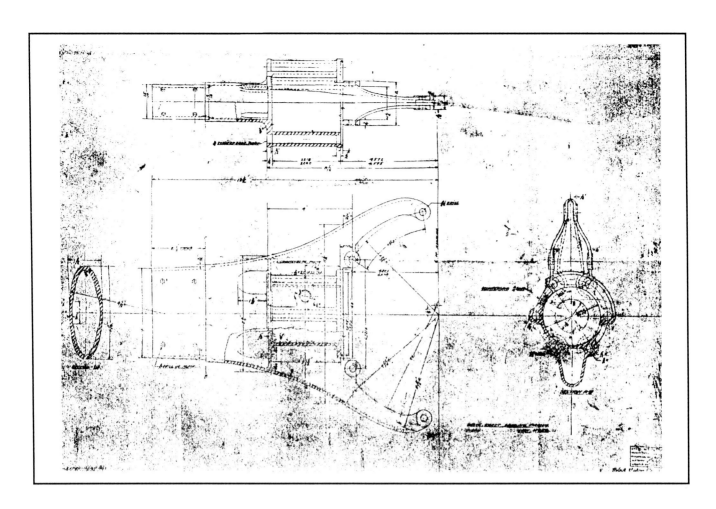

ABOVE: Of passing interest is this copy of a Ford Motor Company blueprint from late 1908. (The original print is of very poor quality.) The device is an assembly to attach to the front of the rear-axle housing which would support a roller pinion bearing. So far as is known it was never used but it indicates that the original babbitt-bearing design was recognized as deficient early in Model T production. A number of modifications were made in the babbitt bearing before the roller bearing was finally adopted in early 1910.

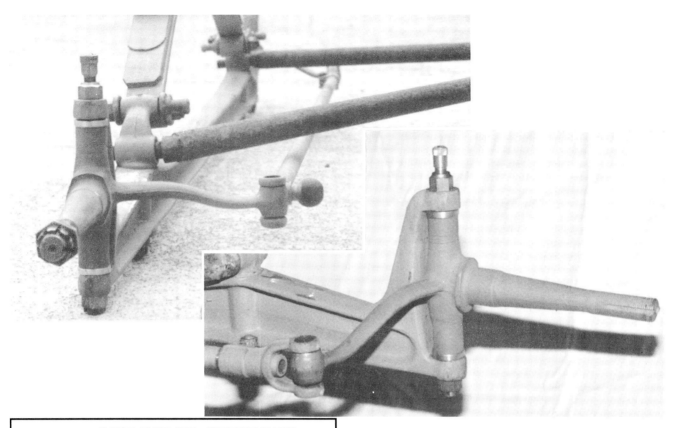

1922 ONE-PIECE SPINDLES

Two types of one-piece spindles were made by Ford, one of which the steering arm bent downwards to allow the tie rod to pass below the radius rods, instead of bending upwards with the tie rod above as in the 1909-1910 cars. The full story is not fully understood but this spindle is listed and pictured in the April 1922 Parts List as part number 2694C (right) and 2695C (left) for use on 1922 cars. The June 1922 Parts List has the illustration but the part number is no longer listed. The usual two-piece spindles (2694B and 2695B) are also shown in these Parts Lists. Apparently this new one-piece spindle proved unsatisfactory and was dropped with little or no production in 1922.

It does not seem likely Ford would have reintroduced a new design at this late date for the replacement of a part used only from 1909 to early 1911, but it is possible. The original one-piece spindles (2702 and 2703) last appeared in the February 1922 Parts List and their factory numbers were 203 and 204. (The numbers given are 203A and 204A but Ford almost always added an "A" to an old factory number when a new design was introduced, as they did here when in 1911 the two-piece spindles came out with factory numbers 203B and 204B.) The factory numbers of these new one-piece spindles were 278D and 279D. The factory numbers for the two-piece spindle and arm assemblies were 278C and 279C (numbers used since 1919) so the number sequence seems to indicate a new design for regular production.

Has anyone seen an original 1922 car with the one-piece spindles?

Typical 1910 Touring

O. E. Houser

The 1909 Ford (right in the photo) is number 8513. O. E. Houser was the dealer in Chillicothe, Ohio, who owned the car when the photo was taken.

The car is now owned by Jim Barnhart, the grandson of the original owner. Jim's father began to restore the car in 1955, and had it together by 1961, but somehow during its life, things got changed; the engine is a 1913, the front wheels are now 30x3-1/2, for example.

The photos on the following pages were supplied, for the most part, by Bill Cassiday of Oakland, California. While not of perfect quality, they do serve to illustrate some of the features of the 1909 and 1910 cars. Other photos are credited where the source is known.

A 1909 or 1910 Tourabout. The rear seat assembly was the same as the front, both seats being the same as on the Runabout. The Tourabout was essentially a Runabout with an added rear seat. Note the Prestolite tank, a common Ford-supplied accessory of the period. The picture was taken at Mt. Pocono, Pennsylvania, in 1912.

An early 1909 Runabout. Note the off-white front floor mat and the curve of the body at the rear deck behind the "mother-in-law" seat. Perhaps not visible in the printed reproduction here, the rear fender irons are of the early type which came up under the aprons, rather than through holes in the apron as in the later 1909 Fords. Some idea of the striping is visible on the body and fender moldings. Note how the body bracket bolt heads appear to also be painted.

A 1909 or early 1910 showing some of the 1910 features such as Jno. Brown lamps. Also a six-rivet rear end shows through the rear wheel (in the original photo). However the front body bracket is still of the two-bolt type. A Kingston coil box with a brass switch is used. The running board has the unbroken ribs, and not a single bit of pinstriping shows anywhere on this car.

1909-1910

A late 1909 or 1910 with E&J lamps. This photo was taken in January 1911 in Campbellsport, Wisconsin.

The Ford in this scene photographed in Missouri in 1910 shows how the script "Ford" was mounted on the radiator core. Note that it is level, not on a bias as we so often see on cars today.

A typical example of the Tourabout but with a later radiator (higher filler neck), perhaps original but likely a replacement. This picture was taken in North Dakota in 1914.

This 1910-style Touring serves as a handy mooring for a rowboat in the Watsonville, California, flood of 1911. This photo was supplied by Bill Austen.

The radiator on this Ford is of the later type, probably made by Ford. Note the reinforcing bar through the bottom of the core, and that the "Ford" script on the core no longer appears, yet the filler neck is still of the low style, typical of the period.

This 1909 Touring is from Augusta, Maine. It has sectioned headlight lenses and these lamps appear to have been modified or changed from the standard 1909-10 lamps unless they might be the "M&E" brand listed on some of the shipping invoices. A narrower than usual filler board is used under the windshield (not as wide as the firewall).

A 1909 or 1910 Touring. Note the snubbing straps between the front crossmember and the axle, a common accessory at the time. This photo was dated July 1911.

1909 Ford Runabout, number 4013, owned by Art Burrichter, Boca Raton, Florida. Note the wooden windshield. Factory invoices show a few Troy wood windshields; this might be one of them, or a later addition. This photo was taken when the car was first acquired, and shows evidence of some modification (wheels, lamps) but note the similarity in painting with the other Runabouts pictured in this coverage.

Art Burrichter's 1909 Runabout after restoration.

1911

Body Type	Factory Price #	Shipping Weight Lbs.	Production Total *	
Touring	$780	1200	26405	
Tourabout	725	—	0	
Runabout	680	—	7845	***
Torpedo R'bt.	725	—		***
Open R'bt.	680	—		***
Town Car	960 ##	—	315	
7P Landaulet	1100 ##	—	0	
Coupe	840 ##	—	45	
Chassis —	940		248	**
Total			34858	

Note: 1200 pounds was the figure given for the Touring car "with others in proportion." The bare chassis weighed about 900 pounds.

\# Prices effective October 1, 1910. Open cars supplied with gas lamps, horn, windshield and top as standard but could be had without this equipment (as in 1910) for $80 less, early in 1911. By about April 1911 the open cars were sold "fully equipped" only.

\## Prices for cars without headlamps! In the January 1911 issue of Ford Times, the Town Cars were shown "fully equipped" at $1200, and the Coupe fully equipped at $1050.

* Fiscal year, October 1, 1910 to September 30, 1911. Ford News, Nov. 1, 1920, gives a figure of 24,528.

** Chassis not shown in catalogs.

*** Runabouts not broken down by types in production figures.

MODEL YEAR DATES: November 1910 through December 1911 approx.

MAJOR MODEL YEAR FEATURES
See component listings for details.

BODY TYPES. Touring, Runabout, Torpedo Runabout, Open Runabout, Town Car.
Note: The Tourabout, Coupe and Landaulet were "1910" models built in late 1910 but a part of Fiscal 1911 production figures. Bodies supplied by several manufacturers. Metal panels over wood frame. Newly-styled Touring cars with more integrated appearance. Torpedo and Open Runabouts all new with different fenders, running boards, hood, etc. Landaulet was listed in catalog but none were built.

COLORS. All cars were painted a very dark, all-but-black, blue. Black is reported as an available color but Ford records do not indicate black as a standard color. A few red Open Runabouts and green Town Cars were built in April 1911. It was possible that there were green early 1911 models; the date of the body change is unknown but both "blue" and "green" cars were built in later 1910 (after the 1910 fiscal year ended). Fenders and aprons were painted body color, although either blue or black might have been used, based on surviving samples. However, records indicate only blue. Striping of fenders and running gear began to be phased out about July on many cars.

UPHOLSTERY. Full leather in the open cars, in a diamond-tufted pattern. Closed cars were also leather, with imitation leather trim on the door panels. The front seats in the Town Car were leather.

FENDERS. Front: redesigned with top section that flared inward and the splash apron area was now a triangular insert. No embossed bead on the apron, or across the wide part of the front fender. Has front bill. **Rear:** similar in style to the front. Support irons were now attached to the body framing, extending out the side of the body, through a hole in the apron of the fender, and were clamped to a single plate under the fender.

SPLASH APRON. Longer than the 1909-10 style, with bulge at the rear to clear the brake and radius rods.

RUNNING BOARDS. Pressed steel with embossed-diamond pattern. The Ford script ran parallel to the board, with no "Made in USA."

HOOD. Aluminum, with no louvers. Hinges separate from the panels, and riveted in place. Hold-down clamps had one "ear" and were of forged steel. The steel hood former no longer had the "notch" on either side.

DASHBOARD (Firewall). Wood, with brass edge trim which now overlapped the wood. Added extension piece of wood used between the top of the dashboard and the windshield.

CHASSIS. Rear body support was now a separate forging bolted to the rear of the frame. Painted body color or black, depending on who you believe (no records indicate the color but black is the preferred choice).

STEERING COLUMN ASSEMBLY. Brass quadrant, brass-plated spark and throttle levers, with hard-rubber knobs. Gear case was bronze, riveted assembly. Wheel was 15" diameter, wood, and painted black. The wheel spider was bronze, either bare or painted black. Column was now 56" long on the standard cars, but 60" on the Torpedo and Open Runabouts, and 51" on the Town Cars. The column was painted body color.

FRONT AXLE. "One-piece" spindles. Tie rod ran above the radius rod, had an integral yoke/ball fitting on right end, and adjustable yoke, with the locking bolt in a horizontal plane (parallel to the road). Drag link threaded 20 t.p.i. at the column end. No oilers on most fittings. Radius rod fastened to the engine pan with cap screws. Early in calendar 1911 the "two-piece" spindles appeared, with a new front axle. The steering tie rod now ran below the wish bone. The drag link now had 13 t.p.i. threads. The new axle had brass oilers at all connections.

REAR AXLE. "Six-rivet" style, like those used in later 1910. Reinforcing rings around the center flanges gave this final type a thicker flange area. Non-tapered axles discontinued in favor of the tapered type early in the year. In July 1911, the "1912" rear axle began to replace the older style. This "12-rivet" housing had a cast center section and is commonly called the "clamshell" rear axle.

DRIVESHAFT HOUSING. Pinion bearing spool was a casting and was held by studs and nuts, the studs being enclosed (not visible) in the housing. Separate front housing for universal-joint assembly.

REAR RADIUS AND BRAKE RODS. Had forged ends. Brake-rod support brackets now folded down along the side of the clamp, then out and wrap up around the brake rods.

WHEELS. Used 30 by 3 tires in front; 30 by 3-1/2 in the rear. Original tires were an off-white color, with no tread. Hub flanges were six inches in diameter, for either the tapered or non-tapered axles. Front wheels used ball bearings. Hub caps had "Ford" in script letters but no "Made in USA." Spokes were somewhat thicker than those of the earlier cars. The rear hub used with the tapered axles was shorter and no longer looked like the front hubs.

SPRINGS. Tapered-leaf, front and rear. "Mac West" style shackles.

1911 (Continued)

RADIATOR. Manufactured by Ford with the standard Ford script, but no "Made in USA." The brass "Ford" on the radiator core was discontinued. Cast filler neck was higher than 1909-10 type.

ENGINE. Open-valve type. Early in the year the block was redesigned to have enclosed valve chambers. The crankshaft main bearings now had babbitt in the block casting.

ENGINE PAN. One-piece type (no inspection door), but wider than the previous types, to accommodate a new, larger magneto. Early in the year (late March) a new pan was introduced which now had a "three-dip" inspection door.

OIL FILLER CAP. The mushroom-shaped cap, of brass, with six flutes and the Ford script, appeared on all models.

ENGINE CRANK. Rubber handle discontinued, and now had an aluminum-formed handle. The crank and handle were painted black.

FAN. Driven by a leather belt from a pulley at the front of the engine. The fan hub was brass (bronze), with the blades riveted in place. The fan blades were not as deeply embossed as the 1909-10 type. Adjustment was by means of a spring between the fan arm and the engine front plate. Later the spring was replaced with a screw and nut in the same location, allowing a fixed adjustment.

FUEL TANK. Cylindrical, under the front seat. Mounting brackets riveted to the tank. Outlet was at the center, above the drive shaft, and screwed into place.

MANIFOLDS. Exhaust was cast iron; pipe fits inside the threaded end and was packed with asbestos and held with a brass nut. Intake was still aluminum but the "dogleg" style was dropped in favor of a straighter design.

CARBURETORS. Kingston "five ball," or Holley. All used a choke and a heating arrangement at the air intake.

CARBURETOR STOVE ASSEMBLY. Generally a tube which ran upwards to the front of the exhaust manifold, and connected to a cast "stove" fitting against the manifold.

MUFFLER. Cast-iron ends, mounted with pressed-metal brackets. Longer, curved rear exhaust pipe extension integral with the rear cover plate. Wrapped with asbestos, secured with three steel straps.

COIL BOX ASSEMBLY. Kingston, Jacobson-Brandow, or Heinze.

TRANSMISSION. Three-pedal standard design. The brake lever operated the clutch as well as the rear brakes. Pedals were marked with "C," "R," and "B." Transmission cover was cast aluminum, and wider than the 1910 cover. The inspection door was held with four screws. Later, a new aluminum cover appeared which used the tapered inspection door, held with six screws. The door on this new cover was embossed with the Ford script.

LAMPS. All lamps were now standard except on the closed cars. Made by Edmond and Jones (E&J) or Jno. Brown.

HORN. Bulb type, double-twist, all-brass. Standard equipment on all cars.

WINDSHIELD. Standard equipment, were either Rands, Mezger (Automatic), or Vanguard. Made of brass.

TOP. (Open cars). Top color was black on all open cars. Oval top sockets now attached to body brackets. Sockets were no longer curved at the bottom. Front support was by means of straps which ran forward to a bracket near the headlights.

SPEEDOMETER. Stewart Model 26.

1911 Touring, owned, at the time this photo was taken, by Gary Hoonsbeen, Minneapolis, Minnesota. This is car (engine) number 64,627 and it has a Pontiac body, number B13974. According to Ford Archives records, this car was assembled August 17, 1911. It features Brown No. 19 headlights, Brown No. 85 side lights and a Brown No. 75 tail light. The Prestolite tank may have been original; Ford records indicate these were sometimes installed at the factory. This car also has the "1912" 12-rivet rear axle.

The Model T Ford Cars for 1911

The "1911" model year is believed to have begun in late October 1910. Existing Ford Factory Shipping records show that, other than for a number of special order cars supplied in a number of colors for various customers, all "1910" Fords were "green." These records also show that beginning about October 25, "blue" Runabouts began to be built along with green Tourings, and about November 19 "blue" Tourings joined the green, both colors being built for a short time.

On October 26, these Ford records show a blue runabout with doors, built with a "sample body" on a chassis which had been assembled October 5. This was, no doubt, the first Torpedo Runabout. A mix of green and blue Tourings continued until early December, then all cars were blue. We presume the blue cars were the 1911 models.

Of course, we don't know if the Touring bodies on the blue cars were "1911" style and the green cars were "1910." Serial numbers in this era were in the 33,000 to 34,500 range and it would be interesting to know if there were blue 1910's and/or green 1911's. In any event, it is believed that the 1911 style year began with the introduction of blue as the standard color.

By 1911 the Model T Ford had become a major success. Ford had orders on the books for every car it could produce but could not build enough cars to keep pace with the increasing orders. Supplying the needs of its market was not a new problem for the Ford Motor Company, however. Sales of the N-R-S models had been much higher than anticipated, and the new Model T was selling at an even greater rate.

Ford had begun construction of its new Highland Park plant in 1909 — the third assembly plant for a company which was just six years old at the time — in anticipation of the growing demand for its products. On January 1, 1910, the company began to move to the still-under-construction Highland Park plant but the move was a gradual one, and major production continued at the Piquette Avenue plant until late 1911.

FORD MODEL T COUPE
$1050
With equipment of 3 oil lamps, horn, and tools only

FORD MODEL T TOWN CAR
$1200
With equipment of 3 oil lamps, horn, and tools only

FORD MODEL T TORPEDO RUNABOUT
Fully Equipped, $725
Unequipped, $645
(Note the "square" fuel tank)

FORD MODEL T ROADSTER
Fully Equipped, $680
Unequipped, $600

FORD MODEL T OPEN RUNABOUT
Fully Equipped, $680
Unequipped, $600

The 1911 Ford line (except for the Touring, which was the same as the Touring shown on the next page) in early 1911. Note that the most expensive cars, the Coupe and the Town Car, did not have gas headlights as standard equipment, or was the speedometer standard. Just forty-five Coupes were made in 1911, and only 315 Town Cars. Interestingly, Town Cars built in the early part of 1911 (at least until April) were painted green. Perhaps these were 1910 bodies that had not been sold. The color of the Coupe is not known but these might have also been green. (We have not found the records which show any Coupes.)

Note, too, that the gas tank on the Torpedo and Open Runabouts is rectangular in shape. Later in the year this tank was replaced with the more common round style. These cars were supplied in blue except for a number of Open Runabouts built in April 1911 which were painted RED!

The picture of the standard Runabout, Coupe, and Town Car are identical to those shown in the 1910 catalog. Little is known about the Coupe and Town Cars, but the standard Runabout in 1911 used the same fenders as the Touring, NOT the 1910 style shown in these catalog illustrations.

5 PASSENGER TOURING CAR
Fully Equipped, $780
Unequipped, $700
(Not sold unequipped after early 1911)

3 PASSENGER ROADSTER
Fully Equipped, $680

6 PASSENGER TOWN CAR
Equipped with 3 oil lamps, tubular horn,
and kit of tools, $960

2 PASSENGER OPEN RUNABOUT
Fully Equipped, $680

2 PASSENGER TORPEDO RUNABOUT
Fully Equipped, $725

2 PASSENGER COUPE
Equipped with 3 oil lamps, tubular horn,
and kit of tools, $840

"Fully Equipped" meant the top, windshield, speedometer, gas lamps, horn, and a kit of tools. "Unequipped" cars came with the oil lamps, horn, and tools only.

Later 1911 Torpedo Runabout, owned by John Mitchell of Irving, Texas. Note that the gasoline tank is now round, replacing the rectangular tank used in the earliest models. The "Ford" script on the radiator should be horizontal rather than on the angle as it is here. This script was discontinued in 1911.

The Highland Park plant was one of the first, if not the first, ever designed exclusively for the manufacture of automobiles. The plant was designed around the machines, instead of the usual method of adapting the machines to the building. Ford's "moving assembly lines" had yet to be developed but the need for the machines to be located where the work was performed had become recognized. Up until this time the usual practice was to have all lathes, for example, in "the lathe department," Ford's new layout was to have the lathe located convenient to the flow of the work in which the lathe was needed.

A major signal for a "full speed ahead" was the final settlement of the Seldon Patent suit, after years of litigation, on January 9, 1911. Had this suit been lost, Ford could have been forced out of business, or at least saddled with tremendous fines and assessments, which would have severely crippled its ability to expand. The court's decision in Ford's favor signaled the beginning of a new era for the entire automobile industry.

On June 22, 1911, Ford purchased the John R. Keim Mills in Buffalo, New York. Keim was the supplier of the large, metal pressings such as the crankcase and rear axle housings for the Ford car. To no small extent, it was Keim that made the Model T possible. These large, metal pressings were major factors in enabling Ford to sell his car at such a low price. Along with the purchase of the company came many of Keim's top men, including William S. Knudsen, John R. Lee, and William H. Smith. The major machinery at the Keim plant was shipped to Highland Park, and the Keim plant was converted for use as the Ford Buffalo assembly plant.

The "1911" Fords are of considerable interest

because of the many major changes in the design of the Model T that were made during the year. Excluding the frame, almost every component of the car was either modified or changed completely. These changes included the engine, transmission cover, engine pan, front and rear axles and the wheels. To say nothing of the bodies themselves.

Using the Touring Car as the typical example, the 1911 style body consisted of metal panels which were attached to a wooden framework, replacing the all-wood construction used in 1910. Much of the body was still wood, such as the lower side panels, the door frames, etc., but the major portions were now metal-skinned — a considerable improvement, not only in durability but also in the reduction of the cost. The new body had the square-shaped doors, the open front compartment, and the "step" (or inset) in the side panels under the seat areas. The body lines were continuous and less abrupt than the 1909-1910 styling. This design continued until early 1912 when it was superseded with the 1912 style which featured a more integrated rear door design and smooth (no-step) side panels, and an enclosed front compartment made possible by the use of removable front "doors." The tool compartment door on the rear seat kick panel, seen on the 1909 and 1910 Tourings, continued on at least some bodies (Hayes, it is believed) until about July.

The Runabout (roadster) was similar to the 1910 in style but did not use the same body as the earlier cars. The Coupe and Town Car bodies had but minor changes, if any. The Coupe had never been a popular model, selling just 187 in 1910, and was phased out in 1911 with a production of just forty-five units. Production of the Town Car was not much better, with just 315 being produced. The Tourabout and Landaulet were discontinued, none being built in fiscal year 1911 (October 1, 1910 to September 30, 1911) according to existing production records.

New for the 1911 model year, and introduced in late 1910, were the Open Runabout and the Torpedo Runabout. Very few were actually assembled in calendar 1910 but for some reason a good number of those built in January and February 1911 used chassis which were assembled in October 1910. These were similar cars, differing mainly in that the Torpedo had an enclosed passenger compartment with doors while the Open Runabout did not. Interestingly, while these models are considered very desirable today, they did not prove too popular then, due to the difficulty in entering and exiting them, and the less comfortable seating position. The design was dropped late in the year in favor of a Torpedo based on the standard Runabout but with doors added. These new models were called "1912."

The 1911 Open Runabout and the Torpedo Runabout were probably the most "racy" Model T Fords ever produced. The seats were moved rearward and lowered by moving the gasoline tank to the rear deck. The hood was made longer by about two inches, and the bottom section of the

Right side of Gary Hoonsbeen's original 1911. The "step" in the side panel under the front seat is quite clear. This style body is typical of all 1911 and 1912 cars built during calendar 1911 and early 1912, although there are many minor variations between individual bodies. Bodies were built by various manufacturers and all were not identical in every detail.

The outward appearance of the 1911-style Ford was almost all new. Aside from the new bodies, the fenders and running boards were a noticeable departure from the previous design. The running boards were now pressed with the familiar diamond pattern (instead of the pressed-in "dashes" of the 1910 type), but with the "Ford" running parallel with the board. The "Made in USA" did not appear on 1911 boards but was added in 1912 before the change to the "1913" style with the "Ford" running crosswise. The splash aprons now extended a bit further to the rear, meeting with the rear fenders. The apron had a noticeable "bulge" at the rear to clear the brake rods. The rear fenders were now wider and flared to match the body lines.

The typical hub caps had the "Ford" script instead of the block letters of 1910, and had no "rim" or circle around the name as did the later caps. Apparently there were a number of suppliers of the hub caps; a number of minor differences in the design of the script have been observed.

windshield sloped back, all of which gave the car a longer and lower appearance. Adding to the style were the lower body, longer and curved front and rear fenders, the shorter running boards, and the lower and longer steering column.

The top support irons on the open cars were now an integral part of the body, rather than being the "add on" frame rail used in 1909-10. The tops on the open cars were still held with the straps which attached to the front of the car at the headlights. During the year, though, the separate eyelet used to accept the top strap hook was dropped in favor of a loop-hole integral with the headlamp fork.

Tops, side curtains, lamps and speedometer were standard equipment on all open cars (as they had been in 1910). Strangely, lamps were not standard on the more expensive closed cars. (Lamps may have become standard on the closed cars, but the 1911 catalogs show them as options.)

Fenders were also redesigned for 1911. While

they followed the same general style as the 1910 cars, they were now of a less complicated design, one which set the general design pattern for all future Model T's. The rear fenders, now nearly mating with the body, fastened to the body with short support irons instead of the complicated and flimsy "butterfly" style used earlier. These new fenders were wider and longer, and had a more "finished" appearance.

New, too, were the running boards. Now with the familiar diamond pattern, they set the pattern for the next fifteen years. The 1911 (and 1912) boards differed from the later ones, though, in that the "Ford" ran lengthwise instead of across the board. (The "Made in USA" was added during 1912.) Interestingly, shipping invoices during June 1911 show the use of "1910 runningboards." It would appear that some old stock was found somewhere, and there was no sense in wasting it.

The splash aprons were longer, greatly reducing

the open look at the rear, and giving the car a more finished appearance. They featured a noticeable bulge at the rear, necessary to clear the brake rods.

Headlights were all brass and were either Brown model 19 or Edmond & Jones (marked "Made by E&J, Detroit, Mich."). The E&J were the model 666, although the older 466 also seemed to have been used in early 1911. Sidelamps were Brown 85 or E&J. The tail lamps were Brown 75 or 78, or E&J. E&J side and tail lamps were marked "Pat. 1908."

Initial 1911 running gear was the same as the later 1910 cars. The rear axle was the six-rivet "1911" type (with the reinforcements around the center flange bolt holes), introduced in October 1910, and continued the use of the non-tapered axles. Wheel hub flanges were increased to six inches diameter, and the wheels themselves were of heavier construction. Tapered-end axles were introduced during 1911, and the entire assembly was changed beginning in July to the "1912 axle."

It is possible that the tapered axle first appeared in the 6-rivet rear end. Internally, the differential spider was modified to have larger arms (5/8" instead of 9/16"), which required new differential gears with 5/8" holes (with bronze bushings) and a new differential carrier. The pinion bearing spool was also changed and now used 13/32" studs instead of the 3/8" used in 1910. The dates of these changes are not known but they may have been at the time of the change to the "1912" axle in July 1911.

The "1912" axle differed from the "1911" in that it had a cast iron center section with the steel axle tubes flared and riveted to the center casting with twelve rivets. The design was thinner than the later types, and is commonly called the "twelve-rivet clamshell" rear axle. Perhaps an improvement, it too had severe flaws and was replaced with the "1913" (1913-1914) type in late 1912 after little over a year in production.

The front axle was redesigned and now used "two-piece" spindles (separate steering arm instead of the one piece forging) beginning in January 1911. This change began at about car number 36,972 on January 31, but did not appear on all cars at once. About August the right hand spindle arm was redesigned to now include a hole for the speedometer swivel assembly.

Many changes were made to the engine and transmission assembly. Initially, the 1910 style continued unchanged. Beginning in February 1911 a "new transmission cover" began to be used, along with a "1911 wide pan." The new cover still had the "square door" but it and the pan were somewhat wider than the earlier type to allow room for a redesigned flywheel magneto. The engine pan was again redesigned and during March the pan with the "removable bottom" (or inspection door) began to be used. Then about June the transmission cover was redesigned again and now had the tapered

inspection hole. The inspection hole cover was heavy pressed steel and was embossed "Ford" in script.

The engine itself started out the same as the 1910 type. In January 1911 the main bearings in the block were given babbitt linings. (1909-10 engines had no babbitt in the block; the crank ran against the cast iron.) Beginning about April, the cylinder casting was also altered to accept metal covers over the valve chambers. In April the first "1911 engine throughout" appeared on the shipping invoices. We presume these were the closed-valve type with the latest inspection-door pan (but with the square-hole transmission cover). Engines of old and new types (open and closed valve) continued until sometime in June, after which time all apparently were "all 1911" engines.

PAINT COLORS FOR 1911

A wise man might respond "no comment" if asked about the colors used on 1911 Fords. Ford specified "blue" on all production other than a few special cars built for special people. Yet black and green "1911" cars are around which appear to be original. Some seemingly original cars seen today have all black bodies (including fenders, etc.) and some have black bodies with blue fenders. Ford's records list no black cars at all, and no green cars built after December 1910, except for a few Open Runabouts and Town Cars built during April 1911.

Most 1911 cars were painted blue according to factory records. This blue was extremely dark, appearing almost black. It is possible this blue oxidized to black, or that the blue was a final coat over black undercoats, and the blue vanished in time. While the shipping invoices of the period did specify "blue" they don't say if the body was blue or the fenders were blue. The situation could have been similar to that in 1926 when Fords came in green and maroon but all had black fenders and running boards. Maybe the fenders were blue and the bodies were black on 1911 Fords. In any event, *according to the Ford records*, all 1911 Fords were "blue," in spite of the appearance of "black" or "green" cars that have survived.

The only exceptions noted in the records were a number of RED Open Runabouts (not Torpedo Runabouts) and GREEN Town Cars, built in early April, 1911. These colors were in addition to the standard blue Open Runabouts and Town Cars built during the same month.

Some striping of the body, fenders and running gear continued until about August. At that time the striping of the fenders, and front and rear axles was discontinued. Body striping continued through most of 1911 and 1912 but apparently not on all cars. All striping was done in French gray. Being a hand operation, by different painters, there are many variations is the style and placement of the striping. In general, the body was striped inside the body moldings, not on them.

The rear fenders now were wider and matched the lines of the body, reducing the large gap seen on the 1909-1910 models. In addition, the fender support iron was now a short rod, fastened to the body instead of the flimsy "butterfly" affair used earlier.

Early 1911 production continued the use of the non-tapered rear axles. Hub flanges on all models were increased to six-inches diameter (from five and one-half inches) but the rear hubs themselves looked similar to the 1910 when the non-tapered axle was used. During the year the tapered axle appeared and the rear hub was redesigned to match. (It is possible the tapered axle and the six-inch hubs appeared in late 1910 on some production. The factory shipping invoices note "1911 axle" on some cars but it is not known if this referred to the axle shafts, the heavier housings, or what.)

The wheels continued in the 1910 pattern, except for the six inch hub flanges and somewhat larger spokes. None of the tires had a tread pattern. It would be several years before Ford supplied tires with treads.

The front fenders, too, were changed. The top section was now wider, flared to match the splash apron, and had a triangular insert which mated with the hood clash strip. Note that there was no bead across the widest part, a change made during 1913. Ford's catalog illustrations do not show the bill on the front fenders but most, if not all, Fords had the bill after early 1909, and continued its use until 1913. 1913 Fords did not have the bill but in 1914 it was reinstated and used until the change to the "black era" in mid-1916.

An early-in-the-year 1911 Touring owned by Dave Lau of Portland, Oregon. The color of this car is a light blue, which is not correct, but shows the typical striping which appeared on some of the 1911 cars. This car has E&J lamps all around: headlamps are Model 666, side lamps and tail lamps are all "Pat Dec. 9, 1908."

The body of this car is by Pontiac Body Co., of Pontiac, Michigan. The coil box is Heinze and the speedometer is Stewart Model 26. The bottom right photo shows the forged "eye" for the top support strap hook, used in early production 1911's.

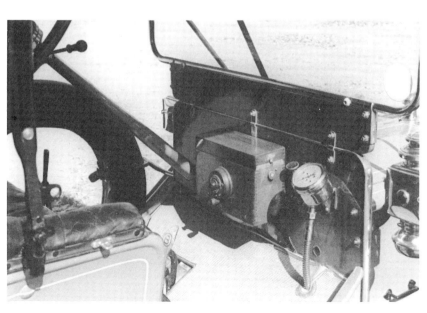

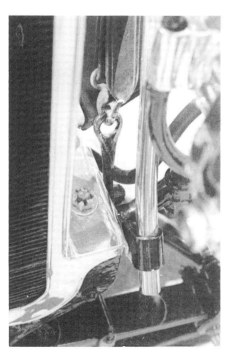

1911

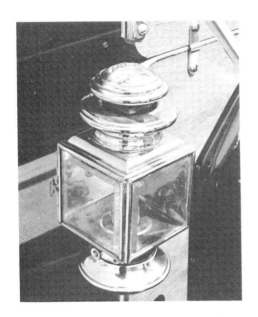

The lamps shown here are from a late 1911. Headlamps are Brown Model 19, side lamps are Brown Model 85, and the tail lamp is Brown Model 75. 1911 Fords used two Jno. Brown tail lights, the Model 75 and the Model 78. They were similar except that the 78 had a round clear lens on the side (like the rear red one) while the 75 had a rectangular clear lens and a round red one. The Model 78, shown below, is believed to be the most common.

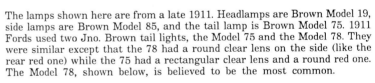

Dave Lau's 1911, shown here, uses all Edmond and Jones lamps. The headlamps are Model 666. Side and tail lamps are marked "E&J Pat. Dec. 9, 1908."

NOTE: The spare tires and tool box are not standard equipment. The "Ford" script attached to the radiator core is believed to have been discontinued in 1910. When used, it appears as shown: horizontal, not on a slant as is often seen.

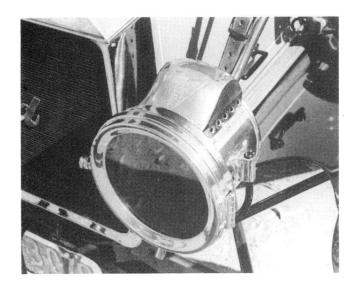

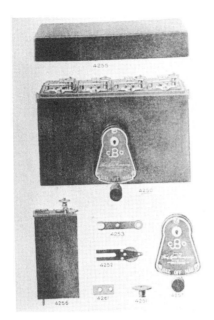

Jacobson-Brandow coil and parts

Heinze Model T Ford Coil

"The Heinze coil gives added efficiency with greater speed to Model T cars and ignition troubles are unknown" say owners who have had experience with other makes of coils on this model.

We are offering an attractive proposition to Model T owners who are not satisfied with their present ignition equipment. This proposition is being accepted all over the country. Write and we will tell you what it is.

HEINZE ELECTRIC COMPANY
Lowell, Massachusetts

Kingston coil box

Heinze coil box

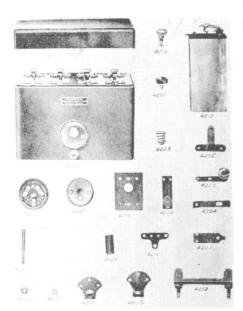

Three brands of coils were used during 1911 production: Jacobson-Brandow, Heinze, and Kingston (two styles). Note the name "Jacobson-Brandow. Ford's parts books show the name as Jacobson-Brandon but the name on the coil is spelled with a "w."

Master vibrators, mounted on the dash, were an accessory and were not installed at the factory — at least according to our research.

Kingston coil box and parts
1910-1911

Kingston coil box and parts
1911-1912

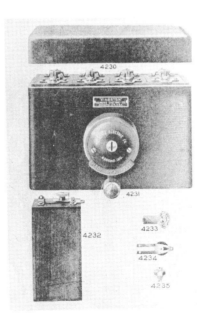

All cars which were sold "equipped," had a speedometer as a part of the standard equipment. Very early 1911 cars used either the Stewart Model 24 or Model 26, but only the Model 26 was used after early January 1911.

The double-twist horn is similar to the 1909-10 types but now has its hose fitting at an angle to better accommodate the body lines and hose routing.

Lower right: Kingston coil unit as used in the later Kingston coil box.

An accessory K-W Master Vibrator can be seen in the photo below. These were accessories, and were never installed at the factory so far as we have been able to determine.

Later 1911 and 1912 front axle assembly. The early 1911's continued the one-piece spindles of the 1910 cars but in January the two-piece design superseded them, a change which also required a new axle with larger forks to allow clearance. Early production of this new design used plain steering arms, but in August a hole was provided in the right arm for the speedometer swivel gears.

The steering "drag link" had the ball socket threaded on. The threads were 1/2" by 13 tpi beginning in early 1911. The earlier models were threaded 1/2" by 20 tpi. This new link was used until about 1913.

Not shown: the radius rods were connected to the engine pan with two bolts instead of the stud, spring, and nut arrangement (which appeared about 1913). Also, the ball caps were metal pressings during this period. The change to the castings (or forgings) is believed to have been in later 1911.

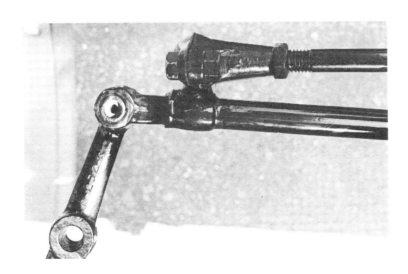

The radiator on the typical 1911 Ford was a bit different from the 1909 and 1910 in that the filler neck is higher and the "Ford" script no longer had the "wings." The filler neck was a machined casting, soldered in place. These changes were probably made during 1910 when Ford began to make all its own radiators (they were made by a number of suppliers earlier) but were typical of the 1911. Note the lack of the "Made in USA," an addition first made during later 1912. Note, too, that there were no holes in the side panels for the headlamp gas hoses, additions also made during 1912.

The method of attaching the front top straps varied during the production year. The earlier cars used a forged bracket which was held by the fender iron bolts, to which the hook of the strap attached. Later an "eye" was forged into the fender iron, as is shown at the left. The actual dates of these changes are not known.

1911

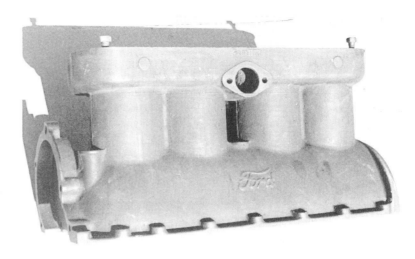

An early 1911 open-valve block. The block at the right is number 49289, cast 2-18-11, and went into a Touring Car on April 24. The block shown below is 46263, cast 2-21-11, which went into another Touring Car on April 6. The casting dates are just above the water inlet. The serial numbers are on a boss just to the rear of the timing gear cover on the right side.

These are the so-called "open-valve" engines. Note the removable valve and push-rod guides. The "closed-valve" engines apparently began to be produced about March and the first, 46326, went into a car on April 7. The removable guides were not used on the engines with the enclosed valve chamber.

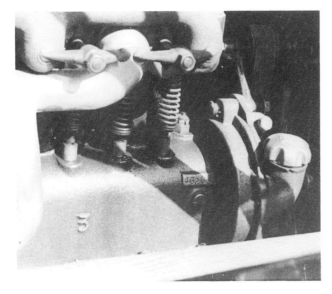

The timing gear cover shown here is not correct. The fan belt tension screw was on the left side in 1911, after the tension spring system was discontinued.

The Present Day Model T Motor

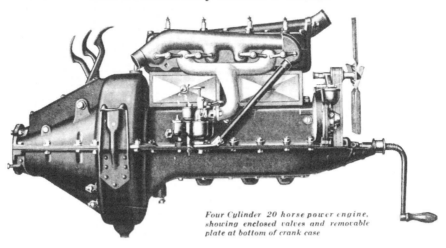

Four Cylinder 20 horse power engine, showing enclosed valves and removable plate at bottom of crank case

The new "1911" engine with the enclosed valve chambers. The cover doors were made of rather heavy metal, embossed with the "X" pattern. The catalog picture above shows the doors in a lighter color, probably to call them to the viewer's attention. The story persists that originally these doors were painted with aluminum paint, but the author has yet to see such on an original car, or has he found anyone with an original car who will substantiate the claim. The only evidence we have found indicates they were not painted at all, or perhaps were painted black. The serial number continued to be located on the right side of the engine until sometime in 1912.

The exhaust manifold on all Model T Fords until 1913 was constructed so that the exhaust pipe fit into it and was sealed with an asbestos packing held in place with the retaining nut.

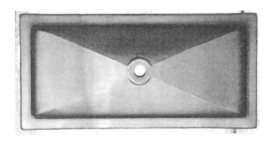

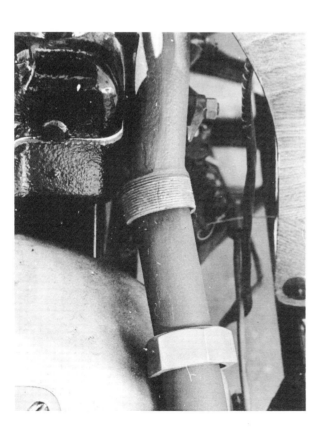

1909 to early 1911 timing gear cover

ABOVE: Typical 1909-1911 timing gear cover. Note the boss at the upper right on which the fan belt tension spring rested. During 1911 this boss was tapped to accept a screw and lock nut which replaced the spring. The "knob" on the fan bracket, which originally kept the spring in place, now rested on the head of the adjusting screw.

Above top: Typical 1909 to 19?? (date unknown) fan bracket. Note the knob at the outer end which either held the tension spring in place, or which rested on the adjusting screw head. This fan bracket arm was used for some time, for the "knob" continued as a part of the arm's design long after the need for it was eliminated. Eventually, the knob was eliminated and the arm shown in the lower picture was used until the 1917 models.

Later 1911 cover with the tapped hole for the fan belt adjusting screw.

Typical 1909 to early 1911 spring loaded fan.

The 1909 to 1911 timing gear cover differed from the later types, too, in that it was designed to accommodate the "two-piece" timer. This early timer was dropped in late 1911 or 1912 and replaced with the one with an integral oil spout, which in turn was quickly superseded with a timer of the "standard" design (which apparently came in more variations than any other part of the Model T).

The fan belt tension arrangement used from 1909 to 1911. Note the spring between the fan arm and the timing gear cover. During 1911 this spring was discontinued and the timing gear cover was given an adjusting screw, with lock nut, and the head of this screw formed the stop for the fan arm, allowing adjustment of the fan belt tension. This arrangement continued through 1911 or early 1912 when the more familiar method, in which the adjusting screw mated with the boss at the lower (pivot) end of the arm, appeared. This later adjustment method continued until the 1926 models.

Above: The timer (commutator) used in the 1909 to 1911 production is quite different from that used in the 1912 and later cars. The timer case was held in place by the rotor; the case cover was then secured to the case with two thumb nuts. The pictures show the front and rear views of this timer.

Two carburetors (perhaps more) were used in 1911. One was the Kingston "Five Ball" which continued from 1910, and the other was the Holley 4500 shown below.

Note the cylindrical housing above the fuel inlet (which contains an air valve). This is the distinguishing feature of the 1911 Holley.

The Kingston "Six Ball" carburetor appeared sometime in late 1911 on some production but is not shown in the parts books. The "1912" Holley H-1 may also have appeared during 1911.

1909-1911 Kingston Five Ball

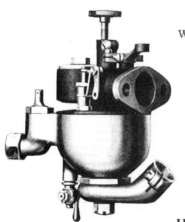

1911 Model T Holley Carburetor

We guarantee this carburetor:

Not to leak.

To start motor on second turn of the crank during the coldest weather.

To enable any owner of a Ford Model T to drive at least 25 miles on a gallon of gasoline.

To give entire satisfaction in every respect.

PRICE $9.00

Holley Brothers Company
Detroit, Mich.

1911 Holley 4500

99   1911

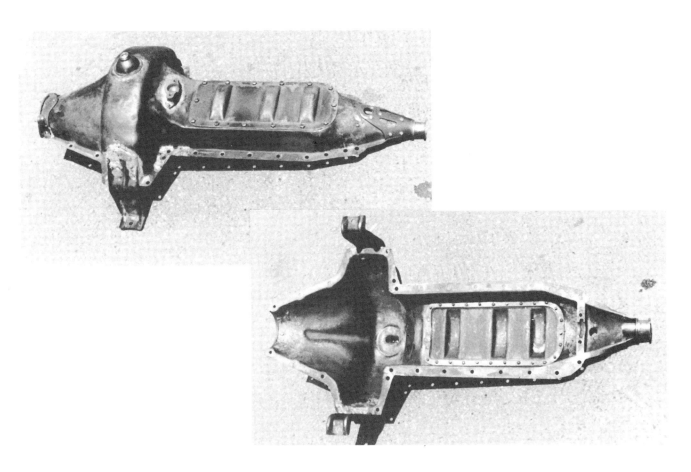

The 1911 pan with the removable inspection plate, used beginning about March 1911. Note how the one-piece bolt ring was riveted in place. The rivets were eliminated early in production but the bolt ring remained a single piece until about 1913.

The pan inspection cover was somewhat heavier than the later type, with deeper and sharper embossed areas. The removable one-piece bolt ring is shown here.

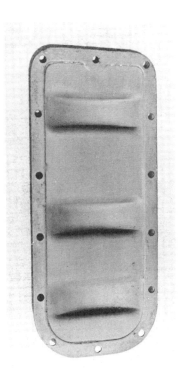

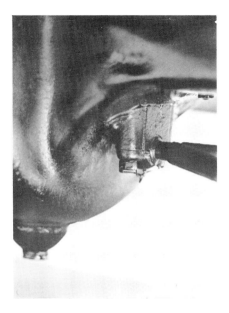

Typical 1910-1911 transmission cover. The late 1910 and 1911 covers were wider than the 1909-10 types (which otherwise looked alike).

The front radius rod was clamped to the crankcase housing with two screws instead of the stud, nut and spring arrangement used beginning sometime in 1913. The two screws were wired together to prevent them from loosening. The oil drain plug was still a slotted screw.

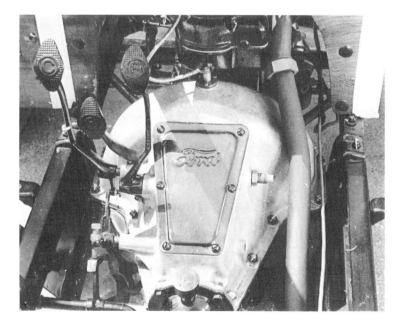

The new transmission cover with the tapered hole. The cover plate was of heavy pressed steel and was embossed with the Ford Script. The larger hole allowed adjustment of the clutch operating "fingers" which could not be done with the square-hole cover. Early 1909 cars did not have adjustments on the clutch fingers, so the larger hole was not really necessary at first, but it took Ford some time to make it easier for the mechanic.

Typical magneto post used during the early years.

1911

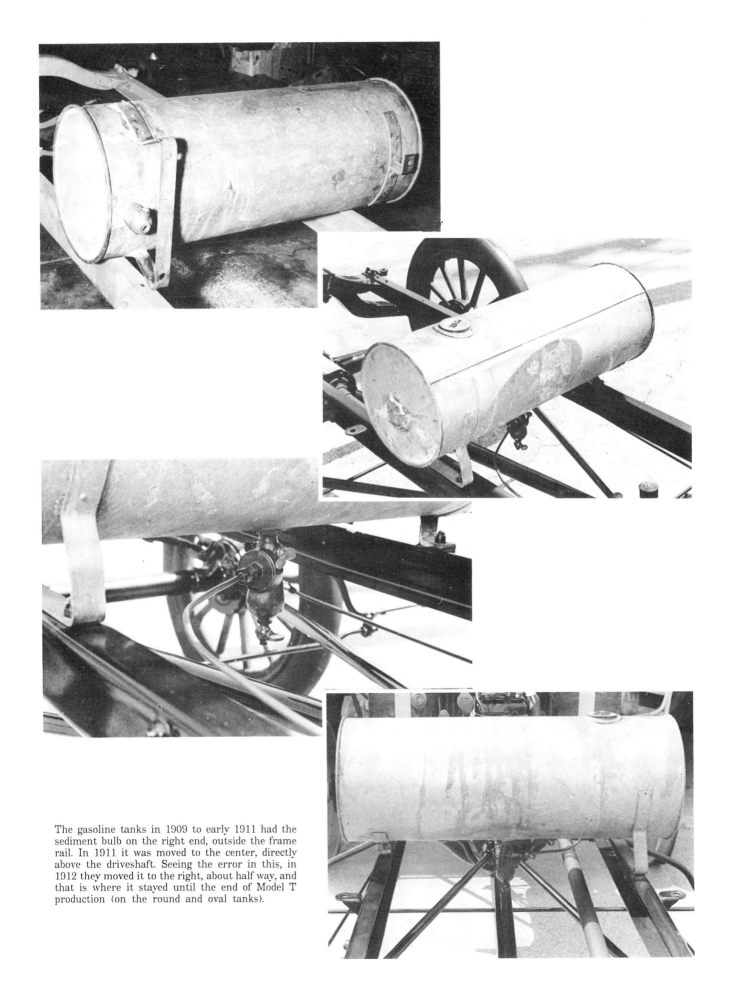

The gasoline tanks in 1909 to early 1911 had the sediment bulb on the right end, outside the frame rail. In 1911 it was moved to the center, directly above the driveshaft. Seeing the error in this, in 1912 they moved it to the right, about half way, and that is where it stayed until the end of Model T production (on the round and oval tanks).

A Close Look
At An Original 1911 Touring

The pictures here and on the following pages are of an original 1911 Touring that was owned by Gary Hoonsbeen, from Minneapolis, Minnesota. Gary purchased the car in August 1974 from a farmer in northern Wisconsin. Gary's story on the car was printed in Volume 10, Number 3 of *The Vintage Ford* magazine. He has since sold the car.

The car is serial number 64,627, assembled on August 17, 1911. The body is number B13974, made by Pontiac. According to the factory records, the car was originally blue, came with Jno. Brown lamps, a Stewart 26 speedometer, a Kingston carburetor, Heinze coils, and a Rands windshield. It has the "1912" (12-rivet) rear axle. Over the years the wheels have been changed, various parts have been switched and/or repaired, and the ravages of time have taken their toll, yet here is a car that is almost as Henry built it.

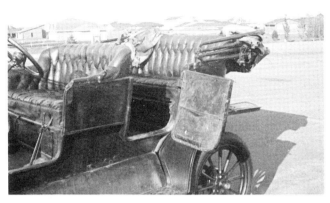

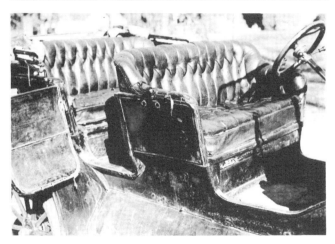

1911

 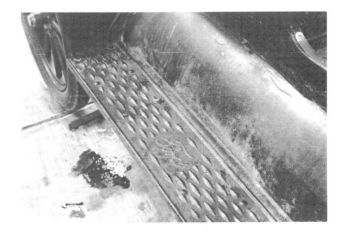

The transmission stub shaft is dated on this car, as it was on most of the early cars. This one uses Roman numerals instead of the usual Arabic. This may have been quicker since they didn't need a set of number stamps; just a sharp chisel. This shaft is dated 8-9-11.

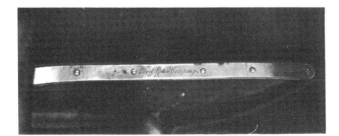

The front brass step plate

Rear brass step plate

Brown Model 78 tail light. The Model 75 was more common. This one appears to be little more than a converted side light (clear lenses on the sides and a red one at the rear).

1911   106

Spring shackles continued in the "Mae West" style, and used brass oilers.

The steering gear case and quadrant are bronze, as is the steering wheel spider. The spark and throttle levers are brass-plated, with hard rubber knobs. The steering wheel is now fifteen inches in diameter and is made of wood, painted black. It is believed that the steering wheel spider was also painted black in the later production but this cannot be confirmed.

The starting crank continued the black hard-rubber style of the 1909 and 1910 cars but was changed to aluminum during 1911. While this picture shows the handle as bare aluminum, handles were always painted black when they left the factory. The license plate bracket is an accessory.

A typical Ford wooden cover over the gasoline tank was made of scrap material, as were the rear floor boards and the rear seat tool box cover. Note the random widths and the cross slats, not at all unusual. This tank cover (or front seat trap door if you like) is chiseled out to clear the gas tank cap. Others seem to have a hole through which the tank could be filled.

NOTE: There is no known foundation for the story, incidentally, that Ford ordered parts in boxes of a certain size so that they could be used for these covers (and other parts). However, it is almost certain that Ford did use the wood from such boxes to make some of the floor boards, etc.

1911

1912

Body Type	Factory Price #	Shipping Weight Lbs.	Production Total *	
Touring	$690	1200	50598	
Torpedo R'bt.	590	—	13376	**
Runabout	590	—		**
Town Car	900	—	802	
Delivery car	700	—	1845	
Coupe	—	—	19	***
Chassis	—	940	2133	***
Total			68773	+

Note: 1200 pounds was the figure given for the Touring car "with others in proportion." The bare chassis weighed about 940 pounds.

\#   Price effective October 1, 1911.
*   Fiscal year, October 1, 1911 to September 30, 1912.
**   Roadster production figures were combined. The total was 13,376.
*** Coupes and the Chassis were not shown in the catalogs.
\+   *Ford News*, Nov. 1, 1920, gave a figure of 78,440.

MODEL YEAR DATES: January 1912 to September 1912 approx.

MAJOR MODEL YEAR FEATURES
See component **Description** section for details.

BODY TYPES. Touring, Runabout, Town Car, Coupe, Torpedo Runabout, Delivery Car. Bodies supplied by several manufacturers. Metal panels over wood frame. Again restyled. While similar to the 1911, the side panels were now relatively smooth and the front compartment was enclosed with removable "fore doors." Torpedo Runabout was now based on the standard Runabout, except for the enclosed front compartment and the fuel tank and tool box on the rear deck (instead of the "mother-in-law" seat). Touring cars came in several variations, depending on the manufacturer and time era.

COLORS. All cars were painted a very dark, all-but-black, blue. Black was reported as an available color but Ford records do not indicate black as a standard color. Delivery cars came in red with the standard blue fenders initially but were offered with unpainted bodies and **black** fenders beginning in early calendar 1912.

UPHOLSTERY. Full leather in the open cars, in a diamond-sewn pattern. Imitation leather began to appear on some cars in some pieces of the upholstery. The front and rear seats in the Town Car were leather.

FENDERS. Front: same as 1911 with top section that flared inward and the splash apron area now a triangular insert. No embossed bead on the apron, nor across the wide part of the front fender. Had front bill. **Rear:** similar in style to the front. Support irons were now attached to the body framing, extending out the side of the body, through a hole in the apron of the fender, and were clamped to a single plate under the fender.

SPLASH APRON. Now longer, with bulge at the rear to clear the brake and radius rods, but less pronounced than in the 1911 cars. Fenders and aprons were painted body color, an almost black blue. They may have been painted black, based on surviving original cars.

RUNNING BOARDS. Pressed steel with embossed diamond pattern. The Ford script ran parallel to the board. "Made in USA" appeared during the year.

HOOD. Aluminum, with no louvers. Hinges were separate from the panels, and riveted in place. Hold-down clamps had two "ears" and were of forged steel. Handles were aluminum.

DASHBOARD (Firewall). Wood, with brass-edge trim which now overlapped the wood. Board on the "1912" bodies was higher and square, eliminating the need for the separate section used on the earlier cars to match the windshield.

CHASSIS. Rear body support was a separate forging bolted to the rear of the frame. Painted black.

STEERING COLUMN ASSEMBLY. Brass quadrant, brass-plated spark and throttle levers, with hard-rubber knobs. Gear case was brass, riveted assembly. Wheel was 15" diameter, wood, and painted black. The wheel spider was bronze at first, then iron and painted black. Column was now 56" long on all cars.

FRONT AXLE. Same as the later 1911 cars. The right steering arm was modified to include a hole for the speedometer gear assembly.

REAR AXLE. "Twelve-rivet" style introduced in July of 1911. The axle housings were again redesigned in late 1912, with the cast center section now being fatter, and with the axle tubes flared and riveted to it. This new axle then continued into early 1915.

DRIVESHAFT HOUSING. Pinion bearing spool was a casting and was held by studs and nuts, the studs being enclosed (not visible) in the housing. Separate front housing for universal joint assembly.

REAR RADIUS AND BRAKE RODS. Had forged ends. Brake-rod support brackets fold down along the side of the clamp, then out and wrap up around the brake rods.

WHEELS. Used 30 by 3 tires in front; 30 by 3-1/2 in the rear. Original tires were an off-white color, with no tread. Hub flanges were six inches in diameter. Front wheels used ball bearings. Hub caps had "Ford" in script letters. "Made in USA" appeared during the year.

SPRINGS. Tapered-leaf, front and rear. "Mae West" style shackles.

RADIATOR. Manufactured by Ford with the standard Ford script on the top tank, but no "Made in USA" until late in the year.

ENGINE. Closed-valve type as in later 1911. Serial number moved to the rear of the water inlet location, at about 100,000, then to a position above the water inlet within a short time (both locations may have appeared at the same time).

ENGINE PAN. Typical "three-dip" with narrow front "snout."

OIL FILLER CAP. The mushroom-shaped cap, of brass, with six flutes and the Ford script appeared on all models.

ENGINE CRANK. Aluminum-formed handle. Handle and crank painted black.

ENGINE FAN. Driven by a leather belt from a pulley at the front of the engine. The fan hub was brass (bronze), with the blades riveted in place. Adjustment was by means of a bolt/nut arrangement now located on the right side of the front plate and bearing against a boss on the mounting end of the fan bracket.

1912 (Continued)

FUEL TANK. Cylindrical, under the front seat. Mounting brackets riveted to the tank. Outlet was at the center, directly above the drive shaft, and screwed into place. Later, the outlet was moved to a location between the center and the right side, between the frame rails.

MANIFOLDS. Exhaust was cast iron; pipe fits inside the threaded end and was packed with asbestos and held with a brass nut. Intake was aluminum of the relatively straight (typical) design.

CARBURETORS. Holley H-1 was common. The Kingston "six ball" was used in limited quantities.

CARBURETOR STOVE. Initially the same as the 1911 cars, then several new designs, all of which rose vertically at the rear of the carburetor and mated with the exhaust manifold at the rear area.

MUFFLER. Cast-iron ends, mounted with pressed-metal brackets. Longer, curved rear exhaust pipe extension integral with the rear cover plate. Wrapped with asbestos, secured with three steel straps.

COIL BOX ASSEMBLY. Kingston of new style, or Heinze. A smaller version of the Jacobson-Brandow box has also been seen on "original" cars but it does not appear in Ford literature.

TRANSMISSION. Three-pedal standard design. Pedals were marked with "C," "R," and "B." Transmission cover was cast aluminum. Tapered inspection door, held with six screws. The door was embossed with the Ford script.

LAMPS. All lamps were now standard equipment except on the closed cars. Made by Edmond and Jones (E&J) or Jno. Brown, they were all-brass initially but changed to the "black and brass" (iron bodies with brass trim) later in the year.

HORN. Bulb type, double-twist, all-brass. Later cars used the single-twist horn, all-brass, and then the black and brass (1913 style) before the 1913 models appeared.

WINDSHIELD. Rands or Vanguard. Generally made of brass.

TOP. (Open cars). Top color was black on all open cars. Top irons were similar to 1911. Front support was now by means of short straps to the center windshield hinge.

SPEEDOMETER. Stewart Model 26.

The Evolving 1912 Model T Fords

The author would like to express his appreciation to a number of special people who donated catalogs, photos, and information on the 1912 Fords. It is not possible to name everyone but the major contributors were Darel Leipold, Ted Aschman, Mitchell Bunkin, Bill Cassiday, John Hale, Donald Lewis, Donald Reichert, John Smith, Mal Staley, and Allen Williams. Without their help, this coverage might not have been possible.

The 1911 Ford Touring. This style was built until mid-January 1912, with the two-piece firewall and with the one-piece firewall. The fore doors (not shown) were added in the "1912" models beginning around December 1911.

The 1912 Fords must qualify as the most varied and perhaps the most interesting of any of the Model T styles. There were at least five different "1912" Touring body types.

Ford's 1912 fiscal year began October 1, 1911. At that time they were producing the typical 1911 style Tourings; the ones with the "step-side" body and the open front compartment. Cars built during October, of this style, could be called "1912" Fords.

By December, 1911, (approximately) this same body was supplied with the add-on front "fore doors." The two-piece firewall (dash) continued, and the front door sections "dipped down" to match the lower firewall. These cars could be also be called "1912" Fords.

During December (again, approximately) the firewall was changed to the one-piece design, and the fore doors no longer had the dip at the front. These cars could be called "1912" Fords.

In late December or early January the new "1912" body appeared. This is the style with the smooth sides, the rear-opening rear doors, the one-piece firewall, the top-support strap which now hooked to the windshield, and with the fore doors. There were at least two of this style: one with outside rear door handles, and the other with inside handles. These two models definitely were "1912" Fords. To add to the confusion, there were numerous variations in these bodies, and it appears that the "1911" style was also used in early calendar 1912.

In addition, the "1913" bodies appeared in late

A restored 1912 Delivery Car. The front wheels appear to be 30 by 3-1/2 instead of the normal 30 by 3 but otherwise the car illustrates the style of this "one year only" model.

The first 1912 Touring was essentially a 1911 body with the fore doors added. It continued the two-piece dash board (firewall). This illustration is from the December 1911 catalog and shows a front-opening rear door. This is believed to be an artist's error, for no such bodies are known to exist. Note the smooth panel at the side of the front seat, and that the doors do not dip at the front where they meet the firewall.

A later 1912 catalog shows another body, similar to the one above, but with the rear door opening at the rear. Still another 1912 body was similar except that the door handle was inside the car. The fore (front) door sections were removable and were not interchangeable between the various body styles, nor between bodies of the same type made by different manufacturers. The top front was supported by short straps which connected to the windshield hinge, instead of the long straps to the front of the chassis, as used in the 1911-style "1912" cars.

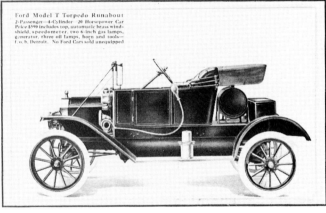

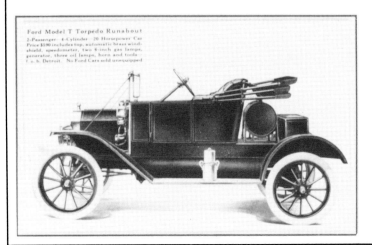

Left above: The earliest catalog illustration of the 1912 Torpedo Runabout. Note the two-piece dash and the fore door which is lower than the seat section side panel. Note the double-twist horn with the bulb outside the body. All 1912 Torpedos were based on the standard Runabout, using standard parts, unlike the 1911 models.

Above: An early 1912 catalog showed the Torpedo with the one-piece dash and the doors the same height as the seat side panel.

Lower Left: The July 1912 catalog showed the Torpedo quite similar to the second type (above) but note the single-twist black and brass horn with the bulb now inside the passenger compartment.

The Commercial Roadster followed an evolution similar to that of the Torpedo except that the horn was outside the body in every picture and, of course, there were no doors. The Commercial Roadster was also shown with the curved rear fenders of the Torpedo. Parts catalogs and existing original cars would indicate that this illustration was also an artist's error, for the Roadsters actually used the same rear fenders as the Touring Cars.

The Town Car and Delivery Car pictures seem to be exactly the same in all the catalogs. These illustrations are, of course, touched up artist's renditions of photographs, and may not reflect the cars as they were actually built.

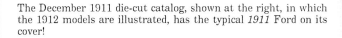

The December 1911 die-cut catalog, shown at the right, in which the 1912 models are illustrated, has the typical *1911* Ford on its cover!

1912, but these are never called "1912" Fords. For the purposes of this study, it is the smooth side, rear-opening-door model that we will call the 1912 Ford.

The Model T Ford for 1912 is perhaps one of the most interesting models produced by Ford. It truly marks the transition from the "old" to the "new" in the evolving Model T.

The 1909 through 1911 cars were all open-front models; there were no doors to enclose the front seat passengers. The 1912 Touring Cars were supplied with "fore doors" as standard equipment. The driver's side did not open on the Touring Car but the passenger side had a door as a part of the add-on assembly. Thus began the three-door style that was to continue until mid-1925, ending with the introduction of the "Improved Fords" for 1926. Interestingly, the Town Car was also given the fore doors but the Runabout (now called the "Commercial Roadster" continued the open-front body of the 1911's. Even more interesting is the fact that there *were* doors on both sides of the Torpedo Runabout.

The changes which marked the beginning of the 1912 models began, perhaps, in August 1911 when Ford began using the right-front steering arm with the integral hole for the speedometer swivel, and referred to it as the "1912 arm." According to factory invoices, the "1912 rear axle" was first used in June 1911. (This is the so-called "clamshell" twelve-rivet rear axle of 1911-12.) Still another clue

was a reference to "1912 rear fenders" on some production of the runabouts, also during September 1911. Ford's fiscal year, at the time, was from October first through September thirtieth, and Ford generally referred to cars made after September as "1912" Fords.

Cars of that period were carryovers of the 1911 models except for the "1912" parts. The 1911 style Touring Cars continued until about December 1911, and then began evolving into the 1912 style, apparently by mid-January 1912. The December 1911 cars generally had the one-piece dash (firewall) and have generally been referred to as the "early 1912" style. Since Ford's records indicate 1912 production began with about engine number 70,000* on October 1, 1911, it seems reasonable to call these 1911 cars "1912s."

The last of the 1911-built "1912" Touring Cars used the typical 1911 body with the "step" in the side panel and the front-opening rear doors, but with the one-piece dash. They retained the 1911 top support straps which extended forward to the front of the chassis. The new 1912 Touring body had the relatively smooth side panels, with rear doors that opened at the rear. As noted, the front compartment was enclosed with matching but removable panels. Similar fore door assemblies were used on the late

* Ford records show the first number of 1912 production to be 69,877 but invoices show numbers above 70,000 built in September 1911.

A family outing in their brand-new 1912 Ford. Note the accessory electric headlights. Photo courtesy Mal Staley.

1911-style bodies to "update" the older style. With these panels in place, the 1912 Ford took on the general appearance that was to typify the Model T for the next decade or so.

Interestingly, the 1912 catalog, dated December 1911, illustrates the 1912 Touring with the smooth sides but with front-opening rear doors. While this style may have been produced, it must have been quite rare. More likely the catalog illustration was an artist's creation, and he just put the door handles on the wrong side. The same catalog illustrates the 1911 Runabout. The Town Car is shown with the fore doors, and the Delivery Car, then new, is pictured. The new Torpedo Runabout, based on the standard Runabout body, completed the line.

The new 1912 Torpedo was announced in a letter to the branches, dated October 27, 1911. This car replaced the earlier Torpedo and Open Runabouts which, while popular today because of their "racy" styling, were not too popular in 1911. The letter points out that this model now has standard height seats. Also, unlike the 1911 Torpedo, this new design used the standard hood, steering column and other chassis and body parts.

The standard Runabout followed the style of the earlier Runabouts. It was called the "Farm" or "Commercial" Runabout, and was supplied with a single "mother-in-law" seat on the rear deck. The December 1911 catalog shows the Commercial Runabout with the flat rear fenders but in all of the 1912 (calendar year) catalogs, the car is shown with the rounded fenders, the same as used on the Torpedo. The author has never seen a 1912 standard Runabout with anything but the flat fenders, and Ford's *Parts Lists* show the cars using the same (flat) rear fenders as on the Tourings. Perhaps both types were used, but more likely the catalog picture is incorrect. In any event, Ford went back to the flat

An early 1912 Touring with the 1911 body, two piece dash, and "dipped" fore doors. Photo courtesy of Bill Cassiday.

"Early" 1912 Touring with the rear door handles and the double-twist horn. Photo courtesy of Bill Cassiday.

rear fenders in their 1913 catalogs.

With the new bodies on the Touring Cars an improvement came in the top support. Instead of having the front support straps running all the way to the front of the chassis, they now hooked to a bracket at the windshield hinge. The tubular metal windshield supports to the front of the chassis were continued, however.

This new 1912 series of cars lasted but a part of the year. In September 1912 (perhaps even a bit earlier) the 1913 body style was introduced. The last of the 1912 Torpedos were "sold out" in October 1912, to be replaced with the 1913 style. (While called "Torpedos" by Ford in later years, the 1912 Torpedo was the last car of this name to have the rear-mounted gasoline tank.) Although the new 1913 Touring was shown in the fall, the older Town Car continued. The Delivery Car was still shown, although none had been built for several months. It had proved to be a poor seller, and it took a little

time to get rid of the stock. 513 Delivery Cars were sold after October 1, 1912, but all were "old stock." The last one was sold in December 1912, and that was the end of the Model T Delivery Car business, although accessory bodies of this style, provided by outside suppliers, were used on the Ford chassis in later years.

Most of the 1912 Fords used the "1912" 12-rivet rear axle which had been introduced in the summer of 1911. Based on seemingly original cars, and from photos of later 1912 cars, it would appear that the "1913" rear axle was introduced in the later part of 1912, before the 1913 models. (The 1913 axle is the type used from 1913 through early 1915, with the "fatter" center section having a shape similar to all later Model Ts.)

The engines in the 1912 cars continued in the 1911 pattern. The serial-number boss was located just behind the timing gear housing on the right side until about number 100,000, when it was

A repainted 1912 Touring. Note the spare tire and tool box; neither were "standard" equipment. Photo courtesy of Bill Cassiday.

An "accessoried 1912 Touring. Note the pointed radiator, the Prestolite tank and the incorrect "one man" top. Photo courtesy of Bill Cassiday.

A typical 1912 Torpedo Runabout. Photo courtesy of Art Volbrecht.

moved to a location just behind the water inlet on the left side. Shortly after that, it was again moved to the standard location above the water inlet. The actual date of these changes is not known; the 100,000 figure is approximate.) 1912 cylinder blocks were not marked with the "Made in USA."

The "Made in USA" on the cylinder head appeared late in the year and is believed to have been before the introduction of the 1913 models. The bulk of 1912 production had only "Ford" cast into the head (plus the usual foundry identification numbers).

The standard carburetor used on the 1912 cars was the Holley H-1 (P/N 4550), introduced in 1911. There were also Kingston "6-ball" carburetors used in limited numbers but Ford did not list the Kingston in the parts books.

Early 1912 production used a new aluminum timer with an integral oil-filler spout. The timing gear cover used with this timer had no oil filler spout. This timer proved to be unsatisfactory and was replaced with another aluminum timer of what

was to become the standard design. The timing gear cover once again had the oil spout. Both of these 1912 covers had the fan adjustment screw on the right side, and this screw bore against a boss at the engine end of the fan support arm, a system which continued until the 1926 models.

The ignition coil box for 1912 was either the Heinze 4600 or the Kingston 4675. The Heinze box used coils which measured 2-5/16 by 3-1/16 by 5 inches. The Kingston used coils which were 2-9/16 by 2-5/16 by 5-3/4 inches. It is possible that some of the earlier Kingston 4660 boxes were used in early 1912 production. This box used the same coils as the 4675 box.

1912 is believed to have been the last year in which dust pans were installed at the factory between the transmission and the frame. The pans at the sides of the engine continued, of course, throughout Model T production.

The fuel tank used in the 1912 cars (other than the Torpedo) continued in the pattern of the 1911's, with the mounting brackets riveted to the tank. The

1912 Touring owned by Donald Reichert, Spokane, Washington. The fore doors are not installed in this picture. The top-support straps run to the front of the frame, as on the 1911 models. Mr. Reichert did not say if this was original or not but if it is, it is quite unusual.

sediment bulb was located to the center of the tank, directly over the universal joint. The tank was again modified during the year, this time to use separate mounting brackets, and with the bulb between the frame rail and the driveshaft — the location used on the round (and oval) tanks until the end of the Model T era.

The aluminum hood continued the pattern of the 1911's. Sometime during this period the hold-down clamps, still forged, were given another "ear," adding to the owner's convenience since he did not now have to look at the clamp to put it in place. Real progress here!

The bulb horn on the 1912's began with the double-twist, all-brass type. Early on, these were superseded with an all-brass single-twist type. Later in the year the black and brass single-twist horn appeared, before the 1913 models. 1912 truly began the "black and brass" era.

Headlamps were generally either E&J 666 with the Ford script, and all brass, or the Brown Model 19. As with the horn, the black and brass lamps appeared later in the year. These were E&J 666 or Brown 16.

Side lamps were all brass E&J "Pat. 1908" or Brown 100. The black and brass E&J 30 or 32, or the Brown 110 (and perhaps the Corcoran and Victor lamps of 1913) appeared later in the year. The tail lamps were E&J "Pat. 1908" or Brown 105, with the E&J 10 or 12, and the Brown 115 (black and brass) appearing later.

The radiator continued in the pattern of the 1911's, with the cast filler neck. There was no "Made in USA" under the Ford script during most of the year but this may have been added before the 1913 models.

Speedometers were standard equipment. They were all apparently Stewart Model 26, in two styles, both all-brass. The first Stewart 26 had round holes in the face for the odometer; five across the upper part, and three across the lower part for the trip odometer. The later Model 26 used a drum-type odometer, with the drums appearing through rectangular holes across the upper half of the face. Black and brass models may have appeared later in the year.

1912 was the last year in which the hard-rubber knobs were used for the spark and throttle levers. These were replaced with levers with flattened ends. It is possible that some early 1913 style cars used the rubber knobs but these were just transitional models.

The steering column itself continued in the style of the 1911's; with the brass gear case, brass-plated levers, the fifteen-inch black-painted steering wheel with the forged iron spider, and the brass quadrant. Earlier production 1912 cars used the bronze steering wheel spider, perhaps being painted black.

Upholstery in the open cars was for the most part leather but some leatherette seems to have been used in later production.

PRODUCTION FIGURES

1912 is the only Model T production year in which no verifiable production figures have been found. The existing records indicate 1912 production began with engine number 68,877 but other records show numbers above 70,000 as having been built in September 1911. (The 1912 Ford fiscal year began October 1, 1911 and ended September 30, 1912.) Our official "guestimate" is that "1912" cars would be in the engine number range of 70,750 to 157,424. The earlier numbers, of course, would be 1911-style cars. The later numbers could be "1913" models. Serial numbers for the calendar year 1912 were from 88,901 to 183,563.

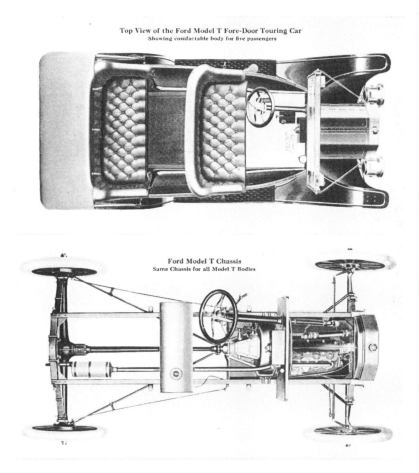

Top View of the Ford Model T Fore-Door Touring Car
Showing comfortable body for five passengers

Ford Model T Chassis
Same Chassis for all Model T Bodies

AN "ALMOST ORIGINAL" 1912 TORPEDO

The 1912 Torpedo Runabout featured on this and the next five pages is owned by Elmer Fox, Doylestown, PA. The photos were supplied by Mitchell Bunkin, Piperstown, PA.

Mr. Fox purchased this 1912 Torpedo in the Pennsylvania Dutch area of the state. It had been purchased originally by a "black bumper" Mennonite. This strict sect permits motorized transportation instead of the well known "Pennsylvania Dutch" buggies, but only if any shiny metal is painted black to eliminate pretentiousness. That is why this car has its original brass radiator and lamps painted black. The car is pretty much the same as it was until it was last driven in 1932 and then "mothballed" in the hayloft of the original owner's barn.

The car was photographed as it was found. The car may have had some modifications over the years (prior to 1932) and some of these may not be "correct" for a 1912 Torpedo. The accompanying captions will point out areas of interest and/or question. The spare tire brackets, for instance, are accessories.

Elmer Fox in his original 1912 Torpedo Runabout, originally owned by a "black bumper" Mennonite farmer.

The body appears to be black with a trace of the original yellow striping.

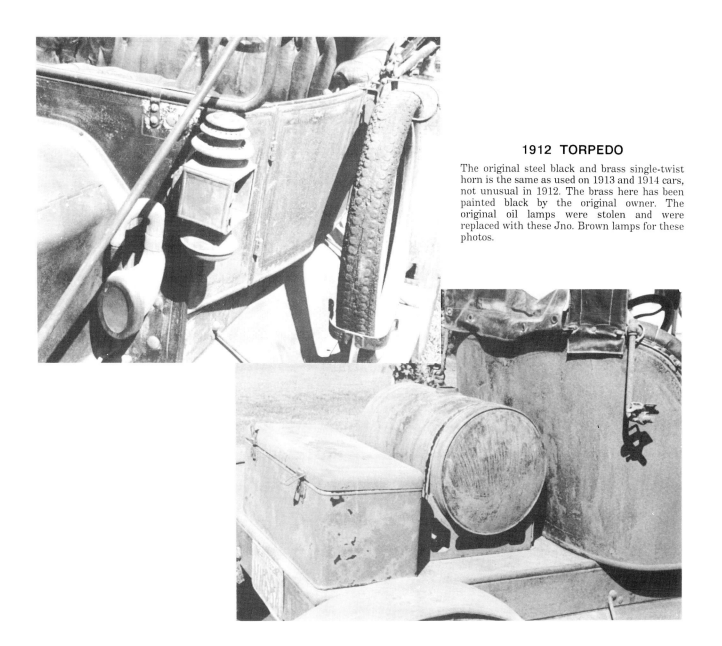

1912 TORPEDO

The original steel black and brass single-twist horn is the same as used on 1913 and 1914 cars, not unusual in 1912. The brass here has been painted black by the original owner. The original oil lamps were stolen and were replaced with these Jno. Brown lamps for these photos.

The serial number of the engine is 129,477, which indicates the car was probably assembled about June 1912. Using this date as a basis, it seems the gradual change to the "black and brass" era had begun. The original lamps on this car were all-brass but the horn was not.

1912 TORPEDO

The steering wheel spider on this car is forged steel and painted black. The rim is wood, with one joint (not pieced together). Earlier 1912 cars had brass spiders; all had black wooden rims.

The metal coil box, while seemingly original, is probably a replacement. Wooden boxes were used well into 1913 and there is no evidence of metal ones being available as early as 1912.

The steering gear box and cover are brass. The spark and throttle levers are steel, and brass-plated. The knobs are hard rubber.

The windshield wiper is an accessory.

1912 TORPEDO

The floor mat was standard for all open cars; an off-white rubber with the "Ford" emblem, and large cutouts for the pedals and brake lever. Many were reversible, being imprinted on both sides for use on either left or right hand drive cars. The hole at the lower left is for an accessory exhaust cutout lever.

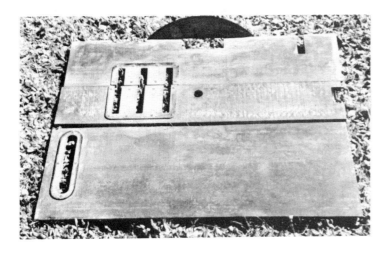

Three-piece floor boards were generally of solid wood. The pedal and brake plates were steel. These were brass plated in the earlier models of 1912 but black here.

Seats and other upholstery was generally leather but imitation-leather material began to be used in 1912 on the door panels (and perhaps elsewhere). Note the inside door handle, typical of all open cars on which the inside handles appeared. Note that the driver's door can be opened, unlike the Touring car.

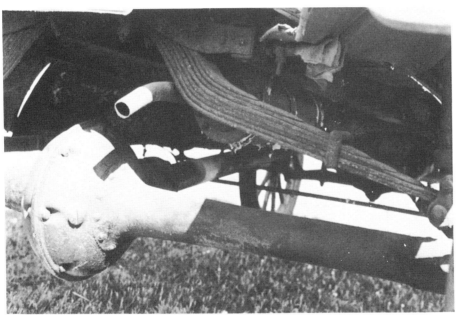

1912 TORPEDO

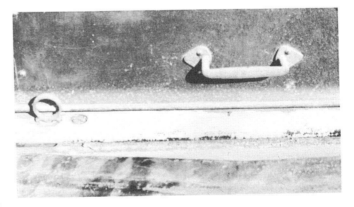

Front and rear wheels had oval-shaped spokes and were usually painted dark (midnight) blue. Note the striping on these; just a rather broad dark line on what appears to be cream or yellow wheels. These wheels may have been repainted but it hardly seems likely since the first owner painted everything else black. Striping was a hand operation and there was considerable variation in the striping on wheels in Ford production.

The rear axle is the typical 1912 twelve-rivet, "clamshell" type. The larger "1913 style" axle appeared a bit later in the year.

Note the tapered and curved exhaust pipe; typical of the period. The muffler was asbestos-wrapped, the wrapping being secured with three iron straps.

Spring shackles, while not visible here, were all of the "Mae West" type, front and rear, with brass oilers.

Hood clamps now had two "ears" instead of just one, for added owner convenience. The hood handle was a forging, riveted to the hood panel. The clash strips were wood.

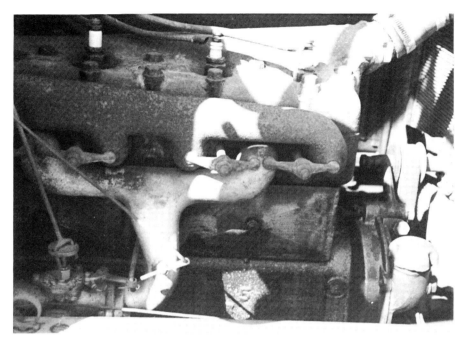

1912 TORPEDO

The Model T engine had now taken on a "standard" appearance, with enclosed valves, standard timer, non-dogleg intake manifold (of aluminum). At about 100,000, the serial number was placed above the water inlet (after a short time of being located to the rear of the inlet).

This was, however, the last of the "high-performance" Model T engines. 1912 was the last year for the higher-compression "low" cylinder head, and the camshaft was reground for a shorter-duration valve timing about 1913.

The carburetor shown here is the Holley H-1, by far the most common one used in 1912.

There is no "Made in USA" on the cylinder head, nor on the block. The water jacket plugs are half-inch pipe.

Note the dash-operated "economizer" valve in the intake manifold; added by the original owner.

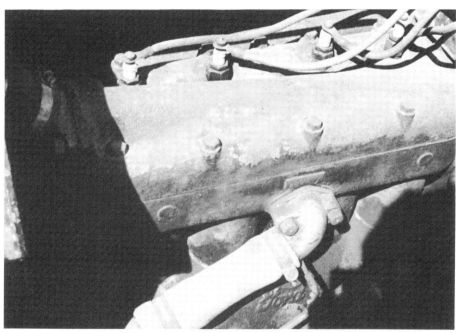

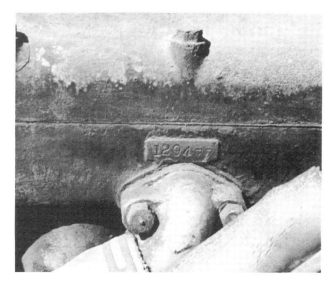

1912

Typical upholstery of 1912 Ford Touring Cars was all leather, in a diamond-tufted pattern as shown. This was the last year of all-leather upholstery; by late 1912 the use of imitation leather began and by the middle of 1913 real leather was a thing of the past except for a few high-wear areas. The wooden panel under the front seat appears to have been made of scrap material; note the various widths and shapes of wood used. (Ted Aschman photo.)

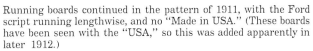

Running boards continued in the pattern of 1911, with the Ford script running lengthwise, and no "Made in USA." (These boards have been seen with the "USA," so this was added apparently in later 1912.)

Early hub caps were the same as 1911: "Ford" in script on a rounded end. During 1912 the design was modified, with the end now flat and with a border around the edge. The "Made in USA" may have appeared on this style cap in later 1912 but this modification is generally considered to have been made in 1913.

Two Stewart Model 26 speedometers were used in 1912 production. The most common is the earlier style (left) with the round odometer holes in the face. The later Model 26 has a drum-type odometer, with rectangular holes. Both types have trip odometers which will read to 99.9 miles. Both types had brass cases. It is possible, even likely, that the Stewart Model 100 appeared in later production, and that the Model 26 came with a black case, with brass trim, in later models.

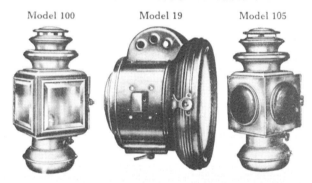

Model 100   Model 19   Model 105

This handsome Lamp equipment with standard Generator, manufactured expressly for Ford Model T cars, by

The Jno. W. Brown Mfg. Co.
Columbus, Ohio, U. S. A.

Headlamps used in 1912 production were for the most part either Brown Model 19 (shown) or E&J Model 666. Side lights could have been Brown 100 (left) or E&J "Pat. 1908." Tail lights were either Brown 105 or E&J "Pat. 1908." A mixture of brands on any given car was not uncommon, although it is unlikely there were mixed headlights, or mixed sidelights.

E&J side and tail lamps had no model number, just the "Pat. 1908" imprint. (Actually, "E&J, Detroit, Mich. Pat. Dec. 9, 1908.") Side lamps had a round lens in front, a square one on the side, and a little jewell at the rear. They came in pairs, left and right, and were all brass.

The E&J tail lamps were marked like the side lamps but had three round lenses; red to the rear, clear on the right, and blue on the left.

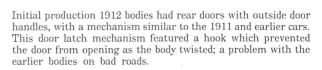

Initial production 1912 bodies had rear doors with outside door handles, with a mechanism similar to the 1911 and earlier cars. This door latch mechanism featured a hook which prevented the door from opening as the body twisted; a problem with the earlier bodies on bad roads.

Later production eliminated the outside door handle and used a lever on the inside of the door to operate the latch mechanism, which no longer "hooked" into the body pillar. This new latch operated vertically, in line with the body, and was designed to overlap the latch plate to prevent the flexing body from allowing the door to open. Most of these inside door handles used a round knob but examples have been seen with a vertical tapered lever, and in one example, both types were used on the same car (bar in front, and knob in the rear).

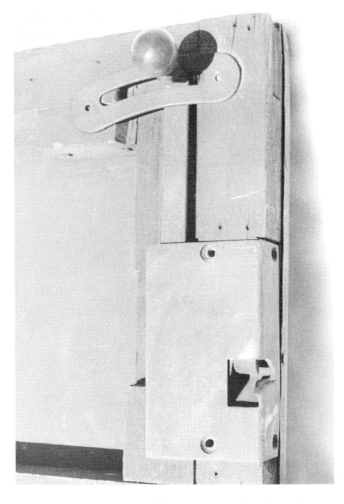

Typical 1912 inside door latch mechanism. Note the plain stamped-metal plate.

Above photos courtesy of Phil Lawrence, San Jose, CA.

The bar type inside door handle. This one is on the left front door on a car with the knob-type latches on the rear doors. Note the trim plate is more finished looking that the other type, appearing to be pressing. It is possible this type of latch was a replacement for the earlier type, or it may have just been a variation due to a different supplier.

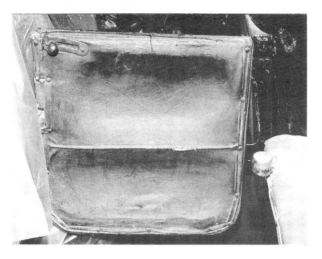

Typical 1912 rear door. Note the door latch escutcheon is slightly different in placement from the others shown, in that it is on an angle rather than horizontal. The doors were upholstered in leather, with an imitation-leather strip tacked in place. (Ted Aschman photo)

Ford Runabout Stolen

FORD Model T 1912 torpedo runabout was stolen at 9 p. m., April 27, 1912, while standing in front of the home of the owner, Dr. C. C. Towle, 24 Prospect Hill Avenue, Somerville, Mass.

The car was new, run 250 miles. Painted black, had top, windshield, speedometer and electric headlights. Mass. registry No. 11545; maker's No. 100163; motor No. 86567.

A suitable reward will be paid for information leading to recovery of car or arrest of thief. Communicate with owner or Charles A. Kendall, Chief of Police,
Somerville, Mass.

What color was the 1912 Ford? All literature, paint lists, etc. found in our research of Ford documents indicates all cars were "blue." Existing cars, on the other hand, seem to indicate bodies could be blue, or black, and that the fenders and splash aprons could be in either color. To add to the confusion, any combination of the two colors might be found (black body with blue fenders, blue body with black fenders, all blue, or all black).

The above clipping from an early *Ford Times* seems to indicate black was indeed a possibility, in spite of the documentation to the contrary.

Rear floor boards were of solid wood, in four pieces of random width; typical of most Model T Fords in that they appear to have been made from scrap material. (There is no evidence that the old wives tale of Ford ordering packing boxes of a certain size for floor boards is valid. They probably used whatever was handy, including packing boxes.)

The three 1912 serial number locations. At about 100,000 (March) the number was placed on a boss to the rear of the water inlet on the left side of the engine. Shortly later, apparently before June, the number was relocated to its final location above the water inlet.

The casting date on the 116,341 engine appears to be 1-30-12, while the serial number would indicate a May engine assembly; quite a spread of time. We have no known-accurate 1912 engine production figures so it is possible these dates are a bit off.

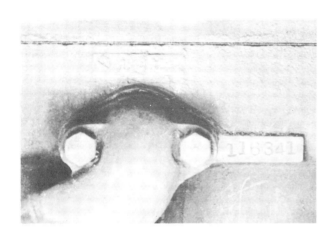

Valve chamber doors were sharply embossed and made of heavier material than those of later production.

Pistons used in the earlier Fords (until about 1914) were flat-topped, generally with three rings above the piston pin, instead of bevel-edged with the oil ring below the pin as in the later engines. The piston overall height did not change, however.

VALVE TIMING

Sometime during later 1912 (Ford records say 1913) the camshaft was modified for shorter duration and this, coupled with a lower-compression cylinder head, somewhat reduced the engine's power. The valve-piston measurements are given below. All dimensions presume the standard 5/16" piston height above the top of the cylinder at top dead center.

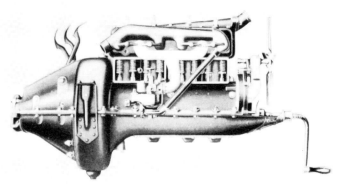

Right side of Model T Motor showing valves, intake and exhaust manifolds. Valve cover plates have been removed to show valve arrangement

1909-1912

		Piston position from top of cylinder
Intake opens	7/64" ATDC	13/64" above
Intake closes	3/8" ABDC	3-5/16"
Exhaust opens	3/8" BBDC	3-5/16"
Exhaust closes	1/16" ATDC	19/64 above

1913 and LATER

Intake opens	1/16" ATDC	1/4" above
Intake closes	9/16" ABDC	3-1/8"
Exhaust opens	5/16" BBDC	3-3/8"
Exhaust closes	TDC	5/16"

ATDC=After Top Dead Center. ABDC= After Bottom Dead Center. BBDC=Before Bottom Dead Center. TDC=Top Dead Center.

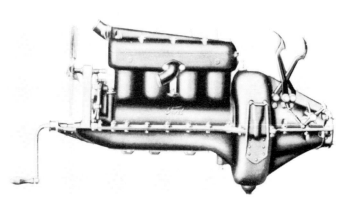

Left side of Model T Motor. Notice the simplicity of the Ford en-bloc motor; the freedom from unnecessary parts

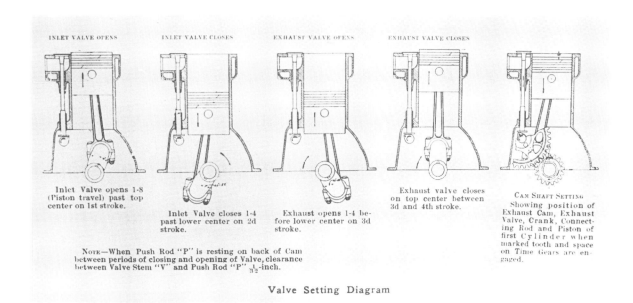

INLET VALVE OPENS — INLET VALVE CLOSES — EXHAUST VALVE OPENS — EXHAUST VALVE CLOSES

Inlet Valve opens 1-8 (Piston travel) past top center on 1st stroke.

Inlet Valve closes 1-4 past lower center on 2d stroke.

Exhaust opens 1-4 before lower center on 3d stroke.

Exhaust valve closes on top center between 3d and 4th stroke.

CAM SHAFT SETTING Showing position of Exhaust Cam, Exhaust Valve, Crank, Connecting Rod and Piston of first Cylinder when marked tooth and space on Time Gears are engaged.

NOTE—When Push Rod "P" is resting on back of Cam between periods of closing and opening of Valve, clearance between Valve Stem "V" and Push Rod "P" 1/32-inch.

Valve Setting Diagram

As if to further confuse matters, this diagram, reprinted from the March 1912 Ford Instruction Book, shows the valve timing to be the same as the later (1913 +) engines. The camshaft change was noted in June 1912 and must have been made in 1912 production; perhaps this illustration predated the actual switch.

1912

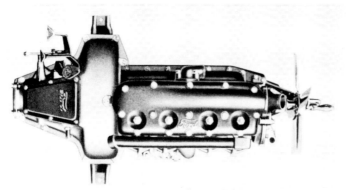

Top view of Model T Motor showing Ford removable cylinder head
This may be removed by taking out the fifteen
bolts shown in the picture

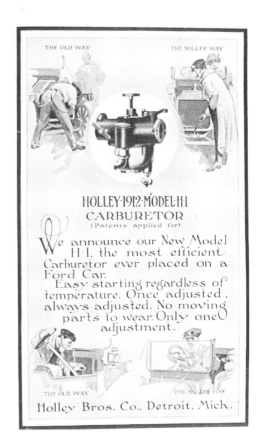

THE OLD WAY   THE HOLLEY WAY

HOLLEY·1912·MODEL·H·1
CARBURETOR
(Patents applied for)

We announce our New Model
H·1, the most efficient
Carburetor ever placed on a
Ford Car.
Easy starting regardless of
temperature. Once adjusted,
always adjusted. No moving
parts to wear. Only one
adjustment.

THE OLD WAY   THE HOLLEY WAY

Holley Bros. Co., Detroit, Mich.

The most common carburetor used on the 1912 Fords was the Holley H-1, which came in three variations. All were quite similar; the first had a two-screw chamber cover, the next had a three-screw cover — both of these having a clamp arrangement on the air intake. The third type was similar to the second except that there was no clamp.

A Kingston carburetor was also used in some production in late 1911 and early 1912. This rare carburetor used a set of six balls for air control; these balls being located inside the casting rather than under screw-in plugs as in the earlier five-ball and later four-ball models. Apparently this model was unsatisfactory because it does not appear in any of the parts books.

It is possible the "1913" Kingston four-ball and the Holley Model S might have appeared in later 1912 production, for these were the typical carburetors used in the 1913 cars which were introduced in the fall of 1912.

The Kingston six-ball was built in the style of the earlier carburetors used by Ford, with the air intake at the bottom center of the float bowl. The new Holleys, though, set the pattern for all future Ford carburetors, with the air intake at the rear, in line with the output (manifold) side.

The late 1911-1912 Kingston "six ball." Apparently not used on too many cars, no reference is made to it in the Ford parts books. The body and float bowl were bronze. The six air valve balls were retained by a staked-in-place retainer, shown in the photo below.

Top view of the "six ball" Kingston.

The underside of the upper part of the Kingston "six ball" carburetor.

The "1912" Model H-1 Holley with the two-screw cover plate. This basic design came in three variations during 1912; the one shown above, one with a three-screw cover and the air pipe clamp, and the three-screw without the clamp.

The two-screw seems quite rare but is the one illustrated in the Ford parts books. The photo here is taken from the November-December 1975 issue of *The Model T Times*, used in an article on Ford carburetors by Cecil Church. Whether the two-screw came first, or if it and the three-screw were used concurrently, is not known. The three-screw without the air pipe clamp seems to have come later.

This design evolved into the "1913" Holley which is quite similar except for the change in the fuel inlet system, and the vertical choke shaft. The 1913 model went back to the two-screw cover but the cover was not the same as the 1912 two-screw.

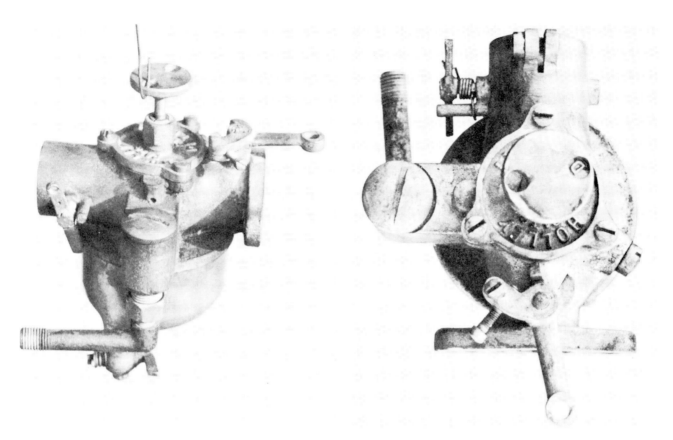

The 1912 Holley H-1 three-screw without the pipe clamp.   The 1912 Holley H-1 three-screw with the pipe clamp.

The two Holley three-screw carburetors, with and without the air pipe clamp.

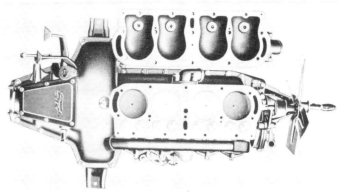

Top view of Motor, with cylinder head removed, showing pistons,
valve setting and water jackets

Access to crank shaft, cam shaft, pistons, connecting rods and bearings
may be had by simply removing a plate in the
lower crank case housing

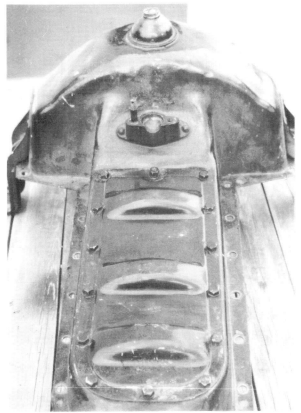

View of the engine crankcase. Note the deep "tea-cup" oil drain
fitting, with the screw-slot drain plug. Note, too, the heavier
and deeply embossed inspection plate. The screws which secure
the plate thread into a one-piece strap affair inside the
crankcase, rather than one of two horseshoe-shaped pieces used
in later Model T engines. Photos courtesy of Allen Williams,
Painted Post, NY.

The early 1912 commutator (timer) and timing gear cover.
Note the integral oil spout on the aluminum timer case, and
the large hole in the cover. Used but a short time, apparently in
late 1911, these were replaced with the standard timer
(aluminum case) and gear cover, which continued with minor
variations until 1919 (and later on non-starter cars).

Side view of the crankcase showing the seven-rivet support arms. Note the lack of a reinforcing "lip" along the outside of the crankcase flange.

The serial number on Allen Williams' engine is located in the now-standard position above the water inlet. Note that the casting date (3-16-12) is upside down.

Side view of the 1912 cylinder block. Note the pipe-plug water jacket plugs. The drain hole was not drilled through in this engine. Oil works up through the valve lifters and is eventually sucked up through the valve guides, greatly increasing oil consumption. We believe this hole was supposed to have been drilled through. Photos courtesy Allen Williams, Painted Post, NY.

1912

The transmission tail shaft had a Woodruff key to prevent the clutch collar from turning. The key-to-collar fit was not tight in order to allow the collar to slide on the shaft. This key was eliminated during 1913, and the collar was allowed to slip, reducing wear on the clutch shift assembly.

While essentially similar to all Model T transmissions, the earlier ones were a bit different in details. The top photo shows the two brake drums; the left being the type used in Ted Aschman's 1912, and the right being the typical later small drum type. Just when this change in construction was made is not known.

Above: Inside view of the transmission brake-drum assembly. The center bushing has a flange which serves as a thrust bearing. This design was modified, apparently during 1912, and the flange was eliminated.

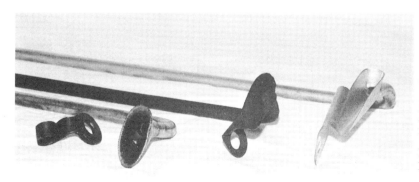

The three engine oil tubes used in Model T production. The left one is brass, with a separate mounting clamp, used from 1909 (after 2500) until about 1915. The center one is steel, with an integral clamp, used from about 1915 until July 1924. The tube on the right is also of steel, with a larger funnel, used after July 1924. Ted Aschman photo.

1912

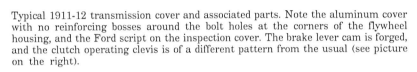

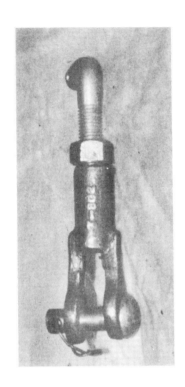

Typical 1911-12 transmission cover and associated parts. Note the aluminum cover with no reinforcing bosses around the bolt holes at the corners of the flywheel housing, and the Ford script on the inspection cover. The brake lever cam is forged, and the clutch operating clevis is of a different pattern from the usual (see picture on the right).

Below: The crankcase inspection plate was of heavier material than on the later cars, and its retaining collar (called "reinforcement") was of one piece instead of the two pieces seen in later production.

Lower right: Typical magneto post used during the era.

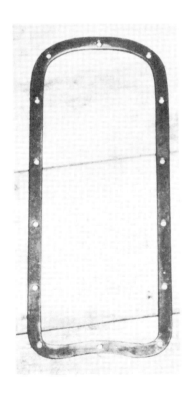

1913

Body Type	Factory Price #	Shipping Weight Lbs.	Production Total *	
Touring	$600	1200	126715	
Runabout	525	—	33129	
Town Car	800	—	1415	
Delivery car	625	—	513	
Coupe	—		1	**
Chassis	—	960	8438	**
Total			170211	+

Note: 1200 pounds was the figure given for the Touring car "with others in proportion." The bare chassis weighed about 960 pounds.

\#   October 1, 1912. The Touring was now the 1913 style.
*   Fiscal year, October 1, 1912 to September 30, 1913.
**   Coupes and the Chassis were not shown in the catalogs.
\+   *Ford News*, Nov. 1, 1920, gives a figure of 168,220.

MODEL YEAR DATES: September 1912 to August 1913 approx.

BODY TYPES: Touring, Runabout, Town Car. The Delivery car was a "1912" model built in late 1912 during the 1913 *fiscal* year.

MAJOR MODEL YEAR FEATURES
See component description section for details.

The "1913" style body appeared in late 1912, and was replaced by the "1914" style later in the year (perhaps October 1913). The Touring body was modified during production in attempts to overcome the weakness of the rear section by means of reinforcing wood strips glued and screwed to the body sill, heavier wood sills, additional support brackets, and reinforcement plates.

The windshield lower section sloped to the rear, with the top section upright. The top section folded forward.

The front compartment was now enclosed. The right front door opened but the left was just a dummy. The doors extended to the splash apron and had a rectangular shape. The Runabout was similar in style to the Touring. The turtle deck was new this year, and had rather sharp corners.

Lamps and horn were black-painted steel with brass trim.

The one-piece driveshaft appeared during 1913, before the 1914 models, but apparently both the old and new types were used for some time.

The bodies were supplied by several manufacturers, with metal panels over a wood frame. Door handles extended through the top surface. Body top sills had a separate metal trim plate. No door on the driver's side.

COLORS. All cars were painted a very dark blue, with either blue or black fenders on the cars built in late 1912. Black became the standard color early in the year. Delivery cars (remaining from 1912 production) were phased out, and could be ordered several colors or in just the primer coat of paint.

UPHOLSTERY. Full-leather in the open cars, in a diamond-sewn pattern. Imitation leather began to appear on the seat backs and side areas, with real leather at the very front of the arm rest.

FENDERS. Front: similar to 1912 style. No embossed bead on the apron, nor across the wide part of the front fender. Front fenders had no front bill but the "lip" on the front tapered outward in early production, becoming straight during the year. Reinforcing bead added across the wide part later in the year. **Rear:** similar in style to the front. Support irons were now attached to the body framing, extending out the side of the body, through a hole in the apron of the fender, and were clamped to a single plate under the fender.

SPLASH APRON. Now longer, with bulge at the rear to clear the brake and radius rods, similar to the later 1912 cars. Fenders and aprons were painted either blue or black, this based on surviving original cars.

RUNNING BOARDS. Pressed steel with embossed diamond pattern. The Ford script now ran across the board. "Made in USA" appeared on all boards.

HOOD. Aluminum, with no louvers. Hinges were separate from the panels, and riveted in place. Hold-down clamps had two "ears" and were of forged steel. Hood handles were now forged steel.

DASHBOARD (Firewall). Wood, with flat, brass edge trim. Board now mated with the body side panels.

CHASSIS. Rear body supports are separate forgings bolted to the rear of the frame. Painted black. Extra body brackets were installed, just ahead of the rear seat, to support the rear section of the touring body. During the year the rear crossmember was lengthened, eliminating the need for the forged body brackets.

STEERING COLUMN ASSEMBLY. Brass quadrant, brass-plated spark and throttle levers, with flattened metal ends replacing the rubber knobs. Gear case was brass, riveted assembly. Wheel was 15" diameter, wood, and painted black. The wheel spider was iron and painted black. Column was 56" long on all cars.

FRONT AXLE. Same as the 1912 cars.

REAR AXLE. Cast center section, introduced in later 1912, with the axle tubes flared and riveted to it. This axle then continued into early 1915.

DRIVESHAFT HOUSING. Pinion bearing spool was a casting and was held by studs and nuts, the studs being enclosed (not visible) in the housing. Separate front housing for universal joint assembly discontinued later in the year.

REAR RADIUS AND BRAKE RODS. Had forged ends. Brake-rod support brackets extended out and wrapped down around the rods.

WHEELS. Used 30 by 3 tires in front; 30 by 3-1/2 in the rear. Original tires had no tread. Hub flanges were six inches in diameter. Front wheels used ball bearings. Hub caps had "Ford" in script letters. "Made in USA" on all caps.

SPRINGS. Tapered-leaf, front and rear. "Figure-eight" style shackles, similar to the earlier type but not so ornate. The use of the brass oilers continued.

RADIATOR. Manufactured by Ford with the standard Ford script. "Made in USA" on all radiators under the Ford script. The filler neck was now a spun brass design, riveted and soldered in place.

1913 (Continued)

ENGINE. Closed-valve type as in 1912. Serial number above the water inlet. Pipe-plug water jacket seals were replaced with press-in welch plugs during the year, with mixed production of both types. New camshaft and slightly-lower-compression cylinder head was introduced in late 1912.

ENGINE PAN. "Three-dip" with narrow front "snout" and "tea-cup" oil drain.

OIL FILLER CAP. The mushroom-shaped cap, of brass, with six flutes and the Ford script appeared on all models. "Made in USA" added.

ENGINE CRANK. Aluminum-formed handle, painted black.

ENGINE FAN. Driven by a leather belt from a pulley at the front of the engine. The fan hub was brass (bronze), with the blades riveted in place. Adjustment was by means of a bolt/nut arrangement now located on the right side of the front plate and bearing against a boss on the mounting end of the fan bracket.

FUEL TANK. Cylindrical, under the front seat. Mounting brackets now clamped to the tank. Outlet was between the center and the right side, between the frame rails.

MANIFOLDS. Exhaust was cast iron; pipe fits inside the threaded end and was packed with asbestos and held with a brass nut. The exhaust manifold and pipe were modified so that the pipe flared at the manifold and was held in place with the brass nut but with no packing. Intake was aluminum and was more curved than the usual design. The iron intake manifold of similar design to the aluminum may have appeared during the year.

CARBURETORS. Two types: the Kingston "four-ball" or Holley Model S.

CARBURETOR STOVE. Several designs, all of which rose vertically at the rear of the carburetor and mated with the exhaust manifold at the rear area.

MUFFLER. Cast iron ends, mounted with pressed-metal brackets. Longer, curved rear exhaust pipe extension integral with the rear cover plate. Wrapped with asbestos, secured with three steel straps. The asbestos was painted black on some production.

COIL BOX ASSEMBLY. Kingston, Heinze, K-W or Ford. The Ford box used the standard-size coils.

TRANSMISSION. Three-pedal standard design. Pedals were marked with "C," "R," and "B." Transmission cover was cast aluminum. Tapered inspection door, held with six screws. The door was now a plain metal plate with no script.

LAMPS. Made by Edmond and Jones (E&J), Brown, Corcoran or Victor. All were painted black with brass trim, replacing the all-brass types used until late 1912.

HORN. Bulb type, single-twist. Black and brass style.

WINDSHIELD. Rands, Vanguard, Diamond, or Standard. Painted black. Lower section leans back, while top section was vertical. Top section folded forward.

TOP. (Open cars). Top color was black on all open cars. Oval top sockets. Front attaches to the windshield hinge with a strap, similar to 1912.

SPEEDOMETER. Stewart Model 26 in black and brass on early cars, then Stewart Model 100.

TURTLE DECK (on Runabout). Similar in style to later types except that its corners were rather sharp. Handles were brass but painted black.

The 1913 Model T Fords

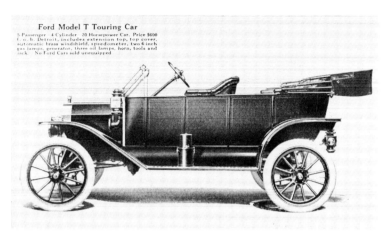

Ford Model T Touring Car

5 Passenger 4 Cylinder 20 Horsepower Car. Price $600 f. o. b. Detroit, includes extension top, top cover, automatic brass windshield, speedometer, two 6-inch gas lamps, generator, three oil lamps, horn, tools and jack. No Ford Cars sold unequipped

The author wishes to thank
Larry Smith
Lomita, California,
for his assistance in this coverage.

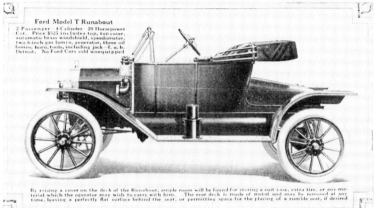

Ford Model T Runabout

2 Passenger 4 Cylinder 20 Horsepower Car. Price $525 includes top, top cover, automatic brass windshield, speedometer, two 6-inch gas lamps, generator, three oil lamps, horn, tools, including jack—f. o. b. Detroit. No Ford Cars sold unequipped

By raising a cover on the deck of the Runabout, ample room will be found for storing a suit case, extra tire, or any material which the operator may wish to carry with him. The rear deck is made of metal and may be removed at any time, leaving a perfectly flat surface behind the seat, or permitting space for the placing of a rumble seat, if desired

The Ford line for 1913. Only three models were offered this year, the Touring, Runabout, and Town Car; the Touring being by far the best seller. Bodies were supplied by several outside firms, and while all appeared similar, there were minor variations in their construction. Typical of the open cars were the rectangular doors which extended down to the splash apron, unique for the year. The windshields on the open cars all folded forward, a feature which appeared only in 1913. Just 1,415 Town Cars were produced in fiscal 1913 (October 1912 through September 1913), and very few have survived.

Early 1913 cars had body striping in gray, as is shown in the catalog illustrations and in the photo of the crated car below. Striping was discontinued early in the model year, probably before calendar year 1913.

(*Lower photo from the Collections of the Henry Ford Museum and Greenfield Village.*)

Introduced in October 1908, the Ford Model T had received unprecedented public acceptance. Fiscal 1909 (October 1908 to October 1909) had seen 10,660 cars assembled; fiscal 1910, 19,050; fiscal 1911, 34,858; and fiscal 1912, 68,773. 1913 was to see sales almost triple to 170,211 cars.[1] Selling the product was not the problem, the problem was that the increasing sales made it difficult to produce the cars needed to fill the orders.

While the year 1913 is generally regarded as the year in which the moving assembly line was "invented," the real beginning had come years earlier, and at Ford no doubt as early as 1903. It is only natural to seek easier and quicker ways of accomplishing an objective. Just as one might wash dishes — you wash all, then dry; not wash one, dry one, etc. The simplification of manufacturing and assembly by implementing logical routines evolved into the step by step placement of men and machines in the order of the operations, and from this evolved the moving assembly line. The Ford Motor Company was in a unique position to fully develop manufacturing and assembly methods to their maximum efficiency; it made just one product and it made enormous quantities of that product.

Increasing production could have been accomplished by adding more workers and more factory space for them but this obvious solution has a number of flaws. Men cost money, as does factory space, and the per-unit cost of the item would remain constant. Ford's aim was to increase production by improving efficiency. In most cases, this effort resulted in far fewer men putting together far more parts. As a consequence, the unit costs were greatly reduced, thereby reducing the cost of the finished product. With the product's cost reduced, its sales price could be lowered, and with the lowered price, more could be sold. With greater sales, a greater profit could be made, and this increased profit could then allow further reduction in price, which increased sales, which demanded further production efficiency, and so on.

Every phase of the manufacturing of the Ford car was analyzed and modified to this end. In the case of the engine, the engine traveled over 4,000 feet during assembly in 1909 but this distance was reduced to just 340 feet in 1914. In October of 1913, it took nine hours and fifty-four minutes of one man's time to assemble the engine, but by May 1914 this time was reduced to five hours and fifty-six minutes.

Machine tools were moved into the production lines so that one operation fed the next with a minimum of handling. Machines were given just

1913 Model T Ford Touring, serial number 249,881, owned by Dan Williams, San Pablo, California.

enough room so the operator could produce with the greatest efficiency; less room would have cramped him, while more room would have meant wasted steps or lost motion. An example of time-saving on just one of the operations was outlined in the July 1914 issue of *The Engineering Magazine*:

To show what can be done by simply dividing an operation seemingly already reduced to its lowest terms, and placing the short work-slide lengthwise of the assembling bench; the first example of the improved Ford practice here illustrated and described is the piston and connecting rod assembling, changed within the past two months, so that now fourteen men assemble 4,000 pistons and connecting rods in one eight-hour day, instead of the twenty-eight men employed to do exactly the same work less than two months ago, and with no change whatever in the tools used, nor in the ultimate operations performed.

In addition to the labor-time saving, the present practice of piston and rod assembling includes an inspector, who gauges and inspects each piston and rod assembly, with the result of no rejections from the motor assembling line. With the former practice, where each man did the whole job of piston and rod assembling, numerous returns were made from the motor assembling line, causing delays in the motor assembling to say nothing of the costs of pulling down and re-assembling the faulty piston and rod assemblies.

The finished weights of Ford pistons vary — maximum, about six ounces. Each piston is weighed and marked on the head by a center-punch used without a hammer, with one, two, three, or four center marks, dividing the pistons into four weight classes, maximum weight variation in each class three-quarters of an ounce. After inspection, the inspector places the assemblies on one or another of four shelves, according to the center

marks on the piston head, and the pistons are paired for weight on opposed crank-throws by the motor assembler.

The pistons and pins come to the piston-and-rod-assembling bench with the pins in the pistons. The rods come to the bench by themselves.

The work bench is covered with sheet metal on top. In the old style, where each man did the entire job (average time about three minutes), each bench had seven piston-holding special vises on each side, with no inspector, and no inclined work-slide over the bench — fourteen men to each bench, two benches, twenty-eight men in all, who assembled 175 pistons and rods, average, in nine hours of one man's time, or about three minutes and five seconds time, each. Operations, tools and benches were the same as now used in working the new methods, save that seven of the fourteen vises are now removed from each bench. The flat-top sheet-metal-covered benches are fourteen feet long and four feet wide.

Here was a three-minute operation, very simple: push pin out of piston, oil pin, slip rod in place, slip pin through rod and piston and tighten the pin-pinching screw in the rod top-end, and place and open the pinching-screw split pins; and although the time was not very small and the work not faultless, no one had studied the job carefully, or held a stop-watch on the operations to find out how the three minutes were actually expended. Finally the motor assembling foreman analyzed the time with a stop-watch and found that four

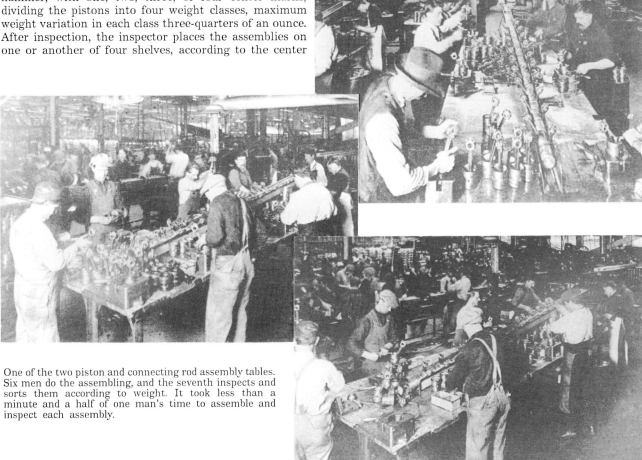

One of the two piston and connecting rod assembly tables. Six men do the assembling, and the seventh inspects and sorts them according to weight. It took less than a minute and a half of one man's time to assemble and inspect each assembly.

The Ford assembly line in late 1913, before the moving assembly line. These are 1914 models, with the metal coil boxes and the longer rear frame crossmember. Careful examination of the original photo, under an magnifying glass, shows these chassis had the reversible firewall (choke rod hole on both sides), the aluminum crank handle (painted black), and that the engines were not painted black. Note the two brace-wrenches on the mounting bolts of the center firewall. Whether this was a standard procedure or they were just left in place for this photo is not known. (The firewall on the left hangs waiting for a chassis but that line is empty.) *Photo from the Collections of the Henry Ford Museum and Greenfield Village.*

hours out of the nine-hour day were spent in walking — that is to say, in body movements of each assembler made by moving his feet.

In a day or two the forman had split the single man into three men and reported to the machine-shop superintendent that he had no use for fourteen of the twenty-eight men on the piston-and-rod assembling job, and the superintendent laughed at him.

Seeing convinced the superintendent that the laugh was misplaced, and he then said that it was surprising that the job had not been changed before.

It is of no use whatever to tell this story without detailing it as minutely as a split second-hand details operation-motion time-losses; therefore three photographs are shown, together with a fairly complete operation-time analysis so that the reader can see for himself much more than he could learn as a mere uninstructed spectator in the Ford shops, watching this piston-and-rod-assembling job in actual work.

OLD STYLE, ONE MAN PERFORMING SIX OPERATIONS

Operation 1.
Drive out pin with special hand-hammer.

Operation 2.
Oil pin by dipping end in box of oil.
Operation 3.
Slip pin in rod-eye. Hand.
Operation 4.
Turn pin to take screw. Screwdriver.
Operation 5.
Turn in pinch-screw. Hand brace.
Operation 6.
Tighten screw with open-end wrench, and put in cotter-pin; spread pin-end with special tool.
Time: Three minutes and five seconds; no inspection; fourteen men on one bench. Average production per man, 175 pistons and rods assembled in nine hours working time.

NEW STYLE, OPERATION SPLIT INTO THREE DIVISIONS

Bench provided with slide, three men on each side of bench, and inspector at end of bench.
Operation 1.
Drive out pin, oil pin, enter pin in piston. Average time, ten seconds.
Operation 2.
Place rod in piston, pass pin through rod and piston, with screwdriver turn pin to position and take screw, turn screw in with brace. Time, ten seconds.

1913   146

Operation 3.

Tighten screw with open wrench, place cotter-pin by hand, spread cotter-pin ends with special tool. Time, ten seconds.

Operation 4.

Inspection. Inspector gauges piston with flat steel gauge, places piston in pin-holding jig, tries rod to see if rod is pinched tight on pin, then holds piston horizontal in both hands and vibrates it slowly in vertical plane to see the weight of the rod free-end will barely rock pin in piston-pin bushes, and that pin has friction enough to keep rod from moving freely, a delicate test for pin-fit in the piston bushes. If rod works either too stiffly or too freely the assembly is rejected, goes back to the assemblers, and has a larger or smaller pin put in, as the case may demand.

Actual inspecting time about eight seconds, leaving inspector two seconds time to place the assembly on the proper shelf, according to the center-punch marks or the marks on the piston head.

The best time record for seven men, six assemblers and one inspector is 2,600 piston and rod assemblies turned out in eight hours, equal to one assembly in 77-1/13 seconds of one man's time. Average time, 2,400 assemblies in eight hours, with seven men, gives one assembly in 84 seconds of one man's time, or better than double the work of one man doing the job with no inspector, and with a saving of 101 seconds of time of assembling.

With inspection, under new style, as said before, there are no returns from the motor assembling line.

The piston-assembling job teaches two lessons of first importance. The first is that there are great savings in labor to be made by splitting operations to such an extent that the workman does not need to change the position of his feet, and the second lesson is that a work-slide so located that the workman can drop his completed operation out of his hand in a certain place, without any search for a place of deposit, and can also reach to a certain place and there find his next job under his hand, is also a very important time saver.

The vises are sixty inches apart, so that there is only thirty inches reach required for the pistons and pins, which are placed on the bench after Operation 1, ready to hand to the man who performs Operation 2, who in turn places the pistons where they are readily reached for Operation 3. The slide is used for the completed assembly only, and delivers the completed assemblies close in front of the inspector so that not a movement need be wasted anywhere.

In commenting on the late change from the old routine of piston and rod assembling to the new method by which fourteen men are made to do more and better work than twenty-eight did before, the foreman of the assemblers said, "We were asleep over that job, asleep and dreaming. I don't see how we came to overlook the possibilities the way we did."

The piston and rod assembly was, of course, just one small part of assembling a Model T. Similar savings were made in every step of assembly. The first major Ford assembly to be given the moving assembly line "treatment" was the flywheel-magneto. Until the moving assembly line was created, one man took about twenty minutes for each one. After the change it took about thirteen minutes and ten seconds. As the methods were further refined, and a chain drive was added to the

line, the time was dropped to about five minutes per man per assembly.

The moving assembly lines for the sub-assemblies for the Model T resulted in a severe problem at the final assembly. While final (chassis to axles to engine, etc.) assembly had been modified and shifted, the actual operations were carried on in more or less static locations. The moving final assembly line was Ford's crowning achievement.

In August 1914, Horace L. Arnold described the chassis assembly lines in *The Engineering Magazine:*

Up to August, 1913, the Ford chassis was assembled on one location. First the front and rear axles were laid on the floor, the chassis frame with springs in place was assembled to the axles, next the wheels were placed on the axles, and the remaining components successively added to complete the chassis. All components needed to make up one chassis had to be brought by hand to each chassis-assembling location. This routine of stationary chassis assembling was, in September 1913, worked with two lines of assembling-floor space, 600 feet long, twelve feet chassis to chassis centers, fifty assembling locations in each 600 foot line, 100 cars in process of assembling in the two lines. Working in this routine 600 men were employed, 500 being assemblers who were supplied with components by 100 men acting as component carriers.

About April 1, 1913, the first sliding assembly line, used for assembling the Ford flywheel magneto, was placed in work and immediately showed a large reduction is assembling labor-cost. Consequently, the possibility of lowering chassis-assembling costs by introducing the moving assembly line for chassis assembling became a

Installing the engine in the chassis in 1914. There can be little question that the engine was not painted black. Photo from *The Engineering Magazine.*

matter of discussion among Ford engineers.

In the month of August 1913 (the dull season), 250 assemblers, with a stationary assembling location for each chassis, the assemblers being served by eighty component carriers, worked nine hours per day for twenty-six days to turn out 6,182 chassis assemblies. Total labor hours 330 x 26 = 77,220 hours, giving twelve hours and twenty-eight minutes for each chassis, about as good as ever done with stationary chassis assembling.

The assembling line was long — 600 feet — but even that did not give enough room, and 12-1/2 hours of labor time seemed altogether too much for one chassis. It was in the dull season, and an experiment was made with rope and windlass traction on a moving assembly line 250 feet long. Six assemblers traveled with the chassis as it was slowly pulled along the floor by a rope and windlass past stationary means of component supply, and the chassis-assembling time was reduced to five hours and fifty minutes of one man's time, over fifty percent saving.

October 7, 1913, on a moving assembly line 150 feet long, with no helpers, components being piled at suitable locations, 140 assemblers in the line completed 435 chassis assemblies in one nine hour day, two hours and fifty-seven minutes of one man's time for each chassis assembling.

The assembling line was lengthened by degrees to 300 feet, giving the men more room, and on December 1, 1913, 177 assemblers working nine hours turned out 606 completed chassis assemblies, about two hours thirty-eight minutes of one man's time on each chassis.

December 20, 1913, working two assembly lines, 191 men completed 642 chassis assemblies in one nine-hour day, a little less than two hours forty minutes of one man's time for each chassis, the cars being pushed along by hand.

January 14, 1914, one assembling line was endless-chain driven, with favorable results.

January 19, four chassis-assembling lines were worked, only one line being chain driven. The wheels were put on as soon as the axles and frames were assembled, and the assemblies in progress ran with their front wheels on the floor and their hind wheels carried on three-wheeled cradles, used to give easy placing of the rear wheels on the motor-starting drive at the end of the line.

February 27, 1914, the first high line of rails with chain drive was used. The chassis slid on its axles as pulled by the chain, and the wheels were applied only a short distance before the motor-starting was reached. This first high line was made with rails 26-3/4 inches above the shop floor, and at once showed great advantages, the best time for one chassis assembling being only eighty-four minutes, while the worst time was two hours. Two other high lines were soon installed, 24-1/2 inches high, with chain drives; tall men worked on the line 26-3/4 inches high, and short men on the other two lines, 24-1/2 inches high.

The Ford engineers make a point of "man-high" work placing, having learned that any stooping position greatly reduces a workman's efficiency. The differing heights on the chassis-assembling high lines are believed to be decidedly advantagous.

Installing the engine in the chassis, circa 1913 before the chain-driven moving assembly line. One man centers the universal joint while the other pushes the engine into place. Note that the engine does not appear to be painted (certainly not black) but that the intake manifold does appear to be black. Note, too, that the four bolts holding the front motor mount/spring clip are apparently bare. Standard practice was to "touch up" the visible pieces that were not painted, so at least the forward nuts would have been painted by the time the chassis left the factory. *Photo from the Collections of the Henry Ford Museum and Greenfield Village.*

1913   148

On these high lines, on April 30, 1914, 1,212 chassis assemblies were completed in one eight-hour day,[2] each chassis being assembled in one hour thirty-three minutes of one man's time, as against twelve hours twenty-eight minutes, the best time with stationary chassis assembling, September 1913; 93 minutes as against 728 minutes – – and it must be borne in mind that the September 1913 Ford practice in chassis asssembling was fully abreast of the best known in the trade. Very naturally this unbelievable reduction in chassis-assembling labor costs gave pause to the Ford engineering staff, and led to serious search for other labor-reduction opportunities in the Ford shops, regardless of precedents and traditions of the trade at large.

In addition to the constant changes in production methods, the design of the car itself was modified to facilitate ease of production or cut the basic cost of the components. The new 1913-style Model T Ford was the result of many of these cost-cutting modifications.

Introduced about October of 1912, the 1913-style Ford had an all-new body of simpler and less-expensive design than those that preceded it. Small details such as the use of all-brass lamps, hard-rubber knobs on the spark and throttle levers, and extensive use of leather all came "under-the-axe" in the economy drive. As the year progressed, the car evolved in cost-cutting design.

One of the minor changes which had a major consequence in cutting costs was the elimination of the separate forged body bracket at the rear of the frame by simply using a longer rear cross member, a modification during calendar 1913. Presume that it took just one minute to install the forged brackets on each chassis. Ford produced about 200,000 cars in 1914; it would have taken 200,000 minutes, or better than 3,300 hours for the installation of these forgings. Each of these brackets was held in place with three screws, three nuts, and three cotter pins; that's six screws and nuts per car — 1,200,000 of each! This saving does not take into account the cotter keys nor the brackets themselves. Each bracket had four holes which had to be drilled — 1,600,000 holes — which took some time as well. If the screws alone were as cheap as ten for a penny, the savings on screws alone would have been $1,200!

The 1913 body (not made by Ford, but purchased outside) followed the general lines of the 1912 cars (as they appeared with their fore doors installed) but was a much simpler design and considerably more modern appearance. The separate fore doors of the 1912 were now integral with the body; the door on the driver's side being eliminated since the brake lever and steering column precluded its practical use anyway.

The wooden dashboard (firewall) was made smaller and a new steel-frame windshield with a sloping lower section was installed. This windshield was braced to the body side instead of using the long rods to the front of the chassis as in the earlier models. The top section could be folded forward.

The cast (actually forged) rear body bracket, last used in 1913 and replaced by a longer rear cross member beginning early in the year. The savings involved in this relatively minor change are described in the text.

Upholstery, possibly all leather initially, evolved to a combination of imitation-leather material and the real thing during 1913 production. The diamond pattern continued with the diamonds being sewn into the seats rather than tufted (a change made, apparently, in the 1912 model year).

The standard color for the initial (and perhaps all) 1913 cars was a very dark almost-black blue, with black fenders and splash aprons, following the same color scheme as the 1912's. No written evidence has been found of all black Model T's prior to 1914, although surviving examples would seem to indicate that there were such cars. A factory list, issued in December 1913, showed the following colors:

F-101 First coat plastic black japan for fenders and shields
F-102 Second coat black japan for fenders and shields
F-103 First coat blue dipping for hoods and rear axles
F-104 Second coat quick-drying black for rear axles
F-105 First coat brushing black japan for front axles
F-106 Second coat brushing black japan for front axles
F-107 Blue black baking for coil box
F-108 First coat black wheel surfacer for wheels
F-109 Second coat blue color varnish for wheels
F-110 Second coat black brushing for frames (the first coat was not specified)
F-111 First coat red baking metal body primer for body
F-112 Second black glaze putty for body
F-113 Second coat blue ground for body
F-114 Solid blue rubbing for body (repairs only)

F-115 Third and fourth coat body spraying blue
       varnish for body
F-117 French gray for striping wheels
F-119 Black engine dipping for finishing crank-
       cases.

Striping (in French gray) appeared on some of
the early 1913 production but was apparently
discontinued early in the year. The use of black
undercoating on the bodies is interesting. Just how
durable the blue final finish was is open to question
but perhaps after a little oxidation and polishing the
blue wore through, giving the appearance of a black
body. Note, too, that there was no paint specified for
the engine — just for the engine pan. Production
photos of 1913 and 1914 (and even later) seem to
indicate the engines were not painted, or if they
were, they were not black. They may have been
coated with some preservative but more likely they
were just bare iron.

The initial 1913 Touring bodies were built on
wooden sills about 2-5/16 inches thick. The front
and rear sections of the body were separate, with the
doors extending to the splash aprons to give the
body a one-piece appearance. These thin sills proved
to be too weak, allowing the doors to open as the
rear of the body flexed, particularly when there were
rear-seat passengers. Early in production the sills
were reinforced with a a strip of wood which was
glued and screwed on top of the existing body sill.
Later a formed-steel bracket which coupled the two
body sections together was installed over the body
sill. Then additional body brackets were installed
ahead of the rear seat section, and finally the sills
were increased to 3-1/4 inches but the problem was
still not solved. The ultimate solution, however, was
the change to smaller doors with a connecting body
panel (the 1914 style body) in later 1913.

Interestingly, later in the year the factory asked
for an inventory count of the reinforcing brackets at
the branches. It seems they were still getting orders
for them and that they had already made and sold

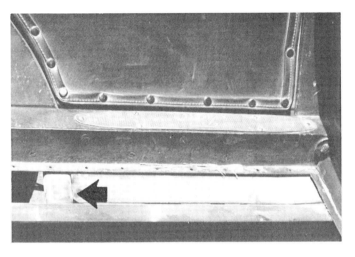

Above: The frame-to-body reinforcing bracket which was
installed at the factory early in calendar 1913.

Below: The sill-reinforcing bracket seen on many but not all
early 1913 Touring bodies. The car illustrated is a January 1913
car.[3]

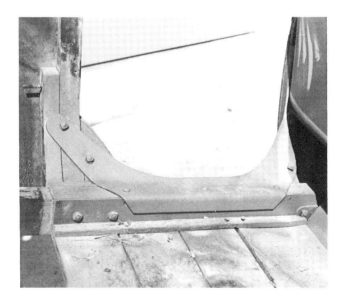

more than enough to fit every body that had been produced prior to becoming standard equipment. Rather than tooling up for more, they hoped the branches could come up with the surplus that just had to be somewhere.[3]

While the square-cornered doors extending to the splash aprons were the main identifying feature of the 1913 body style, the windshields and their supporting brackets were another. The upper half of the windshield folded forward this year and the supporting brackets were relatively straight. The 1914-style windshields looked similar but the top section folded to the rear, and the supporting brackets had a curve to allow clearance for the folded section. The windshield frames were steel and painted black, as were the supporting brackets. Windshields were supplied by Rands, Diamond, Vanguard, and Standard.

The fenders used in 1913 continued in the style used in 1912 except that the front "bill" was eliminated (to be reinstated in the later 1914 cars). Some of the early cars had the lip of the front fenders on an angle (see photo) as if the former bill had been cut off. There were no reinforcing moldings pressed into the triangular splash section of the front fenders, and no cross molding pressed into the wide part of the front fenders (as in the 1914-1916 style).

As mentioned earlier, the chassis frame initially was the same as the 1912, using the forged rear body brackets. During May 1913, at about #271,425, the rear crossmember was made longer, eliminating the need for the brackets.

1913 was the last year in which any parts with the Dodge Brothers name would appear. The Dodges, major stockholders in the Ford Motor Company, had been major suppliers of Ford parts (mainly forgings in later years) since the company had begun in 1903. Until about 1906, the Dodges were the *manufacturers* of the Ford car, exclusive of the body and wheels. The two Dodge brothers, John and Horace, had decided to build their own car about this time. There is little doubt that the highly successful Dodge car got its start from the profits of the Ford company, in which they shared. Dodge Brothers apparently continued to supply forgings to Ford but the "DB" logo did not appear on many of them.

1913 marked the beginning of the "Made in USA" identification either stamped or cast in many parts of the Model T. The practice had begun in 1912 (and on some parts, much earlier), but by 1913 it was wide-spread. Most noticeably, this indentification appeared on the front of the radiator and on the hub caps.

Mechanically, the 1913 car was like the 1912. During 1912, the rear axle had again been redesigned to use the rounder cast center section, with the axle housings flared and riveted to it. This style was introduced, perhaps, about August 1912

Above: The door sill of a 1913 Ford Touring, without the reinforcing plate.

Below: Another 1913 Touring with the reinforcing plate (opposite side from that shown above).

The rear floor was covered with a cocoa mat on all Ford Touring cars until about 1917 when it was replaced with a wool mat.

and continued until early 1915. Other minor changes were:

Brake rod Anti-rattlers. During 1913 these were changed from the welded design which went under the brake rods and folded over, used since 1909, to a simpler pressed type which now went over the brake rods and folded under.

Carburetors. The Kingston Y "four ball" or the two-screw Holley S were supplied by Ford. Later production used the Holley three-screw model G.

Coil Boxes. Early cars used the wooden Kingston and Heinze boxes but during the year the Ford metal box, using the standard-size coils made by Kingston, Heinze, and Ford, became standard. This metal box continued through 1914; differing from the 1915 and later types in that it had a one-piece, non-sloping cover.

Crank. Most 1913 production used the aluminum-handled crank (painted black) introduced in 1912. The simpler steel-handled crank may have appeared later in the year but it is believed to be more typical of the 1914 and later cars.

Driveshaft Housing. 1913 was the last year for the so-called "two-piece" driveshaft housing with the separate U-joint housing. During the year, the U-joint housing was made integral with the front forging.

Engine. 1913 was the last year for the pipe-plug water jacket seals. These were dropped in favor of welch plugs beginning about number 200,000 (February 1913). The flat-top pistons were superseded with the domed type, and the compression ratio was reduced to about 4:1. Many 1913 engines had cylinder heads which were drilled on the left edge for priming cups. The holes were plugged with screws. The early cars (built in 1912) may have used the earlier camshaft which had greater timing overlap (and more power). 1913 was also the last year for the engine pan with the deep "tea-cup" oil drain.

The 1913 Runabout "turtle deck" differed from later types in that it had rather sharp corners. It is not known if the rounded-corner type appeared during 1913 production, or at the change to the 1914 models, or after the 1914's were being produced, but the sharp corners are considered to be typical of "1913" models.

Engine Manifolds. 1913 cars used the aluminum intake manifold as on the earlier cars. The cast-iron manifold may have appeared in later 1913. The exhaust manifold was modified during production to use the flanged exhaust pipe, instead of having the pipe fitting into the manifold and being sealed with asbestos packing.

Front Axle. The steering connecting rod (drag link) now had integral sockets, riveted and welded at each end, replacing the adjustable type used from 1911 to sometime in early 1913. The front radius rod (wishbone) was now held to the engine pan with studs and springs, instead of the screws used earlier (with no springs). The steering connecting rod (from spindle to spindle) now had the locking bolt on the left-hand fork vertical instead of horizontal.

Hood. Aluminum, in the same pattern as the 1912's. During the year the handles were made of forged (or cast) steel (instead of aluminum), riveted in place.

Lamps. First introduced in late 1912 cars, all lamps were of the "black and brass" type; steel bodies with brass trim. Headlamps were either E&J 666, 66, or 656, Brown 16, Victor 1, or Corcoran. Side lamps were E&J 30 or 32, Brown 110, Victor, or Corcoran. Tail lamps were E&J 10 or 12, Brown 115, Victor, or Corcoran.

Muffler. 1913 was the last year for the curved tail pipe, and the separate mounting brackets. Typical 1914 production, which may have appeared in 1913, used the muffler with the straight pipe and mounting brackets cast as a part of the end plate.

Oil Filler Cap. Brass, with Ford script, but now with the "Made in USA" also stamped on the cap.

Radiator. Similar to the 1912 type but with the "Made in USA" under the "Ford" on the upper tank. The filler spout was now spun-brass (instead of cast), riveted and soldered in place.

Rear Axle. Cast, thicker, center section. The brake shoes were now modified to use two springs; the second spring across the mounting bolt side. Since the cast shoes easily broke at this point, the added spring held them in place. By 1913, the hex-head filler plug was standard. Many of the internal bronze bushings (differential spider, gears, etc.) were discontinued and by 1914 all were eliminated.

Running Boards. Similar to the 1912 except that the "Ford" now run across the width of the board, rather than parallel with it. While the style was identical to later boards, the stamped diamonds are deeper and sharper, probably due to the dies being worn down in later years.

Speedometer. Stewart Model 100, of shallow design, with drum-type indicator and a three-digit trip odometer to the right of the regular odometer, both above the speed drum. Trip-reset knob was on the right side of the case. Black case with brass bezel. The larger Stewart 100 with the odometer below the speed drum may have appeared during the year. 1913 was the last year in which the speedometer was supplied as standard equipment on all production.

Splash Aprons. While earlier cars had a pronounced bulge at the rear to clear the radius rods, late 1912 and later aprons had a more gradual taper to the rear, beginning about ten inches before the rear. The rear of the apron now matched the fender line, eliminating the large gap seen on the earlier cars.

Spring Shackles. "Figure-8" style with brass oilers, front and rear.

Steering Column. 1913 was the last full year for the spun brass, riveted gear case. The hard-rubber spark and throttle knobs were discontinued; the arms were now flattened on the ends. The mounting flange (column to firewall) was changed from a forging to pressed steel. The steering wheel had a cast-iron spider and a wooden rim, all painted black.

Transmission. Essentially the same as earlier except that the key was eliminated between the clutch collar and the tail shaft. Minor modifications in the drum bushings, and one additional clutch plate appeared during the year. The transmission cover had a plain steel door, lettered pedals, and was aluminum. During the year, some covers had the cast-in reinforcing ribs at the corners of the flywheel housing to prevent breakage when the corner bolts were tightened.

The Runabout (or Roadster) body with a metal turtle deck was introduced a few months after the new touring. The December 1912 *Ford Times* showed the new style. Apparently Ford continued the 1912 style Runabout with the "mother-in-law" seat for a time, for in February 1913 the company issued a letter in which they stated that only the new style was then available.

The Runabout followed the style of the Touring, with the full-length door that extended to the splash aprons. New, though, was the rear "turtle" deck. Styled in the pattern of all such decks used on Fords until 1923 models, the 1913 was unique in that

instead of the smoothly rounded rear corners, this one had rather sharp corners. The deck lid was hinged at the top (forward side) and used two "L"-shaped handles at the rear.

In addition to simplifying the design of the car, Ford also reduced the number of body styles available. In 1912 they had offered the Touring, Runabout, Torpedo Runabout, Town Car, Delivery car, and a few Coupes. In 1913 the line was reduced to just the Touring, Runabout, and Town Car. Ford did not offer a bare chassis in their catalogs but they did ship a number of them (2,133 in 1912, and 8,438 in 1913). These may have been for export but the records do not indicate their use. Some of the 1913 production may have been available to dealers, though, since the 1914 catalog included the bare chassis.

Like the 1912 style cars, the 1913's were short-lived and were soon superseded by the next year's models. The "1914" style appeared about August or September 1913, and these "new" models began the era of major expansion for the Ford Motor Company. By August 1913 Ford had built about 300,000 Model T's, making the company the major supplier of automobiles in the world.

Henry Ford was little-known outside Detroit, and really not well known in that city. All this was to change dramatically in January 1914 when the Ford Motor Company announced its new five dollar a day pay schedule and at the same time reduced the work day from nine to eight hours. Almost overnight, Ford became a national hero. Just who came up with the idea is still an open question. Charles Sorensen, James Couzens, and Henry Ford (and perhaps others) all took the credit, but as far as the public was concerned, Henry Ford was the greatest benefactor of mankind who had ever appeared on the industrial scene. And in view of Henry Ford's attitude in later years, he must have agreed with the public.

1913 Touring Car

NOTES

1. The figures given are for U.S. car production. Engine production was 11,146 in fiscal 1909, 20,387 in fiscal 1910, 39,217 in 1911, and 86,675 in 1912. Engines were shipped to Britain and Canada during these years for assembly there, and those cars are not included in the car production figures.

2. In January 1914 Ford announced the "Five-Dollar-Day" and at that time also reduced the work day from nine to eight hours, six days a week.

3. In a letter issued by the factory, dated January 28, 1913, Ford announced a reinforcing body bracket for the Touring body. On March 4 another letter said that this reinforcement would be discontinued because the heavier sill was now being used. On June 12, 1913, still another letter indicated the bracket was still in use and hinted that the problem was a bit acute. These letters do not detail this bracket or brackets, but apparently there were more than one type, depending on the manufacturer of the body and/or the thickness of the body sills. None of these parts were listed in the parts books. A Factory Letter dated May 29, 1913, listed the brackets as p/n T-5668 and T-5669 for the body with 2-1/4" sills, and T-5676 and T-5677 for the body with 3-1/4" sills.

4. There appears to have been considerable overlap in 1912 and 1913 production. Original 1912 cars have been seen with black and brass lamps, steel-frame windshields, imitation leather upholstery (in part) and the "1913" rear axle. Some of this may have been due to some cars being assembled at Ford branches as well as at the Highland Park plant.

The accompanying photos illustrating the 1913 Model T Ford come from a number of different cars, collected over many years. There are two main featured cars, however. The first is owned by Larry Smith, from Lomita, California. This is car number 212,526 (February 1913). The second car is owned by Dan Williams, from San Pablo, California, and is serial number 249,881 (April 1913).

Larry Smith has studied the 1913 Ford for more years than he can remember, and probably knows more of the detail differences in this model year than most of the "experts," including the author. Larry made a number of notes on the 1913 Fords and we have reproduced them here.

THE 1913 FORD
(As I See It)
By Larry Smith

My '13 is an original car that I purchased in Irving, Texas, in 1961. I completed the restoration when I was twenty-one years of age so obviously there was and is room for improvement. I didn't restore the car to be a show car, although it truly was when it was finished. My car is driven about 2,000 miles each year and has accumulated well over 30,000 miles by now (in 1977 when this was written). I have added many accessories to get me around better but I have all the correct parts available to make my car truly "authentic."

The 1913 Ford was probably, with the exception

The final chassis assembly line in later 1913. The "1914" models were being built at this time. Note the row of Town Cars behind the Touring Car at the right.

of the 1926 models, the most transitional model year of Model T production. As you have read many times before, Ford used up all the old style parts on the new model, and 1913 was no exception. The 1913 models produced in 1912 were simply 1912's with 1913 bodies. Some of these cars had all-brass lights and windshields although I have yet to see the all-brass horn used.[4]

By the time the 1913 model was into January (1913) production, one thing was very apparent; the body was quite weak. Whether the controversial body supports that were available to strengthen the '13 bodies were genuine Ford, I don't know. This part (the formed metal plate that straddled the sill between the front and rear body sections), as far as I have been able to determine, was not available from Ford but was supplied by dealers from other channels.[3] However, Ford did take a step to alleviate the problem by introducing a special body-to-frame bracket that was attached to both sides of the frame under the rear doors and simply extended from the frame about three or four inches, and was attached with two 5/16" screws and castle nuts as on the controller shaft. These brackets were introduced in January sometime and were continued through the balance of 1913 production on the early *and* late style frames.

There were three frames used in 1913. The 1912 style, the 1912 style with the special body bracket, and the 1914 style with the long rear cross-member. The 1912 style frames were pretty well used up by the end of March 1913, and the new style (1914) frames replaced them.

1913 Touring owned by Larry Smith, Lomita, California. The serial number is 212,526 (February 1913).

There were two types of springs used in 1913 *at the same time*. Some of the early 1913's used a spring clip similar to the later style except that the clip was riveted to the spring leaf, and the bolt went through *under* the spring as the late styles did. The other spring clip was a separate piece, with the clamp bolt above the spring. Both spring types were taper-leaved. Spring shackles were all of the "figure eight" type.

The controversy lingers on but I have seen so many bonafide original 1913's with the one-piece torque tubes (the driveshaft housing with the integral U-joint housing) that I am inclined to believe the new style was introduced as early as January 1913, with the older style being used as well.

Most seem to agree the wheels were painted blue with a "V" stripe on each spoke and a single stripe on the felloe. Wheels were supplied mainly by Pruden but Kelsey and Hayes were also used.

The 1913 bodies were all about the same, although the frame rails were increased in thickness around April or May. I have seen no evidence that body striping was used past the earliest models, and it appears to me that black bodies were supplied along with the blue. Some 1913's had a 1914-style door handle. Just when these were produced is anyone's guess but they were made as evidenced by early photos. I have also seem complete doors at swap meets with the 1914-style latch.

Some of the reproduction lists have a large patent plate listed for late 1912's. I have never seen one of these plates on a 1912 model but have seen them on the 1913 models produced in 1912 and up until about March 1913. These plates are about three times larger than the usual patent plate and have the winged script plus more than the usual number of patent numbers. I have yet to see a patent plate that has a body number that agrees with the engine number. For example, my body number is 198,329 and the engine number is 212,526.

I have evidence that the spark and throttle levers were brass plated, and that the four screws and nuts that hold the windshield brackets were also brass plated.

There were three brands of windshields used in 1913. All fold forward. They were Diamond, Vanguard, and Rands. Rands had two designs; one had a short top as on the Vanguard and Diamond, but the other used two bottoms which made it necessary to make the stay rods shorter and move the top bow back. Also the hinge dimple arrangement is different to accommodate the changed angle of the lower windshield section.

The only speedometer available was a very flat Stewart which is not the usual Stewart 100 as used in part of 1914. It has a "13" stamped on the face and is much thinner than the usual 100. The standard Stewart drive was used, however.

Two types of spring clips were used, not necessarily in just 1913. In one (top photo) the clip was riveted to the spring and the bolt went under the spring. In the second type, the end of the leaf was curled and the bolt went through this curl on top of the spring (lower two photos).

The brass oil filler cap seemed to have followed the same pattern as the radiator — no "Made in USA" up to 1913, and a "Made in USA" under the "Ford" in 1913.

The two wooden coil boxes used in 1913 were the Heinze and the K-W. The photos of a day's production in 1913 clearly bears this out. One difference in the Heinze box over the earlier models is that they seemed to have dropped the cam-action lid locks in favor of the familiar snap latch (brass plated). Metal coil boxes were apparently introduced in 1913 but I have no evidence to prove this.

The early 1913 models used the 1912-style crankcase but have only three rivets on the ears instead of seven. By June, the 1914-style crankcase was introduced. The drain plug was slotted. The engine splash pan was dished deeper than most to clear the Kingston "4-ball" carburetor.

Many early 1913's still used the 1912 exhaust manifold in which the exhaust pipe fit into the threaded section, and which used asbestos packing. The new type with the flared pipe apparently appeared about mid-year. Aluminum intake manifolds were used well through 1913 and I have seen one iron manifold which is exactly the same (as the aluminum one) on a June car.

Crank handles were aluminum and were always painted black.

1913 and 1914 running boards are the same as the 1912 except that the script runs across the board instead of in line with it. The script is entirely different from the later styles.

If you put a 1913 hub cap next to a later style you will see the script is much finer, with a higher "F" in the "Ford."

Three lamps were available in 1913; Victor, E&J and Jno. Brown. I do not believe the Corcoran was introduced until 1914. The big difference was in the Victors; they used a number 1. Headlamps were quite large with an embossed script. Some had steel tops. Sidelamps were embossed as well. The tail lamp was round, like a railroad lamp, and the top was held on by three or four tabs, right through the brass. All had embossed Ford script.

Some of the early models had a special tail light bracket which was attached with three bolts from the corner of the body, and went out towards the fender, rather than straight back as did the later style which carried into 1914 and was attached with just two bolts. Just when this change was made is unknown.

Two types of front fenders were used. The lip on one protrudes out, and the other goes straight down.

The early 1913 models still used many parts produced by Dodge Brothers. Some of the parts I've seen on '13's are the steering gear box, front axle, spindles, steering arms, connecting rods, flywheels, transmission pedals, steering column and spider.

= = = = = End of Larry Smith's comments = = = = =

Larry Smith's 1913 Touring Car.

1913

Three brands and four styles of windshields were used in 1913. Manufacturers were Vanguard, Diamond, and Rands. Most used unequal upper and lower sizes but Rands made one in which both halves were equal, giving the assembly a different slope and requiring a different set of support brackets, and a modification to the front top bow. The car in the photo at the left appears to have the 1914-style support brackets; the 1913-style did not have the "dogleg" needed to clear the upper windshield section when folded back. 1913 windshields folded forward, while 1914 windshields folded back.

Note the "piano hinge" between the sections on the Vanguard windshield (lower left).

The front fenders on the 1913 and early 1914 cars did not have the bill as did the 1911 and 1912 cars. The early 1913 cars had the front lip on an angle (left) but most used the straight-down type shown at the right.

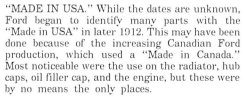

"MADE IN USA." While the dates are unknown, Ford began to identify many parts with the "Made in USA" in later 1912. This may have been done because of the increasing Canadian Ford production, which used a "Made in Canada." Most noticeable were the use on the radiator, hub caps, oil filler cap, and the engine, but these were by no means the only places.

Hub caps in 1913 came in a number of minor variations, two of which are shown here. Note the "F" in "Ford" was much higher than in the later, more common, types.

1913

Except for the elimination of the bill at the front, the fenders of the 1913 cars were similar to those of the 1912's. Note that there was no reinforcing bead across the fender at the widest part (as in the 1914 to 1916 cars) and that there was no embossed bead in the triangular inner panel.

The horn on the 1913 and 1914 models was painted black except for the rim and screen. It was mounted with the bell down, as shown here, not with the bell up. Some of these horns were made of brass (painted black) but most were steel.

1913

Heinze coil box

K-W coil box

1913 was the last year in which the wooden coil boxes were used in the Model T. These were supplied by K-W, Heinze, and a few Kingston. While all were similar in size and shape, the coils in them were not interchangeable. During 1913 Ford began using the metal box and standard-size coil units.

A typical K-W coil unit is shown at the lower right (for the wooden coil box).

BELOW: Typical 1913 front compartment. The correct 1913 Stewart speedometer is shown.

Ford-made standard 1913-14 metal coil box

The running gear was essentially unchanged from that of the 1912 cars. The only major change at the front axle was in the steering connecting rod between the steering arm and the right-hand end of the tie rod. Up until late 1912 the socket at the steering arm end had been threaded on and locked with a nut. Now the socket was riveted and brazed in place.

The brass oil fittings and the spring shackles were typical of the Model T's until around 1916-1917. Note that on the shackles the oilers faced forward on the bottom and to the rear on the top. The axle shown has an additional wishbone under the axle which was an aftermarket accessory and was a common practice to strengthen the axle assembly. Standard production used just the upper wishbone until 1919, then just a lower one.

In 1912 the rear axle was redesigned and had a much 'fatter' center section, with the axle tubes flared and riveted to it. This style axle was used until early 1915.

The driveshaft housing was on the two-piece (separate universal joint housing) type until calendar 1913. The one-piece design with the integral universal joint housing was a running change during 1913 production.

The brake rods and the rear radius rods both had forged forks which were welded to the rods.

The crank handle was aluminum. Most appear bare today but they were originally painted black at the factory.

The major change in the engine compartment was the "Made in USA" on the side of the crankcase, under the "Ford," and also on the cylinder head. The brass oil filler cap also had this identification.

At about number 300,000 the cylinder casting was changed and now used pressed-in (welch) plugs in the water jacket instead of the pipe plugs which had been used since 1909. There was considerable overlap in time when both types of castings were used. in a survey of engines which exist today, the earliest engine with welch plugs was 131,432 (which may have been a renumbered block), then several around the 200,000 era. More and more were listed with the last pipe plugs at around 400,000 (although one 1915 engine was listed with pipe plugs by its owner). Other modifications were made in the cylinder casting which are difficult to date and would be a study in themselves.

The serial number was now located in the standard position just above the water inlet. The casting date, if there was one, generally appeared just to the rear of the water inlet.

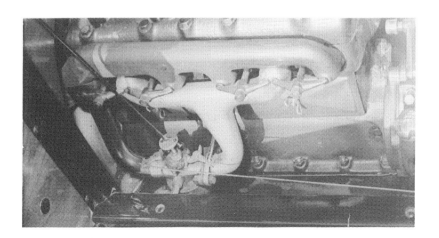

Some of the 1913 cylinder heads were drilled for priming cups on the left side, apparently for ease of starting in the colder climates. Normally these holes were plugged with screws as shown in the photo at the upper left.

The intake manifold on the typical 1913 was aluminum but this was changed to iron by 1914 (again with some overlap when both types were used). Carburetors for 1913 were either the Holley model S (4450) with two screws on the top cover, or the Kingston model Y four-ball.

1913

Two styles of tail lamp brackets were used in 1913. The earlier type mounted with three bolts to the body and went out at an angle toward the left fender, placing the lamp more to the left (this car has an accessory license plate bracket which moves the lamp even further to the left).

The later and more common type mounted with two bolts and extended straight to the rear, placing the lamp in back of the body.

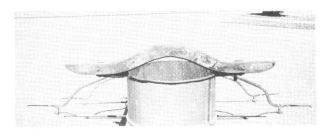

In addition to the body-supporting brackets for the Touring, added to the 1912-style frame, later production used the frame with the longer rear cross-member, eliminating the cast body brackets (shown elsewhere). The early frames with the longer cross-member differed from the later in that the upper surfaces of the cross-member are relatively smooth; not raised at the ends where the body mounts.

Early tail lamp position

Late tail lamp position

View, looking up, at the early tail lamp bracket.

SIDE LAMPS

Corcoran

Victor

E&J

Side and tail lamps for 1913 and 1914 were all of the oil type and were made by Jno. Brown, Corcoran (in 1913 only), Edmond and Jones (E&J) or Victor. All were iron with brass trim, or the so-called "black and brass" type. A few are shown here but there were a number of variations, especially in 1914 when many had integral mounting brackets.

The question arises: Did the cars that had, for instance, E&J headlamps, also have E&J side and tail lamps, or could they have been another brand? We have no definite information one way or the other. Factory invoices for 1909 to 1911 indicate that they were mixed on many cars, and all the same brand on others, and we could presume this could also be true in 1913 and 1914. In the haste of assembly, it is not likely that a worker would check to see which brand he grabbed, and if the brand he did choose was the same as the other lamps that might have already been installed on the car.

TAIL LAMPS

Corcoran

E&J

Brown 115

E&J "666."
The 66 and 656 were similar.

The gas headlamps were supplied by Brown, Victor, E&J, and Corcoran. All were "black and brass," steel bodies with brass tops and rims.

E&J apparently supplied three types, all similar but with different model numbers. They were the 656, 666, and 66. The 66 and 666 were the same lamp; E&J had made a model 666, all brass, for earlier Fords and the new 666 was similar except for the steel shell. Later they eliminated the last '6' leaving the '66' off-center. The 656 apparently followed the 66.

Victor made, apparently, two styles of head, side and tail lamps. The only photo we have of the earliest (we presume) is of the tail lamp. The headlamp was the number 1, with an embossed script instead of the stamped imprint as on the model 2 shown, and was larger than the model 2.

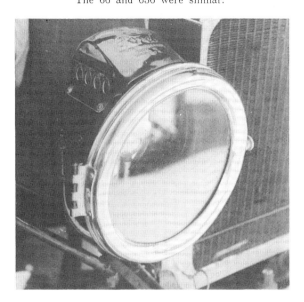

Jno. Brown Model 16

Victor Model 2

Rare Victor tail lamp, used in part of 1913. The top was brass and was held in place by four steel tabs from the chimney which pierced the top and were bent over. The brass top had the "Ford" in script, in addition to "Victor Lamp Co. Cincinnati, O."

Top view of E&J model 66, showing the off-center number.

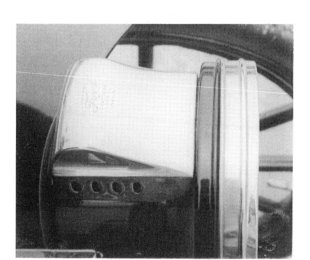

Not too common, the Corcoran headlamp was almost a duplicate of the Victor model 2.

The runningboard-mounted gas generators for the 1913 and 1914 cars were supplied by the same firms that supplied the headlamps. All were similar in appearance, made of steel, and with brass fittings. Inside the lower section was a galvanized-iron basket into which calcium carbide was placed. The upper section was filled with water. The valve on top was opened to allow the water to drip down onto the carbide, creating the gas which was piped to the headlights.

1913

Upholstery varied during 1913 production from all-leather seats to a combination of leather and imitation leather. Door and side panels were imitation leather. Generally the seat cushions were leather but the seat backs became imitation leather except for the forward roll of the arm rest, which was real leather.

Wooden doors covered the gas tank and the tool compartment under the rear seat.

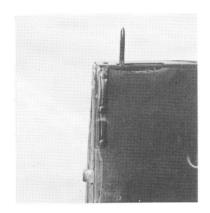

The 1913 cars had large doors that extended down to the splash aprons. There was no sheet metal across the door areas to add support to the body structure, and consequently the bodies were quite weak. Passengers in the rear seat could cause enough flexing to allow the doors to unlatch and open. Note how the door handle extends through the top surface of the door and that the latch moves horizontally. This arrangement was modified later in the year (1914 models?) to a more secure vertical-latching system in which the door handles were inside the car. 1913 bodies were also unique in that the side sheet metal did not cover the top surface of the wooden framing. A separate metal trim strip, screwed in place, added the finishing touch.

Body striping, as shown here, appeared only in the early production 1913 cars; those built during late 1912 and, perhaps, early 1913. Ford records indicate the color was "blue." The blue was a midnight blue, almost black. There has been no documented evidence found which would indicate black cars in 1913, although many seemingly original cars appear to be black.

The 1914 Model T Fords

"ANY COLOR AS LONG AS IT'S BLACK"

Some photos by Bill Cassiday, Bill Austen, and Glenn Embree.

THE FORD LINE FOR 1914

Not much of a selection. Initially just three models; the Touring, the Runabout, and the Town Car. Later the bare chassis was added to the line, ending Ford's hard-fast rule about "non-Ford" bodies (the use of which would void the warranty) and opening the doors for accessory body manufacturers.

Prices: $490 for the Touring, $440 for the Runabout, and $690 for the Town Car, F.O.B. Detroit. (When announced on July 28, 1913, the "1914" prices were $550, $500, and $750, but the above prices were in effect by mid-1914.) When the chassis was introduced, its price was just $20 less than the Runabout!

Old photograph of a later 1914 Ford Touring. Note the smooth tires all around and the bills on the front fenders. Earlier 1914 Fords continued the fender style of the 1913's (no bills) but the bills were added during the production run. Compare this car with the Runabout shown on the next page.

The 1914 Model T Ford style year has created a good amount of confusion. There are many "1914s" around that are called "1913" and the owners can prove that the car was, indeed, made in 1913. Further, the "1914" style was built at some of the branches in calendar 1915, and apparently at the same time that the new "1915" cars were being built at Highland Park. There is some evidence that the 1914 cars were built, at some of the branches, as late as March or April of 1915.

The facts are that the 1914 style began in later 1913, perhaps as early as August, at the Highland Park plant. Ford issued a letter on July 28, 1913, announcing, "1914 prices effective August 1, 1913: Touring, $550; Runabout, $500; Town Car, $750." The letter does not indicate a "new" style, however.

The 1913 Touring body had been somewhat of a disaster. The rear section was a separate unit, supported only by the wooden body sill initially. Early versions were so weak that a reinforcing bracket was made to couple the front and rear sections. Later the sill was made of heavier material, and an additional body bracket was added at the front of the rear seat section. These cars came with and without the reinforcing bracket (which was

supplied by Ford as a repair part). It is quite likely that Ford came up with the modified body with the sheet metal coupling the two sections, typical of the 1914 through 1925 bodies, before September 1913.

In any event, the 1914 style differed mainly from the 1913 in that the doors no longer extended to the splash apron, but now had rounded bottoms and were set into the sides of the body, a characteristic of Ford bodies for years to come. The "1914" style, then, is this "rounded door" body coupled with the wooden firewall/sloping windshield style of the 1913 cars.

The 1914 style year was a time of Ford's greatest changes. The moving final assembly line, the Five Dollar Day, the $50 Rebate, and Ford's first 300,000 unit production record all occurred during this period. And, of course, the car itself evolved considerably.

Perhaps the second most noticeable change in the car was the new but similar windshield. The 1913 type could be folded down but it folded forward towards the front of the car. This arrangement made it difficult, if not dangerous, to fold or unfold the windshield while driving. For 1914 the windshield was made to fold to the rear, or towards the driver,

The 1914 Runabout. Here the fenders are of the earlier style without the front bills. The rear fender appears to have been pushed forward in this right-hand-drive car.

and this operation could be done while driving. In order for the windshield to fold back, the windshield support brackets were given a "bend" to clear the windshield frame when it was folded.

The fenders continued in the 1913 style initially, but during the year they were modified to now include a reinforcing rib across the widest section of the front fender. Still later, the "bill" on the front fenders, dropped for the 1913 models (in 1912), was reinstated, and continued until the introduction of the 1917 models in August 1916. Still later, the triangular beading was added to the apron area of the front fender. That about does it for the major visible differences between a "1913" and a "1914."

"Invisible" changes were many, though. Typical of Ford, nothing was done all at one time. For example, the wooden coil boxes used since 1909 (in the Model T) were discontinued in favor of a metal box during the 1913 model year. Early 1914 style cars used the metal boxes but they were supplied by outside makers; Heinze being one of them. During 1914 Ford began making its own boxes and coils, so a "1914" may have either type.

The so-called "two-piece" driveshaft was dropped during the 1914 style year. Early 1914s used the two-piece type while the later ones used the one-piece style. (It is likely that some 1913s may have used the newer type as well.)

Speedometers, standard equipment on the Model T since early 1909, were discontinued, for a short time at least, because of a shortage in supply. According to a letter dated November 4, 1913, a $6.00 allowance was to be made in the price of the car when there was no speedometer installed.

Ford's increasing sales resulted in a reduction of prices. On August 1, 1914, the following prices were announced: Touring, $490; Runabout, $440; Town Car, $690. These prices did not include a possible $40 to $60 rebate, pending on the sale of 300,000 cars by August 1915.

The engine casting was modified somewhat during the 1913-1914 period. The first 1913 cars used an engine almost identical to the 1912 cars. The major characteristics of this engine were the "lip" at the rear of the cylinder casting, and the screw-in pipe plugs in the water jacket on the right side. During 1913, and probably appearing in the 1913 style year, the lip was eliminated but the pipe plugs continued. Still later, and typical of most 1914 cars, the pipe plugs were replaced with pressed-in welch plugs.

There were, of course, many variations in the

engine castings. It is quite possible that all three types of engines were built at the same time, with the older designs being phased out as new casting cores were made.

Transmission covers were of aluminum, as they had been since 1909. During the 1914 model year, reinforcing ribs were cast into the cover around the bolt holes at the flywheel housing in an effort to strengthen the casting. It had been quite easy to crack the cover when tightening the bolts after changing the transmission bands, and these reinforcements made it a bit stronger. Transmission cover doors were flat steel. Foot pedals continued with the lettered design, to be replaced with a ribbed pattern in early 1915.

Carburetors were either Holley or Kingston. Early production 1914 cars may have come with the Holley Model S (2-screw) as in our feature car, but the most common Holley was the Model G, a similar design but with the cover secured with three screws. The Kingston carburetor was the "four-ball" Model Y. It is possible that the Kingston Model L appeared in 1914 cars in the later production. Intake manifolds were aluminum in early production but the typical 1914 engine used a cast-iron intake manifold of almost identical design.

Late in the 1914 model year the magneto was enlarged and the magnets were now 3/4" thick. This change began with 572,437 on September 4, 1914, and by October (after 598,041) all engines had the new magneto. The new magneto was needed to supply power for the electric headlamps used on the then-new closed cars, introduced in the fall of 1914. (While the Sedan and Coupelet were introduced in 1914, they are considered to be 1915 cars and are not a part of this coverage.) The Touring and Runabouts continued in the 1914 pattern until about February 1915, when the 1915 style began to be produced at the Highland Park plant.

It is believed that all 1914-style open cars used gas headlamps but it is quite possible the later ones came with electric lamps. In a letter to the branches, dated January 12, 1915, Ford noted that they were no longer supplying the gas lamp tube on the

The front compartment of Bill Cassiday's 1914 Touring. The floor mat was originally an off-white and the design was molded on both sides. Done in this manner, the same mat could be used on left or right hand drive cars. The patent plate, located above the steering column, covered a hole in the firewall. The firewalls, too, were reversible so they could be used on RHD cars. The covered hole was for the carburetor adjustment on the RHD installation. (Being drilled on an angle, one hole is lower on one side than the other.) Note the spark/throttle quadrant and steering bear box were brass, as on the 1913 and earlier Fords. The metal coil box, now standard, was made by Heinze in this car.

radiators "as all cars now have electric lights." (A tube, part number T-4052X, was listed for use when the new radiator was used to replace the older type on a gas-lamp car.) Yet it was not until February 1915 that the 1915 style car bodies were being shipped to the branches. Therefore, one would think that 1914 bodies built until about March or April came with electric lights. On the other hand, we have seen a number of pictures of 1915-style Tourings (old pictures of seemingly original cars) with gas lamps. Ford never admitted to using gas lamps on a "1915" and it is possible that owners, unhappy with the poor electric lights, replaced them with the older gas type.

All 1914-style cars used the new chassis frame with the longer rear cross-member. The date of the change from the old frame with the forged body brackets is not known for certain but evidence would indicate the new chassis appeared about May, 1913. A letter to the Ford branches notes that the longer rear member began to be used "after 114,000 1913 cars." Ford, in other records, indicates that "1913" production began with 157,425 on October 1, 1912. Adding the 114,000 to this number puts it at 271,425 and the engine bearing that number was built on May 16, 1913. No doubt both the old and the new frames were used in production until the older style were used up.

1914 is commonly believed to have been the first year of the "any color as long as it's black" policy. Parts Lists all indicate wheels were "blue" but this may have been an oversight on the part of the people who made up the lists. To add even more to the confusion, though, the following list of paints was published on December 2, 1913, well into the "1914" model year:

F-101	1763	1st coat plastic black japan	Fenders and shields
F-102	1001	2nd coat black japan	Fenders and shields
F-103	258	1st coat blue dipping	Hoods and rear axles
F-104	1355	2nd coat quick drying black	Rear axles
F-105	40	1st coat brushing black japan	Front axles
F-106	459	2nd coat brushing black japan	Front axles
F-107	450	Blue black baking	Coil box
F-108	1843	1st coat black wheel surfacer	Wheels
F-109	260	2nd coat blue color varnish	Wheels
F-110	417	2nd coat black brushing	Frame
F-111	488	1st coat red baking body primer	Body
F-112	66	Black glaze putty, 2nd operation	Body
F-113	948	2nd coat blue ground	Body
F-114	619	Solid rubbing body blue	Repairs only
F-115	480	3rd & 4th coat blue color varnish	Body
F-116	908	5th coat black striping color	Not used regularly
F-117	1435	Fine French Gray deep striping	Wheels
F-118	1761	Oil proof steel blue	Painting machines
F-119	896	Black engine dipping	Crankcases

Still further confusion presents itself. In a letter dated March 22, 1917, Ford said, "As we expect to paint all bodies black by April 15th, we ask that you kindly give us an inventory of all the F-113 (blue body paint) you now have on hand, and that you do not requisition any more of this material beyond your needs to April 15th." This letter was mailed to Ford assembly plants and would seem to indicate that there were some blue cars as late as 1917!

To add to the confusion, another letter, dated February 20, 1919, addressed to the branches, said, "As closed bodies are now being painted black, instead of green as heretofore, also carmine striped, it becomes imperative that the branches prepare to repair bodies when needed according to the new color. It is necessary that someone in your paint shop, accustomed to the method of striping, be assigned to this work, as this section of body painting is something new for branches to contend with. Striping pencils and carmine paint for striping will be furnished you for this purpose upon request for same."

In the same letter, Ford goes on with "New paint specifications. . . . These are being sent you at this time and comprise the change in sedan, coupe, touring car and torpedo body painting, according to the latest information. You will note the change in the Symbol number of paint used in painting closed bodies, as well as that for the touring car and torpedo bodies, and wheel paint, as called to your attention in our general letter of the 11th and 12th. F-165 and F-166 will be held for repairs only on closed bodies which were formerly painted green."

There is no indication of just when "formerly painted green" was. There were, of course, no closed bodies in the 1914 line of Fords, but the 1915 Sedan and Coupelet appeared in October 1914. Were these green? Blue? The author has seen very few closed cars of the 1915 to 1919 era, and all have been black. Just a little more confusion to add to the enigmatic Model T story.

Our featured car is an early 1914 Touring, owned by W. E. Cassiday, of Oakland, California. The engine number is 355,995 which was built, according to the records, on October 17, 1913. The engine casting date is 9-18-13. The body date, found under the front seat, is 11-8-13 — which is interesting. Apparently the engine sat around a while or, and most likely, the car was assembled at one of the branches.

The car is NOT the "typical" 1914 in that it came with "1913" front fenders, the non-Ford metal coil box (Heinze), a transitional engine and any number of other oddities. It is this very non-typicalness (the author invents words as they are needed) that makes this car interesting. Ford never dropped everything and began a new model. Style years evolved and there was always a great deal of overlapping of details in assembly. The photographs showing details of the car will illustrate a number of the interesting oddities on this car. All photos were supplied by Bill Cassiday and Bill Austen, also from Oakland.

The Ford assembly line after the installation of the chain driven moving assembly line. These chassis have the extended rear cross member, typical of the later 1913 and all subsequent Fords. These are probably 1914 cars. Photo from the Collections of the Henry Ford Museum and Greenfield Village.

The inside "works" of the carbide generator. Water in the upper compartment is allowed to drip on carbide held in the basket in the lower section, and this creates acetylene gas for the headlamps.

Unpainted Touring Car bodies being delivered to the Highland Park plant. This photo was taken in late 1913 and illustrates an interesting paradox; horses and wagons being used to supply the very industry which rendered them obsolete. Photo from the Collections of the Henry Ford Museum and Greenfield Village.

1914 Touring car bodies, now painted and upholstered, with tops attached, being hand pushed to the assembly line ramp at Highland Park. Note the stack of engine blocks in the background. The left-most body is a Runabout. Photo from the Collections of the Henry Ford Museum and Greenfield Village.

1914

The first 1914 front fenders were a continuation of the 1913 design; four rivets to hold the fender iron bracket, no front bill, and no molding across the wide part of the fender, nor on the triangular apron piece.

The first modification was to add the molding across the widest part of the fender as is shown in the photo of the 1915 fender below.

After the addition of the reinforcing bead, but before the addition of the molding on the triangular section, the front bill, which had been deleted in the 1913 models, was reinstated. Still later, the beads were added to the triangular section, and this final design (beads, bill, and four rivets) continued into early 1915.

The front fenders for early 1915 cars were like those of late 1914 but early in the year the fender iron bracket was changed and the almost identical fender now had just three rivets on the top surface.

It is possible these changes (other than the "1915" style) overlapped. The author has not seen the non-bead fender with the front bill (except in pre-1913 cars) but it may have occurred.

Early 1914 front fender, typical of the 1913 style. Note the lack of beads on the apron, and that there is no bead across the widest part of the upper surface.

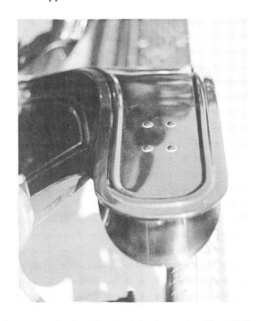

The last 1914 (and early 1915) fender style. The bill had been reinstated and the molded-in beads appear on the apron and across the widest part (which is not visible in this picture).

1915 fender shown here to illustrate the bead across the widest part. 1914 fenders looked the same except that they had four rivets for the fender iron bracket.

Upholstering on our feature car was all leatherette except for the front roll of the arm rests. There seems to be some evidence of the seat bottom cushions being supplied in full leather during this period, so either type of bottom cushion might be correct.

The seat backs were made in three main sections; the two sides and a separate back. The hub cap wrench is shown inserted between the sections. Pictures of Ford assembly lines during the upholstery installation will confirm that the upholstery was not all one piece.

The doors were also covered with leatherette, with tacked-in-place trim strips. There were two major changes in design here, beside the rounded doors. The 1913 cars used a separate metal trim strip along the tops of the doors, while the 1914 (and later) bodies were made with the body metal folded over to cover the edge. The door handles, which extended up through the top edge in 1913 bodies, now were inside the doors, as shown.

Typically, all upholstery jobs were not identical. Note the strip nailed across the center of the door in another (later) 1914 Touring. The seat bottoms in that car were real leather.

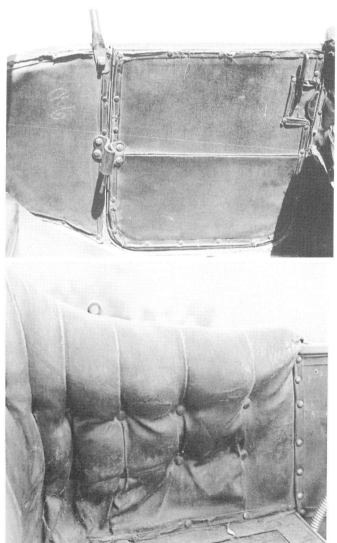

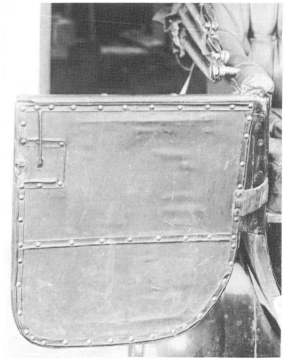

The door check straps were all leather. Note the workmanship on the upholstery. Talk about the "lovin' hands of home."

Both front and rear seat frames were covered with doors made of wood strips of random width. It would appear that Ford used every piece of scrap wood it could find and this, no doubt, began the old-wives tale about Ford ordering parts in boxes of a given dimension (for which no proof is known to exist). The space under the rear seat was given a metal "box" with wood end panels for storage of the side curtains, tools and baling wire. (The two bolts seen at the right rear of the top picture hold the tail light bracket.)

The gasoline tank was galvanized, as were the straps which held it. The tank filler cap was cast iron.

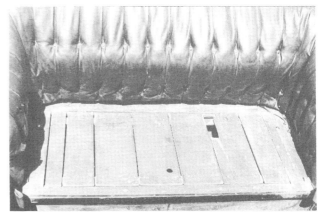

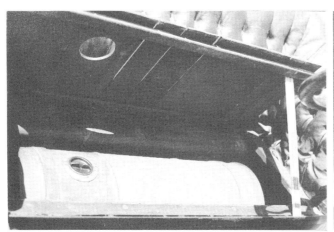

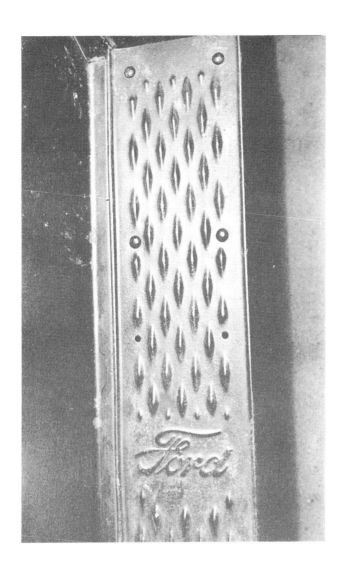

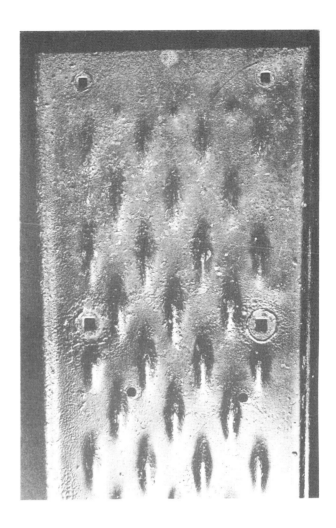

The original running boards on our featured 1914 Ford were both drilled for the carbide generator. Apparently this was done to make them completely interchangeable from side to side, thus eliminating any need for a decision by the man who installed them on the assembly line.

The closeup shows the difference between the holes drilled for the fender bolts and those for the runningboard bracket. While the head size of the two sets of bolts was the same, the shank size for the fender bolts was smaller.

The closeup of the "Ford" shows the "Made in USA" to be upside down. Well, nobody's perfect!

With the advent of the standard metal coil box during 1913, the ignition coils became a uniform size, regardless of the supplier. The coils and box shown here are Heinze. During 1914 production, Ford began making its own coils and boxes but continued the use of outside suppliers as well.

1914 Runabout. The step plate on the runningboard is an accessory, not supplied by Ford.

The engine (#355,995) is an evolution between the "typical" 1913 and the "typical" 1914. This one has the pipe-plug water jacket plugs (1913 and earlier) while the block casting does not have the lip at the rear of the cylinder (1914 and later).

The carburetor here is the Holley "two screw" used in 1913, along with the Kingston "Y" four ball.

The throttle rod, shown at the right, has a screw-on end, typical of 1909 to 1914 Fords. Note that the end is not bent at a ninety degree angle.

The intake manifold is aluminum in this example but the cast iron type was also used during 1914.

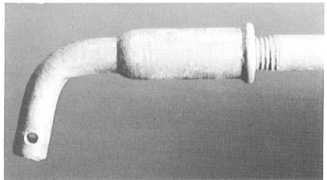

The starting crank on the 1913 cars had an aluminum handle, which was painted black. During 1914 production the handle was changed to one of steel as is shown here. This design continued until the early 1920's.

Note the metal clip used to support the commutator wire. These clips are not found on all cars; perhaps because they were lost or broken off over the years, or perhaps because they weren't used originally on all production.

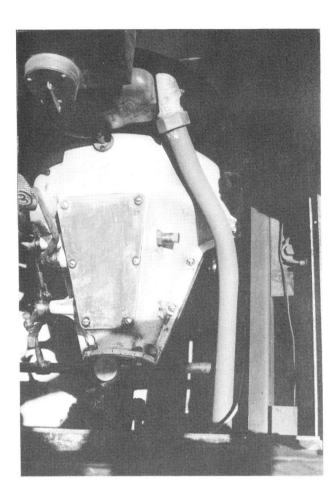

Holley Model S

The transmission cover is of aluminum, as in previous models. During 1913 reinforcing ribs were added around the bolt holes at the front corners, barely visible in this picture. The actual date of this change is unknown. We have seen later 1914 cars with the non-reinforced cover. The cover shown here may be a replacement.

The typical inspection door during this period is as shown here; a flat piece of steel with no "Ford" or other markings.

Above: Kingston Model Y
Below: Holley Model G

The original exhaust pipe, shown in the picture, was made with gentle bends so that the pipe cleared everything and was easy to install, unlike the replacements found today.

This car has the two piece driveshaft housing. The one piece design appeared during 1913 production.

At least three carburetors were used during 1914 production; perhaps more. The first cars used either the Kingston "Y" four ball or the Holley "S" two screw. The Kingston continued through 1914 but the Holley was replaced with the model "G" of similar design but now with three screws to hold its top plate.

It is quite possible that the so-called "1915" Holley "G" (similar to the 1914 model G but with a different air intake horn) and the new Kingston model "L" appeared on some of the later 1914s.

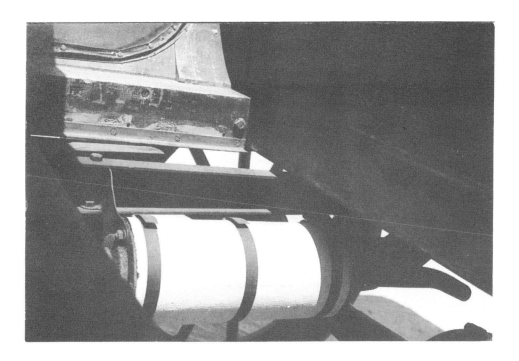

The muffler was asbestos-wrapped; the asbestos being held with three metal straps, the same as those used on heating pipes in buildings. During 1914 the muffler was modified to use a new rear casting with an integral mounting bracket. The exhaust pipe extension also became straight rather than curved as in our example, during 1914 production.

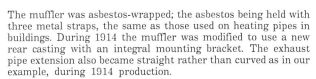

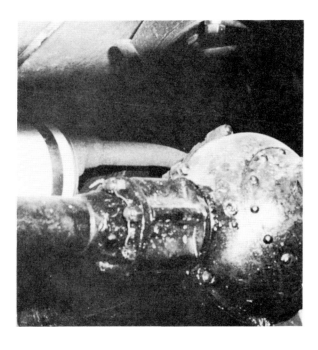

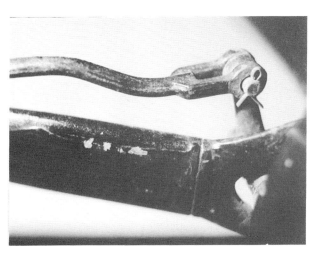

The rear axle continued in the style set in late 1912. The center section was cast iron, similar in size and shape to the axle introduced in 1915 and which continued with but minor modifications until the end of Model T production. The axle housings were flared at the inner ends and held to the center section by twelve rivets on each side. The pinion bearing spool was held with six studs and nuts, secured with a tie wire.

Brake rods and rear radius rods continued the use of the forged ends. The rear radius rods were interchangeable from side to side.

An almost new 1914 Touring owned by Barbara and Stuart Herman, of West Redding, Connecticut. New tires and a top have been installed but otherwise the car is as delivered in 1914 except for the deterioration of the paint.

LAMPS

Head, side and tail lamps continued the styles and models used in 1913 with few changes. Corcoran, one of the minor suppliers in 1913, was apparently dropped, leaving E&J, Brown, and Victor as the manufacturers used in 1914.

In later production some of the side lamps were supplied with integral mounting brackets, eliminating the need for the separate brackets, and resulting in lower manufacturing costs for Ford.

AN ORIGINAL 1914 TOURING
(Photos by David W. Reed)

At the AACA Hershey Meet in 1983 the author met Stuart Herman, from West Redding, Connecticut, who owned an original and unrestored 1914 touring. Stuart was the third owner of the car, and had an interesting story to tell.

A Mr. C. Herrlinger and his son went to purchase an automobile for his daughter. Their choice was a new 1914 Ford touring, from the J.H. Walsh Motor Car Co., a dealer who also sold Oaklands (unusual for the time, as Ford seldom allowed dual dealerships). The car was ordered on August 31 from the Ford Motor Company, and a deposit of fifty dollars was secured. On September 5,

Mr. Herrlinger again visited the dealer and agreed to purchase some additional items with the car, as noted:

One Model T Touring car	$490.00
Freight	21.50
10 gal. gas	2.00
1 gal. oil	.50
	$514.00
1 pr. 30x3-1/2 Ridaskid chains	2.65
1 30x3-1/2 Goodyear tube	3.50
1 30x3 Goodyear tube	2.80
2 spark plugs @ .50	1.00
1 tire fork	.25
1 pair license plate brackets	.80
1 100 Stewart speedometer	12.00
	23.00
Total	537.00
Credit by cash 9/5/14	50.00
	487.00
Less $6.00 for speedometer	6.00
Total due	481.00

On November 11, 1914, Mr. Herrlinger took delivery of his new Ford. Upon bringing the car home, he was disappointed to learn that his daughter was not pleased with the car, and because of this the car saw little use and was subsequently stored in the barn and not driven.

In 1968, Mr. Don Carlson, of Kensington, CT, bought the car from the daughter, and in 1971 Barbara and Stu Herman purchased it from Mr. Carlson.

When the Hermans purchased the car the original top and tires were still on the car. In addition, under the back seat were the tire iron, chains and side curtains. Since the speedometer was purchased with the car (dealer installed), we believe the mileage to be correct. It read 2237 in 1971, the day of the final purchase. About 600 miles had been added when the photos shown here were taken. Other than the new top and tires, the car is as delivered originally to Mr. Herrlinger.

The Herman's 1914 Ford is serial number 557,809. The engine was assembled August 15, 1914. The body is numbered "8.14.20 1914" on the sill of the front seat. Ordered on August 31, the car was delivered on November 11, to Charles A. Herrlinger, Winfield, Long Island, New York.

The car might be called the "typical" 1914 style. It has the fenders with all the moldings, oil lamps with the integral mounting brackets, and other features of a standard 1914 Model T Ford Touring car.

1914

The steering gear case was all brass and of the riveted design. The case was redesigned in 1914 or 1915, as was the quadrant, to a simpler (and cheaper) yet better arrangement. The steering wheel was wood, painted black, and the steering wheel spider was "cast iron," also painted black (as was the retaining nut).

The Stewart Model 100 speedometer was installed by the Ford dealer in 1914 as optional equipment. At that time Ford had discontinued supplying speedometers as standard equipment because of a shortage of supply, and Ford allowed a $6.00 discount on the price of the car for the lack of the factory-supplied speedometer.

Note the black and brass horn and side lamps, typical of 1913-14. These items varied, depending on the supplier and date. Some horns were brass and painted black; others were steel and painted black. Most had the brass rim. Lamps came with the integral mounting brackets (shown here) as well as the usual (earlier) clamp-on arrangement.

The right-hand steering arm was no longer provided with a mounting hole for the speedometer swivel, as in earlier models. The swivel now clamped to the arm. Note the brass oilers on the kingpins, steering rods and shackles. These were replaced (except for the shackles) with cheaper "manhole cover" types in 1915 production (if not earlier).

The typical rear axle housing, used from later 1912 until early in 1915. The center section was cast iron as in the 1912 housings, but was larger and stronger. The axle tubes were flared and secured with twelve rivets. This construction was discontinued because of the tendency to leak oil around the rivets.

1914

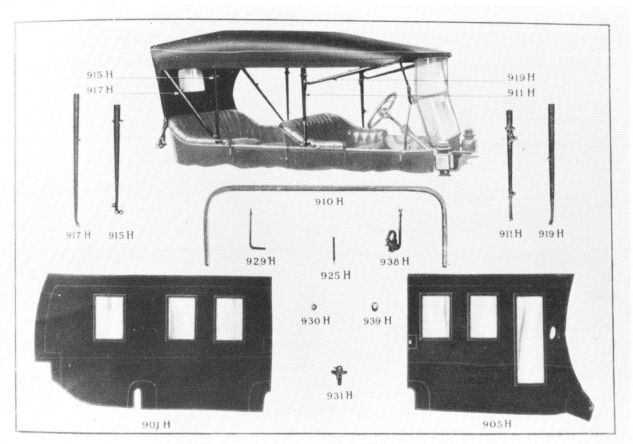

PLATE No. 5—Touring Car Top

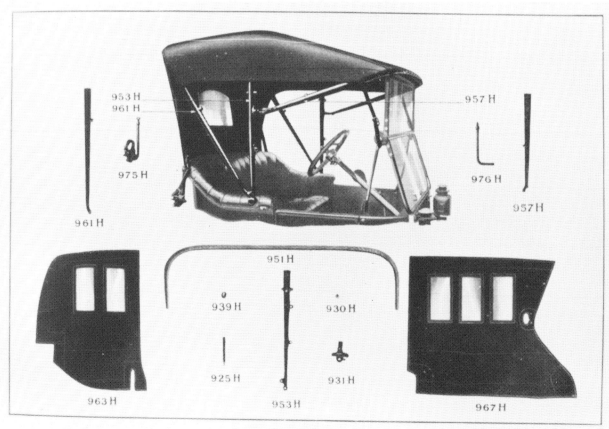

PLATE No. 6—Runabout Top

1915

Body Type	Factory Price #	Shipping Weight Lbs.	Production Total *
Touring	$490	1510	244181
Runabout	440	1395	47116
Town Car	690	—	0
Sedan	975	1730	989
Coupe	750	1540	2417
Chassis	410	980	13459
Total			308162 **

\# August 1, 1914.
* Fiscal year, August 1, 1914 to July 31, 1915.
** *Ford News*, Nov. 1, 1920, gave a figure of 308,213.

MODEL YEAR DATES: September 1914 (Sedan), October (Coupelet) and January 1915 (open cars) to August 1915.

BODY TYPES: Touring, Runabout, Sedan, Town Car, Coupelet, and Chassis.

MAJOR MODEL YEAR FEATURES

Similar to 1914 but now had metal cowl section which tapered down to the hood. Early in production the front seat frame was modified, and a bolt head (or "rivet") appeared in the side panel just ahead of the rear door on the Touring. Windshield was now upright and folded to the rear at the center. Hood was aluminum, but had louvres on the side panels. Rear fenders were curved to follow the wheel outline but had no crown.

Headlamps were now electric, made of steel with brass rims. The brass rims were replaced with black-painted steel in June 1915.

Oil side and tail lamps were steel, with brass trim until mid-year, and were of a new interchangeable (from side to side) design.

The bulb horn, now mounted under the hood, was replaced with magneto powered electric type beginning in January 1915 on some cars, and in all production by October. (There is no evidence of a klaxon horn ever being supplied on a Model T Ford as factory equipment.)

The transmission foot pedals were changed from the "C-R-B" markings to a vertically ribbed pattern. This in turn gave way to the plain pedals during calendar 1915.

Rear axle housings redesigned, taking on the final major exterior change in appearance.

COLORS. All cars were painted black, with black fenders.

UPHOLSTERY. Imitation leather in the open cars. The pattern was a stitched diamond on the seat bottoms, and vertical pleats on the seat backs. Sedan upholstery was gray* with an ornate pattern, and trimmed with an ornate, tapestry-like material as well. The Coupelet had leather seats and the top was leather and trimmed with the same fabric as the Sedan. Trim was imitation leather.
* The parts books show "blue" but existing samples look gray.

FENDERS. Front: continued the style of the later 1914 cars. Mounting bracket changed early in the year and was now held with just three rivets (instead of four as in previous years). **Rear**: similar in style to the front but now curve to follow the wheel outline, and had no crown as did the later fenders. Support irons were attached to the body framing, extending out the side of the body, through a hole in the apron of the fender, and were clamped to a single plate under the fender.

SPLASH APRON. Same as in 1914. Fenders and aprons were painted black.

RUNNING BOARDS. Pressed steel with embossed diamond pattern. The Ford script ran across the board. "Made in USA" appeared on all boards.

HOOD. Aluminum, with louvers for the first time. Hinges were separate from the panels, and riveted in place. Hold-down clamps had two "ears" and were of forged steel. Hood handles were forged steel.

DASHBOARD (Firewall). Wood, fitted inside the front cowl, hidden by the metal hood former.

CHASSIS. Same as 1914 with the longer rear cross-member. Painted black.

STEERING COLUMN ASSEMBLY. Some early production apparently used the "1913" type column with the riveted gear box. Early in the year the new one-piece, brass, gear box with the iron quadrant appeared. There was apparently some overlap in production where both the old and the new types were used. Brass-plated spark and throttle levers, with flattened metal ends, although some black painted rods seem to have appeared. Wheel was 15" diameter, wood, and painted black. The wheel spider was iron and painted black.

FRONT AXLE. Same as the 1914 cars. The right-hand steering arm no longer had the hole for the speedometer swivel, since speedometers were no longer standard equipment. Brass oilers were gradually replaced with pressed steel, "manhole type," types in many locations.

REAR AXLE. Cast center section, same as 1914, and with the axle tubes flared and riveted to it. This axle was replaced with a new design in early 1915. The new type had a cast center section and the axle tubes were inserted into the housing extensions on each side, and riveted in place. This design became the final type except for minor modifications. The brake backing plates continued the "plain" design of the previous type but had reinforcing "ribs" added later in the year.

DRIVESHAFT HOUSING. Pinion bearing spool was a casting and was held by studs and nuts, the studs being enclosed (not visible) in the housing. Integral front housing for universal joint assembly.

REAR RADIUS AND BRAKE RODS. Brake rods had forged ends. Brake-rod support brackets were of the type which go out and wrap down around the rods. Radius rods were of pressed steel with split ends (no forged rear fork).

WHEELS. Used 30 by 3 tires in front; 30 by 3-1/2 in the rear. Original tires had tread on the rear tires. Hub flanges were six inches in diameter. Front wheels used ball bearings. Hub caps had "Ford" in script letters. "Made in USA" on all caps.

SPRINGS. Tapered-leaf, front and rear. "Figure-eight" style shackles.

RADIATOR. Manufactured by Ford with the standard Ford script. "Made in USA" on all radiators under the Ford script.

ENGINE. No major changes from 1914.

ENGINE PAN. Typical "three-dip" with narrow front "snout."

1915 (Continued)

OIL FILLER CAP. The mushroom-shaped cap, now made of steel, with six flutes and with the Ford script as used in 1914. The "Made in USA" did not appear on all steel caps.

ENGINE CRANK. The plain steel-sleeve type as used in later 1914.

ENGINE FAN. Driven by a leather belt from a pulley at the front of the engine. The fan hub was brass (bronze), with the blades riveted in place. Adjustment was by means of a bolt/nut arrangement located on the right side of the front plate and bearing against a boss on the mounting end of the fan bracket.

FUEL TANK. Cylindrical, under the front seat. Mounting brackets clamp to the tank. Outlet was between the center and the right side, between the frame rails. Tank in the Sedan was under the rear seat. The standard round tank was under the seat on the Coupelet.

MANIFOLDS. Exhaust pipe flared at the manifold and was held in place with the brass nut but with no packing. Intake was cast iron in the same pattern of the standard design.

CARBURETORS. Kingston Model L and L2, or Holley Model G.

CARBURETOR STOVE. Pressed steel which rose vertically at the rear of the carburetor and mated with the exhaust manifold at the rear area.

MUFFLER. Cast-iron ends, mounted with brackets integral with the end castings. Exhaust pipe extension integral with the rear cover plate and no longer tapered or bent. Wrapped with asbestos, secured with three steel straps.

COIL BOX ASSEMBLY. Ford. The Ford box used the standard-size coils. The box now had a tapered one-piece top to enable the coils to be changed in the limited space created by the new cowl. The box lid was one-piece. The switch had a brass and black escutcheon plate over the switch housing.

TRANSMISSION. Three-pedal standard design. Pedals were marked with "C," "R," and "B" initially but gave way to pedals with a vertical rib pattern until about mid-1915, then to the plain type used thereafter. Transmission cover was cast aluminum, and had reinforcements around the bolt holes at the widest part. Tapered inspection door, held with six screws. The door was a plain metal plate with no script.

LAMPS. Magneto-powered, electric-type headlights. Brass rims, with clear lens. Side and tail lamps were of new design, also with brass rims. Side lamps were interchangeable from side to side. The brass trim was discontinued during the year. Early headlamps mounted on the same forged forks that were used on the gas lamps, and these lamps varied in style from the usual types. Some were larger in diameter, with "fatter" brass rims. Early side and tail lamps were also made with the larger rims. The standard lamps with the integral mounting post appeared early in the model year.

HORN. Bulb type, single-twist. Black and brass style, mounted under the hood. Beginning in January 1915, the magneto-powered electric horn began to be used on some production, and by October 1915, all cars had the electric horn.

WINDSHIELD. Upright, with top section that folded to the rear. Steel frame was riveted to the mounting brackets. Painted black.

TOP. (Open cars). Top color was black on all open cars. Similar in style to the 1914, with the front still supported by webbed straps to the windshield hinge.

SPEEDOMETER. No longer standard equipment. A number of "Ford Specials" appeared.

TURTLE DECK (on Runabout): Similar in style to the 1914. Handles were painted black.

1916

Body Type	Factory Price #	Shipping Weight Lbs.	Production Total *	
Touring	$440	1500	363024	
Runabout	390	1380	98633	
Town Car	640	—	1972	
Sedan	740	1730	1859	
Coupelet	590	1540	3532	
Chassis	360	980	11742	
Ambulance	—	—	20700	**
Total			501462	***

#	Price effective August 1, 1915. Speedometers no longer supplied as regular equipment.
*	Fiscal year 1916, August 1, 1915 to July 30, 1916.
**	Built for military.
***	*Ford News,* Nov. 1, 1920, gives a figure of 533,921

MODEL YEAR DATES: August 1915 to August 1916.

BODY TYPES: Touring, Runabout, Sedan, Coupelet, Town Car and Chassis.

MAJOR MODEL YEAR FEATURES

Similar to 1915. Hood was now steel with louvers on the side panels. Brass trim on lamps was discontinued. The new all-black style (1917 models) appeared in August.

Transmission cover was now cast iron, replacing the aluminum type used earlier, and used the smooth-surfaced pedals.

The Sedan, while similar in appearance, was redesigned using steel panels and standard fenders and splash aprons. The Coupelet had a collapsible top almost identical to the 1915 except for the addition of small windows in the rear quarter panels.

COLORS. All cars were painted black, with black fenders.

UPHOLSTERY. Imitation leather in the open cars. The pattern was a stitched diamond on the seat bottoms, and vertical pleats on the seat backs. Sedan upholstery was gray and white stripped pattern, less ornate than the 1915's. The front seat upholstery in the Town Car was now imitation leather. The Coupelet was trimmed in green fabric and lace; the rear compartment of the Town Car in blue fabric and lace.

FENDERS. Front: continued the style of the 1915 cars.

SPLASH APRON. Same as in 1915. Fenders and aprons were painted black.

RUNNING BOARDS. Same as 1915.

HOOD. Steel, in same pattern as 1915. Hold down clamps had two "ears" and were of forged steel. Hood handles were forged steel.

DASHBOARD (Firewall). Wood, fitted inside the front cowl, hidden by the metal hood former.

CHASSIS. Same as 1915. Painted black.

STEERING COLUMN ASSEMBLY. Iron quadrant, brass-plated spark and throttle levers, with flattened metal ends, appear to have been used, although black painted rods have been seen. Gear case was brass, one-piece assembly. Wheel was 15" diameter, wood, and painted black. The wheel spider was iron and painted black. Horn button located on top surface, below the steering wheel.

FRONT AXLE. Same as the 1915 cars. Brass oilers were used only on the spring shackles.

REAR AXLE. Same as later 1915. Reinforcing ribs now on the outside of the brake backing plates.

DRIVESHAFT HOUSING. Pinion bearing spool was a casting and was held by studs and nuts, the studs being enclosed (not visible) in the housing. Integral front housing for universal joint assembly.

REAR RADIUS AND BRAKE RODS. Brake rods had forged ends. Brake-rod support brackets were of the type which go out and wrap down around the rods but were of a reinforced (stronger) design, which continued until the end of Model T production in 1927. Radius rods were of pressed steel with split ends (no forged rear fork).

WHEELS. Used 30 by 3 tires in front; 30 by 3-1/2 in the rear. Rear tires now had a tread pattern. Front wheels used ball bearings. Hub caps had "Ford" in script letters. "Made in USA" on all caps.

SPRINGS. Tapered-leaf, front and rear. "Figure-eight" style shackles. Non-tapered front springs began to be used during the year.

RADIATOR. Manufactured by Ford with the standard Ford script. "Made in USA" on all radiators under the Ford script.

ENGINE. No major changes from 1915.

ENGINE PAN. Typical "three-dip" with narrow front "snout."

OIL FILLER CAP. The mushroom-shaped cap, made of steel, with six flutes and the Ford script as used in 1915. During the year the cap was redesigned and now had just three flutes, and no name or other marking. This style continued until the end of Model T production.

ENGINE CRANK. The plain, steel-sleeve type as used in 1915.

ENGINE FAN. Driven by a leather belt from a pulley at the front of the engine. The fan hub was now cast iron, with the blades riveted in place. Adjustment was by means of a bolt/nut arrangement located on the right side of the front plate and bearing against a boss on the mounting end of the fan bracket.

FUEL TANK. Cylindrical, under the front seat. Mounting brackets clamped to the tank. Outlet was between the center and the right side, between the frame rails. The Sedan now had the "square" tank under the driver's seat.

MANIFOLDS. Exhaust pipe flared at the manifold and was held in place with the brass nut, with no packing. Intake was cast iron.

CARBURETORS. Kingston Model L2, or the Holley Model G.

CARBURETOR STOVE. Pressed steel which rose vertically at the rear of the carburetor and mated with the exhaust manifold at the rear area.

MUFFLER. Cast-iron ends, mounted with brackets integral with the end castings. Exhaust pipe extension integral with the rear cover plate and no longer tapered or bent. Wrapped with asbestos, secured with three steel straps.

1916 (Continued)

COIL BOX ASSEMBLY. Ford. The box had a tapered top to enable the coils to be changed in the limited space created by the cowl. The box lid was one-piece. The switch cover was now black painted steel with "Mag-Off-Bat" stamped on the surface, instead of the brass escutcheon plate used earlier.

TRANSMISSION. Three-pedal standard design. Pedals were of the plain type used thereafter. Transmission cover was cast iron. Tapered inspection door, held with six screws, was a plain metal plate with no script.

LAMPS. Magneto-powered electric type headlights, with clear lens. Black steel rims. Side and tail lamps were similar to 1915 but without brass rims.

HORN. Magneto-powered electric. Button on top surface of steering column.

WINDSHIELD. Upright, with top section that folds to the rear. Frame was riveted to the mounting brackets. Painted black. (Unchanged from 1915.)

TOP. (Open cars). Same as 1915.

SPEEDOMETER. No longer standard equipment.

TURTLE DECK (on Runabout). Similar in style to the 1915. Handles were painted black.

A typical early production 1915 Model T Ford Touring. Note the smooth tires and the bulb horn. The photo is blurred around the windshield area, apparently due to the "trick" photography in which the the man doing the cranking is also shown sitting in the front seat of the car.

The Model T Fords for 1915 and 1916

The 1915 Model T Ford model year is difficult to pinpoint. There was considerable overlap in the new "1915 style" and the older 1914 models. In general, we consider the 1915 model year to have begun in about September 1914 for the closed cars, and January 1915 for the open models.

The new Sedan, with the center door, was introduced in September 1914, and the Coupelet with the folding top shortly after. The new Touring and Runabout bodies, though, were introduced at the Highland Park plant in January 1915. Many, if not all, of the Ford assembly plants continued making the 1914 style open cars until about April 1915, so there is considerable overlap in the production of the 1914 and 1915 open cars. The new Touring and Runabout were first shipped from Highland Park in February 1915. At the same time, sample bodies were shipped to the branches; these bodies to be used as models for the changeover to the new style.

The Sedan and Coupelet, though, were the harbingers of the "new" Ford line for 1915. While retaining the straight front fenders of the 1914's, the rear fenders were now curved to follow the wheel outline (roughly), and the cowl section was now metal and flared to join the body to the hood, replacing the flat wooden board which had been used since 1909.

Along with the new styling came another modification to the Ford car: electric lights. While there were examples of early 1915's with gas lamps, the standard issue was electric headlamps, powered by the engine magneto. Not wanting to startle the public too much, though, the side and tail lights continued to be of the oil (kerosene) type, although they were of a new and cheaper design.

Since the 1914 style open cars continued into 1915, and all apparently used the 1914 style black and brass gas headlamps and oil side/tail lamps, there was most certainly a period of mixed production. Early photos have been seen of 1915 cars with the gas lamps. Factory photos of 1914 cars with electric lamps, though, are another matter.

Continued on page 201

1915-1916

The Ford Line in November 1914.

(Except for the Town Car and Chassis). While the open cars continued in the style of 1914, the Sedan and Coupelet were of the new style. Note the front fenders with the bills on the closed cars, and no bills on the open models. These are catalog illustrations and not necessarily representative of the actual cars. All models are believed to have had billed fenders by this time. The older (1914 style) open models continued into early 1915. Highland Park began producing the 1915 style in January and there was considerable overlapping until about April.

Ford Runabout. $440, fully equipped, f.o.b. Detroit.

Ford Touring Car. $490, fully equipped, f.o.b. Detroit.

Ford Sedan. $975, fully equipped, f.o.b. Detroit.

Ford Coupelet. $750, fully equipped, f.o.b. Detroit.

The Ford Line in April 1915

Note that the catalog illustrations still show the bulb horn. The chassis illustration is from a later catalog and shows the horn button on the steering column. The bare chassis was not usually supplied with a horn during the bulb horn era. Typical of Ford catalog illustrations, a number of errors occur. Most illustrations were retouched photos, and Ford used the same pictures in later catalogs when the differences were minor, such as these on the closed cars, which still show the forked headlamp brackets.

Ford Runabout. $440, fully equipped, f.o.b. Detroit.

Ford Town Car. $690, fully equipped, f.o.b. Detroit.

Ford Touring Car. $490, fully equipped, f.o.b. Detroit.

Ford Sedan. $975, fully equipped, f.o.b. Detroit.

Ford Coupelet. $750, fully equipped, f.o.b. Detroit.

1915-1916

The Ford Line for July 1916

Almost the same as that of April 1915. Note that the closed cars now had the magneto horn (the button is visible on the original pictures but may not be on these reproductions). The Sedan picture was almost identical to the earlier one except for the headlamp mounts which were now the standard type. The Coupelet now had the "port holes" in the rear quarter panels. Note, too, the reduction in prices. The new 1917 cars appeared in August of this year.

Ford Touring Car. $440

Ford Runabout. $390

Ford Town Car. $640

New Ford Enclosed Cars

HERE they are—(see next two pages)—two new enclosed Fords, the 5-passenger Sedan and 2-passenger Coupelet, of the first class in appointments—grace and beauty in every line and builded upon the superb qualities of the Ford Vanadium steel chassis—at "Ford" prices.

It is the bodies we ask you to examine; to mark the roomy, comfortable and altogether pleasing interior appointments; the neat, refined appearance of these cars in general. And underneath is the strong, sturdy foundation which has made the Ford record of service with more than 1,000,000 Ford owners.

There's a large demand for the comforts, the conveniences, the snug-coziness, of these trim enclosed cars. We most practically combined those qualities in the Ford Sedan and Coupelet—at moderate selling prices. It's just a question of the desired capacity—the Coupelet for two passengers or the five-passenger Sedan—they're both Fords.

The Coupelet has a handsome perfectly finished body, and a tight-fitting top, raised or lowered in two minutes, with sliding plate glass door panels.

Seat wide, with high back, deeply upholstered, and with liberal room for two passengers. Side windows give the driver the widest possible range of vision. Windshield is of the double ventilating type. Top lined with felt of the highest quality.

All the factors of Ford manufacturing efficiency and quantity production economies have been put forth in establishing the price of the new Ford Coupelet—$590 f.o.b. Detroit.

THE FORD COUPELET
Combines inviting trimness of appearance with the highest degree of utility

Ford Coupelet. $590

With top down the Coupelet is a runabout almost attractive appearance

The Ford Sedan (not shown) was $740.

The 1915 Ford Runabout. *Photo from the Collections of the Henry Ford Museum and Greenfield Village.*

The factory issued a letter on January 12, 1915, which advised that the crossover tube on the radiator, for the gas lamps, was being discontinued "as all cars now have electric lights." This would lead one to believe, then, that the 1914 style cars then being assembled would have had electric lamps. It is believed that all of the 1914 style cars used gas lamps, probably using up the remainder of the radiators with the gas tube, and that where a photo shows the electric type, someone other than Ford made the switch.

The first electric headlamps were designed to mount on the same forks that were used for the gas lamps. By early 1915, though, the standard design with the riveted-in-place post was standard equipment. The earliest 1915 electric headlamps, used on the closed cars in late 1914, were somewhat different from the later. Made by Edmond and Jones, they were a little larger than the "standard," having lenses 8-5/8" in diameter (instead of the standard 8-1/8"). All early 1915 lamps had brass rims, but these earliest lamps had rims that were thicker. The early side lamps, too, had larger lens and brass trim.

MAGNETO

On September 14, 1914, beginning with engine number 578,042, Ford began using the new magneto with the 3/4" magnets. Not only was this new magneto able to supply the additional current for the headlights, its design was such that it reduced the "dead spots" in the spark lever setting that were so noticeable in the earlier design. This was accomplished by also using larger and oval-shaped pole pieces in the magneto coil. Other than casting a "notch" in the base plate to clear the starter shaft in 1919, the magneto remained relatively unchanged through the balance of Model T production.

THE NEW SEDAN

The new Sedan set the pattern for the familiar "centerdoor" style which was used until mid-1923. However, the 1915 Sedan had an entirely different body than that used on the later models. It was made of aluminum panels, with a one-piece lower rear panel (from door to door, with no seams at the rear). The body sat a bit lower on the chassis, and required a different splash apron and rear fenders than the other models. The rear fenders were fastened directly to the body instead of to the usual fender irons. The windshield was a rather complicated three-section affair, with top sections that folded inward and outward (see pictures).

Upholstery was beautiful when compared with the other Ford cars. The front seats were individual

An original 1915 Ford Sedan, owned by Charles White of La Puente, California. This car has the fork-mounted headlights, lettered foot pedals, and the original upholstery. The sidelights are missing and the front wheels have been converted to 30 by 3-1/2".

bucket style, with the passenger seat folding forward to allow better access to the driver's seat. Neither of these seats could be praised for comfort, with the passenger seat being downright uncomfortable, at least to the author. The rear seat, however, was luxurious, with the rear cushion extending around to add side support. The upholstery material was a fancy broadcloth, with elaborate embroidered trimming. The Coupelet used the Sedan's upholstery styling, with minor variations. As in all the closed cars, the cowl area was covered with imitation leather.

The gasoline tank on the 1915 Sedan was located under the rear seat. Being just a few inches above the frame, and about six feet to the rear of the carburetor, fuel flow was a real problem. This problem apparently became known soon after the introduction of the car. During late 1914 Ford advised changing the fuel line to 5/16" and then, in December, announced a new and longer intake manifold which lowered the carburetor. The Kingston carburetor was recommended, since it was claimed to have a better fuel flow than the Holley. The tank was moved to its position under the driver's seat with the 1916 models (which also used a new, but similar, body).

Note the smooth rear panel (with no seam as in the later models and on the Touring Cars of the same year). Note, too, the assist handle on the window post just ahead of the rear side window. This is missing on the right side and we are not certain that the car ever had one there.

THE COUPELET

The Coupelet was the first Ford convertible. The top could be lowered but the doors had glass windows which could be adjusted by means of a strap, as in the Sedans. The top was leather in 1915, then changed to leatherette later in the year. Seats and door panels were of a material similar to the sedan, a gray and white design cloth. The top was lined with a cloth material in gray, trimmed with a lace similar to that used in the sedan. The standard round gas tank on the Coupelet was under the seat. The initial cars had a door on the rear panel of the turtle deck, making access somewhat inconvenient. Apparently the turtle was modified to have the top-opening door during the 1915 model year (before the addition of the "port holes" in the rear quarter panels of the top).

The early Coupelets were quite "blind" since the top sides wrapped around the seat. The top was modified in later production (typical of the 1916 Coupelets) to have a small window on each side quarter.

THE TOWN CAR

The Town Car was modified to conform to the new styling. This model had added rear passenger space but at the expense of the driver's comfort. The front seat was closer to the steering wheel, and its back rest was quite upright and poorly padded. Portly chauffeurs had a real problem! The passenger compartment could seat five in a pinch (and it would have been a pinch), seating three in the seat and using the two folding jump seats. Upholstery in the

(Continued on page 210)

There was certainly nothing shoddy about the upholstery in the 1915 Sedan. The side windows could all be lowered by means of the upholstered straps. The door, rear side, and back windows all had roll-down curtains. The Coupelet and the rear compartment of the Town Cars had similar upholstery.

1915-1916

While the front seats were anything but comfortable, the rear seat was pure luxury. Note the piping around the seats, doors, and inside top. The window straps on the front and rear side windows could be "poked" into holes in the side panels to keep them out of the way.

The gasoline tank in the 1915 Sedans was located under the rear seat, and gave no end of problems in fuel supply to the carburetor. 1916 and later models had the "square" tank under the driver's seat.

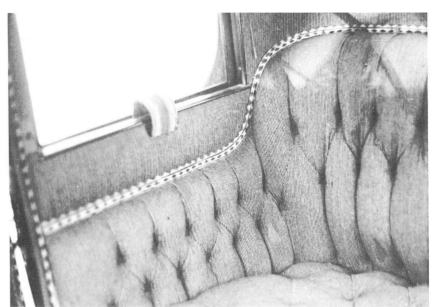

The upholstery in all closed cars extended under the dash to cover all wood and metal, unlike the open cars.

While the original foot pedals were lettered, the brake pedal here has been changed to a later, smooth, one. The coil box cover here is not correct; it should have the smooth and rounded corners.

The car is equipped with a dome light, with the switch near the door on the right side. The wiring is missing on this car, so the location of the batteries is not known. We presume they would be under the rear seat.

The window straps have a leather liner with a series of holes which engaged a peg on the door, allowing several window positions (all of which rattled).

1915-1916

The windshield was an elaborate affair consisting of three separate panes of glass, two of which were at the top. One of these panes folded inward to the ceiling while the other folded outward like a visor. The lower pane could be lifted about an inch and then pulled in at the bottom. With this arrangement, no end of ventilation variations could be achieved.

It's no wonder the Sedan cost almost twice as much as the Touring Car.

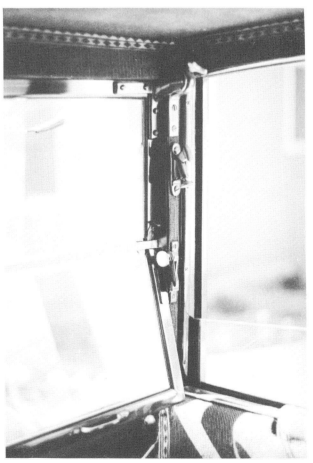

Above: Two new Fords in front of a dealer's showroom in 1915. The Sedan has the assist handle on the right side, unlike our featured car.

Right, and below: The assist handle, the special rear fenders, and the seamless Sedan rear panel.

1915 Coupelet owned by Ron Neave, Kent, Washington. While styled similar to the Sedan, the fenders, aprons, etc. were standard Ford parts. The Coupelet did not have the elaborate windshield of the Sedan, but did have similar upholstery. The inside of the top was lined with a gray cloth, trimmed with a lace similar to that used in the Sedan. Notice the hinged covers on the doors, which doubled as window channels when the glass was up, and as covers for the window slot when the glass was down. The glass was lowered and raised with a strap as in the Sedan. Earlier versions of the 1915 Coupelet had the turtle deck access door on the rear panel, not on the top surface as shown here. In addition, the Coupelets had a more rounded top corner than this example. There was a metal plate inside the top that gave the rounded appearance.

TOP: Note the rounded appearance of
the top rear. This was achieved by the
use of a metal former inside the top, a
piece that is missing in Ron Neave's car
on the opposite page.

RIGHT: The turtle deck on the early
1915 Coupelets had a door on the rear
panel instead of on the top. It didn't
take Ford long to see the error in this
system and so the top became hinged in
later production.

The Ruckstell axle is an accessory; it
was not even available as early as 1915.

1915-1916

1915 Ford Touring, owned by Hugo Richter, now of Aubrey, Texas. This car is what we might call a "typical" 1915 Touring. The standard head, side and tail lamps are used. The Klaxon horn, seen on so many 1915-16 Fords, is an accessory.

Town Car was full leather on the front seat, with either real or imitation leather door panels. The jump seats were upholstered in imitation leather. The rear seat and compartment were upholstered with material similar to that used on the Sedan. The top was imitation leather. Inside the top was lined with a gray cloth, trimmed with a lace similar to that used in the sedans and coupes. The kick panel of the rear seat was covered with a rug-like material.

The Town Car is interesting. Ford's existing records show that none were built during fiscal 1915 (August 1914 to August 1915). Also, Ford generally referred to cars built during a fiscal year as models of that year. 1915 is certainly an exception to this rule, since the cars built during 1914, except for the Sedan and Coupelet, were definitely 1914's. Apparently there were enough unsold 1914 Town Cars to last through the first part of calendar 1915, and the "1915" models were actually built in fiscal 1916 (August 1915 to August 1916). It is also possible the existing Ford records (a relatively recent compilation) are in error. Interestingly, though, of the existing "1915" Town Cars the author knows of, all are dated late in the year.

The closed cars did not sell well. According to Ford Archives figures, just 989 Sedans, 2417 Coupelets, and no Town Cars were produced in fiscal 1915. In February 1915 Ford announced that they would discontinue all advertising because they were backlogged some 50,000 cars. In the same letter, though, they noted that there were plenty of the closed models available and that more effort should be made (by the dealers) to move them.

THE OPEN CARS

The early open models continued the basic bodies of the 1914 cars except for the change in the cowl, windshield, and rear fenders (and other lesser details). The bodies on these models were the same width as the 1914's, and used a slightly wider top bow than the usual 1915 (and later) style. Early in

Open car upholstery was all imitation leather. The seat bottoms had a diamond sewn pattern, with the backs in the plain ribbed style. The front roll of the arm rest was real leather. Door and side panels were cardboard, covered and trimmed with an imitation leather.

Windshields

The windshield on the open cars now stood upright, supported at the cowl by two forged brackets which also supported the side lights. These supports were riveted to the windshield frame, with the rivets going from front to rear. (After the early 1917 models, the brackets bolted to the frame, with the bolts on the side.) The frame is black painted steel, and is hinged in the center so that the top section can be folded back and down. The top and bottom sections of the windshield were of equal size. The top was supported by straps to the windshield hinge, as in the earlier models.

Fenders

As mentioned earlier, the rear fenders were now curved to roughly follow the wheel outline. These fenders were not crowned, however, as were the 1917 and later type. Early production front fenders were the same as the later 1914 cars, with four rivets securing the fender-iron clamp. Early in the year, though, a new clamp arrangement appeared which used just three rivets, and this type remained unchanged through 1916 production. Both fender styles had the front bill, a feature added in later 1914 production.

Hood

The hood, while in the same pattern as the earlier cars, was now given louvers. The 1915 hood was initially made of aluminum but by 1916 hoods

the year, though, the bodies were modified, eliminating some of the wood framing and substituting sheet metal, notably in the seat frames. The new body, in the Touring car, could be identified by the "rivet" on the side panel just ahead of the rear door. This "rivet" is actually the head of a carriage bolt which tied the side panel and the seat frame together.

The cowl section varied, apparently due to a different manufacturer. One cowl section was an assembly of top, side and front panels which were riveted together, with the rivets clearly visible from inside the car, along the top edge. The other cowl was similar, if not identical, to that used in the later bodies in that it was a three-piece affair with a top, and two sides. The front panel was integral with the top section, and there were no rivets. Both of these cowl types appeared at the same time, and both were used into 1916. (The riveted type was apparently dropped in later 1916 but the author is not certain.)

For the first time the Model T was given louvers in the hood. These were necessary because of the location of the horn, not for cooling. The hood was made of aluminum initially, but was changed to steel during calendar 1915.

1915-1916

A 1915 Runabout, owned and restored by Bob Patton, now of Arroyo Grande, California. Bob sold the car some years ago and its present location is unknown. Somewhat over-restored (with diamond tufted upholstery), the car would have been a prize winner in most contests.

were made of steel. The louvers were not added for cooling, although they might have helped. Rather, they were necessary because of the location of the horn. Previous cars had the horn outside the hood, mounted on the firewall. With the new cowl, the horn was placed inside the hood, mounted on the firewall on the inside of the steering column. With no louvers in the hood it would have been almost impossible to hear the horn.

Horns

Horns, incidentally, were still of the bulb-type in most of the 1915 cars. The magneto-powered horn was announced as an experiment in January 1915 and was initially installed on 10,000 cars. It was so much better than the bulb-type that it gradually replaced the bulb horn, and by fall of 1915 the magneto horn was used exclusively. The bulb for the bulb horn was attached to the steering column, with the air hose entering the passenger compartment through a notch in the floorboard just to the right of the steering column. There are pictures, too, of the horn bulb being mounted on the driver's side panel. Is it any wonder we can't say anything for sure about a Model T?

The button for the magneto horn was located on the top surface of the steering column, just below the gear housing, and a metal tube-like piece was added under the column for the horn wire. Early magneto horns had brass-trimmed bells but the later models were black painted steel. There were, of course, variations in the various horns used, due to different suppliers and/or design changes. While it is commonly believed that 1915-16 Fords used a hand operated Klaxon horn, there is no evidence that Ford ever installed such a horn at the factory. Klaxon horns were a very popular accessory, and probably better than the factory equipment.

TOP. The upholstery here is far better than the original. The 1915's came with imitation leather material, with plain seams on the seat backs, and a diamond-sewn pattern on the seat cushions. The only real leather was on the front roll of the arm rests.

The hand Klaxon horn is an accessory. There is no evidence that Ford ever supplied anything other than the bulb horn or the magneto horn in 1915, and the magneto horn was standard by late 1915.

ABOVE. Unique on the Runabouts of this period was the screwed-in-place molding which ran from the top of the body and along the lower edge of the turtle deck, ending at the center of the rear panel where it was met with a similar piece on the other side. This molding was discontinued in later years but is believed to be typical of the 1915's and perhaps even later.

The standard Ford top did not have the roll-up curtain in the rear, nor was it secured with the Murphy fasteners shown here. Rather, it was tacked in place with the tacks covered with a metal strip.

Lamps

Electric headlamps, and oil tail and side lamps, with brass rims were standard equipment on the 1915's. By about June of 1915, the brass trim was discontinued on all lamps. The bulbs of the headlamps were wired in series, and connected to the magneto through a push-pull switch on the firewall just to the right of the coil box.

The side and tail lamps were of a new design. Not only were they cheaper, the side lamps could be interchanged from side to side. The tail lamp had a large red lens on the door, and a clear lens on the side facing the license plate (towards the center of the car). Both types mounted by means of a stud on the rear side.

Tires

1915 was the first year in which Ford began to supply rear tires with a tread pattern as well as the non-tread type, both types being installed depending on the supply. Tires with treads were not new, but Ford wanted to continue to be the last with the newest. (Brass radiators, oil lamps, hand cranks, and bulb horns were all obsolete on most cars by 1915!) A letter dated January 1916 announced that "non-skid tires are to be supplied by U.S. Tire Co." and that the branches were to use up the smooth tires first.

Rear Axle

1915 was a time for another redesign of the rear axle housings. Evolving through several major design changes, and many minor ones, they finally got it "right." Interestingly, the new design was very similar to the type used on the Models N, R and S Fords of 1906-08. The early 1915 models used the 1914 style axle but by April 1915 the new type was standard. This new design used cast center sections, with straight axle tubes inserted into them; the standard design used through 1927. The brake backing plates on the initial 1915 axles, though, were smooth as on the 1914 type. Reinforcing ribs were added later in the year. The last of the internal bronze bushings disappeared during the year. These

The standard horn in early 1915 was the bulb horn, with the bulb mounted on the steering column. The horn itself was mounted in the same location as the magneto type shown. Beginning in January 1915, the magneto horn began to be used on some production, and by October 1915, all Fords had the magneto type. Early magneto horns had a brass trim on the bell but the standard type was as is shown. There were variations in the shape of the horn, depending on the supplier.

The horn button was mounted on the upper surface of the steering column, and continued in this location until sometime about 1918. The horn wire was covered with a metal tube on the underside of the column.

the housing (introduced in about 1913). Sometime during the year, though, the cover was changed to the cast iron style. All 1916's were believed to have had the iron cover.

Beginning on June 17, 1915, a metal disk was installed in the tail shaft of the transmission brake drum in an effort to prevent oil leaks out of the universal joint. This disk was used in all later Model T's.

bushings were in the three spider gears. The bearing surfaces of the spider were made larger to fit the gears without the bushings.

Transmission

Early in 1915 the foot pedals were made without the usual "C, R, and B" cast on their top faces. In place of the letters, the faces now had a ribbed pattern. By late 1915, though, the ribs were also dropped and the pedals were perfectly smooth and were to remain so for all future Model T Fords.

The typical transmission cover in 1915 was aluminum, identical to the 1914, with the reinforcing bosses around the bolt holes at the widest part of

Oilers

Minor items, such as the oilers on the spindles and tie rods, were modified. Initially these oilers were the brass twist-to-open type which had been used for a number of years. Sometime during the year these were dropped in favor of a less expensive brass-capped oiler with a "manhole like" cover. This cover was held in place with an internal spring. These oilers are not the same as the more common "flip-top" type used later.

Springs

Springs, front and rear, were of the tapered style in 1915. 1916 production saw the gradual change to the square-end front springs but the rear springs remained taper-leaf. Shackles were the two-piece figure-eight type with the brass oilers, as used in the 1914 models.

Steering Column

A great improvement was made in the steering column assembly. Early production used the riveted-type gear case of the earlier models, but early in 1915 (apparently) the new one-piece gear case appeared, with the pressed-steel quadrant and iron control rods. The gear case is cast bronze and is not plated. With the addition of the electric horn, a small tube was added to the underside to cover the horn wire. The steering wheel spider was black-painted cast iron (forged steel, actually). The wheel rim was wood, and also painted black.

Ignition Coils

With the new and smaller cowl section, the firewall was also smaller. Since the coil box was mounted on the firewall, it was necessary to redesign the box in order to remove the coils. The top of the box was now cut on an angle, allowing the coils to be tipped forward to clear the top of the cowl. A new box cover was made to fit. While similar to the later covers, the 1915-16 covers were a one-piece stamping with rounded covers, rather than the fabricated three-piece affair used later. The ignition switch on the bulk of the 1915 cars had a black and brass cover plate. Ultimately this plate was dropped in favor of the plain steel one, painted black, which had "Mag-Off-Bat" stamped on the switch cover.

Interestingly, on March 24, 1915, Ford issued a letter to its branches which said, "It has been suggested that the left rear door be eliminated......" and asked for opinions on the matter. Apparently the idea fell on deaf ears.

One should note that not all bodies of the same style during any year were exactly alike. There was more than one supplier of bodies, and there were variations between the different brands. In June 1915 Ford issued a letter to its branches: "Hereafter when ordering body panels for 1915 cars, please give both the car and body numbers. The body number will be found just inside the front door. This number will be preceded by a letter which indicates by whom the body was made. The above information is

(Continued on page 229)

TOP. The coil box cover for the 1915 and 1916 (and perhaps even later) cars was a one-piece stamping with smoothly rounded corners. (Later covers were made of three pieces; the ends being separate, and having relatively sharp corners.)

CENTER. Early 1915 production continued the lettered pedals of the earlier years. Early in the year, though, the letters were dropped in favor of ribbed surfaces. Still later, the ribs were discontinued, and the smooth pedals became standard.

BOTTOM. The handles on the deck lid of the Runabout were castings. They were painted black, not polished as shown here.

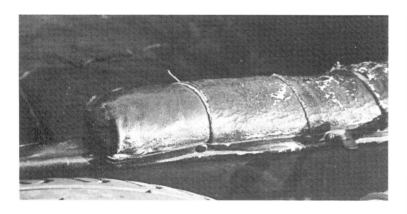

Upholstery on all open cars of this era was quite similar. Imitation leather was used throughout except for the extreme front roll of the arm rest, which was real leather. This upholstery is original and is on a 1916 Ford. Note the diamond pleating on the seat bottoms.

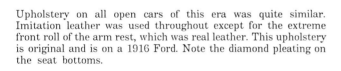

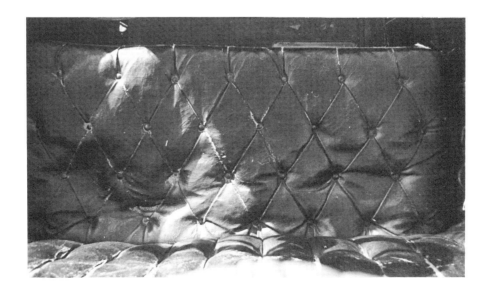

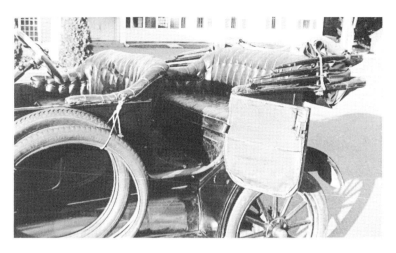

The door panels were leatherette covered with a tacked-on trim strip. Note the attention to detail by the skilled Ford workman.

The 1916 Touring shown here was owned to Ted Doty, of Southampton, Massachusetts. The picture was taken around 1972.

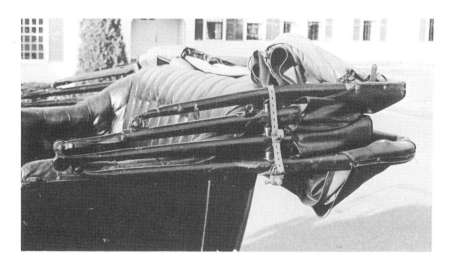

The top sockets shown here are typical; oval in cross section with steam-bent wooden bows across the top. The change to the rectangular sockets occurred about 1918, and are not correct for the cars of this era even though they are often seen on "1915" cars today.

After the initial 1915 production, the Touring bodies assumed a standard construction that was to continue with minor changes until about 1921. The major construction change from the earlier body was in the seat frames, now made of steel. The identifying mark of this body is the "rivet" just ahead of the rear door on each side. (During a period in 1917-18, the seat frames were again made of wood, but the rivet remained.)

The typical 1915 and 1916 touring body had metal covers over the gas tank and tool areas under the seats. During 1916, however, the metal cover under the rear seat was discontinued. The tool box area under the rear seat was originally lined with cardboard.

The toe board at the bottom of the rear side of the front seat back was new; it now had pressed-in beads to add stiffness, and folded up and rearward at the top to enclose the area under the front seat.

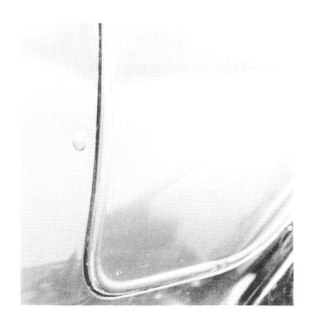

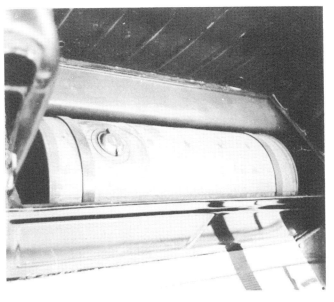

The rear seat compartment was similar to the older wooden style bodies. The metal floor pan was riveted to the front panel and the the rear lip of the body. All cars of this period had the stringer across the compartment under the rear seat. Some were made of metal and others were made of wood with a metal covering.

Most bodies were numbered and dated. Since they were supplied by more than one maker, all were not identical in construction and dimensions. Many replacement parts had to be ordered according to the specific body number, which identified the manufacturer.

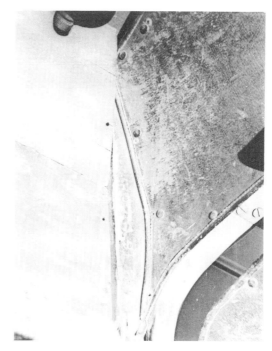

1915-1916

Right Rear

Right Front

The door latches on the 1915 open cars continued in the pattern of 1914. Note that the handles do not "twist" as they come out of the door panel (upper photo). This door latch system operated the bolt in an up-and-down motion, engaging a hook on the body as shown in the upper right photo.

This system required both right and left fittings for each side of the car. During 1916 a new design appeared which was simpler and required fewer parts. The handle now twisted and the bolt operated in a back-and-forth motion, engaging hooks as shown in the lower right photos. The two upper right photos are from the same car, a 1916. The rear doors use the old style latches while the front door uses the new.

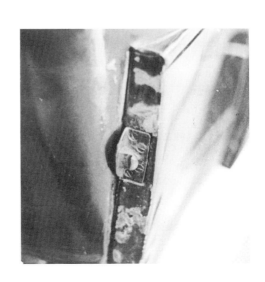

Electric lamps on the early production 1915 models were mounted on the same forks that were used for the gas lamps. Like everything else, the lamps varied. The ones shown here are of the standard (common) size. The early E&J lamps used about a half-inch larger lens. All lenses were clear glass, as shown.

The rims were brass until sometime in mid-1915 when black-painted steel became standard. The 1915 brass rims differed from the 1926-27 (brass with nickel plating) in that they had the manufacturer's name (other than "Ford") stamped on them.

The right angle connection in the upper left photo is correct for cars of this period. The "straight-out" type connector appeared later. Here again, there were variations in the location of the connector, depending on the lamp supplier. The electric lamps were wired in series and powered by the magneto. The light switch was mounted on the firewall, to the right of the coil box, and was of the push-pull type.

221

Side lights were now interchangeable from side to side. The top photos show the earlier type with the thicker brass rims, while the lower pair are typical of most 1915 Fords. The brass trim was discontinued in mid-1915.

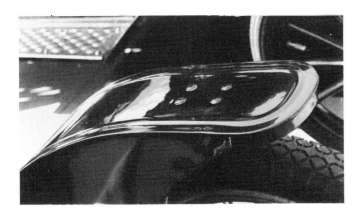

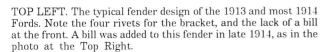

TOP LEFT. The typical fender design of the 1913 and most 1914 Fords. Note the four rivets for the bracket, and the lack of a bill at the front. A bill was added to this fender in late 1914, as in the photo at the Top Right.

ABOVE. During early 1915 the fender bracket was changed and was now attached with just three rivets. This pattern continued until the crowned and curved fenders of the 1917 models. 1915-style fenders have been seen with a rivet pattern similar to that of the rear fender (lower right) but it is believed that these were replacements supplied during the "black era" (1917 and later).

CENTER RIGHT. The rear fenders were new for 1915, now being curved to follow the wheel outline. Note that there was no crown as on the 1917 and later fenders. Early cars had a rivet pattern similar to the three-rivet fender shown above but the bulk of the production had the pattern shown at the bottom right.

BOTTOM RIGHT. Typical four-rivet rear fender used on most 1915 and 1916 Fords.

1915-1916

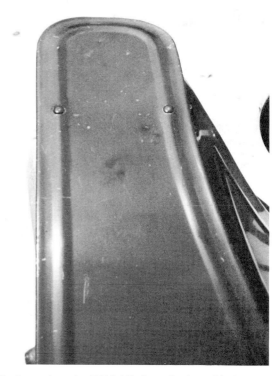

Note the reinforcing rib across the widest part of the front fender. In 1913 the only embossed area was that around the edges of the top surface. In late 1913 or early 1914 the cross rib was added, and still later, beads were added to the triangular insert panel (behind the headlight, below). All of these fenders used the four-rivet fender iron bracket. During 1915, the three-rivet bracket appeared, and continued through 1916.

ABOVE. An early-style (1915-16) front fender with just two rivets securing the fender iron bracket. These are believed to be replacement fenders produced during the "iron era" (1917 and later) and they use a fender iron bracket identical to that used on the 1917 and later fenders.

BELOW. Rear fender of the Runabout and Coupelet. Note the little bracket between the fender and the splash apron. This one is brass but Ford supplied one of pressed steel, riveted to the fender and bolted to the apron.

The windshield used on the 1915, 1916 and early 1917 models differed from that used on later Fords in that the supporting brackets were riveted to the frame. The later brackets were attached with screws.

The windshields hinged at the center, with the top section folding back and down. Note that the hinges had equal length arms, and that when the top was folded it was even with the bottom. Later 1917 models used unequal length arms and with that arrangement, the top section was a bit higher than the lower, as is shown in the bottom right photo.

Note the poor grade of glass used in the bottom section of the original windshield at the top left.

Typical 1917 to 1922 windshield

1915-1916

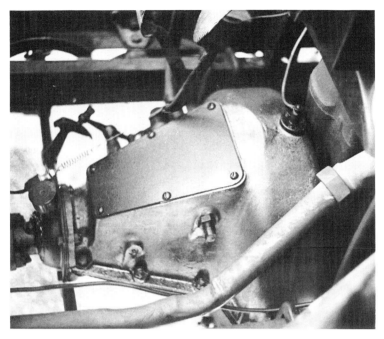

Typical of cars of this era was the plain steel transmission cover door. The aluminum cover, used in 1915, had the reinforcing ribs (introduced about 1913) shown in the upper right photo. The cover was changed to cast iron sometime during later 1915.

The driveshaft universal-joint housing was of the one-piece design introduced in 1914. The brake-light switch shown is a modern item. Ford had not perfected the brake-operated oil stop light.

RIGHT: 1915 and 1916 cars used the pressed-steel spark/throttle quadrant. The date the brass quadrant was discontinued is not known but is believed to have been in late 1914, with perhaps some overlapping when both types were used. The spark and throttle levers are believed to have been painted black but may have been plated brass. Stories conflict on this matter.

The horn button shown is typical of 1915-17.

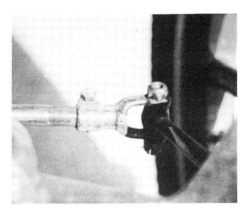

TOP LEFT. Typical front axle, spindle, and speedometer drive assembly used on cars of this era. The spring shackles are correct and have the proper oilers. The oilers on the spindle and tie rods (missing in these photos) were of the "manhole" type; the type with the round lid-like cover which was held in place by a spring.

UPPER RIGHT. The two ends of the steering tie rods were as shown (except for the missing oilers). The tie rod here is typical of all Fords until 1918, and differs from the later cars in that the left side (top photo) was adjustable while the right side was not. In 1918 the right side was made adjustable, using the drag link ball and nut as the locking device.

ABOVE. New in 1915, after some production of the 1914 style rear axle, was this last major modification of the center section. Where the earlier style axle housings were flared at the center and were riveted to the housing, this type used straight axle housings which fit into the center section. Not only cheaper to make, but much better as well. Note that the filler hole is just below the center line. In 1919 it was moved down a bit to prevent over-filling.

RIGHT. Most of the 1915 cars used the brake backing plates which had been used with the 1914 axle. Later, and somewhat typical of the 1916's, reinforcing ribs were cast into the backing plates (bottom right photo). This reinforced style continued until 1926 models.

227

Other than the changes in the transmission, transmission cover, and magneto, the 1915-16 engines were little changed from 1914. The factory-issue carburetor was either a Kingston Model L or a Holley Model G. The Holley G was introduced in 1914 and continued until 1920. The typical 1915-16 G differed from the others in that it had a cast-in groove around the intake, while the 1914, and 1917 and later units had a smooth-surfaced intake horn. The choke arm was changed in 1919 to accomodate the dash-mounted choke. The Kingston L appeared in late 1914, replacing the earlier Model Y "four-ball" Kingston.

The serial number of the engine appeared on a boss above the water inlet, the standard location since 1912. Serial numbers ranged from about 577,000 to 1,363,000 (Mid-September 1914 to August 1916).

Note the cute but almost worthless accessory water pump on the water outlet.

One new item appeared; the steel oil cap with the Ford script. The previous cap, similar in appearance, was made of brass. Note that it has six flutes. During 1916 (a guess) the simpler three-flute style appeared which did not have any script or "Made in USA" on its top.

Holley Model "G"

Kingston Model "L"

ABOVE. A typical 1915 or 1916 Ford Touring Car as it appeared when almost new. This car is no doubt a late 1916; close examination of the original shows the front arm rest has the metal cap instead of the leather roll. This change is typical of the 1917 and later cars and is unusual for 1916's.

RIGHT. The "manhole" oiler (top of the spindle bolt) which was typical for the era. The top cover (cap) is held in place by a small spring inside the oiler. The cap can be lifted from any side (if a circle has a "side").

necessary as panels for bodies made by our various body manufacturers vary somewhat." Incidentally, Ford discontinued noting body numbers in production beginning in May 1915.

As noted above, there is little difference between 1915 and 1916 models, one year just evolving into the next. In general, the major changes for "1916" cars were:

1. Brass trim on the lamps is dropped in favor of black-painted steel.
2. The ribs on the foot pedals were replaced with the smooth-surface type.
3. The iron transmission cover replaced the aluminum type.
4. The hood is steel rather than aluminum.
5. The horns were all magneto type after October 1915.
6. Brake backing plates all had the reinforcing ribs.

1917

Body Type	Factory Price #	Shipping Weight Lbs.	Production Total *	
Touring	$360	1480	568128	
Runabout	345	1385	107240	
Town Car	595	—	2328	
Sedan	645	1745	7361	
Coupelet	505	1580	7343	
Chassis	325	980	41165	
Ambulance	—	—	1452	**
Truck chassis	—	1450	3	***
Total			735020	+

#	Price effective August 1, 1916.
*	Fiscal year 1917, August 1, 1916 to July 30, 1917.
**	Built for military.
***	Apparently a pilot run.
+	*Ford News*, Nov. 1, 1920, gave a figure of 785,432.

MODEL YEAR DATES: August 1916 to August 1917.

BODY TYPES: Touring, Runabout, Coupelet (three types), Sedan, Town Car and Chassis. Note: "1917" trucks were "1918" models built in Calendar year 1917.

MAJOR MODEL YEAR FEATURES

Body was similar to 1916 but fenders were crowned and curved. Radiator shell was now black. Hood was larger eliminating the "step" at the cowl. Hood clash strips now metal, replacing the earlier painted wood type. Set the general style used until 1926 models. Brass trim was eliminated and replaced with nickel plating.

Three Coupelets appeared in 1917. The first was similar to the 1916, with the folding top, except for the new hood and fender styling. The second was a "hardtop" coupe with removable door pillars, similar in style to the earlier, and having a leather-covered solid top. The leather covering included the rear section and top quarter panels, giving the car a "soft top" look. This type was superseded by the "1918" style before the end of 1917. This third type was similar to the second except that just the top (roof) was in leatherette; the sides and rear panels were metal.

New engine pan with wider front area and a new cylinder head (so-called "high" head) were major engine modifications.

The hood and radiator were all new, setting the pattern for all future Model T's. The radiator was now a separate unit, covered with a black-painted shell. The hood was larger and more rounded, blending better with the cowl section.

COLORS. All cars were painted black, with black fenders.

UPHOLSTERY. Imitation leather in the open cars. The pattern was a stitched vertical-pleat design on both seat bottoms and backs. The arm rests now had a metal cap at the front, replacing the leather front roll. Side and door panels were now cardboard with imitation leather-like trim welting. Closed car upholstery was the same as the 1916's.

FENDERS. Curved and crowned, setting the standard used until the 1926 models.

SPLASH APRON. Now smoothly tapered from front to rear, with no bulge at the rear.

RUNNING BOARDS. Unchanged from previous year.

HOOD. Steel, of new rounded design. Hold-down clamps had two "ears" and were of forged steel. Handles were pressed steel. Clash strip was now metal, replacing wood used previously.

DASHBOARD (Firewall). Wood, fits outside the front cowl, hidden by the metal cowl trim strip.

CHASSIS. Same as 1916. Painted black.

STEERING COLUMN ASSEMBLY. Iron quadrant, Nickle-plated spark and throttle levers, with flattened metal ends. Gear case was a brass but nickel-plated, one-piece assembly. Wheel was 15" diameter, wood, and painted black. The wheel spider was iron and painted black. Horn button remained on the top of the steering column, as in the previous models, until late in the year (1918 models).

FRONT AXLE. Same as the 1916 cars. Brass oilers were used only on the spring shackles. During the year all cars used the non-tapered springs in the front.

REAR AXLE. Same as 1916.

DRIVESHAFT HOUSING. Pinion bearing spool was a casting and was held by studs and nuts, the studs being enclosed (not visible) in the housing. Integral front housing for universal-joint assembly.

REAR RADIUS AND BRAKE RODS. Brake rods had forged ends. Brake-rod support brackets were of the type which go out and wrap down around the rods but were of a reinforced (stronger) design, which continued until the end of Model T production in 1927. Radius rods were of pressed steel with split ends (no forged rear fork).

WHEELS. Used 30 by 3 tires in front; 30 by 3-1/2 in the rear. Front wheels used ball bearings. Hub caps had "Ford" in script letters. "Made in USA" on all caps.

SPRINGS. Tapered-leaf at the rear, and non-tapered in front. "Figure-eight" style shackles used but without oilers in the front, and were later replaced with "L" shaped shackles of an assembled design. Oilers were now pressed into the front springs but remained a part of the rear shackles as in previous cars.

RADIATOR. Manufactured by Ford. Shell had the Ford script pressed into the upper part. "Made in USA" was stamped in below the Ford script. Filler neck was nickel-plated. The shell was painted black.

ENGINE. No major changes from 1915 except for an enlarged "high" head with greater water capacity.

ENGINE PAN. "Three-dip" with wider front "snout" which would accommodate the larger fan pulley that didn't appear until 1920.

OIL FILLER CAP. The mushroom-shaped cap, made of steel, with three flutes, as used in later 1916.

ENGINE CRANK. The plain steel-sleeve type as used in 1916.

ENGINE FAN. Driven by a leather belt from a pulley at the front of the engine. The fan hub was cast iron, with the blades riveted in place. Adjustment was by means of a bolt/nut arrangement located on the right side of the front plate and bearing against a boss on the mounting end of the fan bracket. The fan bracket (arm) was now longer and straight. Early models had a fan shroud but this was apparently discontinued during the year.

1917 (Continued)

FUEL TANK. Cylindrical, under the front seat on all cars except the Sedan. Mounting brackets clamp to the tank. Outlet was between the center and the right side, between the frame rails. Sedans used the square tank under the driver's seat.

MANIFOLDS. Exhaust pipe flared at the manifold and was held in place with the brass nut, with no packing. Intake was cast iron.

CARBURETORS. Kingston Model L2, or Holley Model G.

CARBURETOR STOVE. Pressed steel, which rose vertically at the rear of the carburetor and mated with the exhaust manifold at the rear area.

MUFFLER. Cast-iron ends, mounted with brackets integral with the end castings. Brackets were stubbier than previous types. No exhaust pipe extension. Wrapped with asbestos, secured with three steel straps, initially, but wrapping was discontinued during the year.

COIL BOX ASSEMBLY. Ford. The box had a tapered top to enable the coils to be changed in the limited space created by the cowl. The box lid was now an assembly of three pieces.

TRANSMISSION. Three-pedal standard design. Pedals were of the plain type (no embossed letters or other pattern). Transmission cover was cast iron. Tapered inspection door, held with six screws. The door was a plain metal plate with no script.

LAMPS. Magneto-powered electric type. Black steel rims. Side and tail lamps were similar to 1916.

HORN. Magneto-powered electric.

WINDSHIELD. (Open cars) Upright, with top section that folds to the rear. Frame was riveted to the mounting brackets initially, then was modified and bolted to the brackets. During the year the center hinge arms were altered so that one was longer than the other. Using this hinge, the folded windshield was now a bit higher; the upper section in the folded position being somewhat above the lower section. Windshield frame, hinges, and brackets were painted black.

TOP. (Open cars). Top color was black on all open cars. Unchanged from 1916.

SPEEDOMETER. No longer standard equipment.

TURTLE DECK (on Runabout). Similar in style to the 1915. Handles were painted black.

1918

Body Type	Factory Price			Shipping Weight Lbs.	Production Total	
	#	##	###		*	
Touring	$360	360	450	1500	432519	
Runabout	345	345	435	1390	73559	
Town Car	595	645	—	—	2142	
Sedan	645	695	695	1715	35697	
Coupelet	505	560	560	1580	14771	
Chassis	325	325	400	980	37748	
Ambulance					2136	**
Truck chassis		600	600	1450	41105	
Delivery					399	***
Foreign					24000	****
Total					664076	+

#	Price effective August 1, 1917.
##	Price effective October 6, 1917.
###	Price effective February 21, 1918.
*	Fiscal year 1918, August 1, 1917 to July 30, 1918. *Ford News*, Nov. 1, 1920, gave a figure of 706,584.
**	Built for military.
***	Not indicated in catalog.
****	Cars built in foreign plants and Canada (no breakdown by types).
+	*Ford News*, Nov. 1, 1920, gives a figure of 706,584.

MODEL YEAR DATES: August 1917 to January 1919 approx.

BODY TYPES: Touring, Runabout, Coupelet, Sedan, Town Car, Chassis and Truck.

MAJOR MODEL YEAR FEATURES

Until late 1920, open car bodies were built similar to the 1917 bodies. All had the separate rear quarter panels, the "rivet" on the side, etc. Touring Car bodies used wood seat frames in some production during this period. The Coupelet now had the metal top section, and continued the removable door posts of the late 1917 (1918) design. The Town Car was discontinued during calendar 1917.

COLORS. All cars were painted black, with black fenders.

UPHOLSTERY. Imitation leather in the open cars as in 1917. The pattern was a stitched vertical-pleat design on both seat bottoms and backs. Closed car upholstery was same as 1916's, except that the Coupelet now used the same upholstery style and color as the Sedan.

FENDERS. Front: curved and crowned as in 1917.

SPLASH APRON. Smoothly tapered from front to rear, with no bulge at the rear.

RUNNING BOARDS. Unchanged from previous year.

HOOD. Steel. Hold-down clamps had two "ears" and were of forged steel. Handles were pressed steel.

DASHBOARD (Firewall). Wood, fitted outside the front cowl, hidden by the metal cowl trim strip.

CHASSIS. Same as 1917. Painted black.

STEERING COLUMN ASSEMBLY. Iron quadrant, nickle-plated spark and throttle levers, with flattened metal ends. Gear case was brass but nickel-plated, one piece assembly. Wheel was 15" diameter, wood, and painted black. The wheel spider was iron and painted black. Combination horn/light switch on left side of column.

FRONT AXLE. Same as the 1917 cars.

REAR AXLE. Same as 1917.

1918 (Continued)

DRIVESHAFT HOUSING. Pinion bearing spool was a casting and was held by studs and nuts, the studs being enclosed (not visible) in the housing. Integral front housing for universal-joint assembly.

REAR RADIUS AND BRAKE RODS. Brake rods had forged ends. Brake-rod support brackets were of the type which go out and wrap down around the rods but were of a reinforced (stronger) design, which continued until the end of Model T production in 1927. Radius rods were of pressed steel with split ends (no forged rear fork).

WHEELS. Used 30 by 3 tires in front; 30 by 3-1/2 in the rear. Front wheels used ball bearings. Hub caps had "Ford" in script letters. "Made in USA" on all caps.

SPRINGS. Non-tapered, front and rear. "L"-shaped shackles of an assembled design and later of the forged type. Oilers were now pressed into the springs and none were used on the shackles as in previous cars.

RADIATOR. Unchanged from 1917.

ENGINE. No major changes from 1917.

ENGINE PAN. "Three-dip" with wider front "snout" which would accommodate the larger fan pulley that didn't appear until 1920.

OIL FILLER CAP. The mushroom-shaped cap, made of steel, with three flutes as used since late 1916.

ENGINE CRANK. The plain steel-sleeve type as used since 1914.

ENGINE FAN. Driven by a leather belt from a pulley at the front of the engine. The fan hub was cast iron, with the blades riveted in place. Adjustment was by means of a bolt/nut arrangement now located on the right side of the front plate and bearing against a boss on the mounting end of the fan bracket.

FUEL TANK. Cylindrical, under the front seat. Mounting brackets clamped to the tank. Outlet was between the center and the right side, between the frame rails. Sedan tank under the driver's seat. The Coupe tank was still round but was now located in the turtle deck.

MANIFOLDS. Exhaust pipe flared at the manifold and was held in place with the brass nut but with no packing. Intake was cast iron.

CARBURETORS. Kingston Model L2, or Holley Model G.

CARBURETOR STOVE. Pressed steel which rose vertically at the rear of the carburetor and mated with the exhaust manifold at the rear area.

MUFFLER. Cast-iron ends, same as later 1917 type. No exhaust pipe extension. Asbestos wrapping was discontinued.

COIL BOX ASSEMBLY. Ford. Same as used in 1917.

TRANSMISSION. Three-pedal standard design. Pedals were of the plain type. Transmission cover was cast iron. Tapered inspection door, held with six screws. The door was a plain metal plate with no script.

LAMPS. Magneto-powered electric type. Black steel rims. Side and tail lamps were similar to 1917.

HORN. Magneto-powered electric.

WINDSHIELD. (Open cars) Upright, with top section that folds to the rear. Frame was bolted to the brackets. Painted black. Hinge arms of unequal length as in later 1917.

TOP. (Open cars). Top color was black on all open cars. Similar in style to the 1917 but now with rectangular cross-section irons.

SPEEDOMETER. No longer standard equipment.

TURTLE DECK (on Runabout). Similar in style to the 1915. Handles were painted black.

1919

Body Type	Factory Price #	Shipping Weight Lbs.	Production Total *
Touring	$525	1500	286935
Runabout	500	1390	48867
Sedan	875 ##	1875	24980
Coupe	750 ##	1685	11528
Town Car	—		17 ***
Chassis	475	1060	47125
Ambulance			2227 **
Truck chassis	550 ###	1395	70816
" "	590 ####		
Delivery			5847 ***
Total			498342 +

Note: Add 90 lbs. for starter; 45 lbs. for demountable rims and tire carrier on open cars. Starter and rims standard on closed cars.

#	Price effective August 16, 1918.
##	Includes starter and demountable wheels.
###	Price with solid rubber tires.
####	Price with Pneumatic tires.
*	Fiscal year 1919, August 1, 1918 to July 30, 1919.
**	Built for military.
***	Not indicated in catalog.
+	*Ford News*, Nov. 1, 1920, gave a figure of 533,706.

MODEL YEAR DATES: January 1919 to August 1919.

BODY TYPES: Touring, Runabout, Sedan, Coupe, Chassis and Truck.

MAJOR MODEL YEAR FEATURES

Note: Starter was an option on the open cars at $75. (Weight 95 lbs.) Demountable rims were an additional $25. (Weight 55 lbs.) The "1919" model year began in January 1919 with the introduction of the electrical equipment as standard in the closed cars. Until this time, there was little change in style since the 1917 models, due to the war effort. The Coupe was similar to the 1917-18 style but the window posts were no longer removable. Ford used the terms "Coupelet" and "Coupe" interchangeably, but they are the same body style. Generally "Coupelet" should refer to the types with the folding top and/or with the removable side pillars, while the "Coupe" would the those types with the solid pillars.

Instrument panel appeared on the starter cars only for the first time as a factory installed item. Non-electric cars had no instrument panel.

Rear axle assembly modified in several areas; now used a gasket between the halves, different wheel oil seal cups, and the filler plug was located lower on the housing than before to help prevent overfilling.

Front axle assembly modified; used new radius rod assembly which now fastened below the spring perches.

COLORS. All cars were painted black, with black fenders.

UPHOLSTERY. Imitation leather in the open cars. The pattern was a stitched vertical-pleat design on both seat bottoms and backs. Closed car upholstery was the same as 1918 except that the cowl area was no longer enclosed with leatherette on all cars (apparently depending on the manufacturer). Quarter panels were now cloth.

FENDERS. Front: curved and crowned as in 1918.

SPLASH APRON. Unchanged from 1918.

RUNNING BOARDS. Unchanged from previous year.

HOOD. Steel. Hold-down clamps had two "ears" and were of forged steel. Handles were pressed steel.

DASHBOARD (Firewall). Wood, fitted outside the front cowl, hidden by the metal cowl trim strip. This trim strip was redesigned to include a rain gutter to direct water to the sides, away from the coil box.

CHASSIS. Same as 1918 except for the addition of the battery bracket on the starter cars, with the accompanying mounting holes. Painted black.

STEERING COLUMN ASSEMBLY. Iron quadrant, nickle-plated spark and throttle levers, with flattened metal ends. Gear case was brass but nickel-plated, one piece assembly. Wheel was 15" diameter, made of "Fordite" (synthetic material), and painted black. The wheel spider was iron and painted black. Horn/light switch same as 1918 except for starter-equipped cars where the light switch was located on the instrument panel.

FRONT AXLE. Same axle as the 1918 cars. The radius rod now connects below the axle, at the spring perches, making a stronger assembly. Timken roller bearings in front wheels except in the non-starter, non-demountable cars.

REAR AXLE. Same as 1918. The oil filler hole was moved down to a point about 1-3/4" below the centerline. Center section now machined for a paper gasket between the halves. A change in the machining of the axle housing ends required a new oil seal cup of 1/32" larger inside diameter.

DRIVESHAFT HOUSING. Pinion bearing spool was a casting and was held by studs and nuts, the studs being enclosed (not visible) in the housing. Integral front housing for universal-joint assembly.

REAR RADIUS AND BRAKE RODS. Brake rods had forged ends. Brake-rod support brackets rattlers were of the type which go out and wrap down around the rods but were of a reinforced (stronger) design, which continued until the end of Model T production in 1927. Radius rods were of pressed steel with split ends (no forged rear fork).

WHEELS. Used 30 by 3 tires in front; 30 by 3-1/2 in the rear. Front wheels now used taper-roller (Timken) bearings except in the non-starter, non-demountable open cars. Hub caps had "Ford" in script letters. "Made in USA" on all caps. Demountable-rim wheels standard on closed cars, and optional on the open models; used 30 by 3-1/2 tires all around.

SPRINGS. Non-tapered, front and rear. "L" shaped shackles of the forged type. Oilers were now pressed into the springs and none were used on the shackles as in previous cars.

RADIATOR. Same as previous year but had larger mounting holes to fit new spring-mounted arrangement which replaced the older pad method.

ENGINE. Modified to accept starter and generator, now standard on closed cars, and optional on the open models after about June 1919.

ENGINE PAN. "Three-dip" with wider front "snout" which would accommodate the larger fan pulley that didn't appear until 1920.

OIL FILLER CAP. The mushroom-shaped cap, made of steel, three flutes.

1919 (Continued)

ENGINE CRANK. The plain steel-sleeve type as used since 1914.

ENGINE FAN. Driven by a leather belt from a pulley at the front of the engine. The fan hub was cast iron, with the blades riveted in place. Adjustment was by means of a bolt/nut arrangement now located on the right side of the front plate and bearing against a boss on the mounting end of the fan bracket.

FUEL TANK. Cylindrical, under the front seat. Mounting brackets clamped to the tank. Outlet was between the center and the right side, between the frame rails. Sedan and Coupe used the square tank; located under the driver's seat in the Sedan, and in the turtle deck in the Coupe.

MANIFOLDS. Exhaust pipe flared at the manifold and was held in place with the brass nut but with no packing. Intake was cast iron.

CARBURETORS. Kingston Model L2, or Holley Model G. Choke arm had additional lever arm for dash-mounted choke pull rod.

CARBURETOR STOVE. Pressed steel which rose vertically at the rear of the carburetor and mated with the exhaust manifold at the rear area.

MUFFLER. Cast-iron ends, same as 1918.

COIL BOX ASSEMBLY. Ford. Same as used in 1917. Starter cars no longer had the ignition switch on the box; it was moved to the dashboard. The switch on the coil box now was of the fully enclosed pressed steel design.

TRANSMISSION. Three-pedal standard design. Pedals were of the plain type. Transmission cover was cast iron, and modified to accept the starter. Tapered inspection door, held with six screws. The door was now of pressed steel with an embossed "X" pattern.

LAMPS. Magneto-powered electric type on the non-starter cars, and six-volt electric on the starter models. Black steel rims, and clear lens. Side and tail lamps were similar to 1917 on the non-starter cars. Starter cars had a small electric tail light and did not have side lights.

HORN. Magneto-powered electric.

WINDSHIELD. (Open cars) Upright, with top section that folds to the rear. Frame was bolted to the brackets. Painted black.

TOP. (Open cars). Top color was black on all open cars. Unchanged from 1918.

SPEEDOMETER. No longer standard equipment.

TURTLE DECK (on Runabout). Similar in style to the 1915. Handles were painted black.

1920

Body Type	Factory Price #	Shipping Weight Lbs.	Production Total *
Touring	$575	1500	165929
"	675 ##	1650	367785
Runabout	550	1390	31889
"	650 ##	1540	63514
Sedan	975 ##	1875	81616
Coupe	850 ##	1685	60215
Chassis	525	1020	18173
"	620	1255	16919
Truck chassis	600 ###	1380	135002
" "	640 ####		
Total			941042

#	Price effective March 3, 1920.
##	Includes starter and demountable wheels.
###	Price with solid rubber tires.
####	Price with pneumatic tires.
*	Fiscal year 1920, August 1, 1919 to July 30, 1920.
+	*Ford News,* Nov. 1, 1920, gave a figure of 996,660.

Note: Starter was an option on the open cars at $75. Weight 95 lbs. Demountable rims were an additional $25. Weight 55 lbs.

MODEL YEAR DATES: August 1919 to August 1920.

BODY TYPES: Touring, Runabout, Sedan, Coupe, Chassis and Truck.

MAJOR MODEL YEAR FEATURES

Continued in the styles of previous years with but minor changes. Wooden seat frames of the 1918-1919 cars were replaced with metal ones as used in 1915-1917. A new body was announced in June 1920, with parts specified for production, but apparently the new type was not standard until 1921. (See notes under 1921.) Oil lamps discontinued on cars supplied with electrical equipment.

The frame was modified in mid-year and now used the channel type running board brackets, replacing the forged brackets and truss rod assembly used since 1909.

The oval gas tank became standard during the year, except in the closed cars.

New pinion bearing spool (forged, exposed bolts) was a running change in 1920.

COLORS. All cars were painted black, with black fenders.

UPHOLSTERY. Imitation leather in the open cars. The pattern was a stitched vertical-pleat design on both seat bottoms and backs. Closed car upholstery was same as 1919.

FENDERS. Front: curved and crowned as in 1919.

SPLASH APRON. Same as 1919.

RUNNING BOARDS. Same as 1919.

HOOD. Steel. Hold-down clamps had two "ears" and were of forged steel. Handles were pressed steel but were now made in such a way that they can be fastened to the hood without a separate rivet. (A "hole" appears where the rivet was.)

DASHBOARD (Firewall). Wood, fitted outside the front cowl, hidden by the metal cowl weather strip.

CHASSIS. Same as 1919. Painted black.

1920 (Continued)

STEERING COLUMN ASSEMBLY. Iron quadrant, nickel-plated spark and throttle levers, with flattened metal ends. Gear case was brass but nickel-plated, one-piece assembly. Wheel was 16" diameter, made of "Fordite" (synthetic material), and painted black. The wheel spider was now pressed steel and painted black. Horn button on left side of column but light switch was now on instrument panel on starter cars. Non-starter cars used the combination switch used previously.

FRONT AXLE. Same as the 1919 cars.

REAR AXLE. Same as 1919.

DRIVESHAFT HOUSING. Pinion bearing spool was changed to the forged type with the exposed bolts. Integral front housing for universal joint assembly.

REAR RADIUS AND BRAKE RODS. Brake rods now split at the ends, eliminating the forged forks. Brake-rod support brackets rattlers were of the type which go out and wrap down around the rods but were of a reinforced (stronger) design, which continues until the end of Model T production in 1927. Radius rods were of pressed steel with split ends.

WHEELS. Used 30 by 3 tires in front; 30 by 3-1/2 in the rear. Front wheels used taper-roller (Timken) bearings except in the non-starter, non-demountable open cars. Hub caps had "Ford" in script letters. "Made in USA" on all caps. Demountable-rim wheels standard on closed cars, and optional on the open models; used 30 by 3-1/2 tires all around.

SPRINGS. Non-tapered, front and rear. "L"-shaped shackles of the forged type. Oilers were now pressed into the springs and none were used on the shackles.

RADIATOR. Same as 1919.

ENGINE. Same as 1919. Lighter rods and pistons introduced during the year. Starter was still optional on the open cars. Fan pulley was now of larger diameter.

ENGINE PAN. "Three-dip" with wider front "snout" which will accommodate the larger fan pulley that finally appeared.

OIL FILLER CAP. The mushroom-shaped cap, made of steel, with three flutes.

ENGINE CRANK. The plain steel-sleeve type as used since 1914.

ENGINE FAN. Driven by a leather belt from a pulley at the front of the engine. During the year the fan was changed; the hub was now aluminum with a welded-blade assembly bolted to the hub. The pulley was larger to match the larger crank pulley, introduced at the same time. Adjustment was by means of a bolt/nut arrangement located on the right side of the front plate and bearing against a boss on the mounting end of the fan bracket as in the earlier design.

FUEL TANK. Cylindrical, under the front seat. Mounting brackets clamp to the tank. Outlet was between the center and the right side, between the frame rails. The oval tank was introduced during the year and became the standard tank on all models except for the Coupe and Sedan (which continued the square tank under the driver's seat). Some Coupes used this new oval tank under the seat, apparently experimental, but most used the square tank in the turtle deck as in the previous year.

MANIFOLDS. Exhaust pipe flared at the manifold and was held in place with the brass nut, with no packing. Intake was cast iron.

CARBURETORS. Kingston Model L2 or Holley Model G on early cars, then Kingston L4, or Holley Model NH.

CARBURETOR STOVE. Sheet-metal type which rose vertically at the rear of the carburetor and mated with the exhaust manifold at the rear corner, being held by the rear manifold retaining stud/nut.

MUFFLER. Pressed-steel type with no tail pipe. Single mounting bracket on rear head.

COIL BOX ASSEMBLY. Ford. Same as used in 1919. Starter cars no longer had the ignition switch on the box; it was moved to the dashboard.

TRANSMISSION. Three-pedal standard design. Pedals were of the plain type. Transmission cover was cast iron, and modified to accept the starter. Tapered inspection door, held with six screws. The door was of pressed steel with an embossed "X" pattern.

LAMPS. Magneto-powered electric type on the non-starter cars, and six-volt electric on the starter models. Black steel rims, with clear lens. Side and tail lamps were similar to 1917 on the non-starter cars. Starter cars had a small electric tail light and did not have side lights.

HORN. Magneto-powered electric.

WINDSHIELD. (Open cars) Upright, with top section that folds to the rear. Frame was bolted to the brackets. Painted black. Starter cars no longer had the integral mount for the oil side lights.

TOP. (Open cars). Top color was black on all open cars. Same as that used since 1918.

SPEEDOMETER. No longer standard equipment.

TURTLE DECK (on Runabout). Similar in style to the 1919. Handles were now pressed steel and painted black.

The Model T Fords for 1917 to 1920

Model T Fords of the "brass era" are probably the most desirable types to the average enthusiast. Certainly they are the most ornate and spectacular in appearance. Yet the Model T that comes to mind at the mention of the subject is the all-black Ford of the 1917 to 1925 era. More were built during this period than at any other time; about two-thirds of the total Model T production!

The 1917 to 1920 models might be considered the "elite" of the black Fords; not because they were the earliest, but because they represent the period of the greatest changes. Changes not only in the car, but in the Ford Motor Company itself.

James Couzens, the number two man in the company, had resigned in October of 1915, just prior to the "black era." Couzens was probably the one person most responsible for the success of the Ford Motor Company and he, like Henry Ford, was "his own boss" and not about to be directed by someone else. Clashes in policy and principle between the two lead to his leaving the company (he eventually became a U.S. Senator). Couzens' leaving set the stage for events to follow in the next five or so years.

In 1915 the Ford Motor Company had the following stockholders: Henry Ford, James Couzens, John and Horace Dodge, John Anderson, Horace Rackham, the heirs to the Gray estate, and Couzens' sister, Rosetta V. Hauss. Ford and Couzens were the only stockholders who participated in the management of the company, a situation which apparently galled Ford. Couzens' departure left Ford alone.

Henry Ford's displeasure with "unproductive partners" was pretty well indicated when he formed Henry Ford and Son, a separate firm, to manufacture the Fordson tractors, in November of 1915. In this new venture, he had to answer to no one. Ford's philosophy was to put the profits from the Ford Motor Company back into the company to increase

Ford catalog illustrations from the 1917 (upper left) and the 1920 (above) brochures appear identical. The 1920 picture is in error, as it shows the earlier front radius rod, which was changed in 1919. Ford used the same, or almost the same, illustration throughout the 1917 to 1920 era.

production, sales, and of course, profits; rather than distributing these profits among stockholders. This philosophy was not shared by the other stockholders, the Dodges in particular. One consequence was that the Dodges brought suit against Ford to force him to distribute the profits. On February 7, 1919, the Supreme Court ruled in favor of the Dodges; Ford not only had to distribute company profits in the future, he also had to distribute those dating from August of 1916 — with five percent interest! This action was a sizable setback for Ford but he rose to the challenge. He resigned!

Installing his son, Edsel, as president of the Ford Motor Company, Henry Ford let it be known that he was retiring to pursue some of his other interests, one of which was the manufacture of another car, much better and more modern than the Model T, and which would sell at a lower price. One effect of this announcement, or rumor, was a drop in the saleability of Ford Motor Company stock. After all, who would want to invest in a firm whose future was uncertain because of the loss of its leader, with

Ford Touring Car—Price $360 f. o. b. Detroit

Ford Sedan—Price $645 f. o. b. Detroit

Ford Chassis—Price $325 f. o. b. Detroit

The Ford line in the fall of 1916. Note that the chassis continued with the brass radiator for a short time. The Coupelet was replaced with another (fixed top) style sometime in later 1916 or 1917, and the Town Car was discontinued.

Ford Runabout—Price $345 f. o. b. Detroit

Ford Coupelet—Price $505 f. o. b. Detroit

Ford Town Car—Price $595 f. o. b. Detroit

said leader becoming a competitor?

The result was that the Ford stockholders were put in a position where they were willing to sell. Henry Ford was willing to buy! In 1919 Ford borrowed seventy-five million dollars, bought out the stockholders, and became the sole owner of the Ford Motor Company. James Couzens, the last to sell, received $30,000,000 for his interest; the Dodge brothers, Anderson, and Rackham received $12,000,000 each. The heirs to the Gray estate received the sum of $25,000,000. Mrs. Hauss, Couzens' sister, who had invested just $100 in 1903, received $260,000. Now in complete control, Henry Ford merged Henry Ford and Son with the Ford Motor Company; kept Edsel as president; and resumed "command."

At the end of World War I, many in the Ford management wanted to supersede the Model T with a new car. Ford, however, was interested only in production of the Model T — and history indicates that Henry got his way. The frustration of some of the top personnel might be indicated by the exodus of many of the top men between 1919 to 1922. Carl Emde, C. Harold Wills, Charles Morgana, Dean Marquis, Norval Hawkins, and William Knutsen were but a few of the key men to leave the company. Perhaps the best-known was William Knutsen, who left in 1921, joined Chevrolet, led that organization to its position of leadership, and who ultimately became president of General Motors. Of course, not *all* of these men "'quit." Some, no doubt, were eased out of their jobs because of their differences with Mr. Ford.

The Ford Motor Company changed. And so did the Model T.

Engine production figures for the period are interesting. For the fiscal years (August 1 to July 31) they were:

1917	750,512
1918	642,750
1919	521,600
1920	988,484 *

The decline in production was due to Ford's war efforts. A good part of the cars produced no doubt went to the military. Production figures for the calendar years are a little more indicative of the situation:

1916	586,203
1917	834,663
1918	382,247
1919	827,245 *
1920	1, 038,448
1921	1, 978,100

* Does not include 1300 shipped to Manchester, England, in late 1919.

THE NEW FORD CARS
(From a Ford announcement in 1916)

"On August 1st, the Ford Motor Company began its fiscal year of 1916-17 with an announcement of sharp reductions in the prices of Ford cars, the following new prices being placed in effect:

"Chassis, $325; Runabout, $345; Touring Car, $360; Coupelet, $505; Town Car, $595; Sedan, $645. These new prices bring the pleasure and profit of motoring within the reach of added millions.

"This price announcement was followed by the introduction of new models embodying marked changes in the familiar lines of Ford design. The hood is of graceful streamline design. There are sweeping crown fenders both front and rear. The radiator is larger, and with a new enclosed fan construction has a greater cooling efficiency. The new cars are finished in black with nickel trimmings, and are equipped with non-skid tires on the rear wheels.

"The Ford enclosed cars — Sedan, Coupelet, Town Car — represent the same attractive changes in design, equipment and construction that have been made in the open models. In the Sedan, we have also included several refinements in interior appointments. There is a new folded plait upholstery on both front and rear seats, while both rear side windows, as well as the window in the rear of the body, are finished with attractive black and white silk shade curtains in harmony with the color scheme of the upholstery.

"It is a joy to drive the Sedan every day of the year. A year around car it is, with the most comfortable of upholstery and inviting appointments. Cool and breezy in the summer time, it fully protects the occupants from heat and sun. And for the demands of fall and winter driving, one cannot wish for a cozier, more attractive car either for social purposes or general family use. There's generous accommodation for five persons — a broad back seat for three passengers, while both individual front seats have the hinge back, right-hand seat folding out of the way when not in use. Wide doors giving access from either side. Double water-tight windshield, and big plate glass windows are regular features which you will appreciate in an enclosed car.

"The Sedan has the low cost of operation and upkeep that is a feature of all Ford cars, and with its simplicity and easy facility of operation, is an ideal car for a woman to drive. Nothing to puzzle or confuse but, instead, a simple distinctive Ford control that anyone can quickly understand. It is comfort, service, beauty, builded upon Ford quality."

The Coupelet and Town Car have the streamline hood, crowned fenders and new radiator, but are without changes from last year's models in interior appointments.

In the Coupelet there is the same deep, comfortable upholstery, the broad seat with high restful back. And it has that feature which is more generally demanded each day—the instant convertibility at pleasure from an open to a closed car, and the reverse. You can make this change in two minutes. There is both ventilation and protection from the elements in the sliding plate glass windows, while the small windows in each side of the top give the driver a wide range of vision as to travel.

The top is lined with a fine quality of felt, fits neatly when up and folds snugly when lowered. In the rear deck of the body is ample space for luggage, parcels, extra tire, etc.

Women who drive their own cars vouch for the popularity of the Coupelet as a woman's car. Always in favor through its ease of control and the reliability of service which gives the driver confidence in her driving skill and safety. Besides, there is typical Ford economy in the first investment, in operation and upkeep.

With the substantial reductions in the prices of Ford cars there has been no slighting of the materials entering into their construction, no compromise with the established Ford standard of quality. They represent "efficiency savings," the savings which come with production on the scale which Ford cars are built and marketed, refinements in construction, new methods of distribution. It is all contained in the policy of the Ford Motor Company—to build "a better car at a lower price."

You can convert the Coupelet into a most attractive runabout in two minutes

The more you see of the interior appointments of the new Coupelet, the better it looks

1917 was the last year in which the Coupelet with the convertible top was produced. Essentially a restyled 1916 model (same body and upholstery), it continued the side "port holes" of the 1916 models. This model was replaced with a "hard top" coupe which had a padded top during 1917 production.

1917-1920

It is important to remember that the Model T did not truly come in annual models. Changes were made as they were developed. When we speak of, say, a 1917 Ford, this is not to say that all Fords of 1917 were alike. The "typical" car of the period would fit our descriptions, but there could be variations. In many cases we have no accurate data on just when changes were made. An example would be the 1917 cars, which first appeared in August of 1916. The brass-radiator cars built before the change would be called "1916" while the black-radiator cars would be "1917," even though both were made in 1916.

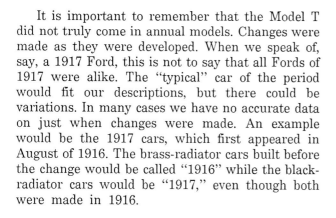

Ford Touring Car

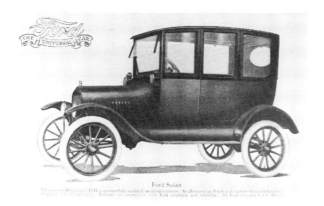

Ford Sedan

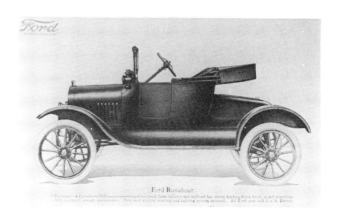

Ford Runabout

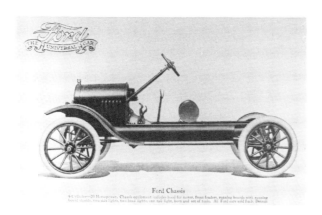

Ford Chassis

Ford Coupe

Illustrations from the 1918 catalog show the same Touring and Runabout as in 1917. There was little change in these models. New were the Coupe and the TT truck chassis. The bare passenger car chassis now had the new radiator and front fenders. Ford catalog illustrations cannot be relied on as being typical of the cars of the catalog year. For example, the Touring and Runabouts show the horn button on top of the steering column but all open cars had the combination horn and light switch on the side of the column by this time. 1918 was the last year in which oil lamps were supplied as standard equipment on the closed cars.

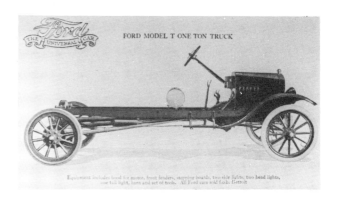

FORD MODEL T ONE TON TRUCK

Ford Sedan

5-Passenger—4-Cylinder—20-Horsepower. Large sliding plate glass windows in doors and sides. Roomy doors. Two unit electric starting and lighting system. Demountable rims. 3½-inch non-skid tires all around. Tire carrier. An all-season car of style and comfort—for social functions, for shopping, for touring, and general uses. Enclosed car comforts with Ford simplicity and reliability. All Ford cars sold f. o. b. Detroit.

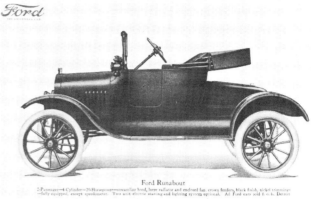

Ford Runabout

2-Passenger—4-Cylinder—20-Horsepower—streamline hood, large radiator and enclosed fan, crown fenders, black finish, nickel trimmings —fully equipped, except speedometer. Two unit electric starting and lighting system optional. All Ford cars sold f. o. b. Detroit.

Ford Coupe

2-Passenger—4-Cylinder—20-Horsepower. Permanent top with sliding plate glass windows. Two unit electric starting and lighting system. Demountable rims. 3½-inch non-skid tires all around. Tire carrier. The ideal type of 2-passenger car where great amount convenience is combined with the highest degree of utility. All Ford cars sold f. o. b. Detroit.

The Fords of 1919 and 1920. While different catalogs were published, they all used the same illustrations. The open cars still show the oil lamps, which seems unusual. Ford made about twice as many starter-equipped open cars as he did the non-starter, and oil lamps were only supplied on the non-starter models.

Ford Chassis

4-Cylinder—20-Horsepower. Chassis equipment includes hood for motor, front fenders, running boards with running board shields, two side lights, two head lights, one tail light, horn and set of tools. Two unit electric starting and lighting system optional. All Ford cars sold f. o. b. Detroit.

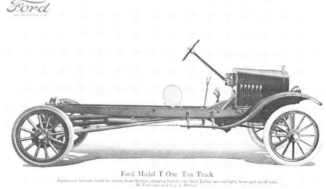

Ford Model T One Ton Truck

Equipment includes hood for motor, front fenders, stepping boards, two head lights, one tail light, horn and set of tools. All Ford cars sold f. o. b. Detroit.

241

The 1917 chassis. A number of differences between this and the 1917 Touring are evident. Note that the steering gear case (under the steering wheel) is nickeled on the chassis but black on the Touring. The caps on both are nickeled. It is believed that the earliest 1917 models used the black-painted case, probably on the remaining stock of the earlier brass type, but most production was nickeled. The rear springs on the chassis are taper-leaf, typical of most if not all passenger cars of 1917. *Photo from the Collections of the Henry Ford Museum and Greenfield Village.*

The coil box cover was now of the three-piece fabricated type instead of the one-piece stamping used in 1915 and 1916.

The attractive arrangement and new appointments of the Sedan are shown in this phantom photograph.

The 1917 Sedan. The same illustrations were used in 1918, 1919, and 1920 (but less the oil lamps).

The 1917 Ford Coupelet

Photos and Story by Don Black, Mesa, Arizona
(Introduction by the Author)

1917 was an "odd" year for the Ford Motor Company, when it came to its Coupelet bodies. There were apparently three different styles.

When the style year began, in August 1916, the Coupelet was a duplicate of the 1916 model except for the change to the new fenders, hood, radiator, etc. of the "iron era." This body was quickly dropped in favor of a transitional style Coupelet, which is featured here. The date of this change is not known but is believed to have been in late 1916 or early 1917.

This body type lasted for just a short time, and was replaced with the familiar Coupe body style at, perhaps, mid-1917, which was probably called a "1918" model. (These 1918 Coupes continued the removable side posts, while the 1919 to 1923 Coupes had solid posts, but the general style was the same.)

We have no data on how many of each of these body styles were made. Ford records available today do not indicate the type of Coupe; all three were grouped under "Coupe" in the production records. A total of just 7,343 "Coupes" were built between August 1916 and August 1917.

It has been only in very recent years that we have been able to confirm that this interim "1917" style coupe was actually ever built. Artists conceptions of the car have appeared in various publications but the Ford catalogs of the era (that we have seen) show only the earlier or the later style, not the style of our featured car. The 1917

Coupelet featured here is the second we have been able to locate but there are probably more out there somewhere. This particular car has been extensively modified, with little, if any, of the original chassis components. Don Black's story points out many of the changes but it appears that even the chassis is not original. Possibly just the body components are "1917." Yet, the body is the most important and

The rear view shows a later spare-tire carrier (it had none when the car was built). Careful inspection will show a handle on the rear deck lid, another "accessory."

interesting part of this rare model. The body appears to be entirely stock. Other than the addition of a 1924-style valence under the radiator core, and the addition of the "Ford" script on the radiator core, it appears to be "correct."

The terms "Coupelet" and "Coupe" are often interchangeable in Ford literature. The Coupelet is generally considered to be the type with either the folding top or the removable pillars, while the Coupe is the type with the solid pillars.

THE 1917 COUPELET
By Don Black

This Ford Coupe originally came to light quite unexpectedly in about 1970. Two spinster sisters, both ex-school teachers, lived in an old and decrepit house outside of Cleveland, Ohio. For years neighbors thought that the two women were in need, and would bring them food regularly, as well as check on them for their safety and other concerns or needs. When one was taken from the house on a cold winter's day, suffering from frost bite, and the other being unable to take care of herself any longer, the property was put up for sale.

When the local sheriff and a court-appointed attorney entered the house, they were amazed at what they found. Under the mattress, in small sealed envelopes found throughout the house, and in hiding places, they found a total of over $360,000 in cash, gold and bonds!

With no relatives to be found, the house was opened to the public. For a one dollar admission price, anyone could look over what was left of the personal belongings which were to be auctioned. Witnesses said that other than for a few pieces of antique furniture, there wasn't really anything of value. Then the garage was opened — and there it was: a very well kept old Ford Coupe. But this Ford Coupe was definitely different from other Ford Coupes. This was one of a very few made with this particular body style during 1917 before the change to the more traditional model Coupe of that era.

Note the non-Ford tail light. Difficult to really determine (from these photos), it appears that the frame is also later style, with the pressed-steel running board supports instead of the forged brackets and tie rods used before 1921. Perhaps the body itself is the only original part of this car.

The difference? The top is rounded and soft on the corners. Subsequent models had a flat, hard top. The car sports the removable pillars which, when removed, open up the area between the windshield and the rear quarter; the first "hardtop" look.

Over the years the ladies had their Ford updated. In 1922 they had the non- starter 1917 engine replaced with a new 1922 starter model. Sometime along the way the accessory dash board, with a speedometer and later style light and ignition switch assembly. Bulbs were added to the oil side lights, with a wire that goes through the cowling. A spotlight was added. The rear axle was replaced with the later (1926) style with the larger brake drums. The front axle now has the later "wishbone" and the wheels were changed to the demountable type. The body is near perfect, as solid as it was when new. Doors and wood are absolutely tight.

An interesting feature of the car is the little compartment behind the seat. This compartment is divided into two sections, allowing storage space for the two removable pillars.

For a car as heavy as it appears, it is a surprisingly good runner, with a totally stock engine except for a water pump.

It was sold at the auction for $200 to a local man, who turned right around and resold it for a huge profit. The second buyer sold it to a third for an even higher price.

So far as this writer has been able to determine, there is only one other Ford with this body style still in existence, on the East Coast.

With the side posts removed, the car becomes a "hardtop." On the 1915 to 1917 Coupelets with the foldable top, the side post was part of the top assembly; there was no rear quarter window as in this body. (The 1916-17 models did have a "port hole" in the quarter, which helped remove a little of the blind spot.) The later 1917 and 1918 Coupes retained the removable pillar of this car but the top sections were metal and somewhat "square" instead of rounded as on this model.

1917-1920

When the door window is lowered, hinged window supports fold down to cover the door sill. The window is lowered or raised with the leather strap. This system was quite common on many lower-priced cars, and standard on Fords until about 1922.

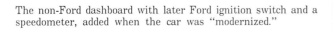

The non-Ford dashboard with later Ford ignition switch and a speedometer, added when the car was "modernized."

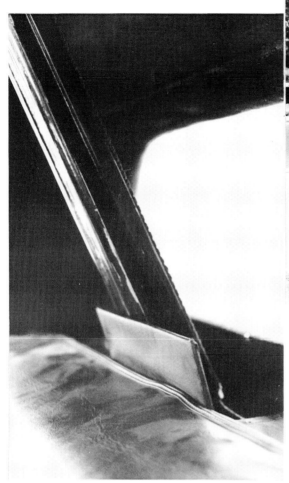

The "updated" 1917 Coupelet as it appeared at the time of its discovery. The spotlight, demountable wheels, "Ford" on the radiator, luggage rack, tool (battery?) box, spare-tire carrier, and the valance under the radiator shell are all later additions. The body itself is just as it appeared in 1917.

Two compartments behind the seat provide storage for the side pillars.

1917-1920

The 1918 Coupelet
*(Photos by Dwight Madsen,
Minneapolis, Minnesota*

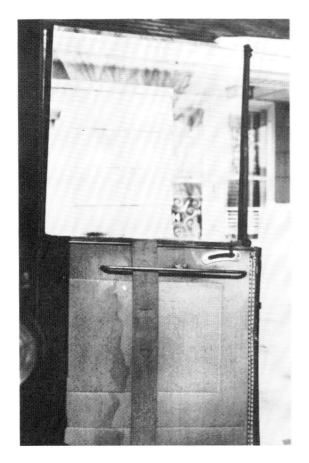

Front view with the doors open. The original upholstery is quite good although water stained.

The left door with the glass raised. Note the strap to raise and lower the window, and the hinged cover which covers the opening in the door when the window is down. The rear quarter windows also lower with a strap so that they are flush with the top of the sill.

The two pillars and the wing nut which locks the pillar to the top inside the car. The wing nuts and the T-bolts are nickle-plated. The posts are solid wood and are quite sturdy.

The door pillars store in a box under the seat and are held in place with a strap.

BELOW: The upholstered area under the cowl, used on many but not all closed cars in the 1917 to 1921 era.

1917-1920

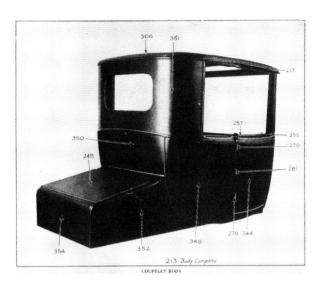

213 *Body Complete*
COUPELET BODY

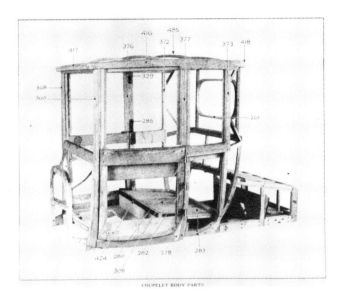

COUPELET BODY PARTS

Right door open with the center pillar installed. All inside window moldings were of wood and were painted black. Note the fancy cut in the pillar for the glass and hinged channel.

The round gas tank almost fills the rear deck, leaving room for little more than a picnic lunch. The later coupes used the square sedan gas tank which was located in the right-front corner of the deck.

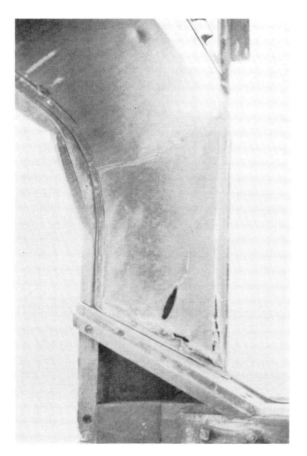

The under side of the cowl area of this example is upholstered in leatherette, unlike some of the later models.

The "1918" Model T Coupelet was unique in that it differed from the year that preceded it as well as the one that followed. The "1917" came in two styles, the "convertible" and the "soft top," and the "1919" did not have the removable posts although otherwise it appeared quite similar.

1918 was the last year in which Ford offered closed cars without electrical starting equipment. All later closed cars came with an instrument panel.

Many of the 1919 and later cars did not have the upholstered under-dash; the introduction of the instrument panel made it unnecessary. Apparently this under-dash covering depended on the body manufacturer.

The 'typical of the year" cars are described in the following:

1917
(Introduced August 1916)

While basically a restyling of the 1915-16 models, the 1917 Model T Ford appeared to be an all-new car. The brass radiator was replaced with a higher one with a black shell. The hood was larger and mated smoothly with the cowl. Fenders, front and rear, were now crowned and curved to follow the wheel outline. The steering column gear box and control levers were nickel-plated, as were the radiator filler neck and the wheel hub caps.

In addition to the major styling changes, there were a number of minor modifications. The front body (firewall) brackets, which had been forgings in the earlier cars, were now pressed steel. The hood clash strip was now a metal stamping instead of wooden as in all the earlier Fords.

The windshield frame and mounting brackets on the open cars were modified during 1917. Similar to the 1915-16 type, the cast support brackets now bolted to the frame rather than being riveted. In addition, the windshield hinge was modified so that the hinge was off-center, making the windshield a little higher when in the folded position. Apparently the change in the mounting (bolts instead of rivets) came first; the new hinge came later.

Along with the new windshield, but not necessarily at the same time, came a restyled top. Rather than the one large window in the rear, three rectangular windows (about 5-1/4 by 9-1/4 inches each) appeared. Otherwise the top appeared similar to the 1915-16 type.

1917-1922 Non-Starter Cars

One of the many changes made in the Model T open cars in the early years of the "black era" was in the windshield support bracket. The 1915 and 1916 cars used a forged bracket as shown in the lower left photo. Note how the windshield frame is riveted in place, with the rivets going from front to rear. The typical 1917 to 1919 (and 1920-21 non-starter) cars used a bracket in which the frame is secured with screws (upper right), from the side. With the introduction of electrical equipment, oil lamps were not used on cars so-equipped, and the bracket was then made without the oil lamp support (lower photo).

NOTE: The horn bulb shown in the lower right photo is incorrect, the bulb was fastened to the steering column on those 1915 cars which used this type of horn. The mirror in the lower right photo is an accessory. Also note the metal cap at the end of the arm rest. This was first used in late 1916 models and continued through the open cars of this era.

1915-1916

1919-1922 Starter Cars

The 1917 Ford Touring as it appeared at introduction. Careful examination of the original photo shows several interesting items, which may indicate that it was a pre-production model. The windshield brackets at the cowl are of the new bolted construction but the bolts are hex-headed instead of the usual screws. The windshield hinge is of the typical 1915-16 type, instead of the usual 1917-style with the unequal arms. The horn button is the same as the 1916. (The combination horn-light switch appeared late in 1917.) The steering gear case is painted black while the case top is nickel, apparently using the brass 1916-style gear case. The two control levers are nickeled. The spring perches, front and rear, have oilers (earlier cars had the oilers on the shackles). Note that the hub caps have a black background. There are no runningboard support brackets showing. The headlights are mounted higher than the normal position, and actually look better in this position. This body style continued with but minor changes until late 1920 (1921 models). *Photo from the Collection of the Henry Ford Museum and Greenfield Village.*

Even the upholstery underwent a modification. The last bit of real leather, at the front roll of the arm rests, was eliminated. In its place was a steel end cap, with the imitation leather now extending to this cap. (This modification was made in the late 1916 cars, before the styling change.

Early production 1917 cars continued to have the light switch on the firewall, just to the right of the coil box. The horn button was located on the top surface of the steering column, as on the 1915-16 models. In late 1917, actually during "1918" production, the light switch was combined with the horn button. Now located on the left side of the column, the button was pushed for the horn, and turned for the headlights.

There was no dashboard at this time; the ignition switch was still located on the coil box. However, when a speedometer was installed, the manufacturer (Stewart and others) supplied a dashboard.

Accompanying the new radiator was a new fan

and fan support arm assembly. The fan itself was similar to the previous type except that it had an iron pulley (which apparently appeared during 1916) instead of one of brass. The support arm no longer had a bend. Early 1917 cars were equipped with a fan shroud, added to aid the cooling. It may have helped but the swinging arm adjustment probably caused the fan to strike the shroud after some wear, and rather than redesigning the fan belt tension system, the shroud was discontinued.

The engine sported a new crankcase with a wider front "snout." This pan design continued until 1924 when a new "four-dip" pan replaced it. While the wider front made room for a larger pulley, the large pulley did not appear until May of 1920. This suggests that it had been planned much earlier.

The so-called "high" cylinder head appeared as a running change during early 1917 production. Of slightly lower compression ratio, it held considerably more water which aided in cooling the engine. Accompanying this new head were longer head bolts, now 3-1/4" long, as compared with 2-9/16" before this change.

A new, longer, water-outlet casting was used on the cylinder head to match the new radiator. The connecting rubber hose was the same as that used with the brass radiators.

The muffler was redesigned and while quite similar to the previous types, still using the cast-iron ends, the tail pipe was eliminated. An oblong hole in the rear casting exhausted the gases directly.

During 1916 production, Ford began to install front springs with non-tapered ends, as well as using the tapered type. Rear springs, according to the Ford Parts List, were tapered in all production until sometime in 1918. There is conflicting information as to whether square or tapered, or both, were used between 1916 and 1919. Seemingly original cars as early as 1917 have been seen with square-end springs front and/or rear, and the tapered rear springs into 1919. However, most cars of the 1917 period seem to have had tapered rear springs and non-tapered front springs.

The front axle assembly underwent a few minor modifications. The spring perches were now drilled to accept an oiler, eliminating the need for oilers on the shackles. New shackles accompanied this change. Initially they were the same "figure-eight" forgings used with the oiler types, but less the oilers. Later, but apparently during 1917, the "L" type shackles, in more than one design, appeared. Spindle bolts used the "trapdoor" type of oiler, similar to those used on the shackles, but larger, instead of the "manhole" style of 1915-1916. The rear spring perches were modified in a similar manner. Both front and rear main leaves were drilled and fitted with oilers.

The body styles of the 1917 cars continued in the pattern of 1915-16, except for the cowl section. This was the last year for the "convertible" Coupelet, and the Town Car; both types being dropped during early 1917 production apparently.

The Sedan had been redesigned during 1916, and now had the fuel tank under the driver's seat. The body was now steel (over a wooden frame) and sat higher on the chassis, allowing the use of the standard rear fenders and splash aprons. While similar in appearance to the 1915 Sedan, this was an all-new design. "1916-style" sedans are extremely rare and the 1917 style is also rather rare. Just 1,859 Sedans were built in fiscal 1916, and 7,361 in fiscal 1917.

After the initial production of the carryover convertible Coupelet, a new Coupelet appeared for 1917. Similar in style to the convertible model, the new one had a solid top and removable door pillars, making it one of the first "hardtops." The top was leather covered above the waistline, therefore looking like a convertible but with a fixed top. This model apparently saw little production; few survive,

Early production 1917 cars were supplied with a fan shroud to aid in cooling. It was discontinued early in production, perhaps because of interference with the fan blades as the belt wore.

The combination horn and light switch, introduced in late 1917 and used until 1922 in the non-starter cars. The steering gear case was nickeled, as were the two control levers, in the production cars.

and the 1918 type appeared before the end of the year.

1918

The 1917 cars evolved into the 1918 with little in the way of changes. Production of civilian passenger cars had been cut drastically because of the war. During 1917 production, and typical of the 1918's, the top irons on the open cars changed from the oval cross-section type to the rectangular.

The Coupelet was superseded by a new Coupe (but still called a "Coupelet" in the Ford catalogs)

The late 1917 and 1918 Coupelet. All new, it featured a solid top but had removable center posts, making it an early "hardtop." This Ford Archives photo shows the car as it first appeared. Note the forward-opening doors; cowl lamps, 30 by 3 tires in front, clear headlamp lenses and early-style front radius rods; all characteristics of the 1917 and 1918 Coupelets. In 1919, the door posts became fixed, oil lamps disappeared, demountable rims with 30 by 3-1/2 tires were standard (on all closed cars), and the radius rod was replaced with the new type which connects below the axle. This style, with minor modifications, continued until mid-1923. *Photos from the Collections of the Henry Ford Museum and Greenfield Village.*

which continued the removable posts between the door and rear quarter windows, as in the short-lived 1917 hardtops, but with a metal-covered top section. The standard round fuel tank was located in the rear turtle deck compartment on these models.

The Model TT truck appeared in the catalogs for the first time in 1918. The truck was not new this year, though. It had been built in 1917 but most, if not all, production went to the war effort. Ford supplied the truck as a chassis only, with a firewall, front fenders and a hood. Bodies were installed by dealers and owners, either home-made or made by one of the many body suppliers for the Ford aftermarket.

During 1918 the steering tie rod was modified. The yoke on the left side, which formerly had been threaded on and used for toe-in adjustment, was now integral with the tie rod. The right-hand yoke was modified to be adjustable and its position was locked in place by the same nut that secured the drag-link ball.

1919

World War I was over, and once again Ford was able to devote all its efforts to the production of the Model T. The new year continued with the 1918 style cars but the engine and running gear underwent major modifications.

The most significant change was the addition of electrical starting equipment, beginning in January 1919, on the closed cars as standard equipment. Open cars and the chassis (both car and truck) did not offer this equipment, even as an option, initially. However, by summer of 1919, production of the electrical components had increased so that it could be made available, as an option, on the open models. (Trucks, apparently, had to wait until about 1921 for this option.) This seemingly innocent change required major modifications of the engine.

In addition to a new cylinder block casting, with a modified front section to accommodate the generator mounting, a new transmission cover had to be made with provision for the starter motor. The generator mounted on the right side of the timing gear case and was gear-driven from the large timing

The off-center windshield hinge used from 1917 until about September 1922 (when the 1923 models appeared). Note that the top half of the windshield was now higher than the lower when folded. The reason for this change is open to speculation; this system allows more clearance between the steering wheel and the windshield top when folding, and offered a bit more protection from the wind when in the folded position. The 1915, 1916, and early 1917 cars used equal-length windshield hinge arms.

Side and tail oil lamps continued in the style introduced in 1915 (but with no brass trim). Cars with electrical equipment were not supplied with oil lamps.

Accompanying the new styling, metal hood clash strips replace the painted wood type used earlier. The hood hold-down clamps were forged, as shown here, until about 1920-21.

New in 1919, and appearing only on those cars equipped with starter and generator, the instrument panel added a bit of finish to the interior. The example shown here is typical of later 1919 through 1922. The speedometer was a dealer/owner installed option. The instrument cluster on the early 1919's used a more expensive ammeter in which the pointer mechanism was more elaborate and exposed, and the switch knob was a casting rather than the pressed-metal type used in the bulk of Model T production. The switch/ammeter assemblies were made by several suppliers, and there were variations in style, lettering, and construction, although the general appearance was the same.

gear. The timing gears were now spiral-cut for quieter operation. The old straight-cut timing gears were discontinued; both gears had to be changed if an older engine needed a new gear.

The flywheel was modified to accept a replaceable ring gear for the starter. The magneto field coil was modified by adding a notch to clear the starter gear assembly. Interestingly, Ford experimented with a flywheel with an integral gear cut in its outer rim, but decided in favor of the separate ring gear.

A battery support bracket was bolted between the frame rails just to the rear of the gasoline tank. The starter switch was mounted near the driver's left heel. Initial production of the starter cars had the generator cut-out mounted on the firewall, but by mid-1919 the cut-out was relocated to the standard location on the generator.

Accompanying the electrical equipment was a dashboard with an ammeter and a combination ignition/light switch. In early 1919 the switch handle was a casting but apparently changed to pressed-steel as production increased. These switch assemblies were bought from outside suppliers, and varied from manufacturer to manufacturer in detail, although they appeared alike to the casual observer. On the non-starter open cars, no dashboard was supplied, and the ignition switch remained on the coil box as in earlier cars. The light switch continued to be in combination with the horn button on non-starter cars until the 1922 models.

Now that the Ford had a battery, new headlights were supplied which had two bulbs; one for the regular "bright" running lights, and the other a 2 candle-power (C.P.) bulb for the "dim" lights. Both bulbs were of the single-contact, six-volt type. Non-starter cars continued the double-contact bulbs, wired in series and powered by the magneto. The starter cars were also supplied with an electric tail light, using a six volt bulb. Non-starter cars continued with the oil tail lamp. Oil side lamps were discontinued on the starter cars, but were standard equipment on the non-starter models.

Above: The early 1919 ammeter. Note the elaborate construction. Apparently these came with and without the "Ford" and with the "Ford" in various styles and locations.

Below: The cast switch lever used in early production. The pressed-metal type, typical of most Model T's, appeared in later 1919 or 1920.

On those cars with the electrical equipment, an inside choke pull rod was installed. This rod operated by means of a bell crank on the firewall in the manner used in all starter-type Fords until 1926 models. Initially, the knob on this control rod was cold-rolled but the more common cast aluminum knob became standard early in 1919.

1917-1920

Initial production of the 1919 cars (those built in 1919) supplied without starters continued to use the old-style cylinder casting and transmission cover. The last of the non-starter cylinder castings was made on May 28, 1919, and from then on, all cars, starter or not, used the starter-type cylinder casting. Cars without electrical equipment had blanking plates over the holes in the transmission cover, and a different casting for the timing gear cover on the right front of the engine.

The front axle assembly was not spared in the sweeping changes. The radius rods were all new and now bolted to the front axle below the spring perches. The perches no longer had the hole where the earlier-design rods connected, and the mounting stud was made longer to accommodate the new radius rod assembly. The spindle arms were given a new "bend" to clear the radius rods, and the tie rod now was located above the radius rods. Timken roller bearings were now used on the closed cars and trucks, replacing the ball bearings used earlier. Roller bearings were used on the open cars later in 1919 when they were supplied with starters. Ball bearings continued on the front wheels on those open cars supplied with non-demountable wheels and no starter until 1926 production. The Timken bearings, being a bit thicker, made another modification of the front spindles necessary; the spindle axle was made a bit longer. The roller bearings could be used with the earlier spindles (and commonly were used as replacements for the ball bearings), but the slightly longer spindle axles made a better fit. The oiler on the spindle bolt was reduced in size and was now the same as the oiler used on the timer.

In 1919 demountable rims were offered as standard equipment on the closed cars, and as an option on the others after early production. These rims and wheels were manufactured by either Hayes or Kelsey, and used 30 by 3-1/2 tires all around. A spare rim and carrier was available for cars with the demountable wheels, but the tire for this rim was not standard equipment.

The rear axle assembly underwent some relatively minor modifications during 1919. The oil filler hole was relocated a bit lower on the center housing. This was done to prevent over filling the differential housing, reducing the leakage at the axle ends. The two center sections were milled to allow for a thin paper gasket between them, helping a small leakage problem at the center seam. A modification in the machining operation at the outer ends of the axle housing made it necessary to use a larger retaining cup for the felt axle seal at the wheel.

In June 1919, the muffler was modified so that the exhaust port was moved slightly to the side, directing the exhaust away from the spare tire.

The method of mounting the radiator was modified on the trucks to now include a thimble on

Above: When the new body style was introduced in mid-1916 (1917 models), the firewall became the support for the rear of the hood, replacing the separate hood former used earlier. Its edges were protected with a metal strip which, in turn was covered with a woven weatherstrip.

Below: In 1919 the metal strip was redesigned to now include a rain gutter which directed water away from the coil terminals. Water could still work its way between the firewall and the body, and Ford recommended the use of a felt seal as a dealer-installed cure. Such a seal apparently was never installed at the factory.

either side of the mounting flange, and a spring to support the radiator assembly. Passenger cars continued the use of the old leather pad for some time, but eventually all cars came with the spring-mounted radiator. The new mounting method required a change in the radiator-mounting bracket; the hole in it was increased from about 1/2 inch to about 1 inch diameter.

During 1919 production, a rain gutter was added to the firewall metal trim strip. This gutter directed water to the sides and therefore kept it away from the coil box terminals on the engine side. (Water could still seep between the firewall and the body, and Ford advised using a felt packing between the two pieces. Such packing, however, was never installed at the factory.)

Body styles for 1919 continued in the 1917-1918 pattern. Late in 1918, perhaps in what might be called 1919 models, the Coupelet no longer had the removable door posts but otherwise was quite similar in style. The square Sedan fuel tank was now used in the Coupelet, replacing the round type, but still located in the rear compartment.

With the introduction of starter equipment on the open cars, the windshield support brackets were made without the integral lamp brackets. From here on, if you wanted oil lamps on a starter car, you had to buy the brackets as well as the lamps. Non-starter cars continued to use the older bracket and the oil lamps for a time, then separate lamp brackets were used.

Body features varied in detail all through Model T production. For one thing, there was more than one supplier, and each had its own methods and parts. In addition, many minor detail changes were made which might make, say, a 1918 sedan differ from a 1919. Such details are beyond the scope of this coverage.

1920

The Ford of 1920 continued in the style of the 1919. Electrical equipment and demountable wheels were standard on all closed cars, and optional on the open models. Trucks apparently were not given the starter option until 1921.

A bracket was added to support the battery cable between the battery and the starter switch, apparently an oversight in 1919. During 1920 the oval gasoline tank appeared. The oval tank was raised to the proper height by means of special adaptor brackets under the tank-mounting straps.

The forged running board brackets and tie rods were dropped during the year and replaced with the channel-type brackets, a considerable improvement

in the rigidity of the running boards.

The cast-steel steering wheel spider was replaced with a new one of pressed steel. In addition, the steering wheel diameter was increased to sixteen inches to give added leverage with the now-common 30 by 3-1/2 front tires (which were harder to turn than the 30 by 3's).

The driveshaft underwent a few modifications. A new pinion bearing housing of forged steel replaced the casting used before. This new housing eliminated the need for the separate bearing sleeve which had been used inside the earlier casting. The new style is easily identified because its retaining bolts are exposed while on the earlier housing, studs were used which were enclosed within the casting. Accompanying this change, the driveshaft flange no longer had the raised area which fit into the older bearing housing. The new pinion bearing housing assembly could be used to replace the earlier type, but it was (is) necessary to grind off this raised area. In addition to the housing change, the pinion thrust bearing was simplified. Instead of the rather complex assembly used before, the new bearing consisted of two identical washers (bearing races) and a ball bearing ring assembly.

A cost-cutting modification was made by a redesign of the brake rods. Instead of the forged fork ends, the metal rod was now split to form the fork.

At last the fan and crankshaft pulleys were enlarged; a change that seemed to be forecast by the wider front pan introduced in 1917. The larger pulleys gave a better "grip" on the fan belt. Along with this change, the fan itself was greatly improved. Rather than the four blades riveted to the pulley, the new fan was made of two pieces, spot-welded together, which bolted to the pulley. A gasket was used between the pulley assembly and the fan blade which now served as an oil retainer for the fan shaft bearing. This new fan assembly was a great improvement since the earlier riveted types were known to "throw" blades from time to time.

During 1920, Ford introduced new light-weight

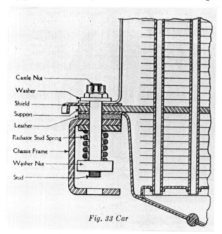

Fig. 33 Car

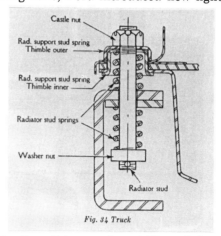

Fig. 34 Truck

During 1919, on the trucks at first, then on all cars, the method of mounting the radiator was changed. The typical 1909-1919 mounting (LEFT) used a leather pad between the radiator support and the frame (left picture) but the new method (RIGHT) used two springs, a thimble and a cup washer. This new mounting allowed greater flexibility without damaging the radiator, and was used in all later Model T Fords.

improvement in the engine's performance and durability.

Overlooked in the past, or forced by legislation, irate Ford owners, or whatever, Ford added two brackets to the front motor mount/spring support assembly which could hold the license plate. Short lived, these brackets gave way to another design in 1921 when the new support with the integral clamping bolts appeared.

In its never-ending search for less expensive components, Ford discovered that money could be saved by making the muffler entirely of pressed steel. And so it was! The new muffler also required a new exhaust pipe. Another area of savings was in the method of securing the hood handles. Previously riveted in place, the handles now were made so that the metal of the handle itself formed the "rivet" and instead of seeing a rivet head on each end of the hood handle, one saw a "hole."

In June 1920, the factory issued a letter announcing a new body for the open cars. This was followed by sample bodies being shipped to the assembly branches as examples. Then began a changeover beginning in November 1920 to the new style. These new bodies were similar in style to the 1917-20 types, but a great improvement in finish and comfort.

1920 ended with severe problems for Ford. His notes for the money he had borrowed to buy the company, would be due in early 1921, but the business recession of the early 1920's created a shortage of cash with which to retire the notes. Ford was up to the situation, though. Late in 1920 he assembled everything he had in parts to make Fords, and shipped them, along with spare parts, to his dealers — C.O.D. He closed the plant in January 1921, cutting costs to the bone, and waited for the money to come in. The plan worked, although not without considerable pain to Ford dealers. By mid-1921 Ford was out of debt, and headed for his greatest era of profits.

The photographs in this article are from the Model T Ford Club of America collection, gathered over many years. We begin here with the new 1917 Ford Touring featured in *The Vintage Ford* in 1978 and again in 1991. This car had just twenty-six miles on the speedometer, and except for the deterioration from years in semi-protected storage, was just as it left the factory. The car is typical of the Touring cars of the 1917 to 1920 era, except for mechanical details of the chassis, and minor modifications in body construction. The photos were taken as the car was pulled from a shed near St. Croix Falls, Wisconsin.

To those who do not have access to the issue in which this car was featured, the story briefly is as follows: In the summer of 1917, Oscar W. Peterson, of Center City, Minnesota, decided that the only way to keep the Ford salesmen away was to buy a new Ford. If he already had a car, he thought, they wouldn't keep pestering him. Mr. Peterson ordered his car from the Lorens Garage in Center City and had them drive it out to his farm, a distance of about 6 miles. The car was put in a prepared barn, put up on blocks, and sat there until 1937 when he passed away. Although he never drove the car, Mr. Peterson purchased new license plates every year, and stored them under the rear seat.

Oscar Peterson lived alone and upon his death, the car was sold at auction. The highest bidder was Eugene R. Princeton, a Ford dealer in St. Croix Falls, Wisconsin, who paid the unheard of sum of $87. Mr. Princeton named it the "Rip Van Winkle Ford" and put it on display at his dealership. In time the car was placed in storage and remained there until vandals broke in and drove it until it ran out of fuel; about twenty miles. Rescued, it went back into storage in several locations, ending up in the barn where we found it.

Mr. Princeton died a few years after we photographed it, and his son, Eugene Princeton Jr., moved it to California and placed it on display in his antique shop. Its whereabouts today is unknown.

About 1920 the rear axle pinion bearing spool was redesigned. The new type used a forged spool with exposed bolts rather than the cast type with the enclosed studs. A new thrust bearing and a modified driveshaft tube accompanied this change. The new forged spool eliminated the need for the separate bearing sleeve used with the earlier cast spool.

Hub caps on the 1917 and later cars were nickel plated. Some were made of brass and others of steel, and some had a black painted background.

The 1917 "Rip Van Winkle" Ford as it was uncovered for photographs. The car had been stored in this open shed for fifteen years, and the leaking roof and exposure had taken its toll of the paint and upholstery. Careful examination proved that it was, indeed, a brand-new Ford, even though its outward appearance might indicate otherwise. The axle stands shown here are the same ones made by the original owner in 1917. Unused license plates for many years were still under the rear seat cushion.

Under the rear seat, in addition to the license plates, were these tools, still in a new-looking tool pouch. Ford script tire patches were included. The duplication of some tools is no doubt due to additions over the years, but the pliers, etc. were still shiny!

1917-1920

The rear tires had been lost due to vandalism and were replaced with new ones after this photo was taken. The only dent in the entire car was a small one on the right rear fender where apparently something was dropped on it. In addition, the fount of the right sidelight was missing.

The accessory Stewart speedometer shows the car's mileage, most of which was put on when the car was stolen some years earlier. The instrument panel was also supplied by Stewart.

Time and weather have severely eroded and tarnished the paint but where it remains it is quite shiny. There are numerous runs in the paint, particularly in areas such as the seat kick panels, indicating that Ford's flow-on painting method was not completely satisfactory.

Note the metal trim strip across the back, covering the rear curtain's bottom edge. These strips have largely disappeared over the years and are seldom seen on cars which have been restored. The strips were apparently standard issue on 1915 through 1920 open cars. The eyelet in the lower center of the rear curtain is for a Murphy fastener on the top boot, for use when the top was folded and the boot installed.

The workmanship on the original top shows the result of the rushed assembly line pace. Note how the rear panel and the top do not match at the upper corner.

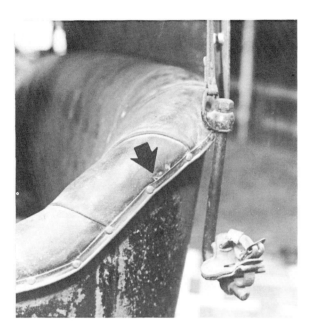

The upholstery is entirely of imitation leather. The installation is crudely done, with tacks visible outside the tack strip. The factory upholsterer who did this car even left a spare tack, with the point sticking out of the trim strip (arrow). Note the door panels. The board-like panel has a hole cut out to clear the handle and the tack strip stops on each side of the latch cutout, rather than being formed around it. Upholstery details varied from car to car, and over the years, but this is how it was done on this car in June of 1917.

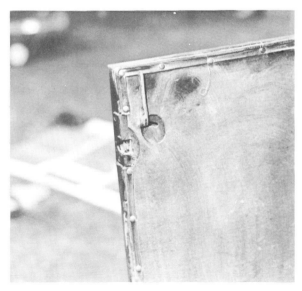

The front floor mat is black rubber. Note that it does not cover the entire front floor; just the floorboards. The mat is still notched just to the right of the steering column for the pipe from the bulb horn, which was last used in 1915!

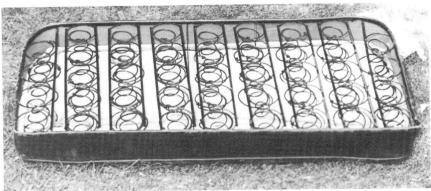

The upholstery on the front seat cushion of this original 1917 was beyond repair. Time, weather and rats had done it in. The rear seat, however, was in excellent condition even though it is dried and cracked. The underside is like new; the springs are shiny-black and the material almost white. The bottom edges are held in place with a crimped-on metal strip.

The rear seat box has no covering lid, as did the 1916 cars. It is lined with a cardboard sheet which is curved upward at the rear, meeting the underside of the seat frame, which holds it in place. The license plates shown are all like new and were purchased each year by the original owner, even though he never drove the car during the twenty years he owned it.

The kick plate at the bottom of the front seat is a study in Ford's quality control. Here, and on the kick panel behind the front seat, there are many runs in the paint, probably a result of the "garden hose flow-on" painting method used. The stains on the floorboard were made later, we presume.

The rear floor mat is wool and is quite thick. The edges are bound all around as shown.

The rear floor boards are fastened permanently in place and further held with quarter-round strips on each side.

The top is made of a pebble grain material. The underside is cloth-like and of a much lighter color (tan here but perhaps white when new, as under the seats).

The top straps are all cloth webbing. The only leather straps are those at the top saddles, used to hold the top when it is folded.

The original timer case is cast iron and uses a bronze roller assembly. It shows no wear and appears just as it did when it was new.

It is important to remember that the car featured here is a June 1917 model. The general features are similar for all Touring Cars built by Ford from mid-1916 until about 1921, but there are differences which should be kept in mind.

The top sockets on this car are oval in cross section, as they had been since 1909. In late 1917 (1918 models?) the rectangular sockets became standard, and that style continued through 1927.

Oil side lamps were standard on all cars until 1919, then on the non-starter models only. The headlights all used clear lenses until 1921, but the headlamp housings varied in minor details because of the various suppliers.

Front wheels and tires continued to be of the 30 by 3 size, but only on the non-electric cars after 1918. Demountable rims and electric starters became standard on the closed cars in 1919, and most if not all open cars supplied with starters also had the demountables. Such cars used 30 by 3-1/2 tires all around.

Instrument panels appeared only on starter-equipped cars until 1922. Speedometers were always accessories after 1915.

Other than minor details, all 1917 to 1920 Ford Touring Cars were almost identical to the 1917 car shown here. Crude as it may appear, this is the way it came from the Ford factory! Except for the deterioration, *this is a NEW car!*

A metal panel under the front seat covers the gasoline tank, typical of the earlier Fords. The tank itself is galvanized and was as clean on the inside as it appears on the outside. The filler cap is cast iron.

The steering wheel is wood and is painted black. The spider is malleable cast iron, and the gear case and control levers are nickel-plated. The horn button is of the type used since 1915; the change to the combination horn/light switch came later in the year.

The front tires are original, with no tread pattern, and white walls. Front tires are 30 by 3 and in this case have "Ford" script on the sidewalls. These were made by the United States Tire Company.

1917-1920

Of particular interest to all of us when this original car was first seen was the engine. Was it painted? The first view, above, would not indicate there was any paint but a close look, particularly on the left side, removed any doubt. The engine was at one time "painted" with a very thin coat of shiny black paint. Heat and moisture had entirely eliminated any trace from the cylinder head but the engine block itself still had traces of the original paint.

The engine splash pans were in place, and on both sides the two screws at the rear corners were missing. Apparently these were too difficult to install on the assembly line and were therefore left out.

The carburetor is a Holley Model G.

A number of details can be seen in these pictures. The placement of the wires, the hose clamps, horn mounting, etc.

The radiator top tank was not painted; still shines like new.

The final inspector's number is stamped on the top of the left front head bolt (arrow). It this case it is either a "6" or a "9."

The hood clamps are cast and have two "ears."

The engine pan has the wide front "snout," first used in 1917. Note the straight fan support arm (first used with the black radiator cars), and the iron fan pulley.

The engine is as produced, with the inspection numbers stamps visible on some of the head bolts. The engine was originally painted in a thin black coating but most of it has fallen away over the years. The splash pans are in place, but on both sides the rear screws are missing. Perhaps they were too difficult to install on the assembly line, so were just left out. The carburetor is a Holley Model G.

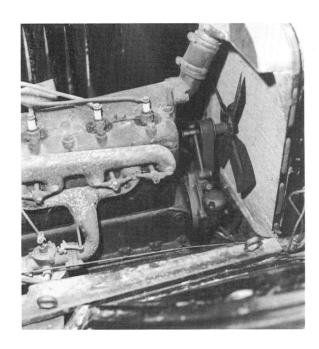

The magneto horn on this 1917 has a cone-shaped rear housing, and its electrical connections come out of the cover.

Note the transmission inspection plate is a flat piece of steel (as it had been for a number of years), and the larger than usual reinforcing web on the clutch shaft bearing boss (arrow).

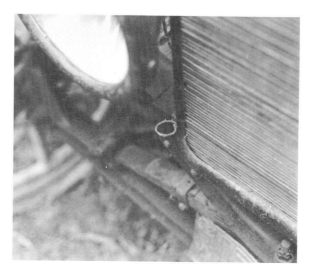

The choke pull wire has a round loop, with the loop horizontal. The wire is bent to form the loop, with just one turn to hold it in place. Whether or not all loops were horizontal is unknown; they can easily be bent to any position.

One of the interesting things found on this car was the mixture of spring shackles. Note that the fronts are of the fabricated design (the shaft is riveted to the loop). The rear shackles still have the oilers and are of the figure-eight design used since 1913. Later, the oilers were eliminated but the shape remained the same. After some evolution, both of the types seen here were replaced with the forged "L" shaped type used until about 1923.

Springs were mixed; tapered-leaf at the rear, and non-tapered in the front. This was common during the period until the change to all non-tapered about 1918.

The front hubs, as well as the hub caps, were packed full of grease.

Headlights had clear glass lenses until about 1921. The bulbs are large, single filament, and powered by the engine magneto until the starter cars of 1919.

1917-1920

FORD SCRIPT TIRES — Made by the United States Tire Company, these tires were obviously made especially for Ford. They recommend sixty pounds pressure. Time and weather have taken their toll; alas, the original air had escaped. The old original innertubes rejected our modern air when we tried to pump them up. Note the "white" sidewalls.

1920 Touring, owned by Fred Lau of Portland, Oregon. The wheel rims are painted black on this car, which is incorrect. All demountable rims were zinc plated (galvanized, not cadmium) which turns black after some exposure to the elements. New, zinc looks somewhat like silver paint.

Our second feature car is a 1920 Touring, owned by Fred Lau of Portland, Oregon. This example is a bit over-restored but all the parts are correct so far as is known. The restoration began with a complete and original car.

The 1920 touring is essentially the same as the 1917 except for the addition of the starting equipment, demountable wheels, and minor details which will be pointed out. 1920 was the last year of this body type; it was superseded with a new but quite similar body in 1921.

1920 was also the last year for the sheet metal door over the gasoline tank under the front seat. The new oval tank not only allowed the seat to be lowered (in the 1921 models) but it also pretty well filled the underseat area, making the door (actually a dust shield) unnecessary.

Also shown are pictures of the side curtains and top assembly which show the location and type of fasteners used.

Steering wheel rims were wood, painted black, until about 1919. At that time Ford began using "Fordite," a plastic-like material, for the rims. The steering wheel spider was forged until about June 1920 when it was changed to pressed steel and at the same time the rim diameter was increased from fifteen to sixteen inches.

1917-1920

ABOVE: Ford script upholstery! This sample, the original upholstery in Fred Lau's 1920 touring, has a series of "F's" embossed in the material at random locations. Note the pebble graining on the imitation leather material. While the "F" imprint did not appear on all cars, the basic material is the same for all open cars of this period.

RIGHT: The top support straps were black woven cotton on all open cars. The date of the change from leather is not known but was apparently before 1917.

BELOW: Oil lamps with the large red lens to the rear and a small clear lens to the right were used on all cars which were not equipped with a starter. Those cars with a starter used a small electric lamp with a clear panel on the side to illuminate the license plate, and which was mounted on the spare-tire carrier. No starter-equipped cars came with oil lamps as original equipment.

LOWER RIGHT: In 1917 the muffler was modified, eliminating the tail pipe. The end plates were still cast iron, though, until 1920 when the pressed-steel type appeared. This example is of the 1917 to 1919 muffler. Early in 1919 the exhaust hole was moved ten degrees from the bottom center to direct the exhaust away from the spare tire.

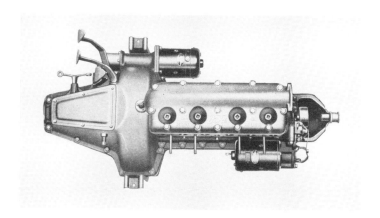

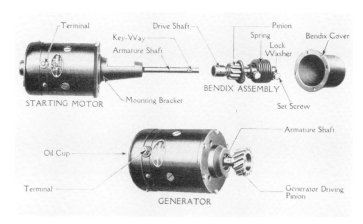

The big change in 1919 was the introduction of electric starting equipment. Available at first only on the Coupe and Sedan (as standard equipment), by mid-1919 it could be had as an option on the Runabout and the Touring. Trucks, however, had to wait until about 1921 for a factory-installed starter.

Factory photos show the starter and generator with identification plates (F.A. Starter, Liberty Starter Co., Detroit) but it is doubtful if these plates appeared in production.

The wiring diagram (left) shows the old-style horn button (on top of the steering post) and the magneto horn, but the button was actually located on the side of the post. The battery-operated horn did not appear until during 1922.

Initial production had the generator cutout mounted on the firewall. Early in 1919, though, it was moved to the generator. The earlier generater-mounted cutouts were rectangular in shape, as shown at the lower left.

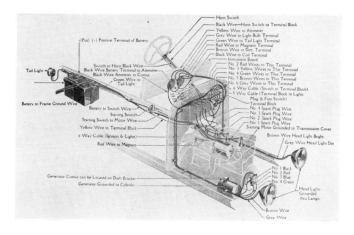

The starter switch (below) and its extension, used in the first starter cars (1919 and 1920) differed considerably from the later types.

The 1919 generator and cutout (right). Initial 1919 production had the cutout mounted on the firewall but during 1919 it was moved to the standard location on the generator. Note that it is rectangular, not round as in the later types.

The firewall terminal block on a 1919 sedan is shown here, along with the usual wooden type for comparison. Machine screws are used which thread into a brass insert; a much better arrangement that the later type which used wood screws.

Ford experimented with a number of Bendix covers in 1919. One of them is shown on the right in this picture. This is an assembled cover with a seam on the side and with the bottom welded in place. Note that it is longer than the usual type shown on the left.

The "production" ammeter and switch. Note that the switch handle is a casting, not the pressed-steel type of later years. Early production ammeters were more elaborate than this one (which may have been changed at some time).

Another interesting enigma on a 1919 sedan; the car has the earlier-style front radius rods with an accessory lower brace. This car (engine) was built in July 1919, at which time it is believed that all cars had the newer (below the axle) radius rods. Possibly the car was built at a branch and used up the last of the old stock, or the front axle assembly has been changed. The accessory brace has been seen on many Fords from 1917 to 1919 and could have been a Ford-supplied item.

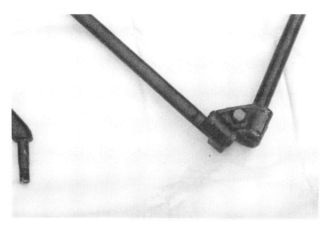

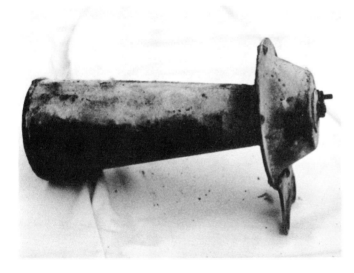

The magneto horn, typical 1915 to 1922, which mounted on the firewall. Not all such horns were alike, differing between suppliers. Some had two terminals while others had just one. Generally, the two-terminal horns were used on cars where the horn was mounted on the firewall, while the one-terminal horn mounted on the side of the engine (1922-1926 non-starter cars). This one came on the 1919 sedan.

RIGHT. The starter switch and its mounting bracket.

In 1919 the front axle assembly was improved by a redesign of the radius rod, relocating its attachment to the underside of the axle below the spring perch, instead of above the axle through the perch. (About 1922 the hole in the radius rod was modified to accept a tapered nut, making the assembly a bit more solid.) All 1919 and later Fords used the new steering tie rod with the fixed yoke on the left (driver's) side, and a combination yoke, ball and adjustment on the right (above left). This modification was made during late 1918. The older style is shown at the right. Note: The top right photo illustrates the left end of the tie rod only. The axle, radius rod, and shackles are 1923 and later.

BELOW: Spring shackles came in four types during the 1917 to 1921 era. The first was the figure-eight type with the oilers (not shown) which had been used for several years. When the oilers were moved to the perches and springs, beginning in 1916, the same basic shackle was used but without the oilers (left). In 1917 the fabricated steel shackle (center) appeared, along with the earlier forged type (perhaps due to the war effort and the availability of forgings). About 1920 a new forged design (right) became standard and continued until about 1923 when the "U" style (not shown) came out.

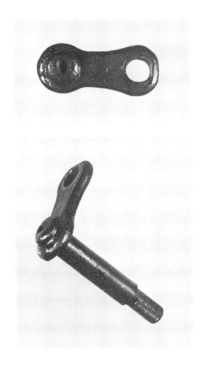  

1917-1920

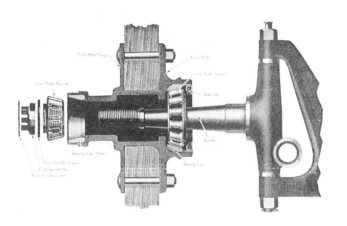

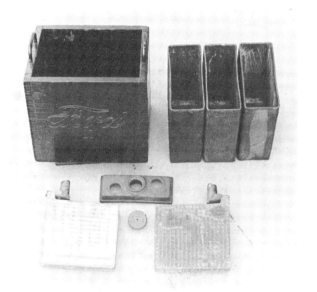

TOP LEFT: Roller bearings became standard on all cars with demountable rims beginning in 1919. The standard wheels (non-demountable) continued using the ball bearings until about 1925.

TOP RIGHT: Nickeled hubcap with the black-painted background. All caps were not necessarily painted, being plain nickel.

LEFT: Batteries were not just replaced, they were repaired. All parts could be ordered from the Ford dealer, and dealers were all equipped to make battery repairs. Shown are the major components.

BELOW: The 1920 Holley NH carburetor. Note the cast arms for the choke and throttle, the brass screw for the air bleed, and the almost straight-through air passage. These carburetors used the cork float as in the Model G. Later versions used steel control arms, a brass plate over the air bleed hole, and had a smaller venturi area.

The demountable rims and wheels used in 1919 were different from those of later years. Kelsey was the major supplier. Note the locating lug on the rim and the matching hole in the wheel felloe, and the unusual retaining clamps. (All wheels were painted black, not the natural finish shown here, incidentally.) Rims were zinc-plated (not cadmium).

Engines were painted a thin black in some cases, and not painted at all in others. Fred Lau's engine had no sign of paint on it, and it was not painted when restored.

Standard carburetors on the Model T were the Holley model G or the Kingston model L-2 from 1915 until about 1920. The Holley NH replaced the "G" in 1920 and the Kingston L-4 replaced the L-2 in 1921. The Holley seems to have been the most common, and the NH was probably the best Ford-supplied carburetor ever offered on the Model T. The featured 1920 Ford has the Holley NH.

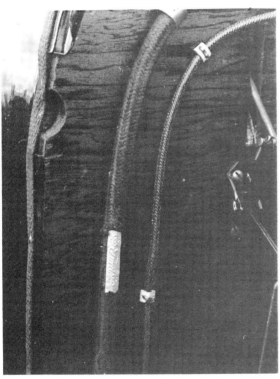

Note the "extra" wire on the firewall, to the right of the main loom in this photo. This was the wire from the generator. It became a part of the loom wiring during 1920. Note, too, the aluminum label on the loom, found on the original wiring and added to the replacement loom shown here.

Ford experimented with a number of different timers and brushes in 1919 and 1920. The standard brush in 1919 was like the one shown at the right but Ford went back to the roller type after a short time. The common timer was made in aluminum, brass, and steel during the period, with brushes of the same materials, apparently in any mix.

The top and the side curtains are exact copies of the originals, using the originals as patterns. The placement of the fasteners, tacks, etc., may be used as a guide for the restoration of Ford touring cars from 1915 through 1922.

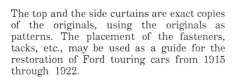

Ford Sedan
5-passenger — 4-cylinder — 20 Horsepower — style, class, convenience. The Ford de luxe for social functions, shopping and general uses. $975 f. o. b. Detroit

The 1915 Ford "Centerdoor" Sedan as it appeared in the 1915 catalog. Note the fork-mounted headlamps, the handle at the rear quarter window, and the windshield brace for the upper panel. The 1915 Sedan had an aluminum body and was unlike the later Sedans except in general appearance.

"Centerdoor" Sedans

Featuring photos and data supplied by Dave Huson and David Simmering

The Model T Ford Sedan built from late 1914 until mid-1923 is perhaps the rarest of all the common Ford body types. (The Town Car, of which very few exist today, is not considered a "common" body type.) It's not that they didn't build many; it's mainly because they weren't too popular and that they found their way to the junk yard a bit faster than the other models.

The Ford Sedan was announced in a letter to Ford branches dated September 23, 1914. Photos released at that time illustrated a car that saw little, if any, production. It featured carriage lamps on the side and gas headlights. Later photos show the same or similar car with large electric headlamps and oil cowl lamps. The Sedan, in production form, had a body made of aluminum panels over a wooden frame, and a design unlike the Sedans of 1916 and later. The "1915" Sedan required special rear fenders and splash aprons; had the gasoline tank under the rear seat, and is almost a study in itself. (See coverage under the 1915-16 models.) The price in 1915 was $975, a sizable sum in those days. Just 989 Sedans were built in fiscal 1915 (August 1, 1914 through July 31, 1915); this out of a total of 308,162 Fords, or just three tenths of one percent of the production.

1916 Sedans (those with the brass radiator) seem to have been of the steel-panel type which was typical of all later models. Few 1916's have survived; the author has yet to see a "real" one. Ford

produced 1,859 Sedans during fiscal 1916, just four tenths of one percent of the 501,462 Fords built that year.

Fiscal 1917 saw the production of Sedans grow to one percent of the total; 7,361 out of 735,020. Sedan production for later fiscal years was: 1918, 35,697 (5.4%); 1919, 24,980 (5%); 1920, 81,616 (8.7%). Ford records changed to the calendar year in 1921. 53,903 Sedans were built from August 1, 1920 until December 31, 1920 (11.6%). Calendar 1921 production was 125,831 (13%) and in 1922, 146,060 (11%). 1923 figures reflect some Tudor Sedans (introduced about June 1923) since Ford grouped all Sedans with two doors together in the production figures. 89,535 of both types were built during 1923 but just how many of these were the centerdoor type is not known. (Ford referred to the Tudor Sedan as a "1924" model, incidentally.

It is no secret that the public was not too impressed with closed cars during the late 'teens. Not only did they seem top-heavy and unstable, they had a lot of glass — and this was before safety glass had been developed. People may have considered them unsafe but Ford did sell a lot of Coupes during the period, so price may have been the major factor.

Ford, of course, was not unique in offering a Sedan with the doors in the center of the body. Dodge and Chevrolet, to mention just two, had similar designs. The center door seemed quite practical at the time. Had the door been at the front,

1915-1923 Sedans

"An interior view of the Ford Sedan reveals its qualities as a car ideal for the family or social demands. The price is $740 f.o.b. Detroit." So reads the caption under this picture taken from the 1916 Ford catalog. By this time the steel body was apparently used, along with the standard splash aprons and rear fenders, unlike the 1915 models of the Sedan.

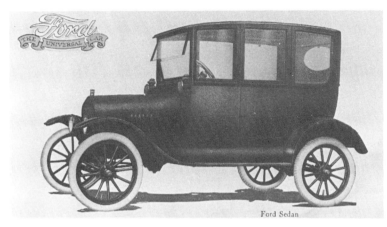

Ford Sedan

In August 1916, the "1917"-style had appeared. "5-passenger, 4-cylinder, 20 horsepower, streamline hood, large radiator and enclosed fan, crown fenders, black finish, nickel trimmings, fully equipped except speedometer. An all-season car of style and convenience, for social functions, shopping and general use. Price $645 f.o.b. Detroit." This illustration, from the 1917 catalog, shows the car appearing a bit lower than it was; a common feature of automotive ads until relatively recent times.

The charm of the new Ford Sedan as a family car and for all social purposes is apparent in this phantom photograph

"The charm of the new Ford Sedan as a family car for all social purposes is apparent in this phantom photograph." (1917 catalog)

the front passenger would have to be the last person to get in the car, and the first to get out. With the center door, anyone could enter and exit without disturbing another passenger. The later Tudor, of course, changed this but apparently by that time the inconvenience was not considered serious.

The Centerdoor Sedan (which Ford never called a "centerdoor") remained relatively unchanged during its eight year life span after the 1915 models. There were changes in the upholstery materials during the years; exposed wooden areas were covered with metal about 1922; the door handles changed from the bail type to "T" bar around late 1921, then to the "L" type about 1922. The strap window adjusters were changed to a ratchet type in 1922 in the front quarter and door windows. (The rear quarter windows continued with the strap.)

Being the "premium" car in the Ford line, the Sedan, along with the Coupe, got all the latest improvements before the open cars did. Beginning in January 1919, both closed-car types (Coupe and Sedan) came standard with electrical starting

Photos from the Collections of the Henry Ford Museum and Greenfield Village.

Upper photos: the Centerdoor Sedan as it appeared in October 1920. With the introduction of electrical starting equipment in 1919, the oil side and tail lamps were discontinued on cars so equipped. All Sedans and Coupes came standard with starter and demountable-rim wheels beginning in January 1919.

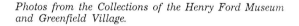

The Sedan in January 1921. Note the new "T" shaped door handles and the visored lens in the headlights. Ford was noted for drastic changes such as these!

LEFT: A sales flyer from early 1923. Note the older style coupe (front-opening doors), the Centerdoor Sedan, and the new Fordor Sedan. In early summer of 1923 the new Tudor Sedan and new Coupe superseded the older models and the Fordor was given the new higher radiator and other features of the new models. The Runabout and Touring had been introduced in late 1922 with the one man top and sloping windshield. These models were also given the higher radiator in early summer 1923. Ford generally referred to the high radiator cars as "1924" models, even though they appeared in mid-1923.

1915-1923 Sedans

Ford Archives photo dated June 25, 1922. This was the last version of the Centerdoor Sedan. While it looked exactly like the 1917-1921 models, most of the wooden parts were now covered with metal panels, and the front quarter and door windows had the ratchet arrangement for raising and lowering, instead of the straps. This design continued until mid-1923 when the model was discontinued. *From the Collections of the Henry Ford Museum and Greenfield Village.*

equipment and demountable-rim wheels. The oil side and tail lamps were discontinued at that time on these models. Open cars did not get these advancements until mid-year. The closed cars (and trucks) got the new roller front wheel bearings in 1919, also before the open models.

Prices of the Sedans changed as production increased. The price dropped from $975 to $740 in August 1915; to $645 in August 1916; then up to $695 in October 1917 (due to the World War); then to $875 in 1919 but this included the starter and demountables. The price went up again to $975 in March 1920, then down to $795 in September 1920. Following were a series of price decreases; to $660 in September 1921; $645 in January 1922; to $595 in October 1922 — where it remained until the body type was replaced by the Tudor Sedan in mid-1923.

Ford Sedan bodies were not made by Ford. Apparently they were made by either Fisher or Wadsworth, and perhaps others. Not all parts were interchangeable between the different suppliers, so the manufacturer had to be specified when ordering body parts. This, coupled with the complex nature of the body, makes restoration of a Sedan a real challenge today.

The upholstering in the Sedans also varied, not only with the body maker but also during the production runs. In general the pattern was similar between the makers. From 1916 until 1919 it seems to have been a gray, white-striped material. The underside of the cowl was upholstered as well. The cowl upholstery was discontinued on some cars in 1919 but continued on others until 1922, being replaced with side panels similar to those used on

the open cars. This upholstery material continued until about mid-1922 when a gray cloth with thin white stripes on the seats, doors, etc., was used. In mid-1922 the color was changed to brown, with and without stripes. (Generally, the seats and door used the striped material, while the headliner and body panels were plain brown.) There were many variations, judging from existing examples, and the subject of upholstery could be a study in itself.

Until about 1920, the Sedan was supplied with pull-down curtains over the rear window and the two rear quarter windows. In 1920 the quarter window curtains were discontinued.

The gasoline tank (after the 1915 models) was located under the driver's seat, and had to be filled through the front quarter (driver's) window. The single seat cushion was removable.

The front passenger seat, perhaps the most uncomfortable design ever produced, could be folded forward to allow the driver easier access. The rear seat was quite comfortable, particularly when compared with the front seats.

The body was considerably updated in mid-1922. Metal covers were added over the door posts, both on the body and on the door. The window moldings, which had been painted bare wood, were also covered with metal. It was at this time that the rail-type door pull handle inside the car was replaced with a finger grip pressed into the bottom window molding. Whether this was or was not an improvement is open to question; it was certainly less expensive. While the style of the car appeared unchanged, many of the body parts were different from those of the pre-1922 models.

By 1922 the centerdoor design was quite "old fashioned." Other manufacturers were beginning to make inroads into the Ford market with Sedans of a more modern design. The public was becoming aware of the comforts offered by the closed car design, and as we now know, Sedans were to become the most popular of the body types.

The demand grew and Ford announced a new four-door Sedan in late 1922. Initially the four-door Sedan was sold only to customers who would not buy the older Sedan, and where a sale might be lost to another make of car. The centerdoor Sedan's appeal declined, and by mid-1923 the new two-door (Tudor) Sedan, and a slightly modified four-door (Fordor) Sedan replaced the older models.

Ford's Tudor and Fordor Sedans were a great improvement over the Centerdoor, but the older style has a certain "charm" which is lacking in the later cars.

Two Sedans are featured in this coverage, with some additional photos from the files of the Model T Ford Club of America. The first car is a 1922 Sedan owned by David Simmering of Contoocook, New Hampshire. The second, beginning on page 297, is a 1919 owned by Dave Huson of Akron, Colorado.

David Simmering's 1922 Sedan, a classic example of why one can't absolutely define a certain year Ford. This one has the earlier body with the painted wood window sills and the strap-type window lifts on all side windows. This car has engine number 5,699,521 which has a casting date of January 21, 1922, and which was assembled February 8, 1922. This would be considered "mid-year" since Ford generally introduced "new" models about August each year. In any event, this car is typical of the 1919-1922 Sedans before the "1922 updating."

NOTE: This car has many non-Ford accessories; the bumper, Hassler shock absorbers, and front fender brace being most evident.

1915-1923 Sedans

The rain gutter ran from the back of the rear side window, around the front to the rear of the opposite rear side window.

The window sills and surrounds were black-painted wood. During 1922 these were covered with metal.

VARIATIONS IN THE SEDAN
1916 to 1923

The 1915 Centerdoor Sedan was a unique model, using an aluminum body and many other variations from the later types covered in this study. Details on the 1915 Sedan can be found in the 1915-1916 coverage elsewhere in this book.

Most of the parts in the Sedan body were unchanged from 1916 until the end of production in mid-1923. Many but not all of those that changed are listed here. It should be noted that there were alway minor variations during the years which made parts "different" yet they remained interchangeable. Such variations are not noted here, or in the Ford parts books. Furthermore, there are similar variations between manufacturers of the bodies.

Accompanying this data are Ford drawings of the Sedan bodies, taken from the *Body Parts List*. There are two sets; the 1916 to 1922, and the mid-1922 to 1923. The major difference is in the window lifts, door handles, and the metal coverings over some of the exposed wooden parts which had been just painted prior to 1922.

For ease in listing here, the "1922" models will refer to the later 1922 and 1923 bodies, while the other references will be to the 1916 through early 1922 cars. The Ford factory numbers are shown in parentheses.

Door anti-rattlers (5052 female and 5053 male).

New in the 1922 models.

Door lock anti-rattlers. 8320A used beginning in 1919; changed to 8320B in 1921.

Window anti-rattlers (9455). Used from 1916 until the 1922 models.

All parts related to the window lifters, unless noted elsewhere, were different after the 1922 cars in which the latching arrangement replaced the lift-strap system.

Driver's and passenger's seats came in malleable-iron type or a pressed-steel type during production. 9681 (iron) and 9681B (steel) were used until 1922. 9681C (iron) was used in 1922-23, and two types of steel frames; 9681D (1922) and 9681E (1923). The last new numbers vary only in the color of the upholstery. These part numbers are for the frames with the upholstery and are for the driver's seat back, but similar changes were made in the driver and passenger seat bottoms, and the passenger seat back.

The instrument panel was modified. 10134 was used from 1919 until 1922, 10134B was used in 1922-23.

The metal body door hinge pillar brace was 9535 until 1922 (left and right). A new design came with the 1922 body; 9553 (right) and 9554 (left).

Floor carpets varied through the years, being essentially alike from 1916 until 1921, another color and pattern in 1921, and still another in 1922-23.

The front panel carpeting was discontinued in 1920.

In a major step towards luxury, the passenger seat bottom and rear kick panel were given carpeting in 1922.

Two thicknesses of rear window glass were used, requiring different window channels, during production. 9506 was for the thin glass; 9506B for the thicker. Apparently either might have been used at any time.

Upholstery cloth varied all through production. Where the same general color may have been standard, the actual pattern of the material evolved. It appears that there is no "correct" type for a give year since the variations seem to have been dependent on the suppliers. In general, though, the styling and overall pattern was similar from 1916 to 1921, changed in 1922 and again in 1923. The colors were some type of gray until 1922, then brown in 1922-23. Some of the browns were striped and others were plain, depending on the use. Likewise, there were two (or more) shades of gray trimming material used.

The metal covering over the window frames, etc., appeared in 1921 on some production, with the older type (bare painted wood) being made at the same time. Whether the metal covers appeared before the change in the window lifts, or at the same time is unknown to the author but the parts books seem to indicate the covers came first.

Seat cushions varied through the years, not only in color and pattern, but in general design. The rear seat cushion was 9509 in 1916, 9635 in 1917, 9682 in 1918 and 1919, 9621B in 1920 and 1921, 9621C in 1922, and 9621D in 1923. Similar changes were made in the driver and passenger seats.

Doors varied in details. 9560 (right) and 9561 (left) were used 1916-1918. 9560B and 9561B were used 1919-1921. 9560C and 9561C in 1922. 9560D and 9561D in 1923.

Door handles are listed at 9058 (black) 1915-1918, 9058B (nickel) 1919-1920, 9058C ("T" handle) in 1921, and 9058D ("L" handle) in 1922-23.

Various body moldings changed over the years. For example, the roof drip molding was 9297 from 1915 to 1921, 9297B (side) and 10290 (front) in 1922-23.

Most body wood pillars changed with the change of 1922. Variations in such parts depended on the manufacturer and with the type of door lock. In general, aside from differences between Fisher and Wadsworth bodies, parts were similar from 1916 to 1919, or 1916-1921 depending on the manufacturer, and apparently the 1922-23 parts were all alike.

Window curtains came in four types, depending on the supplier. Curtains were manufactured by Fisher, Curtain Supply Co., Stewart Hartshorn, and Ford.

The upper windshield hinge and clamp assembly. Note that the glass swings outward at the top.

The lower windshield hinge and clamp. This window panel swings inward.

1915-1923 Sedans

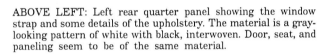

ABOVE LEFT: Left rear quarter panel showing the window strap and some details of the upholstery. The material is a gray-looking pattern of white with black, interwoven. Door, seat, and paneling seem to be of the same material.

ABOVE RIGHT: Details of the windshield hinges, typical of the post-1915 centerdoor Sedans. Both sections open; the top out, and the bottom in. Note the fancy edging trim around the top and doors.

BELOW: The door on this 1922 Sedan still has the window strap. This car was made in early February 1922; later in the year the "lever and notch" system replaced the straps in the doors and front quarter windows. The door pull rail is typical 1916 through early 1922.

TOP: Underside of the front passenger seat, showing the folding support mechanism.

CENTER: Right front side window molding and upholstery. The metal plate was added by the Ford dealer; "Sold by Stipphen Motor Company, 395 Columbia Rd., Dorchester, Mass."

BOTTOM: The driver's seat is placed over the gas tank which is surrounded by a sheet metal box covered with leatherette. The original floor boards are hard wood. The cover behind the driver's seat hides the battery. Snaps in the corners secure the carpet.

1915-1923 Sedans

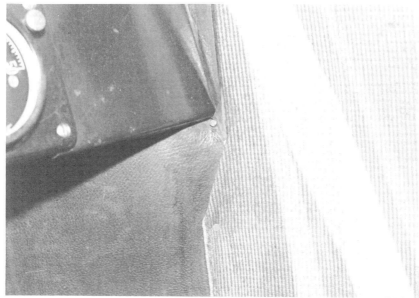

LEFT: Note how the cowl area is covered with leatherette. This upholstery was apparently discontinued during 1922, perhaps with the other body changes, and was replaced with the panels similar to those used on the open cars.

BELOW: The upper windshield area showing the overhanging top which forms a small visor.

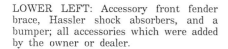

LOWER LEFT: Accessory front fender brace, Hassler shock absorbers, and a bumper; all accessories which were added by the owner or dealer.

LOWER RIGHT: Engine compartment, typical of the Model T Ford. The magneto horn, mounted on the firewall as shown here, was standard equipment until late 1922 when the battery horn was introduced. The battery horn, and the later magneto horns, mounted on the side of the engine over the water inlet. For the nit-pickers: the hose clamps are modern and not "correct."

Our second featured car is a 1919 Sedan owned by Dave Huson. This car is quite similar to the 1922 in most respects but Dave has supplied a number of photos of minor details.

The car was originally sold in Kansas, and eventually ended up in a museum in Canon City, Colorado. It was purchased from the museum by a farmer in Nebraska years ago, and Dave bought the car in 1985.

The engine number is 3,288,543, with a casting date of 8-4-19. According to Ford records, the engine was assembled on August 7, 1919 — proof again that Ford "aged" his engine blocks before machining them — at least long enough to cool so they could be handled!

The doors on the 1919 car are similar to those on the 1922. The major difference is in the outside handles, which are the bail type instead of the "T" type. The bail handles were used from 1915 until about 1921; the "T" type in 1921 to 1922; then the "L" type from 1922 on.

The window strap has a series of holes punched in it to allow several positions for the window. When the window is fully raised, it is pushed outward and then it rests in a channel, holding it in the closed position. To lower it you must pull upward on the strap to get the glass out of the channel, and then allow it to drop into the door. Yes, the windows rattled. Any number of devices were marketed to stop the rattles but none were too satisfactory. The later "notch" system was just slightly better.

1915-1923 Sedans

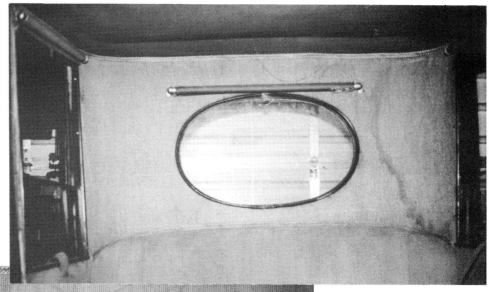

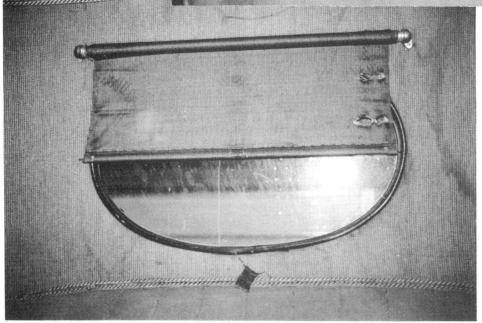

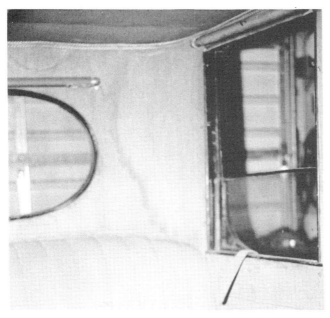

All three rear windows were supplied with curtains until about 1920, at which time just the rear window had a curtain. All upholstery material except for the trim, seems to the the same.

The passenger seat, which folds forward to allow easier access to the driver's seat. Note that the back rest folds down and the bottom seat then hinges toward the front, and that the rear supporting leg also folds out of the way.

299   **1915-1923 Sedans**

The driver's seat is similar to the passenger seat except that it does not fold forward. It sits on a metal frame over the gasoline tank, and this metal frame is covered with leatherette. The seat back will fold forward.

The kick panels on the 1919 are leatherette covered cardboard, unlike the 1922 featured. Apparently there was some variation between cars of the same period. Perhaps Fisher bodies were one way and Wadsworth bodies were another.

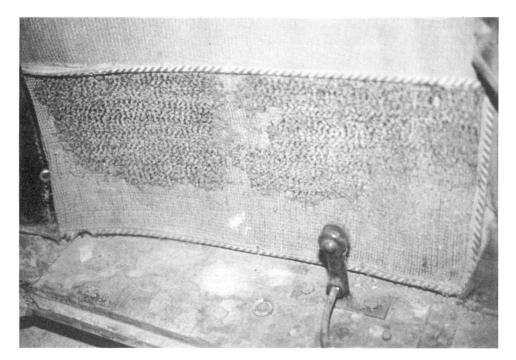

The doors on Huson's 1919 Sedan have carpet at the bottom. Not all Sedans had this feature, perhaps due to different suppliers. The front quarter panels also have this carpeting on this car.

1915-1923 Sedans

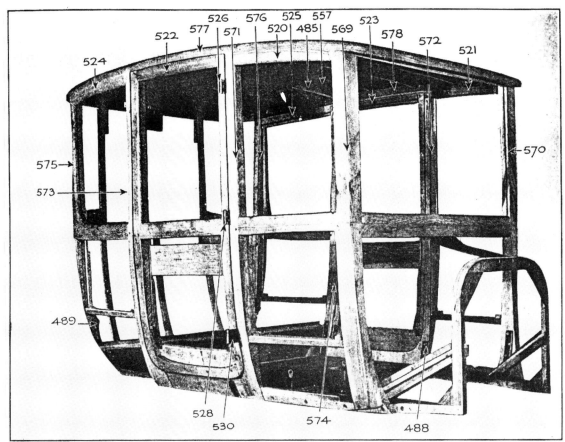

SEDAN BODY PARTS

1916-1922

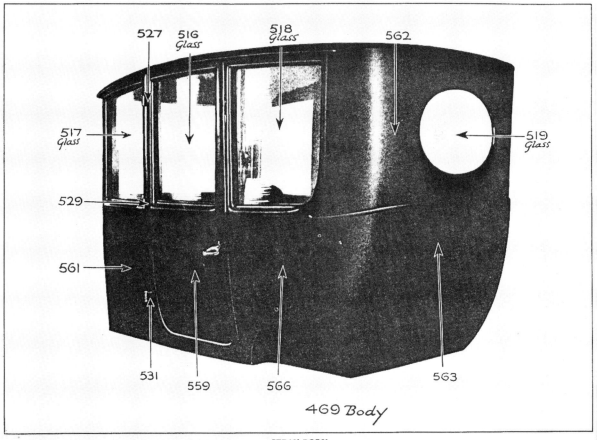

469 Body

SEDAN BODY

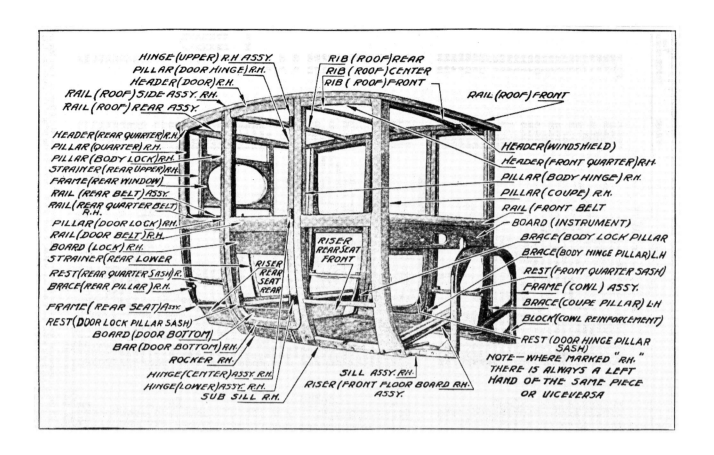

HINGE (UPPER) R.H. ASSY.
PILLAR (DOOR HINGE) R.H.
HEADER (DOOR) R.H.
RAIL (ROOF) SIDE ASSY. R.H.
RAIL (ROOF) REAR ASSY.

RIB (ROOF) REAR
RIB (ROOF) CENTER
RIB (ROOF) FRONT

RAIL (ROOF) FRONT

HEADER (REAR QUARTER) R.H.
PILLAR (QUARTER) R.H.
PILLAR (BODY LOCK) R.H.
STRAINER (REAR UPPER) R.H.
FRAME (REAR WINDOW)
RAIL (REAR BELT) ASSY.
RAIL (REAR QUARTER BELT) R.H.
PILLAR (DOOR LOCK) R.H.
RAIL (DOOR BELT) R.H.
BOARD (LOCK) R.H.
STRAINER (REAR LOWER
REST (REAR QUARTER SASH) R.
BRACE (REAR PILLAR) R.H.
FRAME (REAR SEAT) ASSY.
REST (DOOR LOCK PILLAR SASH)
BOARD (DOOR BOTTOM)
BAR (DOOR BOTTOM) R.H.
ROCKER R.H.
HINGE (CENTER) ASSY. R.H.
HINGE (LOWER) ASSY. R.H.
SUB SILL R.H.

RISER
REAR SEAT
REAR

RISER
REAR SEAT
FRONT

SILL ASSY. R.H.
RISER (FRONT FLOOR BOARD R.H. ASSY.

HEADER (WINDSHIELD)
HEADER (FRONT QUARTER) R.H.
PILLAR (BODY HINGE) R.H.
PILLAR (COUPE) R.H.
RAIL (FRONT BELT
BOARD (INSTRUMENT)
BRACE (BODY LOCK PILLAR)
BRACE (BODY HINGE PILLAR) L.H
REST (FRONT QUARTER SASH)
FRAME (COWL) ASSY.
BRACE (COUPE PILLAR) L.H
BLOCK (COWL REINFORCEMENT)
REST (DOOR HINGE PILLAR SASH)
NOTE—WHERE MARKED "R.H."
THERE IS ALWAYS A LEFT
HAND OF THE SAME PIECE
OR VICEVERSA

1922-1923

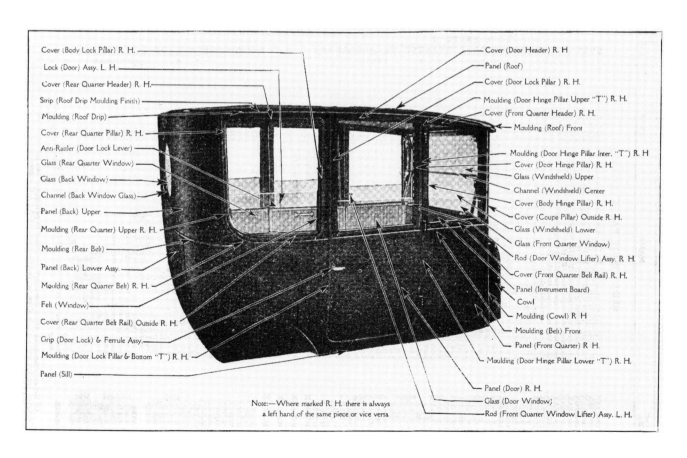

Cover (Body Lock Pillar) R. H.
Lock (Door) Assy. L. H.
Cover (Rear Quarter Header) R. H.
Strip (Roof Drip Moulding Finish)
Moulding (Roof Drip)
Cover (Rear Quarter Pillar) R. H.
Anti-Rattler (Door Lock Lever)
Glass (Rear Quarter Window)
Glass (Back Window)
Channel (Back Window Glass)
Panel (Back) Upper
Moulding (Rear Quarter) Upper R. H.
Moulding (Rear Belt)
Panel (Back) Lower Assy.
Moulding (Rear Quarter Belt) R. H.
Felt (Window)
Cover (Rear Quarter Belt Rail) Outside R. H.
Grip (Door Lock) & Ferrule Assy.
Moulding (Door Lock Pillar & Bottom "T") R. H.
Panel (Sill)

Cover (Door Header) R. H
Panel (Roof)
Cover (Door Lock Pillar) R. H.
Moulding (Door Hinge Pillar Upper "T") R. H.
Cover (Front Quarter Header) R. H.
Moulding (Roof) Front
Moulding (Door Hinge Pillar Inter. "T") R. H
Cover (Door Hinge Pillar) R. H.
Glass (Windshield) Upper
Channel (Windshield) Center
Cover (Body Hinge Pillar) R. H.
Cover (Coupe Pillar) Outside R. H.
Glass (Windshield) Lower
Glass (Front Quarter Window)
Rod (Door Window Lifter) Assy. R. H.
Cover (Front Quarter Belt Rail) R. H.
Panel (Instrument Board)
Cowl
Moulding (Cowl) R. H
Moulding (Belt) Front
Panel (Front Quarter) R. H
Moulding (Door Hinge Pillar Lower "T") R. H.
Panel (Door) R. H.
Glass (Door Window)
Rod (Front Quarter Window Lifter) Assy. L. H.

Note:—Where marked R. H. there is always
a left hand of the same piece or vice versa

303   1915-1923 Sedans

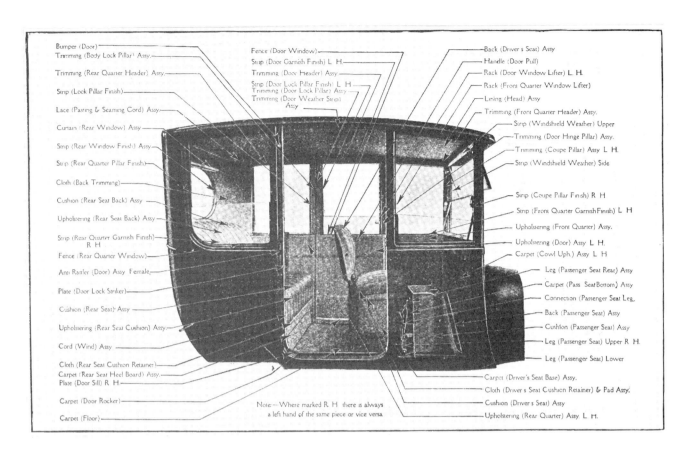

Bumper (Door)
Trimming (Body Lock Pillar) Assy.
Trimming (Rear Quarter Header) Assy.
Strip (Lock Pillar Finish)
Lace (Pasting & Seaming Cord) Assy.
Curtain (Rear Window) Assy
Strip (Rear Window Finish) Assy.
Strip (Rear Quarter Pillar Finish)
Cloth (Back Trimming)
Cushion (Rear Seat Back) Assy
Upholstering (Rear Seat Back) Assy
Strip (Rear Quarter Garnish Finish)
            R H
Fence (Rear Quarter Window)
Anti Rattler (Door) Assy Female
Plate (Door Lock Striker)
Cushion (Rear Seat) Assy
Upholstering (Rear Seat Cushion) Assy.
Cord (Wind) Assy
Cloth (Rear Seat Cushion Retainer)
Carpet (Rear Seat Heel Board) Assy.
Plate (Door Sill) R H
Carpet (Door Rocker)
Carpet (Floor)

Fence (Door Window)
Strip (Door Garnish Finish) L H
Trimming (Door Header) Assy.
Strip (Door Lock Pillar Finish) L H
Trimming (Door Lock Pillar) Assy
Trimming (Door Weather Strip)
            Assy

Back (Driver's Seat) Assy
Handle (Door Pull)
Rack (Door Window Lifter) L. H.
Rack (Front Quarter Window Lifter)
Lining (Head) Assy
Trimming (Front Quarter Header) Assy.
Strip (Windshield Weather) Upper
Trimming (Door Hinge Pillar) Assy.
Trimming (Coupe Pillar) Assy L H.
Strip (Windshield Weather) Side
Strip (Coupe Pillar Finish) R H
Strip (Front Quarter Garnish Finish) L H
Upholstering (Front Quarter) Assy.
Upholstering (Door) Assy L. H.
Carpet (Cowl Uph.) Assy L H
Leg (Passenger Seat Rear) Assy
Carpet (Pass Seat Bottom) Assy
Connection (Passenger Seat Leg.
Back (Passenger Seat) Assy
Cushion (Passenger Seat) Assy
Leg (Passenger Seat) Upper R H.
Leg (Passenger Seat) Lower
Carpet (Driver's Seat Base) Assy.
Cloth (Driver's Seat Cushion Retainer) & Pad Assy.
Cushion (Driver's Seat) Assy
Upholstering (Rear Quarter) Assy. L. H.

Note:—Where marked R H there is always
a left hand of the same piece or vice versa

1922-1923

1921

Body Type	Factory Price #	##	Shipping Weight Lbs.	Production Total *
Touring	$440	415	1485	84970
"	535	510	1620	647300 **
Runabout	395	370	1380	25918
"	490	465	1515	171745 **
Sedan	795	760	1875	179734 **
Coupe	745	695	1685	129159 **
Chassis	360	345	1070	11356
"	455	440	1205	23436 **
Truck	545 ###	495	1430	118583
Foreign & Canada				***
Total ***				1477409

#	Price effective September 22, 1920.
##	Price effective June 7, 1921.
###	Price with pneumatic tires.
*	August 1, 1920 to December 31, 1921. (Ford began calendar year figures in 1921).
**	Includes starter and demountable wheels.
***	Canadian production from August 1920 to December 1920 not available. During calendar 1921, Canada produced 42,348 units and foreign plants produced 42,860 units of all types. The figures shown do include all foreign (other than Canada) production.

Note: Starter was an option on the open cars at $70. Weight 95 lbs. Demountable rims were an additional $25. Weight 55 lbs.

MODEL YEAR DATES: August 1920 to August 1921.

BODY TYPES: Touring, Runabout, Sedan, Coupe, Chassis and Truck.

MAJOR MODEL YEAR FEATURES

A new body for the Tourings had been announced in June 1920. Similar to the earlier style, the rear section was now three pieces (instead of 5), with no vertical seam on the rear quarter side panel. Seats were lower and had higher backs. The older style body continued for a time before the new one became standard, perhaps into 1921. (Some sources even say late 1921.) The Runabout continued in the earlier style until late 1922 (1923 cars). The Sedan was relatively unchanged from previous years, except for a solid roof panel, replacing the open-padded assembly which had been used until late 1920.

The oval gas tank was standard (introduced during calendar 1920).

Top support irons now came through the side panels instead of being the "L" shaped brackets used previously. The Coupe continued with minor modifications.

COLORS. All cars were painted black, with black fenders.

UPHOLSTERY. Imitation leather in the open cars. The pattern was a stitched, vertical-pleat design on both seat bottoms and backs. Closed car upholstery was gray cloth with a lined pattern as in 1920. The new Touring body had the tack strips inside the metal, resulting in a smoother appearance and a smaller metal end cap on the front edge of the arm rests.

FENDERS. Curved and crowned, unchanged since 1917.

SPLASH APRON. Same as previous years.

RUNNING BOARDS. Same as previous years.

HOOD. Steel. Hold-down clamps had two "ears" and were of pressed steel. Handles were pressed steel but were now made in such a way that they can be fastened to the hood without a separate rivet. (A "hole" appears where the rivet was.)

DASHBOARD (Firewall). Wood, fitted outside the front cowl, hidden by the metal cowl weather strip.

CHASSIS. Same as 1920 except that the running board brackets were now steel channels running from side to side and were much stronger than the forged bracket and tie rod arrangement of previous models. Painted black.

STEERING COLUMN ASSEMBLY. Iron quadrant, nickle-plated spark and throttle levers, with flattened metal ends. Gear case was brass but nickel-plated, one-piece assembly. Wheel was 16" diameter, made of "Fordite" (synthetic material), and painted black. The wheel spider was now pressed steel and painted black. Horn button same as in 1920.

FRONT AXLE. Same as the 1920 cars.

REAR AXLE. Same as 1920.

DRIVESHAFT HOUSING. Same as 1920.

REAR RADIUS AND BRAKE RODS. Same as 1920.

WHEELS. Used 30 by 3 tires in front; 30 by 3-1/2 in the rear. Front wheels used taper-roller (Timken) bearings except in the non-starter, non-demountable open cars. Hub caps had "Ford" in script letters. "Made in USA" on all caps. Demountable-rim wheels standard on closed cars, and optional on the open models; used 30 by 3-1/2 tires all around.

SPRINGS. Non-tapered, front and rear. "L"-shaped shackles of the forged type.

RADIATOR. Supplied by Ford. Same as previous years.

ENGINE. Same as 1920. Starter was still optional on the open cars.

ENGINE PAN. "Three-dip" with wider front "snout."

OIL FILLER CAP. The mushroom-shaped cap, made of steel, with three flutes.

ENGINE CRANK. The plain-steel sleeve type as used since 1914.

ENGINE FAN. Same as 1920.

FUEL TANK. Elliptical, under the front seat. Mounting brackets clamped to the tank. Outlet was between the center and the right side, between the frame rails. The Sedan continued the square tank under the driver's seat. The Coupe used the sedan tank located in the turtle deck.

MANIFOLDS. Exhaust pipe flared at the manifold and was held in place with the brass nut but with no packing. Intake was cast iron.

CARBURETORS. Kingston Model L4, or Holley Model NH.

CARBURETOR STOVE. Sheet-metal type which rose vertically at the rear of the carburetor and mated with the exhaust manifold at the rear corner, being held by the rear manifold retaining stud/nut.

MUFFLER. Pressed steel type with no tail pipe.

COIL BOX ASSEMBLY. Ford. Same as used in 1920. Starter cars no longer had the ignition switch on the box; it was moved to the dashboard.

1921 (Continued)

TRANSMISSION. Three-pedal standard design. Pedals were of the plain type. Transmission cover was cast iron, and modified to accept the starter. Tapered inspection door, held with six screws. The door was of pressed steel with an embossed pattern.

LAMPS. Magneto-powered electric type on the non-starter cars, and six-volt electric on the starter models. Black steel rims. A green-visored lens replaced the clear type for a short time, then the visored lens was superseded by the Ford "H" fluted lens which became the standard through 1927. Side and tail lamps were similar to 1917 on the non-starter cars. Starter cars had a small electric tail light and did not had side lights.

HORN. Magneto-powered electric.

WINDSHIELD. Upright, with top section that folded to the rear. Frame was bolted to the brackets. Painted black. Same as 1920.

TOP. (Open cars). Top color was black on all open cars. Sockets were the same as those used since 1918.

SPEEDOMETER. No longer standard equipment.

TURTLE DECK (on Runabout). Similar in style to the 1919. Handles were pressed steel and painted black.

1922

Body Type	Factory Price #	##	###	Shipping Weight Lbs.	Production Total *
Touring	$355	348	298	1485	80070
"	450	443	393	1620	514333 **
Runabout	325	319	269	1380	31923
"	420	414	364	1515	133433 **
Sedan	660	645	595	1875	146060 **
Fordor			725	1950	4286 **
Coupe	595	580	530	1760	198382 **
Chassis	295	285	235	1060	15228
"	390	380	330	1195	23313 **
Truck	445	430	380	1477	135629
"			475	1577	18410 **
Totals (Excluding Canada)					1301067 ***

#	Price effective September 2, 1921.
##	Price effective January 16, 1922.
###	Price effective October 17, 1922.
*	January 1, 1922 to December 31, 1922. (Includes foreign production.)
**	Includes starter and demountable wheels.
***	An additional 50,266 units were made in Canada.

Note: Starter was an option on the open cars at $70. Weight 95 lbs. Demountable rims were an additional $25. Weight 55 lbs.

MODEL YEAR DATES: August 1921 to September 1922.

BODY TYPES: Touring, Runabout, Sedan, Coupe, Chassis and Truck.

MAJOR MODEL YEAR FEATURES

New body construction on Touring Cars (introduced in 1921 models). Rear section was now three pieces with quarter panels integral with the side panels. Seats were lower; the top irons now extended through the quarter panel (instead of the "L" iron previously used).

Instrument panel supplied on all cars. A blanking plate was used to cover the hole where the ammeter would be, on the non-electric models.

Centerdoor Sedans had solid roof panel, latch-type window lifts, and metal over the door and window posts.

The Coupe was modified to now have the latch-type window raisers. In addition, the previously exposed window and door sills were now covered with metal, as on the Sedan.

FORDOR SEDAN: Introduced in December 1922, the all-new four-door sedan had an aluminum body. No cowl vent, low radiator. This was a "1923" model, as were the Touring and Runabouts built in 1922 after September.

The engine casting was modified in November 1921 to use the one-piece valve door, and by April 1922, all engines were of the new type.

COLORS. All cars were painted black, with black fenders.

UPHOLSTERY. Imitation leather in the open cars, as described under 1921. The pattern was a stitched vertical pleat design on both seat bottoms and backs. Closed car upholstery was gray cloth with a lined pattern but was changed to a brown color during the year.

FENDERS. Unchanged since 1917.

SPLASH APRON. Unchanged since 1917.

RUNNING BOARDS. Unchanged since 1914 except that the diamonds were not as sharp, probably due to wear on the dies that pressed them.

1922 (Continued)

HOOD. Steel. Hold-down clamps had two "ears" and were of pressed steel. Handles were pressed steel but were now made in such a way that they can be fastened to the hood without a separate rivet. (A "hole" appears where the rivet was.)

DASHBOARD (Firewall). Wood, fitted outside the front cowl, hidden by the metal cowl weather strip.

CHASSIS. Same as 1921. Painted black.

STEERING COLUMN ASSEMBLY. Iron quadrant, nickle-plated spark and throttle levers, with flattened metal ends. Gear case was brass but nickel-plated, one-piece assembly. Wheel was 16" diameter, made of "Fordite" (synthetic material), and painted black. The wheel spider was now pressed steel and painted black. Horn button no longer the combination light/horn type since all cars now had the light switch on the instrument panel.

FRONT AXLE. Same as the 1921 cars.

REAR AXLE. Same as 1921.

DRIVESHAFT HOUSING. Same as 1921.

REAR RADIUS AND BRAKE RODS. Radius rods now were of seamed construction, requiring a right and left side (the seam must face down to allow water to leak out).

WHEELS. Used 30 by 3 tires in front; 30 by 3-1/2 in the rear. Front wheels use taper-roller (Timken) bearings except in the non-starter, non-demountable open cars. Hub caps had "Ford" in script letters. "Made in USA" on all caps. Demountable-rim wheels standard on closed cars, and optional on the open models; use 30 by 3-1/2 tires all around.

SPRINGS. Non-tapered, front and rear. "L"-shaped shackles of the forged type. Oilers were pressed into the springs.

RADIATOR. Same as that used since 1919.

ENGINE. Same as 1920. In November 1921 the valve chambers were altered and the engine now had one long cover plate instead of the two used since 1911. Starter was still optional on the open cars.

ENGINE PAN. "Three-dip" with wider front "snout."

OIL FILLER CAP. The mushroom-shaped cap, made of steel, with three flutes.

ENGINE CRANK. The plain steel-sleeve type as used since 1914 was replaced with the one-piece type with the rolled-in-place sheet metal handle sleeve.

ENGINE FAN. Same as 1920.

FUEL TANK. Elliptical, under the front seat, on all cars except the Centerdoor Sedan and the Coupe. Mounting brackets clamp to the tank. Outlet was between the center and the right side, between the frame rails. The Centerdoor Sedan continued the square tank under the driver's seat. The Coupe used the sedan tank located in the turtle deck.

MANIFOLDS. Exhaust pipe flared at the manifold and was held in place with the brass nut but with no packing. Intake was cast iron.

CARBURETORS. Kingston Model L4, or Holley Model NH.

CARBURETOR STOVE. Sheet-metal type which rose vertically at the rear of the carburetor and mated with the exhaust manifold at the rear corner, being held by the rear manifold retaining stud/nut.

MUFFLER. Pressed steel type with no tail pipe.

COIL BOX ASSEMBLY. Ford, same as used in 1920, but no longer had the ignition switch on the box. The switch was on the dashboard on all cars.

TRANSMISSION. Three-pedal standard design. Pedals were of the plain type. Transmission cover was cast iron, and modified to accept the starter. Tapered inspection door, held with six screws. The door was of pressed steel with an embossed pattern.

LAMPS. Magneto-powered electric type on the non-starter cars, and six volt electric on the starter models. Black steel rims, with Ford "H" lens. Side and tail lamps were similar to 1917 on the non-starter cars. Starter cars had a small electric tail light and did not have side lights.

HORN. Magneto-powered electric on non-starter cars, but six-volt battery operated on starter models, new this year.

WINDSHIELD. Upright, with top section that folds to the rear. Frame was bolted to the brackets. Painted black. Unchanged from 1921.

TOP. (Open cars). Top color was black on all open cars. Unchanged from 1921.

SPEEDOMETER. No longer standard equipment.

TURTLE DECK (on Runabout). Similar in style to the 1921. Handles were pressed steel and painted black.

1923

Body Type	Factory Price			Shipping Weight Lbs.	Production Total
	#	##	###		*
Touring	$298	295	295	1500	136411
″	393	380	380	1650	792651 **
Runabout	269	265	265	1390	56954
″	364	350	350	1540	238638 **
Sedan	595	590	590	1875	96410 **
(Includes both Centerdoor and new Tudor)					
Fordor	725	685	685	1950	144444 **
Coupe	530	525	525	1760	313273 **
Chassis	235	230	230	1060	9443
″	330	295	295	1210	42874 **
Truck	380	370	370	1477	197057
″	475	435	455	1577	64604 **
Trk/Body			490	—	***
Totals					2090959

#	Price effective October 17, 1922.
##	Price effective October 2, 1923.
###	Price effective October 30, 1923.
*	January 1, 1923 to December 31, 1923. (Includes foreign and Canada production.)
**	Includes starter and demountable wheels.
***	Not listed separately from chassis figures. See production charts.

Note: Starter was an option on the open cars at $65. Weight 95 lbs. Demountable rims were an additional $20. Weight 55 lbs.

"C" type truck cab, $65. Truck rear bed, $55.

MODEL YEAR DATES: September 1922 to July 1923.

BODY TYPES: Touring, Runabout, Sedan, Fordor Sedan, Tudor Sedan (which Ford called a "1924" model), Coupe, Chassis and Truck.

MAJOR MODEL YEAR FEATURES

The "1923" Touring car style was introduced in September 1922, with a one-man top and sloping windshield, but otherwise the body was the same as the 1922. The Runabout followed in November, with a new body and turtle deck as well. A new "Fordor" sedan appeared in December 1922, which used aluminum panels throughout the body. The cowl section and lower body section were changed to steel during the year. There was no cowl vent in the early Fordor sedans but the vent was added during early 1923, before the change to the larger hood.

The Coupelet and Sedan (Centerdoor) continue into 1923 with minor modifications that were introduced in 1922, but were both replaced with the new Coupe and Tudor Sedan in about June 1923.

The front section of the car was revised in mid-year, with a new and higher radiator, larger hood, valence under the radiator, and revised cowl section to match. These cars were generally referred to as "1924" models in Ford literature, although some were built in fiscal 1923 (before August). The Coupe and Tudor Sedan were all new, with coupe doors opening at the rear. Body construction continued with the metal panels over a wood frame design.

New steering column support bracket connected the instrument panel to the column for added rigidity, apparently during later 1923 (1924 models) production.

All cars had an instrument panel with the ignition-light switch.

COLORS. All cars were painted black, with black fenders.

UPHOLSTERY. Imitation leather in the open cars. The pattern was a stitched, vertical-pleat design on both seat bottoms and backs. Closed car upholstery was brown cloth with a lined pattern.

FENDERS. Front: curved and crowned as in 1922. In June 1923, the "1924" style appeared. The front fenders now had a lip on the front apron to match the new valence under the radiator.

SPLASH APRON. Same as earlier until June, then unchanged except for a hole for the rear hood clamp.

RUNNING BOARDS. Unchanged from 1922.

HOOD. Same as 1922 until the higher radiator style introduced in June 1923. The hood was then larger (higher and wider). Handles were pressed-steel in the pattern of the 1922 type. The hood clash strip now "doglegs" out at the rear, with the rear hold-down clamp extending through the splash apron.

DASHBOARD (Firewall). Wood, fitted outside the front cowl, hidden by the metal cowl weatherstrip. In early 1923 a new metal firewall replaced the wood one for a short time, then in June a new larger metal firewall was used to match the larger hood.

CHASSIS. Same as 1922. Painted black.

STEERING COLUMN ASSEMBLY. Iron quadrant, nickle-plated spark and throttle levers, with flattened metal ends. Gear case was brass but nickel-plated, one-piece assembly. Wheel was 16" diameter, made of "Fordite" (synthetic material), and painted black. The wheel spider was pressed steel and painted black. Horn button on left side of column.

FRONT AXLE. Same as the 1922 cars.

REAR AXLE. Same as 1922.

DRIVESHAFT HOUSING. Same as 1922.

REAR RADIUS AND BRAKE RODS. Radius rods were of seamed construction, requiring a right and left side (the seam must face down to allow water to leak out).

WHEELS. Used 30 by 3 tires in front; 30 by 3-1/2 in the rear. Front wheels used taper-roller (Timken) bearings except in the non-starter, non-demountable open cars. Hub caps had "Ford" in script letters. "Made in USA" on all caps. Demountable-rim wheels standard on closed cars, and optional on the open models; used 30 by 3-1/2 tires all around.

SPRINGS. Non-tapered, front and rear. "L" shaped shackles of the forged type. Oilers were pressed into the springs. The final "U" shaped shackles appeared during the year.

RADIATOR. Manufactured by Ford. Shell had the Ford script pressed into the upper part. "Made in USA" was stamped in below the Ford script. The shell was painted black. In June the slightly higher (5/8") radiator appeared, along with the new hood and the shell with the valence at the bottom.

ENGINE. Same as 1922. Starter was still optional on the open cars.

ENGINE PAN. "Three-dip" with wider front "snout."

1923 (Continued)

OIL FILLER CAP. The mushroom-shaped cap, made of steel, with three flutes.

ENGINE CRANK. Same as later 1922 one-piece type with the rolled-in-place handle sleeve.

ENGINE FAN. Same as 1920.

FUEL TANK. Elliptical, under the front seat, on all models except for the Centerdoor Sedan and the Coupe. Mounting brackets clamped to the tank. Outlet was between the center and the right side, between the frame rails. The Centerdoor Sedan continued the square tank under the driver's seat. The Coupe used the Sedan tank located in the turtle deck until the new bodies (1924 models), which used the standard oval tank under the seat.

MANIFOLDS. Exhaust pipe flared at the manifold and was held in place with the brass nut but with no packing. Intake was cast iron.

CARBURETORS. Kingston Model L4, or Holley Model NH.

CARBURETOR STOVE ASSEMBLY. Sheet-metal type which rose vertically at the rear of the carburetor and mated with the exhaust manifold at the rear corner, being held by the rear manifold retaining stud/nut.

MUFFLER. Pressed-steel type with no tail pipe.

COIL BOX ASSEMBLY. Ford, same as used in 1922. The switch was on the dashboard on all cars.

TRANSMISSION. Three-pedal standard design. Pedals were of the plain type. Transmission cover was cast iron. Tapered inspection door, held with six screws. The door was of pressed steel with an embossed pattern.

LAMPS. Magneto-powered electric type on the non-starter cars, and six-volt electric on the starter models. Black steel rims. Side and tail lamps were similar to 1917 on the non-starter cars. Starter cars had a small electric tail light and did not have side lights. The oil tail lamp now had a large clear lens facing the license plate, and a small red lens to the rear. It had the mounting bolt on the side, rather than on the rear. This lamp probably appeared earlier; the date is unknown.

HORN. Magneto-powered electric on non-starter cars, but six-volt battery operated on starter models.

WINDSHIELD. Square, with slight rake to the rear. Top section opens outward. Painted black. Unchanged when the "1924" style appeared in June.

TOP. (Open cars). "One-man" style, attached to the top of the windshield at the front. Top color was black on all open cars. Top sockets were rectangular cross-section.

SPEEDOMETER. No longer standard equipment.

TURTLE DECK (on Runabout). Larger, shaped to mate with the rear of the body. No longer had any handles; must be opened with a large key. The new Coupe had an integral turtle deck.

1924

Body Type	Factory Price #	##	###	Shipping Weight Lbs.	Production Total *
Touring	$295	290	290	1500	99523
"	380	375	375	1650	673579 **
Runabout	265	260	260	1390	43317
"	350	345	345	1540	220955 **
Tudor	590	580	580	1875	223203 **
Fordor	685	660	660	1950	84733 **
Coupe	525	520	520	1760	327584 **
Chassis	230	225	225	1060	3921
"	295	290	290	1210	43980 **
Truck	370	365	365	1477	139435
"	435	430	430	1577	88700 **
Trk/Body	490	485	485	—	***
" "	555	550	550	—	***
Trk/Stake body		495		—	***
Total					1993419

#	Price effective October 30, 1923.
##	Price effective December 2, 1923.
###	Price effective October 24, 1924.
*	January 1, 1924 to December 31, 1924. (Includes foreign production.)
**	Includes starter and demountable wheels.
***	See production charts. Truck figures above include all types of trucks.

Note: Starter was an option on the open cars at $65. Weight 95 lbs. Demountable rims were an additional $20. Weight 55 lbs.

"C" type truck cab, $65. Truck rear bed, $55 if ordered separately.

MODEL YEAR DATES: July 1923 to August 1924.

BODY TYPES: Touring, Runabout, Tudor and Fordor Sedans, Coupe, Chassis and Truck.

MAJOR MODEL YEAR FEATURES

Same models as the later 1923 (which Ford referred to as "1924's"). The Fordor sedan now had steel lower panels although aluminum continued in the upper sections; doors on the closed cars changed to steel during the year, eliminating the wood framework used in the previous doors. Cowl vent in the closed cars.

A new tail lamp/license plate assembly appeared during the year and became the "standard" through 1927. "Four-dip" pan introduced.

COLORS. All cars were painted black, with black fenders.

UPHOLSTERY. Imitation leather in the open cars. The pattern was a stitched, vertical-pleat design on both seat bottoms and backs. Closed car upholstery was brown cloth with a lined pattern.

FENDERS. Front: curved and crowned as in 1923. In late 1924 the front fender was given a wider appearance by moving the embossed bead to the inside edge (it now ran under the splash apron). The rear fender was made slightly wider and now flared outward at the junction with the running board. (This "new" style appeared late in the year and such cars were properly called "1925" models.)

SPLASH APRON. Same as later 1923 type.

RUNNING BOARDS. Same as 1923.

HOOD: Same as later 1923.

DASHBOARD (Firewall). Steel, same as in that used in the later 1923 production.

CHASSIS. Same as 1923. Painted black.

1924 (Continued)

STEERING COLUMN ASSEMBLY. Iron quadrant, nickle-plated spark and throttle levers, with flattened metal ends. Gear case was brass but nickel-plated, one-piece assembly. Wheel was 16" diameter, made of "Fordite" (synthetic material), and painted black. The wheel spider was pressed steel and painted black. Horn button of left side of column.

FRONT AXLE. Same as the 1923 cars.

REAR AXLE. Same as 1923.

DRIVESHAFT HOUSING. Same as 1923.

REAR RADIUS AND BRAKE RODS. Same as 1923.

WHEELS. Used 30 by 3 tires in front; 30 by 3-1/2 in the rear on non-demountable-equipped open cars. Front wheels used taper-roller (Timken) bearings except in the non-starter, non-demountable open cars.. Hub caps had "Ford" in script letters. "Made in USA" on all caps. Demountable-rim wheels standard on closed cars, and optional on the open models; used 30 by 3-1/2 tires all around.

SPRINGS. Non-tapered, front and rear. "U" shaped shackles.

RADIATOR. Same as the later 1923 high style.

ENGINE. Same as 1923. Starter was still optional on the open cars. Light-weight pistons and the oil tube with the larger funnel were introduced during the year.

ENGINE PAN. "Four-dip" pan was introduced as a running change during 1924.

OIL FILLER CAP. The mushroom-shaped cap, made of steel, with three flutes.

ENGINE CRANK. Same as 1923 one-piece type with the rolled-in-place handle sleeve.

ENGINE FAN. Same as 1923.

FUEL TANK. Elliptical, under the front seat. Mounting brackets clamped to the tank. Outlet was between the center and the right side, between the frame rails. The Tudor Sedan continued the square tank under the driver's seat.

MANIFOLDS. Exhaust pipe flared at the manifold and was held in place with the brass nut but with no packing. Intake was cast iron.

CARBURETORS. Kingston Model L4, or Holley Model NH.

CARBURETOR STOVE. Sheet-metal type which rose vertically at the rear of the carburetor and mated with the exhaust manifold at the rear corner, being held by the rear manifold retaining stud/nut. Less expensive design eliminates the separate mounting tab which was riveted to the previous type.

MUFFLER. Pressed-steel type with no tail pipe.

COIL BOX ASSEMBLY. Same as 1923.

TRANSMISSION. Three-pedal standard design. Pedals were of the plain type. Transmission cover was cast iron. Tapered inspection door, held with six screws. The door was of pressed steel with an embossed pattern.

LAMPS. Magneto-powered electric type on the non-starter cars, and six-volt electric on the starter models. Black steel rims. Side and tail lamps were similar to 1917 on the non-starter cars. The oil tail lamp was turned sideways with a small red lens on the side (now the rear) and a large clear lens on the door to illuminate the license plate. Starter cars had a redesigned tail light which was mounted on the license plate bracket. This new style was used through 1927.

HORN. Magneto-powered electric on non-starter cars, but six-volt on starter models. Mounted on the left side of the engine, over the water inlet.

WINDSHIELD. Same as 1923.

TOP. Same as 1923.

SPEEDOMETER. No longer standard equipment.

TURTLE DECK. Same as 1923.

1925

Body Type	Factory Price			Shipping Weight	Production Total	
	#	##	###	Lbs.	*	
Touring	$290	290	290	1500	64399	
"		375	375	375	1650	626813 **
Runabout	260	260	260	1390	34206	
"		345	345	345	1536	264436 **
Pickup		281	281	1471	—	****
"		366	366	1621	—	****
Tudor	580	580	580	1875	195001 **
Fordor	660	660	660	1950	81050 **
Coupe	520	520	520	1760	343969 **
Chassis	225	225	225	1060	6523	
"		290	290	290	1210	53450 **
Truck	365	365	365	1477	186810 ***
"		430	430	430	1577	62496 ** ***
Trk/Body	485	485	485	—	***
"		550	550	550	—	*** **
Trk/Stake	495	495	495	—	***

Totals (Including all foreign)   1990995

#	Price effective October 24, 1924.
##	Price effective March 4, 1925.
###	Price effective December 31, 1925 (unchanged from March).
*	January 1, 1925 to December 31, 1925. (Includes foreign production.)
**	Includes starter and demountable wheels.
***	U.S. production only. See production charts. Truck figures include all types of trucks
****	Pickups not separated from Runabouts. Ford produced 33,795 pickup beds.

Note: Starter was an option on the open cars at $65. Weight 95 lbs. Demountable rims were an additional $20. Weight 55 lbs.

21" tires and rims $25 extra. Weight 65 lbs.
"C" type truck cab, $65. Truck rear bed, $55 if ordered separately. Pickup body for Runabout, $25.

MODEL YEAR DATES: August 1924 to August 1925.

BODY TYPES: Touring, Runabout, Coupe, Tudor and Fordor Sedans, Chassis and Trucks.

MAJOR MODEL YEAR FEATURES
Trucks supplied with cabs and bodies beginning in 1924. Roadster-Pickup and Closed-Cab truck in late 1925 (early calendar year 1925, before "1926" models) production. Passenger cars similar in style to the 1924 cars but more steel used to replace wood framework in the open car bodies.

COLORS. All cars were painted black, with black fenders.

UPHOLSTERY. Imitation-leather in the open cars. The pattern was a stitched, vertical-pleat design on both seat bottoms and backs. Closed car upholstery was blue cloth.

FENDERS. Same as late 1924 (the fenders with the wider appearance). In late 1925 models the rear fenders on the Coupe and Runabout were given larger splash aprons, reducing the gap between the body and fenders.

SPLASH APRON. Same as 1924. Near the end of production, aprons were "square-shaped" on some of the Sedans, somewhat in the style of the 1926 models. This apron does not appear in the parts books, however, and it may not have been used on all production.

RUNNING BOARDS. Same as 1924.

HOOD. Same as 1924.

DASHBOARD (Firewall). Steel, same as 1924.

CHASSIS. Same as 1924. Painted black.

STEERING COLUMN ASSEMBLY. Iron quadrant, nickle-plated spark and throttle levers, with flattened metal ends. Gear case was brass, nickel-plated, one-piece assembly. Wheel was 16" diameter, made of "Fordite" (synthetic material), and painted black. The wheel spider was pressed steel and painted black. With introduction of balloon tires, the gear ratio was increased to 5:1.

FRONT AXLE. Same as the 1924 cars.

REAR AXLE. Same as 1924.

DRIVESHAFT HOUSING. Same as 1924.

REAR RADIUS AND BRAKE RODS. Same as 1924.

WHEELS. Used 30 by 3 tires in front; 30 by 3-1/2 in the rear on non-demountable-equipped open cars. Front wheels used taper-roller (Timken) bearings except in the non-starter, non-demountable open cars. Hub caps had "Ford" in script letters. "Made in USA" on all caps. Demountable-rim wheels standard on closed cars, and optional on the open models; used 30 by 3-1/2 tires all around. 21" balloon tires and wheels were available as an option.

SPRINGS. Non-tapered, front and rear. "U" shaped shackles.

RADIATOR. Same as 1924. Nickle shell offered as an option late in production, before the 1926 models. A trim valence over the crank area was used as in the 1924 models.

ENGINE. Same as 1924. Starter was still optional on the open cars.

ENGINE PAN. "Four-dip" pan was standard.

OIL FILLER CAP. The mushroom-shaped cap, made of steel, with three flutes.

ENGINE CRANK. Same as 1924 one-piece type with the rolled-in-place handle sleeve.

ENGINE FAN. Same as 1924.

FUEL TANK. Elliptical, under the front seat. Mounting brackets clamped to the tank. Outlet was between the center and the right side, between the frame rails. The Tudor Sedan continued the square tank under the driver's seat.

MANIFOLDS. Exhaust pipe flared at the manifold and was held in place with the brass nut but with no packing. Intake was cast iron.

CARBURETORS. Kingston Model L4, or Holley Model NH. The Holley Vaporizer was used on some later 1925 models (before the 1926 style cars). The choke rod with the integral carburetor adjustment was introduced late in the model year (before the 1926 models). These cars then used the U-joint type carburetor adjustment.

CARBURETOR STOVE ASSEMBLY. Same as 1924. Not used on Vaporizer-equipped cars.

MUFFLER. Pressed-steel type with no tail pipe.

COIL BOX ASSEMBLY. Same as 1924.

TRANSMISSION. Three-pedal standard design. Pedals were of the plain type. Transmission cover was cast iron. Tapered inspection door, held with six screws. The door was of pressed steel with an embossed pattern. "Quick change" bands introduced in calendar 1925.

1925 (Continued)

LAMPS. Magneto-powered electric type on the non-starter cars, and six-volt electric on the starter models. Black steel rims. Side and tail lamps were similar to 1917 on the non-starter cars. The oil tail lamp was turned sideways with a small red lens on the side (now the rear) and a large clear lens on the door to illuminate the license plate. Starter cars had a redesigned tail light which was mounted on the license plate bracket. This new style was used through 1927.

HORN. Magneto-powered electric on non-starter cars, but six-volt on starter models.

WINDSHIELD. Same as 1924.

TOP. (Open cars). Same as 1924. In late 1925 many Touring Cars appeared with the rectangular window which was used in the 1926 models.

SPEEDOMETER. No longer standard equipment.

TURTLE DECK. Same as 1924.

The 1921 to 1925 Model T Fords

Certain parts of this coverage are based on information gathered at the Ford Archives in Dearborn, Michigan. The author is grateful for the cooperation of the Archives staff in allowing him to spend a few days in search of Model T photos and information. Other photos are not necessarily of one car, but are used to illustrate a particular feature or features.

Pre-production photo of the new four-door Sedan, taken in September of 1922. Note the lack of the cowl vent and the non-standard running boards. The body was made almost entirely of aluminum panels over a wood frame, and weighed less than the then-current centerdoor sedan. Interesting, too, is the pin striping which runs across the vertical moldings, unlike the regular production models. The starting crank is of the early, pre-1922, style (with the separate handle). *Photo from the Collections of the Henry Ford Museum and Greenfield Village.*

Why cover such a wide range of Ford models in one chapter? Wasn't there a big change in body styles with the introduction of the 1923 models?

While the appearance of the Ford models did change with the introduction of the one-man top and sloping windshield in late 1922, the basic body structure did not, and all (open) cars of this period were quite similar. Closed cars continued in the previous style until mid-1923, at which time the "1924" models appeared. The evolution of the Model T Ford during the 1920's is one of natural progression, unlike the major revisions often made in prior years. For this was truly the "golden era" for the Ford Motor Company. Over two-thirds of the Model T's ever built were built after 1920!

1921 began with a groan as far as the Ford Motor Company was concerned. Ford had, in 1919, borrowed some seventy-five million dollars (figures vary in differing sources) to purchase the stock of the other holders in the company. Sales were increasing when the loan was negotiated, and the prospects of paying these notes out of company profits within the next few years looked very good.

Unfortunately, sales dropped as a result of the business recession of 1920. In typical fashion, Ford dropped the price of the Model T — a plan that had worked many times in the past — but to no avail. Not only did the sales fail to increase, with the reduction in the price Ford was selling cars at a loss. Ford was in a tight squeeze at the end of 1920 and his notes were due in early 1921!

William S. Knudsen, said to have been the one man that Henry Ford had ever regretted losing, was at that time Ford's production manager, although titles meant little in the company. During this period he spent time in making cost-cutting changes in many departments in an effort to same money for the impending crisis. As the day of reckoning approached, though, it was obvious that something drastic had to be done. In December 1920, a decision was made to close the plant for a short time in order to take inventory. Prior to the closing, every part available was assembled into new cars or shipped out as "needed replacement stock" to Ford dealers.

The new cars and the parts were shipped to the dealers on sight drafts — a sort of C.O.D. billing. The dealers had to pay upon delivery, making it necessary in many cases for some dealers to borrow the money and thus shifted the Ford Motor Company debt from Ford to the Ford dealers. No doubt quite a few threw in the towel and went into business selling other brands, or just got out of the automobile business.

The Highland Park plant closed through January 1921, as the money began flowing in. The result of this plan was that Ford was able to pay his debts by April 1921. Sales rebounded in 1921, along with profits, for Ford and his dealers.

In March 1921, Knudsen offered a letter of resignation. He had been unhappy with the situation at Ford for some time. He was one of the men who had tried to interest Henry Ford in producing a new car after the war — and failed. Knudsen differed with Henry Ford, too, in the methods of operation at the plant. He was in favor of decentralization of the manufacturing operations, while Ford wanted "everything under one roof." This was the time during which the Rouge River plant was being constructed. Furthermore, Knudsen found his orders being countermanded behind his back by Henry Ford. The frustration he must have felt can only be imagined. His resignation from the company was reluctantly accepted.

Knudsen later moved to Chevrolet and led that company from a position of selling one car to every thirteen Fords in 1921, to one for every two Fords in 1926. While Ford closed for conversion to the Model

The 1921 Ford Touring and Runabout. Note the visored headlight lenses. Both cars here are equipped with electric starting equipment and demountable rims. The Touring featured the all-new body while the Runabout continued in the style set in 1917. *Photos from the Collections of the Henry Ford Museum and Greenfield Village.*

A in 1927, Chevrolet became number one. While Ford regained first place in 1929, the company soon lost it (in 1931) and began the down-hill slide that was to make the Ford Motor Company number three (after General Motors and Chrysler) in 1940.

1921 was a banner year for the Ford Motor Company, and began the period of its greatest sales and profits. While the shock of seeing Chevrolet become the sales leader in 1927 may have been severe, no one even gave it a thought in 1921. In fact, at Chevrolet at this time, a sales management team had suggested to General Motors that they drop the Chevrolet because "it could never compete with the Ford."

The Model T for 1921 was an almost all-new car, yet looked the same as the models that preceded it. The beginning of the 1921 models might be said to have been in November 1919 when in a Factory Letter (a letter circulated among various departments at the Highland Park plant), a new oval gasoline tank was described, with the comment that it would not be used in the present cars but would wait for a redesign of the Touring and Torpedo bodies to be completed. This change, the letter continued, would occur in "about four months."

The oval tank would allow the lowering of the seats, resulting in a better driving position and seats of greater comfort. This oval tank was first used in the 1920 open cars (before the body was redesigned).

The next step towards the 1921 models was in January 1920 when in another letter the new pressed-steel running board brackets were described. We do not believe that these new brackets

The Sedan and the Coupe for 1921, 1922, and early 1923. Electric equipment and demountable rims were standard on the closed cars. Again, note the visored headlight lenses, typical of the early 1921 models. *Photos from the Collections of the Henry Ford Museum and Greenfield Village.*

were seen in production this early but the design was completed and the tooling apparently available. (This type of bracket had been used on the truck chassis since 1917.) Typical of Model T production changes, they were not begun until "present supplies of the older parts are exhausted."

In June of 1920 another Factory Letter described the new Touring body "for 1921 production." No date for the introduction was specified. In July the Torpedo and Touring body parts lists for 1921 models was published.

A modification in the design of the hood and hood handles was made about July of 1920, and specified for future production. This change was in the design of the handle; the holes were punched in such a manner that the punched metal could be used as a replacement for the rivet which had formerly secured the handle to the hood. Now, instead of the two rivet heads, two holes appeared at the ends of the handles.

The all-steel muffler appeared in late summer of 1920. The design was specified, in a Factory Letter of August 13, for use in 1921 models. In this letter the muffler ends were specified as being two pieces, made from scrap fender stock, instead of one piece as had been used in early production of the all-steel muffler. Apparently the single-sheet ends rusted or burned out easily.

Interestingly, the company experimented with a number of different timer types. In 1919 a new design using a plunger brush instead of a roller was tried and later discontinued. After this type they tried timers with aluminum, cast iron, brass, and pressed-steel cases, and roller assemblies made of aluminum, bronze, and steel. In November of 1920 (approximately) the steel case was standardized but experiments continued with the various roller assemblies. We have been unable to determine just what the final design was.

In September of 1920 the oval gasoline tank was specified for certain Coupe bodies, described as "Coupe bodies with leather trimming." "Coupe bodies with cloth trimming will continue to use the square tank." This odd Coupe configuration was

The new (1921-25) body design placed the upholstery tack strip on the inside of the metal panels, extending above the panels. This modification eliminated the overhanging lip which had been characteristic of the cars for years. Holes were provided in the top of the metal panels to accept the nails which held the tack strips.

The result of this modification was a more finished appearance although the arm rests were somewhat less comfortable since they were less rounded and less padded. The seats themselves were greatly improved; the bottom cushions were lowered and the rake of the seat backs increased, giving the effect of a higher seat back.

1915-1920

1917-1920

1921-1925

1921-1925

NOTE: Photos here were selected to show body details. The upholstery, tacks, etc., are not necessarily correct.

1921-1925   316

discontinued in early 1921 because of the reduced head clearance with the oval tank under the seat. (The square tank was located in the rear turtle deck.)

In our research it has not been possible to pinpoint the actual date of introduction of the new 1921-style open cars. Our best guess is that it was about the first of the year (1921) in spite of the numerous references to the new bodies during the latter part of 1920. Furthermore, there is little doubt that the earlier-type bodies continued in production at the branches for some time after the Highland Park plant had made the changeover.

The new open-car bodies were anything but a radical change in style. In fact it takes an "expert" to see the difference from any distance. Continuing the general lines of the Model T that were established in the 1917 models, this new body was but a refinement of previous models, adding a touch of "finish" here and there. Most noticeable were the new rear quarter panels. No longer did the rear panels have the vertical bead on the side where the old side panel and the corner panel joined. The new quarter panel was a one-piece stamping making the section a continuous piece of metal from the door to the rear panel. In addition, the top support iron which held the top saddle now came through the quarter panel, eliminating the L-shaped forged bracket which had been bolted to the top of the body.

A further refinement was that of installing the upholstery tack strip on the inner surface of the seat panels instead of the outer surface. The tack strip extended above the panel to accept the upholstery nails, and a series of holes along the top edge of the panels allowed the "hide-em" welt to cover the seam. The result of this change was the elimination of the overhang of upholstery around the sides and back of the front and rear seats, giving a more finished appearance. Unfortunately the new design resulted in narrower and less padded arm rests, but this was of minor concern.

The new body was constructed so that the seat frames were much lower (made possible by the oval gas tank), giving the effect of a higher seat back. The result here was a more comfortable seat. In addition, the seat backs were modified for a little more slope, adding to passenger comfort.

The top irons and bows continued in the pattern of the previous cars. In the factory specifications a number of changes were shown in the top assemblies but these changes were in detail rather than general style. Tops were mechanically interchangeable from 1915 through 1922.

The Coupe and Sedan bodies for 1921 were the same as in the 1919 and 1920 cars except for minor changes in the upholstery and trim.

The 1921 models came with the new pressed-steel running board brackets, mentioned earlier. These replaced the forged type with the tie rods that

Typical 1913-1920

The major changes in the external construction of the 1921-1925 Touring body can be seen here. The one-piece rear quarter panel no longer has the seam above the fender, nor the bead which followed the fender line. The "L" shaped top saddle brackets have been replaced with straight rods which thread into an internal structural member through holes in the quarter panel. The upholstery tack strip is now inside the metal panel, extending above it, and the upholstery no longer overlaps the body, resulting in a more finished appearance but with narrow, less comfortable arm rests. The "rivet" just ahead of the rear doors on the 1915-1920 bodies has now disappeared.

1921-1925

had been used since 1909. These new brackets were considerably stronger than the old type. The holes in the side of the frame rails, where the old forgings were riveted, were still present and were to continue for some time.

Sometime in late 1920 or early 1921 the front motor mounting bearing was changed to the one-piece type with the integral U-bolt. Interestingly, Ford claimed the new mount improved the ride by allowing more flexibility at the front spring. Along with this new bearing came a one-piece license plate bracket.

A great improvement was made in the cylinder block casting. Ever since 1911, when the valves were enclosed, the Ford engine had used two valve chamber covers. The design of the car was such that the throttle control rod passed through the engine between numbers two and three cylinders where a hole was provided and the two valve covers left this hole open. The new design, introduced in 1921, had but one large valve chamber, with a single cover door, held in place with two screws. A hole was provided in the door for the throttle rod. One would suppose this would be an improvement. Certainly it must have saved assembly time. The major "improvement," though, was in the ease in which oil could leak out, not only through the throttle rod hole, but along the edges of the cover. Being larger, the new cover could bend when the screws were tightened, making a poor fit against the engine block. This modification continued until about 1927

During 1922 the spark adjustment rod was changed to eliminate the little swivel at the lower end (above). Now just a bent wire, it was cheaper and seemed to do the job just as well.

when the hole in the cylinder block was eliminated as well as the hole in the valve cover. (These later cars used the "hot plate" manifold/carburetor with which the throttle rod passed over the engine.) The elimination of the hole in the cover at least stopped *that* leak. (One should not judge too harshly. The Model T had so many chronic oil leaks that this minor addition really didn't make much difference anyway.)

Late in 1920, in response to new laws regarding headlight glare, Ford introduced a new headlight lens with a green "visor" at the top. This lens continued until about June 1921 when the fluted

(Continued on page 324

About 1922 the closed cars were given a more positive window adjustment. The old pull-strap system was still used for the quarter windows but this lever and notch method was used on the door windows.

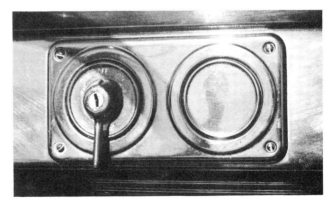

Blank switch panel used on non-electric cars, 1922-1925.

Typical closed cars, 1919 to 1923. Many minor modifications were made, such as the change of the door handles from the bail type to the bar type about 1922, and the addition of metal covers for the wooden window frames about the same time, but the general appearance remained about the same. *Photos from the Collections of the Henry Ford Museum and Greenfield Village.*

319   **1921-1925**

6511-EX

6594-X

6576-BX

6511-HX

6594-HX

6576-HX

All Ford headlight lenses were clear glass until late 1920, when a green-visored lens appeared for a short time. These visored lenses were superseded in early 1921 by the familiar Ford "H" lens with the fluted-rib pattern, and this type was used until the demise of the Model T in 1927.

These changes were made to conform with newly-enacted laws which had been made to cut headlight glare. The pie-shaped visor helped but the molded-in pattern of the "H" lens was far superior as it modified the distribution of light, making the beam eliptical in pattern; wider than it was high.

1921-1925

The "Ford-O" tail lamp, used from about 1923 to 1926 on non-electric cars. This photo shows the lamp but the bracket is home-made and the lamp is on the wrong side of the car. The Ford installation used special brackets which held the lamp on an angle so that the clear lens would illuminate the license plate (i.e., the clear lens faced a bit back to direct the light to the license plate) leaving the red lens pointing a bit to the right as viewed from the rear.

These brackets are 3662 (1926 runabouts), 3662-B (1923-26 touring), and 3660-E (1923-26 with spare-tire carrier) in the catalog illustrations below.

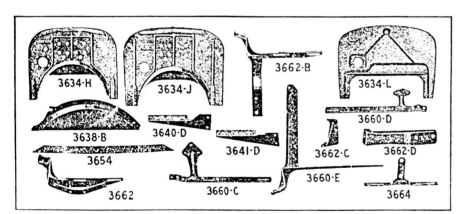

Typical electric tail lamp, used from 1919 to 1924.

Typical oil side light, late 1915 through early 1926.

Tail lamp and bracket assembly, typical of the 1924-25 cars. The same assembly was used in 1926-27 but it was mounted on a bracket on the left rear fender.

321

SIDE AND TAIL LIGHTS: Those cars which were supplied without electrical equipment were equipped with oil side and tail lights, typical of all Fords from 1916. The tail light was similar to the side lights except for the red lens and a smaller clear lens on the side to illuminate the license plate. About 1923 the tail light was modified as described on the previous page.

Those cars with a starter came with a small electric lamp with a clear lens on the side and such cars did not come from the factory with side lamps.

In 1924 the electric tail lamp was furnished with an integral license plate bracket, a style that continued through the 1927 models.

Magneto-powered horn, typical 1915 to 1927

HORNS: The magneto-powered horn was supplied on some production beginning in early 1915, and on all cars from late 1915 until about mid-1922. Beginning in 1922, the electric (battery) horn was installed on those cars with electric equipment, while the magneto horn continued on the non-starter cars. (The date of introduction of the battery horn is not known; 1922 is an educated guess.)

Battery-powered horn, typical 1922 to 1925. The same horn, with a different bracket, was used in 1926 and 1927.

Right top: The gasoline tank on all 1916 to 1925 two-door sedans was located under the driver's seat.

Right center: The Sedan gasoline tank was located in the rear deck in the 1919 to 1923 Coupes., except for a few built in 1920 which used the standard round tank under the seat. With the advent of the 1924 models in June 1923, the round tank was used on all cars except the Tudor Sedans

Right bottom: The firewall was of wood on all cars until early calendar 1923 when it was changed to a metal stamping. With the advent of the new high-radiator 1924 models, a similar but larger metal firewall was used.

Left bottom: The standard horn on all Fords until sometime in 1922 was the magneto-powered type, mounted on the firewall as shown. Sometime in 1922 the battery-operated horn appeared on starter-equipped cars. The battery horn was mounted on the left side of the engine, as was the magneto type in later models.

Ford "H" lens, a vast improvement, appeared. This new "H" lens continued until the end of Model T production in 1927.

The Ford open cars were still available (and advertised because of the lower price) without the electric starter equipment, and with the magneto-powered headlights plus the oil side and tail lights. These "standard" cars were furnished with square felloe non-demountable wheels using 30 by 3 tires in the front and 30 by 3-1/2 in the rear. Demountable rims, standard equipment on the closed cars, were offered as an option, and these used the 30 by 3-1/2 tires all around.

The open cars supplied without electrical equipment did not have an instrument panel until 1922. The ignition switch was located on the coil box, and the light switch was in combination with the horn button on the steering column as it had been since late 1917. When electric equipment was supplied, the instrument panel was part of the package. The instrument panel in 1920-21 may have been metal or leatherette covered wood, depending on the supply at the time.

Another change made during 1921 was in the design of the rear radius rods. Now of folded sheet metal design, with a seam along the edge, they came in rights and lefts so that the seam could be at the bottom, allowing any water that might enter to easily leak out.

The front radius rods were modified to accept a tapered nut at the point of attachment to the spring perch stud under the front axle. This tapered nut design provided a much more rigid assembly.

Windshields on the open cars came in two styles. Those cars which came from the factory with electrical equipment were not supplied with oil side lamps, so the windshield mounting brackets had no provision for the lamps. Non-electric cars were supplied with oil lamps and so had the mounting brackets as an integral part of the windshield mounting brackets. Somewhere in this era, separate lamp brackets were used, eliminating the need for two windshield bracket types.

The 1922 open models were but a continuation of the 1921 cars except for minor changes noted below.

The starting crank was changed from the type with the roller-type handle which was held in place with a long screw, to the simpler type in which the handle was sheet metal rolled into place over the crank end.

Closed cars were further improved by the addition of metal cover plates over the wood window frames. The exposed wood had been a problem for some time; no matter how well they were painted, in a short time the paint peeled off. The metal covers solved the problem. Another modification was in the method of raising and lowering the windows. Up until this time, straps were provided for the purpose. While the straps continued on the rear side windows of the Sedan, the door and front side windows were provided with a latching arrangement. While far from being as nice as the later crank system, this was much better than the straps. In addition to the above modifications in the closed cars, numerous changes in trim and upholstery were made.

Among the many changes made during the year was the elimination of the little ball joint at the bottom of the steering column on the spark adjustment rod. After twelve years of production, someone discovered that a bent wire would work just as well if enough clearance was left at the points of attachment. Clearance between parts was one of Ford's strong points, so this modification was a natural.

Later in 1922, perhaps at the time of introduction of the 1923-style Touring bodies in the late summer, the dashboard became standard equipment in all cars. Those without electrical equipment had a blank panel where the ammeter would have appeared but the ignition and light switch was on the instrument panel on all cars.

The magneto-powered horn continued on all cars until late in 1922 when the battery-powered type appeared on starter-equipped cars. Non-electric cars used the magneto horn until the end of the Model T.

Typical of the 1921 and later cars was the new one-piece front motor mount and spring clamp. This design continued until the end of production in 1927 with minor modifications. The crank handle shown here is the later design which appeared in later 1922 and continued through 1927. The handle sleeve is held in position by just rolling the edge over the end of the crank and also into a groove near the bend. Many cranks of this design have been seen in which the sleeve has rusted to the crank itself, and won't turn. Such a feature makes cranking somewhat less of a pleasure.

FORD TOURING CAR

Five-Passenger. May be purchased either with or without Ford Starting and Lighting System, and with or without Demountable Rims.

Demountable Rim Equipment includes 30x3½ Non-Skid tires all around, extra rim and tire carrier.

FORD RUNABOUT

Two-Passenger. May be purchased either with or without Ford Starting and Lighting System, and with or without Demountable Rims.

Demountable Rim Equipment includes 30x3½ Non-Skid tires all around, extra rim and tire carrier.

FORD COUPE

Two-Passenger. Standard equipment includes Ford Starting and Lighting System, Demountable Rims, Non-Skid tires all around, extra rim and tire carrier. Interior finished in grey whipcord. Permanent top with sliding plate glass windows.

FORD SEDAN

Five-Passenger. Standard equipment includes Ford Starting and Lighting System, Demountable Rims, Non-Skid tires all around, extra rim and tire carrier. Interior finished in grey whipcord. Permanent top with sliding plate glass windows.

The Ford line in the Fall of 1922. The Touring Car now sports the sloping windshield and the one-man top, while the Roadster continued in the 1922 style. The Roadster was modified into the 1923 style later in 1922 but the closed cars continued with no significant changes until about June 1923 when the "1924" models appeared. The Fordor Sedan was introduced also in later 1922 but was not shown in the catalog of the period.

The early 1923 (late 1922) Ford line. The Sedan and Coupe were unchanged from the 1922 cars but the Touring and Runabout (Roadster) had the new windshield and one-man top. The Runabout also sports a new and larger turtle deck. Note the top on the Touring in the lower right photo; that it does not taper down at the rear. The first 100,000 1923-style tops were of this pattern, then the tops were given a gentle curve down at the rear. *Photos from the Collections of the Henry Ford Museum and Greenfield Village.*

1921-1925

The 1923 Model T Ford Touring car as it looked at the time of its introduction in August 1922. Note the straight line of the top assembly. Other than the new top and the sloping windshield, the car was almost exactly like the 1922 models. After the first 100,000 of this model, the top was modified to curve down at the rear about 2-5/8 inches. *Photo from the Collections of the Henry Ford Museum and Greenfield Village.*

The 1923 model year began in the late summer of 1922 with the introduction of the one-man top and the sloping windshield on the touring cars. These two changes gave the appearance of a new car but the basic body was the same as that used in 1921 and 1922. The Torpedo (Runabout) appeared a bit later in 1922 and the closed cars continued with no significant changes.

The tops of the initial 1923-style Touring cars differed from the later production in that the lower edge line was straight from the windshield to the rear bow. After the first 100,000 cars, this line was modified to have a slight downward curve at the rear (dropping 2-5/8 inches at the rear bow), giving the car a lower appearance. This curved design was used in the styling of the Runabouts as well.

The Runabouts received the new body styling about October 1922 (the date is uncertain). Also at this time the Runabout also received the new turtle deck which was considerably larger and flared upward to match the rear of the body.

In a notice dated October 10, 1922, Ford described a new four-door Sedan which was to be added to the line. It was noted that it was not meant to supersede the centerdoor; at least that's what the

letter said. The letter reads:

OCT 10   (Letter from Louisville Branch)
New Fordor Sedan described. Price: $725, FOB Detroit. Dealers asked to not advertise it and to sell it only when the standard (centerdoor) sedan could not be sold to a customer.

"A new four-door, five-passenger sedan body has been added to the line of standard Ford body types. This body is an entirely new development in design and construction, and does not in any way displace the present two-door sedan, which will continue to come thru.

"While this new four-door body will go into production within the next several weeks, the output will necessarily be limited for some time to come; therefore your sales effort on the present two-door type should be increased rather than relaxed. This present type still represents one of the best automobile values on the market, and the new type of body will simply broaden the field of sedan prospects, so far as Ford business is concerned.

"The price of the new four-door sedan is ($725.00) Seven hundred and twenty-five dollars, F.O.B. Detroit, and the differential between it and the two-door type is large enough to prevent competition between the two models. There is no reason why you should lose a single sedan order because of inability to deliver the new type,

The early 1923 Fordor Sedan. This model has the low radiator and a body made with aluminum panels. Note the whitewall tires. *Photo from the Collections of the Henry Ford Museum and Greenfield Village.*

WHICH SHOULD ONLY BE MENTIONED TO PROSPECTS WHO HAVE PREVIOUSLY GIVEN CAREFUL CONSIDERATION TO THE PURCHASE OF A FOUR-DOOR SEDAN, AND WILL NOT BE SATISFIED WITH ANY OTHER TYPE. (sic)

"Continue pushing the sale of the two-door sedan, and only accept orders for the four-door type to prevent actual loss of business.

"VERY LITTLE PUBLICITY ON THE NEW SEDAN IS BEING GIVEN OUT. THEREFORE, FOR THE PRESENT, PREPARE NO ADVERTISING COPY ON IT, AND SEND OUT NO LITERATURE. IN THIS WAY YOUR SELLING PROBLEM WILL BE GREATLY SIMPLIFIED.

"Attached is a description of the features of the new four-door sedan, and a little later it is expected that a descriptive folder with illustrations will be ready for use."

FEATURES OF THE FOUR-DOOR SEDAN

"The body is approximately three inches longer than the two-door type Sedan, the extra length providing additional leg room for the occupants of the rear seat.

"All body panels are of aluminum with embossed molding, the metal extending up around the window sills and runways so that there are no wood parts exposed on the entire body. This feature insures a uniform finish and will largely prevent checking or other paint trouble.

"The body though longer that the present design weighs approximately 80 lbs. less. The saving in weight is gained by the use of aluminum panels in place of steel and also a lighter roof construction.

"The roof is of the soft type with artificial leather reinforced and padded, making it as durable and substantial as the old fiber board type, and eliminating

the possibility of vibration noises. The overall height of the body is one inch less that the present design. With the straighter roof line the car has the appearance of greatly increased length.

"A permanent leather visor above the windshield adds greatly to the appearance of the car while protecting the driver from the glare of the sun.

"The tire carrier is of a new and improved design which permits the spare tire to set at an angle that corresponds with the lines of the body.

"The front door openings are 23-4/8 (sic) inches and the rear door openings are the same width as on the present two-door sedan.

"Door handles are of the straight bar type made from hard black rubber with nickel tips and fittings. All doors are equipped with locks. Three of the locks are operated by levers from the interior of the body while the right front door is operated by a key from the outside.

"All doors are equipped with special Ford design double roller dovetail guides at center as well as rubber bumpers top and bottom to prevent rattling.

"The upper sash of the windshield is adjustable either outwardly or inwardly to provide the proper degree of ventilation. An improved design of clamp permits it to be easily adjusted and securely fastened in any position. The lower section of the windshield is stationary which is a factor in preventing rain from leaking into the body.

"The windows in all four doors are operated by means of crank type window regulators, while the rear windows are operated by the present lever type used in the two-door Sedan.

"All interior fittings, including window regulators, door pull handles, door latch levers, etc., are finished in oxidized silver.

"A dome light is operated by a button on the right rear body pillar.

"Upholstery material is of improved design with a fine dark stripe on a brown background of a shade that will not easily show dust and dirt. Silk window curtains to harmonize are provided for the three rear windows.

"The rear seat cushion is 46-1/2 inches by 20 inches, or one inch wider than in the two-door Sedan. The front seat is 42-1/2 inches by 19 inches and will accommodate a third person if necessary. The front seat cushion is divided in the center making it necessary to raise but one-half of the cushion to fill the gasoline tank. Therefore, the driver may have the tank filled without leaving his seat.

"Seat cushions are held in position by means of dowel pins in place of the covered binding strip used on our two-door Sedan.

"The price of the new Sedan is $725.00 F.O.B. Detroit."

A red pin stripe was specified for all Sedans. This stripe was to be no less than 3/32" and no more than 1/8" wide, and was to run across the cowl and no more than 3/8" or less than 5/16" below the belt molding.

The Centerdoor Sedan continued until about June 1923 and was replaced with a new two door Sedan. The Coupe continued in the 1922 pattern as well until June and was then replaced with a new

design based on the Tudor Sedan.

The aluminum-bodied four-door Sedan which was described earlier used the same hood and "low" radiator that was used on the other Fords when it was first introduced. As production increased, the use of aluminum was phased out on the lower body panels but was retained for the top sections.

In about March 1923 a metal sill cover was specified for the rear doors on the Touring body. This sill cover was to be painted black. The rear floor mat was changed from wool to rubber.

During 1923 production the spring shackles were again changed; this time to the "U" type with the single tie strap. This final design continued until the end of Model T production.

Sometime during this period the oil tail lamp was altered. The typical lamp up to this time had a large red lens to the rear and a smaller clear lens facing the right (license plate) side. Apparently this type did not give enough light to the license plate so the lamp was modified by turning it so that the large lens, now clear, faced the right, and the smaller lens, now red, was moved to the other side and now faced the rear. The mounting stud is now on the side of the lamp opposite the red lens. The electric tail lamp was unchanged.

The 1923 Runabout, introduced in October of 1922. A new top design, sloping windshield, body, and turtle deck make this an almost all new car. Note that spare tires were an extra on all Fords even though a spare rim was furnished as a part of the demountable wheel package. *Photo from the Collections of the Henry Ford Museum and Greenfield Village.*

1921-1925

The 1923 Fordor Sedan shown here is owned by Dave Lau, of Portland, Oregon. The serial number of this car is 7,891,398, indicating June 1923. The lower body panels of this car are all steel but the upper sections and moldings are aluminum. Note that by now the Sedan was supplied with the higher radiator and larger hood, as were the other body types. Ford referred to these cars as "1924" models. The Centerdoor Sedan and the Coupe with the front-opening doors had been discontinued by this time.

Early in 1923 (perhaps March or April) the firewall, which had been wood since 1909, was changed to one of steel. This firewall matches the "low" hood style, and is different from the steel firewall used when the car was restyled in June.

In June 1923 the entire Ford line was restyled somewhat and this new series was referred to as "1924 models" in Ford parts lists. The Centerdoor Sedan and the Coupe with the front-opening doors were discontinued. These were replaced with the two-door Sedan (called "Tudor") and a new Coupe with doors that opened at the rear. Both these cars were based on the same design and many parts were interchangeable. The four-door Sedan (called "Fordor"), Touring and Runabout were given the new "high" radiator and larger hood that was a feature of the Coupe and Tudor but were otherwise little changed. The general restyling consisted of the following changes:

1. The height of the radiator was increased.
2. The firewall (called the "dash" by Ford) was made larger and the body cowl section was modified to match.

Continued on page 335

1921-1925   330

The instrument panel on the open cars was redesigned for the 1923-25 models, having a slight slope upwards at the bottom outer ends. It also was set at a slight angle (slope) and the end mounting bolts were now behind the panel instead of in front of it as before. The speedometer was optional equipment, generally installed by the dealer. The bracket which holds the steering column to the panel was used only on the high-radiator cars of 1923 and later (1924 models).

The valance below the radiator added a note of finish to the front of the car. Note that the front edges of the fenders had a folded lip to match the valance. This photo shows a later valance (1926-7) with the hole below the crank for a retaining screw but otherwise this is typical of the 1924-25 models.

LEFT. Typical 1924 Touring. Oil side lamps were used only on the non-starter cars.

1921-1925

LEFT. From 1914 until late 1922 the turtle deck on the runabouts appeared as shown, although the handles were pressed-steel in the later models, rather than the cast type shown here.

CENTER. In late 1922 (1923 models) a larger deck appeared. No handles were used; the lid was provided with a key which served as a handle. This type deck continued until the appearance of the 1926 models in the summer of 1925.

All closed cars used roll-down door windows beginning with the 1924 models in June of 1923. The side windows continued the latching arrangement used in 1922-23. A number of door window regulators were used and are shown at the right. The 17200A and 17201A show the design of the A-type regulator. They were interchangeable. There were rights and lefts of the 17200 A, B, and C but 17200D could be used on either side.

| 17200A | 17200B | 17200C | 17200D |
| 17201A | 17201B | 17201C | |

Ford
RUNABOUT
Two-Passenger

A practical business utility furnishing individual transportation at a minimum cost. Like the touring car, it may be purchased either with or without starting and lighting equipment and with or without demountable rims. Demountable rim equipment includes 30 x 3½" non-skid tires, all around, extra rim and tire carrier.

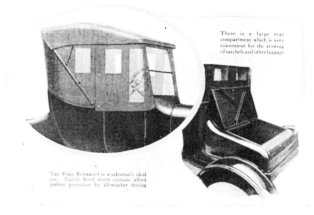

There is a large rear compartment which is very convenient for the stowing of satchels and other luggage

THE FORD RUNABOUT is a salesman's ideal car. Tightly fitted storm curtains afford perfect protection for all-weather driving

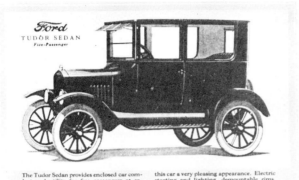

Ford
TUDOR SEDAN
Five-Passenger

The Tudor Sedan provides enclosed car comfort and utility for five passengers at exceptionally low cost. The straight roof line and well proportioned windows give this car a very pleasing appearance. Electric starting and lighting, demountable rims, non-skid tires, all around, extra rim and tire carrier are standard equipment.

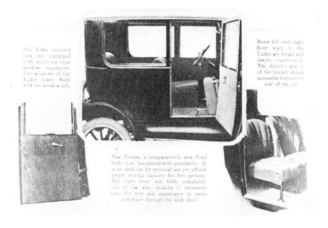

ALL FORD enclosed cars are equipped with revolving type window regulators. The windows of the Tudor lower flush with the window sills

Both left and right front seats in the Tudor are broad and deeply cushioned. The driver's seat is of the bucket design accessible from either side of the car

THE TUDOR, a comparatively new Ford body type, has gained wide popularity. It is an ideal car for personal use yet affords ample seating capacity for five persons. The right front seat folds completely out of the way, making it extremely easy for rear seat passengers to enter and leave through the wide door

Ford
FORDOR SEDAN
Five-Passenger

The Ford Fordor Sedan is designed and built to meet all normal, enclosed car requirements. It is sturdy in construction and appropriate for any use. The purchase price includes electric starting and lighting equipment, demountable rims, 30 x 3½" non-skid tires, all around, and extra rim and tire carrier.

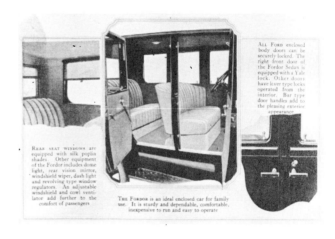

REAR SEAT WINDOWS are equipped with silk poplin shades. Other equipment of the Fordor includes dome light, rear vision mirror, windshield wiper, dash light and revolving type window regulators. An adjustable windshield and cowl ventilator add further to the comfort of passengers

ALL FORD enclosed body doors can be securely locked. The right front door of the Fordor Sedan is equipped with a Yale lock. Other doors have lever type locks operated from the interior. Bar type door handles add to the pleasing exterior appearance

THE FORDOR is an ideal enclosed car for family use. It is sturdy and dependable, comfortable, inexpensive to run and easy to operate

Ford
COUPE
Two-Passenger

The Ford Coupe covers a wide range of usefulness. It is well adapted for the personal requirements of the business or professional man, salesman or any member of the family. Standard equipment includes starting and lighting system, demountable rims, non-skid tires, all around, extra rim and tire carrier.

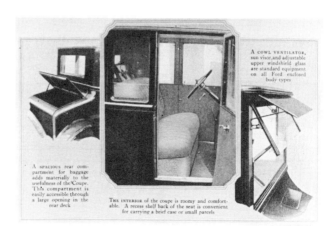

A SPACIOUS rear compartment for baggage adds materially to the usefulness of the Coupe. This compartment is easily accessible through a large opening in the rear deck

A COWL VENTILATOR, sun visor, and adjustable upper windshield glass are standard equipment on all Ford enclosed body types

THE INTERIOR of the coupe is roomy and comfortable. A recess shelf back of the seat is convenient for carrying a brief case or small parcels

1921-1925

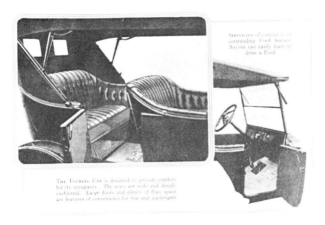

The Touring Car is designed to provide comfort for its occupants. The seats are wide and deeply cushioned. Large doors and plenty of floor space are features of convenience for rear seat passengers.

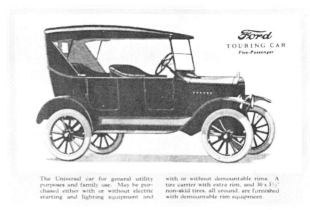

Ford
TOURING CAR
Five-Passenger

The Universal car for general utility purposes and family use. May be purchased either with or without electric starting and lighting equipment and with or without demountable rims. A tire carrier with extra rim, and 30 x 3½" non-skid tires, all around, are furnished with demountable rim equipment.

ONE-TON
TRUCK

In commercial activities the adaptability of the Ford One-Ton Truck Chassis to a wide range of uses makes it the most economical and efficient of haulage units.

With varied types of bodies, the one-ton truck chassis may be suited to the transportation of farm products and to the needs of large or small industrial customers.

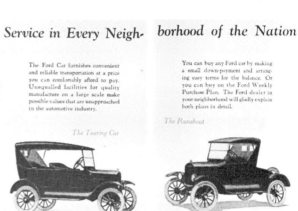

Service in Every Neigh- borhood of the Nation

The Ford Car furnishes convenient and reliable transportation at a price you can comfortably afford to pay. Unequalled facilities for quality manufacture on a large scale make possible values that are unapproached in the automotive industry.

You can buy any Ford car by making a small down-payment and arranging easy terms for the balance. Or you can buy on the Ford Weekly Purchase Plan. The Ford dealer in your neighborhood will gladly explain both plans in detail.

The Touring Car

The Runabout

ABOVE and previous page: The late 1923 (1924 models) and 1925 Ford line.

Unchanged in general style, numerous modifications were made during this period. The new four-dip pan appeared in 1924. Balloon tires were offered in 1925 and were accompanied by a new five-to-one steering gear ratio — which later became standard regardless of tire size.

The trucks were finally offered with bodies. A "C" cab appeared at first, in 1924, and was followed later with a closed cab and several variations of a rear platform. The stake body and cab shown in the illustration were not made or supplied by Ford.

Ford had for some time been offering time payment plans. These differed from present day methods in that you paid a little each week until you had enough in the kitty, and then you took delivery of the car. The advertisement at the left tells you all about it.

By 1925 sales were beginning to take real effort. Accessories, Ford Service, Easy Terms and other pitches were employed to woo the buyer. Yet, in spite of the built-in Ford quality at a low price, sales were slipping. The wild ride was nearing the end.

1921-1925

334

3. A new and larger hood made the front of the car appear much more massive.
4. New hood clash strips to mate with the wider hood were installed.
5. An apron was added below the radiator. This apron covered the front motor mount and frame, adding a more finished look to the car.
6. The front edges of the fenders were given a lip which matched the lines of the radiator apron, adding further to the finished appearance.

The new Coupe was described as follows by the Ford sales department:

"New rear fender curving outward at end with rear fender apron bolted to sill of body.
"Ventilator in cowl operated by quick action lever under the dash.
"Windshield visor supported to body by two steel rods. Has pull-to brackets on lower side of windshield frame.
"Bottom windshield does not open.
"Upper windshield is wider and lower windshield is narrower, bringing the division and the rubber strip below the vision of the driver.
"Seat divided. Gas tank opening under right half of seat.
"Check straps on doors are rubber.

"Revolving door window regulators.
"Inside door latch and regulators nickeled.
"Pull rods on doors eliminated. New arrangement on window sill (embossed finishing strip).
"Turtle back rear deck with increased carrying capacity.
"Upholstery of soft brown cloth with mahogany stripe. Head lining plain brown mixed.
"Yale lock on right hand door.
"Inside lock on other door.
"Rear side windows operated by rod and knob.
"Silk curtain on rear window. No curtain on side windows.
"Curtain brackets nickeled.
"Broad, square back window, stationary.
"Battery held in bracket under rear deck and is accessible through trap door of rear compartment.
"Door handles black with nickel trimming.
"Top of body covered with leather.
"Anti-rattling device on both doors. Slot in frame with steel piece in door which fits in the slot.
"Heavy covered hinges on doors.
"Recess shelf at back of seat for carrying small parcels.
"Doors hinged at front."

This new Coupe was quite a change from the previous design. In addition to the items mentioned above, the turtle deck was now an integral part of

The "1924" Coupe, introduced in mid-1923. This photo is not dated (on our copy) but the license plate shows 1922! This may have been a prototype or just may have had the older plate installed at the time of the photo. *From the Collections of the Henry Ford Museum and Greenfield Village.*

the body. Note that the doors opened at the rear (hinge in front).

The new Tudor Sedan followed the general pattern of the Coupe except for the addition of the rear seat and the lack of a turtle deck. The same cowl section and windshield was used for both types.

The restyled Fordor Sedan had a new cowl section to match the larger hood. The doors continued in the previous style; wood framing with aluminum panels.

These "late 1923" models were, in fact, the 1924 Fords. A number of minor mechanical modifications were made in addition to the larger hood. One such change was the addition of a brace for the steering column. This brace fastened to the instrument panel and gave the steering wheel a more solid feeling. Later in 1924 production, most significant was the introduction of the new, so called, "four-dip" engine pan which made it much easier to adjust the number four rod, and the rear main bearings. Other modifications were the use of new, lighter pistons (1 lb., 12 oz.) and a new, shorter front camshaft bearing. The camshaft itself was modified to accept the shorter bearing — essentially just the lengthening of the front cam lobe.

Late in 1924 the oil pipe in the engine was given a larger funnel to collect oil for circulation to the front of the engine.

The tail light on the electric-equipped cars was changed to the type in which the lamp is an integral part of the license plate bracket. (Typical "1926" type.) Non-electric cars continued the oil lamps.

The 1924 Fordor Sedans were changed during the year to use all-steel doors instead of the wood and aluminum types used earlier.

The 1924 models evolved into the 1925 models, essentially unchanged. Late in 1924 the fenders were modified for a more massive appearance. The bead on the front fenders, which had matched the splash apron front curve, now ran under the splash apron. This gave the fender a wider appearance. These fenders have often been called "truck fenders" but they were the standard 1925 type. Rear fenders were made a bit wider and now flare out at the front where they meet the running board.

During the 1925 model year balloon tires were offered as an option. The standard equipment on the closed cars was the 30 by 3-1/2 tire mounted on demountable rims, and on the open cars the same tires mounted on non-demountable rims (wheels). The demountable wheels were optional on open cars. The new balloon tire size was 4:40 by 21 and they were mounted on demountable rims. They were optional on all models.

Electrical equipment remained standard on closed cars, and optional on open models.

1925 models continued with little or no changes from the 1924 other than in the construction details, such as the use of more and more metal framing in the body, replacing wood parts. Ford's efforts were apparently being directed to the production of the "Improved Ford" of 1926, which was introduced in August 1925.

A minor change was in another modification of the rear fenders of the Coupe and Roadsters. Here the inner apron was extended further to the rear, improving the appearance of these models considerably from the back. A number of closed cars were apparently produced with a new running board splash apron, late in the model year. These aprons were somewhat "square," similar to the 1926 style. They may have been used only on some production.

The Model T Ford chassis of 1924; typical of 1921 to 1925 except for the hood-radiator size and minor details. *Photo from the Collections of the Henry Ford Museum and Greenfield Village.*

The late 1923 to 1925 Fordor Sedan as it appeared in October 1924. Note that the striping ran all around the body but did not cover the door moldings. Ford's Factory Letter regarding striping of the Sedans made this quite clear. Notice, too, the door handles with the nickel trim all around. These and the type with just the nickel ends both appeared on cars at the same period, apparent y depending on the supply. *Photo from the Collections of the Henry Ford Museum and Greenfield Village.*

Introduced on the Fordor Sedan, the cowl ventilator and the visors became standard on all closed cars when the new styles were introduced in mid-1923. The visor was offered by the factory as a dealer-installed accessory for previous closed cars for just three dollars.

While the pre-production four-door Sedan did not have the cowl ventilator, it is believed that all actual production models were so equipped.

While the upper section of the windshield could be opened, the lower section was fixed.

The Centerdoor Sedan and the earlier Coupe windshields were similar but the lower section could be raised and pulled inward, making the cowl ventilator unnecessary. The old windshield tended to leak water, though, so the fixed bottom section was an improvement.

The "1925" Ford closed cars as they appeared on November 2, 1924. Note they all had the wider fenders at the rear and the front fenders on which the molding ran under the splash apron. *Photos from the Collections of the Henry Ford Museum and Greenfield Village.*

The late 1923, 1924 and 1925 Tudor Sedan and Coupe. Striping was similar to that on the Fordor Sedan, and was in bright red paint. *Photos from the Collections of the Henry Ford Museum and Greenfield Village.*

Typical 1924-1925 Runabout and Touring cars. Note that neither had top support irons and saddles. The holes were there but they were covered with rubber plugs. Presumably the irons and saddles came with the car, to be installed by the dealer or owner if he needed them. *Photos from the Collections of the Henry Ford Museum and Greenfield Village.*

1917 to late 1924   **1925**

The front fenders on the Fords from 1917 until 1925 were all of the same pattern except for the lip at the front, added with the introduction of the high radiator. Note how the bead on the upper surface followed the outline of the splash apron.

During late 1924 (1925) production the fender beading was modified and now ran under the splash apron, as shown in the top right photo. (This fender is mounted on an earlier model in this photo. Note the hole in the apron; a feature of all models using the larger radiator and hood. This fender type has often been referred to as a "truck fender" but all Fords came with them in 1925, as well as on the trucks of 1926 and 1927.

The lower right picture shows the last style of splash apron before the "Improved Fords" of 1926. Little is known of this "square" type apron other than it appeared on many of the Tudor and Fordor Sedans (and only these types so far as can be determined) in the last of the 1925-style cars. This apron may have been added after the appearance of the 1926 models in an effort to "up date" the older body style as a sales aid. These aprons are not listed in any of the parts books in our files but they are far too common to have been accessories.

Press Release Announcing
THE RESTYLED FORDS
Dated August 27, 1923

Detroit, Mich., August. Introduction of a higher radiator, bringing new and improved body lines to all Ford cars, is announced today by the Ford Motor Company.

The changes have just gone into effect and the various types are now in production.

While the larger radiator has been made standard on all types and while it has made possible other betterments in body design, there is no radical departure in construction, but rather a general improvement which has resulted in more graceful lines.

The new radiator sets an inch and a half higher than the former and has an apron at the bottom which joins a similar apron effect of the fender on either side, giving a highly finished appearance to the front of the car. The larger radiator also increases cooling efficiency.

Most conspicuous among the new types is the Ford Coupe which is of entirely new body design and construction, resulting in a more trim exterior appearance, more comfortable seating arrangement and a greater luggage carrying capacity.

From the dash there is a graceful sweep in the cowl to the radiator bringing a pleasing effect to the front. The doors are wide and open forward making access and exit easy. They are heavily framed for rigidity and strength. The compartment at the rear has been enlarged to afford increased carrying capacity. The gasoline tank is under the seat, with divided cushions to afford easy filling of the tank from the right side making in unnecessary for the driver to leave his seat. Ventilator in the cowl and a visor over the windshield add much to the attractiveness of the car. A new rear fender of more sturdy construction is also a feature.

Interior fittings are of choice material and the arrangement of the deeply cushioned seat has been effected so that at the rear there is a small recess shelf for carrying parcels. The rear vision window is much larger and oblong in shape. Door windows have been equipped with revolving type window regulators and door locks are provided. Side windows are equipped with the lever type lifters.

Marked, too, is the improvement in the four door sedan. Highly popular since its introduction a year ago, because of its low, graceful lines, the car now provides even much better lines and a sturdier appearance.

This has been brought about by the installation of an entirely new cowl and a graceful sweep from the dash blending into a larger hood and radiator. The change also affords an increase in leg room for occupants of the front seat.

In the open types, the Touring Car and the Runabout, the cowl has been enlarged and flows in a graceful curve to the higher hood.

The result brings a most pleasing effect to the exterior appearance of both types. The improvement in the Touring Car which came when the one man top and slanting windshield were introduced, is greatly enhanced by the larger radiator, the car appearing lower and more attractive than ever. The effect on the Roadster is likewise most appealing, giving it a more rugged and sturdy appearance.

The new radiator is also extended to the Ford Truck chassis, affording improved appearance and better cooling to delivery services.

These new Ford types and the generally recognized performance ability of the Ford under all motoring conditions, promise to bring greater demand than ever before as the public becomes more fully acquainted with the higher standards and greater values which have been incorporated. No changes are contemplated in prices.

Graceful lines; finished appearance; low, graceful lines — is this the Model T Ford they are describing? Note that no mention is made of the Tudor Sedan. This suggests that that body style did not appear until later in the year (after August 1923).

INTERIOR COUPE VIEW

Photos from Ford literature extolling the virtues of the 1925
Fords for business and pleasure.

343

Hardly noticeable unless compared side by side with the earlier type, the subtile changes in the rear fenders in 1925 models created a more massive and stronger appearance. Note how the fender was now wider, curving outward from the running board. The inner skirt on the Coupe and Runabout fender was larger and curved outward to the body, covering more of the open space at the rear.

Note, too, that the rear tip had a very gentle rearward flare, adding a dash of raciness to the car.

1917-1924 style. (Runabout shown, but typical of the Coupe.)   1925 style. (Coupe shown but the Runabout was identical.)

In late 1925, perhaps at about the time of introduction of the 1926 models, the splash apron on some of the closed cars was modified. Rather than the gentle curve from the running board to the body, the apron was more "square," similar to that of the 1926-27 Fords.

This "square" style has been seen by the author on Tudor and Fordor sedans. It may have been used on the coupes as well but it has not been seen on any of the open cars.

1925 Fordor Sedan with the late "square" splash apron. Owner: Larry Bechard, Wheat Ridge, Colorado.

 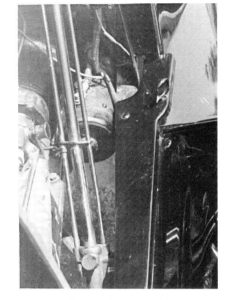

1917-1923   **June 1923-1925**

The larger hood, introduced in mid-1923, required new hood clash strips to match. Notice the "dogleg" at the rear. The splash apron had to be modified as well. A hole was now provided to allow the rear hood clamp to pass through.

Firewalls on all Fords until early 1923 were made of wood. Early in calendar year 1923 a metal firewall of the same overall dimensions replaced the wooden one. This "low radiator" metal firewall was used only a few months and was then replaced with a similar but larger metal firewall to match the new hood. This larger type continued until the introduction of the 1926 models on the passenger cars, and until the end of production in 1927 on the trucks.

Spring shackles were of the later "L" type (right photo) until about 1923 when the "U" type (bottom photo) became standard. These continued until the end of Model T production in 1927.

Demountable rims were supplied by Hayes, Kelsey, and Ford (the Ford rim did not appear until about 1922). All rims were zinc (galvanized, not cadmium) plated.

The oiler on the king pin bolt above is not standard production, nor is the speedometer drive.

April 14, 1924 saw the introduction of a new camshaft and camshaft front bearing. The new design had a shorter front bearing and a wider cam lobe. Just what the advantage of this modification was is not clear but perhaps it made for longer wear on the front cam since it probably receives less oil than the others.

In June 1924, engines began to be built with 1/32" babbitt in the front and center mains, and by July 16 all engines had the thinner bearings.

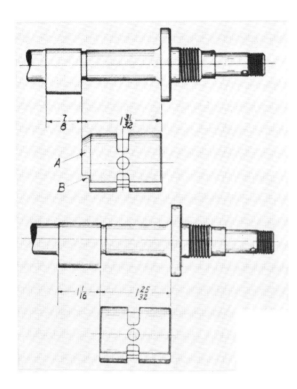

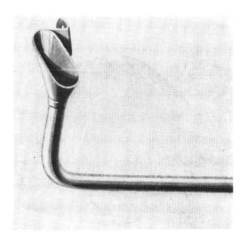

July 17, 1924, was a "red letter" day at the Ford plant. Two major modifications were made to the Ford engine. One was the addition of a cast-in projection (or rib) in the transmission cover which directed oil to the rear for better lubrication of the transmission bands (upper right illustration). The second was in the modification of the oil tube in which a larger funnel was installed, collecting more oil for the front of the engine (illustrations at the right).

Next day, July 18, the new "four-dip" engine pan appeared. This long-overdue improvement made adjustment of the rear connecting rod and the rear main bearing much easier.

In 1925 Ford finally did what owners had been doing for years; they installed "quick change" bands in the transmission as standard equipment. These bands had removable "ears" so that the bands could be changed without removing the transmission cover.

Production of the 1926-type engine began in early summer of 1925. The last "old style" engine came off the line on July 27, 1925. That engine was number 12,218,728 and it was completed at 5:51 P.M. that day.

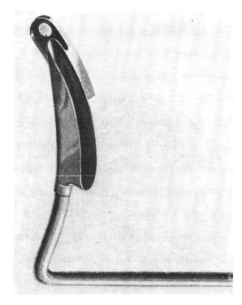

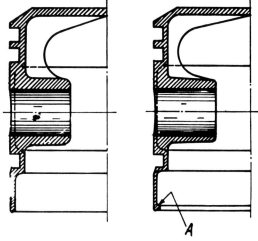

Light-weight piston (right). Note the thinner casting and the ridge at the skirt ("A").

ENGINE

In general, the engine and running gear of the Model T continued in the pattern set in 1919. Numerous modifications were made, of course, and of these the major ones were:

Beginning on November 1, 1921, engines were produced with the one-piece valve door. This new engine was built while supplies of the older cylinder castings were used up and it was not until April 3, 1922 that all production was of the new type.

Late in 1921 a new light weight connecting rod was put into production. During this period, too, pistons were machined to reduce their weight.

On March 31, 1922, Ford began using rolled-thread cylinder head bolts. These were thinner than the older bolts, yet much stronger. Both types of bolts were used until July 14 when the stock of the older bolts ran out.

On March 12, 1924, the pistons were redesigned to further reduce their weight, as shown in the upper right illustration. The new piston was of thinner construction and can be identified by the ridge around the inside of the skirt ("A" in the illustration).

The front camshaft bearing was changed in 1924. The new bearing was shorter and the front cam lobe was longer. While the new camshaft and bearing could be used in the earlier engines, one could not use the old bearings with the new shaft, or the new bearings with the old shaft.

In June 1924 the front and center main bearings were built with thinner babbitt, just 1/32-inch thick. By July 16, all engines had the thinner bearings.

The Ford oiling system was simplicity itself. When all was new and clean it could hardly fail. However, in time lint and sludge tended to clog the oil line and stop the flow of oil to the front of the engine. Accessory manufacturers offered a number of effective solutions to the problem but Ford remained aloof. Finally, on July 17, 1924, a new oil line with a larger funnel began to be used. While the larger funnel could collect more oil, only so much could flow through the pipe, and the larger funnel did nothing to prevent clogging.

In 1925 production, Ford altered the carburetor adjustment system. By installing a "U-joint" on the adjustment needle, the choke rod could be used to also adjust the mixture, eliminating the separate adjuster and bell crank system. This new system was similar to that used on the 1926-27 cars except for the length of the choke rods used. Ford also began installing the Vaporizer carburetor on some 1925 models (prior to the 1926 cars).

(The vacuum line from the intake manifold is not Ford equipment.)

The 1925 Model T Roadster. Balloon tires were added to the list of options this year. While retaining the general style of the 1923 models, late in 1924 and in 1925 a good many of the body parts were redesigned or modified, generally in an effort to make the bodies lighter yet more durable. *Photo from the Collections of the Henry Ford Museum and Greenfield Village.*

PRODUCTION FIGURES
(February 1, 1921 to July 1, 1925)

Note: These engine serial numbers are for the calendar year, not the "style year" of the cars.

1921 (4,698,420 to 5,638,071)	939,652
1922 (5,638,972 to 6,953,071)	1,315,000
1923 (6,953,072 to 9,008,371)	2,055,300
1924 (9,008,372 to 10,997,941)	* 1,989,570
1925 (10,997,942 to 12,062,486)#	* 1,064,545

*Figure is approximate. Because of the changeover from Highland Park to the Rouge plant, there was some overlapping of engine numbers in late 1924 and early 1925.

#January 1925 until July 1, 1925. 1926 production began in July and some 1926 engines will be a part of these figures.

Total production of the calendar year 1925 was 1,992,135, which included 1926 models. While almost as good as 1924, the automobile market was expanding and Ford was getting a smaller percentage of the total than he had been enjoying in the past.

Among the changes in the open car body design was the use of pressed-steel floor risers instead of wood. Seat frames, top body sills, general construction of the front quarter sections, door hinges and other parts were all new in the late 1924 and 1925 open bodies.

Three New Sales Opportunities

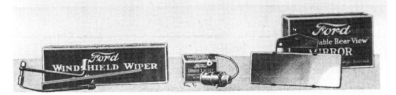

Accessories, a long-neglected segment of the automotive market so far as the Ford Motor Company was concerned, became a part of the sales pitch. Mirrors, offered as an option, then standard on the closed cars, were made available for the open cars (as an option) as well. Dash lamps, windshield wipers, tire pumps and repair kits were now promoted by the factory. Even the windshield visor, standard on closed cars since 1923, was offered to owners of earlier models at just three dollars. (Not so cheap — the average working man was lucky to make six dollars a day at that time.)

1924-25 Ford. Later models had a one-piece rear window, like the 1926 models. *Ford Archives photo.*

The Late 1925 Model T Coupe

This featured 1925 Coupe is owned by Milton Webb, from Lakeview Terrace, California. The front and rear bumpers are non-Ford accessories.

The car is a later 1925 model which is equipped with balloon tires (4:40x21), which were first offered as an option by Ford in 1925. The 21" wheels were offered in either black or natural finish. The use of the larger tires made steering even more difficult and so Ford changed the steering gear ratio from four-to-one to five-to-one, and increased the steering wheel diameter an inch, from sixteen to seventeen inches.

Note that the rear fenders are of the later style with the larger inner splash aprons which gave the rear a more finished appearance.

Milt Webb's Coupe has the large-drum (1926 style) rear axle which he says is the one that came with the car when new. This is not the first late 1925 car (that is, built just before the 1926 style in summer of 1925) we have seen with the later axle but we have not been able to establish its "authenticity."

Because of the overlap in production of cars between the Highland Park plant and Ford's many branches, no doubt the 1925 style continued to be assembled at the branches while the main plant was building the new models. It is therefore quite likely that later-style parts appeared on early-style cars. We know for certain that this had happened in previous years.

A running change made during the 1924 model year was a new tail light and license plate bracket. The light is now in the center of the plate instead of to the left, and the bracket forms an integral part of the lamp. The tail light assembly continued through the 1927 models, unchanged except that it was mounted on the left rear fender beginning with the 1926 cars.

The second lamp to the right has been added by the owner and is not typical of cars of this period.

Photo from the Collections of the Henry Ford Museum and Greenfield Village.

The Ford Model TT truck chassis had been only offered as a bare chassis (no cab or body) until 1924. In January of 1924 the "C" cab plus a number of rear platform variations were made available.

In April 1925 the all-steel closed cab was added to the line. The 1925-style trucks continued until the end of Model T production in 1927.

Photos from the Collections of the Henry Ford Museum and Greenfield Village.

ONE-TON
TRUCK

In commercial activities the adaptability of the Ford One-ton Truck Chassis to a wide range of uses makes it the most economical and efficient of haulage units.

With varied types of bodies, the one-ton truck chassis is alike suited to the transportation of farm products and to the needs of large or small industrial concerns.

When the bare TT chassis was supplied with electrical equipment, the switch panel was mounted on a pressed-metal bracket, shown above. Electrical equipment was apparently first offered on the truck chassis in 1921.

On the trucks supplied with a Ford-made cab, a regular instrument panel, similar to that used on the passenger cars, was used.

When the TT was supplied with electrical equipment, the battery was mounted between the running board brackets on the left side.

Note that the closed cabs did not have roll-down windows as did the passenger cars. Windows were adjusted with the strap shown, a method used in the passenger cars until 1924 models. Window regulators may have been made available in later years but the author has not seen them on the trucks he has viewed.

The 1925 Ford Roadster Pickup. The bed differs from the 1926 type in that the sides are not embossed for the fenders (as in 1926). The 1925 bed has a reinforcing plate to which the fender iron is bolted. This photo is dated December 12, 1924 but the pickup was not offered until 1925. *Photo from the Collections of the Henry Ford Museum and Greenfield Village.*

1921-1925

THE 1925 ROADSTER PICKUP

BASED ON PHOTOS AND DATA FROM STEVE CONIFF
Colorado Springs, Colorado

The 1925 Roadster Pickup is probably the rarest of the passenger car body styles. While the roadster body itself was the standard model for 1925, the pickup bed was unique to 1925, and was built for just a few months before the introduction of the "Improved Ford" 1926 models about August.

The featured car is owned by Steve Coniff of Colorado Springs, Colorado, who supplied the photos and many of the caption notes. The serial number is 12,146,071, indicating an engine assembly date of July 15, 1925. No doubt the car itself was assembled a short time later since this was just about the end of the line for this body style. In viewing many of the pictures you might note some of the "1926" features on this car, such as the universal joint carburetor adjustment and the eight-leaf front spring (both features of many 1925 models).

The pickup box for the 1925 model, while appearing quite similar to the more common 1926-27 style, was unique. The side panels were not embossed and drilled for the rear fenders as on the 1926-27 models. Rather, an internal bracket was supplied, to which the fender iron was riveted. The pickup used standard Roadster rear fenders. The front panel of the bed was unique to 1925, but the rear door (drop gate) was the same for 1925 through 1927. (Early production may not have had the "Ford" script.) The bottom (floor of the bed) boards were also different from the 1926-27 style, due to the higher rear cross-member and the installation of a

metal cover over the cross-member area of the floor.

Whether or not Ford offered the pickup box as a separate item for in-the-field conversions of existing Roadsters in 1925 is not known. The pickup box was offered during 1925 for $25.00 but we do not know if this was for 1925 or 1926 cars. The roadster pickup from the factory, in 1925, cost $21.00 more than the standard Roadster.

The deck floor boards were not the same as the 1926-27 boards. Ford listed four different boards: left, right, center, and intermediate. The 1926-27 models had a metal plate over the rear cross-member, due to the greater crown of the cross-member.

The spare-tire carrier, side lamps, and extra tail lights appear to have been added later. Holes in the end of the turtle deck platform would indicate the the tail light was mounted to the left of center under the bed. The original top had just one large window, as in the 1926 models, but Steve ordered the usual 1923-25 top in error. The rear spring has nine leaves, as in the Sedans, instead of the usual eight leaves used in the Touring, Roadster, and Coupe.

The inside view of the right side wall. Note the reinforcing plate for the fender mount, and how crooked it is. Automobile assembly line men were no more careful in 1925 than they are today!

The front spring is of the low crown type as used on the 1926-27 cars, and has eight leaves. The front axle is dated 6-27-25.

The battery box hole appears to be the same as on the 1926-27, and the *Factory Parts* book lists the same door for all years. There is a major difference, though. The front bed panel has a much shallower depression stamped in it. If you look closely you can see the turtle deck platform under the bed floor. The *Parts Lists* show different part numbers for the Pickup and Roadster battery cover doors, incidentally.

Eighteen bolts are used to secure the bed to the car. The bed floor is bolted through the turtle deck platform with ten bolts. Metal angle pieces straddle the sill and are held in place by four carriage bolts on each side.

The right rear fender brace, riveted to the bed side panel.

1925

Apparently added by a previous owner, the car has two wooden side boxes at the rear sides of the pickup box. Both have padlocks as shown. Note the piece of felt on the edge of the fender to stop the rattle.

The door upholstery has metal trim around the lever hole and the door latch cutout.

The original "hide-em" welting was reused when the top was replaced. The top material shown is not like the original, which was more of a "pebble" grain than the type shown here.

A rubber plug seals the hole where the top rests would be. These were pretty much standard equipment, it seems, for if you look at most original factory pictures, there are no support irons installed and the holes are plugged on most open cars.

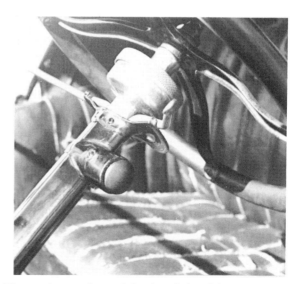

The steering gear box and the throttle/spark levers were nickel-plated, as on all Model T Fords of the era.

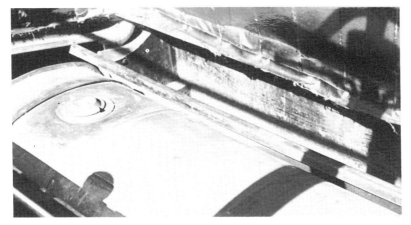

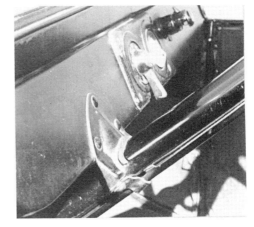

There is a tool compartment behind the gasoline tank.

The steering column support brace has a rubber pad between the upper part and the column, but no pad on the lower part.

Original Photos of the 1925 Roadster Pickup

From the Collections of the Henry Ford Museum and Greenfield Village.

There are two sets of these original Ford photos. The first (the ones with the railroad tank cars in the background) are dated December 12, 1924, and the others (with the brick pavement) are dated February 28, 1925. All these photos show a different bed from that in Steve Coniff's car in that these do not have the Ford script on the tailgate, while Coniff's does. Otherwise, the beds appear identical.

Another interesting observation. The front fenders on the 1924 photos are of the type with the bead that runs outside the splash apron, while those on Coniff's car have the bead that runs under the apron. This latter style is typical of the 1925 cars. Factory photos of the various Sedan and Coupe models, dated November 1924, show the newer style fender; yet these dated December have the old type. There was no doubt some overlap in the style change. In addition, the 1924 photos of the "1925" line, dated October 1924, show the rear fenders which flare out from the running board, while these pictures show the earlier style without the flare. It is also quite possible that these photos are of a "1924" Runabout on which the new "1925" pickup box has been installed.

1926

Body Type	#	##	###	####	Shipping Weight Lbs.	Production Total *	
Touring	$290	310	—	—	1633	+	
"	375	—	380	380	1738	364408	**
Runabout	260	290			1550	+	
"	345	—	360	360	1655	342575	**
Pickup	281	—	—	—	+	N/L	
"	366	—	381	381	1736	75406	**
Tudor	580	520	495	495	1972	270331	**
Fordor	660	565	545	545	2004	102732	**
Coupe	520	500	485	485	1860	288342	**
Chassis	225				1167	+	
"	290		300	300	1272	58223	**
Truck	365		325	325	1477	228496	***
"	430		375	375	1577	**	***
TRUCK BODIES ONLY							
Open cab			65	65		***	
Closed cab			85	85		***	
Express body			55	55		***	
Platform body			50	50		***	
Expr. w/Roof/Screen			110	110		***	
Totals (Including foreign)					1655107		

Price effective January 1, 1926.
Price effective February 11, 1926.
Price effective June 6, 1926.
Price effective December 31, 1926 (unchanged from June).
* January 1 to December 31, 1926. (Includes foreign production.)
** Includes starter and 21" demountable wheels.
*** Chassis production figures are for U.S and foreign, of all body types. See production charts for production figures of the various truck bodies. Starter models not listed separately.
+ Early models with 30 x 3-1/2 non-demountable wheels and no starter. Available only on special order by calendar 1926.

Starter was optional on the truck.
Pickup body for Runabout, $25.

NOTE: Starter and 21" demountable wheels were standard on all cars after early calendar 1926. Early 1926 cars with 30 by 3-1/2" demountables (then standard equipment) were 10 pounds lighter than the later cars. Wire wheels available beginning January 1926 in limited quantities as optional equipment, although they were announced in August 1925.

MODEL YEAR DATES: August 1925 to August 1926.

MAJOR MODEL YEAR FEATURES

All-steel construction except for the Fordor Sedan. The Fordor was steel over wood frame, a modification of the 1925 body. Completely new styling; colors offered on the closed cars. Larger and heavier fenders and running boards. Touring and Runabout given doors on driver's side for the first time in U.S. production.

New chassis frame with longer front and rear cross-members. Larger rear wheel brakes. Engine/transmission modified with new pedals, a larger brake drum, different fan mount, coil box mounted on the engine, etc. Fuel tank now in the cowl except on the Fordor Sedan and truck.

COLORS. All cars were painted black, with black fenders initially, in spite of the announcement of colors on the closed cars. Closed cars then offered in colors: green for the Tudor and Coupe, and Maroon for the Fordor. Other options offered later in 1926, perhaps for the "1927" models.

UPHOLSTERY. Imitation leather in the open cars. The pattern was a stitched, vertical-pleat design on both seat bottoms and backs. Closed car upholstery was gray cloth with green stripe on the green cars, and gray with a red stripe on the maroon cars.

FENDERS. All new and of much larger design, front and rear. The trucks continued the previous (1925) type.

SPLASH APRON. All new, rectangular in cross section, now mated with the fenders and body to give the appearance of a more finished product.

RUNNING BOARDS. Pressed steel with embossed diamond pattern but with much smaller diamonds than before. The "Ford" now appeared along the edges instead of in the center. Much wider than the previous design.

HOOD. All new to match the new bodies.

DASHBOARD (Firewall). Steel, now a part of the body cowl (except in the Fordor).

CHASSIS. Similar to the 1925 but with new front and rear cross-members to accommodate the new bodies and fenders.

STEERING COLUMN ASSEMBLY. New design although quite similar to the 1925. Wheel was 17" diameter, made of "Fordite" (synthetic material), and painted black. The wheel spider was pressed steel and painted black. 5:1 gear ratio.

FRONT AXLE. Same as the 1925 cars. Front spindles had the axle located higher on the spindle in order to lower the chassis a bit.

REAR AXLE. Same as 1925 but with larger brakes.

DRIVESHAFT HOUSING. Same as 1925.

REAR RADIUS AND BRAKE RODS. Radius rods were of seamed construction, requiring a right and left side (the seam must face down to allow water to leak out). New design to accommodate the larger rear brakes. Brake rods were shorter than the previous type.

WHEELS. Open cars used 30 by 3-1/2 tires all around. Non-electric open cars used non-demountable rims but all others used the demountables as standard. By calendar 1926, non-demountables were discontinued. Front wheels used taper-roller (Timken) bearings on all models. Hub caps had "Ford" in script letters. 21" demountable wheels standard on closed cars, and optional on the open models. Welded wire wheels offered as an option, apparently beginning in January 1926 according to factory letters to the branches. Standard wire wheel color was black but colors were available as dealer-installed options.

SPRINGS. Non-tapered, front and rear. "U" shaped shackles.

RADIATOR. Same as 1925. Nickle shell offered as an option; became standard on the closed cars. Radiator valence had nickel trim strip to match the nickel shell. Radiators offered in several designs; three and four row round-tube, and flat-tube types.

ENGINE. Similar to 1925 but modified in many ways. Transmission cover now bolted to the rear of the cylinder block. Water outlet served also to mount the fan.

ENGINE PAN. "Four-dip" pan was standard.

OIL FILLER CAP. The mushroom-shaped cap, made of steel, with three flutes.

ENGINE CRANK. Same as 1923 one-piece type with the rolled-in-place handle sleeve.

1926 (Continued)

ENGINE FAN. Now mounted on the water outlet and was adjusted by an eccentric arrangement. Early adjustment was by a "worm screw" cross bolt but this was changed to a new design in which the eccentric was adjusted by a lever (a screwdriver) and held in adjustment by a clamping arrangement. Aluminum pulley of different dimensions from the 1925 type.

FUEL TANK. Mounted in the cowl on all cars except for the Fordor and truck. The Fordor and the truck continued the oval tank under the driver's seat.

MANIFOLDS. Exhaust pipe flared at the manifold and was held in place with the brass nut but with no packing. Intake was cast iron. Vaporizer carburetor had integral intake and exhaust manifolds.

CARBURETORS. Kingston Model L4, or Holley Model NH, and the Holley Vaporizer. Carburetor adjustment was integral with choke and the adjustment needle now had a universal joint intead of the "T" fitting. The Holley Vaporizer, first used in some 1925 models, was installed on many 1926 cars and became standard in late 1926.

CARBURETOR STOVE ASSEMBLY. Same as 1925. Not used on Vaporizer-equipped cars.

MUFFLER. Pressed-steel type with no tail pipe.

COIL BOX ASSEMBLY. Redesigned and now mounted on the left side of the engine. Used the same coils as previously.

TRANSMISSION. Three-pedal standard design. Pedals were of the plain type but the clutch and brake pedals were much wider. The brake drum was made wider, allowing more lining area. The cover was cast iron, and was somewhat wider. The cover had two "ears" which were bolted to the rear of the cylinder block. Tapered inspection door, held with six screws. The door was of pressed steel with an embossed pattern. Bands now had removable ears to allow changing without removing the transmission cover.

LAMPS. Magneto-powered electric type on the non-starter cars, and six-volt electric on the starter models. Nickle-plated rims. Side and tail lamps were similar to 1924 on the non-starter cars. The oil tail lamp was turned sideways with a small red lens on the side (now the rear) and a large clear lens on the door to illuminate the license plate. Starter cars had a tail light which was mounted on the license plate bracket, the same as introduced in 1924, but mounted on the left rear fender. This new style was used through 1927. Electric equipment became standard during 1926 and oil lamps were discontinued.

HORN. Magneto-powered electric on non-starter cars, but six-volt on starter models. Mounted on the left side of the engine, below the coil box, on the water inlet.

WINDSHIELD. Open cars used two-piece, similar to 1925 (but not the same), with new stanchions. Both sections could be opened outward. Tudor and Coupe had one-piece windshield which opened at the bottom, pushing outward. The Fordor Sedan continued the 1925 (and earlier) style.

TOP. (Open cars). Similar to 1925. Top socket had a slight curve at the bottom where it fastened to the body iron.

SPEEDOMETER. No longer standard equipment.

TURTLE DECK. (Runabout) Much larger than before, blending with the body yet still removable. Had no handles and used a larger key than the 1925 style.

1927

Body Type	Factory Price	Shipping Weight Lbs.	Production Total *
Touring	$380	1738	81181
Runabout	360	1655	95778
Pickup	381	1736	****
Tudor Sedan	495	1972	78105
Fordor Sedan	545	2004	22930
Coupe	485	1860	69939
Chassis	300	1272	19280
Truck chassis	325	1477	83202 ***
" "	375	1577	**
TRUCK BODIES ONLY			
Open cab	65		***
Closed cab	85		***
Express body	55		***
Platform body	50		***
Expr. w/roof & Screen	110		***

Total (Includes foreign) 450415

*   January 1, 1927 to December 31, 1927. (Includes foreign production.)
**   Includes starter and demountable wheels.
***   Chassis production figures are for U.S and foreign. Truck figures include trucks of all body types. See production charts. Starter production was not listed separately.
****   Pickups not listed separately from Runabouts. 28,143 pickup bodies were produced in 1927.

Note: Starter and 21" demountable wheels were standard on all cars. Starter was optional on the truck. Wire wheels an option but became standard equipment on some closed cars at some branches during the last few months of production.

Pickup body for Runabout, $25.

Automobile production ended May 26, 1927 but trucks continued for some time.

MODEL YEAR DATES: August 1926 to May 26, 1927.

BODY TYPES: Same as 1926.

MAJOR MODEL YEAR FEATURES
Chassis in passenger cars made of heavier metal; minor construction changes during the year, but generally the same as the 1926 models. Color options on all cars. Wire wheels standard on closed cars made at some assembly plants in 1927 calendar year. Hot-plate carburetor was standard in 1927 models.

COLORS. All cars had black fenders. Various color options, ultimately on all models. Black no longer available except on special order.

UPHOLSTERY. Imitation leather in the open cars. The pattern was a stitched, vertical-pleat design on both seat bottoms and backs. Closed car upholstery was gray cloth with green stripe on the green cars, and gray with a red stripe on the maroon cars, then became gray with a white strip on all closed models.

FENDERS. Same as 1926.

SPLASH APRON. Same as 1926.

RUNNING BOARDS. Same as 1926.

HOOD. Same as 1926. Painted body color.

DASHBOARD (Firewall). Steel, now a part of the body cowl (except in the Fordor).

1927 (Continued)

CHASSIS. Same as 1926. Later models used heavier steel and a stronger rear cross-member. Shock absorbers offered as a dealer installed option, front and rear (mounted at the center of the axle).

STEERING COLUMN ASSEMBLY. Same as 1926.

FRONT AXLE. Same as 1926.

REAR AXLE. Same as 1926. Later versions used a pipe plug filler screw.

DRIVESHAFT HOUSING. Same as 1925.

REAR RADIUS AND BRAKE RODS. Same as 1926.

WHEELS. 21" demountable wheels were standard, wire wheels optional on all models. Late in the model year, black wire wheels became standard on some closed cars in some areas. Wire wheels in colors were dealer-installed options.

SPRINGS. Non-tapered, front and rear. "U" shaped shackles.

RADIATOR. The three-tube and flat-tube radiators were discontinued and the four-tube type became standard. Nickel shell offered as an option on most open cars, was standard on the closed cars.

ENGINE. Similar to 1926. Cylinder head bolts (and some others) were given nickel-plated heads, apparently to "dress up" the car.

ENGINE PAN. "Four-dip" pan was standard.

OIL FILLER CAP. The mushroom-shaped cap, made of steel, with three flutes.

ENGINE CRANK. Same as 1923 one-piece type with the rolled-in-place handle sleeve.

ENGINE FAN. Now mounted on the water outlet and was adjusted by an eccentric arrangement. Aluminum pulley of different dimensions from the 1925 type. Adjustment was made by rotating the eccentric, using a screwdriver (or other type of bar).

FUEL TANK. Mounted in the cowl on all cars except for the Fordor and truck. The Fordor and the truck continued the oval tank under the driver's seat.

MANIFOLDS. Exhaust pipe flared at the manifold and was held in place with the brass nut with no packing. Intake was cast iron, integral with the Vaporizer carburetor which was now standard on all cars.

CARBURETORS. The Holley Vaporizer was standard. A few Kingston Regenerators were also used on some production during calendar 1927.

CARBURETOR STOVE. Not used on Vaporizer-equipped cars.

MUFFLER. Pressed-steel type with no tail pipe.

COIL BOX ASSEMBLY: Same as 1926.

TRANSMISSION. Same as 1926.

LAMPS. Six-volt electric on all cars. Stop light offered as an option. Nickle rims on the headlights, which were now mounted on a tie bar between the front fenders on all cars. (Trucks continue the 1925 style.)

HORN. Six-volt electric now standard.

WINDSHIELD. Same as 1926 but with stronger stanchions.

TOP. (Open cars). Same as 1926.

SPEEDOMETER. No longer standard equipment.

TURTLE DECK (on Runabout). Same as 1926.

The Improved Fords for 1926 and 1927

The TOURING
$310
F. O. B. Detroit

Color Black. All steel body with pronounced streamline effect. Low deeply cushioned seats. Double ventilating windshield. One man top. Standard equipment includes weatherproof side curtains opening with all four doors, windshield wiper, nickeled headlamp rims and four cord tires. Starter and demountable rims $85 extra. Balloon tires $25 extra.

The RUNABOUT
$290
F. O. B. Detroit

Color black. All steel body with streamline treatment. Large compartment under the sweeping rear deck. Double ventilating windshield. Standard equipment includes weatherproof storm curtains opening with both doors, windshield wiper, nickeled headlamp rims and four cord tires. Starter and demountable rims $85 extra. Balloon tires $25 extra.

The FORDOR SEDAN
$565
F. O. B. Detroit

Color Windsor Maroon with upholstery to harmonize. Composite body. Nickeled radiator and headlamp rims. Double ventilating windshield. Plate glass windows with rotary lifts. Standard equipment includes silk curtains on rear windows, dome light, hooded sun visor, windshield wiper, rear view mirror, dash lamp, starter, demountable rims and four cord tires. Balloon tires $25 extra.

By 1925 the records showed that Ford's greatest production year had been 1923, during which 2,032,759 cars and trucks had been assembled. Sales dropped in calendar 1924 to 1,825,646 cars and trucks. During 1925 Ford began an extensive advertising campaign to boost its sagging market share. Competition was snapping at the heels of the company which had dominated the market for so many years. In particular, Chevrolet was capturing more and more of Ford's customers.

Chevrolet and other cars in the same price field offered luxuries and styling, and a level of standard equipment that could not be had in the Ford at any price. All of these cars offered a three-speed, selective-gear transmission and a starter as standard equipment. Many offered a choice of colors. In sheer styling, Ford wasn't even in the same league. No one questioned the quality of the Ford car; mechanically it was as good as most, and better than some — including the Chevrolet — but people were beginning to buy cars because of their styling and other features, rather than on their reputation.

Time had long passed for an all new car if Ford was to continue the exceptional market lead it had enjoyed for so many years. Yet, in spite of the urging of some of his top men, including his son Edsel, Henry Ford had been insistent on retaining the Model T as "the car for the masses."

Henry Ford may have been stubborn but he was no fool. The increasing resistance encountered in the sale of the Ford car did not escape his attention. As usual, his immediate reaction was to blame his declining market on a lack of salesmanship on the part of his dealers. But he finally had to relent; he allowed his engineers to develop a new model. Not a new car — a new model.

This new model was introduced to the public in newspaper and magazine ads on August 26, 1926 as the "Improved Ford." No attempt was made to disguise the fact that his was just a restyling of the previous Fords. In fact dealers were instructed to point out to prospective customers that this was a restyled and more comfortable version of the tried and true Model T that everyone knew and loved. A sales bulletin to the dealers, dated August 30, 1925, reads:

"We do not want the impression to prevail that we are producing new Ford cars.
"Bodies of Ford cars have been materially improved

but the Model T chassis remains unchanged except for lowering the frame and a few other important changes ...."

In an early sales booklet, Ford said:

"Note also that Ford bodies have been entirely redesigned for greater comfort, convenience and added beauty. Yet it important to remember that these cars are in no sense NEW cars. It is advisable to avoid using the word 'NEW' in discussing them. The word 'NEW' implies a redesigning of the chassis as well as the body. While it is true that certain refinements have been added to the chassis and that these are more radical and therefore more conspicuous than any which have heretofore been made, the Model T chassis (though lower) remains the same in design and construction as it has been since 1908. It is the same Ford car, now as always noted for economy, performance and reliability; only the bodies have been redesigned. Do not forget this point and do not fail to stress it in talking to prospective car owners. It is a strong selling point."

There is little question that this "improved" Ford looked a good deal like "more automobile" than the one it replaced. Lower, longer, heavier, more streamlined — and a choice of colors! Well, not really a choice. Initial production offered the Fordor Sedan in "Windsor Maroon." The Coupe and Tudor Sedan were offered in "Channel Green." There were no options; maroon Fordors and green Tudors and Coupes. Period. The Touring and Runabout were available in your choice of black.[1]

All cars featured new nickel-plated headlight rims as standard equipment. In addition, all closed cars came with a nickeled radiator shell as standard, with this being an option on the open cars.[2]

In late 1926, perhaps for the "1927" models, the available colors were expanded. The closed cars were all available in a choice of Royal Maroon, Highland Green or Fawn Gray. The open cars could be had in Phoenix Brown or Gunmetal Blue. Black was no longer listed as a body color. The Roadster Pickups, when ordered from the factory with the pickup bed installed, came in "Ford Commercial Green." According to a factory letter dated March 21, 1927, if a commercial user ordered the pickups on a special order, Ford would paint them all black "to match the color of the existing fleet of Ford cars."

All cars, regardless of body style or color, came with black fenders, splash aprons and running boards. (Running gear was, of course, also black.)

At their introduction, all closed cars came with electrical equipment (starter and generator), windshield wiper (hand operated), rearview mirror, dash light, and demountable rims with 30 by 3-1/2 *cord* tires as standard equipment. It should be noted that *cord* tires were new; the previous tires of that size were *fabric* construction. The cord construction was considerably stronger. While the spare rim was supplied, the tire for that rim was optional equipment. Balloon tires with black-painted wooden wheels were an additional option at $25. Natural-finish wood wheels were available from the factory for installation by the dealers.

"The Ford Tudor Sedan with all steel body, five wire wheels and four balloon tires. Pyroxylin finish in Fawn Gray, Highland Green or Royal Maroon."

"The Ford Fordor Sedan with five wire wheels and four balloon tires, Pyroxylin finish in Fawn Gray, Highland Green or Royal Maroon."

"The Ford Coupe with all steel body, five wire wheels and four balloon tires. Spacious luggage compartment under rear deck. Pyroxylin finish in Fawn Gray, Highland Green or Royal Maroon."

"The Ford Touring Car will all steel body, one-man folding top and weatherproof storm curtains opening with all doors. Four balloon tires. Pyroxylin finish in Gun Metal Blue or Phoenix Brown."

"The Ford Runabout with all steel body. Roomy luggage compartment under rear deck. Weatherproof storm curtains opening with both doors. Four balloon tires. Pyroxylin finish in Gun Metal Blue or Phoenix Brown.

The 1927 Ford line in late 1926

The open cars came standard with 30 by 3-1/2 *cord* tires on non-demountable wheels, no electrical equipment, and no luxuries like a mirror or a dash light. For an additional $85 you could have demountable rims for those 30 by 3-1/2 tires, and the electrical equipment. Balloon tires were $25 on top of that.

Wire wheels (21"), painted black, were listed as a factory-installed option in the initial literature but apparently were delayed until early calendar 1926. Black wire wheels were apparently the standard color option, but after a time they could be ordered in green, straw, Casino red and English vermilion as well, as dealer-installed options. Wire wheels were not standard equipment on any models until late 1926 and early 1927 when black wire wheels became standard on closed cars in some areas, at varying dates, on various models, depending on the assembly plant. For example, the Chicago branch announced black wire wheels as standard equipment on the Fordor Sedan in a letter dated October 28, 1926, noting that the colors could be installed by the dealer at a suggested $10 exchange price. The Fargo, North Dakota branch announced black wire wheels as standard on the Tudor in January 1927, and on the Coupe on February 14, 1927.

1. In spite of the initial announcement of maroon and green closed cars, it seems that these cars were also supplied in black if surviving examples of original cars are used as evidence. Perhaps some of the assembly plants could not be geared up for the new colors initially, in spite of the ads to the contrary.

2. As with the paint colors, seemingly original 1926 cars have been seen with black headlight rims, and closed cars with black radiator shells. While these could have been changed in later years, it doesn't seem likely since there are so many examples.

THE FORDOR SEDAN

THOUSANDS of families who could readily afford to pay more than Ford prices, prefer to drive the Ford Fordor Sedan—because of the additional motoring satisfaction its dependable performance assures.

THE rich moleskin gray body is in pleasing contrast with the black fenders and polished nickel radiator. The upholstery fabric is of a pleasing tone. All in all, the Fordor presents a striking appearance.

IT embodies, of course, Ford reliability—in addition to numerous features that contribute to comfort and convenience. Its beauty may be further enhanced by the addition of special equipment at an extremely moderate cost.

[*545⁰⁰ F. O. B. DETROIT]

Early in the "improved model" production the 30 by 3-1/2 tires and wheels were discontinued and all cars came with balloon tires and black wooden wheels with demountable rims as standard equipment, with natural-finish wood wheels as an option. Electrical equipment apparently also became standard on all cars, although non-starter open cars could be ordered from the factory.

During 1926, two "new" models were shown in the catalogs; the Sports Touring and the Sports Runabout. These were the standard Touring and Runabout but with the addition of five wire wheels (a spare was standard) and the nickeled radiator shell, plus windwings, nickel-plated bumpers front and rear, and a tan top boot.

The list of options available from the factory grew and grew in an effort to stimulate a dying Model T market. Speedometers, shock absorbers, stop lights, automatic windshield wipers, top boots, and so on, plus a number of apparently factory-authorized items of outside manufacture such as the Ruckstell axle.

The "Improved Ford" did stimulate sales for a time. 2,145,787 cars and trucks were manufactured in 1925 (this including the 1925 cars made until August), but dropped to 1,730,514 in 1926, then to just 478,558 in the first five months of 1927 when the end of the era was announced. Sadly, the 1926-27 Fords were somewhat out of style when they were introduced; looking remarkably similar to the Chevrolet models of 1923! The newer look was like a "shot in the arm" but the patient died anyway.

An interesting sidelight: Ford's records show the last Model T to be built (on May 31, 1927) was number 15,007,033 but other Ford records show the

engine with that number was the first one built June 1, 1927, the day following the end of car production.

Oddly, the entire "improved" line of Fords had all-new, all-steel bodies — except for the Fordor Sedan. The Fordor continued in a style similar to that introduced in 1922 as a new 1923 model, except for a new cowl section and a change in the front to the "coupe pillar" styling which had been dropped in mid-1923 (used on the centerdoor sedan and coupe until the "1924" models).

For the first time in its long history the Model T looked like an integrated car. The fenders, splash aprons, running boards and body all fit together so as to look like one unit. Gone were the gaping holes, and the flapping fenders of the previous models. The styling was contemporary — similar to the competition which had a similar style for years — and then changed, when Ford caught up. The fenders were fuller, and more gracefully curved. The running boards were wider. The bodies, except for the Fordor, lower and much more attractive.

The radiator shell, which Ford said was "higher" was the same as that which had been used since mid-1923. The nickel-plated shells were made of brass but otherwise interchangeable with the earlier type. (The black-painted shells continued being made of steel.) From the radiator shell on back, though, it was all new. The hood was larger, longer, and had more louvers. The windshields were further to the rear, the seats were lower, and the bodies themselves were lower. The cars appeared more "streamlined" but, alas, all this was at the expense of comfort (in spite of Ford's words to the contrary). In the open cars in particular, the front seat

THE TUDOR SEDAN

THE UNPARALLELED demand for the Ford Tudor Sedan definitely establishes it as America's most popular enclosed family car—bought and used by people from every walk of life.

WITH ample room for five passengers, with all-steel body, and with the performance for which Ford cars are famous everywhere—the Tudor offers the greatest Sedan value the world has ever seen. It is priced far lower than any other Sedan on the market and for a small additional cost it may reflect the owner's taste by the addition of colored wheels and other special features as illustrated.

UTMOST riding ease is assured by the deeply-cushioned seats, set at the most comfortable angle. Both front seats tilt forward, giving easy access to the rear seat through either door.

DEEPLY cushioned upholstery harmonizes with exterior finish. Nickeled radiator and headlamp rims, windshield wiper, beaded sun-visor, rear view mirror, dash lamp, starter and four balloon tires are standard equipment.

[$495 f.o.b. Detroit Special Equipment Extra]

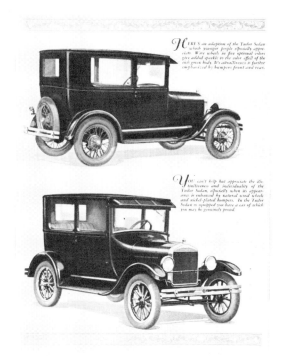

HERE'S an adaption of the Tudor Sedan which younger people especially appreciate. Wire wheels, in five optional colors, give added sparkle to the color effect of the inch green body. Its attractiveness is further emphasized by bumpers front and rear.

YOU can't help but appreciate the distinctiveness and individuality of the Tudor Sedan, especially when its appearance is enhanced by natural wood wheels and nickel-plated bumpers. In the Tudor Sedan so equipped you have a car of which you may be genuinely proud.

passenger compartment was cramped and difficult to enter and leave. Ford had at last provided a door on the driver's side but the company left the brake lever in its normal position. With the lowered steering wheel and cramped compartment, it took some maneuvering to get seated. A tall man would find his knees against the instrument panel.

The new bodies were all metal except for the floorboards. Upholstery was nailed into place by using tack strips of a cardboard-like material. The cars were very solid when compared with the previous design, so much so that the Model T gained a new personality.

When introduced in late 1908, the Model T was over-powered when compared with its competition. Through the years it gained weight and suffered from some engine detuning. The 1926 models were almost the last word in weight addition, although they would become even more obese before the end, and this was just about the final blow to "peppy" performance.

The "improved" Fords were lower in height than the previous models. This height reduction was accomplished by not only reducing the height of the bodies themselves (except for the Fordor) but also by lowering the frame by a redesign of the front spindles, and a reduction of the crown in the front spring. The rear cross-member had a deeper curve which lowered the chassis somewhat as well. These modifications lowered the chassis height one and one-half inches.

The chassis frame, while basically the same as the previous models, had a new rear cross-member, and steel brackets replaced the forgings which supported the front fenders. Initially, the rear cross-member was a channel section similar to the earlier

design except for being longer and with a higher crown. During production it was modified to have flanges (or lips) on the underside, and then still later the entire frame was made of heavier gauge steel.

The rear axle was changed from the previous design by the addition of larger rear brake drums, and backing plates which supported larger brake shoes, now lined with an asbestos material. The new brakes used eleven-inch diameter steel drums, and were effective enough to have been used as the regular service brakes, had they been so connected. Ford preferred the transmission brake, however, so the new brakes were still operated by the hand lever. Internal leather seals were used at the outer rear axle bearings, in addition to the usual external felt seals, to eliminate rear axle oil leaks. Apparently little faith was placed in the new seal because provision was also made for oil which might bypass the seals to leak out without soaking the brake linings. Experience proved that oil would, indeed, leak out, the linings did get soaked, and the rest leaked out on the wheels. Later production rear end housings used a half-inch pipe-plug drain plug instead of the usual hex-head screw. The date of this change is not known but is believed to have been in late 1926 or in calendar 1927. Aside from these modifications, and new radius and brake rods, the rear axle was the same as the earlier models.

The engine, while basically the same, had a number of modifications. Most noticeable was the new fan mounting; now a part of the water outlet casting. Initial production of this new mounting had a "worm-gear" adjustment; the fan shaft bolted to an eccentric collar and the belt tension was adjusted by rotating this collar by means of a clamp screw which engaged this collar like a worm gear. Turning the clamp screw also turned the collar and when the adjustment was correct, the adjusting screw was locked with a nut. Unfortunately, tightening this lock nut could easily break the casting. Later versions had a more simplified design in which the eccentric was rotated by means of a tool which engaged two cast-in lugs, and the adjustment was locked by a washer and nut on the end of the fan bearing shaft. With this new fan mounting, the front timing gear cover was slightly modified to eliminate the old fan adjusting arrangement.

The ignition coil box, mounted on the firewall since 1908, was moved to a position on the left top of the engine. This location required a redesign of the horn mounting bracket. Instead of being mounted on the upper-left side of the engine, the horn bracket now was mounted on the two water inlet mounting screws below the coil box.

Initial production used a Holley NH or Kingston L-4 carburetor with the universal joint fitting on the adjustment screw. During 1925 Ford had combined the carburetor adjustment with the choke pull rod, and this feature was carried over into the new models. Also supplied during the year was a new carburetor system called a Vaporizer. Designed by Holley, and used earlier on some 1925 cars, this carburetor system drew fuel past a thin steel plate which was heated by exhaust gasses, giving better vaporization of the poor fuels of the day. This system had been used on the Fordson tractor, which was designed to run on kerosene (after being started on gasoline). The Vaporizer did give better performance on the poor fuels but general engine power was decreased still further. For pure fuel economy, though, the Vaporizer was hard to beat. Used in an ever-increasing portion of production, by mid-July

1926 the Vaporizer was used on all production. Holley was the major supplier of these carburetor systems but Kingston also supplied a similar unit called a "Regenerator."

All 1926-27 engines used the so-called "four-dip" pan. This engine pan had been standard equipment since 1924. Interestingly, all these pans were made (beginning in 1924) with sufficient room for the larger transmission brake drum introduced in the 1926 models, which might suggest that Ford had been planning this change for over a year before it appeared.

The transmission now had a brake drum which was 5/8 inch wider than the previous models. The added surface aided transmission band life but this advantage was somewhat offset by the increased weight of the cars. Internally, steel "shoes" were installed over the cast-iron bosses on which the metal clutch plates rode. This gave much better wear and resulted in better clutch operation, even after considerable use. Demountable-ear transmission bands, introduced by Ford in 1925 production, were standard. The new transmission cover, which also featured larger brake and clutch pedals, was somewhat larger, allowing easier band changing. The magneto post now screwed into the cover like a spark plug (1/2 inch pipe threads) instead of being held with the three screws which had been used since the introduction of the Model T.

A further modification of the engine-transmission assembly was the modification of the cylinder block casting and the transmission cover so that the two now were bolted together at the top, resulting in a much more rigid assembly. Added, too, were steel brackets which ran from these bolts to the chassis at the rear engine mounting, relieving the strain on

THE COUPE

DISTINCTIVE features include nickeled radiator and headlamp rims, one-piece windshield, beaded cowl visor and a roomy luggage compartment. Standard equipment includes starter, windshield wiper, rear view mirror, dash lamp and balloon tires.

THE COUPE is one of the most popular of Ford cars, combining an unusually smart appearance with exceptional utility.

It is extensively used by commercial and professional men who demand extraordinary closed car service at the lowest possible cost. The sturdy all-steel body is designed to afford the maximum riding and driving comfort, while many unusual features have been provided to increase the car's utility.

In common with all Ford cars, the Coupe embodies those basic features of Ford design which have maintained Ford leadership throughout the years. And for those who want the dash and vigor of added color, the Coupe may be equipped with wire wheels in five optional colors, or natural wood wheels, and other special equipment shown. There is no other Coupe on the market that offers such value—as thousands of owners will testify.

[$485 F. O. B. DETROIT Special Equipment Extra]

ALWAYS a smart car, the Coupe assumes a new air of distinction when equipped with natural wood wheels. This form a pleasant contrast with rich coloring of the body, a feature which people of good taste are among the first to recognize and appreciate. The spare tire and wheel mounted at the rear also add to the car's attractiveness.

To the standard Coupe are sometimes added colored wire wheels contrasting with the rich green body, a lively touch which adds to the appearance of grace and flashiness. Bumpers front and rear are the final item of equipment, leaving nothing to be desired for comfort, convenience and driving safety.

the mounting "ears" which had a tendency to break in the earlier design.

All cars except for the Fordor Sedan now had the gasoline tank mounted in the cowl. The filler was located under a door similar to the cowl vent. (In the Fordor, the cowl "vent" was a *vent*; on the other models very little air could pass the fuel tank.) This location greatly aided fuel flow, eliminating the flow problems the T had on steep hills. The fuel sediment bulb was now located on the firewall inside the engine compartment, making it much easier to drain. The Fordor's tank was located under the driver's seat as in the previous models.

Initially, the headlights were mounted on flanged posts which bolted to the fender apron. In later 1926 production, several types of tie bars were added between the fenders which served two purposes: (1) tying the fenders together made the front assembly more rigid, and (2) The introduction of front bumpers as optional equipment had created a problem by obscuring the license plate. Law enforcement agencies complained and the license plate was moved up to this headlamp tie bar. Later 1926, and all 1927 production used a revised tie bar on which the headlamps were mounted directly.

Alas — all this was to be in vain. In spite of the "improvements," the public continued its swing away from the Ford offering. Chevrolet had risen like the Phoenix from the ashes in the early 1920's to a close second in 1926. Model T production was halted in May of 1927 and the Ford plant was closed down for the first time in its history (except for the month of January, 1921). To most, it was the end of an era — almost like a death in the family.

Ford continued producing Model T engines while the plant was "closed," and the changeover to the all-new Model A began. Dealers were left stranded, with no product to sell for the better part of a year. Many switched to other makes of automobiles but the majority made-do by selling used cars and servicing Model T's.

The new Model A was an instant success. Chevrolet had gained first place in sales in 1927, mainly because there was no Ford competition during most of the year, but Ford regained the first place position in 1928. Unfortunately, while the Model A was an excellent car — far superior to the Model T — it was obsolete when it was born. Chevrolet countered with its "six" in 1929 and in 1931 again became first in sales, a position it then held for almost thirty years.

Ford had lost its position of leadership. There have been a few years when the Ford (brand) car was the first in sales but General Motors rose to the dominant position in the U.S. market. Even the upstart Chrysler Corporation outsold Ford during some of the Thirties and Forties.

But it was Ford's Model T that put the world on wheels. When the 'T' was introduced, the world traveled for the most part on horseback or in horse-drawn vehicles. The Model T Ford changed all that almost in the "twinkling of an eye" of man's history. The Model T may have had its faults, but the ability to gain almost universal love and respect was not one of them. The Model T had truly been "the Universal Car."

THE RUNABOUT

THE FORD RUNABOUT is an attractive car with all-steel body of graceful lines and with many features of convenience and utility. The doors are wide and give easy access; the seat is low, deep-cushioned and extremely comfortable. Under the sweeping rear deck is a large dust and rainproof luggage compartment.

THIS type of body mounted on the standard Ford chassis gives a car that is light in weight, fast in traffic and inexpensive to operate.

THE Runabout is the ideal personal car, either for business or social use, available at a price that almost anyone can afford. It can be made a car of extreme individuality by equipping it as shown in these illustrations.

[$360 00 F. O. B. DETROIT
Special Equipment Extra]

The catalog illustrations shown above, as well as those on the previous pages, show the 1926 models prior to the use of Pyroxylin paints and the use of colors on the open cars.

There is no clear date of a change to "1927" models but Ford traditionally began its fiscal year on August 1. As a consequence, those cars built after July 1926 have been considered "1927" models. The availability of colors on the open cars was announced in August 1926 and using the August date as the beginning of the "1927" models, all "1926" open cars were black and the "1927" open cars were in color. As with almost everything else regarding the Model T, though, there were probably exceptions.

The 1926 Ford Coupe as it appeared in late 1925. There is a very thin stripe running about one-half inch below the belt line molding, beginning at the front of the door and extending around the back to the front of the opposite front door. No stripe is visible (in the original photograph) across the cowl as in other original photos. Ford claimed the Coupes were all green but there seems to be no difference in the shading between the body and the fenders or splash apron in this black and white photo. *Photo from the Collections of the Henry Ford Museum and Greenfield Village.*

1926-1927

The 1926 Model T Ford Coupe at the time of its introduction. Note the lack of the tie bar between the headlights, the odd position of the license plate, and the use of the rear axle with the small-drum brakes. Note, too, that the striping runs around the belt line but not down the front pillars. This photo probably was taken before production really got under way. It's hard to tell from the original black and white photo, but there doesn't seem to be a difference in shading between the fenders, aprons and running boards, so the car may have been all black. *Photo from the Collections of the Henry Ford Museum and Greenfield Village.*

FORD'S INTRODUCTORY ANNOUNCEMENT
(August 1925)

The following is a direct copy of the text from Ford's announcement to its dealers in August 1925. Keep in mind that a number of features were later modified or changed entirely. This reproduction is for interest only and should not be used as a guide as to what should or should not appear in the 1926 and 1927 Model T Fords.

Information for Ford Dealers and Salesmen on Improved Ford Cars

Beauty of design is so conspicuously evident in the improved Ford cars that this improvement immediately impresses itself upon everyone who sees them. Open and closed body types have been redesigned with modern stream-line treatment. Many other important changes in bodies and chassis contribute to comfort and convenience as well. These changes include the following:

Chassis frame lowered
Bodies lower and longer (except Fordor)
Bodies redesigned (except Fordor)
Closed cars in color
Improved upholstery with lower, deeper cushioned seats
Nickeled radiator shells on closed cars.
One piece windshield on Tudor and Coupe
Larger, better looking fenders
Fuel tank under cowl (except Fordor)
Added accessories on all cars
Coil box and sediment bulb more conveniently located
Improved brakes in rear axle and transmission
Two doors on Runabout; four doors on Touring Car.

It is of particular importance that the bodies of all closed and open cars are all-steel throughout, except the Fordor which has a composite body. All-steel bodies mean added strength and durability.

1926-1927   380

The early 1926-style Touring Car. Furnished in black only until August 1926, all 1926 models came standard with nickel-plated headlight rims. The black radiator shell was standard on all open cars but the nickeled shell could be had as an option. This car was equipped with the optional balloon tires and wheels (and electric equipment) which became standard equipment, probably before calendar 1926. *Photo from the Collections of the Henry Ford Museum and Greenfield Village.*

Note also that Ford bodies have been entirely redesigned for greater comfort, convenience and added beauty. Yet it is important to remember that these are in no true sense NEW cars. It is advisable to avoid using the word "NEW" in discussing them. The word "NEW" implies a redesigning of the chassis as well as the body. While it is true that certain refinements have been added to the chassis and that these are more radical and therefore more conspicuous than any which have heretofore been made, the model T chassis (though lower) remains the same in design and construction as it has been since 1908. It is the same Ford car, now as always noted for economy, performance and reliability; only the bodies have been redesigned. Do not forget this point and do not fail to stress it in talking to prospective car owners. It is a strong selling point.

In telling your customer of these changes, it is not necessary to emphasize the details. Your prospect is more interested in the beauty of the car, to which especial thought has been directed, and in the added comfort and convenience than he is in how these improvements were achieved. However, the detailed information given in the following pages is intended to prepare you fully to answer any and all questions which are likely to be asked concerning the improved Ford cars.

APPEARANCE

A pronounced stream-line treatment has been effected in all body types. The best way to appreciate this is to actually see the cars. If you can get your prospect into your showroom, you will find that little salesmanship is necessary as far as the beauty feature of these cars is concerned. They are so conspicuously different in design that they speak for themselves.

Many other factors contribute to appearance of the improved body designs. The chassis frame is lower. The bodies are longer and lower.

The actual figures are comparatively unimportant. The big fact is that the top of the body has been lowered and the seats have been lowered.

The beauty of the bodies has been further enhanced by the slightly raised radiator, larger hood, nickeled head lamp rims and in the case of closed cars nickeled radiator shells.

Fenders — Changes in fender design are of particular importance. Like the bodies, Ford fenders have been completely redesigned to give added

The 1926 Sport Touring announced in early calendar 1926. This was the standard Touring, but with a nickel radiator shell, windwings, a tan top boot, and bumpers. The top and body were still black but a khaki top boot (and gypsy curtains) soon became available as options. Wire wheels, announced at the introduction of the Improved Fords, apparently did not become available until about January 1926. *Photo from the Collections of the Henry Ford Museum and Greenfield Village.*

beauty to the cars. They are now of the crown type, wider, larger and more attractive. They extend lower both front and rear, affording maximum protection against splashing mud and water.

Running boards are also wider and nearer the ground.

Closed Cars in Colors — Ford closed body types are now finished in attractive colors. The Tudor and Coupe are a deep Channel Green, and the Fordor Sedan is in rich Windsor Maroon. Open cars remain black.

Accessories — Standard equipment on all closed cars include windshield wiper, rear view mirror, windshield visor and dash light. The Fordor Sedan has, also, the dome-light, as before. Windshield wiper is standard on open cars.

Windshields — On the Tudor Sedan and the Coupe, the plate glass windshield is of one piece opening forward. A passage way at the base of the windshield directs the ventilation downward into the front compartment when the windshield is slightly opened. Plate glass windshield in the open body types are of the double ventilating type both halves opening. The windshield on the Fordor has been redesigned to conform with the improved cowl. Lower half is stationary and there is a cowl

ventilator as before.

Radiator and Hood — The radiator is 5/8" higher and the hood larger, more louvres (side openings) in the hood permit freer circulation of air.

Radiator shells of bright nickel, polished and buffed are standard on closed cars.

Windows — All windows in all closed body types are of Ford plate glass and lower flush with the molding. They operate by lifters set conveniently within reach.

Doors — All doors open forward on all body types except rear doors on the Fordor Sedan.

Seats — All seats in the Tudor Sedan, Coupe, Touring and Runabout have been lowered and set further back and with improved cushion effect, providing greater comfort.

Tire Carrier — A newly simplified design of arm type tire carrier accommodates either the Ford wire wheel or demountable rim. It is set at the most attractive angle to add to the appearance of the car.

Tires — Standard equipment on all Ford cars includes cord tires in place of fabric as formerly.

Headlights — The headlights have polished nickel rims, are set higher and further apart and are attached to pressed fender supports.

The 1926 Fordor Sedan. From the coupe pillar in front to the rear it was the same body as the 1924-25 cars. The front pillars and cowl section were new to match the new hood and styling of the rest of the Ford line. The nickel radiator shell and headlight rims were standard on the closed cars. The standard color for the Fordor was Windsor Maroon, with black fenders, splash aprons and running boards, although in this photo, dated November 30, 1925, it appears to be all black. *Photo from the Collections of the Henry Ford Museum and Greenfield Village.*

Taillight and License Bracket — On all body types the taillight and license plate bracket are now located on the rear left fender.

CHASSIS CHANGES

Chassis Frame — The chassis frame has been dropped one and one-half inches. This has been accomplished without materially affecting the road clearance by lowering the crown of the springs one inch. The spindle has been raised on the spindle body one-half inch.

Coil Box — The coil box is now mounted on the left-hand side of the motor. This change is a great convenience for servicing as access to the coil box may now be had by simply raising the hood. The mechanic need no longer enter the car to make coil box adjustments.

Fan — The fan has been raised to add to its cooling efficiency. Fan belt adjustments are now more quickly and simply made. This is due to a special fan belt bracket and eccentric adjustment. The bracket is designed as an integral part of the cylinder head outlet.

Transmission Brake Band — The transmission brake band has been increased from 1-1/8 inches to 1-3/4 inches wide, an improvement which contributes to the ease and smoothness of braking. In addition, the wider brake band lining requires infrequent adjustment and will last much longer than heretofore. All transmission bands now have removable ears to facilitate changing and band lining. Hardened steel shoes have been placed over clutch casing keys to prevent wear.

Hand Brakes — Brake drums in the rear axle have been increased from 8 inches in diameter to 11 inches in diameter and the width has been increased from 1-5/32 inches to 1-1/2 inches. Brake shoes are now covered with asbestos composition, eliminating the old method in which braking was effected by direct contact of cast iron shoes on the steel brake drum. Being of the self energizing type, these new improved brakes render braking smooth and positive.

Pedals — Brake and clutch pedals are farther apart and have wider surfaces with flange at the side to prevent the driver's foot from slipping.

Steering Wheel — The steering wheel on open and closed cars was recently increased from 16 to 17 inches in diameter. In all types except the Fordor Sedan the wheel has been set three inches lower for

A pre-production 1926 Runabout. Note the 1925 (small drum) rear brakes and the position of the license plate (which is the same plate that is on the Touring car shown elsewhere). *Photo from the Collections of the Henry Ford Museum and Greenfield Village.*

greater comfort and ease of driving as seats have been moved back and lowered. There is a 5 to 1 reduction in the steering mechanism to accommodate balloon tires.

Gasoline Tank — In the Tudor Sedan, Coupe, Touring and Runabout the fuel tank is now placed beneath the cowl in front of the instrument board. This is a marked improvement, the importance of which cannot be over estimated. The gasoline now flows from the tank to the carburetor at an abrupt angle, even when negotiating the steepest hills. The tank can be readily filled from outside. The filler cap is located in the middle of the cowl under a rain proof cover, having the appearance of a cowl ventilator. A large trough and overflow pipe has been provided to carry any spillage directly to the ground.

There is a marked convenience in having the gas tank located under the cowl for it brings the sediment bulb, usually so difficult to access, to a convenient location under the hood where water can easily be drained from the gasoline which is so necessary in freezing weather as all automobile owners already know. Any Ford salesman can readily see that the hazard has not been increased, for the ventilation and overflow provided has been a distinct improvement. The dash provides an

adequate separation from the motor. Vacuum tanks containing a quart of gasoline and being suspended almost over the motors have not been considered dangerous, and the location of our gasoline tank is much improved over these.

TUDOR SEDAN

Body in Color — The Improved Tudor Sedan is finished in deep Channel Green.

New Upholstery — The upholstery fabric is especially strong and durable. It is of a gray tone with a fine green stripe to harmonize with the exterior color of the car. The headlining is a fabric of gray mixture and the floor carpet is gray with a suggestion of green. The back curtain is of gray silk.

Driver's Seat Tilts — The driver's seat, in addition to the other front seat, is of the full bucket type, tilting forward with much deeper cushioning, giving added comfort. When tilted forward, rear seat passengers may either enter or leave the car without disturbing occupant of the other front seat, which is also deeper cushioned with higher back. Rear seat also is lowered and deeper cushioned. All occupants of the car have greater riding comfort, being seated nearer the road and having more leg room.

Visibility — Visibility for the driver has been materially increased by new design front pillars on either side of the one-piece windshield. They are narrower, this giving the driver better vision in every direction.

Visor — Another marked contribution to driving comfort is the redesigned leather cloth sun visor which is closed completely at both ends. It is of much better appearance.

Accessories — The Tudor Sedan now comes equipped with windshield wiper, rear view mirror and dash lamp. Starter and demountable rims are included as standard equipment.

Changes in Dimensions — Following are the approximate changes in dimensions between the former and the improved Ford Tudor Sedan:

Body — 4 inches lower from top to road. 3-1/2 inches longer

Seats — 2-1/2 inches lower from top of seat to floor. This with 1-1/2 inch drop in chassis brings the seat 4 inches nearer the ground.

Distance from back panel of front seats to front of rear seat increased 2 inches, affording more knee room. Foot room also is increased.

COUPE

Color — The improved Coupe is finished in a deep Channel Green.

New Upholstery Fabric — The upholstery fabric in the Coupe, is the same as in the Tudor Sedan. The back curtain is of gray silk.

Beauty — Improvements in the Coupe are most pronounced. The sweep of the body lines from the radiator cap back to the spare tire carrier is startling. By no means the least important feature is the rear deck which is full width of the body enclosure and extends well back over the rear spring with fenders bolted to the body. The rear deck compartment is not only wider and longer, but deeper as well. Rust-proof compartment lid hinges are concealed at the juncture of the rear deck and

body enclosure. The wide double steel panel lid sweeps backward and down almost to the floor level of the compartment. When opened, access to the compartment is extremely easy. An automatic catch fixes the lid firmly opened. This compartment is waterproof and dustproof. Hidden channels carry any rain or moisture leakages around the lid to the ground.

Seat — Redesigned with deeper cushion and windshield same as in the Tudor Sedan.

Recess Shelf — The shelf at the back of seat is 5 inches wider than in the former Coupe and affords more room to accommodate parcels or small luggage.

Door — Door is wider, making it easier to enter and leave the car.

Accessories — Same as Tudor Sedan

Changes in Dimensions — Following are the approximate changes in dimensions between former and Improved Ford Coupe:

Body — 4-1/2 inches lower from top to road. 3-1/2 inches longer.

Seats — 2-1/2 inches lower from top of seat to floor. This with 1-1/2 inch drop of body on chassis brings seat 4 inches nearer the ground.

FORDOR SEDAN

Color — The improved Fordor Sedan is finished in rich Windsor Maroon.

New Upholstery — The upholstery fabric is especially strong and durable. It is of a gray tone with a fine red stripe to harmonize with the exterior coloring of the car. The headlining is a fabric of gray mixture to harmonize with the upholstery cloth. Floor carpet is gray with a suggestion of red. The window curtains are of gray silk.

Seats — Same as former Fordor Sedan.

Gasoline Tank — Under the front seat as before.

Changes in Dimensions — Following are the approximate changes in dimensions between the former and the Improved Ford Fordor Sedan:

Body dropped 1-1/2 inches on the chassis. No other changes.

RUNABOUT

Color — The improved Ford Runabout is finished in black. The upholstery is of Ford leather cloth.

Appearance — The sweep of the body lines from the radiator cap back to the spare tire carrier suggests the sports car more conspicuously perhaps than the other improved body types. By no means the least important feature of the improved Runabout is the rear deck which is now the full width of the body and extends well back over the rear spring with fenders bolted to the body. The rear deck compartment is not only wider and longer, but deeper as well. Rustproof compartment lid hinges are concealed at the juncture of the rear deck and the body. The wide double steel panel lid sweeps backward and down almost to the floor level of the compartment. When opened, access to the compartment is extremely easy. An automatic catch fixes the lid firmly opened and it must be released by hand in order to close down the lid which locks. This compartment is actually waterproof and dustproof. Hidden channels carry any rain or moisture leakages around the lid to the ground.

Two Doors — An additional door is provided at the driver's left, a new convenience. Both doors open forward and are wider than before.

Storm Curtains — are on uprights and open with the doors.

Seat — has been completely redesigned for increased comfort.

Changes in Dimensions — The following are the approximate changes in dimensions between the former and the Improved Runabout:

Body — 4-1/2 inches lower from top to road. 7-3/4 inches longer.

Seat — 2-1/2 inches lower from top of seat to floor. This with 1-1/2 inch drop in chassis brings the seat 4 inches nearer the ground. Seat is 3 inches wider.

TOURING CAR

Color — The improved touring car is finished in black. The upholstery is of Ford leather cloth.

Four Doors — An additional door is provided at the driver's left which is of genuine convenience both to driver and passenger. All four doors open forward and are wider than before.

Storm Curtains — are on uprights and open with the doors.

One Man Top — The top is a genuine one man top of Ford leather cloth. Improved design makes it extremely easy for one man to raise or lower the top.

Compartments — are provided under both front and rear seats for tools and curtains.

Seats — have been completely redesigned for increased comfort.

Changes in Dimensions — Following are the approximate changes in dimensions between the former and the Improved Ford Touring Car:

Body — 4-1/2 inches lower from top to road. 3-1/2 inches longer.

Seats — 2-1/2 inches lower from top of seat to floor. This with 1-1/2 inch drop in chassis brings the seats 4 inches nearer the ground. Front seat is 3 inches wider. Rear seat is 5 inches wider. Distance between back panel of front seat and the rear seat is increased 3-1/2 inches, giving more room for passengers. This increased width also provides additional floor space between the seats to accommodate a bushel basket, an advantage for farmers.

Another rattle gone! An improvement in the 1926-27 cars was the modification of the front motor mount/spring clip, in which a tapped hole was added. A screw through the radiator apron which mated with this hole cured all. The photo above is without the apron; below with the apron in place.

At the time of the introduction of the "improved " Fords, the headlights were mounted on flanged posts which were bolted to the fenders as shown in the upper left photo. During 1926 several types of tie rods were used between the fenders, three of which are shown here. Note the variations is design. The upper right has a channel-type cross rod, the center left has a rolled-steel rod, and the center right has a solid rod which is threaded into the castings under the lamps and provides some adjustment. Whether these are accessory or genuine Ford is not known. The final design, shown in the lower photo, has the headlamps mounted on the tie rod. The front license plate was mounted on the tie rod in front of the radiator, after early 1926 production.

1926-1927

The radiator shell on all closed cars (after early production) was nickel plated. The lower radiator apron had a nickel trim strip to match the shell. Open cars and trucks were furnished with a black steel shell and had no trim on the apron, but the nickeled parts could be ordered as an option.

Running boards were completely new, wider, and had a smaller diamond pattern. They were interchangeable from side to side.

The fenders and aprons were also all new, of much more substantial construction, better looking and larger. The fenders, aprons, and runningboards fit together tightly and gave the cars a much more finished look.

Excluding the initial production on which 30 by 3-1/2 tires (with and without demountable rims, non-demountable on the non-starter open cars only), were used, the standard wheel was as shown above. These "balloon" wheels used 4:40 by 21 tires. The standard color for the wood wheels was black but beginning in early 1926 natural-finish spokes were also offered.

Wire wheels were an option (after the early production cars in 1925) until very late 1926 when black wire wheels became standard on the Fordor, and later on the Coupe and Tudor, at some assembly plants. Optional colors available in wire wheels were red, straw, and two shades of green.

Spare tires were carried on either a flanged post (Coupe and Runabouts) or a tubular bracket (Sedans and Touring). The same bracket was used for either the wooden wheels or the wire wheels. A "Y" bracket adapter held the rims of the wooden wheels to the bracket flange while the wire wheels fit the bracket directly.

1926-27 Spindle Design

In order to lower the chassis, the front spring was given less arch and the spindle was moved up one-half inch on the steering knuckle. The two upper photos show the new spindle while the lower shows the older style for comparison. The rear frame cross-member had a deeper arch, which lowered the chassis at the rear by allowing the chassis to sit lower on the spring.

The rear axle now had the larger brake drums and backing plates. The backing plates came in several types. The brake shoes were supported by little clips on the backing plate. Some designs used clips which were riveted in place, other had the clips pressed out of the plate itself. Both types came with or without embossed reinforcing ribs. Internally, a leather oil seal was added just inside the outer bearing (shown in the lower right photo) but there were no other changes. In very late production the oil filler plug was changed from the hex-head screw to a 1/2 inch pipe plug with a square hole for a special wrench.

Spindle Design Prior to 1926

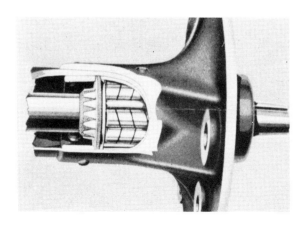

1926-1927

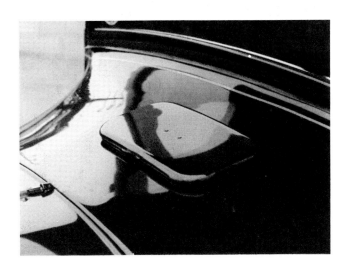 

The cowl vent on all cars except the Fordor opened to expose the gasoline tank filler cap. The filler was surrounded by a drip pan which would collect any spilled fuel and direct it outside the passenger compartment by means of a pipe to the ground. The location of the gasoline tank blocked any flow of air through the vent for cooling, and in this respect, the vent on the Fordor was more effective.

The instrument panel in the Coupe was identical to that in the Tudor (and these two body styles had many other parts in common). The panel was painted the same as the body color. The dash light was standard equipment in the closed cars, and optional on the Touring and Roadster. (The "gear shift" lever in the center photo is an accessory, used with the Ruckstell rear axle.)

1926-1927

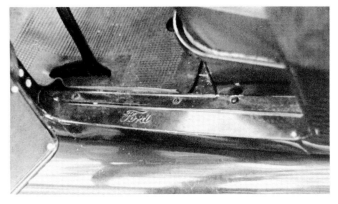

A minor change was made in the body sill. Early production cars used an aluminum step plate over the sill, adding a bit of "flash" as shown below. This was discontinued in later cars; the steel sill plate now being embossed with the "Ford" script as shown in the photo at the upper left.

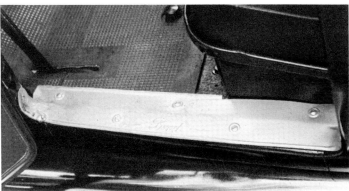

The top bows and sockets were quite similar to those of the 1923-1925 models except for the curve at the bottom where they fasten to the body. Side curtains, supplied as standard equipment, were new and designed to open with the doors. This was made possible by the use of a metal rod which fit into a hole in the doors and which supported the door sections of the curtains.

1926-1927

Subtle changes were made in the Touring and Runabout body construction during production in 1926. Note the "step" in the door jamb in the earlier bodies, near the top where the front cowl panel joins the front side panel (in both the Touring and the Runabout). This was "smoothed out" in later production as shown in the photos at the right.

1926-1927

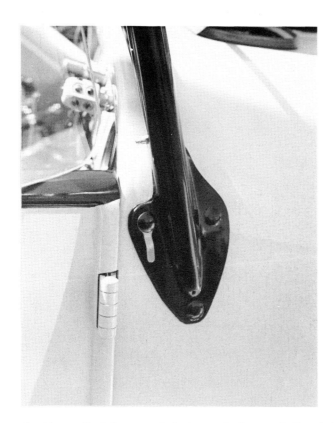 

A seldom-noticed change made during production was in the windshield stanchion of the open cars. The earlier type, shown at the left, proved to be somewhat weak at its mounting point. The Later version appears as at the right. Notice how the rear side of the mounting flange of the later style is flared into the post, similar the front side, while the earlier style was not.

The Roadster Pickups initially had no provision for carrying a spare wheel or rim but by 1927 Ford offered this side-mount bracket as an "added convenience" (a term often used to describe such improvements in the Model T).

Commercial vehicles (the Roadster Pickup and the TT trucks) used a special taillight bracket which mounted below the bed or pickup box. This bracket had been used in 1925 models as well. While this bracket could have been used on those Roadsters which were converted to pickups later, most of the converted types used the standard passenger car bracket on the left rear fender.

Rear view of the Ford combination stop and taillight, offered as an option in 1926 and 1927.

The standard taillight for all models other than the early open cars which did not have electrical equipment (and used an oil lamp) is shown here. This was the same license plate bracket and lamp that was introduced in 1924, but it was now mounted on a bracket which bolts to the left rear fender.

The taillight lens, inside the metal housing, was cup-shaped and of clear glass. A slot in the bottom side of the housing allowed illumination of the license plate, while a red plastic disk over the "bottom" of this cup provided the red color to the rear.

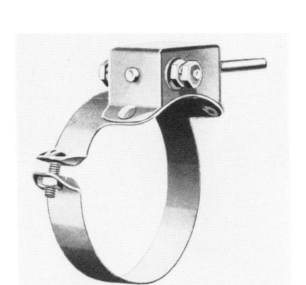

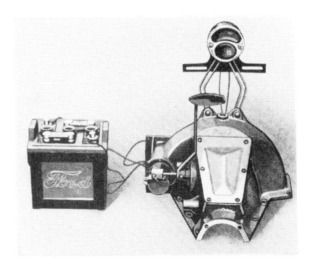

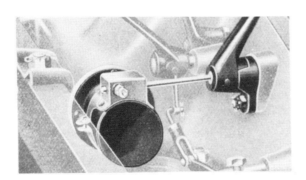

Ford offered a combination tail and stop light as a dealer-installed option. The stop light switch, taillight assembly and dealer display arrangement is shown here.

A number of changes were made in the engine compartment. The most noticeable change was the coil box, now located on the upper-left side of the engine. The horn, previously in this position, was moved down and now mounted on the water inlet fitting. The fan was moved up to the water outlet and was adjusted by means of an eccentric mounting.

Early production cars used either the Holley Vaporizer, the Holley NH or Kingston L-4 carburetor, as did the last of the 1925 models. All used the universal joint needle valve to accommodate the combination dash adjuster/choke pull rod. As the supply increased, the Vaporizer began replacing the standard carburetors, and by late 1926 all Fords used the Holley Vaporizer.

1926-1927

The Vaporizer, or "hot-plate" carburetor systems used the heat of the exhaust to vaporize the fuel prior to its being mixed with air. The system was quite economical and allowed the use of low-grade fuel, but performance in terms of power was inferior to that of the older carburetor systems.

The Vaporizer carburetors required a relocation of the throttle and choke rods. The throttle rod now came across the top of the engine, eliminating the need for the hole between the two center cylinders. This hole was closed off in later engines, and the corresponding hole in the valve cover door was also eliminated.

Very late in engine production, perhaps even after the end of car production, a new connecting rod with an oil dipper was used. All-steel valves (one piece, without the cast iron separate head) also became standard. (Engine production continued for several years after the end of car production.)

The 1926-27 electric horn. The only change from the earlier design was in the mounting bracket, now designed to mount on the water inlet. Early non-electric open cars used a magneto horn on a similar bracket.

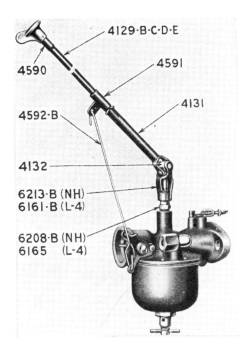

4129-B-C-D-E

4590

4591

4131

4592-B

4132

6213-B (NH)
6161-B (L-4)

6208-B (NH)
6165 (L-4)

LEFT: The 1926 Holley NH carburetor assembly with the combination choke pull rod and needle valve adjuster. This system was also used in the later 1925 models (before the 1926 style cars) as well, but used a different pull rod. A Kingston L-4 carburetor was also used in a similar configuration.

Several 4129 adjusting rods were used over the years. 4129 (same as 4129A) is the standard carburetor adjusting rod used on all cars up until mid-1925. This is the "adjusting" rod, not the "choke" rod. These came in a number of variations over the years.

4129, 4129A (various lengths) used on all cars prior to the "universal joint" system.

4129B (24-1/8" long) was used on the 1925 open cars and trucks.

4129C (25-3/4" long) was used on the 1925 closed cars.

4129D (15-5/8" long) was used on the 1926 chassis and truck chassis (no instrument panel).

4129D1 (18-11/16" long) was used on the T and TT chassis with the Vaporizer carburetor.

4129D2 (18-11/16" long) was used on the T and TT commercial models (with bodies).

4129E (27-3/8 or 27-9/16" long) was used on the closed cab trucks.

4129F (27-13/16" long) was used on the 1926 Coupe and Tudor, standard carburetor.

4129G (26-1/4" long) was used on the 1926 Fordor, Runabout and Touring with the standard carburetor, and on the Open Cab truck with with the Vaporizer.

4129H (31-1/16" long) was used on the Coupe, Tudor and Closed Cab truck with the Vaporizer.

4129I (29-9/16" long) was used on the Touring, Roadster and Fordor with the Vaporizer.

4129J (28-15/16" long) was used on the 1925 Coupe, Tudor and Fordor with the Vaporizer.

4129K (27-5/8" long) was used on the 1925 Roadster and Touring with the Vaporizer.

With natural wood wheels the standard run about is a little more conservative than the sport, yet considered by many as classier. All special and standard equipment shown on the other models is included here. It is a vigorous, youthful car, especially appreciated by young people. It is smart in every detail as well as economical to buy and drive.

Kingston Vaporizer Parts

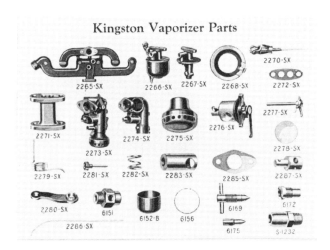

2265-SX   2266-SX   2267-SX   2268-SX   2270-SX   2272-SX

2271-SX   2273-SX   2274-SX   2275-SX   2276-SX   2277-SX   2278-SX

2279-SX   2281-SX   2282-SX   2283-SX   2285-SX   2287-SX

2280-SX   6151   6152-B   6156   6169   6172

2286-SX   6175   S-1232

The Kingston Vaporizer was used in some 1927 production. The Kingston came in at least two types, one called the "Regenerator," which is different from the parts shown here and was probably an accessory item. The Holley Vaporizer was by far the most common, and was the standard carburetor system on the 1927 models.

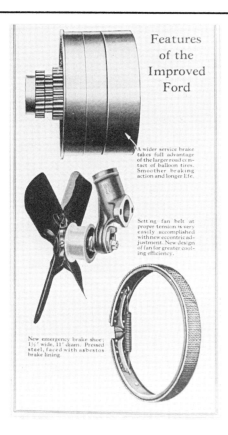

Features of the Improved Ford

"A wider service brake takes full advantage of the larger road contact of balloon tires. Smoother braking action and longer life.

Setting fan belt at proper tension is very easily accomplished with new eccentric adjustment. New design of fan for greater cooling efficiency.

New emergency brake shoe; 1½" wide, 11" diam. Pressed steel, faced with asbestos brake lining.

Features of the Improved Ford

By mounting the wheels higher on the axle, the improved Ford sets closer to the ground.

The coil box has been placed on the left hand side of the motor making it unnecessary for anyone to get inside the car when making adjustments.

The gasoline tank of greater capacity—instead of being under the front seat is now beneath the cowl, where it affords an even flow of gasoline on any incline. It can be filled from the outside, making it unnecessary for the front seat occupants to get up. The new position makes it possible to provide lower and roomier seats.

Some features of the Improved Ford are shown here. The wider transmission brake drum, the new fan mounting arrangement (the later type is shown here), and the larger, lined, rear brake shoes were definite improvements.

TOP. "By mounting the wheels higher on the axle, the improved Ford sets closer to the ground."

TOP RIGHT. "The coil box has been placed on the left side of the motor making it unnecessary for anyone to get inside the car when making adjustments."

BOTTOM. "The gasoline tank, of greater capacity, instead of being under the front seat is now beneath the cowl, where it affords an even flow of gasoline on any incline. It can be filled from the outside, making it unnecessary for the front seat occupants to get up. The new position makes it possible to provide lower and roomier seats.

"The width of the transmission brake band has beeen increased to 1-3/4 inches, a feature which contributes to ease and smoothness of braking. All bands have removable ears to permit changing of lining in a few minutes, should occasion require it."*

"Pedals are generously spaced for driving convenience, with flanges to prevent the foot from slipping. Weather strip, fitting snugly around the pedals, shuts out drafts, dirt and heat."

* This may come as a shock to those of you who have spent more than "a few minutes" changing bands. . . "should the occasion require it."

The new instrument "cluster" is smaller and nickel-plated. The ammeter is of a new and smaller design as well. The switch and handle assembly is similar to the previous design. Most switch handles were painted black but nickel-plated ones, such as shown here, were also supplied. Whether the nickel handles were used in later production, or perhaps just in the closed cars, is unknown.

1926-1927

400

ABOVE. Two steel straps, one on each side of the engine, were used to add support to the engine and aid in the prevention of crankcase arm breakage. These were apparently not used in all early production but became standard on all cars by mid-November 1925. These braces ran from the two new transmission mounting bolts at the upper rear of the cylinder block to the upper engine mounting bolts on the top of the frame.

RIGHT (Top and center). Two types of fan mounting brackets were used. Early production, shown in the upper right picture, used a bolt at the bottom which acted as a worm gear to turn the eccentric fan mounting adjustment casting. Turning the bolt rotated the casting which moved the fan in an eccentric path. The adjusting bolt was then locked into position by a lock nut which, if tightened too much, could easily break the mounting collar.

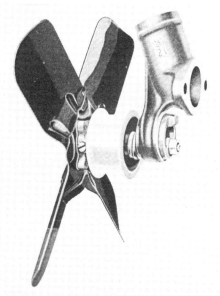

The second type, shown in the lower picture, eliminated the worm screw adjustment. A lug was now provided in the eccentric casting and by using a lever between it and the fan shaft nut, the casting could be turned within the outer collar. Tightening the fan mounting shaft nut locked everything securely. This new design was not only less likely to break, but it was also cheaper to make!

LOWER LEFT. The transmission cover, in addition to being a bit wider to accommodate the larger brake drum, and having the new wider pedals, now had two "ears" which were bolted to the rear of the cylinder casting. (Shims are used between the two for proper alignment.) This modification made the engine-transmission assembly much more rigid.

ABOVE. The larger transmission brake drum now used steel caps or shoes on the clutch plate lugs which greatly reduced wear at this point and improved clutch operation.

LEFT. The magneto post now threaded into the transmission cover (1/2 inch pipe threads) instead of being held with three screws as it had since the 1909 models.

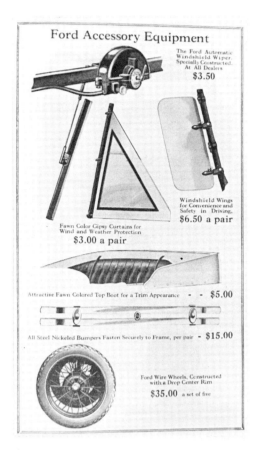

Ford Accessory Equipment

The Ford Automatic Windshield Wiper. Specially Constructed. At All Dealers
$3.50

Windshield Wings for Convenience and Safety in Driving,
$6.50 a pair

Fawn Color Gipsy Curtains for Wind and Weather Protection
$3.00 a pair

Attractive Fawn Colored Top Boot for a Trim Appearance - - $5.00

All Steel Nickeled Bumpers Fasten Securely to Frame, per pair - $15.00

Ford Wire Wheels, Constructed with a Drop Center Rim
$35.00 a set of five

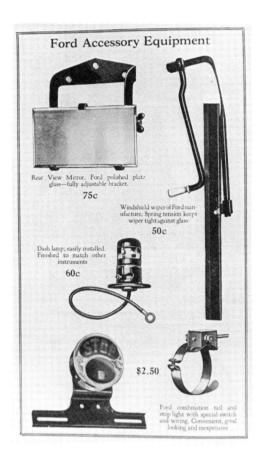

Ford Accessory Equipment

Rear View Mirror. Ford polished plate glass—fully adjustable bracket.
75c

Windshield wiper of Ford manufacture. Spring tension keeps wiper tight against glass
50c

Dash lamp; easily installed. Finished to match other instruments
60c

$2.50

Ford combination tail and stop light with special switch and wiring. Convenient, good looking and inexpensive.

Ford Accessories. For years Ford had ignored the accessory market. In fact, in the early years, Ford would void the warranty if non-Ford accessories were added to the basic car. By 1926 the Model T needed all the help it could get to remain competitive, and not only did Ford supply accessories, they encouraged others. The Ruckstell axle parts list even became a part of the Ford parts catalogs!

A new and smaller Stewart speedometer could be had for the Ford. The Stewart drive system came in more than one type. Some used a pressed-metal wheel gear with a small spur gear, in a manner similar to the common type used earlier. The ultimate system is shown here. Using a worm-type gear arrangement, it was much quieter than the other designs.

Ford bumpers were nickel-plated and added greatly to the appearance of the car. In the center was a small medallion which served no purpose other than as a bit of decoration. The bumper supporting irons were painted black.

COLORS

After the initial announcement in which the Fordor Sedan was shown as being Windsor Maroon, the Tudor and Coupe as being Channel Green, and the open cars as being black, a number of changes occurred.

Existing samples of 1926 models, which appear to be original, seem to indicate that in spite of the colors listed for the closed cars, all body types also appeared in black in early production.

By mid-1926 the Fordor Sedan color was listed as "Moleskin" which should be a gray. By the fall of 1926 (1927 models?), all closed cars were apparently painted in a choice of three colors: Royal Maroon, Highland Green and Fawn Gray. Whether the "Windsor" and "Royal" maroons were alike; the "Channel" and "Highland" greens were alike; or the "Moleskin" and "Fawn Gray" were alike is open for question but evidence seems to indicate they were not. The differences may have been due to the different paints used. The 1926 cars were initially painted in enamel, but later production used the new Pyroxylin paint.

BODY COLORS
ENAMELS
Black, Channel Green and Windsor Maroon
PYROXYLIN
Black, Highland Green, Royal Maroon, Fawn Gray, Gunmetal Blue, Phoenix Brown, Commercial Green, Moleskin and Drake Green.

WIRE WHEEL COLORS
ENAMELS
Casino Red, Emerald Green and Straw
PYROXYLIN
Casino Red, Emerald Green, Straw, Drake Green and Black
Note: While not listed under the enamels, Black was the *standard* wire wheel color. The other colors were optional and often dealer-installed.

STRIPING COLORS
Champagne, Cream, Emerald Green, Orange and Vermilion

Apparently the Pyroxylin paints were introduced after the initial introduction of the 1926 cars. The "enamel" colors listed in the Ford Parts List concur with the colors in the introductory line folders. It would appear that at the time the Pyroxylin paints were used in place of the enamels, the Fordor Sedan body color became Moleskin (gray) and that after a time all the closed cars could be had in a choice of colors (maroon, gray or green). The actual dates of the changes are not known but it seems the Pyroxylin finish became available during 1926, and that the three-color option came in the fall of 1926

("1927" models). Further study seems to indicate that the open cars were all black until late 1926 when black was dropped in favor of the Gunmetal Blue and the Phoenix Brown options.

The bodies of the closed cars were striped at the factory. The stripe was quite thin and appeared just below the body molding. On some of the cars another stripe was added on the front body pillar; this stripe beginning at the front edge of the upper body stripe and following the curve of the pillar down to the bottom near the splash apron. The striping colors were Vermilion or orange on the maroon cars, champagne on the gray cars, and cream or emerald green on the green cars. Some open cars were seen with stripes but it is believed that these were dealer options and that such striping did not come from the factory.

When supplied as standard equipment, wire wheels were black. Any of the available colors could be ordered on any car. Ford offered an exchange program for the dealers who installed wire wheels in place of the wooden ones, or colored wire wheels for the black ones.

Fenders, running boards and splash aprons, as well as most hardware (bumper brackets, for example) were painted black on all cars.

ENGINE COLOR
The generally accepted "pitch" has been that the engines on the 1926 and 1927 cars were painted green. In our research at the Ford Archives, and after examining a good many original cars, we have yet to prove this to be true. The only reference to engine paint we have found was in the engine number record books, where on July 27, 1926 a note was entered which read, "Began painting engines in Pyroxylin." Drake Green was specified. Whether all engines were black, unpainted, or green cannot be determined with certainty. We have seen original engines in black, and also unpainted but have yet to see a green one that seemed "original." Yet, it is quite possible that Drake Green was used on at least some engines after mid-1926.

UPHOLSTERY
Upholstery in the closed cars was listed as gray with a red stripe in the maroon cars, and gray with a green stripe in the green cars in the introductory Ford descriptions. By mid-1926 the green cars were listed as having "Rich dark green wool fabric with carpets and curtains to match." The moleskin cars had a "rich dark brown wool fabric, with carpets and curtains to match." All open cars were upholstered in a black leatherette fabric.

The Ford body catalogs list no options other than the gray with the red or green stripe until "1927" models when gray with a white stripe was the only color. Original samples of cars seen by the author seem to indicate these three fabrics only, and no doubt the gray with white stripe came into use when the cars could be ordered in optional colors. Gray with a white stripe would "match" any of the possible exterior colors.

MODERN PAINTS

What is the modern equivalent of the original paint colors? Probably there are none. Maroon, in particular, was an unstable color until fairly recent times. Beautiful when new, it soon oxidized into a dirty brown. Some years ago one of our members gave the author three samples of original paint from new old stock, unopened Ford Motor Company cans. When these samples were painted on a sheet of aluminum foil, I could not tell them apart! They all looked black!

Original Model T Ford paint colors are all but impossible to duplicate accurately today. The paints used in the very early cars were varnishes, and had a relatively short life. This was also true of the later enamels and Pyroxylins, although they were a good bit better than the earlier varnishes. The original early greens and blues were all but black, and could easily be taken as black. Consequently, original cars seen today no longer have the same color they had when they were new. Today, batches of the same paint formula will vary in color, and it is certain the variations were even more pronounced more than sixty years ago. Suggested equivalents for the original colors are listed under *Paints* in the *Descriptions* chapter.

The Ford commercial line continued the types introduced in 1924 and 1925 with no styling changes. Other than a few prototypes, there is no verifiable evidence that the trucks ever used the "improved" style hood and fenders. The pickup is the standard Runabout with the box instead of the turtle deck.

There are two types of rear seat panels used on the Runabouts; one with embossed moldings to match the turtle deck, and one which does not have the embossing. One might presume the non-embossed type would have been supplied with the factory-built pickup.

The pickup box was available as a separate item for conversion of Roadsters to Pickups. Such boxes were painted black at the factory. The 1927 Roadster Pickups came from the factory painted Ford Commercial Green (body and box), the same color that was used on the TT trucks. Black was offered as an option, on special order, on these models

A stainless steel Ford truck, apparently used at the Dearborn airport. *Photo from the Collections of the Henry Ford Museum*

LEFT. This photo shows the perhaps-never-produced "improved" Model TT truck. This photo may have been a prototype of a truck which never reached production due to the demise of the Model T in 1927. The cab seems different from the standard TT closed cab, and is also different from the later Model AA cab. No authentic TT trucks with this styling are known (by the author) to exist. *Photo from the Collections of the Henry Ford Museum and Greenfield Village.*

The 1927 Roadster Pickup in Ford Commercial Green (with black fenders). This Ford Archives photo is dated February 15, 1927. *Photo from the Collections of the Henry Ford Museum and Greenfield Village.*

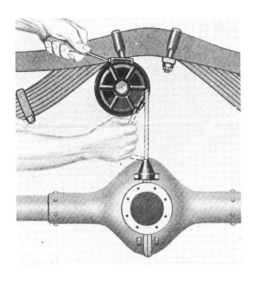

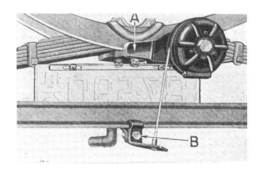

Ford-supplied, and dealer-installed, optional equipment included shock absorbers in 1927, and shown here. These were "one-way" absorbers which tended to prevent rebound action of the springs. As the axle moved upwards, a spring reeled in the cable and a friction device resisted its being pulled out on the rebound.

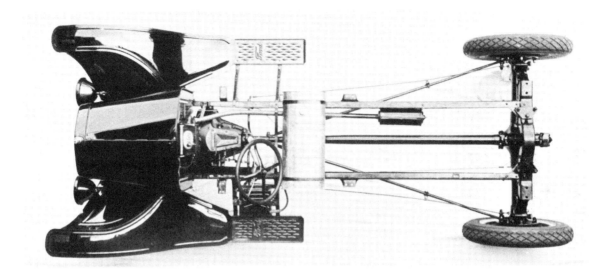

The Model TT chassis. The upper photo is dated July 29, 1926, and the lower photo is dated November 18, 1926. Both photos show the pre-1926 style front fenders, running boards, and firewall. The lower photo shows the coil box mounted in the firewall instead of on the engine as in the passenger cars, which seems unusual. This style TT chassis continued until the end of Model T production in 1927. *Photos from the Collections of the Henry Ford Museum and Greenfield Village.*

The new "Improved" Model T Ford as it appeared on August 6, 1925. This is no doubt a pre-production example, judging from the wrinkles in the splash apron. Note: the nickel radiator shell was not standard equipment on the open cars at the time, but was optional even on the 1925 models. *Photo from the Collections of the Henry Ford Museum and Greenfield Village.*

The 1926 Ford Tudor Sedan. The Tudor and the Coupe shared many body parts and were all new in the 1926 models. While advertised as being available in green, surviving examples of the early 1926 closed cars indicate that many came in black. *Photo dated October 22, 1925. From the Collections of the Henry Ford Museum and Greenfield Village.*

1926-1927

The 1927 Ford Coupe. The striping design is quite clear in this photo, and is typical of the striping on all the closed cars. Striping was a hand operation so there are minor variations from car to car. This Ford Archives photo is dated December 31, 1926. Note the use of wooden wheels at this late date. Black wire wheels became standard equipment in some areas about February 1927 on the Coupe. *Photo from the Collections of the Henry Ford Museum and Greenfield Village.*

The Fifteen Millionth Model T Ford as it appears today. This car is on display at the Henry Ford Museum in Dearborn, Michigan. *Photo from the Collections of the Henry Ford Museum and Greenfield Village.*

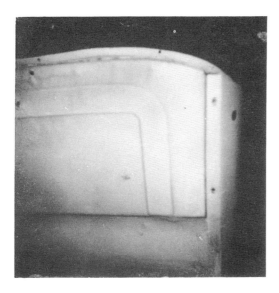

The rear body panel of the standard 1926-27 Roadster. Note the embossed area on the panel and the holes for the turtle deck retaining bolts.

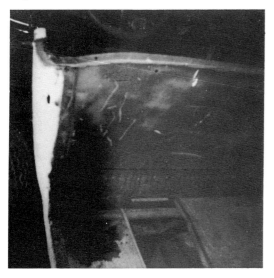

Compare the rear panel here with the one in the upper photo. This panel is on a Roadster which came from the factory with a pickup bed installed. There are no bolt holes and there is no embossed area.

Closeup view of the taillight assembly used on the Roadster Pickups and trucks.

Door handles on the closed cars were nickel-plated with a black hard-rubber insert, continued from prior years.

Oil lamps on the 1926? Indeed. The very early 1926 open cars could be had with no electrical equipment, and these cars came with an oil tail lamp and oil side lamps. Electric equipment became standard in late calendar 1925 (1926 models) and oil lamps were discontinued.

1926-1927

Upholstery in the closed cars followed the same pattern in all body types; Tudor, Fordor, or Coupe. All used a gray woolen cloth with a striped pattern on the seats, doors and lower side panels, and a plain gray material on the upper side panels and the head liner.

There were minor variations in the pattern of the upholstery during 1926 and 1927 production. Initially, the gray material used on the seats, doors and lower panels had a stripe which matched the body colors; a red stripe for the Fordors which were painted maroon, and a green stripe on the Coupes and Tudors which were painted green. In late 1926 when these cars could be ordered in several colors, the stripes were white in all body styles since white would not "clash" with any of the body colors. In addition, the gray, green-stripe, and red-stripe material came in two textures which Ford called "hard" (early 1926 cars) and "soft" (later 1926 cars). Later 1927 Fordor sedans also had narrower pleats in the seat upholstery than did the earlier 1927 models, both types using the gray with white stripe material.

The Coupe and Tudor used the same instrument panel, and the Fordor panel was similar. The speedometer, gear shifter, and flower vase shown here are accessories.

Original upholstery in the Coupe. The Tudor and Fordor were similar.

While the 1926-27 Fordor body was essentially the same as the 1925 models, the cowl section and front pillars were modified to conform with the styling of the Coupe and Tudor and to match the new hood line. Unlike the Coupe and Tudor, the gas tank in the Fordor is under the driver's seat, which makes the cowl ventilator functional as a "ventilator" instead of just an access door for the gasoline tank.

Door handles on all the closed cars were nickel-plated with a hard-rubber insert as shown.

The late 1926 and 1927 Fordor Sedan. This example was restored by John Smith who lived at Edwards Air Force Base when these photos were taken many years ago. The car was painted maroon and the upholstery was gray with the thin red stripe, typical of the 1926 models. The headlight tie bar did not appear until mid-1926 production, and this car's serial number indicated a July 1926 date of manufacture, just prior to the "1927" models.

Note the windshield on the Fordor is two piece while that on the Coupe and Tudor was one piece. The Fordor was a carry-over body from 1925 while the Coupe and Tudor were all new for 1926.

1926-1927

The striping on this car is typical of the factory pattern except that it is a bit wider than original. The original stripe was about one-sixteenth inch wide. Note that it just runs around the belt line, under the bead, and runs down the side of the coupe pillar, then back toward the door.

The spare-tire carrier was the same for the wire or the wooden wheels. The mounting bolt pattern fit the wire wheels directly while the wood wheel demountable rims fit a "Y" bracket which bolted to the carrier bolt pattern.

Wood wheels were standard on all Fords until very late calendar 1926 when black wire wheels became standard on some closed cars at some assembly plants. Colored wire wheels were apparently optional throughout production, and were generally dealer-installed.

The 1926 Fordor Sedan in a pre-production photo dated August 4, 1925. The Fordor sedan continued the same body as that used in 1924-25 except for modifications in the cowl section. *Photo from the Collections of the Henry Ford Museum and Greenfield Village.*

Sun visors were standard equipment on all closed cars. They are made of top material over a metal frame.

1926-1927

COMPONENT DESCRIPTIONS

The year-to-year coverage in the first chapters of this book has attempted to show the major changes in the Model T Ford over its nineteen-year life span. It is not practical to show every change, in every year. Indeed, it is not even *possible!* There are many differences in certain parts of the Model T which were due to varying suppliers, as well as those modifications made to improve the quality or lower the cost.

The following pages list, in alphabetical order, the major components of the car, the *approximate* dates these components were used, and the general nature of any changes. Be aware that there was considerable overlapping in the use of a part while it was being superseded by a new or different design.

Where applicable, page numbers, indicating where a part is illustrated in this book, are given. These are shown as "[##]" where ## is the page number. Not every part is so indicated; sometimes there is no good illustration, or sometimes there are many. You also might find a picture of the part or assembly under the model year coverage even though a page number is not indicated.

Every effort has been made to have this information as accurate as is possible. Even so, errors or omissions no doubt will occur; such is the nature of the Model T Ford story.

AXLES (See FRONT AXLE or REAR AXLE)

BODIES

(Also see Top, Windshield, Aprons, Fenders, etc.)

1909

Unless noted otherwise, the fenders, aprons, chassis, running gear and wheels were painted the same color as the body. Striping varied somewhat from car to car, this being a hand operation done by different painters and suppliers.

TOURING

COLORS: Red at first, Brewster Green added by March. Both colors used until June when red was discontinued. A few gray tourings were shown on early shipping invoices. Pontiac supplied bodies with both all wood and wood with aluminum panels. Wilson bodies were all wood only. Open front compartment. Front-opening rear doors with external handles. Door on rear seat kick panel for storage of curtains, tools, etc. Pontiac aluminum body discontinued in September 1909. Separate irons to hold top sockets.

ROADSTER (Runabout)

COLORS: Mostly gray but a few green and red cars were also indicated. After June, all were Brewster Green. Manufactured by Pontiac and Wilson, wood panels only. Open front compartment. Rear deck had either a tool box or a "mother-in-law" seat on top of the tool box. "Scalloped" seat back.

COUPE

COLORS: Green. Manufactured by Wilson. Generally supplied without head lamps.

TOWN CAR

COLORS: Generally green but a few gray were indicated. Manufactured by Pontiac and Wilson. Generally supplied without head lamps.

LANDAULET (Similar to Town car but with open driver's compartment)

COLORS: Green but some gray. Manufactured by Pontiac and Wilson.

TOURABOUT

COLOR: Green. Apparently first appeared about July. Similar to Touring except for open front and rear compartments (no doors). Manufactured by Pontiac.

1910

Same styles as 1909. All body types were painted Brewster Green.

TOURING

Manufactured by Pontiac and KH (or KA, perhaps Kelsey Hayes, or Hayes American.) Wilson apparently did not supply any bodies in 1910. All-wood panels until 1911 production. Touring bodies had a hinged door on the rear seat kick panel.

ROADSTER (Runabout)

Manufactured by Pontiac, wood panels only. Open front compartment. Rear deck had either a tool box or a "mother-in-law" seat in place of the tool box. "Scalloped" seat back.

COUPE

Manufactured by Pontiac and KH. Generally supplied without head lamps. Body was a bit wider than the 1909 Coupe.

TOWN CAR

Manufactured by Pontiac. Generally supplied without head lamps.

LANDAULET (Similar to Town Car but with open driver's compartment)

Manufactured by Pontiac.

TOURABOUT Similar to Touring except for open front and rear compartments (no doors). Manufactured by Pontiac.

1911 (Introduced about November 1910)

All cars painted a very dark blue except for a few red Open Runabouts and green Town Cars built in April 1911, according to factory invoices. Existing cars seem to indicate black bodies with blue fenders, as well as all black cars. Striping of fenders and running gear began to be discontinued in July on some production.

TOURING

Manufactured by Pontiac, KH, and American Body. Continue open front compartment but body panels were now steel over wood frame. "Square" rear doors with outside handles, open at the front. "Step" in side panels under front and rear seats. Door in rear seat kick panel was discontinued after early production of the new bodies.

RUNABOUT

Pontiac bodies, generally in the style of the 1910 cars.

TORPEDO RUNABOUT

Introduced in December 1910. Bodies made by Pontiac. Enclosed front compartment with lower seat, longer steering column, longer hood, and windshield with sloping lower section. Curved fenders, unique to this body and the Open Runabout. Gas tank and tool box on rear deck. Early production used a rectangular gas tank, but most production used a round one. The Torpedo and Open Runabout use different pedals and a different brake lever than the other cars.

OPEN RUNABOUT

Bodies by Pontiac and Hayes. Similar to the Torpedo but no doors.

TOWN CAR

Relatively few made. In the same style as the 1910.

1912

All painted blue (see comments under 1911)

TOURING

Made in several styles. All supplied with front door assemblies which were removable. Early cars had a "stepped down" fore door, apparently using the same bodies as the 1911 cars which used the two-piece dashboard, but the standard production used door assemblies of the same height as the seat sides. The second style body was similar but with a one-piece dash. The third "typical 1912" style had relatively smooth sides (without the added-on look of the 1911's) and rear-opening doors at the rear, with outside handles. The fourth style was similar to the third except that the rear door handles were inside the car. The two last types may have been supplied at the same time, the variation being perhaps due to differing suppliers.

Descriptions

BODIES (Continued)

RUNABOUT

Similar in style to the 1911 Runabout. Early versions may have used the curved rear fenders of the Torpedo Runabout but later versions used the same fenders as the Touring. All were supplied with front "fore doors." Early cars had a "stepped-down" fore door, as on the Tourings, but the standard production used door assemblies of the same height as the seat sides.

TORPEDO RUNABOUT

Now based on the standard Runabout, and using standard chassis components, the Torpedo had front doors, curved rear fenders, and the round gas tank at the rear as on the 1911's. Early versions used the two-piece dash and had lower door sections. Later models used the one-piece dash and the side door panels were the same height as the seat section.

TOWN CAR

Similar to the 1911, the front compartment now had the "fore doors."

DELIVERY WAGON

Introduced in late 1911. These were initially painted red, with the standard blue fenders. In January Ford announced that fenders would be black and the bodies unpainted. A poor seller, production was discontinued early in the year. The last were sold in December 1912.

1913

An all-new design, setting the general pattern for all Fords to come until 1925 (1926 models), was announced in early November 1912 but may have appeared earlier. Early models (built in 1912) were apparently still blue and some, if not all, were striped. Striping was discontinued early in production. Black cars quite possible but Ford didn't indicate it. Lamps and horn now "black and brass" (brass and steel construction) instead of all-brass.

TOURING

Doors extended to the splash apron and were somewhat "square" in shape. Windshield slopes back on the lower section, with the top section folding forward, with support straps from the center hinge to the body. Door handles extended through the upper door. Top surfaces of body side panels were covered with a separate metal trim strip. Early production used uncovered lower body sills which tended to break. During production, these sills were reinforced with a formed metal bracket extending across the rear door opening and/or additional body-to-frame brackets. Later, even heavier wooden sills were used, apparently with and without steel reinforcements which connected the front and rear sections together under the rear doors. The "1914" style appeared in about August 1913.

RUNABOUT

In the same pattern as the Touring. First year for the rear turtle deck, which was unique in that it had rather sharp rear corners. [152]

TOWN CAR

Generally in the style of the 1912 Town Cars.

1914

TOURING

Similar to the 1913 bodies, the doors now were shorter, with rounded bottom corners, setting the door style used through 1925. Door handles were inside the car and operate a vertical-moving latch arrangement. This style was introduced in late summer of 1913 and continued into early 1915. Windshield is similar to the 1913 but the top section now folded to the rear. The windshield support bracket now had a bend to allow the folded windshield to clear. Late production had many "1915" features (billed fenders, hood with louvres).

RUNABOUT

As in the Touring, the doors were now rounded. The turtle deck now had the standard rounded corners.

TOWN CAR

An evolution of the 1913 Town Cars.

CHASSIS

For the first time Ford now offered the bare chassis in the catalog. Prior to this time Ford said the use of non-Ford bodies would void their warranty. Production figures indicate that chassis were produced earlier.

1915

TOURING

(Introduced in January 1915 but 1914-style cars were still produced at the branches, perhaps as late as April.) While initially using the same body section as the 1914's, a new metal cowl section was added, eliminating the flat board firewall which had been a feature of Fords since 1909 (and even earlier). This cowl section on some open car bodies differed from the other types in that it was made up of four (instead of three) pieces; the front "lip" being riveted to the cowl. While the rivets were hidden by the hood former, they can be easily seen from inside the car. This oddity was apparently seen on bodies made by only one of the Ford suppliers, and it continued into the 1916 models. The hood was now louvred, but still made of aluminum. The windshield was vertical and was riveted to the support brackets, which also held the oil side lamps. Later production, while appearing the same, had more metal in the internal seat area and now sported a "rivet" just ahead of the rear doors. Rear fenders were now curved with no crown on all body styles.

RUNABOUT

Styled in the pattern of the Tourings. Same turtle deck as the 1914's, with black-painted, cast handles.

COUPELET

Ford's first "convertible." A Coupe with a folding top. Glass in the doors raised and lowered by a strap. Top was almost blind to the side since there were no windows in the quarter panels. Turtle deck on early models had the door at the rear panel but later versions had the door on the upper surface.

SEDAN (Centerdoor)

Introduced in September 1914, the Sedan (and the Coupe) were the first "1915" models. Aluminum body with unique aprons and rear fenders. Three-piece windshield of elaborate design. Gas tank under the rear seat. No seams in the rear quarter panels. Door handles were of the bail type. This Sedan was almost completely unlike those that followed, even though it was of the same general pattern.

BODIES (Continued)

TOWN CAR

Styled in the pattern of the Tourings; an evolution of the earlier Town Cars.

1916

Generally continued the 1915 styles. The Coupelet was given small port holes in the quarter panels. The Sedan evolved into the standard type described under the 1917 Sedan. Brass trim on side, tail and head lamps discontinued. Hood was made of steel instead of aluminum. Door lock assemblies changed from a vertical latching to a horizontal latching bolt, with many cars being made with combinations of both types. Door handles on the closed cars were of the bail type.

1917

Revised styling using the same basic bodies of 1915-16. Open cars now had a small metal cap at the front end of the arm rests, instead of the rolled leather front covering. Brass radiator and small hood was dropped in favor of the black shell and larger hood. All fenders were now curved and crowned on all models. Bail type door handles on the closed cars.

SEDAN

Revised design apparently first used in 1916, the body was now steel and used standard aprons and rear fenders. The gas tank was now under the driver's seat. Complicated windshield of 1915 was replaced with a simple two-piece design. Windows still adjusted with straps. Top was solid panel, not padded.

COUPELET

Initially a restyled 1916, the convertible coupe was replaced with a "hardtop" coupe during the year. This coupe had removable door posts so that when the windows were lowered the opening extended from the windshield to the rear quarter panel. The top section was leather covered, somewhat in the style of the convertible type. The "1918" metal top Coupelet replaced it, apparently, before the end of 1917.

1918

Generally a continuation of the 1917 cars. Body construction on the open cars reverted to the 1914-style wooden seat frames during the War years 1918-1919. The Model TT truck chassis (introduced in late 1917) was added to the line. The Coupelet now had a metal top section instead of the leather-covered type of mid-1917, but continued the removable door posts. The Town Car was discontinued in the 1917 catalog but production records (if correct) indicate they were built during 1918.

1919

Same as 1918. Electric equipment and demountable rims standard on closed cars. This equipment became optional on the open cars about June 1919. Oil lamps not supplied on cars with electrical equipment.

COUPE

Removable door posts discontinued but coupe otherwise similar in style to the earlier model.

1920

Same as 1919. Open cars again constructed using metal seat frames as in 1915 to 1917. Side window curtains in the sedans discontinued about 1920.

1921-1922

Generally similar to 1919 except as noted.

TOURING

A new body design with lower seats of much more comfortable design was announced on October 15, 1920, and is properly called a "1921" model. Rear quarter panel is now one piece instead of the two-piece design used since 1913. Upholstery tack strips were now inside the body panels, extending above them for the tacks. Metal cap on arm rests was now somewhat narrower. Top iron support post now came through the quarter panel instead of the "L" bracket used earlier. Instrument panel standard on all models, starter or not, in 1922. Oval gas tank was standard. The lid over the gas tank was discontinued.

RUNABOUT

Continued in the style of the 1920 cars until late 1922 (1923 models).

Note: The "1923" style open cars were introduced in September (Touring) and October (Runabout) of 1922. While these were "1923" models, Ford often refered to them as "1922" in the parts books.

SEDAN and COUPE

Door handles changed to the "T" bar type in 1921, then to the "L" type about 1922. Later 1922 cars had a new latch arrangement for lowering the door windows, although the rear quarter windows still had the straps. Metal plates cover the door and window sills (which were painted wood earlier) in later 1922 and 1923 Sedans and Coupes. Brown upholstery replaced former gray about April, 1922, and this color continued into 1923.

1923

Similar bodies to the 1921 but restyled as noted. Firewalls were wood, as in the earlier cars, but were changed to steel in early 1923, before the appearance of the higher radiator.

TOURING

New sloping windshield (introduced in September 1922) along with a new "one-man" top gave the 1923 Ford a new look. Otherwise the body was the same as before.

RUNABOUT

Restyled with the new windshield, and a new body in the same general pattern as the Touring, and a turtle deck of much larger size, and with no handles. (The key served as the handle.)

FORDOR SEDAN

Introduced in late 1922, the new four-door sedan is added to the line. It did not replace the older centerdoor sedan. The new body was aluminum. The cowl, still made to match the low radiator, had no ventilator until early 1923, about the time of the low steel firewall apparently.

SEDAN and COUPE

Similar to the 1922. Upholstery was now brown (instead of the gray striped material). The centerdoor Sedan and the Coupe with the forward-opening doors were discontinued in June 1923.

BODIES (Continued)
1923-1924

About June or July 1923 the cars were again restyled. The radiator was made a bit higher, as was the cowl area and hood, giving the front of the car a more massive appearance. Front of fender lip is folded down to mate with a new valence at the bottom of the radiator, giving the front a more finished look. Other than as noted, the cars were like the earlier 1923's. During the early part of 1923, a metal firewall replaced the wooden one. With the mid-year styling (high radiators), all cars used a new larger metal firewall. Window regulators were introduced on the door windows of the closed cars.

COUPE
An all new design. Doors now opened to the rear. Vent in the cowl. An integral rear deck gave the Coupe a more massive appearance. Door windows now had regulators.

TUDOR SEDAN
All new but based on the new Coupe design. Doors were at the front of the body, opening to the rear. All steel panels over a wooden framework.

FORDOR SEDAN
In the pattern of the earlier 1923 Fordor but with the larger front cowl as in the Coupe and Tudor, with the adjustable vent. Steel lower body panels replaced the aluminum, though upper panels remained in aluminum.

TRUCK
On January 9, 1924 a "C" cab truck body was added to the line. Also announced on this date was the availability of an "express" bed with and without stakes and canopy, finally enabled Ford to offer a complete truck.

1924-1925

A continuation of the 1924 cars. Doors on the Coupe, Tudor and Fordor Sedan were now all metal instead of the wood-frame construction. Open cars now had more steel in the body framing, as well as a steel firewall. A nickel radiator shell was offered as an option in late 1925 production (just prior to the "1926" models in July). Fenders were redesigned to have a wider appearance in late 1924 and during 1925 (depending on the model and fender). Some, but not all, later production 1925 Sedans had splash aprons of a "square" design, similar to that used in the 1926 models.

PICKUP
A pickup body for the Roadster chassis was announced in late 1924 but apparently not delivered until early 1925. All steel except for the flooring. The rear door did not have the Ford script in early production. Fenders fastened to rods which extended from reinforcing plates on the side panels.

TRUCK
A platform body for the TT was announced on December 24, 1924. On March 4, 1925 the pickup bed for the Roadster was announced. Then on April 9, the closed cab for the TT chassis.

1926-1927

All new bodies in style and construction except for the Fordor Sedan which continued with minor modifications. New bodies were all steel except for the floorboards. Closed car bodies available in color after initial production. Window garnish moldings (inside the car) were black regardless of the body color. 1926 open car sill plates were aluminum but these were dropped in favor of an embossed steel sill integral with the body in later (1927 but perhaps late 1926 as well) production.

Sloping windshield on the open cars now could be opened at either half (the lower half of the 1923-25 cars was fixed, only the top could open). Fenders were all new, as were the splash aprons and hood. The radiator shell was the same except that it could now be had with a nickel finish (standard equipment on the closed cars). Chassis (and car) height was lowered by several modifications in the frame, springs, and front spindles.

TOURING
Now with four doors, all opening at the rear. Gas tank was in the cowl (as in all other 1926-7 cars except for the Fordor Sedan and the truck).

RUNABOUT and PICKUP
All new, in the style of the Touring. Larger turtle deck. Also available was the Runabout with the pickup bed factory installed. Many factory-made pickups used a rear seat panel which was not embossed to match the turtle deck.

The pickup box was a modification of the box introduced in 1925. The major differences were in the side panels, to which the rear fenders now bolted directly, and in the floor boards. The floor boards differed in that there was now a metal panel over the rear frame crossmember and the wooden boards were cut to accommodate this panel. Factory made pickups were painted Commercial Green in 1927 production but if the pickup box was ordered separately, it was supplied in black.

COUPE
All new, similar to the 1925 Coupe in general style, but all steel.

TUDOR SEDAN
Again based on the Coupe design but all new steel construction.

FORDOR SEDAN
Basically the same body as the 1925 (using wood framing) except for the front pillars and cowl area which were redesigned to match the new hood. Gas tank remained under the seat on the Fordor.

TRUCK
Continued in the same styles as the 1924-25 trucks. Ford Archives photos show a restyled TT, looking similar to the 1926-27 passenger cars but few, if any, were produced. None are known to exist today.

BRAKE LEVER (and Trim Plates)

1909-1910
Lever was steel, brass-plated on some early cars. Clutch cam was forged steel. Trim plates on floorboard were brass, or brass-plated steel.

1911-1915
Lever was steel, painted black but otherwise similar to 1910. Trim plates black steel after sometime in 1911 or 1912.

1915-1927
Lever was steel, painted black. Clutch cam made of pressed steel, replaced the earlier forging. Trim plates were black steel.

BRAKE RODS

1909-1920
Forged fork ends. [187]

1920-1925
In August 1920 the forged ends were eliminated and the rod was split to make the fork at the rear end.

1926-1927
Similar to the 1925, rods were shorter and shaped differently for the new larger brake drums.

BRAKE ROD SUPPORTS

1909
Pressed metal bracket with hole in end through which the brake rods passed. Clamped around the radius rod. [64]

1909-1913
Relatively simple pressed "U" shaped design in which the support arm was folded down and then out, rolling up and over the brake rods. These came in at least two designs. One, believed to have been used in 1909-10, had the extension arm bent out about 1/3 of the way from the top of the clamp, and angling down. The other had the arm about 2/3 down, angling up. [32]

1913-1915
Similar to the 1913 style but the support arm is not folded back on the "U" section but instead extended out and rolled over the brake rod.

1916-1927
Similar to the 1915 but a stronger and reinforced type, with a shorter support arm which goes over the brake rod and folded under. The date of the change is not known. The parts books show the same (earlier) bracket until about 1924. Trucks used a similar but larger part.

BRAKE SHOES

Early 1909
Made of bronze, used one spring. [31]

1909-1913
Made of cast iron, used one coil spring. The spring was p/n 2570 and about 1-1/4" long. An additional flat metal spring clip was used across the anchor point.

1913-1925
Cast iron but now used two springs, each about 3-3/8" long. The flat spring was discontinued.
Note: These shoes were cast and machined in one piece but were supposed to be broken at the anchor point when installed.

1926-1927
Pressed steel, with riveted-in-place lining, to match new 11" drums. Used one coil spring.

CARBURETORS

Part #	Factory #	Description
1909		Early production
—	553	Kingston 5-ball, no choke [50,424]
1909		
4100	553	Kingston, same as above
—	—	Buffalo, used until about June [51,424]
1910		
4100	553	Kingston, with choke in hot air pipe to front of exhaust manifold. [50,424]
—	—	Buffalo, used from November 1909 until about March 1910 [424]
4150		Holley. ("1910 Holley") Both "pot metal" and bronze castings. With choke in hot air pipe to front of exhaust manifold. [50,427]
1911		
4100	553	Kingston, same as 1910
4500	—	Holley An oddly-shaped model with a single air valve located in a cylindrical housing at the rear of the upper casting. Air intake similar to the 1910 model (at the bottom). [99,428]
4550	553	Holley H-1 Two-screw top cover plate. Early versions had a built-in clamp for the hot air stove. The clamp was eliminated in later production 1911. [135, 428]
1912		
—	—	Kingston "Six-Ball" [134,425] used in limited numbers.
4550	553	Holley H-1 (Same as late 1911) Later versions had three screws on the top cover plate, and came with and without the hot air pipe clamp at the intake. The "1913" Model S may have appeared in later 1912 production. [125,136,428]

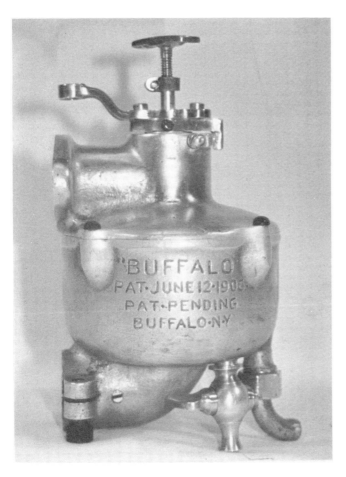

Top Left: This is believed to be the early 1909 Buffalo carburetor, used on some production until about April 1909. Unlike the Kingston, this unit had a choke valve in the air intake. Photo courtesy Russ Potter, Bismarck, Illinois.

Lower Left: Another Buffalo carburetor, believed to be the 1910 model, of which very few were used. The adjustment at the top is probably incorrect; it should be similar to the type used on the Kingstons and Holleys, to accept the dash adjuster.

Below: The 1909 Kingston 4100 "Five-Ball." There was no choke, and there was no heating stove. The carburetor was "choked" by depressing a plunger on the top which pushed the float down and flooded the carburetor.

Top Left. The 1910 - 1911 Kingston "Five-Ball." Similar to the 1909 version, the air intake now had a choke valve and was angled to accept a tube which led to the hot air stove at the front of the exhaust manifold.

Center Left. The seldom-used Kingston "Six-Ball." This carburetor does not appear in any of the Ford parts books.

Bottom Left. The 1913-1914 Kingston 4400 "Four-Ball" Model Y.

Bottom Right. The 1915-1917 Kingston "L"

Descriptions

"1917" Kingston "L-2." The arrow shows the location of the air bleed hole.

The "1918" Kingston "L-2." Similar to the earlier version, the air bleed hole was now located in the cast-in bulge just ahead of the air valve hinge screw. The choke arm had just one lever.

The Kingston "L-2" after 1918. The only significant change from the "1918" is that this model had the double choke arm, needed for the dashboard choke.

The early Kingston "L-4" which had a bronze body.

The second version of the Kingston "L-4." This model had a cast iron body. Note the size of the bowl retaining nut, and compare with the nut on the 1925-1926 version (below).

The Kingston "L-4" used from about 1921 to late 1925. About 1924 the carburetor was modified somewhat but the major difference was in the shape of the bowl and the larger retaining screw in this version.

The late 1925 and 1926 version of the Kingston "L-4." The adjusting valve screw with the universal joint was the only difference between this model and the 1924-1925 model. The larger retaining screw can be seen here.

The 1910 Holley 4150. These came in two versions; one with a bronze body and the other with a "pot metal" body. Otherwise they were alike.

Descriptions

CARBURETORS (Continued)

1913

Part #	Factory #	Description
4400	553D	Kingston "Y" (Four-ball) [186,425]
4450	553D	Holley "S" [186,429]

Two-screw top cover plate. Choke shaft was vertical with lever on the top of the air inlet.

1914

Part #	Factory #	Description
4400	553D	Kingston "Y" [186,425] Same as 1913 Kingston
4450	553D	Holley "G" [186,228,429]

Three-screw top cover plate. 1914 production had "Pats. Pend." cast in the brass cover plate.

1915

Part #	Factory #	Description
6100	553E	Kingston "L" [228,425]

Bronze casting. Fuel inlet at the bottom of the float bowl. Air valve hinge pin cover on side away from the engine.

| 6100 | 553E | Kingston "L2" [426] |

Bronze casting. Steel float bowl. Fuel inlet was now at the side of the body where the hinge pin cover was on the model L. The hinge pin cover screw was moved to the engine side of the body.

| 6040 | 553D | Holley "G" [270,429] |

Three-screw top cover plate. Most production had "Pat. Dec. 22, 1914" cast in the cover plate.

1916-1920

Part #	Factory #	Description
6100	553E	Kingston "L2" [426]

Double choke arm after 1918.

| 6040 | 553E | Holley "G" [270,429] |
| 6040 | 553A2 | Holley "G" |

Brass casting until about 1919, then cast iron, including the cover plate. Minor modifications over the years. The iron models had an extended choke arm for the choke pull rod used in the starter cars, and the word "Detroit" no longer was cast in the cover plate.

1920-1922

Part #	Factory #	Description
6150	553A1	Kingston "L4" [425,427]

Early versions had a bronze body and a rather rounded float bowl. Later versions were cast iron.

| 6200 | 553A3 | Holley "NH" [281,429] |

Off-center fuel drain. Early design used cork float and had a brass vent screw. The air passage was larger and more direct than in the later models. The later design had a "dip" in the air passage, had a bare vent hole under the brass nameplate, and a brass float.

The "1911" Holley 4500. An air valve was under the cylindrical housing behind the needle valve.

The "1912" Holley "H-1" with the two-screw cover plate. The "H-1" came in three versions; the one shown, another with a three-screw cover plate, and a third with the three-screw plate, but without the air pipe clamp.

The 1913 Holley Model S. Back to the two-screw cover but of a less complicated design than that of the 1912 model.

The Holley Model NH, typical 1921 to about 1923. The "1920" NH was similar but the venturi area did not have the "dip" at the needle valve area, and had a brass air breather fitting located on the top surface in place of the brass label in this version. About 1923 the carburetor was redesigned and had the drain valve integral with the bowl retaining nut, as in the 1926 version (below).

The Holley Model G of 1914. Similar in design to the 1912 and 1913 Holleys, the choke arm shaft was now horizontal, and the float bowl was somewhat larger. This model continued until 1920 with minor variations. In 1919 the casting was changed from bronze to cast iron, and the choke arm had two levers (the casting and the levers not necessarily being changed at the same time).

The late 1925 and 1926 version of the Holley NH. The major change was in the universal joint needle valve.

Descriptions

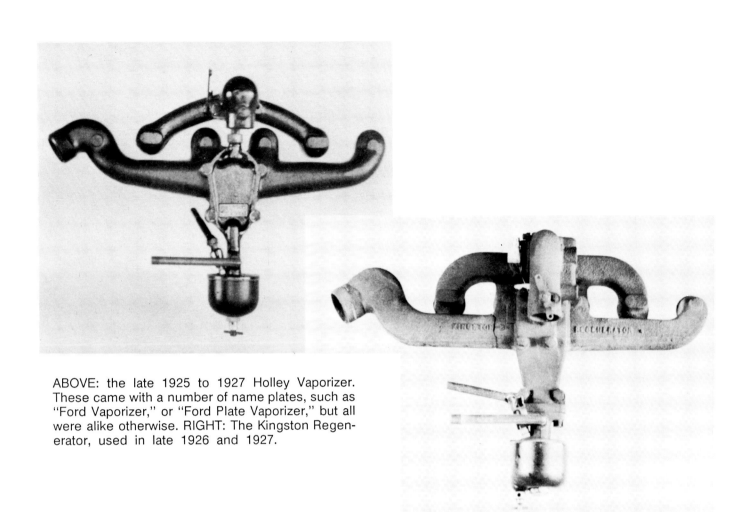

ABOVE: the late 1925 to 1927 Holley Vaporizer. These came with a number of name plates, such as "Ford Vaporizer," or "Ford Plate Vaporizer," but all were alike otherwise. RIGHT: The Kingston Regenerator, used in late 1926 and 1927.

CARBURETORS (Continued)

1922-1925

6150   553A1 Kingston "L4" [425,427]
Around 1924 the L4 was given a new float bowl with a more cylindrical appearance (the bottom corners were "squarer") and a larger retaining nut.

6200B   553A4 Holley "NH" [429]
               Center fuel drain.
This carburetor was also made by Ford, under license from Holley and with the "Ford" name on the plate.

Late 1925-1927

6150B   553B1 Kingston "L4" [429]
               With "U-joint" needle valve.

6200C   553B2 Holley "NH" [397,399,429]
               With "U-joint" needle valve.
6250   2201S Holley Vaporizer * [397,430]
               (Limited number of cars in 1925)

—   —   Kingston Regenerator [430]
               Limited use, in 1927.
* Standard in 1927 models. Also made by Ford, under license. These units came with varying nameplates but were otherwise alike.

CARBURETOR STOVES

1909
No hot air pipe used.

1910-1911
A cast "stove" of apparently two styles and attached to the front of the exhaust mainfold, was connected to a pipe which ran down to the air intake of the carburetor. Carburetors were now supplied with an angled air inlet to match this pipe, and also now had integral choke valves.

1912-1920 (Approximately)
A simple pipe and stove combination which fit under the rear part of the exhaust manifold and clamped to the air intake at the rear of the carburetor. The pipes were castings of iron in 1912-13 but most production was sheet metal. [270]

1920-1924 (Approximately)
A sheet metal type which fitted over the rear of the exhaust manifold and   was secured with a steel arm which was held by the rear manifold stud nut.

1924-1926
Similar in style and location to the previous type except that the metal was formed in such a manner that the need for the separate support arm was eliminated. A hole in the metal now fitted over the manifold stud. [397]

1926-1927
Cars supplied with the Vaporizer carburetors did not use hot air intake pipes.

CHASSIS (Frame)

1909 (Early)
Side rails had riveted reinforcing plates inside the channel. Otherwise similar to regular 1909 production. Painted body color. [70]

1909-1910
Short rear cross-member with forged brackets for body and fender support. Painted body color.

1910-1913
Same as 1909, painted body color until sometime in 1910, then painted black thereafter. (Date unknown.) After 1910 the body support was no longer a part of the fender irons. [149, 156]

1913-1920
Initially the same as the 1911 chassis. About January 1913 two additional rear body brackets were added for the Touring body, under the rear door ahead of the rear seat. These brackets were used only in 1913 and only on the Touring bodies. Longer rear cross-member, beginning about 271,425 (May 1913), eliminating the forged body brackets. Early rear cross-members were relatively flat across the top surface; not raised as in the later versions. While using the same parts, holes were added for the battery brackets beginning in 1919. [150,164]

1920-1925
Same as earlier but pressed-steel running board brackets replaced the riveted-in-place forgings used earlier. The holes used for the forged brackets continued at least until 1923. Beginning in June 1920 the front cross-member was made of heavier steel.

1926-1927
Rear cross-member much longer to accommodate new body and fenders. Rear cross-member was a simple channel in early production, then were made with a flanged design. In 1927 heavier steel was used for increased strength. The front cross-member had added brackets to support the fenders.

COIL BOXES

Part #	Factory #	Description

1909
1520 — Heinze [47]
Early 1909 with terminals on the bottom of the box. This was the same box that was used on the later Model S Fords. Part number is an N-R-S number. This box was discontinued before car number 2500.

1909 to Early 1911
4200 — Kingston [48,49]
Used 4215 coils. Rear terminals.

4250 — Jacobson-Brandow [48]
Used 4256 coils
Note: Ford parts books show the name as Jacobson-Brandon but the actual name was Jacobson-Brandow.

1911
4660 — Kingston [92]
Used 4238 or 4713 coils, 2-9/16 x 2-5/16 x 5-3/4".

4250 — Jacobson/Brandow [92]
Used 4256 coils

4600 — Heinze [92]
First used in 1911. Uses 4611 coils 2-5/16 x 3-1/16 x 5"

1912
4660 — Kingston
(Few used. May have been superseded by 4675 in 1912. Used 4713 coils, 2-9/16 x 2-5/16 x 5-3/4"

4675 1383 Kingston

4600 — Heinze

— — Jacobson-Brandow
Not cataloged. Smaller than 1911 type.

1913
4706 1383 Kingston
Used 4713 coils, 5-3/4 x 2-9/16 x 2-5/16"

4600 — Heinze [161]
Used 4611 coils, 5 x 3-1/16 x 2-5/16"

4725 1383 K-W [161]
Used 4681 coils, 5-3/8 x 3-1/4 x 2-1/4"

4725 1383 Ford [161,176,184]
Metal box, non-sloping lid. Individual coils supplied by Kingston, Heinze and Ford. Used 4732 or 5007 standard-size coils, 5 x 3-1/2 x 2-1/8"

1914
4725 1383 Ford [161,176,184]
Same as 1913 Ford box. Used standard Ford coils, 5 x 3-1/2 x 2-1/8", supplied by Kingston, Heinze or Ford. Switch cover was brass with black background.

1915-1919
4725 1383 Ford [205,215]
Sloping lid. Lid was one-piece in 1915 and 1916 but was changed to assembled type during 1916. Switch had brass escutcheon plate as on the 1914 but was changed to a black steel plate by 1916. The steel cover plate was stamped "Mag-Off-Bat."

1919
4725 1383 Ford
Non-starter cars. The switch is redesigned so that the cover plate covers the top and sides of the switch, same as "1916."

4725B — Ford [331]
Starter cars (no switch on box).

1919-1922
5000 1383 Ford
Same as 4725, non-starter cars.

5001 1383B Ford
Same as 4725B, starter cars.

1922-1925
5001 1383B Ford [331]
All cars (switch was on dashboard)

COIL BOXES (Continued)

1926-1927

    5001B   1383C Ford [397,398]
        Mounted on the engine, except for 1926 TT trucks.

COLORS

See BODIES, PAINTS, or information under specific part or assembly.

CONTROL RODS

(Also see Steering Column)

CARBURETOR

1909-1915 [185]

    "L" shaped adjuster, threaded on, at carburetor end.

1915-1927

    Adjuster eliminated, rod now just a bent piece.

CHOKE (Instrument panel)

1919

    Knob was cold rolled.

1919-1925

    Knob was aluminum casting on steel rod. [331]

Late 1925-1927

    Aluminum knob which now turned to adjust the needle valve. A sliding sleeve arrangement closed the choke when the knob was pulled. [391,399]

COMMUTATOR

1909-1922

    Ball joint swivel joint at steering column end, threaded on control rod. [67,318]

1922-1927

    Swivel eliminated; now just a plain rod, bent to fit.

CRANK

Early 1909

    Wooden handle [67]

1909-1911

    Handle was hard rubber, secured with a long bolt. [67]

1911

    Handle changed to aluminum during production year. Painted black *including handle*. [107,162]

1912-1914

    Aluminum handle the same as the later 1911 type (All black, including handle.) [162]

1914-1921

    Handle changed to an iron sleeve, held with a rivet-like bolt. Later versions have been seen which used a riveted-in-place pin instead of the bolt. [185]

1922-1927

    Handle a thin steel sleeve rolled into place on a formed crank. [324]

DASHBOARD (Firewall)

1909

    Brass trim on edges did not overlap the wood. Additional piece added on top if windshield was used, this piece varying in design and shape.

1910

    Same as 1909 but all had windshield and added piece.

1911

    Similar in design to 1910 but brass trim now overlaped the wood panel. Continued the separate top section.

1912

    One-piece design eliminated the add-on top section used earler, beginning about April 1912. **NOTE:** Many boards of this era were made for right or left-hand drive, with the carburetor adjustment hole drilled on both sides. The patent plate covered the hole. The board was just reversed for right-hand drive; and the components mounted on the rear-facing side.

1913-1914

    One piece design. Flat brass trim. Now mated with the body metal.

1915-1923

    Wood, painted black, outside cowl. Rain gutter added at cowl in 1919.

1923

    Steel, used with low hood for short time in early 1923.

1923-1925

    Steel, larger for higher hood.

1926-1927

    Steel, integral with the body. Trucks continued the 1925 type.

DRIVESHAFT

1909

    Babbitt pinion bearing. "Two-piece" housing (with separate u-joint housing). Driveshaft pinion riveted to non-tapered shaft, using a Woodruff key, until #7,000 (July). At that time the shaft was modified to secure the gear with a nut, but was still not tapered at the gear.

1910 [32]

    Roller pinion bearing housing, with 3/8" studs after 18,000 (March 17). "Two-piece"housing. Pinion thrust bearing is P/N 2589, an assembly of 2589 cup, 2590 race, 15 2592 or 2811 balls, and a 2590 snap ring. Driveshaft now had tapered end for the pinion gear.

1911-1913 [187]

    Similar to 1910, pinion bearing housing now used 13/32" studs.

1913-1920

    U-joint housing integral with shaft housing. Used cast pinion bearing housing with enclosed stud mount (same as 1911-1913). In July 1919 Ford introduced a 4:1 ring and pinion set using a 12-tooth pinion and a 48-tooth ring gear.

1920-1927

    A new forged pinion bearing spool identified by the exposed mounting bolts (instead of enclosed studs). Rear flange of driveshaft housing was machined to match the new spool (no longer had the lip that fit the earlier spool). The pinion thrust bearing was of the three-piece type, using two 2591 races, and a 2591 ball bearing assembly. These changes were made during 1920. In January 1920, the ten tooth pinion was introduced, and the previous 12 and 48 tooth gears were discontinued. The ten tooth pinion worked with the standard ring gear.

DRIVESHAFT HOUSING

Part #	Factory #	Description

1909-1910
2533   153   Babbitt pinion bearing.

1910-1911
2582   74C   After 18,000
Drilled for 3/8" studs. (March 17)

1911-1913
2582   153D   Drilled for 13/32" studs.

1913-1920
2582   153D   "One-piece" type.

1920-1927
2582   153D
Flange modified for new pinion bearing.

ENGINE

General Specifications:

Bore/Stroke	3-3/4 by 4"
Displacement	176.7 cu"
Brake H.P.	22 at 1600 R.P.M.
	20 at 1600 after 1912
N.A.C.C. H.P.	22.5
Torque	83 ft/lbs at 900 R.P.M.
Compression Ratio	4.5:1 approx.
	4.1:1 after 1912
	3.98:1 after 1916

1909 (Early water-pump engines) [34-37]
Ser. # 1 to 309   Calendar year 1908
1 to 2500   Model year
(Oct. 1908 to May 1909)
S/N (serial number) located between center exhaust ports. Gear driven water pump and fan. Oil pipe on left front side. 3/8" head bolts on first 500, 7/16" later. No babbitt in upper main or camshaft bearings. Open valve chambers. Flat-top pistons with three or four rings, some with all rings above the pin and some with one ring below. Piston pin was held in the piston with one bolt. The connecting rods had bronze bushings for the pin, and oil dippers as an integral part of the crankshaft end.

1909 [37]
Ser. # 310 to 14,161   Calendar year 1909.
2501 to 8,100   Model year
(May 1, 1909 to July 31, 1909).
Note: Ford's published data shows 1 to 11,100 built between Oct. 1, 1908 and Sept. 30, 1909.

S/N on boss behind cam gear housing on right side of engine. No babbitt in upper main or camshaft bearings. Thermo-syphon cooling. Piston pin now turned in the piston and was clamped in the rod. Oil dippers were dropped.

VALVE TIMING:
Intake opened with piston down 7/64" After T.D.C.
(13/64" above) *
Intake closed with piston up 3/8" After B.D.C.
(3-5/16") *
Exhaust opened with piston up 3/8" Before B.D.C.
(3-5/16") *

Exhaust closed with piston down 1/16" After T.D.C.
(19/64" above) *
     * Piston position from top of cylinder.

1910
Ser. # 14,162 to 34,901   Calendar 1910.
8,101 to 31,500 approx., Model year
(Aug. 1, 1909 to Oct. 1, 1910).
Note: Ford's published data shows 11,101 to 31,900 between Oct. 1, 1909 and Sept. 30, 1910.

Same as 1909. In March the magneto magnets were enlarged from 1/2 to 9/16" (beginning about 17,501). In April the magnets were again changed to 5/8" (beginning with 20,501).

1911 [96]
Ser. # 34,902 to 88,900 approx.
Calendar year 1911.
31,500 to 70,750 approx.
Fiscal year (Oct. 1, 1910 to Oct. 1, 1911).
Note: Ford's published data shows 31,901 to 69,876 built between Oct. 1, 1910 and Sept. 30, 1911.

Same as 1910 until 38,263 (February 14) when babbitt began to be used in the upper main bearings. This may have occurred along with the enclosed valve chambers, also introduced about this time. Beginning with 46,326 (April 7) all engines were the new type with the enclosed valve chambers. Valve doors were secured with wing nuts initially but these were replaced with T517 hex nuts about November 7, 1911. The inspection plate was heavier and had a sharp embossing pattern. It was secured with a one-piece bolt collar.

1912 [125,132,138]
Ser. # 88,901 to 183,563
Calendar year 1912.
70,750 to 157,424 approx.
Fiscal year (Oct. 1, 1911 to Oct. 1, 1912)
Note: Ford's published data shows 69,877 to 157,205 built between Oct. 1, 1911 and Sept. 30, 1912.

VALVE TIMING (Revised during 1912, and typical through 1927)
Intake opened with piston down 1/16" After T.D.C.
(1/4" above) *
Intake closed with piston up 9/16" After B.D.C.
(3-1/8") *
Exhaust opened with piston up 5/16" Before B.D.C.
(3-3/8") *
Exhaust closed with piston at Top Dead Center.
(5/16") *
     * Piston position from top of cylinder.
Same general design as later 1911. Serial number boss moved to position behind the water inlet at about 100,000, then to the standard position above the inlet a short time later (both types appearing simultaneously for a time). By the end of 1912 all were in the final location.

1913 [163]
Ser. # 183,564 to 408,347
Calendar year 1913.
157,425 to 348,735 approx.
Fiscal year (Oct. 1, 1912 to Oct. 1, 1913).
Ser.# B-1 to B-12,247 built in Detroit.
Note: Ford's published data shows 169,452 to 370,147, plus B1 to B12,247 built between Oct. 1, 1912 and Sept. 30, 1913.

ENGINES (Continued)

1913 (Continued)

Same as 1912 type. Last year the screw-in pipe plugs were used to seal the water jackets. Welch plugs were used beginning about 200,000 (February) and in all production after about 450,000. Compression ratio lowered to about 4:1. Brake H.P. now 20. Last year for flat-top pistons. Inspection plate bolt collar was now two pieces. Some cylinder heads drilled on left side for priming cups; these holes being filled with 1/8" pipe plugs.

1914 [185]

Ser. # 408,348 to 656,063
    Calendar year 1914.
    348,736 to 670,000 approx.
    Model year (Oct. 1, 1913 to Mid-Jan. 1915).
Note: Ford's published data shows 370,148 to 570,790 built between Oct. 1, 1913 and July 31, 1914

Redesigned cylinder casting. Slightly larger water jackets with holes covered with welch plugs. Magneto magnets increased to 3/4" beginning with 572,437 (Sep. 4) and on all engines after 598,042 (Oct. 2).

1915 [228]

Ser. # 656,064 to 1,028,313
    Calendar year 1915.
    670,000 to 856,513 approx.
    Model year (Jan. 1915 to Aug. 1, 1915).
Ford's published data shows 570,791 to 773,487 built between Aug. 1, 1914 and Apr. 30, 1915, and 773,488 to 855,500 built between May 1, 1915 and July 31, 1915.

Connecting rods redesigned for lighter weight. Babbitt now 1/16" thick instead of 1/8".

1916

Ser. # 1,028,314 to 1,614,516
    Calendar year 1916.
    856,514 to 1,362,813 approx.
    Fiscal year (Aug. 1, 1915 to Aug. 1, 1916).
Note: Ford's published data shows 855,501 to 1,362,200 built Aug. 1, 1915 to July 31, 1916.

1917 [270]

Ser. # 1,614,517 to 2,449,179
    Calendar year 1917.
    1,362,814 to 2,113,501 approx.
    Fiscal year (Aug. 1, 1916 to Aug. 1, 1917).
New "high" head with larger water jacket introduced. Compression ratio slightly lower to 3.98 to 1.

1918

Ser. # 2,449,180 to 2,831,426
    Calendar year 1918.
    2,113,502 to 2,756,251 approx.
    Fiscal year (Aug. 1, 1917 to Aug. 1, 1918).

1919 [277,283]

Ser. # 2,831,427 to 3,659,971
    Calendar year 1919.
    2,756,252 to 3,277,851 approx.
    Fiscal year (Aug. 1, 1918 to Aug. 1, 1919).
Beginning with 2,815,891 (December 11, 1918) the first starter type engines were built. Regular production of starter engines began January 1, 1919, used in the closed cars only. All engines built were starter type after June, but used blanking plates at the starter, and a different casting at the timing gear on non-starter cars. Magneto post had metal retaining collar around its base.

1920 [283]

Ser. # 3,659,972 to 4,698,419
    Calendar year 1920.
    3,277,852 to 4,233,351 approx.
    Fiscal year (Aug. 1, 1919 to Aug. 1, 1920).
New light weight rod with 1/16" babbitt introduced. A lighter piston was also introduced which had no reinforcing bosses at the pin and no boss at the bottom. The larger fan pulleys started on "truck engines" on May 1, 1920.

1921

Ser. # 4,698,420 to 5,568,071
    Calendar year 1921.
    4,233,352 to 5,377,545 approx.
    Fiscal year (Aug. 1, 1920 to Aug. 1, 1921).

1922

Ser. # 5,568,072 to 6,953,071
    Calendar year 1922.
    5,377,546 to 6,344,196 approx.
    Fiscal year (Aug. 1, 1921 to Aug. 1, 1922).
Beginning with about 5,530,000 (November 1921) the cylinder casting was altered to use the single valve chamber door. Beginning with 5,812,609 (April 3, 1922) all engines used the single door.

1923

Ser. # 6,953,072 to 9,008,371
    Calendar year 1923.
    6,344,197 to 8,122,674 approx.
    Fiscal year (Aug. 1, 1922 to Aug. 1, 1923).

1924 [348]

Ser. # 9,008,372 to 10,994,033
    Calendar year 1924.
    8,122,675 to 10,266,471 approx.
    Fiscal year (Aug. 1, 1923 to Aug. 1, 1924).
New lightweight pistons introduced March 12. Beginning April 14 the camshaft was modified to use a shorter front bearing. On July 17 the oil tube was given a larger intake funnel, and by August 12 all had the new tube. On July 18 the crankcase was changed to the "four-dip" type. Began 1/32" babbitt in front and center mains in June and in all cars beginning July 16.

1925

Ser. # 10,994,034 to 12,990,076
    Calendar year 1925.
    10,266,472 to 12,218,728 approx.
    Model year (Aug. 1, 1924 to July 27, 1925, the start of 1926 models).

1926 [397]

Ser. # 12,990,077 to 14,619,254
    Calendar year 1926.
    12,218,729 to 14,049,029 approx.
    Fiscal/Model year (July 27, 1925 to Aug. 1, 1926).
Cylinder casting again modified to have boss at rear to mate with new transmission cover which bolted to the cylinder beginning July 27, 1925 with S/N 12,218,729. Beginning in July 1926 the engines were painted a Drake Green Pyroxlyn.

ENGINES (Continued)

1927

Ser. # 14,619,255 to 15,076,231
January 1 to December 31, 1927.
14,049,030 to 15,006,625 approx.
(August 2, 1926 to May 26, 1927).

Beginning in August 1926 the felt front crankshaft seal was changed to the asbestos type with the rubber core. During 1927 the hole between the center cylinders was closed. Since all cars used the Vaporizer type carburetor, the throttle rod passed over the engine instead of through it.

NOTE: Model T car production ended at Highland Park May 26 with #15,006,625. (Records show the last number to be 15,007,032 but according to the engine production figures, only engines (no cars) were built on May 31, 1927. There was no production from May 27 to May 31, then engines and/or trucks began on May 31 (15,006,626 to 15,007,032).

1927-1941

15,007,033 to 15,176,888 (Last number built on August 4, 1941. Seven T engines built in 1941). 169,855 Model T engines built after the last Model T car.

ENGINE COLOR (Painting)

Little written evidence exists that indicates engines were painted any color. If painted, early cars (1909) were painted chassis (body) color, and all were black if painted after the early production. Ford records do not indicate an engine paint. In general, if the engine was painted, the oil pan and transmission cover was also painted, except in the case of the aluminum transmission covers, which were bare aluminum. The late 1926 and 1927 engines were painted green. The green was called (by Ford) Drake Green, and was the same color as the green used on the closed cars. The story persists that the green was the same color as the later Model A engines, but there is some question as to whether or not this is true. Perhaps the very late 1927 engines were this color, and most certainly those T engines built after the Model T era could have been "Model A Green."

ENGINE MOUNT

(Front bearing and spring clip)

1909 (320) (Early water pump engines) [40,67]
Unique design with crank-holding arrangement.

1909-1921 3076 (320B)
Two "U" bolts used to clamp mount to frame. There were a number of variations in the design. The 1910 to 1911 had rather extended mounting "ears," and the late 1911 and later were relatively even-sided. between the bolt eyes. There were minor variations in the general shape as well. [40,67,107,162,268]

1921-1925 3076B (320C)
Forged design with two integral studs, secured with a clip under the spring, two nuts and cotters. [324]

1926-1927 3076B2 (320D)
Similar to previous but has threaded hole in front to which the radiator apron is fastened. [386]

ENGINE SPECIFICATIONS

Note: These dimensions are from the Ford Service Course, and relate to new engines built after 1913. There may be variations over the years. Some dimensions will not apply to modern replacement parts (pistons, valves, etc.).

Crankshaft dimensions

Length of bearings	Front	2"
	Center	2-3/16"
	Rear	3-1/8"
	Rods	1.505"
Bearing diameter (all)		1.248"
Overall length		25-5/32"

Camshaft dimensions

Length		22-23/32"
Bearing diameters (all)		.748"
Bearing lengths	Front	1.967"
	Center	2-7/16"
	Rear	1.750"
Width of cams		7/8"
Diameter of heel of cam		13/16"
Greatest diameter of cam		1-1/16"
Flange diameter		1-3/4"
Flange width		1/4"
Dowel holes		.3120-.3125"
Thread	Large	13/16 x 16 USF
	Small	9/16 x 18 SAE

Cylinder bores   3.750" dia.
   6.752" long
Cylinder head bolt holes   7/16 x 14
Camshaft bearing holes

	Front	1.374-1.375"
	Center	1.372-1.373"
	Rear	.9985-1.000"

Main bearings   1.248-1.249"
Manifold ports   1-1/8"
(With 1-1/4" countersink, 1/8" deep)
Pistons

Diameter	Skirt	3.748-3.749"
	2nd ring	3.743-3.745"
	Top	3.738-3.740"
Ring grooves		1/4 x 13/64 deep
Pin bushing diameter		.740-.741"
Wrist pin diameter		.740-.741"
Wrist pin length		3-1/2"
Ring gaps (original rings)		
	Top	.003"
	Center	.005"
	Bottom	.008"
Push rods	Length	2-11/32"
	Diam.	.4355-.4365"
	Head dia.	1"

Push rod guide holes   .437"
Valves

Diameter of head & upper edge of seat	1-15/32"
Diameter of lower edge	1-17/64–1-9/32"
Width of valve seat	3/32"
Angle of valve seat	45 degrees
Thickness of head	3/16"
Stem diameter	.3105-.312"
Overall length	4.974" +
Retainer pin hole	.110-.113"
4-19/32" from valve seat line	

Valve lift   7/32"
Valve tappet to stem clearance   .022-.032"
Valve ports   1-5/16"
Valve stem guide holes   .3125"

Descriptions

ENGINE PAN

1909 (3069) F/N 800 Early 1909
One-piece with long front bearing in which the rear bearing rivet was located behind the front oil seal, inside the crankcase area. The rear flange had no reinforcement. Had oil dam behind fourth cylinder. Rather deep oil troughs under rods. [41]

1909 3069 (1526B)
One-piece with no inspection plate on bottom. Had oil dam at rear cylinder. Shorter front bearing with rear rivet now outside the crankcase area. Dust pans on side of engine and transmission. [42]

1910
Similar to 1909. Reinforcement added at the rear flange early in the year. Later the oil dam was dropped. [42]

1911 3100 (800D)
Similar to 1910. Beginning in February a new magneto was used and a new, wider, square-hole transmission cover and pan was introduced. This new pan was still "one-piece" but had shallower troughs than the 1909-10 type. About 44,400 (March), the pan with the removable bottom plate appeared. The inspection plate was of heavier metal than the common type, had deeper troughs (7/8" vs 11/16") than the later types, and was embossed around the edges. The inspection plate retaining collar was one piece and was riveted in place. The riveting is believed to have been discontinued during the year. Deep "teacup" oil drain. [42,100]

1912 3100 (1526C)
Similar to the later 1911 type with removable bottom. The 1911 type inspection plate may have been replaced by the thinner, shallower, "standard" type during this period (date unknown). 1912 is believed to have been the last year for transmission side dust pans but engine side pans continued until the end of Model T production. [137,140]

1913-1916 3100 (1526C)
Early 1913 cars used the 1912-style pan except that the mounting ears were held with just three rivets (instead of seven). The slotted drain plug was still used. About June 1913 the now-standard design (no deep drain cup, and 15/16" drain plug) appeared. Narrow front "nose" continued until 1917. The two piece inspection plate screw retaining collar appeared in 1913.

1917-1924 3100 (1526E)
Wider front nose to allow larger crank pulley (which didn't appear until 1920).

1924-1927 3100 (1526E)
(No part number change from earlier style.) Similar to 1917-24 but now with larger "four-dip" inspection plate. (New pan began in July 1924.) Pressed-steel reinforcing brackets used at the engine/transmission junction corners sometime later. By November 1925, all engines also had the support straps from the motor mount to the transmission bolts at the rear of the cylinder block (1926 models and later).

FAN

1909 (First 2500 water pump engines)
The fan was gear driven from an extension of the water pump shaft. Unique to these early engines. [36]

1909-1910
Brass hub. Blades riveted to hub. Fan blades had a deeper embossed groove than the blades of the later (1911 on?) type. Belt tension by a coil spring against cast-in "knob" on the short, bent fan bracket. [38]

1911
Same fan assembly as 1910 but belt tension by a screw in the same location as the old spring, the head of which rested on the old cast-in knob on the fan bracket. [38,98]

1912-1916
Similar fan assembly but tension screw now pressed against a boss at the pivot end of the arm. The cast-in "knob" on the fan bracket was discontinued around 1913. [98]

1916-1920
Similar to earlier type but hub was now cast iron. In 1916 (1917 cars) the fan bracket was changed to the longer and straighter type, which was used until the 1926 models. Early production 1917 cars used a fan shroud behind the radiator but this was apparently discontinued after a short time. [254,271]

1920-1925
Beginning May 1, 1920 a larger aluminum hub with one-piece blade assembly (two blade pieces welded together as an assembly) began on trucks at first, then all cars. [364]

1926-1927
Similar to 1925 but shorter hub to allow water outlet mounting of fan assembly. Early production used a "worm screw" fan adjustment on the water outlet. About February 1926 this was changed to a simpler and less fragile eccentric which was locked in place by the fan bearing bolt nut. [397, 400-401]

FAN BELTS
(All 1-1/8" wide by 7/64" thick, length +/- 1/8")

1909-1916
23" long (inside circumference)

1917-1920
25-3/4" long

1920-1925
26-5/16" long

1926-1927
31-3/4" long

FENDERS

1909-1910

Type with uniform width upper sections and one-piece inserted aprons. Early 1909 types had square fronts and no bills. Later ones were rounded at the front and had bills. Rear fenders supported by irons that ran under the apron on the early 1909 cars; later the irons passed through holes in apron. Painted body color.

1909

Early Production, All body types. [59,62]
(red, green or gray)

Part #	Factory #	Description	
			(red, green or gray).
—	1413	L/F	Square front, no bill.
—	1414	R/F	
—	1415	L/R	No hole in apron.
—	1416	R/R	Supported with irons that ran under the apron.

1909-1910

All body types [59,62-66]
Green only after June 1909

2925	1413A	L/F	Round front with bill.
2926	1414A	R/F	
2927	1415B	L/R	Hole in apron
2928	1416B	R/R	fender iron,

1911-1912

New style fenders with a flared top panel and inserted splash panels. The front fenders were billed, had no reinforcing ribs on the apron. Rear fenders now secured to the body with a single post extending from the body panel (tourings). Fenders were blue, even on now-extant original "black" cars. During 1911 the front fender irons had a "cast-in" eye for the top straps, but this was dropped for 1912 and later. [88]

1911 Touring, Roadster, Town Car (blue)

4801	1413B	L/F	With bill.
4800	1414B	R/F	
4803	1415C	L/R	
4802	1416C	R/R	
4821	1716B	L/F	60" Tread
4820	1715B	R/F	
4823	1748	L/R	
4822	1749	R/R	

1911 Torpedo Roadster and Open Runabout (blue)

4841	2562	L/F	
4840	2561	R/F	
4843	2554	L/R	Curved rear fenders
4842	2555	R/R	
4861	2707	L/F	60" Tread
4860	2706	R/F	
4864	2709	L/R	
4863	2708	R/R	

1912 Touring, Roadster, Torpedo, Town Car [88]

Part #	Factory #	Description	
4801	1413B	L/F	
4800	1414B	R/F	
4821	1716B	L/F	60" Tread
4820	1715B	R/F	
4803	1415C	L/R	
4802	1516C	R/R	
4823	1748	L/R	60" Tread
4822	1749	R/R	

1912 Torpedo, Curved (Also used on earlier standard runabout.)

3783	5218	L/R	or
4803B	5218		
3782	5206	R/R	or
4802B	5206		
4881	—	L/R	or
4823B	2732		60" Tread
4880 or	—	R/R	or
4823C	2733		60" Tread
4414	5212	L/R	or
4803C	5212		Delivery Car
4413	5209	R/R	or
4802C	5209		Delivery Car

1913

Similar to 1912 but front bill was eliminated. Earlier front fenders had a front lip which flared outward, as if the bill had been just cut off. No embossed moldings in the triangular splash apron area. [159]

Touring, Roadster

4801	1413B	L/F	Same part number but
4800	1414B	R/F	now with no front bill.
4803	1415C	L/R	
4802	1416C	R/R	
4821B	2743	L/F	60" Tread
4820B	2742	R/F	
4823D	2740	L/R	
4822B	2741	R/R	

1914

Similar to 1913 but with reinforcing beads added across widest part and in apron area on both front and rear fenders. Later versions appeared with the embossed moldings in the splash apron area and with a front bill. Front fender bracket secured with four rivets (as in all previous fenders). Used from late 1913 to early 1915. [180]

Touring. Roadster

4801	1413C	L/F	
4800	1414C	R/F	
4803	1415C	L/R	
4802	1416C	R/R	
4821B	2743	L/F	60" Tread
4820B	2742	R/F	
4823D	2740	L/R	
4822B	2741	R/R	

Descriptions

FENDERS (Continued)

1915-1916

Similar in style to the late 1914 type; front bill, three rivets now used to secure the front fender iron bracket. Rear fenders were now curved to follow the wheel outline; have no crown. Bracket added between splash apron and rear fender. [223-224]

Touring, Roadster, 1916 Sedan, and Coupelet

Part #	Factory #	Description
4801	1413C	L/F With bill.
4800	1414C	R/F
4803D	1415D	L/R Curved rear fenders.
4802D	1416D	R/R
4821B	2743	L/F 60" Tread
4820B	2742	R/F
4823E	2759	L/R
4822C	2758	R/R

1915 Sedans (1916 Sedan same as above) [207]

4803E	7925	L/R
4802E	7924	R/R
4823F	5724	L/R 60" Tread
4822D	5723	R/R

1917-1923

Front and rear fenders now curved and crowned.
Touring, Roadster, Sedan and Coupe

4801B	7977	L/F
4800B	7976	R/F
4803F	8851	L/R
4802F	8850	R/R

Fordor Sedans only, 1922-1923

4803G	7731	L/R
4802G	7730	R/R

1923-1924

Lip added to front fender apron to match new radiator apron.
Touring, Roadster, Tudor, Fordor and Coupe

4801C	7977B	L/F
4800C	7976B	R/F
4803F	8851	L/R
4802F	8850	R/R
4803G	7731	L/R Tudor & Fordor Sedans
4802G	7730	R/R
4803H	8851B	L/R Coupe
4802H	8850B	R/R

1925

Beginning in late 1924: similar to 1923 style but bead on front fenders now ran under the splash aprons. Rear fenders made a bit wider; now flared out from the running board. There seems to have been some overlap; both types having been used until about the first of 1925. Coupe and Roadster rear fenders had larger skirts in late 1925. [344]

Touring, Roadster, Tudor, Fordor and Coupe

4801C	7977B	L/F
4800C	7976B	R/F
4803F	8851	L/R
4802F	8850	R/R

Part #	Factory #	Description
4803G	7731	L/R Tudor & Fordor Sedans
4802G	7730	R/R
4803H	8851B	L/R Coupe
4802H	8850B	R/R

NOTE: In late 1925 production the rear fender aprons on the coupe and roadster were made larger to cover more of the running gear. These two body styles used the same fender. [344,351]

1926-1927

Completely new design (except for trucks which continued the 1925 style).

Touring, Roadster, Tudor, Fordor and Coupe

4801D	40109	L/F
4800D	40108	R/F
4803J	40124	L/R Touring, Tudor, Fordor
4802J	40123	R/R
4803K	40131	L/R Roadster, Coupe
4802K	40130	R/R

FLOOR BOARDS

Floor Board Hinge

—	1043	Early 1909

Floor Board Hinge Screw

—	1044	Early 1909

Front Floor Board (First or top board)

1909

—	1098	First 800 (2-pedal cars)

1909-1914

3626	1098B	9/16 x 7-1/4 x 29-5/8"

1911 Torpedo

3706	2610	9/16 x 6-5/8 x 26-1/8"

1915-1925

3626B	7296	
3626C	4200	With pedal plate
3626C2	4200BR	With pedal plate, for use with 1926 engine in earlier cars.

Note: 1915 boards had a notch to clear the bulb horn tube, just to the right of the steering column. While unused by 1916, this notch continued for some time, at least into 1917.

1926-1927

45331X	45331	With plate

Front Floor Board (Second)

1909 First 800 (2-pedal cars)

—	1401	Left half
—	1092	Right half
—	1402	Both halves

1909-1914

3627	1402B	9/16x5-21/32x29-5/8" (1909)

1911 Torpedo

3707	2611	9/16 x 5-3/4 x 27-1/4"

1915-1925

3626B	7297	
3627C	4201	With pedal plate
3627C2	4201BR	With pedal plate, for use with 1926 engine in earlier cars.

FLOOR BOARDS (Continued)

Front Floor Board (Second, Continued)
1926-1927

45332X	45332	With plate

Front Floor Board (Third)
1909 First 800 (2-pedal cars)

—	1404

1909-1912

3628	1404B	9/16 x 11-5/8 x 29-5/8"

1911 Torpedo

3708	2612	9/16 x 11-7/16 x 29-3/16"

1913-1925

3628	1404 or 1404B	Specify size
3628B	7104	With plate

1926-1927

45332X	45332	With plate

Front Floor Board (Fourth)
1909 First 800 (2-pedal cars)

—	1403

1909-1912

3629	1403B	9/16 x 3-15/16 x 29-5/8"

1911 Torpedo

3709	2613	9/16 x 5-3/8 x 29-9/16"

1913-1914

3629	1403	Specify size

Front Floor Board (Fifth)
1911 Torpedo

3710	2629	9/16 x 5-3/8 x 30"

NOTE: Judging from original cars, it appears that floor boards were often not painted. The author has new old stock front and rear boards which have never been painted, although they may have been coated with some sort of preservative. Owners of original cars find that some are painted black and others are bare.

FLOOR MATS

NOTE: The size and pattern of the floor mats evolved to suit the body. In addition, many front mats were embossed on both sides so that the same mat could be used on right or left hand drive cars. Closed cars used a wool mat, front and rear.

1909-1910 [68]
Off-white rubber in front; wool carpet in rear of tourings. White rubber mat on rear of mother-in-law seat roadsters.

1911-1912 [105,123]
Off-white rubber in front; cocoa mat in rear of tourings.

1912-1916
Black rubber front mat; cocoa mat in rear of tourings.

1917-1922 [266-267]
Black rubber front mat; wool mat in rear of tourings.

1923-1927
Black rubber front and rear of tourings.

FRAME (See Chassis)

FRONT AXLE

1909-1910 [28]
Style with one-piece spindles. Tie rod above the wishbone, with integral ball/yoke fitting on right end, and adjustment yoke at the left end. The locking bolt of the adjustment yoke is at right angles to the steering arm bolt (was in a horizontal position as installed on the car). The drag link was threaded at the column end with a fine (20 T.P.I.) thread. No oilers on most 1909 production tie rods, etc. Radius rod ball cap secured with studs and nut in early 1909, then with a bolt from 1909 until 1913. Drag link and radius rod used pressed-steel end caps.

1911 [94]
On January 31 (#36,972) the new axle with the two-piece spindles appeared. The tie rod now was below the wishbone. The steering drag link was threaded at the column end with a coarse thread (13 T.P.I.). Brass oilers on all joints except the drag link.

1911-1912
Same as later 1911. The steering arm with the hole for the speedometer, introduced in August 1911, was standard. Radius rod and drag link caps changed to forged type sometime in this era.

1913-1914 [162,191]
Steering drag link had integral ball sockets riveted and braced in place at each end. During 1913 the radius rod ball was secured with stud, spring, and nut, replacing the bolt used since 1909. The steering tie rod adjusting yoke now had its locking bolt parallel to the spindle arm bolt (vertical as installed on the car).

1915-1917 [227,229]
Similar to 1914 but the right steering arm no longer had the hole for the speedometer gear assembly. Oilers evolved from the brass type to the pressed metal type.

1918 [280]
The drag link now had integral forged ends, replacing the riveted-brazed type used since 1913. The steering tie rod was changed to the type with the integral left socket; the adjustment was now at the right end and was locked by the ball nut.

1919-1920
The front radius rod now fastened below the axle at the spring perch studs. Steering arms modified so that the tie rod now was above the wishbone. Oilers were all of the flip-top type. Spindles made a bit longer to better accommodate the new Timken roller wheel bearings.

1921-1925 [346]
Similar to 1920 but mounting holes in the radius rod now bored to fit a tapered nut for a tighter grip at the front axle. Early 1922 *Parts Lists* show spindles with integral arms (one piece) but whether or not they were used is unknown. [73]

1926-1927 [390]
Similar to 1925 but spindles are higher on the spindle body to lower the chassis. New steering drag link which is about an inch shorter than the previous type.

Descriptions

FUEL TANK

1909-1911 [65]

Cylindrical with sediment bulb at right end. Brackets were an integral (riveted in place) part of the tank. Sediment bulb was riveted in place after the early 1909 production (which screwed in).

1911-1912 [102,121]

Same design as earlier 1911 but sediment bulb moved to center of tank, over the driveshaft. Sediment bulb was brass and screwed into the tank.

1912-1915 [218]

Brackets now separate and clamp around tank. Drain now right of center, between the frame and driveshaft. Sediment bulb was brass. 1915 sedan used rectangular tank under rear seat. [204] Coupelet used the standard tank under the seat.

1916-1920 [218,251]

Same as 1915 type but sediment bulb was now iron. Sedans used "square" tank with sloping top, under driver's seat. The Coupelet used the standard round tank under the seat until about 1918, then the round tank was moved to the rear compartment. Around 1919 the Coupelet tank was replaced with the square sedan tank, but still located in the rear compartment.

1920-1925 [323,364]

Oval shaped tank replaced round type. Construction was similar to previous tank except for oval cross-section. Two door sedans and coupes continued the square tank, but oval tank was used in a number of coupes in late 1920, apparently as as experiment. All coupes of the 1924-25 style used the oval tank under the seat.

1926-1927 [400]

Tank now mounted under the cowl except for the Fordor Sedans and the trucks, which continued the oval tank under the seat.

HOOD

1909

Steel, with no louvres. Hinges were integral with the panels in early 1909. [64]
Later production hood hinges were separate, shorter, and riveted to the panels, which were now aluminum. The hood former in all 1909 and 1910 production had a notch to clear the original hinge rod but the notch continued until about 1911. [39]

1910

Aluminum, with no louvres. Clamps were forged with one "ear." Clash strip was wood, painted body color. [51,64]

1911

Similar in style to the late 1910. Aluminum handles, riveted in place.

1912

Same as 1911. Hold-down clamps now had two ears. [124,185]

1913-1914

Similar to 1912. Handles changed to iron, riveted in place.

1915-1916

Similar to 1914 but now with side louvres. Made of steel in later 1915 and 1916. [211]

1917-1920

New style with design to match the "all black" look. Hood handles were pressed steel, riveted in place. Hood clash strip changed from wood to steel.

1920-1923

In July 1920 the handle design eliminated the rivets by using an extrusion of the handle as a "rivet."

1923-1925

Similar to 1917 style but larger to match new higher radiator and body cowl. Hood clash strip larger and swept outward at the rear. [346]

1926-1927

All new styling but of similar construction to 1925.

HORN

1909-1911 [51,93]

Rubes or Non-Pareil double-twist. By 1911 the hose connection pointed down at an angle so that the hose did not interfere with the "door" opening.

1912 [93,160]

Rubes or Non-Pareil double or single-twist. Late production used some 1913 styles.

1913-1914 [160,190]

Rubes or Non-Pareil single-twist. Now made of steel with brass trim.

1915 [214]

Early production used the bulb horn, mounted under the hood. This was superseded by a magneto-powered horn, with a brass-trimmed bell, beginning in some production in January 1915. Both horns mounted under the hood by the steering column. All electric, with no brass trim, by October 1915.

1916-1922 [214,272,279,322]

Magneto horn standard on all cars. Mounted on firewall near steering column.

1922-1925 [322]

Electric vibrator-type horn used on cars with battery. Magneto type continued on non-electric cars. Both types mounted on left side of the engine.

1926-1927 [398,401]

Same horn as 1925 but with new bracket to mount on water inlet, below the coil box. Magneto type used in non-electric cars.

HUB CAPS (See WHEEL, Hub Caps)

INSTRUMENT PANEL

1909-1918

None used. Instruments, if any, were attached to the dashboard (firewall). Accessory instrument boards were supplied by accessory manufacturers, not by Ford.

1919

Boards were wood with "leather" covering in early closed cars, and wood with metal covering later. Open cars, when equipped with starter, used wooden panels initially. The ammeter was of large (about 2" diameter glass) size and had a more elaborate movement than the later meters. Initially, the ammeter had no script but early in the year "Ford Motor Company" was specified. Then in about April, just "Ford" was used on the face. The light switch handle was cast, and painted black. The meter and switch was mounted on a rectangular panel which, in turn, was mounted on the instrument panel.

1919-1922

Metal panel of near uniform width from side to side. The end mounting ears were exposed and were fastened to the rear windshield post support bolt. Instrument panels on open cars only when supplied with electrical equipment. Ammeter about the same size but of simple design. The switch handle was now pressed steel. Handle, mounting board, and switch were all black.

1922-1923

Metal panel now had slope, with lower mounting bolts behind the panel. The width tapers upwards at each side. Non-electric cars used a blanking plate at the ammeter location. [318,331]

1924-1925

Similar to 1923 but now had a support bracket for the steering column. [364]

1926-1927 [391,400,412]

Metal panel built to appear more integral with the cowl. The ammeter was smaller and mounted in an oval, nickel-plated escutcheon. The handle on the light switch was nickel-plated on some of the later production, although most seemed to have been painted black. A dash lamp was an accessory supplied by Ford (and others). The dash was painted body color.

LAMPS

NOTE: Cars supplied with gas lamps were also supplied with gas generators, made by the same firms that supplied the lamps. Generators were brass in the 1909-1912 era, then black and brass in late 1912 through 1914. The generator was not necessarily the same brand as the lamps on any one car. Some 1909 and 1910 (and probably later) cars were also supplied by the factory with Prestolite tanks instead of the generator.

1909 [52-54,91,127-128]

HEADLAMPS E&J 466, Atwood Castle 84, Brown 15 (after about 10,000).

SIDE LAMPS E&J "Pat. Pend." or "Pat. 1908," Atwood Castle 204, Brown 60.

TAIL LAMPS E&J "Pat. 1908," Atwood Castle 204, Brown 60.

1910 [52-54]

HEADLAMPS E&J 466, Brown 15.
SIDE LAMPS E&J "Pat. 1908," Brown 60.
TAIL LAMPS E&J "Pat. 1908," Brown 75.

1911 [90-91,106]

HEADLAMPS E&J 666, Brown 19.
SIDE LAMPS E&J "Pat. 1908," Brown 85.
TAIL LAMPS E&J "Pat. 1908," Brown 78 or 75.

1912 [90,128]

HEADLAMPS E&J 666 with Ford script, Brown 19.
SIDE LAMPS E&J "Pat. 1908," Brown 100.
TAIL LAMPS E&J "Pat. 1908," Brown 105.

1913 (Lamps were now steel, painted black, with brass tops and rims.) [166-167]

HEADLAMPS E&J 666, 66 or 656, Brown 16, Victor 1, Corcoran.

SIDE LAMPS E&J 30 or 32, Brown 110, Victor, Corcoran.

TAIL LAMPS E&J 10 or 12, Brown 115, Victor, Corcoran.

1914 [165]

HEADLAMPS E&J 656, Brown 16, Victor 2, Corcoran.
SIDE LAMPS E&J 32, Brown 110, Victor, Corcoran.
During production side lamps were provided with integral mounting brackets, eliminating the need for the separate brackets used previously.

TAIL LAMPS E&J 10 or 12, Brown 115, Victor, Corcoran.

1915 [217]

(All lamps appeared alike, regardless of make. Early production 1915 lamps varied; made by E&J, they had larger brass rims and lenses (8-5/8 vs 8-1/8") than later standard style lamps. Lamps were supplied by E & J, Brown, Victor and, perhaps others. Headlamp lenses were clear glass until 1921.) Steel headlight rims specified in a letter dated June 19, 1915.

HEADLAMPS 6511X with large brass lens rim. (E&J 456)
6511X with brass lens rim. (standard)
During the latter part of 1914 and early 1915, headlamps were fork-mounted, on the same forks as used by the carbide lamps. Early in 1915 the lamp with the riveted-in-place post became the standard. All were electric, powered by the magneto with the bulbs wired in series. Brass rims discontinued about June 1915.

SIDE LAMPS 6561X with large brass top and lens rim.
(E&J #6 on early cars)
6561X with brass top and lens rim. (standard)
Interchangeable from side to side. Clear lens. Mounted from rear by means of an integral stud.

TAIL LAMPS 6568X with brass top and large lens rim. (E&J 7 early cars)
6568X with brass top and lens rim. (standard)
Similar in style to the side lamps, the large lens in the door was red, with a small clear lens on the side facing the license plate. Mounted from the rear. Side and tail lights were kerosene.

1916-1917 [256,273,276]

Identical to the later 1915 lamps except for the elimination of the brass trimming. Painted all black.

441

LAMPS (Continued)

1917-1919 [256,273,276]

HEADLAMPS 6511BX

In late 1917 a dimmer was added to the light switch on the magneto-powered lamps. The lamps appeared the same as the 1916 style except for the use of bulbs with two contacts (6-8 volt, 16 C.P.) instead of the older single contact type (8-9 volts, 18 C.P.).

SIDE AND TAIL LAMPS

Same as 1916 on non-starter cars.

1919-1920

HEADLAMPS 6511CX

Same appearance as the 1918 lamps but now provided with sockets for two 6-8 volt lamps on those cars supplied with electrical equipment. The main bulb was 6-8 volt, 16 C.P. and the "dim" bulb located in the upper part of the reflector was 2-1/4 C.P. (the same bulb used in the tail light). Magneto lamps were dimmed with a resistor or inductance and were the same as the 1918 type.

SIDE LAMPS 6561X

Oil lamps the same as earlier but used only on non-electric cars. Starter cars had no side lamps.

TAIL LAMPS 7669X (Electric) and 6568X (Oil)

Electric was small round type with red lens and clear lens on the side to illuminate the license plate. Used 2-1/4 C.P. single-contact bulb. Non-electric cars used the oil tail lamp used earlier.

1921-1923 [320]

HEADLAMPS   6511DX, 6511EX, and 6511HX (Battery); 6511KX (Magneto)

The 6511DX used a frosted "Tu-Lite" bulb with a clear lens. Early in 1921 the 6511DX clear lens was replaced with the 6511EX which had green "visor" and used a clear "Tu-Lite" bulb. The " Tu-Lite" bulb was 6-8 volt, 18 and 2-3/4 C.P.. About June 1921 the 6511HX with the Ford "H" fluted lens became standard, and continued through 1925 in the passenger cars. The 6511KX used in non-starter cars used a double contact 6-8 volt, 21 C.P. bulb. The dimming inductance is mounted behind the area where the ammeter would be.

SIDE LAMPS and
TAIL LAMPS   Same as for 1920.

1923-1925

HEADLAMPS

Same as 1923. Nickel-plated lens rims available as an option in late 1925 (before the 1926 models).

SIDE LAMPS   Same as 1923.

TAIL LAMPS

7669X (Electric), 8786CX (Electric in 1924 and later), 6568X (Oil) in early 1923, then 6568BX (Oil) about mid-1923 and later. Electric tail lamp changed to a similar style but mounted as an integral part of the license plate bracket in 1924 (8786CX). This style continued through 1927. The oil tail lamp, 6568BX, introduced in early 1923, was similar in style to the earlier but now had the large lens facing the license plate, with a small red lens on the side, facing the rear. This lamp had the mounting stud on the side opposite the red lens.

1926 [387,396,409]

HEADLAMPS   6501AX and 6502AX (Right and Left) magneto type.
6501CX and 6502CX (Right and Left) battery type.
6511NX magneto type, bar mount.
6511MX battery type, bar mount.

The 6501/6502 types were similar in shape to the 1925, but now mounted on posts that in turn mounted on the fender. The right and left lamps differed mainly in the positioning of the lens, and could be interchanged. Later 1926 production lamps (6511 M,N) were mounted on the fender to fender rod. Standard lamps were all black but nickel-plated rims were optional. Nickel became standard during the year.

SIDE LAMPS

Oil lamps an option on non-starter cars in early 1926 only (those built in 1925) and were the same as the earlier lamps.

TAIL LAMPS [396]

Same as the 1925 styles. A stop light combination became an option by March 1926. Oil tail lamp used only on non-starter cars and was the same as the 1925 type.

1927

Same as later 1926. All had nickel rims. No oil lamps.

MAGNETO — See Engine

MANIFOLDS

1909-1911 [38,97]

Intake was "dog-legged" aluminum. Exhaust pipe fitted into exhaust manifold and had asbestos packing, secured with usual nut.

1911-1913 [97,163]

Intake manifold changed to straighter aluminum type. Exhaust same as 1910 type.

1913 [163]

Intake same as 1912 but in July 1913 the exhaust manifold was made for the flanged exhaust pipe. This new design remained standard until 1926.

1914

Cast iron intake manifold in the same pattern as the 1913. This gave way to the "standard" intake manifold used until late 1926.

1914-1926 [228,271,283,397]

Same as later 1914 type. The 1915 sedan which had the fuel tank under the rear seat used a longer intake manifold (which lowered the carburetor) for better fuel flow to the carburetor.

1926-1927 [397]

Vaporizer carburetor with integral manifolds became standard in late 1926.

MUFFLER

1909-1910 [70]

Cast-iron end plates. Mounted with sheet metal brackets. Straight, longer tail pipe. Asbestos wrapping secured with three iron bands.

1911-1914 [105,187]

Similar to 1910 but tail pipe curved downward.

MUFFLER (Continued)

1914-1916
Cast end plates now had integral mounting brackets. Pipe was now straight and not tapered. Mounting brackets were longer than 1917 type.

1917 [276]
Similar to 1916, with and without tail pipe. No asbestos wrap, painted with F-140 paint. Shorter cast mounting brackets.

1918-1920
Same as 1917 but no tail pipe. In June 1919 the outlet was moved 10 degrees from the bottom to direct the exhaust away from the spare tire.

1920-1927 [395]
Pressed-metal design. No tail pipe.

MUFFLER PARTS

Part #	Factory #	Description

MUFFLER COMPLETE
1909-1920

| 4025 | 1200B | |

1921-1927

| 4025B | 1200C | |

FRONT HEAD
1909

| 4026 | 1202 | Early 1909 |

1909-1914

| 4026 | 1202B | Steel mounting brackets |

1914-1920

| 4026B | 1202C | Integral mounting bracket. Cast bracket is long, thin casting 1914-1917. 1917-20 has a short, stubby casting. |

1921-1927

| 4026C | 1202D | Pressed steel, no mounting bracket. |

REAR HEAD
1909

| — | 1201 | Separate tail pipe, F/N 1213. |

1909-1910

| 4040 | 1221 | Steel brackets, straight pipe |

1911-1914

| 4040 | 1221 | Steel brackets, curved pipe |

1914-1917

| 4040 | 1221B | Integral bracket, straight pipe with no taper. |

1917-1920

| 4040B | 1201D | Integral bracket, no pipe. Shorter mounting bracket. In June 1919 the exhaust opening was moved 10 degrees to direct exhaust away from the spare tire. |

1921-1926

| 4040C | 1201E | Pressed steel, no pipe. Integral mounting bracket was on the rear cap only. |

1926-1927

| 4040D | 1209 | |

OUTER SHELL (5 x 12")
1909-1927

| 4027 | 1203 | |

MIDDLE SHELL (3-1/2 x 13")
1909-1927

| 4028 | 1204" | |

INNER SHELL (2 x 14")
1909-1927

| 4029 | 1205 | |

TIE ROD (5/16 x 13-3/8")
1909-1917

| 4030 | 1206 | |

1917-1920

| 4030B | 1206B | |

REAR BRACKET
1909

| — | 1208 | (Early 1909) |

1909-1914

| 4032 | 1217 | |

FRONT BRACKET
1909

| — | 1209 | (Early 1909) |

1909-1914

| 4033 | 1218 | |

EXHAUST PIPE
1909-1913

| 4037 | 1214 | Non-flared, engine to muffler |

1913-1920

| 4037B | 1214 | Flared at manifold |

1920-1927

| 4037C | 1214B | For pressed steel muffler. Longer and punched for muffler retaining cross piece at rear. |

ASBESTOS WRAP (1/32 x 12-1/4 x 31-3/4")
1909-1917

| 4038 | 1215 | |

MUFFLER BANDS (1/32 x 3/4 x 18" steel)
1909-1917

| 4039 | 1216 | These were the same bands that were used for heating ducts in buildings. They had a loop at one end through which the other end was threaded, then folded over. |

OIL FILLER CAPS

Early 1909 [37-38]
Apparently there was no "standard" cap used on the early (first 2500) engines on which the oil filler pipe was located at the front left of the engine. Several types have been observed but apparently no one is certain which is correct. In general, though, all had a cup-like funnel at the top of the filler tube. Early ones had a screen over the funnel but no cap. Later, a screw-on cap was added to the pipe in the center of the funnel.

1909 [37-38]
A thin brass "pipe" with a screen at the top, which fitted into the oil filler spout.

1909-1912 [96,97]
Brass cap with "Ford" with six flutes (notches) around the top.

1913-1914 [163]
Brass. Similar to the earlier but "Made in USA" added. The style of the "Ford" and of the "Made in USA" varied, perhaps because of different suppliers.

1915-1916 [228]
Steel with Ford script, in the same pattern as the earlier type. The "Made in USA" did not appear on all caps.

1916-1927 [271,397]
Steel. No script. Simpler design, somewhat larger, and with just three flutes around the top. This type did not have any lettering on the top. Examples have been seen with lettering but these are believed to be reproductions.

PAINTS

Original Model T Ford paint colors are all but impossible to duplicate accurately today. The paints used in the very early cars were varnishes and had a relatively short life. This was also true of the later enamels and Pyroxylins, although they were a good bit better than the earlier varnishes. **The original early greens and blues were all but black, and could easily be taken as black.** Consequently, original cars seen today no longer have the same color they had when they were new. Even today, batches of the same paint formula will vary in color, and it is certain the variations were even more pronounced more than sixty years ago.

The paints listed below are acceptable equivalents for the original colors. The numbers are current replacements for older Ditzler nitrocellulose lacquer numbers shown in previous lists. The "DDL" number is Acrylic Lacquer and the "DAR" number is Acrylic Enamel. There is not always a perfect match between the two types of paints so one should not mix the paint types unless slight differences are acceptable. Some of the Ditzler numbers are the same for either the lacquer or the enamel. The full number, of course, would be, say, DDL-71969 (lacquer) or DAR-71969 (enamel) for Brewster Green. We are told that Ditzler dealers can match DDL colors with DAR equivalents where there is no DAR number listed here; they have the formulas but they are not ready-made stock colors.

These paints are by no means the "only" possibilities, and the author will welcome any additions, comments, or corrections to this list.

BODY COLORS
(Paint numbers are Ditzler unless noted otherwise)

VARNISHES (Used 1909 to 1914)

Color	Modern name	DDL #	DAR #
Red	Carmine	71969	71969
Green *	Brewster Green Medium	1017	44328
Gray	Gray	72092A	Dupont
Blue *	Midnight Blue	32663	32663
		81501A	Dupont
Black	Black	9381	9000

* Note: The original blue and green were almost black. Often the color cannot be detected except in bright sunlight, and even then seeing the "color" can be difficult. Surviving original cars substantiate this observation. Red and gray were only used prior to June 1909. Green was used from early 1909 (before June) through 1910. Blue was used from 1911 to early 1913. Black was the standard color from 1913 until the 1926 models.

ENAMELS (1926)

Channel Green	Use paints listed under Pyroxylin		
Windsor Maroon	Use paints listed under Pyroxylin		

PYROXYLIN (Late 1926-1927)

Commercial Green	Rock Moss Green	117	44496
Channel Green	Green	546	45176
	Hillcrest Green	41131	
Drake Green	Vagabond Green	122	44350

Sherwin Williams formula:
(Mixed to match original paint sample

L4 E 317	5 grams
L4 G 311	15 grams
L4 Y 337	30 "
L4 Y 332	50 "
L4 M 318	65 "
L4 Y 303	120 "
L4 B 320	235 "
L4 W 301	335 "
L4 B 325	535 "

Highland Green	Dark Green	42850	42850
	Dark Green	4190A	Dupont
Phoenix Brown	Rosewood Beige	20064	- - -
	Hollywood Tan	20017	- - -
Gunmetal Blue	Gunmetal Blue	436	- - -
	Niagara Blue	438	13637
Moleskin	Moleskin Brown	544	- - -
Royal Maroon	Ford Maroon	1011	50742
Fawn Gray	Granite Gray	30575	- - -

PAINTS (Continued)

WIRE WHEEL COLORS

Note: Based on letters from the factory to the dealers at the time, the standard wire wheel color supplied by the factory was black. The color options were dealer-installed on an exchange basis.

ENAMELS (1926)		DDL #	DAR #
Casino Red	Orange	1166	60449
Emerald Green	Apple Green	519	44783
Straw	Straw	526	82302

PYROXYLIN (1926-1927)		DDL #	DAR #
Casino Red	Orange	1166	60449
Emerald Green	Apple Green	519	44783
Straw	Straw	526	82302
Orange	Orange	1166	60449
Vermillion	Vermillion Red	1412	72204

STRIPING COLORS

Carmine *		- - -	
Champagne *		- - -	
Cream	Medium Cream	125	- - -
Emerald Green	Apple Green	519	44783
Orange	Orange	1166	60449
Vermillion	Vermillion Red	1412	72204
French Gray	French Gray	586	31759

* Carmine and Champagne were used on the black closed cars during the "iron" era (1917-1926). The exact color is not known at the time of this writing.

PAINTING

Exposed parts of Model T Fords were generally painted the body color. Early red cars, for example, had red fenders, aprons, hoods, running boards, axles, and wheels. The same is true of the Brewster Green and blue cars but here these is some question. Since these greens and blues were extremely dark, if not black, it is often difficult to determine if the parts were the body color or actually black paint. The consensus is that the above parts were originally the body color, not black.

Nuts, bolts, and small assemblies which could be seen easily, were also painted, even though such parts were installed after the painting process. Ford had people with paint and brush in hand to "touch up" such parts. While there may be exceptions, all exposed pieces were painted, and this includes the cotter keys in these pieces.

Engines, engine pans, and splash shields (at the side of the engine) may or may not have been painted. Again, the consensus is that most engines were not painted but that some were during the Model T era. Late 1926 and 1927 engines were painted Drake Green, at least at the main factory. Even here, though, there were exceptions. Engine pans follow the same pattern. The dust shields were probably painted body color in the early years, and black through 1927. Floor boards were generally not painted but may have been given a coat of linseed oil or similar.

Indeed, there are no hard and fast rules on what was and what was not painted on any Model T. There were too many variations.

PICKUP BOX (For Roadster Pickup)

1925 [357-362]

First shown in factory photos dated December 12, 1924, the first pickup boxes did not have the "Ford" script on the rear door. The script was added in early 1925. Side panels had reinforcements to which the fender irons mounted.

1926-1927 [405]

Similar in style to the 1925, the side panels were embossed to match the rear fenders which were now mounted directly to the panels. Later (perhaps 1927) the bed was slightly altered and the front reinforcing post was moved forward a few inches, and the embossed molding changed to match. The vertical molding above the fender, which extended from the top molding to the bottom (curved) molding, now only went part way down from the top molding and did not connect to the curved molding. In addition, the floor boards (bottom of the box) were altered to accommodate the metal cover plate over the rear frame crossmember, new with the 1926 models.

RADIATOR

1909 [66]

"Winged" Ford script on front. Brass "Ford" script on the core on most cars. Filler was machined brass, rather low, soldered to the top. Cap had higher fins than usual type. No hole in side for lamp hoses. General design differs from 1911 and later types in that there were fewer seams in the construction. Radiators were supplied by Briscoe from the beginning to about 2500, McCord beginning with about 2500, and Detroit Radiator beginning about 8500. Early production (but after 2500) used screws to mount the radiator, rather than studs. "Paris" radiators were shown on very early (pre-2500) invoices; may have been another brand. Some of the first (Briscoe or Paris?) radiators had separate shells, soldered to an inner core at the top.

1909-1910 [66]

Same as 1909. Standard Ford script used in addition to "winged." Supplied by McCord and Detroit until about 17,000. Ford began making radiators beginning about 12,000, and supplied all after about 17,000. It may be the Ford brand that began the standard "Ford" script on the upper tank. Mounted with studs instead of screws.

1911-1912 [95]

Higher cast filler neck. Standard "Ford" script without "Made in USA." Newer seamed construction, typical of all later brass radiators. Radiators now all made by Ford. The "Ford" on the radiator core was not used after late 1910. There was now a hole in the side for the gas lamp hose, with a soldered-in-place pipe from side to side for the gas.

1913-1916 [159]

Spun-brass filler neck, riveted and soldered in place. "Made in USA" under "Ford" script. In 1915 the gas tube for the lamps was eliminated. Filler cap had short fins.

Descriptions

RADIATOR (Continued)

1917-1919 [261]
Black metal shell over new radiator. Assembly mounted on pads on the frame. Filler neck and cap now nickel-plated. Water outlet hose increased in length to 3-1/2" (from 2-3/4").

1919-1923
Similar to 1917 but mounting holes larger for cushion spring mount. Outlet hose length increased to 4" for better fit.

1923-1924 [331]
Higher radiator. Outer shell now had skirt at the bottom, over engine mount area.

1924-1926 [388]
Some flat tube radiators used during this period. Beginning in late 1925 an optional brass, nickel-plated, shell was offered. During 1926 three and four-row round tube radiators were used in addition to the standard five-row. The bottom skirt was secured to the engine mount/spring clip with a screw. Skirts used with the nickel shell had a nickel trim strip.

1927 [388]
Four and five-row, round-tube, radiators used. Nickel plated-shell now standard.

RADIUS RODS - See Front or Rear
Axles

REAR AXLE
(Also see Driveshaft)

1909 [30-32]
Initial design of 1907 used pressed-steel brake backing plates. These were changed to cast iron in November 1908. It is not known if the pressed-steel type ever saw production. No-rivet style. Non-tapered axles. Babbitt axle (inner) and pinion bearings. Bronze bushings throughout the differential gear assembly. No wires to hold differential nuts in early axles (with the riveted-in-place ring gear). Instead they used slotted nuts which were peened down to lock them. Filler plug was slotted screw. Brake and radius rods had forged ends.

Only the major parts of the rear axle assembly are listed here.

REAR AXLE HOUSINGS
1909 (Early)

Part #	Factory #	Description
2501	1	Right
2502	2	Left

3/8" D.S. studs until about 12,000 (October 1909). Babbitt inner axle bearings. Smooth brake backing plates. Pressed-steel housing with no rivets and no reinforcements.

1910

2501	1B	Right
2502	2B	Left

Similar to above. Reinforced brake backing plates. Slotted filler plug.

1910
Six-rivet style. Non-tapered axles. Roller inner axle (after 12,000, October 1909) and pinion (after 18,000, March 1910) bearings. Later 1910 housings had reinforcing washers around the flange bolt holes, and still later, a ring brazed around center section. By 1911 two such rings were used, one on each half, inside the housing, making the center seam much thicker. Pinion bearing housing drilled for 3/8" studs. Brake backing plates changed from smooth to those with reinforcing ribs in drawing dated November 12, 1909. Otherwise similar to 1909.

1910-1911

Part #	Factory #	Description
2501	1B	Right
2502	2B	Left

1911-12 The brake backing plate was again revised in a drawing dated October 18, 1910. The 1910 style continued until July 13, 1911 when new "1912" rear axle (12-rivet, clamshell design with cast center section) appeared. Tapered axle shafts standard after early 1911 and appeared before the housing change in July. New housing used 13/32" studs for driveshaft pinion bearing spool. Slotted filler plug.

2501-1/2	1E	Right
2502-1/2	2E	Left

1912 [90,105,124]
Same as late 1911 "1912" axle. The newer "1913" axle appeared later in the year, perhaps as early as September (date unknown) but definitely by November. Slotted filler plug.

2501B	1E	Right (Same as 1911)
2502B	2E	Left

NOTE: The roller bearing sleeves used in the earlier axles differed from the later in that the locating dimple was about 3/4" from the end, while the later one had the dimple at about 1/2". Whether both types were used, or just when the change was made is not certain, but is believed to have been in late 1911 or 1912.

1913-1914 [162,187,191]
Introduced in about October 1912. Larger cast center section, similar in shape to later types, but with the axle tubes flared and riveted to the center section. In 1914 the forged-end radius rods were replaced with the less expensive split-end type. These were seamless and interchangeable from side to side. Brake shoes modified to use two springs instead of one; the second spring being across the mounting bolt side of the brake shoe. Hexagon filler plug now standard.

2501D	2835B	Right
2502D	2836B	Left

1915-1919 [227]
New "standard" design adopted about March 1915. Tubular axle housings inserted into center section. Early 1915 brake backing plates did not have reinforcing ribs (added in October 1915). Oil filler hole just below centerline.

1915

2501E	2835C	Right
2502E	2835C	Left

1916

2501E	2835C	Right
2502E	2836C	Left

Reinforcing ribs on brake backing plates (beginning October 1915).

REAR AXLE (Continued)

1917-1918 [273]

Part #	Factory #	Description
2501	2835C	Right
2502	2836C	Left

Same as 1916 except for part number change.

1919-1921

Similar to 1918 above but now machined for a gasket between the two halves. Oil filler now 1-3/4" below the centerline. Driveshaft modified in 1920 to use new forged bearing sleeve. Outer oil seal cups larger in diameter due to machining change in the axle tubes. 4-1 gears became available in July 1919. At first these were a 48-tooth ring and a 12-tooth pinion but by January 1920 the 10-tooth pinion which could be used with the standard ring gear replaced the first type.

1919

2501	7635	Right
2502	7636	Left

1920-1923

2501	7635C	Right (Same as 1919)
2502	7636C	Left

1923-1925

2501	7635D	Right
2502	7636D	Left

Beginning about 1922 the rear radius rods were of seamed construction. Lefts and rights were required so that the seam will be down for drainage.

1926-1927 [390]

Identical to 1925 except for larger brake backing plates. An oil seal was added at the outer axle bearings. Oil plug changed to type with recessed square hole instead of hex head during late 1927.

At least four brake backing plates were used. Some had riveted-on brake shoe retaining clips. Others had clips that were pressed from the backing plate, with and without a spot-welded cover over the pressed-in area on the outside surface. The latter type (with the pressed clips) came with either smooth backing plates or with an embossed "C" shaped molding and an oil vent on the bottom half. The riveted type is believed to be the earliest, but those noted had the embossed bottom area and used the old hex-head filler screw. The plates with the pressed clips seem to be later production but all may have been used simultaneously.

During 1926 the radius rods were modified to eliminate the rearward nut at the universal joint. The nut was replaced with a forged-in collar which located the radius rod on the U-joint housing.

2501B	7635B	Right
2502B	7636B	Left

REAR AXLE PARTS

AXLE HOUSING GASKET (Paper, .009")
1919-1927

Part #	Factory #	Description
2504	139	(None used before 1919.)

REAR AXLE SHAFTS
1909-1910 [31]
2503	48	Non-tapered

Axle gear held with small woodruff key and a pin.

1910-1911
2505A	48B	Non-tapered

Axle gear held with large woodruff key and a collar.

1911-1917
2505D	2818	Tapered

Axle gear held with large key and collar (2 pieces).

1917-1927
2505	2828	Tapered

Same as 1916 except for part no.

THRUST WASHER (Fiber, between axle shafts)
1909-1927
2506	39	1-1/32" diameter

AXLE BEARINGS
1909
2507	51	Babbitt inner bearings.
2508	97	Hyatt roller outer bearings

1910-1920
2508	97	Hyatt roller (Inner/outer)

1920-1927
2508	253	Hyatt roller (P/N change)

AXLE BEARING SLEEVES
1909-1911
2509	170	Right*
2509B	161	Left

* Outer only in 1909. Locating dimple further from the end than later design.

1911-1927
2509	170	Right (Dimple nearer the end)
2509B	161	Left

REAR AXLE SEAL CAPS
1909-1919
2510	56	2-13/32" i.d.

1919-1927
2510-1/2	56B	2-7/16" i.d.

DIFFERENTIAL GEAR CASE
1909 (Early)
—	10	Left (For riveted ring gear)
—	11	Right

1909-1911
2512	10B	Left (9/16" spider arms)
2513	11B	Right

Uses 2517 axle gear bushings.

1911-1913
2512B	10C	Left
2513B	11C	Right

5/8" spider arms, bushing for axle gears.

REAR AXLE PARTS

DIFFERENTIAL GEAR CASE (Continued)
1913-1915

Part #	Factory #	Description
2512C	10D	Left
2513C	11D	Right

5/8" spider arms, no bushing. Uses 2514 stud.

1915-1927

Part #	Factory #	Description
2512C	84	Left Final design.
2513C	81	Right Uses 2514B stud.

DIFFERENTIAL GEAR CASE STUD
1909-1915

2514	52	3/8 x 2-3/4"

1915-1920

2514B	52B or	3/8 x 2-1/4"
2514B	2865	

1921-1927

2414C	52C	Now a cap screw.

DIFFERENTIAL GEAR CASE BUSHING
1909-1913

2517	19	Bronze

1-9/16" I.D., 1-13/16" O.D.

RING GEAR (40 tooth)
1909

—	12	Riveted to gear case.

1909-1927

2518	12B	Threaded holes

DIFFERENTIAL GEAR (Axle Gear, 24 teeth)
1909-1911

2520	13	Drilled for pin #2522

1911-1927

2520B	13B	For key and collars.

DIFFERENTIAL GEAR THRUST WASHER
1909-1914

2523	32	3-1/16" dia. Fiber.

DIFFERENTIAL PINION GEAR (3 used)
1909

2524	14	

1909-1911

2524	14B	9/16" bushing.

1911-1914

2524B	14C	5/8" bushing.

1914-1927

2524C	14D	No bushing.

DIFFERENTIAL GEAR SPIDER
1909

2526	15	

1909-1911

2526	15B	9/16" arms, axle bushing.

1911-1914

2526B	15C	5/8" arms, axle bushing.

1914-1927

2526B	15D	5/8" arms, no bushing.

DIFFERENTIAL GEAR SPIDER BUSHING
1909-1914

Part #	Factory #	Description
2527	18	1-1/16", brass.

DIFFERENTIAL THRUST BEARING (2 used)
1909-1915

2528	30	Bronze

1915-1927

2528	30	Babbitt

DIFFERENTIAL THRUST BEARING WASHER (4 used)
1909-1927

2529	31	Steel, 3-3/4" diameter.

DIFFERENTIAL THRUST WASHER PIN
1909-1916

2530	17	13/32" long.
2531	37	7/32" long.

1917-1927

2531B	7640	

Dual diameter pin, larger of which fits into housings.

DIFFERENTIAL OIL DRAIN PLUG
1909-1912

2532	817	Screwdriver slot.

1913-1927

2532	817	3/4" x 24 Hex head.

1927 (Late)

2532B	2824	1/2" pipe.

Recessed square socket pipe plug.

DRIVESHAFT HOUSING (Also see Driveshaft)
1909-1910

2533	153	Babbitt pinion bearing

1910

2582	74C	Drilled for 3/8" studs.

Used beginning at 18,000

1911-1914

2582	153D	Drilled for 13/32" studs.

1914-1920

2582	153D	"One-piece" type.

1920-1927

2582	153D	Flange modified for new pinion bearing.

RUNNING BOARDS

1909 (Early Production) [63]

Part #	Factory #	Description
—	1410	R/H Linoleum covered
—	1411	L/H

NOTE: This board was made up of 1412 Rubber Matting; 1421, 1422, 1423, 1425, 1486, 1487 and 1488 Brass Trim pieces. (Factory numbers.)

1909-1910 [59,63]

(First 15,000 cars, until January 1910)

2941   1410B   R/H & L/H

Steel with uninterrupted ribs running lengthwise. No Script. Painted body color.

1910 [63]

Steel with interrupted ribs running lengthwise, beginning with 15,000 in January 1910. Painted body color.

2941   1410C   R/H & L/H

1911-1912 [86,105,126]

Steel with typical diamond pattern. Ford script ran lengthwise. "Made in USA" added in later production 1912. Painted body color.

4812   2530   R/H Blue
4813   2531   L/H

1911 TORPEDO RUNABOUT

4846   2551   R/H Blue
4847   2552   L/H

1913-1921 [183]

1913 to 1925 running boards were steel, similar to 1912 but script now ran across the width. Earlier boards had much sharper diamonds that later, apparently due to wear on the dies that pressed them. There were minor variations in the "Ford" script, the placement of holes, etc. during the years but the basic boards were identical. Painted black after 1912.

4812   5418   R/H & L/H

"Ford" script now ran across the board.

1918-1925 TRUCK

1129   TT5418   R/H & L/H

P/N changed to 4830 in 1920.

4830   TT5418   R/H & L/H

1922-1925

4812   5418   R/H
4813   5480   L/H

Same as earlier boards but drilled differently.

1925-1927 TRUCK

4830B   TT5418   R/H (21-29/32" long)
4830C   TT5480   L/H

1926-1927 [388]

Wider board with much smaller diamonds. Ford script now much smaller and was imprinted along the outer edges of the boards.

4813B   5418B   R/H & L/H

SEDIMENT BULBS

(Gasoline tank)

EARLY 1909 [65]

Small brass type which screwed into the tank on the right side.

1909-1911

Brass, larger than above, and riveted to the tank on the right side.

1911-1915

Brass, larger than the previous type, screwed into the tank.

1915-1925 (and 1926-27 Fordor Sedans and trucks)

Similar in style to the 1914 type but now made of cast iron. Often supplied without the drain cock (just a pipe plug).

1926-1927

Smaller design which was now located on the engine side of the firewall.

SPEEDOMETERS

1909

Speedometers were optional in early 1909 and a number of brands were supplied by Ford, perhaps more than those listed.

Stewart Model 11

Brass case 60MPH with 4-digit odometer plus 3-digit trip odometer. Similar in style to the Model 24 and 26. $25 extra cost.

Stewart Model 12

Stewart Model 24 [49]

Dial pointer 60MPH. 5-digit odometer using small disk dials seen through holes across the face above the speed pointer. All-brass case, mounted on the firewall. Almost identical to the Model 26 except that it did not have the trip odometer.

Jones Model 20

50MPH brass case with 4-digit Veeder odometer and 3-digit Veeder trip odometer mounted below the main body of the unit.

Jones Model 21

Similar to the Model 20 but 60MPH.

National

5 to 60MPH brass case. Dial scale almost 360 degrees, beginning and ending near the top of the face. Veeder 4-digit and 3-digit trip odometers on the right side of the main body. $30 extra. Another model with a 5 to 50 mph face was $25.

Descriptions

SPEEDOMETERS (Continued)

1911-1912 Stewart Model 26

1913 Stewart Model 100

1910
Stewart Model 24 (Described under 1909)

1911
Stewart Model 24 (Early production) [89]
Stewart Model 26 (Pictured above) [127]
   Dial pointer 60MPH. 5-digit odometer using small disk dials seen through holes across the face above the speed pointer. 3-digit trip odometer of similar construction wss below the speed pointer. All-brass case, mounted on the firewall.

1912 and early 1913 [127]
Stewart Model 26 (Same as Model 26 above)
Stewart Model 26 (Pictured below)
   Similar case but odometer now had 5-digits on the left upper half of the face, and a 3-digit odometer on the right, with drum type dials seen through rectangular holes.

1913
Stewart Model 100
   Drum type 60MPH. 5-digit odometer above the speedometer drum. 3-digit trip odometer to the right of the regular odometer, with reset knob on the right side of the case. Black case with brass bezel. The case was about one-half inch shallower than the 1914 model 100.

1914
Stewart Model 100
   Drum type 60MPH. Brass bezel and black case. Similar to 1913 type but deeper case. 5-digit odometer with 3-digit trip odometer to the right, both below the speed indicator drum. Mounted on the firewall.

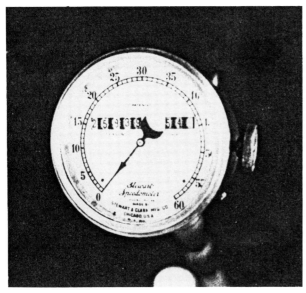

1912 Stewart Model 26

1914 Stewart Model 100

Descriptions

450

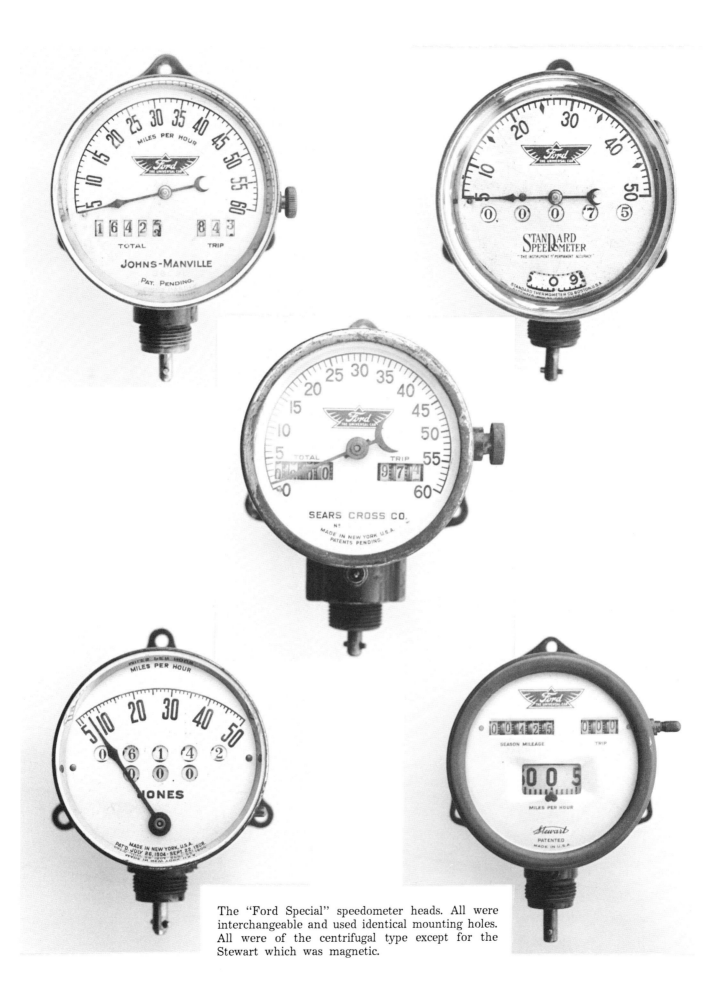

The "Ford Special" speedometer heads. All were interchangeable and used identical mounting holes. All were of the centrifugal type except for the Stewart which was magnetic.

451

Descriptions

SPEEDOMETERS (Continued)

1914 FORD SPECIALS

Johns Manville

Dial pointer 60MPH type. 5-digit odometer plus 3-digit trip odometer, with reset button on the right side of the case.

Standard

Dial pointer 50MPH. 5-digit odometer just below the speedometer needle. Trip odometer was a disk-type dial appearing through an opening in the face at the bottom.

Sears Cross

Dial pointer 60MPH. 4-digit odometer at left of face, with 3-digit trip odometer at the right.

Jones

Dial pointer 50MPH. 5-digit odometer with numbers on small disks which appeared through holes in the face. The 3-digit trip odometer was also the disk type and was just below the regular odometer.

Stewart

Drum type 60MPH. 5-digit odometer above the speedometer, at the left, with 3-digit trip odometer to the right.

1915

The Ford Specials described above were supplied until speedometers were discontinued as standard equipment during 1915.

ACCESSORY SPEEDOMETERS
(Not supplied by Ford Motor Company)

1915-1918

Stewart Model 102

Similar to the Model 100 but all-black finish. 5-digit odometer with 3-digit trip odometer to the right, both above the drum speedometer dial. Reset button was on the side of the case above the centerline. Mounted on the firewall or on a Stewart-supplied instrument panel. [266]

Johns Manville

Many other brands.

1919-1925

Stewart Model 160

This was the most common of the Ford speedometers. Mounted in a rectangular escutcheon which in turn mounted on the right end of the instrument panel. Drum type 75MPH. Had 5-digit odometer plus a 3-digit trip odometer with reset knob at the right.

AC (First Series)

Similar in dimension and mounting to the Stewart. Drum type 80MPH. 3-digit trip odometer was below the 5-digit odometer. Reset button was on the lower face below the trip odometer.

AC (C Series)

Similar to the First Series but with less ornate face design. Trip reset button out the side of the case behind the dash.

1926-1927

Stewart Model 490A (Passenger Cars)
Stewart Model 490J (Trucks)

Small (about 2-1/2" face without a trip odometer. The two styles differ only in the mounting.

Stewart Warner Model 160

Stewart Warner Model 490

SPLASH APRONS

1909-1910 [60,63]

Straight from front fender to rear. Curved cut at rear to clear brake rods. Later 1909 had a straight cut at the rear (angled to the rear and upwards). Painted body color.

Part #	Factory #	Description

1909 EARLY PRODUCTION

—	1408	L/H
—	1409	R/H
3881	1718	L/H 60" tread
3880	1717	R/H
2952	1731	L/H Town Cars (green)
2953	1732	R/H
3885	1731	L/H 60" tread
3884	1732	R/H

1909-1910

Straight from front to rear. Curved cut at rear to clear brake rods. Later 1909 had a straight cut at the rear.

2942	1408	L/H
2943	1409	R/H
2981	1718	L/H 60" tread
2980	1717	R/H
2952	1731 or	
2952	1620	L/H Town Cars (Green)
2953	1732 or	
2953	1621	R/H
3885 or	1731	Town Cars (Green)
2985	1731	L/H 60" tread
3884 or	1732	
2984	1732	R/H

1911-1913 [86]

Bulge at rear to clear rods until mid-1912, then a gradual taper at the rear to a point about 10" ahead of the rear fender. Now matched the rear fender line. Painted black after 1912.

4815	1408B	L/H
4814	1409B	R/H
4827	1718B	L/H 60" tread
4826	1717B	R/H

1911 Torpedo Runabout

4849	2556	L/H
4848	2557	R/H
4868	2710	L/H 60" tread
4867	2703	R/H

1912-1916 [117]

Aprons now tapered gently to the rear fender from a point about 10" from the rear fender, reducing the apparent bulge.

1913-1916 [224]

4815	1408C	L/H
4814	1409C	R/H
4815B	7497	L/H 1915 Sedans [207]
4814B	7496	R/H

1917-1923

Similar to 1916 but patterned to fit new fenders. In early 1917 the aprons were modified to smoothly taper from front to rear, with no bulge at the rear.

4815C	7987	L/H
4814C	7986	R/H
4815D	7748	L/H 1922-23 Fordor Sedans
4814D	7747	R/H

1923-1925

Similar to prior style but patterned to fit wider hood clash strips when higher radiator appeared about June 1923. (Had hole for hood clip.) In later 1925 models (perhaps on cars built at the time of the change to the 1926 models) the aprons on some of the Tudor and Fordor sedans were given a new "square" shape, similar to the 1926-27 style.

4815C	7987	L/H
4814C	7986	R/H
4815E	7748B	L/H SEDANS [345]
4814E	7747B	R/H

1926-1927 [392]

Entirely new design to match new body styles. "Square" rather than earlier rounded design.

4815F	40128	L/H
4814F	40127	R/H

SPRINGS

1909-1915

All taper-leaf. 7 leaves in the front. 8 leaves in the rear, except for the 1911 Torpedo which used 7. Several types appeared. In one the spring clip was riveted to the leaf, with the bolt running under the spring. On another, the leaf was curled upwards and the clip bolt passed through the curl above the spring. Still another used a separate clip assembly.

1916-1917

FRONT: Springs slowly changed to non-taper design beginning in late 1915 or 1916 on some production. This was a 6-leaf, non-tapered type until late 1917 when a seventh leaf was added. Main leaf not drilled for oilers until 1917 (approximately).
REAR: 8-leaf tapered.

1918-1921

FRONT: 7-leaf non-tapered. Main leaf drilled for oilers.
REAR: 8-leaf, non-tapered, with main leaf drilled for oilers.

1922-1923

FRONT: Same as 1921.
REAR: Same as 1921 plus 9-leaf spring added for the Sedans.

1923-1925

FRONT: Same as 1921.
REAR: Same as 1922 but 6-leaf spring added for the Runabouts.

1926-1927

FRONT: New 8-leaf spring used on all cars.
REAR: 8-leaf spring for all cars except the Sedans which used a 9-leaf, both the same as used in 1925. The 6-leaf was discontinued.

SPRING SHACKLES

1909-1912 [29,31,32,64,107]
"Mae West" shape with brass oilers.

1913-1917 [273]
"Figure eight" type with brass oilers. "L" style began at front around mid-1916.

1917-1923 [268,280,346]
"Figure-eight" style at first and then "L" shaped shackles of several designs, without oilers. The oilers were now located on the spring perches and on the main leaf of the spring. The front spring was apparently changed first; then the rear.

The second type was a two-piece steel "riveted" design. This was superseded by the forged "L" shaped style used until around 1923.

1923-1927 [346]
"U" shaped type with tie strap now standard.

STEERING COLUMN

1909-1910 [67]
3500 (900). (Cars under 34,600, December 19, 1910) 50" long. Brass gear housing was a riveted assembly with the column fitting. Brass quadrant. Levers brass-plated with black hard-rubber knobs. The pitman arm was oval in cross-section, and shorter than the later types used with the two-piece spindles.

1911 [107]
3500C (5005). Now 56" long but similar to 1910.
3500B (900B). For Town Cars, 51" length.
3500D (979). For Torpedo Runabouts, 60" length.

1912-1914 [122,190]
3500C (5005). 56" long, on all cars. Brass quadrant, riveted gear case. 1912 was the last year for the hard-rubber spark and throttle knobs. These were eliminated and the ends of the brass-plated control rods were flattened for "handles." Around 1913 the bottom mounting flange was changed from a forging to pressed metal.

1915 [214,226]
3500C (5042). The 1914 column seems to have been used in very early production, with some overlap when both the old and new types appeared at the same time. The new gear case was now one-piece rather than riveted design. Quadrant was pressed steel, painted black. Gear case was brass, not plated. Cover was much flatter than previous cone-shaped type. Levers were steel with flattened ends, and brass-plated (although some black-painted rods seem original).

1915-1917 [226,269]
Similar to previous type but small tube added for horn wire. Horn switch mounted on the top surface, just below the steering wheel. The horn bulb, when used, clamped to the column. Quadrant was painted black.

1917-1920 [254,269]
Gear case now nickel-plated. Levers nickel-plated, with shorter flattened ends. Wire tube made larger to accept light wires. In late 1917 the horn button was now a two-function type with fluted sides. Turning it operated the lights. The button now mounted in a housing on the left side of the column, where it remained for the remainder of Model T production.

1921-1922

3500C (5044). Similar in appearance to 1920 but a longer pin was used for one of the planetary gears. This pin extended down into a groove milled in the case to act as a stop, preventing the steering going "over center."

1922-1925 [363]
Similar to 1917 but horn button no longer doubled as the light switch on non-starter cars. (Dash board with switch was now standard.) Column support bracket (to instrument panel) added in 1924.

1926-1927
3500D (5044B). Similar in style to earlier but now had flange to mate with new body types. Gear ratio changed to 5:1 in 1925 when balloon tires were introduced.

STEERING WHEEL

1909-1910
Brass spider and nut. 14-1/4" O.D. wood rim was painted black. Note: most recent data shows the wheel to be 13" O.D. but this is apparently the result of latter-day reproduction wheels. No original 13" wheels have been found on Ford cars.

1911-1912
Brass spider. 15" O.D. wood rim painted black. Brass spider believed to have been painted black in later production.

1912-1920
Forged-steel spider, painted black. 15" O.D. wood rim painted black until about 1919, then made of "Fordite" composition material.

1920-1925
Pressed-steel spider, painted black. 16" O.D. wheel. (June 1920)

1925-1927
Similar to 1925 but now 17" O.D.

TIMER (Commutator)

NOTE: Ford experimented with many timers during Model T production. Aluminum, brass, iron and steel were used, with varying types of contact (brush) assemblies. There may be no "correct" timer for any given year.

1909-1911 [49,99]
"Two-piece" type. (Until October 1911.) Made of brass.

1911-1913
For a short time in 1912 a new aluminum timer with a built in oil spout was used, along with a new timing gear cover. These were changed to the "standard" timer with a cast aluminum case and another, now standard, timing gear cover.

1914-1919 [267,283]
Similar style to 1913 but cast-iron case in addition to aluminum, and all cast iron beginning around 1915.

1919-1920
Roller type brush replaced with a wiper brush for short time, then back to the roller type. Iron, aluminum, bronze and steel cases used throughout this period, as well as a number of different, experimental, brush assemblies.

1921-1927
Pressed-steel case with roller brush.

TIMING GEAR COVER

1909-1910 3009 (403B) (After first 2500) [39,98]
Designed to use the two-piece timer. The fan belt was held under tension by a spring between the cover and a "knob" on the fan support arm.

1911 3009 (403B) [98]
Similar to 1910 but the tension spring was dropped and replaced with an adjustment screw, the head of which mated with the "knob" on the support arm previously used to locate the spring.

1912 3009B (690) [137]
3009B (690B)
First used a timer with an integral oil spout. Later (apparently in late 1911 or early 1912) the standard type replaced it. Fan adjustment screw was now on the right side of the engine.

1913-1916
Similar to the 1912 but the filler spout was a bit longer and pointed at the bottom, allowing the resulting hole to be larger.

1917-1925
Similar to 1916 but with heavier casting, most noticeable on the bottom edge. (Similar to the later, starter-type casting but without the generator mount.) The filler spout was made even longer. Used on non-starter cars only after 1918.

1919-1925 3009C (690C)
Similar to above but modified to allow for generator mount.

1926-1927 3009D (690D)
Similar to 1925 but no boss for fan adjustment screw. (Early production engines had the screw boss but it was not drilled and tapped.)

TOOLS (Supplied with the car)

NOTE: The design of Ford-supplied tools changed through the years. While the same part numbers were used, all of the same number were not necessarily exactly alike.

1909-1913
T1349 hub cap wrench. T1387 adjustable wrench. T1902 screwdriver. T1903 pliers. T1904 spark plug wrench. T1917 wrench. T2336 tool roll. T2337 oil can. T2338 tire pump. T2340 tire iron.

1914-1916
T1349, T1387, T1902, T1903, T1917, T2335 cylinder head wrench, T2336 T2337, T2338, T2340

1917-1920
Same as 1916 but T2343 jack added.

1921-1927
T1903 pliers modified to have screwdriver blade on one handle and the T1902 screwdriver was dropped. Otherwise the same as 1920. T2344 jack handle added in late 1925. In 1926 and 1927 cars with wire wheels were supplied with a P/N 2891 "T" shaped wrench for the lug nuts.

For complete tool list and descriptions, see pages 573-587.

TOPS (Open cars)

NOTE: All open cars supplied with tops were also supplied with side curtains throughout production. These were made of the same material as the top, with "isinglass" windows sewn in place. Side curtains were somewhat crude in workmanship, with minor variations in dimensions, location of windows, etc.

1909-1910
Fastened to forged rail which in turn was fastened to the body. Bows had curve outward, unique to 1909 and 1910 style cars. Material was imitation leather with pebble grain. Some versions in 1909 lined, others were not, depending on manufacturer. Some tops had a front windshield curtain which rolled up, even on cars supplied with a glass windshield. Rear window 17 x 9-1/4 with 3" biased corners. On early cars, and perhaps even the later ones (into late 1909 or 1910), the top sockets were painted body color. The support rail and the landau irons, however, were black. Rear curtain rolled up. Most were black but some were gray in 1909.
Supported by strap which ran to front lamp bracket, hooked in place.

1911
Top irons and bows now straight and mounted to body brackets. Front was supported by strap to front as in 1910. Style and rear window similar to 1910.

1912
Similar in style to 1911 but top support strap now connected to center windshield hinge.

1913
Rear window now curved on top, measured 16-1/2 x 7-1/2" at the sides, with the curve rising about 1-1/2" more at the center. New bows and top to match sloping windshield. Front straps to windshield hinge.

1914
Similar to 1913 but slightly different shape.

1915-1917
Similar to 1914 but rear no longer rolls up. Metal sockets are oval in cross section, as in earlier cars. Metal tack cover strip at rear of body where top rear curtain is nailed. 1916 was the last year for Murphy fasteners for the side curtains.

1917-1922
Similar in style to 1916 but rear window now three separate pieces, each 9-1/2 x 5-1/4" with 3" between them. Sockets in early 1917 were oval in cross section but were changed to rectangular cross section by 1918. "Lift the Dot" fasteners replaced the Murphy type in some locations. The leather top support straps to the windshield were changed to cotton webbing, and the buckle-type hook now had a loop only for the strap.
About 1920 the top was redesigned to include a "visor" above the windshield for a better weather seal.
In 1921, the open car bodies were redesigned and at that time the top rest support was changed from the "L" bracket bolted to the top body frame to a plain rod extending through the rear quarter panel.

TOPS (Continued)

1923-1925

"One-man" top. When introduced in September 1922 the Touring top lower edge was a straight line from front to rear. After 100,000, the rear was given a gentle curve downward. Two rear windows, each 8-1/2 x 5-1/2", with up to 8" between them (there seems to be no standard, they have been seen with anywhere from 3 to 8 inches between them). Now clamped to the top of the windshield posts, eliminating the support straps used earlier. Later 1925 tops had one rear window, as in the 1926-27 models.

1926-1927

Similar in style to 1925. Single rear window, 16-3/4 x 7". Rear socket curves at the bottom. A letter from the Fargo, ND branch to its dealers, dated March 22. 1926, announced the availability of khaki or black top boots with matching gypsy curtains, for dealer installation.

TRANSMISSION

1909-1916

No adjust screws on early 1909 clutch fingers. Clutch sleeve keyed to brake shaft to prevent turning (but loose enough to slide fore and aft). This key was discontinued in early 1913. 13 small and 13 large plates after early production. During this period there were numerous changes in bushings, and small details but the basic design remained the same. Beginning June 17, 1915 a round disk plug was installed in the tail shaft to reduce oil leaks out through the universal joint.

1916-1925

Similar to 1915 but the brake drum was machined to eliminate the 3330 spacer and only 12 small disks were used in the clutch. About 1917 the one-piece triple gear was introduced but the older riveted three-piece type continued for several years as well. Bands with removable ears (Quick Change) introduced during 1925 production, and remained standard through 1927.

1926-1927

Wider brake drum with steel shoes over the clutch bosses.

TRANSMISSION COVER

1909
(826) First 500-800 cars. [43-45]

Initially pressed-steel in at least two types, it was quickly superseded by an aluminum "two-pedal" type, all three types apparently being used concurrently. Square door held with a clip rotated by a large hex-head bolt in the center. While similar in design to the later 4-bolt cover, this cover would not fit the engine pan due to varying bolt hole locations. Beginning at about car 500 the three-pedal system began to be installed on some production, and by 800 all cars were of the three-pedal type.

1909-1910
3361 (826B) [43-45]

Aluminum in two types; the first being similar to the earlier aluminum cover but with three pedals. The later type had a "rectangular" door held with four screws. Lettered pedals (C, R, B)

1911
3361 (826C) Rectangular hole
3376 (826D) Tapered hole

Wider "square-hole," introduced in at about 37,300 (February 1911), used until June when the tapered type with embossed door (Ford script) became standard. [45,101]

1912-1913
3376 (826D) [140]

Continued in the style of the later 1911. No reinforcing bosses at the bolt holes.

1913-1915
3376 (826D) [186,215,226]

Reinforcing bosses added around the bolt holes to prevent breaking. This modification began as early as 1912 according to factory data but apparently was only used in some production until late 1913. In late 1914 the lettered pedals were replaced with pedals with a ribbed surface. Door was now plain steel.

1916-1919
3376 (826D) [272,274]

Cast iron cover replaced aluminum. Pedals were now smooth surfaced on both the aluminum and iron covers. In 1917 the clutch fork shaft was made shorter and the exposed shaft end on the right side was now enclosed.

1919-1925
3376B (826E) [347]

Cast iron, similar to 1918 but now made for starter. Door was the pressed steel embossed design. "Ford" added to the casting during 1919, just above the inspection door. Oil slinger cast in cover beginning July 17, 1924. BENDIX cover was zinc plated in 1919-1920, then painted black. Some early Bendix covers were three-piece assemblies.

1926-1927
3376C (826F) [401]

New larger cover with new, wider pedals. Bolts to rear of engine block.

UPHOLSTERY (Open Cars)

1909-1910 [61]

Leather, diamond tuft design. Black color.

1911 [108]

Leather. Diamond tuft on seat backs but diamonds sewn on the cushions.

1912 [123,126]

Leather with tufted and sewn diamonds on backs and cushions. Imitation leather may have appeared before the 1913 models.

1913-1927 [168,181,216,265,316,410-411]

Leather phased out and replaced with imitation material. Seat bottoms were leather until about mid-1913, with seat backs and sides in imitation leather beginning earlier (perhaps as early as 1912). In general, the cars with leather upholstery had diamond-tufted seats. The imitation leather seats had a sewn diamond pattern until about 1914 when the seat backs became pleated. The seat bottoms continued the sewn diamond pattern until 1917 models. 1917 and later cars used only the pleated design.

The front roll of the arm rest was leather until around 1916. 1917 and later cars had a small metal cap on the arm rest, and no longer used the leather.

Door and side panels were covered with imitation leather until about 1917 when the side panels were changed to a black cardboard-like material, with a trim welting around the edges. 1926 and 1927 cars came with and without buttons in the seat upholstery.

UPHOLSTERY (Closed Cars)

1909-1914

Coupe: black leather seats with imitation leather door panels and trim.

Town Car: black leather seats and door panels, with fabric lining and trim.

1915

Sedan: gray and white striped pattern in wool. Trim was bright and elaborate. Seats were diamond tufted in the rear, but comparitively plain in front.

Coupelet: black leather seats and door panels. Folding top had blue lining and trim.

Town Car: see 1916

1916-1917

Sedan (Centerdoor): gray and white striped pattern in wool but less ornate than the 1915. Seats were pleated instead of diamond-tufted. Trimmed in gray lace.

Coupe: seats, door panels and straps were changed to imitation leather during this period. The top also changed to imitation leather, and was now lined and trimmed with green fabric and lace.

Town Car: the seats, front and rear were real leather. The jump seats and door panels were covered with imitation leather. The top also changed to imitation leather and was lined and trimmed with the same blue/gray fabric used on the 1915 sedan. Later (mid-1916 and on) used a less ornate cloth top lining.

1918

The Sedan and Town Car continued as in 1917. The Coupelet used gray whipcord fabric and lace previously used in the Sedan. The cowl area was trimmed in imitation leather.

1919-1922

Sedan: continued as in 1917. With the introduction of the starter (1919) came a dashboard and gray whipcord quarter panels.

Coupelet: continued the gray whipcord fabric and lace trim introduced in 1918 and, like the sedan, had whipcord quarter panels.

1922-1923

Centerdoor Sedan and Coupe: brown wool. Carpet at the bottom of the doors.

1923-1924

Tudor, Fordor and Coupe: brown wool. No carpet on the bottom of the doors in later production.

1925

Tudor and Coupe: brown wool as in 1923. Fordor dark-blue wool. Tudor and Coupe may have been blue in later 1925.

1926

Gray with red stripe on maroon cars, gray with green stripe on green cars. Headliner and body panels were gray with no stripe.

1927

Gray with white stripe on all cars. Headliner and body panels with no stripe.

WHEELS

1909-1910

Part #	Factory #	Description
2800	291	Front, red
2801	291	Front, green
2802	291	Front, gray
2812	99	Rear, red
2813	99	Rear, green
2814	99	Rear, gray

30 x 3 tires in front, 30 x 3-1/2 at rear. Hubs had 5-1/2" flanges. Front and rear hubs appeared similar, unlike 1911 and later style. Ball bearings in front hubs. Round-felloe, painted body color, with and without striping. Striping varied but generally was an open "V" on the spokes, and a single ring on the felloe. Hub caps were brass with "Ford" in block letters. Thin oval spokes.

1911-1916

2800	291	Front, blue
2814B	99	Rear

For non-tapered axle. (Early 1911)

2814C	2815	Rear, blue, tapered axle

Same tire size but heavier construction and 6" flanges. Rear hub heavier with change to tapered axles, no longer looked the same as the front hubs. Painted blue, with and without striping as on the earlier cars. Hub caps had "Ford" in script, with "Made in USA" added in 1913. The "F" in the "Ford" was higher in the early caps, and there seems to have been some variation in size and placement of the lettering, perhaps due to different suppliers.

1917-1918

2800	291	Front
2814C	2815	Rear

Hub caps of the same pattern were now nickel-plated. The front hubs were made with a longer shoulder. Rear tires now had tread pattern. (The front tires remained smooth. The treaded rears began appearing during 1916.) Spokes now round in cross section.

1919-1924

2800	291B	Front
		Non-demountable
2800B	291D	Front
		Kelsey demountable (1919-1924)
2800C	291E	Front
		Hayes demountable (1921-1923)
2800G	291G	Front
		Ford demountable (1922-1926)
2814C	2815	Rear
		Non-demountable
2814G	2815B	Rear
		Kelsey demountable (1919-1924)
2814H	2815C	Rear
		Hayes demountable (1921-1923)
2814J	7698C	Rear
		Ford demountable (1922)
2814J2	7698D	Rear
		Ford demountable (1923)
2814K	2815E	Rear
		Ford Demountable (1924-1925)

Demountable rims available as an option, using 30 x 3-1/2 tires all around. Several manufacturers supplied wheels, so there were variations in the style. The rims were zinc plated.

WHEELS (Continued)

Non-demountable wheels continued as standard equipment. By 1920 the square-felloe wheels were used in some production, along with the round felloe type. 30 x 3 tires were used in front when the car had the standard wheels. By 1925 all wheels had the square felloe.

Hub caps were nickel-plated but about 1923 they were made of steel, rather than brass. (Steel had been used as far back as 1918 but brass replaced the earlier steel for a time.)

Beginning in 1919, front wheel bearings were changed to roller on trucks and, later, closed cars. By 1920 they were standard on all cars with demountable wheels but apparently the ball type were used on open cars with non-demountable wheels until 1925.

1925

Same wheels as above but 21" balloon tire/wheels an option.

```
2800I    291H   Front 21"
           Balloon, black (1925-1927)
2800J    291I   Front 21"
           Balloon, natural (1925-1927)
2814N    2815F  Rear 21"
           Balloon, black (1925)
2814P    2815G  Rear 21"
           Balloon, natural (1925)
```
21" wheels finished in natural wood were available in addition to the standard black.

1926

```
2800A1 291J   Front 30x3-1/2
           Non-demountable (1926)
2800I  291H   Front 21"
           Balloon, black (1925-1927)
2800J  291I   Front 21"
           Balloon, natural (1925-1927)
2814F2 7698H  Rear 30x3-1/2
           Non-demountable (1926)
2814N2 2815J  Rear 21"
           Balloon, black (1926-1927)
2814P2 2815M  Rear 21"
           Balloon, natural (1926-1927)
2881   2846   Front/Rear
           21" Wire (1926-1927)
```
Early production continued the options available in 1925 but the 30 x 3-1/2 (all around) demountable wheels became standard after a short time. 21" wood wheels were the same as 1925 except for the 11" rear brake drums. Wire wheels, introduced in January 1926 in black only at first, then in several colors, became optional. These used the same 21" tires as the wooden balloon wheels. New hub caps, nickel-plated steel, were used with the wire wheels.

1927

Standard wheels were the 21" demountables, with the wire wheels an option. Wire wheels became standard equipment in the last production on closed cars made in some assembly plants.

WIRE WHEEL COLORS: (Late 1926 and 1927):

Casino Red, Emerald Green, Straw, Drake Green (1927) and Black.

FRONT WHEEL HUBS

1909-1910 2803 (200)
Flange diameter 5-1/2". Used ball bearings.

1911-1916 2803C (232)
Flange diameter 6". Used ball bearings. Hubs had short outer shoulder (about 7/8") with a 11/16" threaded section for the cap.

1916-1919 2803C (232) Ball bearing
2803B (219) Roller bearing
Similar to 1915 type but now had longer (about 1-1/2" in the 2803B) outer shoulder for greater strength, with shorter (about 3/8") threaded section.

1919-1926 2803 (200) Ball bearing
2803B (219) Roller bearing
Similar to 1918 style but now fitted with Timken roller bearings on all cars except the open models without electrical equipment and with non-demountable wheels, which continued the ball bearings until about 1925.

1926-1927 2803B (219)   Wood wheels
2882   (2841)   Wire wheels
Wood wheels used same hubs as 1925. Wire wheels had entirely different design hub with five studs to secure the wheel.

REAR WHEEL HUBS

1909-1910 2815 (102) [31]
Designed for non-tapered axle with pin through the diameter to hold the wheel. 5-1/2" diameter flanges. The general shape of the hub was like that of the front hubs.

1911 2815B (40B) [88]
Non-tapered axle continued into early 1911. 6" flange style hubs for these axles.

1911-1927 2815C (2819)
Tapered axle. Flanges are 6" diameter. Shorter, near uniform diameter hub section.

1926-1927 2815C (2819)   Wood wheels [281]
2887   (2842B) Wire wheels (with brake drum)
Wood wheels used same hubs as 1925. Wire wheels had entirely different design hub with five studs to secure the wheel.

WHEEL HUB CAPS

1909-1910 [63]
Brass, with "Ford" in block letters.

1911 [86]
Brass, with "Ford" in script. No "Made in USA." Had rounded-end style, in the same pattern as the 1909-10.

1912 [126]
Brass, with "Ford" in script. "Made in USA" in later production. Ends were now flat, with a border, similar to the later types.

1913-1916 [159]
Brass, similar to 1912 but with "Made in USA." Earlier versions had the "Ford" with a higher than usual "F."

MODEL T FORD PRODUCTION (August 1, 1919 to June 30, 1927)

	Touring	Touring Starter	Roadster	Roadster Starter	Tudor	Fordor	Coupe	Chassis	Chassis Starter	Truck	Truck Starter	Total
8-1-19 to 7-31-20	165,929	367,785	31,889	63,514	81,616		60,215	18,173	16,919	135,002		941,042
8-1-20 to 12-31-20	44,036	209,105	5,796	47,891	53,903		36,180	3,087	9,666	53,787		463,451
1-1-21 to 12-31-21	40,934	438,195	20,122	123,854	125,831		92,979	8,269	13,770	64,796	42,860*	928,750
1-1-22 to 12-31-22	80,070	514,333	31,923	133,433	146,060	4,286	198,382	15,228	23,313	135,629	18,410	1,301,067
1-1-23 to 12-31-23	130,326	767,446	55,896	234,884	89,535	143,884	305,437	8,548	28,332	184,053	62,784	2,011,125
1-1-24 to 12-31-24	95,026	654,016	42,663	217,706	213,926	82,679	320,473	2,929	33,512	166,731	92,387	1,922,048
1-1-25 to 12-31-25	57,829	605,218	33,545	259,954	184,929	79,496	335,520	4,723	44,058	186,810	119,624	1,911,706
1-1-26 to 12-31-26		332,619		332,205	253,304	99,026	279,743		43,654		213,914	1,554,465
1-1-27 to 6-30-27		64,960		90,583	68,660	21,197	66,024		13,966		74,335	399,725

* In 1921 42,860 cars and trucks were made in foreign (other than Canada) plants, which brings to total for 1921 to 971,610. Later year's figures include this foreign production.

Figures compiled by Ford Motor Company, August 3, 1927. Total Model T production: 14,690,510

MODEL T FORD PRODUCTION (Calendar 1921)

	Touring	Touring Starter	Roadster	Roadster Starter	Tudor	Fordor	Coupe	Chassis	Chassis Starter	Truck	Truck Starter	Total
Atlanta	20	527	5	121	43		44	19	1			780
Buffalo	1,481	21,143	1,162	6,145	9,240		5,265	476	1,044	4,219		50,175
Cambridge	727	13,860	657	4,603	7,579		3,274	520	1,859	3,134		36,213
Chicago	1,161	24,885	852	5,885	11,215		5,291	878	1,055	4,422		55,644
Cincinatti	2,153	24,682	825	5,671	4,204		3,581	355	608	2,562		44,641
Columbus	2,606	21,465	903	5,523	4,579		3,118	202	572	2,457		41,425
Dallas	515	12,167	219	3,821	1,267		2,107	85	266	1,332		21,779
Denver	51	407	68	343	190		242	21	8	68		1,398
Des Moines	1,432	11,784	746	3,073	2,643		3,636	41	14	974		24,343
Houston	1,063	13,750	262	2,790	1,277		1,182	553	293	1,807		22,977
Indianapolis	2,900	21,951	1,344	4,929	5,300		4,091	327	309	2,621		43,772
Kansas City	4,751	22,035	2,685	6,251	3,676		5,792	309		2,550		48,049
Kearny	2,239	39,321	720	11,213	17,201		6,168	1,350	5,691	9,506		93,409
Louisville	2,589	8,239	569	1,724	1,213		1,462	156	142	531		16,625
Memphis	989	11,092	312	2,695	986		1,101	161	46	1,055		18,437
Milwaukee	1,395	17,264	1,429	5,216	5,465		4,319	161	107	2,180		37,536
Minneapolis	1,662	18,179	894	4,367	4,121		4,008	92	115	2,329		35,767
Oklahoma City	498	10,093	304	5,049	764		1,851	17	10	994		19,530
Omaha	2,479	13,189	945	4,437	2,848		3,387	53	671	1,363		29,372
Philadelphia	2,110	22,779	749	6,405	11,329		5,526	708	1,862	4,861		56,329
Pittsburgh	2,448	15,465	1,436	6,698	2,203		3,279	318	96	2,548		34,491
San Francisco	336	20,312	453	8,373	1,529		1,868	370	5,984	3,389		42,614
Seattle	103	8,409	101	2,814	1,718		1,793	45	168	1,136		16,287
St. Louis	4,180	24,185	1,563	5,962	4,131		5,097	522	392	2,952		48,984
Highland Park	1,046	40,663	919	9,729	13,732		7,120	530	8,578	5,856		88,173
Converted from chassis:		349		17	7,378		8,377		(16,121)			
U.S. Totals	40,934	438,195	20,122	123,854	125,831		92,979	8,269	13,770	64,796		928,750
Walkerville	24,944		2,969		4,056		2,703	3,468		4,208		42,348
TOTALS	65,878	438,195	23,091	123,854	129,887		95,682	11,737	13,770	69,004		971,098

TRACTORS

River Rouge	29,188	Kearny	285
St. Louis	4,304	Cork	1,443
Des Moines	1,562		
TOTAL TRACTOR	36,782		

FOREIGN CAR PRODUCTION

Bordeaux	2,078	Cadiz	1,375
Copenhagen	5,517	Manchester	26,657
Sao Paulo	1,072	Buenos Aires	6,161
TOTAL FOREIGN	42,860		

Production Statistics

MODEL T FORD PRODUCTION (Calendar 1922)

	Touring	Touring Starter	Roadster	Roadster Starter	Tudor	Fordor	Coupe	Chassis	Chassis Starter	Truck	Truck Starter	Total
Atlanta	1,125	16,426	155	2,184	1,066	105	2,455	147	177	2,557	36	26,433
Buffalo	2,103	21,496	1,570	6,363	8,576	299	9,583	765	1,114	6,267	912	59,048
Cambridge	725	15,150	521	4,578	8,875	144	6,434	673	3,644	4,827	1,498	47,069
Chicago	2,736	20,735	1,361	5,974	11,131	329	11,250	1,203	1,451	6,544	727	63,441
Cincinatti	3,282	24,509	1,047	5,575	4,431	165	6,408	436	1,473	4,839	363	52,528
Columbus	4,138	20,563	1,431	5,356	4,453	156	6,527	394	1,655	3,921	319	48,913
Dallas	1,478	17,191	484	5,634	1,830	111	5,472	116	73	2,639	164	35,192
Des Moines	6,207	13,360	2,218	2,107	3,756	176	8,629	92	347	3,060	67	40,019
Houston	3,099	17,614	584	3,356	1,995	116	3,022	1,064	165	3,913	12	34,940
Indianapolis	4,716	19,419	1,928	4,070	5,546	117	7,966	397	619	3,826	215	48,819
Kansas City	5,588	21,739	2,887	5,764	3,773	211	11,584	138	84	4,122	218	56,108
Kearny	4,092	44,891	1,314	12,649	20,508	275	12,303	1,479	8,741	19,258	3,295	128,805
Louisville	3,669	10,461	1,167	2,457	1,569	67	3,202	292	356	1,770	18	25,028
Memphis	1,616	15,404	450	3,223	1,395	100	2,967	305	146	2,345	72	28,023
Milwaukee	2,664	16,195	1,958	4,300	5,206	158	7,154	271	2,303	3,467	186	43,862
Minneapolis	5,796	21,667	1,984	4,601	6,652	190	11,676	206	230	5,430	285	58,717
Oklahoma City	1,050	15,923	500	8,571	1,511	172	5,694	33	200	2,740	80	36,474
Omaha	6,023	10,796	2,119	2,540	3,622	212	7,363	991	4,403	2,617	60	40,746
Philadelphia	3,329	22,744	1,076	6,438	11,499	252	9,261	1,336	2,727	7,710	1,235	68,107
Pittsburgh	2,715	16,812	1,711	6,392	2,511	98	7,172	310	351	4,376	297	42,745
San Francisco	410	14,602	585	6,951	2,276	194	3,801	347	12,857	4,598	596	47,217
Seattle	264	11,900	166	3,028	3,270	106	4,872	90	229	1,913	301	26,139
St. Louis	5,449	23,410	1,907	6,078	4,310	225	9,889	517	1,190	4,666	440	58,081
Highland Park	3,899	40,804	2,057	9,534	15,487	115	16,400	974	14,827	10,092	1,566	115,755
Converted from chassis:	1,146	11,728	582	4,281	7,552	193	16,404	(187)	(44,804)	3,077	28	
U.S. Totals	77,319	485,539	31,762	132,004	142,800	4,286	197,988	12,389	14,558	120,574	12,990	1,232,209
Buenos Aires	1,194	8,683	40	95	185		10	263	317	849	235	11,871
Copenhagen	165	5,459	10	129	1,206		139	69	204		3,171	10,552
Manchester	753	6,654	23	474	1,176		144	1,757	5,083	10,350	780	27,194
Cadiz	256	2,406	8	72	267		11	41	187	1,677	406	5,331
Sao Paulo	269	2,064	9	67	26		7	38	80	755	47	3,362
Bordeaux	144	3,528	71	592	400		83	671	2,884	1,424	781	10,548
Totals	80,070	514,333	31,923	133,433	146,060	4,286	198,382	15,228	23,313	135,629	18,410	1,301,067
Walkerville	2,378	21,524	661	2,968	4,042		4,028	626	7,394	5,138	1,507	50,266

TRACTORS
River Rouge   66,752
Cork   2,233   Total: 68,985

	Touring	Touring Starter	Roadster	Roadster Starter	Tudor	Fordor	Coupe	Chassis	Chassis Starter	Truck	Truck Starter	Total
Atlanta	3,941	35,666	622	5,264	977	1,826	5,140	244	421	7,217	56	61,374
Buffalo	2,659	32,140	1,740	9,643	5,113	7,146	13,269	503	1,474	9,286	1,418	84,391
Cambridge	2,263	30,627	923	9,475	7,781	7,694	11,212	257	3,210	6,105	4,688	84,235
Chicago	3,400	24,692	1,520	8,202	6,357	12,076	16,337	570	1,174	8,924	770	84,022
Cincinatti	4,523	25,211	1,603	7,163	2,075	3,800	9,382	225	596	4,929	674	60,181
Cleveland	443	12,092	413	5,274	1,725	3,877	10,791	148	1,088	2,313	1,454	39,618
Columbus	5,734	29,666	2,211	8,974	2,756	4,745	10,018	210	444	6,647	636	72,041
Dallas	2,964	21,661	982	7,442	589	1,740	5,778	48	26	4,171	141	45,542
Denver	2,104	12,142	1,273	4,467	1,049	2,295	6,140	74	89	2,511	100	32,244
Des Moines	10,889	21,999	4,750	6,578	2,292	4,519	13,586	93	2,429	6,745	75	73,955
Houston	5,778	25,543	1,236	5,354	850	2,450	4,607	341	250	6,036	58	52,503
Indianapolis	7,460	31,202	3,343	8,948	3,765	6,830	13,948	783	788	8,001	327	85,395
Kansas City	7,194	25,524	5,393	9,769	2,046	3,975	15,271	227	153	5,411	270	75,233
Kearny	10,683	76,456	3,517	23,081	11,132	17,478	20,529	979	9,372	29,925	12,084	215,236
Los Angeles	22	4,416	23	2,288	519	1,046	5,517	16	442	941	170	15,400
Louisville	6,946	21,366	2,001	5,520	1,026	2,532	6,627	353	490	4,774	44	51,679
Memphis	1,998	16,873	601	3,823	658	1,185	3,324	122	252	3,352	100	32,288
Milwaukee	3,896	21,293	2,690	6,895	3,242	5,466	9,771	234	763	4,559	306	59,115
Minneapolis	14,377	29,909	5,062	7,822	4,828	6,459	16,388	226	183	7,376	333	92,963
New Orleans	1,870	19,373	192	4,335	531	1,718	3,280	221	526	4,729	23	36,798
Oklahoma City	1,625	18,737	933	12,770	785	1,914	7,507	14	13	3,678	63	48,039
Omaha	8,700	12,607	3,876	3,353	2,191	3,097	9,438	268	432	3,876	52	47,890
Philadelphia	3,878	29,967	1,411	10,912	6,938	10,193	15,390	721	3,247	8,750	2,797	94,204
Pittsburgh	2,765	21,542	2,133	11,212	1,394	2,577	11,254	312	761	5,355	708	60,013
Portland	183	6,005	118	2,043	340	973	2,612	15	151	896	80	13,416
San Francisco	422	20,471	717	11,894	750	2,807	7,117	227	4,423	4,866	893	54,587
Seattle	205	13,859	149	4,836	1,179	2,823	6,545	40	249	2,576	365	32,826
St. Louis	7,168	35,064	2,890	10,623	2,398	4,631	15,269	591	870	7,624	657	87,875
Highland Park	4,597	41,594	2,914	13,498	8,969	13,004	21,522	486	2,524	11,294	2,020	122,422
Converted from chassis:	1,639	6,400	570	1,986	1,048	1,620	7,456		(21,991)	1,186	86	
U.S. Totals	130,326	724,097	55,896	233,444	85,303	142,496	305,025	8,548	14,849	184,053	31,448	1,915,485
Barcelona		2,698		116	139	398	1		118		2,423	5,893
Bordeaux		2,813		448	240	68	40		4,943		4,382	12,934
Buenos Aires		14,243		204	127	279	5		917		2,811	18,586
Copenhagen		8,791		145	2,336	459	200		396		5,059	17,386
Cork		510		30	33	32	6		78		353	1,042
Manchester		8,053		393	1,320	112	139		6,889		13,792	30,698
Sao Paulo		6,241		104	37	40	21		142		2,516	9,101
Totals	130,326	767,446	55,896	234,884	89,535	143,884	305,437	8,548	28,332	184,053	62,784	2,011,125
Walkerville	4,285	25,205	1,058	3,754	6,875	560	7,836	895	14,542	13,004	1,820	79,834
Totals	136,411	792,651	56,954	238,638	96,410	144,444	313,273	9,443	42,874	197,057	64,604	2,090,959

LINCOLNS 7,825
TRACTORS
River Rouge 101,898

Production Statistics

MODEL T FORD PRODUCTION (Calendar 1924)

	Touring	Touring Starter	Roadster	Roadster Starter	Tudor	Fordor	Coupe	Chassis	Chassis Starter	Truck	Truck Starter	Total
Atlanta	3,717	33,862	743	5,365	2,019	1,289	7,150	105	298	7,723	107	62,378
Buffalo	966	18,850	757	8,281	11,844	3,478	13,255	296	1,238	4,905	1,568	65,438
Cambridge	695	20,812	349	6,397	15,592	4,276	10,224	121	2,747	2,895	4,150	68,258
Chicago	2,711	28,853	1,317	10,003	21,288	9,312	20,062	549	1,388	10,055	1,162	106,700
Charlotte	1,506	4,860	451	1,514	222	275	1,614	9	12	1,100	11	11,574
Cincinatti	3,974	22,119	1,494	7,378	4,802	1,807	10,353	177	506	4,690	777	58,077
Cleveland	356	11,934	289	8,018	7,744	3,272	14,751	69	778	2,163	2,338	51,712
Columbus	3,358	16,938	1,583	7,990	6,556	1,596	9,782	297	2,499	4,628	574	55,801
Dallas	2,518	22,318	616	6,974	1,342	1,296	6,991	15	11	4,560	160	46,801
Denver	1,675	11,595	1,200	4,324	2,577	1,436	7,435	88	107	3,801	214	34,452
Des Moines	6,926	10,194	3,644	2,881	6,011	1,914	9,480	68	83	2,851	79	44,158
Houston	5,037	30,901	1,527	7,485	2,251	1,817	6,808	328	233	10,801	169	67,357
Indianapolis	3,651	22,105	1,907	7,738	7,152	3,303	13,550	303	338	6,590	307	66,944
Jacksonville	38	886	3	163	105	159	361		87	431	1	2,234
Kansas City	6,749	26,340	4,659	10,994	6,214	2,255	17,380	104	142	6,735	380	81,952
Kearny	5,913	51,477	1,588	16,886	21,590	7,585	19,995	689	9,490	19,883	14,728	169,824
Los Angeles	33	10,360	80	7,410	3,285	1,301	11,055	39	664	3,197	761	38,185
Louisville	5,738	24,803	1,780	6,088	2,503	1,409	7,967	220	424	6,011	84	57,027
Memphis	1,277	18,440	381	3,976	965	753	3,457	63	101	3,794	165	33,372
Milwaukee	2,013	13,305	2,110	5,834	6,899	3,545	10,274	163	249	3,115	308	47,815
Minneapolis	11,262	18,471	4,103	4,026	12,428	3,994	14,389	253	193	6,789	408	76,316
New Orleans	2,631	24,319	325	5,694	2,210	1,886	5,555	233	654	6,384	212	50,103
Oklahoma City	1,344	21,198	844	11,286	1,728	1,150	9,279	3	1	5,475	108	52,416
Omaha	6,439	11,513	3,654	3,146	5,127	1,642	9,173	183	97	3,003	83	44,060
Philadelphia	3,876	24,937	1,260	10,321	13,606	5,039	15,720	464	2,968	8,397	3,472	90,060
Pittsburgh	1,189	12,987	953	9,148	3,488	1,469	11,345	174	624	4,224	1,289	46,890
Portland	74	4,487	61	2,188	1,023	326	3,056	8	139	976	241	12,579
San Francisco	114	7,935	271	5,737	1,949	756	5,834	133	789	2,756	1,120	27,394
Seattle	40	6,424	45	2,471	2,566	850	5,007	28	153	1,674	578	19,836
St. Louis	5,911	33,927	2,508	11,214	6,949	2,957	15,132	339	563	7,737	626	87,863
Highland Park	1,742	29,983	1,623	13,786	24,372	7,988	21,311	290	1,070	8,597	1,940	112,702
Converted from chassis:	1,553	5,133	538	1,578	481	263	1,999	(2,882)	(9,454)	791		
U.S. Totals	95,026	602,266	42,663	216,294	206,888	80,425	319,744	2,929	19,192	166,731	38,120	1,790,278
Antwerp		4,683		321	3,020	462	356		1,871		14,493	25,206
Barcelona		1,402				5			49		2,926	4,382
Bordeaux		4,188		258	363	352	73		4,767		6,160	16,161
Buenos Aires		17,412		250	173	258	28		1,151		3,938	23,210
Copenhagen		8,448		132	1,810	598	75		378		6,274	17,715
Cork		1,563		75	77	75	6		339		595	2,730
Sao Paulo		8,885		153	53	58	22		190		5,500	14,861
Manchester		5,169		223	1,542	466	169		5,575		14,381	27,505
Totals	95,026	654,016	42,663	217,706	213,926	82,679	320,473	2,929	33,512	166,731	92,387	1,922,048
Walkerville	4,497	19,563	654	3,249	9,277	2,054	7,111	992	10,468	11,544	1,962	71,371
Totals	99,523	673,579	43,317	220,955	223,203	84,733	327,584	3,921	43,980	178,275	94,349	1,993,419

LINCOLNS 7,116
TRACTORS
River Rouge 83,010

MODEL T FORD TRUCK PRODUCTION (Calendar 1924)

	Chassis	"C" Cab Non-Starter	Cab/Body	Total	Chassis	"C" Cab Starter	Cab/Body	Total	Total (all)
Atlanta	5,726	831	1,166	7,723	38	31	38	107	7,830
Buffalo	4,189	339	377	4,905	1,363	69	136	1,568	6,473
Cambridge	2,895			2,895	4,150			4,150	7,045
Charlotte	774	183	143	1,100	7	1	3	11	1,111
Chicago	8,235	839	981	10,055	906	42	214	1,162	11,217
Cincinatti	3,191	615	884	4,690	564	50	163	777	5,467
Cleveland	1,469	377	317	2,163	1,674	248	416	2,338	4,501
Columbus	2,700	1,209	719	4,628	318	119	137	574	5,201
Dallas	2,937	1,069	554	4,560	72	55	33	160	4,720
Denver	1,427	1,023	1,351	3,801	60	51	103	214	4,015
Des Moines	2,289	210	352	2,851	40	11	28	79	2,930
Houston	6,993	1,986	1,822	10,801	82	43	44	169	10,970
Indianapolis	4,870	1,078	642	6,590	251	21	35	307	6,897
Jacksonville	355	69	7	431	1			1	432
Kansas City	4,223	1,337	1,175	6,735	312	45	23	380	7,115
Kearny	17,175	930	1,778	19,883	13,562	171	995	14,728	34,611
Los Angeles	2,295	467	435	3,197	452	152	157	761	3,958
Louisville	4,129	883	999	6,011	42	8	34	84	6,095
Memphis	2,428	702	664	3,794	83	52	30	165	3,959
Milwaukee	3,115			3,115	308			308	3,423
Minneapolis	6,789			6,789	408			408	7,197
New Orleans	6,384			6,384	212			212	5,583
Oklahoma City	5,475			5,475	108			108	5,583
Omaha	1,804	688	511	3,003	36	11	36	3,472	11,869
Philadelphia	7,119	534	744	8,397	3,174	80	218	3,472	11,869
Pittsburgh	2,918	337	969	4,224	983	58	248	1,289	5,513
Portland	371	367	238	976	64	80	97	241	1,217
San Francisco	2,756			2,756	1,120			1,120	3,876
Seattle	737	608	329	1,674	175	170	233	578	2,252
St. Louis	4,357	1,891	1,489	7,737	452	66	108	626	8,363
Highland Park	7,218	892	487	8,597	1,454	196	290	1,940	10,537
Converted from chassis:	548	80	163	791					
U.S. Totals	127,891	19,544	19,296	166,730	32,471	1,830	3,819	38,120	204,851
Antwerp					14,493			14,493	14,493
Barcelona					2,926			2,926	2,926
Bordeaux					6,160			6,160	6,160
Buenos Aires					3,938			3,938	3,938
Copenhagen					6,274			6,274	6,274
Cork					595			595	595
Sao Paulo					5,500			5,500	5,500
Manchester					14,381			14,381	14,381
Totals					86,738			92,387	259,118
Walkerville	11,544			11,544	1,962			1,962	13,506
Totals	139,435	19,444	19,296	178,275	88,700	1,830	3,819	94,349	272,624

Production Statistics

MODEL T FORD PRODUCTION (Calendar 1925)

	Touring	Touring Starter	Roadster	Roadster Starter	Tudor	Fordor	Coupe	Chassis	Chassis Starter	Truck	Truck Starter	Total
Atlanta	944	25,172	238	4,183	1,423	1,109	5,821	33	237	7,069	292	46,521
Buffalo	379	12,902	617	8,328	9,090	3,342	12,499	255	1,124	3,673	3,393	55,602
Cambridge	46	11,977	160	5,634	10,261	2,963	8,648	138	2,455	1,828	5,233	49,298
Chicago	1,470	19,506	1,150	9,785	17,503	8,267	21,101	400	1,511	9,160	2,012	91,855
Charlotte	4,609	24,101	1,881	9,551	1,910	1,254	8,176	25	201	8,282	42	60,032
Cincinatti	1,782	18,832	848	7,697	3,763	1,772	10,197	132	530	4,448	828	50,839
Cleveland	45	7,048	107	8,894	5,430	2,453	13,252	79	836	1,240	3,264	42,648
Columbus	792	12,219	614	6,198	5,066	1,294	7,677	78	440	2,987	958	38,323
Dallas	1,253	23,199	424	9,007	1,831	1,139	9,754	48	84	7,832	337	54,908
Denver	438	7,797	541	4,526	2,356	1,178	6,837	77	98	3,615	663	28,126
Des Moines	4,947	8,475	3,605	3,927	5,717	2,217	10,478	96	62	3,683	125	43,332
Houston	1,661	21,514	624	5,603	1,431	1,450	6,115	210	130	9,418	195	48,351
Indianapolis	1,489	11,867	1,116	6,649	5,872	2,716	10,909	218	375	4,107	390	45,708
Jacksonville	109	15,072	80	3,426	1,747	1,296	4,131	19	896	8,613	298	35,687
Kansas City	4,512	26,782	3,964	14,594	5,988	2,362	18,739	165	142	9,114	432	86,794
Kearny	2,074	41,921	339	13,610	13,213	5,237	13,803	757	10,386	13,317	22,664	137,321
Los Angeles	3	9,620	6	10,772	2,301	925	11,186	1	584	569	3,911	39,878
Louisville	4,841	32,952	1,577	8,983	2,757	1,903	9,768	156	470	8,088	112	71,607
Memphis	2,206	33,347	512	8,714	2,057	1,490	7,711	42	235	10,136	277	66,727
Milwaukee	1,118	9,717	1,448	5,696	7,286	3,496	11,382	115	475	3,792	447	44,945
New Orleans	1,189	20,785	149	5,753	2,201	2,011	6,039	89	710	7,489	844	47,259
Norfolk	2,087	12,240	740	4,534	1,421	565	3,693	6	165	4,004	64	29,519
Oklahoma City	776	19,451	583	11,742	1,781	1,348	10,004	27	30	6,692	206	52,640
Omaha	4,787	10,004	3,408	4,270	5,256	1,765	9,892	133	88	4,027	354	43,984
Philadelphia	1,128	19,138	710	13,324	10,867	4,516	15,038	331	3,085	6,982	5,330	80,449
Pittsburgh	343	11,373	404	10,090	2,513	1,252	10,689	130	680	3,887	1,195	42,556
Portland	13	4,467	28	3,178	978	360	3,900	5	107	1,361	626	15,023
San Francisco	20	8,123	114	8,472	1,846	803	7,007	31	698	2,023	2,966	32,103
Seattle	6	4,521	23	3,031	1,655	720	5,624	16	245	2,044	674	18,559
St. Louis	3,349	23,956	1,918	10,519	6,304	2,700	14,792	203	562	6,455	927	71,685
Twin City	8,531	18,898	4,440	6,603	14,752	6,404	17,932	449	326	12,514	699	91,548
Detroit	872	26,898	1,177	21,404	20,460	6,000	22,096	259	1,153	8,361	2,738	111,418
U.S. Totals	57,829	553,874	33,545	258,697	176,991	76,280	334,880	4,723	29,120	186,810	62,496	1,775,245
Antwerp		3,049		220	2,195	663	186		1,037		7,672	15,022
Barcelona		2,513		21	60	390	5		161		2,632	5,782
Bordeaux		4,951		182	364	527	57		7,260		10,898	24,239
Buenos Aires		16,336		281	193	399	36		1,202		6,489	24,936
Copenhagen		12,026		159	4,118	484	162		630		7,000	24,579
Cork		1,253		39	169	128	51		156		613	2,409
Sao Paulo		8,424		186	111	218	47		361		7,828	17,175
Manchester		2,792		169	728	407	96		4,131		13,996	22,319
Totals	57,829	605,218	33,545	259,954	184,929	79,496	335,520	4,723	44,058	186,810	119,624	1,911,706
Walkerville	6,570	21,595	661	4,482	10,072	1,554	8,249	1,800	9,392	10,580	4,334	79,289
Totals	64,399	626,813	34,206	264,436	195,001	81,050	343,969	6,523	53,450	197,390	123,958	1,990,995

LINCOLNS 8,415
TRACTORS
River Rouge 104,168

MODEL T FORD TRUCK PRODUCTION (Calendar 1925)

	Chassis	Chassis Starter	Total	Open Cab	Cl. Cab	Express Body	Stake Body	Platform Body	Pickup Body	Canopy Body	Scr.Side Body	Grain Body
Atlanta	7,069	292	7,361	2,056	936	1,021	1,093	455	642	68	5	
Buffalo	3,673	3,393	7,066	872	2,411	802	1,704	5	1,288	77	41	
Cambridge	1,828	5,233	7,061	890	1,774	713	794	75	805	86	23	
Charlotte	8,282	42	8,324	2,530	1,089	1,043	1,547	530	960	52	34	
Chicago	9,160	2,012	11,172	670	3,627	1,000	1,120	323	1,227	161	112	98
Cincinatti	4,448	828	5,276	1,759	1,206	1,006	834	4	616	64	24	
Cleveland	1,240	3,264	4,504	642	1,496	574	728	14	820	56	21	
Columbus	2,987	958	3,945	921	1,261	673	694	264	566	49	24	
Dallas	7,832	337	8,169	2,426	2,836	523	2,116	338	1,189	6	11	
Denver	3,615	663	4,278	1,248	2,287	1,038	1,084	338	1,501	67	33	
Des Moines	3,683	125	3,808	509	1,780	366	504	329	903	29		
Houston	9,418	195	9,613	2,429	2,168	1,073	1,961	9	1,253	187	125	
Indianapolis	4,107	390	4,497	690	1,563	356	911	306	827	40	25	
Jacksonville	8,613	298	8,911	2,135	950	854	1,712	2	704	24	19	
Kansas City	9,114	432	9,546	2,093	3,535	1,421	1,517	718	1,752	47	35	
Kearny	13,317	22,664	35,981	2,413	2,626	2,297	1,956	26	1,858	236	127	
Los Angeles	569	3,911	4,480	1,916	882	696	1,092	260	1,431	94	26	
Louisville	8,088	112	8,200	2,705	1,911	1,256	1,476	401	1,055	61	31	
Memphis	10,136	277	10,413	2,977	2,607	936	2,307	201	1,087	51	5	
Milwaukee	3,792	447	4,239	593	1,139	482	679	135	961	19	16	
New Orleans	7,489	844	8,333	1,228	1,185	575	1,009	6	827	63	48	
Norfolk	4,004	64	4,068	1,205	679	353	750	14	461	19	11	
Oklahoma City	6,692	206	6,898	1,755	3,293	858	2,383	579	1,053	24	12	
Omaha	4,027	354	4,381	681	2,054	432	267	566	556	9	4	
Philadelphia	6,982	5,330	12,312	1,557	1,973	1,214	1,409	97	1,224	139	94	
Pittsburgh	3,887	1,195	5,082	1,297	1,494	1,332	805		726	114	22	
Portland	1,361	626	1,987	696	822	263	453	7	616	47	15	
San Francisco	2,023	2,966	4,989	1,771	1,193	565	1,110	83	1,199	69	33	
Seattle	2,044	674	2,718	1,049	1,119	332	604	80	693	65	11	
St. Louis	6,455	927	7,382	2,202	1,864	1,166	1,339	57	1,391	48	10	
Twin City	12,514	699	13,213	493	8,141	2,400	715	2,791	2,123	44	24	
Detroit	8,361	2,738	11,099	693	4,450	646	2,051	2	1,481	125	25	
U.S. Totals	186,810	62,496	249,306	47,101	66,351	28,266	38,722	9,015	33,795	2,240	1,046	98

NOTE: See Passenger Car listing for foreign truck production (chassis only).

Production Statistics

MODEL T FORD PRODUCTION (Calendar 1926)

	Touring	Roadster	Chassis	Coupe	Tudor	Fordor	Truck	Total
Atlanta	10,479	5,333	383	3,871	2,349	1,459	4,254	28,128
Buffalo	6,783	11,451	1,259	11,915	13,035	3,614	4,565	52,622
Cambridge	8,251	7,431	2,287	8,052	14,502	3,675	5,196	49,394
Chicago	7,033	11,642	1,803	13,032	18,867	6,826	7,464	66,667
Charlotte	12,470	11,049	350	7,544	3,357	2,225	5,466	42,461
Cincinatti	9,161	8,675	719	7,294	5,104	2,032	3,761	36,746
Cleveland	3,681	9,861	848	11,166	8,740	2,691	3,314	40,301
Columbus	6,601	8,773	533	6,870	7,549	2,099	3,229	35,654
Dallas	7,216	9,295	281	9,423	2,196	2,254	4,386	35,051
Denver	4,693	6,164	285	5,738	3,946	1,333	3,102	25,261
Des Moines	6,235	6,367	154	6,154	7,255	2,986	2,843	31,994
Houston	12,865	9,554	539	7,196	2,818	2,428	8,120	43,520
Indianapolis	5,578	8,563	735	8,811	9,926	3,618	3,437	40,668
Jacksonville	7,966	8,197	684	5,140	2,593	2,409	4,855	31,844
Kansas City	15,367	18,570	572	15,913	9,162	4,548	7,421	71,553
Kearny	24,566	15,602	12,174	13,003	17,125	5,637	24,477	112,584
Los Angeles	5,296	13,237	434	9,339	3,369	1,318	3,429	36,422
Louisville	18,325	11,271	645	7,955	3,924	2,611	5,606	50,337
Memphis	19,233	12,995	249	7,024	3,341	2,546	8,468	53,856
Milwaukee	5,449	8,652	494	7,382	8,396	4,149	2,780	37,302
New Orleans	10,140	8,166	750	5,785	3,069	2,799	6,648	37,357
Norfolk	12,847	10,145	779	7,261	5,171	2,448	5,533	44,184
Oklahoma City	6,060	11,558	237	9,836	2,440	2,177	4,568	36,876
Omaha	6,816	7,847	355	8,129	7,109	2,640	3,100	35,996
Philadelphia	8,146	13,751	2,763	11,700	13,533	4,256	7,004	61,153
Pittsburgh	5,174	10,278	762	8,023	3,537	1,588	3,610	32,972
Portland	3,291	4,591	259	3,471	1,746	408	1,229	14,995
San Francisco	4,426	8,814	615	6,036	2,748	895	3,066	26,600
Seattle	3,165	4,419	332	4,577	2,884	652	1,857	17,886
St. Louis	15,414	14,907	1,032	11,240	7,564	3,603	5,305	59,065
Twin City	11,109	12,507	393	13,706	17,886	8,575	5,938	70,114
Detroit	7,907	19,837	1,376	16,315	27,645	7,075	9,393	89,548
U.S. Totals	291,743	329,502	35,081	278,901	242,886	97,574	173,424	1,449,111
Antwerp	1,219	239	676	237	2,124	267	4,348	9,110
Asnieres	1,462	113	1,862	45	484	117	3,779	7,862
Barcelona	2,473	150	99	13	536	49	2,096	5,416
Buenos Aires	15,813	1,142	754	57	274	228	5,164	23,432
Copenhagen	9,118	349	536	199	4,767	366	3,770	19,105
Cork	951	139	140	62	365	79	473	2,209
Sao Paulo	6,215	336	155	41	98	41	4,715	11,601
Berlin	350	30	273	43	831	40	1,110	2,677
Mexico	879	10	10		5	9	614	1,527
Yokohama							524	524
Manchester	2,395	195	4,068	145	934	256	13,889	21,882
Walkerville	31,790	10,370	14,569	8,599	17,027	3,706	14,590	100,651
Totals	364,408	342,575	58,223	288,342	270,331	102,732	228,496	1,655,107

LINCOLNS   8,829
TRACTORS
River Rouge   88,101

MODEL T FORD TRUCK PRODUCTION (Calendar 1926)

	Total Trucks	Open Cab	Cl. Cab	Express Body	Stake Body	Platform Body	Pickup Body	Canopy Body	Scr.Side Body
Atlanta	4,254	839	755	242	583	3	737	73	16
Buffalo	4,565		2,651	202	1,142	18	4,301	73	23
Cambridge	5,196		2,476	373	523	22	2,699	138	58
Charlotte	5,466		2,332	401	663	7	1,207	49	34
Chicago	7,464	110	3,536	403	480	672	3,568	180	110
Cincinatti	3,761	587	1,117	386	492	117	1,056	40	16
Cleveland	3,314		2,190	336	579	49	2,457	54	23
Columbus	3,229		2,098	439	512	60	1,231	34	24
Dallas	4,386		2,809	63	832	379	2,055	41	39
Denver	3,102		2,747	327	773	72	2,600	75	31
Des Moines	2,843		2,086	32	80	803	1,434	13	9
Houston	8,120	1,400	1,703	400	1,482	661	2,718	165	58
Indianapolis	3,437	245	1,741	145	558	117	1,687	36	22
Jacksonville	4,855	1,310	715	189	957		1,677	47	34
Kansas City	7,421		5,759	600	683	2,124	3,136	33	21
Kearny	24,477	1,016	2,816	1,432	1,397	1,420	5,667	443	254
Los Angeles	3,429	1,068	1,278	418	1,104	29	3,553	113	49
Louisville	5,606		2,670	309	921	46	1,236	62	17
Memphis	8,468		3,894	345	1,555	1,579	1,882	66	17
Milwaukee	2,780		1,785	254	591	279	2,775	27	14
New Orleans	6,648		2,664	382	1,007	2	1,489	88	27
Norfolk	5,533		2,641	409	888	9	971	72	61
Oklahoma City	4,568	722	3,194	388	820	1,044	1,708	26	20
Omaha	3,100		1,873	67	41	664	789	12	7
Philadelphia	7,004		2,657	459	882	9	2,314	221	110
Pittsburgh	3,610	445	1,663	865	456	88	2,441	181	30
Portland	1,229		997	89	291	18	1,306	31	7
San Francisco	3,066		2,453	392	905	137	3,594	163	53
Seattle	1,857	388	985	174	164	104	1,353	76	28
St. Louis	5,305		3,349	608	1,128	207	2,309	83	35
Twin City	5,938	25	2,978	405	454	1,721	3,868	30	19
Detroit	9,393	242	6,874	540	2,958		5,588	368	155
U.S. Totals	173,424	8,397	79,486	12,074	25,901	12,460	75,406	3,113	1,421

NOTE: See Passenger Car listing for foreign truck production (chassis only).

MODEL T FORD PRODUCTION (Calendar 1927)

	Touring	Roadster	Chassis	Coupe	Tudor	Fordor	Truck	Total
Atlanta	2,108	1,230	91	885	759	388	1,106	6,567
Buffalo	1,523	4,919	586	3,539	4,128	928	1,923	17,546
Charlotte	2,984	3,152	145	2,054	1,187	649	1,617	11,788
Chester	1,151	4,585	856	2,691	3,825	843	2,406	16,357
Chicago	912	3,424	720	2,845	4,254	1,426	2,954	16,535
Cincinatti	1,717	2,511	307	1,522	1,239	430	1,167	8,893
Cleveland	594	3,256	298	2,003	1,970	615	1,143	9,879
Columbus	691	2,599	164	1,574	1,632	359	979	7,998
Dallas	924	2,576	100	2,605	812	528	1,041	8,586
Denver	582	1,386	89	1,236	1,060	349	612	5,314
Des Moines	768	1,719	56	1,746	2,289	514	956	8,048
Houston	2,608	2,493	148	2,112	1,154	845	1,435	10,795
Indianapolis	978	2,700	215	2,047	2,938	698	1,445	11,021
Jacksonville	1,280	1,394	44	839	539	392	655	5,143
Kansas City	2,795	4,802	180	4,248	3,361	1,223	2,156	18,765
Kearny	5,932	5,701	2,677	3,199	4,484	1,398	9,422	32,813
Los Angeles	1,289	4,117	149	2,678	959	473	1,294	10,959
Louisville	1,961	1,769	63	1,170	667	455	1,246	7,331
Memphis	924	1,716	75	1,325	534	350	1,404	6,328
Milwaukee	793	2,861	193	1,957	2,951	883	1,121	10,759
New Orleans	1,118	1,868	187	1,289	789	512	1,552	7,315
Norfolk	2,661	3,198	320	1,912	1,842	706	1,707	12,346
Oklahoma City	712	3,007	101	2,853	874	566	1,468	9,581
Omaha	727	1,542	93	1,824	1,732	524	866	7,308
Pittsburgh	1,047	2,908	221	1,699	797	275	828	7,775
Portland	658	1,312	42	702	685	118	422	3,939
San Francisco	1,068	2,111	217	1,413	785	217	891	6,702
Seattle	670	1,395	147	1,599	1,172	272	563	5,818
Somerville	1,438	2,033	583	1,671	3,060	432	1,829	11,046
St. Louis	2,009	3,243	273	2,551	1,972	618	1,193	11,859
Twin City	1,178	2,784	203	2,981	4,269	1,321	1,314	14,050
Detroit	1,037	5,033	339	2,830	5,427	1,069	2,842	18,577
U.S. Totals	46,837	89,344	9,882	65,599	64,146	20,376	51,557	347,741
Antwerp	399	142	274	155	778	48	1,527	3,323
Asnieres	1,811	88	875	9	410	26	1,690	4,909
Barcelona	1,210	40	116	14	535	104	1,058	3,077
Berlin	733	116	389	75	1,170	100	1,681	4,264
Buenos Aires	9,043	766	495	34	320	148	3,140	13,946
Copenhagen	3,745	150	358	151	1,892	174	2,258	8,728
Cork	583	86	118	32	186	93	409	1,507
Sao Paulo	2,126	104	102	2	11	1	1,727	4,073
Mexico City	943	31	9	6	37	27	1,626	2,679
Yokohama	2,657	29	369		122	178	3,088	6,443
Manchester	1,041	105	2,538	34	304	49	8,341	12,412
Walkerville	10,053	4,777	3,755	3,828	8,194	1,606	5,100	37,313
Totals	81,181	95,778	19,280	69,939	78,105	22,930	83,202	450,415

LINCOLNS	7,247
TRACTORS	
River Rouge	93,972

MODEL T FORD TRUCK PRODUCTION (Calendar 1927)

	Total Trucks	Open Cab	Cl. Cab	Express Body	Stake Body	Platform Body	Pickup Body	Canopy Top	Scr.Side Body
Atlanta	1,106	1	434	131	213	4	335	11	6
Buffalo	1,925	2	1,266	119	616	315	2,136	20	5
Charlotte	1,617		318	81	142	6	334	11	7
Chester	2,406		986	161	258	7	1,335	42	16
Chicago	2,954	7	1,379	122	284	458	1,266	44	8
Cincinatti	1,167	1	626	130	316	21	589	8	5
Cleveland	1,143		684	135	231	14	895	18	7
Columbus	979		678	90	161	35	475	3	2
Dallas	1,041		563	12	137	51	706	3	3
Denver	612		527	146	207	21	871	21	2
Des Moines	956		783	5	23	331	431	1	
Houston	1,435		439	76	264	261	974	12	1
Indianapolis	1,445		894	38	182	74	660	10	1
Jacksonville	655	8	327	14	234	2	527	8	5
Kansas City	2,156		1,405	79	233	631	1,177	11	8
Kearny	9,422		1,923	762	835	862	2,743	626	216
Los Angeles	1,294		739	112	545	47	1,347	50	24
Louisville	1,246		576	67	189	16	343	8	
Memphis	1,404		434	82	120	123	412	13	11
Milwaukee	1,121		737	39	344	33	1,442	7	
New Orleans	1,552		294	40	129		420	15	
Norfolk	1,707		706	177	194	4	464	20	9
Oklahoma City	1,468		1,125	94	258	455	851	11	4
Omaha	866		511	22	17	237	329		
Pittsburgh	828	2	522	224	143	8	834	32	9
Portland	422		322	40	101	8	505	18	4
San Francisco	891		586	160	271	26	1,226	56	17
Seattle	563	4	336	55	30	31	586	16	2
Somerville	1,829	57	1,050	170	227	9	1,086	28	16
St. Louis	1,193		794	128	260	80	726	19	10
Twin City	1,314		383	6	59	167	1,126	1	1
Detroit	2,842	9	1,539	70	632	7	970	8	3
U.S. Totals	51,557	91	23,888	3,587	7,855	4,344	28,143	1,151	402

NOTE: See Passenger Car listing for foreign truck production (chassis only). The total number of trucks (51,557) is less than the total number of the body types (69,461). The body types no doubt include roadster pickup beds built on the passenger car chassis.

Production Statistics

SHIPPING INVOICES

During a visit at the Ford Archives in Dearborn, Michigan, in 1980, the author uncovered a number of 16mm reels of microfilms of original shipping invoices for Model T Fords, beginning in early 1909 and ending in late 1911. Over the next few years we returned from time to time, filling in details missed in earlier visits, and adding more records to our data file.

The records begin with engine/car number 1,119 (March 3, 1909) and end with number 70,750 (October 5, 1911), although there are a few hand-written notes after that date. It would seem that originally these records began in 1903 and continued through at least the 1920's, but most were apparently lost in a fire at the Archives many years ago.

It would take a lifetime to study each and every one of the existing records. During a visit in 1982 the author began by looking at every invoice, then every tenth one. It became obvious that there would not be time for every tenth one, so the author began looking at every hundredth, filling in between these numbers where there might have been some particular interest.

The material was published in an issue of *The Vintage Ford*, and after publication a number of letters were received from members who had "original black Fords." On later visits these particular cars were looked up, and in every case the cars were listed as either green or blue, depending on the year. **No evidence was uncovered of black Fords** except for one roadster, #3,019, in 1909.

The microfilms are of very poor quality. It would appear that the original invoices (no longer extant) were carbon copies. Many were unreadable; none were very clear. All entries on the printed forms were hand-written, apparently by the shop foreman or supervisor. The original invoices were not all alike, nor did they all list the same items. For example, the earliest did not indicate the manufacturer of the lamps; just a check mark to indicate that lamps were supplied. In general, though, they listed the body type, manufacturer, color, carburetor, ignition coil, brand of tires, and other accessories. On some invoices the body number was shown, and on some were notes reflecting some change in production such as "three slot," referring to the three-pedal floorboards used after the original two-pedal cars. (By this time, of course, all production was three-pedal.) Comments, such as "paint finish quality," always got a "fair" grade.

In examining these invoices, one gets the feeling that then, as is the case today, it was more important to put the check mark down on the sheet than it was to be accurate. Because of this it is quite possible, even likely, that there are some errors in the information entered originally. It is just as possible, and likely, that some errors were made when the author took his notes.

In 1909, for a time, they listed "optional equipment" which could be ordered from the factory. Options included robe rails, foot rests, tire chains (Weed for the most part), Prestolite tanks, tire carriers, bumpers, Dragon horns, auto chimes, car covers, and top hoods. Also optional (in 1909) were the headlights, speedometer, windshield, and top. Interestingly, a number of cars were supplied without gas lamps as late as 1911; closed cars for the most part after 1909. Of course, there is no way of knowing if a car on which no note was made did or did not have certain equipment.

Tire manufacturers were indicated as Firestone, Fisk, Diamond, and Goodrich. There may have been others that were missed.

The author has always taken the stand that there is no *written* evidence of any black Fords in the early years of Model T production. The author may have been in error. If the records are correct, car/engine number 3,019, a 1909 roadster, was black. At least that's what the shipping invoice says. In the many invoices sampled (many more than are indicated in the following pages), that was the **only** black Ford listed in the first three years!

As noted earlier, every "original black" car looked up was shipped in either green or blue, depending on the year. In checking with the present owner of one black 1911 touring, he said he even had the paint analyzed and found "lamp black" in it. He said that the original fenders were blue, but not the body. The invoice clearly says the color was blue. It would seem strange if the man who filled out the invoice confused the body color with the fender color, but it could have happened. It is the author's belief that the original greens and blues were so black that they looked "black." Personal observation of original cars confirms this belief. Unless the color is viewed in bright sunlight, it is almost impossible to detect the "green" or "blue" tint in the essentially black car. A comment in the reminisces of E. G. Liebold in July 1909 confirms this observation. (See the chapter on Documentation.)

In early 1909 two types of tops were listed for the touring cars: lined and unlined. Both were apparently interchangeable. Roadsters were supplied with similar tops in either gray or black. When lined, the lining was a dark red wool material.

Colors available in 1909 were:

TOURING: red at first, then either red or green. A few gray tourings were also noted.

ROADSTER: mostly gray, but a number of green and at least one red (#2,585), plus the one black one noted above.

COUPE: Apparently all were green

TOWN CAR and **LANDAULET**: either green or gray.

By late 1909 all body styles were Brewster Green. Green continued until late 1910 as the only color, when blue became the standard color.

We do not know if the red, green, gray, or blue colors were all exactly the same shade of the particular color. It is likely there were variances just as there are today.

Contrary to popular belief, the aluminum Touring bodies (supplied only by Pontiac Body Co.) were quite common until September 1909. All other bodies were wood and were supplied by Pontiac or Wilson for the most part.

Production changes were noted on some but not all of the invoices. Whether the changed occurred only on the cars noted, or the notes were entered at random, is not known. Among these notes the following items appeared:

The first thermo-syphon engine was NOT 2,501 as believed. It was 2,448. The second was 2,455 and the third was 2,456. Engine number 2,500 was the new thermo-syphon type and it went into a gray Roadster with a Pontiac body, equipped with a Kingston coil and carburetor. It was shipped to a Mr. R.W. Finney of Fall River, Massachusetts, on May 4, 1909.

The first green Touring was 2,547, made on April 29.

Car number 3,131 was originally a green Roadster, made on May 14, and was used by Henry Ford. It was returned and converted into a green Coupe on October 27, 1909, then returned again on November 1, 1910 when it was converted to a chassis only. Nothing is said about where that chassis went.

Beginning in March 1909, perhaps even earlier, a number of Buffalo carburetors were installed at the factory. These were used on many cars until early 1910. There seems to have been a period during only which the Kingston was supplied, in 1909, but then the Buffalo reappeared. The last Buffalo carburetor was used in February 1910.

Beginning around number 13,000 (December 1909), "roller bearing rear axle" began to appear on some invoices. This referred to the inner axle bearings, which had been babbitt, not to the roller pinion bearing.

Beginning with 16,278 a number of invoices were marked "special flywheel." Then with 17,985, "new magneto." These may have referred to the 9/16" magneto magnets, a change made at about this time according to other data on file. (According to published information, the 1/2" magnets were used on the first 17,500 cars, then 9/16" magnets until 20,501, at which time the magnet size was increased to 5/8".)

Beginning in April 1910, "new style crankcase" appeared. This may have been due to the change to the new magneto with the larger magnets, to the addition of the reinforcing flange at the rear, or to the discontinuance of the internal oil dam.[1]

Lamps were often mixed in production. Side lamps could be a different brand than the tail lamp, and the headlamps could have been still another brand. It was, of course, possible for all three to be of the same brand. Gas generators may or may not have been the same brand as the headlamps.

Until 1910 all cars were supplied with Kingston coils. In January, though, Jacobson-Brandow coils were also installed. Both of these brands continued through 1910, then in February 1911 Heinze coils were added to the options. (Heinze coils had been used in the N-R-S and very early 1909 Model T Fords, but were discontinued before the earliest existing records.)

Interestingly, In July 1909 a number of Model S Fords were made. One wonders if they discovered some leftover parts and decided to get rid of them.

Cars were assembled, obviously, after engines were assembled. The dates shown are the dates of the body-to-chassis assembly, a short time after the engine date. In addition, chassis were assembled sometimes days before the bodies were installed. Add this to the fact that there were several assembly areas, and a general mix-up of dates versus serial numbers occurs. Where an "engine only" is indicated, the date shown is the shipping date, not the manufacturing date.

The invoice for car 15,675 was the first to be marked "reinforced housing." We presume this to be the rear axle housing with the reinforcement around the two center flanges, but it could refer to the pinion bearing mounting reinforcement.

During October 1910 a number of invoices were marked "1911 rear axle." This was probably the six-rivet housing with the reinforcing rings around the center section bolt holes, but not certain. The reference was **not** to the much later "1912" axle.

In late 1910 a number of special-bodied cars were made for John Wanamaker of New York. These were "delivery" or "service" cars, and were painted red, blue, or yellow!

The first blue cars appeared in November 1910. It is not clear if the body styles were "1910" or "1911," or if the green cars during this period were 1910 while the blue ones were 1911. The author has not seen an original blue 1910, or an original green 1911 Model T, but that doesn't mean they weren't made.

The change to the closed-valve 1911 engine, along with the new pan and transmission cover, did not occur at any one time. One cannot be certain but it appears the transmission cover (with the tapered door) came first, then the new pan (with the "removable bottom"), and then the new engine with the enclosed valves. It also appears that any mix of the new and old components may well have appeared on a car well into 1911. A similar situation occurs with the "1912" (12-rivet) rear axle.[2]

The first note on a "seamed style radiator" was on car 35,400 (January 9, 1911). The author is not sure just what this change was but believes the change to the standard Ford script had occurred much earlier. Ford had been making its own radiators and had been using them exclusively since about April 1910 (all of which are believed to have had the standard, non-winged, script). 1909 and 1910 radiators were somewhat smoother in appearance; perhaps this signaled the introduction of the regular construction used until mid-1916.

Car 37,378 (February 4, 1911) was one of the earliest marked "1911 front axle" and "new transmission cover," although a "new transmission cover" was noted on some invoices in December 1910. The author believes this "new" cover was the wider, square-hole cover to match the wider but still one-piece crankcase. Number 37,427 (February 8, 1911) was the first invoice we noted which said, "1911 wide pan and transmission cover." The first mention of another "new transmission cover" was on car 57,421 (June 1, 1911) and this may have been the newer tapered-hole cover.

38,263 (February 14, 1911) was marked "babbitt bearing motor." Earlier engines used babbitt only in the main bearing caps, not in the cylinder block (upper half of the main bearings). 44,420 (March 28, 1911) was the first "removable bottom." The first car noted to have an "all 1911 motor" was 46,326 on April 7. Various mixtures of these engine components continued well into 1911.

Roadsters, other than the Torpedo and Open Runabouts, built during early 1911 were usually marked "1910." They were built on earlier chassis, although all were painted blue.

In June 1911 a number of cars were made which were marked "1910 runningboards." Apparently they found a few under the pile.

Beginning in July 1911 the apparently standard striping of the fenders and running gear began to be discontinued. Body striping, however, continued until early 1913 production (in late 1912).

The first "1912" Delivery Wagon (that the author found) was 68,900 (September 15, 1911). Initially these were painted red, with the standard blue fenders.

The following lists the manufacturers of various components used during this period.

BODIES
1909: Pontiac (wood and aluminum), Wilson
1910: Pontiac, KH (Kelsey-Hayes?),
Fox Brothers
1911: Pontiac, KH, Hayes, American, Wilson
There may have been others we might have missed.

WINDSHIELDS
1909: Rands, Troy (wood and brass),
Mezger (Automatic), Smith
1910: Rands, Troy, Mezger
1911: Rands, Vanguard, Mezger

LAMPS
1909: Brown, E&J, Atwood-Castle, M&E
1910-1911: Brown, E&J

SPEEDOMETERS
1909: Jones, Stewart 11, 12, 24, "50 mph,"
National 50
1910: Stewart 24
1911: Stewart 24, 26

CARBURETORS
1909: Kingston, Buffalo
1910: Kingston, Buffalo, Holley
1911: Kingston, Holley

COILS
1909: Heinze (very early), Kingston
1910: Kingston, Jacobson-Brandow
1911: Kingston, Heinze, Jacobson-Brandow

RADIATORS
1909: Briscoe, Paris, Detroit, McCord, Ford
1910: Detroit, McCord, Ford
1911: Ford (after April 1910)

NOTES

1.   One-piece pans were not all the same. The first, used on the earliest water-pump engines, had a long front bearing with a rivet inside the sump area. The front bearing was modified (made shorter) so that this rivet was outside the sump area. Both these pans had a rather plain rear flange (no reinforcement).
   The third type, introduced in early 1910, was similar to the second except that the rear flange now had the brazed-in-place forging, similar to the later pans. All three of these pans had an oil dam the the rear of the fourth cylinder to hold oil in the crankshaft area.
   The fourth type, late 1910 or early 1911, was wider than the first three, to match the wider transmission cover. This type did not have the oil dam.

2.   Rear axles evolved about as much as did the oil pans. The earliest no-rivet housings were used in most of 1909. Late in the year the babbitt inner axle bearings were changed to the roller type, and the six-rivet housing was born. (The rivets secured the inner roller bearing support.)
   Still later, in early 1910, the roller type driveshaft (pinion) bearing was installed, and now a forged reinforcement appeared at the driveshaft mounting area. During early 1911, the tapered rear axles were introduced
   The "1912" 12-rivet "clamshell" housings appeared in the summer of 1911.
   The first axle housings were just pressed metal at the seam where the two halves join. Later, reinforcing washers were brazed around the bolt holes. Still later a reinforcing ring of metal was brazed around the circumference, on the outside of the flange, and the washers were eliminated. The final (six-rivet) design had a reinforcing ring INSIDE the flanges, requiring a modification of the center sections, and making the center flange noticeably thicker. Whether these changes were made at the same time as the internal axle changes, or at differing times, is not known.

1909

NOTE: "Old" (lined) and "New" style tops listed. Prestolite tanks, "Dragon" horns were options, in addition to lamps, windshield, tops, etc.

Ser#	Mfg.	Body Style	Color	Mfgr	W/S	Carb	Coil	Speed-ometer	Gas Lamps	Radiator	
1	Sep 27, 1908 (Shipped Oct 1)										
		—	-	-	-	K	K	-	E&J	Briscoe	

Equipped with Prestolite tank, Firestone tires, Dragon horn and American top. Shipped to Ford Motor Co. in New York. Body type not specified but believed to be a Touring. A note on the original invoice says "Motor changed to —(illegible)"

Ser#	Mfg.	Body Style	Color	Mfgr	W/S	Carb	Coil	Speed-ometer	Gas Lamps	Radiator	
1,119	Mar 3										
1,120	Mar 2	Touring		P	**	B	K		Yes	BR	** Mfgr. not listed
1,125	Mar 2	Touring		P	D	K	K	ST-12	Yes	BR	
1,130	Mar 2	Touring		P	D	K	K		Yes	BR	
1,135	Mar 3	Landaulet		P	D	K	K		Yes	BR	
1,140	Mar 3	Touring		P	D	K	K			BR	
1,141	Mar 3										
1,144 to 1,147		Chassis only									
1,150	Mar 3	Touring		P	D	K	K			BR	
1,153	Mar 3	Touring		Pontiac					"New style top"		
1,155	Mar 3	Coupe		Wilson		K	K		No		K=Kingston
1,160	Mar 4	Touring		P	Mezger (Automatic)				Yes		
1,165	Mar 3	Landaulet		W	D	K	K			BR	
1,168	Mar 4	Touring		P	D	B	K		No	BR	American top
1,169	Mar 4	Touring		P	D	K	K		No	BR	Lined top
1,170	Mar 4	Touring		P	D	B	K	ST-50	Yes	BR	American top
1,175	Mar 4	Town Car		W	D	K	K		No	BR	
1,180	Mar 4	Touring		W	D	K	K			BR	American top
1,182	Mar 4	Touring		W				J($25)	Yes		J=Jones
1,183	Mar 4	Landaulet		W					No		
1,185	Mar 4	Touring		P	D	K	K	N 50	No	BR	
1,190	Mar 4	Touring		P	D	K	K		Yes	BR	
1,195	Mar 5	Touring		P	D	K	K		Yes	BR	
1,199	Mar 5	Touring		P		K	K	ST "50 mph'			ST=Stewart
1,200	Mar 5	Touring		P	D	K	K	ST "50 mph"			
1,205	Mar 5	Touring #		P		K	K	–	Yes	BR (Briscoe)	

"New Style" American top. ## Prestolite tank.

Ser#	Mfg.	Body Style	Color	Mfgr	W/S	Carb	Coil	Speed-ometer	Gas Lamps	Radiator	
1,207	Mar 5	Touring		W		K	K		Yes		
1,210	Mar 5	Touring		P	D	K	K		Yes	BR	
1,215	Mar 6	Touring #		P		K	K	–	Yes	BR	
1,216	Mar 5	Landaulet		P		K	K	–	Yes	BR	##
1,220	Mar 5	Touring		P	D	K	K		Yes	BR	
1,225	Mar 6	Runabout		P	M	K	K	N 50	Yes	BR	Gray AM top. ##
1,230	Mar 5	Runabout		P	D	K	K		Yes	BR	##
1,235	Mar 6	Touring #		P		B*	K	–	Yes	BR	
1,240	Mar 6	Touring		P	D	K	K	ST-11	Yes	BR	# ##
1,244	Mar 8	Touring #		W		K	K	ST	Yes	BR	
1,245	Mar 3	Touring		PA		K	K	–	No	BR	"old style head"
1,250	Mar 6	Touring		P	D	K	K		Yes	BR	
1,255	Mar 8	Landaulet		P		K	K	–	Yes	BR	##
1,260	Mar 8	Touring		P	D	K	K		Yes	BR	
1,265	Mar 8	Touring		P		K	K	–	Yes	Lined American top	
1,270	Mar 8	Touring		P	D	K	K	ST-11	Yes	BR	
1,275	Mar 8	Landaulet		P		K	K	–	Yes	Metal body. ##	
1,280	Mar 8	Touring		P	D	K	K		Yes	BR	
1,285	Mar 8	Touring #		P	M	K	K	–	Yes	BR	
1,290	Mar 8	Engine only									
1,295	Mar 9	Touring #		P		K	K	–	Yes	BR	
1,300	Mar 9	Roadster		P		K	K	ST-12		BR	##
1,305	Mar 10	Landaulet		P		K	K	–	Yes	BR	
1,310	Mar 9	Touring		P		B*	K		Yes	BR	*B=Buffalo
1,315	Mar 10	Touring #		P		K	K	–	Yes	BR	
1,320	Mar 9	Touring		W		K	K		Yes	BR	
1,325	Mar 10	Touring #		P		K	K	–	Yes	BR	
1,330	Mar 9	Coupe		W		K	K		No	BR	
1,335	Mar 10	Chassis only to Walkerville									
1,337	Mar 9	Roadster		P	R**	K	K	ST-11	Yes	BR	**R=Rands

1909

Ser#	Mfg.	Body Style	Color	Mfgr	W/S	Carb	Coil	Speed-ometer	Gas Lamps	Radiator
1,340	Mar 10	Touring		P		K	K		Yes	BR
1,345	Mar 11	Touring		P		K	K	—	No	BR
1,350	Mar 10	Touring		P		K	K		Yes	BR
1,355	Mar 11	Touring #		P	S+	K	K	ST-11	Yes	BR + Smith windshield
1,360	Mar 11	Touring		P		K	K		Yes	BR
1,365	Mar 11	Landaulet		P		K	K	—	Yes	BR ##(large)
1,370	Mar 11	Town Car		W		B	K		Yes	BR
1,375	Mar 10	Touring #		P		B	K	—	Yes	BR
1,380	Mar 11	Landaulet		P		K	K		Yes	BR
1,382	Mar 12	Landaulet		P		B	K		No	BR
1,385	Mar 12	Touring #		W		K	K	—	Yes	BR
1,390	Mar 12	Touring		P		B	K		Yes	BR
1,395	Mar 12	Touring #		P		K	K	—	Yes	BR
1,400	Mar 12	Touring		P		B	K		Yes	BR
1,405	Mar 13	Touring #		W		K	K	—	Yes	BR
1,409	Mar 13	Race Car (for Scott)				K	K			BR
1,410	Mar 13	Touring		W		K	K		Yes	BR
1,415	Mar 13	Touring #		P		K	K	—	Yes	BR
1,420	Mar 13	Touring #		P	D	K	K		Yes	BR
1,425	Mar 13	Runabout		P		K	K	—	Yes	BR Gray American top
1,430	Mar 13	Touring #		P	D	K	K		Yes	BR
1,435	Mar 15	Runabout		P		B	K	—	Yes	BR Gray American top
1,440	Mar 15	Touring		P		B	K		No	BR
1,445	Mar 15	Touring #		P		K	K	—	Yes	BR
1,450	Mar 15	Landaulet		W	R	K	K		Yes	BR
1,455	Mar 15	Runabout		P		K	K	ST-12	Yes	BR Gray American top
1,460	Mar 15	Landaulet		P	R	K	K		Yes	BR
1,465	Mar 16	Touring #		P	M	K	K	—	Yes	BR
1,470	Mar 15	Touring		P		K	K	ST-11	Yes	BR
1,474	Mar 16	Landaulet		P	M	K	K		Yes	BR
1,475	Mar 16	Touring #		P	M	K	K	—	Yes	BR
1,480	Mar 16	Touring		P		K	K		Yes	BR
1,485	Mar 16	Touring #		P		K	K	—	Yes	BR
1,486	Mar 16	Touring #		P	D	K	K		Yes	BR
1,490	Mar 16	Landaulet		P		K	K			##
1,495	Mar 16	Touring #		P		K	K	—	Yes	BR
1,500	Mar 16	Chassis (to Canada)								
1,505	Mar 17	Landaulet		P		K	K	—	Yes	BR ##
1,510	Mar 16	Touring		P		K	K		Yes	BR
1,515	Mar 17	Touring		P		K	K	—	Yes	BR Old style lined top
1,516	Mar 17	Touring #		P	M	K	K	ST-11	Yes	BR
1,519	Mar 17	Touring		P		K	K		Yes	BR
1,520	Mar 17	Touring		W	M	K	K		Yes	BR
1,523	Mar 17	Runabout		P	BO?	K	K	—	Yes	BR Gray American top
1,524	Mar 17	Touring		P	BO?	K	K	—	Yes	BR $80 Am. rubber top
1,525	Mar 17	Touring #		P		K	K	—	Yes	BR
1,530	Mar 17	Touring		P		K	K		Yes	BR
1,535	Mar 17	Landaulet		W		K	K	—	Yes	BR ##
1,540	Mar 18	Roadster	Gray	P		K	K		Yes	BR
		(First listing of colors)								
1,550	Mar 17	Roadster	Gray	P		K	K		Yes	BR
1,558	Mar 17	Coupe	Green	W		K	K		Yes	BR
1,560	Mar 18	Roadster	Gray	P						
1,563	Mar 18	Landaulet	Green	P		K	K		Yes	BR
1,570	Mar 18	Roadster	Gray			K	K		Yes	BR
1,579	Mar 18	Town Car	Green							
1,580	Mar 18	Roadster	Gray	P		K	K		No	BR
1,590	Mar 18	Roadster	Gray	W		K	K	N	Yes	Paris? N=National
1,600	Mar 18	Touring	Red			K	K		Yes	Paris?
1,610	Mar 19	Landaulet	Green	P	M	K	K		No	Paris?
1,620	Mar 19	Touring	Red			K	K			Paris?
1,630	Mar 20	Landaulet	Green	P		K	K		Yes	BR
1,640	Mar 20	Roadster	Gray	P	M	K	K		Yes	BR
1,650	Mar 20	Roadster	Gray	P	M	K	K			BR

Ser#	Mfg.	Body Style	Color	Mfgr	W/S	Carb	Coil	Speed-ometer	Gas Lamps	Radiator
1,660	Mar 20	Roadster	Gray	P		K	K		Yes	BR
1,670	Mar 22	Roadster	Gray	P		B	K		Yes	BR
1,680	Mar 22	Roadster	Gray	P		K	K		Yes	BR
1,690	Mar 23	Roadster	Gray	P		K	K		Yes	BR
1,700	Mar 23	Roadster	Gray	P		K	K		Yes	BR
1,710	Mar 23	Town Car	Gray	P		K	K		Yes	BR
1,718	Mar 23	Roadster	Gray	P		K	K		Yes	BR
1,720	Mar 23	Roadster	Gray	P		K	K		Yes	BR
1,730	Mar 23	Roadster	Gray	P		K	K		Yes	Paris?
1,740	Mar 24	Roadster	Gray	P		K	K		Yes	BR
1,747	Mar 24	Landaulet	Green	W		B	K		Yes	BR
1,750	Mar 24	Landaulet	Green	W		B	K			BR
1,760	Mar 24	Roadster	Gray	P		B	K		Yes	BR
1,766	Mar 24	Touring	Red	W	R	B	K		Yes	BR
1,767	Mar 24	Touring	Green	W	R	B	K		Yes	BR

(First Green Touring?)

Ser#	Mfg.	Body Style	Color	Mfgr	W/S	Carb	Coil	Speed-ometer	Gas Lamps	Radiator
1,770	Mar 24	Roadster	Gray	P		K	K		Yes	BR
1,774	Mar 24	Touring	Red	W		K	K			BR
1,780	Mar 24	Roadster	Gray	P		B	K		Yes	BR
1,790	Mar 25	Roadster	Gray	P		K	K		Yes	BR
1,800	Mar 25	Roadster	Gray	P		B	K		Yes	BR
1,810	Mar 25	Touring	Red	P		K	K		Yes	BR
1,820	Mar 25	Roadster	Gray	P	M	B	K		Yes	BR
1,826	Mar 26	Touring	Red	P		B	K		Yes	BR
1,830	Mar 26	Landaulet	Green	P		B	K			BR
1,831	Mar 26	Town Car	Green	W		K	K			BR
1,840	Mar 26	Roadster	Gray	P		K	K		Yes	BR
1,850	Mar 26	Roadster	Gray	P		K	K		Yes	BR
1,860	Mar 26	Touring	Red			K	K		Yes	BR
1,862	Mar 26	Touring	Red	W		B	K		Yes	BR
1,870	Mar 27	Roadster	Gray	P		K	K		Yes	BR
1,880	Mar 27	Landaulet	Green	P		K	K		Yes	BR
1,890	Mar 27	Roadster	Gray	P		K	K		Yes	BR
1,897	Mar 29	Coupe	Green	W		K	K		Yes	BR
1,900	Mar 29	Roadster	Gray	P		K	K		Yes	BR
1,914	Mar 29	Touring	Red	P		K	K		Yes	BR
1,919	Mar 29	Coupe	Green	W		K	K		Yes	BR
1,920	Mar 29	Coupe	Green	W		K	K		Yes	BR
1,924	Mar 29	Touring	Red	W	M	K	K		Yes	BR
1,925	Mar 29	Roadster	Gray	P		K	K		Yes	BR
1,950	Mar 30	Roadster	Gray	P					Yes	BR
1,975	Mar 30	Touring	Red	W		K	K		Yes	BR
2,000	Mar 31	Touring	Red	W	M	K	K	N	Yes	BR	Gabriel horn
2,015	Mar 31	Roadster	Gray	P	M	K	K	N	Yes	BR
2,026	Mar 31	Touring	Gray	PA		K	K		Yes	BR

PA=Pontiac aluminum. (First Gray Touring noted.)

Ser#	Mfg.	Body Style	Color	Mfgr	W/S	Carb	Coil	Speed-ometer	Gas Lamps	Radiator
2,027	Mar 31	Touring	Red	PA	M	K	K	N	Yes	BR
2,035	Apr 1	Touring	Red	PA		K	K		Yes	BR
2,050	Apr 1	Landaulet	Green	P	M	K	K		No	BR
2,075	Apr 2	Roadster	Gray	P		K	K		Yes	BR
2,100	Apr 2	Touring	Red	PA		K	K	N	Yes	BR
2,100	Apr 2	Touring	Red	PA			K			BR

(May 17, 1911, this same serial # "Touring car for Mr. Hawkins, same as old car."

Ser#	Mfg.	Body Style	Color	Mfgr	W/S	Carb	Coil	Speed-ometer	Gas Lamps	Radiator
2,175	Apr 7	Roadster	Gray	P	M	B	K		Yes	BR
2,200	Apr 7	Touring	Red	PA		K	K		No	BR
2,250	Apr 10	Chassis (to Canada)								

NOTE: Black and Gray roadster tops used, mixed during production.

Ser#	Mfg.	Body Style	Color	Mfgr	W/S	Carb	Coil	Speed-ometer	Gas Lamps	Radiator
2,300	Apr 13	Landaulet	Green	P					Yes	
2,350	Apr 15	Touring	Red	PA					Yes	
2,400	Apr 17	Roadster	Gray	P		B	K		Yes	BR
2,436	Apr 21	Touring	Red	PA		B	K		(RHD to Australia)	
2,448	Apr 22	Touring	Red	PA		B	K			BR

2,448 was the first thermo-syphon engine

Ser#	Mfg.	Body Style	Color	Mfgr	W/S	Carb	Coil	Speed-ometer	Gas Lamps	Radiator
2,455	May 1	Roadster	Gray	P		K	K			2nd Thermo-syphon

Ser#	Mfg.	Body Style	Color	Mfgr	W/S	Carb	Coil	Speed-ometer	Gas Lamps	Radiator
2,456	May 5	Roadster	Gray	P		K	K			McCord 3rd Thermo-syphon
2,478	May 4	Touring	Red	PA		K	K		Yes	McC
2,493	May 4	Roadster	Gray	P		K	K		Yes	McC
2,494 to 2,498		All engines only.								
2,499	May 4	Roadster	Gray	P		K	K		Yes	McC (AC=Atwood-
2,500	May 4	Roadster	Gray	P		K	K	AC-84		McC Castle)

"Thermo-syphon" shipped to R.W. Finney, Fall River, MA. Car # 62605.

Ser#	Mfg.	Body Style	Color	Mfgr	W/S	Carb	Coil	Speed-ometer	Gas Lamps	Radiator
2,501	May 4	Roadster	Gray	P		K	K	AC-84		McC
2,518	May 4	Roadster	Gray	P	R	K	K	AC-84		McC
2,541	May 3	Coupe	Green	W		K	K	AC-84		McC
2,547	Apr 29	Touring	Green	PA		K	K			McC
2,548	Apr 29	Touring	Red	PA		K	K		AC-84	McC
2,549	Apr 29	Touring	Green	PA	R	K	K		AC-84	McC
2,550	Apr 29	Roadster	Gray	P		K	K			McC
2,551	Apr 29	Roadster	Gray	P	R	B	K			McC
2,553	Apr 29	Touring	Red	PA		B	K	ST-11	AC-84	McC
2,555	Apr 29	Touring	Green	PA		K	K			McC
2,556	Apr 29	Touring	Red	PA		K	K			McC
2,585	Apr 27	Roadster	Red	P		K	K			McC
2,600	Apr 13	Touring	Red	PA	R		K			McC
2,657	Apr 22	Touring	Green	PA		K	K			McC
2,658	Apr 22	Touring	Red	W		B	K		Yes	McC
2,659	Apr 22	Touring	Red	PA		K	K		Yes	McC
2,660	Apr 22	Touring	Green	PA		K	K			McC
2,661	Apr 22	Touring	Green	PA	M	K	K		Yes	McC
2,662	Apr 22	Touring	Green	PA	M	K	K	ST-11	Yes	McC
2,663	Apr 22	Touring	Green	PA	*	K	K		Yes	McC *"Brass"
2,664	Apr 22	Touring	Green	PA	M	K	K	ST-11	Yes	McC
2,665	Apr 22	Touring	Green	PA		K	K		Yes	McC
2,666	Apr 22	Touring	Red	PA	M	K	K	J **	Yes	McC **"50 mph"
2,677	Apr 26	Touring	Green	PA		K	K		Yes	McC
2,700	Apr 27	Touring	Red	W	R	K	K		AC-84	McC
2,702	May 5	Roadster	Gray	P		K	K			McC
2,707	May 5	Roadster	Gray	P	Troy	K	K	ST-24	BRN	McC
2,709	May 5	Town Car	Green	W		K	K		AC-84	McC
2,710	May 5	Town Car	Green	W		K	K			McC
2,713	May 5	Touring	Red	PA		B	K		AC-84	McC
2,714	May 5	Touring	Red	PA		K	K	ST-12		McC
2,715	May 5	Landaulet	Green	W		K	K			McC
2,737	May 5	Touring	Red	PA		K	K		E&J	McC
2,800	May 7	Engine only (to Canada)								
2,831	May 7	Touring	Green	PA	M	K	K	N-50	E&J	McC
2,850	May 10	Touring	Red	W		K	K			McC
2,880	May 11	Touring	Green	PA		K	K	J $25	AC-84	McC

(Optional equipment listed on invoices: robe rails, foot rests, Weed chains top hood, Dragon horn, auto chimes, car cover, Prestolite tank, jack, tire carrier, bumper rail. All supplied by Ford, if ordered.)

Ser#	Mfg.	Body Style	Color	Mfgr	W/S	Carb	Coil	Speed-ometer	Gas Lamps	Radiator
2,888	May 10	Roadster	Gray	P	M	K	K	ST-11	E&J	McC
2,900	May 11	Roadster	Gray	P		K	K		E&J	McC
2,902	May 11	Roadster	Green	P		K	K			McC
2,914	May 11	Roadster	Gray	P	M	K	K	N	E&J	McC
2,917	May 11	Roadster	Gray	P		K	K			McC
2,920	May 11	Touring	Green	P	M	K	K		E&J	McC
3,000	May 12	Touring	Red	PA	M	K	K	ST-11	E&J	McC
3,019	May 13	Roadster	**Black**	P	R	K	K	ST-11	E&J	McC

===== This was the ONLY black car found in the first 69,000 Model T Fords! =====

Ser#	Mfg.	Body Style	Color	Mfgr	W/S	Carb	Coil	Speed-ometer	Gas Lamps	Radiator
3,050	May 13	Touring	Green	PA		K	K	No equipment		McC
3,065	May 14	Touring	Green	PA	R	K	K			McC
3,100	May 14	Touring	Green	PA		K	K	Lined top		McC
3,112	May 14	Roadster	Gray	P		K	K		E&J	McC

Shipping Invoices

1909

Ser#	Mfg.	Body Style	Color	Mfgr	W/S	Carb	Coil	Speedometer	Gas Lamps	Radiator	
3,115	May 14	Landaulet	Green	P		K	K			McC	
3,131	May 14	Roadster	Green	W		K	K			McC	

Henry Ford's personal car. Converted to a Coupe on October 27, 1909, then to a chassis only on November 1, 1910.

Ser#	Mfg.	Body Style	Color	Mfgr	W/S	Carb	Coil	Speedometer	Gas Lamps	Radiator	
3,187	May 17	Touring	Red			K	K	No equipment		McC	
3,200	May 17	Roadster	Gray	P		K	K	No equipment		McC	
3,300	May 19	Landaulet	Green	W		K	K	No equipment		McC	
3,332	May 20	Touring	Green	P		K	K			McC	
3,358	May 19	Roadster	Gray	P		K	K		E&J	McC	
		(Listed as Touring on one page, Roadster on another.)									
3,374	May 20	Touring	Green	PA		K	K			McC	
3,400	May 20	Touring	Green	PA	R	K	K	No equipment		McC	
3,430	May 21	Touring	Gray	PA		K	K		AC-84	McC	
		(No doubt as to color on invoice.)									
3,434	May 21	Touring	Gray	P	R	K	K		AC-84	Pruden	
3,461	May 21	Touring	Gray	P		K	K			McC	
3,477	May 21	Touring	Green	PA	R	K	K	J-20	AC	McC	
									Prestolite tank		
3,500	May 22	Roadster	Gray	P		K	K	Gray top		McC	
3,553	May 24	Touring	Gray	PA	R	K	K	J	AC	McC	
3,600	May 24	Touring	Green	PA	R	K	K		AC	McC	
								(With robe rail)			
3,601	May 24	Touring	Green	PA		K	K			McC	
3,606	May 24	Touring	Green	PA		K	K		AC	McC	
3,643	May 25	Touring	Red	W		K	K		AC	McC	
3,700	May 25	Roadster	Gray	P		K	K	Black top		McC	
3,709	May 25	Roadster	Gray	P		K	K		AC	McC	Gray top
3,709	Jul 20	**Model S L**	Red	P		K	H		M&E	McC	
3,710	Jul 20	**Model S R**	Red			K	H		M&E	McC	
3,711	Jul 20	**Model S R**	Red								
3,719	Jul 20	**Model S R**	Red	P		K	H		M&E	McC	

R=Roadster, L=Laundalet. All used McCord oilers
No explanation as to why these were built at this late date.

Ser#	Mfg.	Body Style	Color	Mfgr	W/S	Carb	Coil	Speedometer	Gas Lamps	Radiator	
3,711	May 25	Roadster	Gray	P		K	K		E&J		
3,719	May 25	Touring	Green	P		K	K		AC		
3,800	May 27	Touring	Green	PA	R	K	K		AC		
3,900	May 27	Touring	Green	PA		K	K		AC		
3,916	May 28	Roadster	Green	P		K	K		AC		
3,980	May 29	Touring	Green	PA		K	K		AC		
4,000	May 29	Touring	Red	PA		K	K		Yes		
4,041	Jun 1	Roadster	Gray	P	R	K	K		AC		Gray top
4,100	Jun 1	Touring	Green	PA	R	K	K		AC		
4,189	Jun 3	Roadster	Gray	P		K	K		AC		
4,200	Jun 3	Engine only									
4,300	Jun 5	Engine only									
4,310	Jun 5	Touring?	Green	P	R	K	K				
4,380	Jun 7	Touring	Green	PA		K	K		AC		
4,400	Jun 8	Touring	Green	PA	R	K	K	N	AC		
4,500	Jun 9	Touring	Green	PA	R	K	K	No equipment			
4,586	Jun 10	Touring	Red	PA		K	K	No equipment			
4,590	Jun 10	Roadster	Gray	P		K	K			McC	
4,597	Jun 10	Roadster	Gray	P	R	K	K				Gray top
4,600	Jun 10	Roadster	Gray	P		K	K	No equipment			Gray top
4,650	Jun 11	Engine only									
4,660	Jun 11	Touring	Green	PA		K	K				
4,670	Jun 11	Touring	Green	PA		K	K				
4,680	Jun 11	Roadster	Gray	P		K	K	N	AC		Gray top
4,690	Jun 12	Roadster	Gray	P		K	K				
4,700	Jun 12	Touring	Red	PA		K	K		E&J		
4,710	Jun 12	Touring	Green	PA		K	K		E&J		

1909

Ser#	Mfg.	Body Style	Color	Mfgr	W/S	Carb	Coil	Speed-ometer	Gas Lamps	Radiator
4,720	Jun 12	Touring	Green	PA		K	K			No top
4,750	Jun 12	Touring	Green	PA		K	K		E&J	
4,775	Jun 12	Touring	Green	PA		K	K			
4,800	Jun 14	Touring	Green	PA		K	K	No equipment		
4,825	Jun 14	Touring	Red	PA		K	K		AC	
4,850	Jun 14	Touring	Red	PA	R	K	K	ST-12		
4,875	Jun 15	Touring	Green	PA		K	K			
4,888	Jun 15	Touring	Green	PA		K	K	No equipment		
4,900	Jun 15	Roadster	Gray	P		K	K			
4,925	Jun 15	Touring	Red	PA		K	K		AC	No top
4,950	Jun 15	Roadster	Gray	P		K	K		AC	Gray top
4,960	Jun 16	Roadster	Gray	P	R	K	K		AC	Gray top
										Prestolite tank
4,975	Jun 16	Touring	Green	PA	Troy	K	K			No top
4,991	Jun 16	Touring	Red	PA	R	K	K		AC	Prestolite
4,993	Jun 15	Touring	Red	PA		K	K		AC	No top
5,000	Jun 16	Touring	Green	PA	Troy	K	K		AC	
5,001	Jun 16	Touring	Red	PA	Troy	K	K			
5,025	Jun 16	Roadster	Gray	P		K	K			Gray top
5,026	Jun 16	Touring	Green		Troy	K	K		AC	No top
5,050	Jun 17	Touring	Red	PA		K	K			No top
5,075	Jun 17	Touring	Red	PA		K	K		AC	
5,078	Jun 17	Touring	Red	PA	Troy	K	K	ST-12	AC	
				Shipped with robe rail and top hood						
5,100	Jun 17	Touring	Red	PA		K	K	ST-11	AC	No top
5,125	Jun 18	Roadster	Gray	P		K	K			Gray top
5,150	Jun 18	Touring	Green	PA		K	K		AC	No top
5,175	Jun 18	Touring	Green	PA		K	K			No top
5,200	Jun 18	Roadster	Gray	P		K	K			
			"Asbestos bands" appeared on some invoices beginning in June.							
5,208	Jun 19	Roadster	Green	P		K	K			Gray top
			(Color was actually Gray according to owner today.)							
5,225	Jun 19	Touring		PA	M	K	K		AC	
5,250	Jun 19	Engine only								
5,275	Jun 21	Roadster	Gray	P		K	K		AC	Gray top
5,300	Jun 21	Touring	Red	PA		K	K		E&J	No top
5,325	Jun 21	Town Car	Green	P		K	K		E&J	
5,327	Jun 21	Engine only (Canada)				K				
5,350	Jun 22	Touring	Green	PA		K	K		E&J	No top
5,357	Jun 22	Touring	Green	P		K	K		E&J	
5,375	Jun 22	Roadster	Gray	P		K	K	ST-11	E&J	Gray top
5,387	Jun 22	Touring	Green	W		K	K		E&J	Gray top
										"Asbestos bands"
5,400	Jun 22	Touring	Green	W		K	K		E&J	
5,425	Jun 23	Touring	Green	PA		K	K		E&J	
5,450	Jun 23	Roadster	Gray	P	Troy	K	K		E&J	
5,475	Jun 23	Touring	Green	PA		K	K		E&J	
5,500	Record missing									
5,501	Jun 23	Engine only								
5,525	Jun 23	Roadster	Green	P	Troy	K	K	ST-12	E&J	Black top
5,550	Jun 24	Touring	Green	PA	R	K	K	ST-12		No top
5,575	Jun 24	Touring	Green	PA		K	K		"AM"	
5,595	Jun 24	Touring	Green	PA	Troy	K	K		"AM"	No top
5,600	Jun 24	Touring	Green	PA		K	K			No equipment
5,612	Jun 23	Touring	Green	PA	TW*	K	K			*Troy wood.
5,625	Jun 25	Touring	Green	PA		K	K	ST-11	E&J	No top
5,636	Jun 25	Touring	Green	PA	R	K	K	ST-11	E&J	
5,650	Jun 25	Touring	Green	PA		K	K		E&J	
5,675	Jun 25	Engine only								
5,700	Jun 25	Touring	Green	PA		K	K			
5,800	Jun 28	Touring	Green	PA		K	K			No lamps
5,831	Jun 27	Touring	Green	P		K	K		AC	
5,900	Jun 29	Roadster	Green	P		K	K			No lamps

Shipping Invoices

1909

Ser#	Mfg.	Body Style	Color	Mfgr	W/S	Carb	Coil	Speed-ometer	Gas Lamps	Radiator
6,000	Jun 29	Roadster	Green	P		K	K		E&J	
6,006	Jul 1	Roadster	Green	P		K	K			No lamps
6,100	Jul 2	Roadster	Green	P		K	K			No lamps
6,200	Jul 2	Engine only								
6,291	Jul 6	Touring	Green	PA		B	K			
6,300	Jul 6	Touring	Green	PA		K	K	ST-11	E&J	
6,400	Jul 7	Touring	Green	PA		K	K			No lamps
6,500	Jul 8	Roadster	Green	P		K	K			No lamps
6,600	Jul 9	Touring	Green	PA		K	K		E&J	
6,700	Jul 11	Roadster	Green	P		K	K			
6,800	Jul 13	Touring	Green	PA	M	K	K	ST-11		
6,900	Jul 14	Roadster		P	R	K	K		M&E	
6,901	Jul 14	Roadster	Green	P		K	K			
6,910	Jul 14	Roadster	Green	P	Troy	K	K	ST-11	E&J	
6,925	Jul 14	Roadster	Green	P	R	K	K		M&E	
6,950	Jul 14	Roadster	Green	P		K	K		E&J	
7,000	Jul 15	Touring	Green	PA	R	K	K		M&E	
7,100	Jul 16	Touring	Green	PA		K	K		M&E	
7,200	Jul 19	Touring	Green	PA	Troy	K	K		M&E	
7,300	Jul 20	Touring	Green	PA	R	K	K		M&E	
7,319	Jul 20	Touring	Green	PA		K	K		M&E	
7,400	Jul 21	Touring	Green	PA		K	K		M&E	
7,426	Jul 21	Touring	Green	PA		K	K			No lamps
7,500	Jul 23	Touring	Green	PA		K	K		E&J	
7,600	Jul 24	Roadster	Green	P		K	K			
7,700	Jul 26	Touring	Green	PA		K	K		M&E	
7,800	Jul 28	Touring	Green	PA		K	K		M&E	
7,900	Jul 28	Touring	Green	PA	Troy	K	K			
7,984	Jul 30	Tourabout	Green	P		K	K	ST-11	E&J	
7,994	Jul 30	Touring	Green	PA	Troy	K	K		M&E	
7,998	Jul 30	Touring	Green	PA		K	K		M&E	
				"Special Bushing"						
8,000	Jul 30	Touring	Green	PA	Troy	K	K		M&E	
8,009	Jul 30	Tourabout	Green	P		K	K		M&E	
8,021	Jul 30	Tourabout	Green	P		K	K		M&E	
8,044	Jul 30	Town Car	Green	P		K	K		M&E	
8,100	Jul 31	Roadster	Green	P		K	K			"For Mr. Wills"
8,109	Aug 2	Touring	Green	P		K	K		M&E	
8,143	Aug 2	Tourabout	Green	P		K	K		No lamps or equipment	
8,200	Aug 2	Engine only								
8,300	Aug 4	Tourabout	Green	P		K	K			
8,400	Aug 4	Touring	Green	PA		K	K			
8,500	Aug 5	Touring	Green	PA		K	K			
8,600	Aug 6	Touring	Green	PA		K	K	ST-12	M&E	
8,700	Aug 9	Touring	Green	PA		K	K		M&E	Detroit radiator
8,800	Aug 10	Touring	Green	PA		K	K		M&E	Det.
8,900	Aug 11	Touring	Green	PA		K	K			Det.
8,909	Aug 11	Touring	Green	PA		K	K		M&E	Det.
9,000	Aug 12	Touring	Green	PA	Troy	K	K	ST-12	M&E	Det.
9,100	Aug 13	Touring	Green	PA		K	K		E&J	McC
9,200	Aug 16	Touring	Green	PA		K	K		E&J	Det.
9,300	Aug 17	Touring				K	K		E&J	Det.
9,400	Aug 19	Touring	Green	PA		K	K			McC
9,455	Aug 19	Touring	Green	PA		K	K			Det.
9,500	Aug 19	Touring	Green	PA		K	K			McC
9,600	Aug 23	Touring	Green	PA		K	K		E&J	Det.
9,613	Aug 23	Touring	Green	PA		K	K		E&J	Det.
9,700	Aug 25	Touring	Green	W		K	K		E&J	Det.
9,800	Aug 30	Touring	Green	W	Troy	K	K	ST-12	M&E	McC.
9,900	Aug 31	Touring	Green	PA	R	K	K	ST-11	E&J	Det.
9,926	Sep 2	Touring	Green	PA		K	K		E&J	Det.
9,982	Sep 7	Engine only (to Canada)								
10,000	Sep 9	Touring	Green	PA	M	K	K		E&J	

1909

Ser#	Mfg.	Body Style	Color	Mfgr	W/S	Carb	Coil	Speed-ometer	Gas Lamps	Radiator
10,100	Sep 10	Tourabout	Green	P		K	K			Det.
10,200	Sep 11	Touring	Green	PA		K	K		M&E	Det.
10,204	Sep 11	Touring	Green		TW	K	K		M&E	Det.
		(Troy wood) "Roadster top"								
10,300	Sep 13	Touring	Green	PA		K	K	–	M&E	Det.
10,400	Sep 14	Touring	Green	PA	–	K	K	–	M&E	McC
10,441	Sep 15	Touring	Green	PA	–	K	K	–	–	McC
10,500	Sep 16	Touring	Green	W	T(W)	K	K	–	M&E	Det.
10,600	Missing invoice									
10,601	Sep 20	Touring	Green	PA	–	K	K	–	M&E	McC
10,700	Sep 21	Touring	Green	W	R	K	K	ST-24	BRN	McC
10,800	Sep 25	Town Car	Green	P	–	K	K	–	E&J	McC
10,900	Sep 25	Touring	Green	P	R	K	K	–	E&J	McC
11,000	Sep 29	Touring	Green	W	–	K	K	–	?	McC
11,100	Jan 30	Touring	Green	P	–	K	K	–	?	McC
	NOTE: No aluminum bodies listed after September 1909.									
11,110	Sep 30	Touring	Green	P	T(W)	K	K	ST-24	BRN	McC
11,146	Oct 2	Engine only	(Only Kingston coils and carburetors used during							
		((T(W) = Troy wood T = Troy brass))							this period.)	
11,200	Oct 4	Town Car	Green	P	–	K	K	–	–	McC
11,300	Oct 6	Touring	Green	P	T	K	K	ST-24	BRN	McC
11,400	Oct 7	Touring	Green	P	T	K	K	ST-24	BRN	Det.
11,500	Oct 7	Touring	Green	P	M	K	K	ST-24	?	Det.
11,600	Oct 12	Town Car	Green	P	–	K	K	–	–	Det.
11,700	Oct 14	Engine only								
11,756	Oct 15	Touring	Green	P	T	K	K	ST-24	BRN	Det.
11,800	Oct 16	Touring	Green	P	T	K	K	ST-24	BRN	Det.
11,900	Oct 18	Touring	Green	P	Troy	K	K	ST-24	E&J	
12,000	Oct 21	Touring	Green	P	T	K	K	ST-24	E&J	Ford
12,100	Oct 23	Touring	Green	P	T	K	K	ST-24	E&J	Ford
12,200	Oct 26	Touring	Green	P	T	K	K	ST-24	BRN	McC
12,300	Oct 28	Touring	Green	P	T	K	K	ST-24	E&J	Ford
	NOTE: During October "New style Pontiac tops" appeared on some Touring car invoices.									
12,400	Oct 29	Touring	Green	P	T	K	K	ST-24	BRN	Ford
12,438	Nov 1	Touring	Green	P	T	K	K	ST-24	BRN	Ford
12,499	Nov 2	Touring	Green	P	T	K	K	ST-24	BRN	Ford
12,500	Invoice missing									
12,501	Nov 2	Touring	Green	P	T	K	K	ST-24	BRN	Ford
12,600	Nov 4	Touring	Green	P	R	K	K	ST-24	E&J	
12,700	Nov 9	Touring	Green	P	T	K	K	ST-24	E&J	
12,800	Nov 12	Touring	Green	P	T	K	K	ST-24	E&J	McC
12,900	Nov 17	Touring	Green	P	T	K	K	ST-24	BRN	Fisk tires
	"Roller bearing rear axle" (Inner axle bearings)									
13,000	Nov 22	Touring	Green	P	T	K	K	ST-24	BRN	Ford
13,100	Nov 29	Touring	Green	P	R	K	K	ST-24	BRN	McC
	"Roller bearing rear axle"									
13,200	Nov 30	Engine only (to Canada)								
	NOTE: "Roller bearing rear axle" appeared on some invoices during this period									
13,240	Dec 1	Touring	Green	P	R	K	K	ST-24	BRN	Ford
13,300	Dec 3	Touring	Green	P	R	K	K	ST-24	BRN	McC
	(RHD, metric spark plugs, to Scotland)									
13,400	Dec 7	Touring	Green	P	T	B	K	ST-24	BRN	McC
13,500	Dec 9	Engine only (to Canada)			K					
13,600	Dec 11	Touring	Green	P	T	K	K	ST-11	E&J	Ford
13,700	Dec 15	Touring	Green	P	T	B	K	ST-24	E&J	McC
13,800	Dec 17	Touring	Green	P	T	B	K	ST-24	E&J	Ford
13,900	Dec 23	Touring	Green	P	Troy	K	K	ST-24	BRN	F
14,000	Dec 29	Touring	Green	P	R	B	K	ST-24	BRN	F
14,017	Dec 30	Touring	Green	P	T	B	K	ST-24	BRN	F
14,100	Dec 30	Touring	Green	P	R	K	K	ST-24	BRN	F
14,151	Dec 31	Roadster	Green	P	R	K	K	ST-24	BRN	F

Ser#	Mfg.	Body Style	Color	Mfgr	W/S	Carb	Coil	Speed-ometer	Gas Lamps	Radiator	

Ford, Detroit and McCord radiators used during this period, with Ford finally making all radiators.

Ser#	Mfg.	Body Style	Color	Mfgr	W/S	Carb	Coil	Speed-ometer	Gas Lamps	Radiator	
14,165	Jan 3	Touring	Green	P	R	K	K	ST-24	BRN	F	

(First number in 1910)

14,179	Jan 3	Touring	Green	P	R	K	K	ST-24	BRN	F	RHD, metric
14,200	Jan 3	Touring	Green		R	K	K	ST-24	BRN	F	
14,300	Jan 5	Tourabout	Green	P	R	K	K	ST-24	BRN	F	
14,400	Jan 6	Touring	Green	P	R	K	K	ST-24	BRN	F	
14,436	Jan 6	Roadster	Green	P		K	K	ST-24	BRN	F	
14,500	Jan 6	Engine only (to Canada)									
14,533	Jan 6	Engine only (to Canada)									
14,600	Jan 7	Touring	Green	P	Troy	K	K	ST-24	BRN	F	
14,700	Jan 10	Touring	Green	P	R	K	K	ST-24	BRN	F	
14,800	Jan 12	Coupe	Green	P		K	K		No lamps		
14,900	Jan-14	Touring	Green	P	R	K	K	ST-24	BRN	F	
15,000	Jan 15	Touring	Green	P	R	K	K	ST-24	BRN	F	RHD, metric (Jackson top)
15,100	Jan 19	Roadster	Green	P	R	K	K	ST-24	BRN	Det.	
15,200	Invoice missing										
15,201	Illegible invoice										
15,202	Jan 21	Touring	Green	P	R	K	K	ST-24	BRN	Det.	
15,300	Jan 24	Engine only (to Omaha)									
15,394	Jan 27	Touring	Green	P	R	K	K	ST-24	BRN	Det.	
15,400	Jan 26	Touring	Green	P	R	K	K	ST-24	BRN	McC	
15,500	Jan 31	Tourabout	Green	P	R	K	JB	ST-24	BRN	Det.	
15,517	Feb 1	Tourabout	Green	P	R	K	K	ST-24	BRN	Det.	
15,600	Jan 31	Engine only									
15,667	Feb 1	Chassis assembly, RHD, shipped to Canada on Jan 31! The shipping date is a rubber stamp imprint. Perhaps they forgot to change the date.									
15,675	Feb 1	Town Car	Green	P		K	K		E&J	F	

First invoice marked "**REINFORCED HOUSING**" (rear axle). Perhaps this refers to the new roller pinion bearing rear axle.

15,700	Feb 2	Roadster	Green	P	R	H	JB	ST-24	BRN	Det.	
15,800	Feb 4	Touring	Green	P	R	K	K	ST-24	BRN	Det.	
15,900	Feb 7	Touring	Grn ?	P	R			ST-24	BRN		
15,797	Feb 21	Touring	Green	P	R	K	JB	ST-24	E&J	Det.	
16,000	Feb 9	Tourabout	Green	P	R	K	JB	ST-24	E&J	Det.	
16,100	Feb 10	Touring	Green	P	R	K	JB	ST-24	E&J	F	
16,200	Feb 15	Touring	Green	P	R	K	JB	ST-24	E&J	F	
16,267	Feb 15	Touring	Green	P	R	K	JB		E&J	F	

(Metric, kilometer speedometer, shipped to Russia)

16,278	Feb 15	Touring	Green	P		H	JB	ST-24	E&J	F	

(First invoice marked "**SPECIAL FLYWHEEL**.")

16,300	Feb 18	Touring	Green	P	R	H	JB	ST-24	E&J	F	
16,335	Feb 18	"Show Motor"									
16,400	Feb 23	Tourabout	Green	P	R	B	JB		E&J	McC	
16,500	Feb 25	Touring	Green	P	R	K	JB	ST-24	E&J	F	
16,591	Mar 1	Touring	Green	P	R	K	JB	ST-24	E&J	F	
16,597	Mar 1	Touring	Green	P	R	K	JB		E&J	F	
16,600	Mar 1	Town Car	Green	P		K	JB		None	Det.	
16,700	Engine only, to Canada, among many this date.										

NOTE: Bodies mostly Pontiac but some KH. Wheels were Pruden, KH. Carburetors were Kingston, Holley and Buffalo. "Special Flywheel" noted on many but not all cars.

16,704	Feb 23	Motor only (Canada)				K					
16,800	Mar 1	Engine only (to Canada)									
16,900	Mar 2	Touring	Green	P	R	K	JB	ST-24	BRN	F	
17,000	Mar 4	Touring	Green	KH*		K	JB		E&J	F	

* KH or KA (invoice not clear)

17,100	Mar 5	Touring	Green	KH	R	K	JB	ST-24	E&J	F	
17,200	Mar 7	Touring	Green	KH	R	K	JB		E&J		
17,300	Mar 9	Town Car	Green	P		K	K	ST-24	E&J	F	
17,400	Mar 9	Roadster	Green	P	R	K	JB	ST-24	E&J		
17,500	Mar 10	Touring	Green	P	R	K	JB	ST-24	E&J	F	
17,565	Mar 11	Touring	Green	P	R	K	JB	ST-24	E&J	F	
17,600	Mar 11	Touring	Green	KA	R	K	JB	ST-24	E&J	F	

Ser#	Mfg.	Body Style	Color	Mfgr	W/S	Carb	Coil	Speed-ometer	Gas Lamps	Radiator
17,700	Mar 14	Roadster	Green	P	R	K	K	ST-24	E&J	F
17,800	Mar 15	Touring	Green	P	R	K	K	ST-24	BRN	F
17,900	Mar 16	Touring	Green	P	R	K	K	ST-24	BRN	F
17,985	Mar 17	Touring	Green	P	R	K	K	ST-24	BRN	"New Magneto"
18,000	Mar 17	Touring	Green	P	R	K	K	ST-24	BRN	
18,100	Mar 18	Touring	Green	P	R	K	K	ST-24	BRN	

NOTE: E&J and Brown gas lamps mixed during production. Brands were also mixed on the same car; that is, E&J side, Brown tail, both the same, or vice-versa, with either brand of gas lamps, and alternate brands of generators. "New magneto" not shown on all invoices. "Roller Bearing D.S." and "Jackson top" noted on many invoices.

Ser#	Mfg.	Body Style	Color	Mfgr	W/S	Carb	Coil	Speed-ometer	Gas Lamps	Radiator
18,200	Mar 19	Touring	Green	P	R	K	K	ST-24	E&J	
18,300	Mar 21	Touring	Green	P	R	K	JB	ST-11	E&J	
18,400	Mar 22	Touring	Green	KH	R	K	K	ST-24	E&J	
18,500	Mar 23	Touring	Green	P	R	K	K	ST-24	E&J	
18,600	Mar 24	Engine only (to Canada).								

Numbers 18,600 thru 18,796 were all engines only.

Ser#	Mfg.	Body Style	Color	Mfgr	W/S	Carb	Coil	Speed-ometer	Gas Lamps	Radiator
18,800	Mar 23	Tourabout	Green	P	R	K	JB	ST-24	E&J	
18,900	Mar 24	Touring	Green	P	Troy	K	JB	ST-24	E&J	
19,000	Mar 25	Touring	Green	KA	R	K	JB	ST-24	E&J	
19,100	Mar 26	Touring	Green	P	R	K	JB	ST-24	E&J	
19,200	Mar 28	Tourabout	Green	P	R	K	JB	ST-24	BRN	
19,300	Mar 29	Touring	Green	P	R	K	JB	ST-24	BRN	
19,400	Mar 30	Touring	Green	P	R	K	JB	ST-24	BRN	
19,500	Mar 31	Touring	Green	KH	R	K	JB	ST-24	BRN	
19,600	Mar 31	Touring	Green	KA	M	K	JB	ST-24	BRN	
19,647	Apr 1	Touring	Green	P	R	K	JB	ST-24	BRN	
19,700	Apr 1	Touring	Green	KA	R	K	K	ST-24	E&J	
19,800	Apr 2	Touring	Green	KA	R	K	JB	ST-24	BRN	
19,900	Apr 4	Touring	Green	P	R	K	JB	ST-24	BRN	
20,000	Apr 5	Touring	Green	KH	R	K	JB	ST-24	BRN	
20,002	Apr 4	Touring	Green	P	R	K	JB	ST-24	BRN	

"NEW STYLE CRANKCASE" =NSC

Ser#	Mfg.	Body Style	Color	Mfgr	W/S	Carb	Coil	Speed-ometer	Gas Lamps	Radiator
20,100	Apr 6	Roadster	Green	P	R	K	JB	ST-24	BRN	
20,200	Apr 6	Touring	Green	P	R	K	JB	ST-24	BRN	
20,300	Apr 7	Touring	Green	P	R	K	JB	ST-24	BRN	
20,400	Apr 8	Touring	Green	P	R	K	JB	ST-24	BRN	
20,500	Apr 8	Touring	Green	KH	R	K	JB	ST-24	E&J	
20,600	Apr 11	Roadster	Green	P	R	K	JB	ST-24	E&J	
20,700	Apr 11	Touring	Green	KH	R	K	JB	ST-24	E&J	
20,800	Apr 12	Touring	Green	KH	R	K	JB	ST-24	E&J	
20,900	Apr 13	Touring	Green	P	R	K	JB		E&J	
21,000	Apr 15	Touring	Green	KA	R	K	JB	ST-24	E&J	
21,100	Invoice missing									
21,101	Apr 15	Touring	Green	P	R	K	K	ST-24	E&J	
21,200	Apr 16	Touring	Green	P	R	K	K	ST-24	E&J	
21,300	Apr 18	Tourabout	Green	P	R	K	K	ST-24	E&J	

Jacobson-Brandow coilboxes the most common during this period

Ser#	Mfg.	Body Style	Color	Mfgr	W/S	Carb	Coil	Speed-ometer	Gas Lamps	Radiator
21,400	Apr 19	Touring	Green	P	R	K	K	ST-24	E&J	
21,500	Apr 19	Touring	Green	P	R	K	K	ST-24	E&J	
21,600	Apr 20	Touring	Green	P	R	K	K	ST-24	BRN	
21,700	Apr 20	Touring	Green	P	R	K	K	ST-24	BRN	
21,800	Apr 21	Touring	Green	P	R	K	K	ST-24	BRN	Ford
21,900	Apr 21	Touring	Green	P	R	K	K	ST-24	BRN	F
22,000	Apr 22	Touring	Green	KH	R	K	K	ST-24	BRN	F
22,100	Apr 22	Touring	Green	KH	R	K	JB	ST-24	BRN	F
22,200	Apr 23	Coupe (For Henry Ford)	Green	KH		K	K			F
22,300	Apr 25	Touring	Green	P	R	K	JB	ST-24	BRN	F
22,400	Apr 25	Touring	Green	KH	R	K	JB	ST-24	BRN	F
22,500	Apr 26	Touring	Green	KH	R	K	JB	ST-24	BRN	F
22,600	Apr 26	Engine only (to Canada)								
22,700	Apr 26	Touring	Green	KH	R	K	JB	ST-24	BRN	F
22,800	Apr 27	Touring	Green	P	R	K	JB	ST-24	BRN	F

Shipping Invoices

1910

Ser#	Mfg.	Body Style	Color	Mfgr	W/S	Carb	Coil	Speed-ometer	Gas Lamps	Radiator	
22,900	Apr 28	Tourabout	Green	P	R	K	JB	ST-24	BRN	F	
		Jackson tops used during this period.									
23,000	Apr 28	Touring	Green	P	R	H	JB	ST-24	BRN	F	NSC
23,001	Apr 28	Touring	Green	P	R	K	JB	ST-24	BRN	F	NSC
23,002	Apr 28	Touring	Green	P	R	K	JB	ST-24	BRN	F	NSC
23,003	Apr 28	Touring	Green	P	R	H	JB	ST-24	BRN	F	NSC
23,004	Apr 28	Touring	Green	KH	R	H	JB	ST-24	BRN	F	NSC
23,005	Apr 28	Touring	Green	KH	R	K	JB	ST-24	BRN	F	NSC
23,006	Apr 28	Touring	Green	KH	R	K	JB	ST-24	BRN	F	NSC
23,007	Apr 28	Touring	Green	P	R	H	JB	ST-24	BRN	F	NSC
23,008	Apr 28	Runabout	Green	P	R	K	JB	ST-24	BRN	F	NSC
23,009	Apr 29	Runabout	Green	P	R	H	JB	ST-24	BRN	F	NSC
23,010	Apr 28	Touring	Green	KH	R	H	JB	ST-24	BRN	F	NSC
23,056	Apr 28	Touring	Green	P	R	H	JB	ST-24	BRN	F	NSC
		NSC = "New style crankcase"									
23,100	Apr 29	Touring	Green	KH	R	K	JB	ST-24	BRN	F	
23,200	Apr 29	Touring	Green	P	R	K	JB	ST-24	BRN	F	
23,219	Apr 29	Touring	Green	KH	R	K	JB	ST-24	BRN	F	
		"New magneto"									
23,300	Apr 30	Touring	Green	KH	R	K	JB	ST-24	BRN	F	
23,348	May 2	Tourabout	Green	P	R	K	JB	ST-24	BRN	F	
23,400	May 2	Touring	Green	P	R	H	JB	ST-24	BRN	F	
23,500	May 3	Touring	Green	P	R	H	JB	ST-24	BRN	F	
23,600	May 3	Touring?	Green								
23,700	May 4	Touring	Green	KH	R	K	JB	ST-24	E&J	F	
23,799	May 6	—	Green	P	R	K	JB	ST-24	BRN	New style C.C.	
23,800	May 6	Touring	Green	KA	R	K	JB	ST-24	BRN		
23,862	May 6	Tourabout	Green	P	R	K	JB	ST-24	BRN		
23,900	May 6	Touring	Green	P	R	H	JB	ST-24	BRN		
24,000	May 7	Roadster	Green	P	R	K	JB	ST-24	BRN		
24,100	May 7	Touring	Green	KA	R	K	JB	ST-24	BRN		
24,200	May 9	Touring	Green	KH	R	K	JB	ST-24	BRN		
24,300	May 9	Touring	Green	P	R	K	JB	ST-24	BRN		
24,334	May 10	Touring	Green	KH	R	K	JB	ST-24	BRN	KH wheels	
24,400	May 10	Touring	Green	KH	R	H	JB	ST-24	BRN		
24,500	May 11	Town Car	Green	P		K	JB	—	No lamps		
24,600	May 11	Touring	Green	KH	R	K	K	ST-24	BRN		
24,627	May 11	Touring	Green	KH	R	H	K	ST-24	BRN	F	
24,700	May 12	Touring	Green	P	R	H	K	ST-24	BRN		
24,800	May 12	Touring	Green	KH	R	H	K	ST-24	BRN		
24,900	May 13	Touring	Green	P	R	K	K	ST-24	BRN		
25,000	May 13	Touring	Green	P	R	H	K	ST-24	BRN	F	
25,100	May 16	Touring	Green	KA	R	K	K	ST-24	BRN	F	
25,134	May 16	Touring	Green	KA	R	K	K	ST-24	BRN	F	
25,200	May 16	Touring	Green	KH	R	H	JB	ST-24	BRN	F	
25,300	May 17	Touring	Green	KH	R	K	JB	ST-24	BRN	F	
25,400	May 18	Touring	Green	KH	R	K	JB	ST-24	BRN	F	
25,500	May 18	Touring	Green	KH	R	K	JB	ST-24	BRN	F	
25,600	May 19	Touring	Green	KH	R	K	JB	ST-24	BRN	F	
25,700	May 19	Touring	Green	KH	R	K	JB	ST-24	BRN	F	
25,800	May 20	Touring	Green	P	R	K	JB	ST-24	BRN	F	
25,900	May 21	Touring	Green	P	R	K	JB	ST-24	BRN	F	
26,000	May 23	Touring	Green	P	R	K	JB	ST-24	BRN	F	
26,100	May 23	Touring	Green	P	R	K	JB	ST-24	BRN	F	
26,200	May 24	Touring	Green	P	R	K	JB	ST-24	BRN	F	
26,300	May 25	Touring	Green	P	R	H	K	ST-24	BRN	F	
26,306	May 25	Touring	Green	KH	R	K	K	ST-24	BRN	F	
26,364	May 23	Touring	Green	Fox Bros.		H	K			F	
		Henry Ford's car, rebuilt for stock. Metal body. Returned Dec. 1, 1910.									
26,364	May 25	Touring	Green	P	R	H	K	ST-24	BRN	F	
		NOTE: Two different cars with the same engine number.									
26,400	May 25	Touring	Green	P	R	K	K	ST-24	BRN	F	
26,500	May 25	Touring	Green	KH	R	H	K	ST-24	BRN	F	
26,600	May 27	Touring	Green	KH	R	H	K	ST-24	E&J	F	

Ser#	Mfg.	Body Style	Color	Mfgr	W/S	Carb	Coil	Speed-ometer	Gas Lamps	Radiator	
26,700	May 27	Touring	Green	P	R	K	K	ST-24	BRN	F	
26,800	May 28	Touring	Green	KH	R	H	K	ST-24	BRN	F	
26,900	May 31	Touring	Green	P	R	K	K	ST-24	E&J	F	(RHD)
26,933	Jun 1	Touring	Green	P	R	H	K	ST-24	E&J	F	
27,000	Jun 1	Touring	Green	P	R	H	K	ST-24	E&J	F	
27,074	Jun 1	Touring	Green	KH	R	H	K	ST-24	E&J	F	
27,100	Jun 2	Touring	Green	P	R	H	K	ST-24	E&J	F	
27,200	Jun 2	Touring	Green	KH	R	H	K	ST-24	E&J	F	
27,300	Jun 3	Roadster	Green	P	R	H	JB	ST-24	E&J	F	
27,400	Jun 3	Touring	Green	P	R	H	JB	ST-24	E&J	F	
27,500	Jun 4	Touring	Green	KH	R	H	JB	ST-24	E&J	F	
27,600	Jun 6	Touring	Green	KH	R	H	JB	ST-24	E&J	F	
27,700	Jun 6	Touring	Green	P	R	H	JB	ST-24	E&J	F	
27,755	Jun 7	Touring	Green	P	R	H	JB	ST-24	E&J	F	
27,799 to 27,801 missing											
27,802	Jun 7	Touring	Green	KA	R	H	JB	ST-24	E&J	F	
27,900	Jun 8	Tourabout	Green	P	R	H	JB	ST-24	E&J	F	
28,000	Jun 8	Touring	Green	KH	R	H	JB	ST-24	E&J	F	
28,100	Jun 9	Touring	Green	P	R	K	JB	ST-24	E&J	F	
28,200	Jun 10	Touring	Green	KH*	R	H	JB	ST-24	BRN	F	*Metal
28,300	Jun 11	Touring	Green	KH	R	H	JB	ST-24	BRN	F	
28,367	Jun 13	Touring	Green	P	R	H	JB	ST-24	BRN	F	
28,400	Jun 13	Touring	Green	P	R	H	JB	ST-24	BRN	F	
28,500	Jun 14	Roadster	Green	KA	R	H	JB	ST-24	E&J	F	
Both JB and Kingston coils used in this period.											
28,600	Jun 16	Touring	Green	P	R	H	JB	ST-24	E&J	F	
28,700	Jun 16	Touring	Green	P	R	H	JB	ST-24	E&J	F	
28,800	Jun 17	Touring	Green	P	R	H	JB	ST-24	E&J	F	
28,900	Jun 20	Touring	Green	P	R	H	JB	ST-24	E&J	F	
29,000	Jun 21	Touring	Green	P	R	H	JB	ST-24	E&J	F	
29,100	Jun 22	Touring	Green	KA	R	H	JB	ST-24	E&J	F	
29,200	Jun 23	Touring	Green	KA	R	H	JB	ST-24	E&J	F	
29,300	Jun 23	Touring	Green	P	R	H	JB	ST-24	E&J	F	
29,400	Jun 29	Touring	Green	KH	R	H	JB	ST-24	E&J	F	
29,500	Jun 29	Engine only (to Canada)									
29,565	Jul 1	Touring	Green	KH	R	H	K	ST-24	BRN	F	
Kingston coils for the most part during July.											
29,600	Jul 6	Touring	Green	KH	R	H	K	ST-24	BRN	F	
29,700	Jul 8	Touring	Green	KA	R	H	K	ST-24	BRN	F	
29,800	Jul 12	Touring	Green	P	R	H	K	ST-24	BRN	F	
29,900	Jul 13	Touring	Green	P	R	H	K	ST-24	BRN	F	
											All Ford radiators
30,000	Jul 20	Touring	Green	P	R	H	K	ST-24	BRN		Body #10984
30,072	Jul 25	Touring	Green	P	R	H	K	ST-24	BRN		Body #11350
30,100	Jul 22	Touring	Green	KH	R	H	K	ST-24	BRN		
30,200	Jul 26	Touring	Green	P	R	K	K	ST-24	BRN		Body #9531
30,300	Jul 28	Touring	Green	P	R	H	K	ST-24	BRN		Body #11059
"Special Low Compression Head" on many invoices.											
30,357	Aug 1	Touring	Green	KH		K	JB	ST-24	E&J		Body #3446
30,400	Aug 2	Touring	Green	P	R	K	JB	ST-24	E&J		Body #12909
30,480	Aug 2	Touring	Green	P	R	H	JB	ST-24	BRN		
(Many invoices noted with "Special O.O.P") ??											
30,500	Aug 12	Touring	Green	KH	R	H	JB	ST-24			Body #11782
30,600	Aug 17	Touring	Green	P	R	H	JB	ST-24	BRN		
30,700	Aug 19	Touring	Green	P	R	H	K	ST-24	BRN		
30,800	Aug 23	Touring	Green	P	R	H	K	ST-24	BRN		
30,863	Aug 25	Touring	Green	P	R	H	K		BRN		Body #12500
30,900	Aug 25	Touring	Green		R	H	K	ST-24	BRN		Body #11207
31,000	Aug 29	Touring	Green	KH	R	H	K	ST-24	BRN		Body #3618
31,100	Aug 31	Touring	Green	P	R	K	K	ST-24	BRN		Body #11672
31,132	Sep 1	Touring	Green	KH	R	K	K	ST-24	BRN		Body #3660
31,200	Sep 7	Touring	Green	F-B*	R	K	K	ST-24	BRN		*F-B = Fox Bros.
31,300	Sep 9	Touring	Green	KH	R	K	K	ST-24	BRN		Body #3595
"1911 Radiator"											

Shipping Invoices

1910

Ser#	Mfg.	Body Style	Color	Mfgr	W/S	Carb	Coil	Speedometer	Gas Lamps	Radiator
31,400	Sep 13	Touring	Green	P	R	K	K	ST-24	BRN	Body #11566
31,500	Sep 20	Touring	Green	P	R	K	K	ST-24	BRN	Body #11674
31,533	Oct 3	Touring	Green	P	R	K	K	ST-24	BRN	
		(Numbers and dates mixed, apparently due to different assembly lines.)								
31,600	Oct 11	Touring	Green	F-B	R	H	K	ST-24	BRN	
31,673	Oct 26	Torpedo	Blue		R	H	JB	ST-24	E&J	
		Note: First Runabout with doors, sample metal body. "Pipd" (or Pepd) Blue. Chassis built October 5								
31,679	Feb 9*	Roadster	Blue	P	R	K	JB	ST-26	E&J	*1911.
		Chassis built Oct. 3, 1910.								
31,700	Oct 7	Touring	Green	P	R	K	JB	ST-26	E&J	
31,733	Oct 17	Coupe	Green	P			K	JB	ST-24		Chassis built 10-7
31,734	Oct 15	Coupe	Green	P				ST-24		
31,782	Oct 15	Touring	Green	KH	R	K	JB	ST-24	BRN	
31,800	Jan 26*	Roadster	Blue	P	R	K	–	ST-26	E&J	*1911.
		Chassis built Oct. 11, 1910.								
31,810	Dec 19	Service Car	Red	Melbourn		K	JB	ST "30 mile"		
		Chassis built Oct. 11 (for J. Wanamaker)								
31,811	Dec 21	Svc. Car	Red	Melbourn		K	JB	ST "30 mile"		
		Chassis built Oct. 11 (for J. Wanamaker)								
31,812	Dec 21	Svc. Car	Red	Melbourn		K	JB	ST "30 mile"		
		Chassis built Oct. 11 (for J. Wanamaker)								
		Above special order cars built with "1911 rear axle."								
31,848	Dec 21	Del.Wag.	Red	Melbourn		K	JB	ST "30 mile"		
31,900	Oct 15	Touring	Green	KH	R	K	JB	ST-24	BRN	
31,918	Jan 4	Roadster	Blue	P	R	K	K	**	E&J	** ST Kilometer
		Chassis built October 14.								
32,000	Oct 16	Engine only				K				
32,006	Oct 19	Touring	Green	P	R	K	JB	ST-24	BRN	
32,100	Oct 21	Touring	Green	P	R	K	JB	ST-24	E&J	
32,146	Mar 6*	Roadster	Blue	P		K	JB	ST-24	E&J	
		*1911. Chassis built October 24								
32,200	Oct 26	Touring	Green	KH		K	JB	ST-24	BRN	Body #4206
		1911 metal body								
32,201	Oct 25	Roadster	Blue	P	R	H	JB	ST-26	E&J	Body #5918
32,209	Oct 25	Roadster	Blue	P		K	JB			L/H metric
32,211	Oct 25	Roadster	Blue	P		K	JB			
32,216	Jan 3*	Del. Car	Red			*1911. Chassis built Oct. 25 (for J. Wanamaker)					
32,229	Oct 25	Roadster	Green	P		K	JB	ST "30 mile"		
		NOTE: A number of invoices are marked "1911 axle." Whether this refers to the front or rear axle is unknown.								
32,300	Oct 27	Touring	Green	P	R	K	JB	ST-24	BRN	
32,400	Oct 31	Roadster	Green	P		K	JB			
32,404	Nov 1	Touring	Green	P	R	K	JB	ST-24	BRN	
32,500	Nov 2	Touring	Green	P	R	K	K	ST-24	BRN	
32,600	Nov 4	Touring	Green	P	R	K	K	ST-24	E&J	
32,700	Nov 7	Town Car	Green	P		K	K	ST-26	E&J	Body #222
32,800	Nov 9	Touring	Green	P	R	K	K	ST-24	E&J	Body #11838
32,900	Dec 2	Town Car	Green	P		K	K	ST-24	E&J	
		(Chassis assembled Nov. 11)								
32,934	Nov 11	Touring	Green	KH	R	K	K	ST-24	E&J	
32,983	Nov 14	Roadster	Green	P	R	K	K	ST-24	E&J	
33,000	Nov 15	Touring	Green	KH	R	K	K		E&J	
33,100	Nov 17	Touring	Green	P	R	K	K	ST-24	E&J	
33,103	Nov 16	Touring	Green	P	R	K	K	ST-24	E&J	
33,113	Nov 16	Roadster	Blue	P	R	K	K	ST-24	E&J	
		(Blue Roadsters had French Gray striping)								
33,200	Nov 17	Engine only (to Canada)								
33,209	Nov 17	Engine only (to Canada)								
33,300	Nov 19	Roadster	Blue	P	R	K	K	ST-24	E&J	
33,327	Nov 19	Touring	Blue	P	R	K	K	ST-24	E&J	
33,400	Nov 21	Engine only (to Canada)				K				
33,500	Nov 23	Roadster	Blue	P	R	K	K	ST-24	E&J	
33,600	Nov 25	Engine only (to Canada)				K				

1910

Ser#	Mfg.	Body Style	Color	Mfgr	W/S	Carb	Coil	Speed-ometer	Gas Lamps	Radiator
33,700	Nov 28	Touring	Green	KH	R	K	K	ST-24	E&J	
33,800	Nov 28	Engine only (to Canada)				K				
33,900	Nov 30	Touring	Green	P	R	K	K	ST-24	E&J	
33,933	Dec 1	Touring	Green	KH	R	K	K	ST-24	E&J	
34,000	Dec 1	Engine only (to Canada)				K				
34,100	Dec 2	Touring	Green	P	R	K	K	ST-24	E&J	
34,200	Dec 6	Touring	Green	KH	R	K	K	ST-26	E&J	
34,250	Dec 8	Roadster	Blue	H	R	K	K	Kilo	E&J	
		"1911 Roadster" shipped to Italy.								
34,300	Dec 8	Chassis only					"1911 Kingston carburetor"				
34,301	Dec 8	Roadster	Blue	P	R	H	K	ST-26	E&J	
34,333	Dec 10	Torpedo	Blue	H	R	K	K	ST-24	E&J	
		"Runabout with doors" (First Torpedo?)								
34,346	Dec 10	Touring	Blue	H	R	H	K	ST-26	E&J	
		First Blue (1911?) touring								
34,377	Dec 11	Roadster	Green	P	–	K	K	–	–	
		(With French Gray stripe, to Havana, Cuba.)								
34,399	Dec 21	Touring	Green	KH	R	K	K	ST-26	BRN	
		(Chassis assembled Dec. 12.)								
34,400	Dec 15	Touring	Blue	FB	R	K	K	ST-26	BRN	"1911"
		NOTE: Blue and Green Touring and Roadsters built in December. Most, if not all, had "1911" rear axles, speedometers, and CLOCKS!									
34,500	Dec 13	Engine only (to Canada)				K				
34,600	Dec 19	Touring	Blue	H	R	K	JB	ST-26	BRN	(Metal body)
34,672	Jan 3	Svc. Car	Blue	Ford		K	K		(for J. Wanamaker)	
34,673	Jan 3	Svc. Car	Yel	Milburn	Cabinet				(for J. Wanamaker)	
34,674	Jan 3	Svc. Car	Yel	Milburn			K		(for J. Wanamaker)	
34,678	Jan 12	Delivery	Yel	Milburn			K		(for J. Wanamaker)	
34,700	Dec 28	Touring	Blue	P	R	K	JB	ST-26	BRN	
34,800	Dec 21	Engine only (to Canada)				K				
34,899	Dec 30	Torpedo	Blue	H	R	K	JB	ST-26	BRN	
34,700	Dec 28	Touring	Blue	P	R	K	JB	ST-26	BRN	
34,800	Dec 21	Engine only (to Canada)				K				
34,899	Dec 30	Torpedo	Blue	H	R	K	JB	ST-26	BRN	
1911										
34,900	Jan 3	Roadster	Blue	H	R	K	JB	ST-26	BRN	
35,000	Dec 29*	Touring	Blue	P	R	K	K	ST-26	BRN	*1910
35,040	Jan 4	Torpedo	Blue	H	R	K	K	ST-26	E&J	
35,048	Dec 30*	Touring	Blue	P	R	K	K	KILO	E&J	
35,059	Dec 31*	Touring	Blue	P	R	K	K	ST-26	BRN	
35,060	Jan 3	Touring	Blue	P	R	K	K	ST-26	BRN	
35,072	Dec 30*	Touring	Blue	P	R	K	K	ST-26	BRN	
35,073	Jan 5	Touring	Blue	P	R	K	K	ST-26	BRN	
35,077	Dec 30*	Touring	Blue	P	R	K	K	ST-26	BRN	
35,078	Jan 4	Touring	Blue	P	R	K	K	ST-26	E&J	
35,087	Dec 31*	Touring	Blue	P	R	K	K	ST-26	E&J	
35,088	Jan 5	Touring	Blue	P	R	K	K	ST-26	E&J	
35,097	Dec 31*	Touring	Blue	P	R	K	K	ST-26	BRN	
35,100	Jan 6	Touring	Blue	P	R	K	K	ST-26	E&J	
35,200	Jan 4	Runabout	Blue	H	R	K	K	ST-26	BRN	
35,300	Jan 6	Touring	Blue	P	R	K	JB	ST-26	E&J	
35,400	Jan 9	Torpedo	Blue	H	R	K	JB	ST-26	BRN	
		"Seamed style radiator" (first used in Dec. 1910)									
35,500	Jan 11	Touring	Blue	P	R	K	JB	ST-26	E&J	
35,600	Jan 14	Torpedo	Blue	H	R	K	JB	ST-26	E&J	
35,700	Jan 14	Touring	Blue	P	R	K	JB	ST-26	E&J	
35,800	Jan 17	Touring	Blue	P	R	K	K	ST-26	E&J	
35,900	Jan 18	Touring	Blue	P	R	K	K	ST-24	E&J	
36,000	Invoice missing									
36,001	Jan 19	Touring	Blue			H*	K			*1911 Holley
36,100	Jan 20	Touring	Blue			H	(Heinze, first used)			
36,200	Jan 23	Runabout	Blue	H	R	K	K	ST-26	E&J	
36,233	Jan 23	Touring	Blue	P	R	K	K	ST-26	E&J	
36,300	Jan 24	Touring	Blue	P	R	K	JB	ST-26	E&J	
36,400	Jan 24	Torpedo	Blue	H	R	K	JB	ST-26	E&J	

1911

Ser#	Mfg.	Body Style	Color	Mfgr	W/S	Carb	Coil	Speed-ometer	Gas Lamps	Radiator
36,500	Jan 25	Runabout	Blue	H	R	K	JB	ST-26	E&J	
36,600	Jan 26	Touring	Blue	KH	R	K	JB	ST-26	E&J	
36,700	Jan 27	Touring	Blue	P	R	K	JB	ST-26	E&J	
36,800	Jan 30	Touring	Blue	P	R	K	JB	ST-26	E&J	
36,900	Jan 31	Runabout	Blue	H	R	K	JB	ST-26	E&J	
36,972	Jan 31	Touring	Blue	P	R	K	JB	ST-26	E&J	
		First "1911 front axle"								
36,989	Feb 1	Torpedo	Blue	H	R	K	JB	ST-26	E&J	
37,000	Jan 31	Touring	Blue	P	R	K	JB	ST-26	E&J	
37,023	Jan 31	Touring	Blue	P	R	K	JB	ST-26	E&J	
37,025	Feb 1	Touring	Blue	P	R	K	JB	ST-26	E&J	
37,100	Feb 2	Torpedo	Blue	H	R	K	JB	ST-26	E&J	
37,200	Feb 2	Roadster	Blue	P	–	K	JB	–	–	"1910 roadster"
37,300	Feb 3	Touring	Blue	P	R	K	JB	ST-26	E&J	
37,311	Feb 3	Torpedo	Blue	H	R	K	JB	ST-26	E&J	
		First "1911 transmission pan"								
37,378	Feb 4	First invoice marked "1911 Front Axle" and "New Transmission Cover."								
37,380	Feb 6	Town Car	Blue	P	–	K	JB	–	–	"1910"
37,381	Feb 6	Town Car	Blue	P	–	K	JB	–	–	"1910"
37,400	Feb 6	Torpedo	Blue	H	R	K	JB	ST-26	E&J	
37,417	Feb 8	First invoices marked "1911 **Wide Pan and Transmission Cover.**"								
37,433	Feb 6	Touring	Blue	KH	R	K	JB	ST-26	E&J	
		(Chassis assembled Jan 4)								
37,492	Feb 6	Touring	Blue	KA	R	K	H	ST-26	E&J	"1911 front axle"
37,500	Feb 7	Touring	Blue			K	H			1911 fr.ax. & tr.cov.
37,600	Feb 7	Touring	Blue	KH	R	H	H	ST-26	E&J	
37,700	Feb 8	Touring	Blue	KA	R	K	H	ST-26	E&J	
37,800	Feb 9	Touring	Blue	KA	R	K	H	ST-26	E&J	
37,900	Feb 10	Roadster	Blue	P	R	K	H	ST-26	E&J	
		"1910" (All Roadsters are marked "1910")								
38,000	Feb 10	Touring	Blue	KH	R	K	H	ST-26	E&J	
38,100	Feb 13	Touring	Blue	KH	R	H	H	ST-26	E&J	
38,164	Feb 15	Op. Rbt.	Blue	H	R	K	H	ST-26	E&J	1911 fr.axle
38,200	Feb 14	Touring	Blue	P	R	K	H	ST-26	E&J	1911 fr.axle
38,263	Feb 14	Touring	Blue	P	R	K	H	ST-26	E&J	Body #4073
										"Babbitt bearing motor"
38,300	Feb 14	Touring	Blue	KH	R	K	K	ST-26	E&J	Body #795
38,400	Feb 15	Touring	Blue	P	R	K	K	ST-26	E&J	Body #2038
38,471	Feb 16	Touring	Blue	P	R	K	K	ST-26	E&J	Body #1336 WT*
		* NOTE: WT = "1911 wide transmission cover."								
38,500	Feb 16	Touring	Blue	P	R	K	H	ST-26	E&J	Body #895
38,575	Feb 17	Roadster	Blue	P	R	K	K	ST-26	E&J	Body #5705 WT
38,600	Feb 17	Touring	Blue	KH	R	K	H	ST-26	E&J	Body #1557
38,700	Feb 18	Touring	Blue	P	R	K	H	ST-26	E&J	Body #458
38,800	Feb 20	Touring	Blue	KH	R	K	H	ST-26	E&J	Body #2628
38,900	Illegible	invoice								
38,901	Feb 21	Runabout	Blue	H	R	K	H	ST-26	E&J	Body #152
38,996	Feb 21	First marked "1911 New Transmission Cover." (NT)								
		("New" and "Wide" probably the same cover.)								
39,000	Feb 21	Touring	Blue	KH	R	K	H	ST-26	E&J	Body #2717 NT
39,100	Feb 22	Touring	Blue	KH	R	K	H	ST-26	E&J	Body #2470 WT
39,200	Feb 22	Touring	Blue	KH	R	K	H	ST-26	E&J	Body #2540 WT
39,300	Feb 23	'10 Rdstr	Blue	P	R	P	H	ST-26	E&J	Body #4938 WT
39,400	Feb 23	Touring	Blue	P		K	H			Body #4048 WT
39,500	Feb 24	Torpedo	Blue	H	R	K	H	ST-26	E&J	WT
39,600	Feb 24	Engine only				K				
39,700	Feb 24	Touring	Blue	KH	R	K	H	ST-26	E&J	Body #2771 WT
39,800	Feb 25	Touring	Blue	P	R	K	H	ST-26	E&J	Body #4667 NT
39,900	Feb 27	Touring	Blue	KH	R	K	H	ST-26	E&J	Body #2928 NT
40,000	Feb 28	Touring	Blue	KH	R	K	H	ST-26	E&J	Body #2970 NT
40,001	Feb 28	Touring	Blue	KH	R	K	H	ST-26	E&J	"Babbit bearing motor"
40,013	Feb 27	Touring	Blue	P	R	K	H	ST-26	E&J	NT
40,100	Feb 28	Touring	Blue	P	R	K	K	ST-26	E&J	
40,200	Feb 28	Touring	Blue	KA	R	K	K	ST-26	E&J	

1911

Ser#	Mfg.	Body Style	Color	Mfgr	W/S	Carb	Coil	Speed-ometer	Gas Lamps	Radiator
40,232	Mar 1	Touring	Blue	P	R	K	H	ST-26	E&J	
40,292	Feb 28	Touring	Blue	P	R	K	K	ST-26	E&J	
		"Babbitt bearing motor"								
40,300	Feb 29	Touring	Blue	KA	R	K	K	ST-26	E&J	
40,400	Mar 1	Touring	Blue	P	R	K	H	KILO	E&J	Metric
		(Shipped to France)								
40,500	Mar 2	Touring	Blue	P	R	K	H	ST-26	E&J	
40,600	Mar 2	Touring	Blue	P	R	K	H	ST-26	E&J	
40,700	Mar 3	Touring	Blue	KA	R	K	H	ST-26	E&J	
40,800	Mar 3	Engine only (Canada)				K				
40,861	Mar 3	Touring	Blue	P	R	K	H	ST-26	E&J	
		"Jackson top"								
40,900	Mar 4	Touring	Blue	P	R	K	H	ST-26	E&J	
41,000	Mar 6	Torpedo	Blue	P	R	K	H	ST-26	E&J	
41,100	Mar 6	Touring	Blue	KA	R	K	K	ST-26	E&J	
41,200	Mar 7	Touring	Blue	KA	R	K	K	ST-26	E&J	
41,300	Mar 8	Torpedo	Blue	P	R	K	K	ST-26	E&J	
41,400	Mar 8	Touring	Blue	KA	R	K	H	ST-26	E&J	
41,500	Mar 9	Op. Rbt.	Blue	H	R	K	JB	ST-26	E&J	
41,600	Mar 9	Touring	Blue	KA	R	K	H	ST-26	E&J	
41,700	Mar 9	Engine only				K				
41,706	Mar 9	Torpedo	Blue	P	R	K	H	ST-26	E&J	
41,800	Mar 10	Op. Rbt.	Blue	H	R	K	H	ST-26	E&J	
41,900	Mar 11	Torpedo	Blue	P	R	K	JB	ST-26	E&J	
42,000	Mar 11	Touring	Blue	KA	R	K	H	ST-26	E&J	
42,100	Mar 13	Touring	Blue	P	R	K	H	ST-26	E&J	
42,200	Invoice missing									
42,201	Mar 13	Touring	Blue	KA	R	K	H	ST-26	E&J	
42,256	Mar 14	Touring	Blue	AM	M	K	H	ST-26	E&J	
		First "New style fan belt"								
42,258	Mar 14	Touring	Blue	P	M	K	H	ST-26	E&J	
42,300	Mar 15	Torpedo	Blue	P	M	H	H	ST-26	E&J	
42,400	Mar 14	Engine only								
42,412	Mar 14	Roadster	Blue	P	R	H	H	ST-26	E&J	NT
42,500	Mar 15	Touring	Blue	P	–	H	H	ST-26	E&J	
42,600	Mar 15	Touring	Blue	P	–	H	H	–	–	
42,700	Mar 17	Touring	Blue	P	M	H	H	ST-26	E&J	
42,800	Mar 17	Touring	Blue	KA	M	H	H	ST-26	E&J	
42,900	Mar 17	Touring	Blue	P	M	H	H	ST-26	E&J	
43,000	Mar 20	Touring	Blue	P	M	H	JB	ST-26	E&J	
43,100	Invoice missing									
43,101	Mar 20	Torpedo	Blue	P	M	H	JB	ST-26	E&J	
43,200	Mar 20	Touring	Blue	P	M	H	JB	ST-26	E&J	
43,300	Mar 21	Touring	Blue	AM	M	H	H	ST-26	E&J	
43,400	Mar 21	Touring	Blue	AM	M	H	H	ST-26	E&J	
43,500	Mar 22	Op. Rbt.	Blue	H	–	H	H	–	–	
43,600	Mar 22	Touring	Blue	P	M	H	H	ST-26	E&J	
43,700	Mar 22	Touring	Blue	P	M	H	H	ST-26	E&J	
43,800	Invoice missing									
43,801	Mar 24	Touring	Blue	P	M	H	H	ST-26	E&J	
43,900	Mar 24	Touring	Blue	AM	M	H	H	ST-26	E&J	
44,000	Mar 24	Touring	Blue	P	M	H	K	ST-26	E&J	
44,001	Mar 24	Op. Rbt.	Blue	H	M	H	K	ST-26	E&J	
44,100	Mar 25	Touring	Blue	P	M	H	K	ST-26	E&J	Body #6795
44,200	Mar 27	Torpedo	Blue	P	M	H	K	ST-26	E&J	Body #6839
44,300	Mar 27	Touring	Blue	KH	M	K	K	ST-26	E&J	
44,400	Mar 28	Touring	Blue	KA	M	K	JB	ST-26	E&J	
44,420	Mar 28	Touring	Blue	P	M	H	JB	ST-26	E&J	Body #6228
		FIRST "REMOVABLE BOTTOM"								
44,500	Mar 28	Torpedo	Blue	P	M	K	JB	ST-26	E&J	Body #6946
44,600	Mar 29	Touring	Blue	KA	M	H	JB	ST-26	E&J	Body #5755
44,700	Mar 29	Touring	Blue	AM	M	H	JB	ST-26	E&J	Body #5030
44,800	Mar 30	Op. Rbt.	Blue	H	M	H	JB	ST-26	E&J	Body #801
44,900	Mar 30	Touring	Blue	P	M	H	H	ST-26	E&J	Body #6287
45,000	Mar 31	Op. Rbt.	Blue	H	M	H	H	ST-26	E&J	

Shipping Invoices

1911

Ser#	Mfg.	Body Style	Color	Mfgr	W/S	Carb	Coil	Speed-ometer	Gas Lamps	Radiator
45,030	Mar 31	Torpedo	Blue	P	M	H	H	ST-26	E&J	Body #6314
45,100	Mar 31	Torpedo	Blue	P	M	H	H	ST-26	E&J	Body #7107
45,200	Mar 31	Touring	Blue	P	M	H	H	ST-26	E&J	Body #4984
45,204	Apr 1	Torpedo	Blue	P	M	H	H	ST-26	E&J	
45,300	Apr 1	Torpedo	Blue	P	R	H	H	ST-26	E&J	Body #5886
45,400	Apr 3	Op. Rbt.	Blue	H	M	H	H	ST-26	E&J	
45,500	Apr 3	Engine only (to Canada)								
45,592	Apr 3	Torpedo	Blue	P	M	H	JB	ST-26	E&J	
45,600	Apr 3	Touring	Blue	AM	R	H	JB	ST-26	E&J	
45,694	Apr 4	Touring	Blue	P	R	H	H	ST-26	E&J	Body #7226
45,700	Apr 4	Touring	Blue	P	R	H	H	ST-26	E&J	Body #6424
45,800	Apr 4	Op. Rbt.	Blue	P	R	H	JB	ST-26	E&J	Body #5509
45,900	Apr 5	Touring	Blue	P	R	H	H	ST-26	E&J	Body #6477
46,000	Apr 5	Torpedo	Blue	P	M	H	H	ST-26	E&J	Body #7561
46,100	Apr 6	Torpedo	Blue	P	M	H	H	ST-26	E&J	Body #7584
46,200	Apr 6	Touring	Blue	P	R	H	H	ST-26	E&J	Body #6764
46,263	Apr 6	Touring	Blue	P	R	H	H	ST-26	E&J	Body #6726
46,300	Apr 6	Torpedo	Blue	P	M	H	H	ST-26	E&J	Body #7740
46,326	Apr 7	Torpedo	Blue	P	M	H	H	ST-26	E&J	Body #7528
		First "1911 motor throughout"								
46,400	Apr 7	Touring	Blue	P	R	H	H	ST-26	E&J	Body #7378
46,500	Apr 7	Touring	Blue	P	R	H	H	ST-26	E&J	"All 1911"
46,541	Apr 28	Op. Rbt.	Red	P		H	H	ST-26	BRN	Chassis 4-8-11
46,542	Apr 28	Op. Rbt.	Red	P		H	H	ST-26	BRN	Chassis 4-8-11
46,600	Apr 8	Touring	Blue	AM	R	H	JB	ST-26	E&J	Body #5998
46,683	Apr 10	Twn. Car	Green	P		H	JB			
46,686	Apr 10	Twn. Car	Green	P		H	JB		E&J	
46,700	Apr 10	Touring	Blue	AM	R	H	JB	ST-26	E&J	#6327
46,727 to 46,806 all engines to Walkerville, Canada										
46,807	Apr 10	Torpedo	Blue	AM	M	H	JB	ST-26	E&J	#7693
46,880	Apr 28	Op. Rbt.	Red	P		H	H	ST-26	BRN	
46,882	Apr 28	Op. Rbt.	Red	P	R	H	H	ST-26	E&J	Chassis 4-10-11
46,892	Apr 28	Twn. Car	Green	P		H	H		E&J	Chassis 4-10-11
46,900	Apr 10	Touring	Blue	AM	R	H	H	ST-26	E&J	#6195
47,000	Apr 11	Op. Rbt.	Blue	H	M	H	H	ST-26	E&J	R.B.
		"Square Dash" (S.D.)			"Removable bottom" (R.B.)					
47,100	Apr 11	Roadster	Blue	P	R	H	H	ST-26	E&J	S.D.
47,105	Apr 28	Op. Rbt.	Red	P		H	H	ST-26	E&J	Chassis 4-11-11
47,107	Apr 28	Op. Rbt.	Red	P		H	H	ST-26	E&J	Chassis 4-11-11
47,200	Apr 12	Touring	Blue	P	R	H	H	ST-26	E&J	#6482 S.D.
47,300	Apr 12	Touring	Blue	P	R	H	JB	ST-26	E&J	#7545 R.B.
47,347	Apr 12	Twn. Car	Green	P		H	K			To Bucharest.
47,383	Apr 28	Op. Rbt.	Red	P		H	H	ST-26	BRN	Chassis 4-12-11
47,384	Apr 28	Op. Rbt.	Red	P		H	H		BRN	Chassis 4-12-11
47,389	Apr 12	Twn. Car	Green	P		H	K			
47,400	Apr 13	Touring	Blue	AM	R	H	H	ST-26	E&J	"All 1911"
47,418	Apr 13	Touring	Blue	AM	R	H	H	ST-26	E&J	R.B.
47,478	Apr 13	Torpedo	Blue	P	M	H	JB	ST-26	E&J	"All 1911"
47,500	Apr 14	Op. Rbt.	Blue	P	R	H	H	ST-26	E&J	
47,503	Apr 17	Del. Wgn.	Blue	P	R	H	H	ST-26	E&J	
47,504	Apr 17	Del. Wgn.	Blue	P	R	H	H	ST-26	E&J	
47,505	Apr 17	Del. Wgn.	Blue	P	R	H	H	ST-26	E&J	
47,506 to 47,519 all Delivery Wagons like those above										
47,600	Apr 13	Op. Rbt.	Blue	H	M	H	JB	ST-26	E&J	#424
47,634	Apr 28	Op. Rbt.	Red	P		H	JB	ST-26	BRN	Chassis 4-13-11
47,635	Apr 27	Op. Rbt.	Red	P		H	JB	ST-26	BRN	Chassis 4-12-11
47,700	Apr 14	Touring	Blue	KA	R(?)	H	JB	ST-26	E&J	#5982 R.B.
47,800	Apr 14	Touring	Blue	KA	R	H	K	ST-26	E&J	#5999 R.B.
47,900	Apr 14	Torpedo	Blue	P	M	H	H	ST-26	E&J	"All 1911"
48,000	Apr 15	Torpedo	Blue	P	M	H	H	ST-26	E&J	"All 1911"
48,100	Apr 17	Torpedo	Blue	P	M	H	H	ST-26	E&J	"All 1911"
48,200	Apr 17	Torpedo	Blue	P	M	H	JB	ST-26	E&J	
48,204	Apr 17	Twn. Car	Green	P		H	JB	ST-26	E&J	
48,300	Apr 18	Torpedo	Blue	P	M	H	H	ST-26	E&J	
48,400	Apr 18	Touring	Blue	P	M	H	JB	ST-26	E&J	

1911

Ser#	Mfg.	Body Style	Color	Mfgr	W/S	Carb	Coil	Speed-ometer	Gas Lamps	Radiator
48,500	Apr 19	Touring	Blue	AM	R	H	H	ST-26	E&J	
48,600	Apr 19	Touring	Blue	AM	R	H	H	ST-26	E&J	
48,700	Apr 19	Touring	Blue	P	R	H	H	ST-26	E&J	"All 1911"
48,800	Apr 20	Torpedo	Blue	P	M	H	H	ST-26	E&J	
48,900	Apr 20	Touring	Blue	KA	–	H	H	ST-26	E&J	R.B.
48,955	Apr 21	Twn. Car	Blue	P		J	JB		E&J	

Invoice marked "**Worm steering gear.**"   Sent to Germany.

Ser#	Mfg.	Body Style	Color	Mfgr	W/S	Carb	Coil	Speed-ometer	Gas Lamps	Radiator
49,000	Apr 21	Torpedo	Blue	P	M	H	H	ST-26	E&J	R.B.
49,100	Apr 21	Torpedo	Blue	P	M	H	H	ST-26	E&J	R.B.
49,200	Apr 22	Torpedo	Blue	P	M	H	H	ST-26	E&J	R.B.
49,240	Apr 22	Twn. Car	Blue	P		H	H			
49,289	Apr 24	Touring	Blue	AM	R	H	H			Body # 7402

"Square dash." To Los Angeles, Calif.

Ser#	Mfg.	Body Style	Color	Mfgr	W/S	Carb	Coil	Speed-ometer	Gas Lamps	Radiator
49,300	Apr 22	Engine only (To Canada)								
49,311	Apr 22	Torpedo	Blue	P	M	H	H	ST-26	E&J	R.B.
49,400	Apr 24	Torpedo	Blue	P	M	H	H	ST-26	E&J	"All 1911"
49,500	Apr 24	Touring	Blue	KH	R	H	H	ST-26	E&J	R.B.
49,600	Apr 25	Touring	Blue	P	R	H	H	ST-26	E&J	"All 1911"
49,700	Apr 26	Engine only (to Canada)								
49,723	Apr 25	Touring	Blue	KH	R	H	H	ST-26	E&J	"All 1911"
49,747	Apr 25	Touring	Blue	AM	R	H	H	ST-26	E&J	"All 1911"
49,800	Apr 25	Touring	Blue	P	R	H	H	ST-26	E&J	"All 1911"
49,900	Apr 26	Touring	Blue	P	R	H	H	ST-26	E&J	"All 1911"
49,936	Apr 26	Touring	Blue	KH	R	H	H	ST-26	E&J	"All 1911"
50,000	Apr 26	Touring	Blue	P	R	K	K	ST-26	E&J	"All 1911"
50,100	Apr 26	Torpedo	Blue	P	M	H	K	ST-26	E&J	"All 1911"
50,183	Apr 27	Touring	Blue	P	R	H	K	ST-26	E&J	
50,200	Apr 27	Touring	Blue	KH	R	H	K	ST-26	E&J	
50,300	Apr 27	Touring	Blue	P	R	H	K	ST-26	E&J	
50,364	Apr 27	Touring	Blue	P	R	H	K	ST-26	E&J	"All 1911"
50,385	May 1	Touring	Blue	P	R	H	K	ST-26	E&J	
50,400	May 16	Roadster	Blue	P	M	K	H	ST-26	BRN	"Spec. 1911"
50,500	Apr 28	Touring	Blue	KH	R	H	K	ST-26	E&J	Body #7305
50,600	Apr 28	Touring	Blue	P	M	H	K	ST-26	E&J	Body #8648
50,700	Apr 29	Op. Rbt.	Blue	P	M	H	H	ST-26	E&J	
50,800	Apr 29	Engine only (to Canada)								
50,880	Apr 29	Touring	Blue	P	R	K	H	ST-26	E&J	Body #8879
50,881	May 1	Torpedo	Blue	P	M	K	H	ST-26	E&J	Body #5085
50,894	Apr 29	Touring	Blue	P	R	K	H	ST-26	E&J	"All 1911"
50,900	May 1	Touring	Blue	AM	R	K	H	ST-26	E&J	Body #7666
51,000	May 1	Touring	Blue	P	R	K	H	ST-26	E&J	Body #8631
51,100	May 1	Touring	Blue	P	R	K	K	ST-26	E&J	Body #8904
51,200	May 2	Touring	Blue	P	R	K	H	ST-26	E&J	Body #8496
51,300	May 2	Touring	Blue	KH	R	K	H	ST-26	E&J	Body #7113
51,358	May 3	Touring	Blue	P	R	K	H	ST-26	E&J	Body #8640
51,400	May 3	Touring	Blue	AM	R	K	H	ST-26	E&J	Body #7753
51,500	May 3	Engine only (to Canada)								
51,600	May 3	Touring	Blue	KH	R	K	H	ST-26	E&J	Body #7640
51,700	May 3	Touring	Blue	AM	R	K	H	ST-26	E&J	Body #8001
51,800	May 4	Touring	Blue	AM	R	K	H	ST-26	E&J	Body #8633
51,900	May 4	Op. Rbt.	Blue	P	M	K	H	ST-26	E&J	Body #372
52,000	May 5	Touring	Blue	AM		K	H			Body #7980
52,100	May 5	Touring	Blue	P	M	K	H	ST-26	E&J	Body #9342
52,200	May 5	Touring	Blue	P	M	K	H	ST-26	E&J	Body #9038
52,300	May 6	Touring	Blue	KH	M	K	H	ST-26	E&J	Body #7729 P*

* NOTE: During this period engines were supplied in a mix of (P)artial and (A)ll 1911 types.

Ser#	Mfg.	Body Style	Color	Mfgr	W/S	Carb	Coil	Speed-ometer	Gas Lamps	Radiator
52,400	May 6	Touring	Blue	P	M	K	H	ST-26	E&J	Body #9678 A
52,500	May 10	Roadster	Blue	P	R	K	H	"Spec. 1911 body"		#303
52,506	May 8	Touring	Blue	AM	M	K	H	ST-26	E&J	Body #8003
52,568	May 8	Touring	Blue	AM	M	K	H	ST-26	E&J	"All 1911"
52,600	May 8	Torpedo	Blue	P	M	K	H	ST-26	E&J	Body #4447
52,700	May 9	Touring	Blue	KH	M	K	H	ST-26	E&J	Body #7127 A
52,800	May 9	Op. Rbt.	Blue	P	M	K	H	ST-26	E&J	Body #455
52,900	May 9	Touring	Blue	P	M	H	H	ST-26	E&J	Body #8863 A
53,000	May 10	Touring	Blue	AM		H	H	ST-26	E&J	Body #9508 P

Shipping Invoices

1911

Ser#	Mfg.	Body Style	Color	Mfgr	W/S	Carb	Coil	Speed-ometer	Gas Lamps	Radiator	
53,100	May 10	Touring	Blue	AM		H	H	ST-26	E&J	Body #9437	
53,200	May 10	Op. Rbt.	Blue	P	M	K	H	ST-26	E&J	Body #325	A
53,300	May 11	Op. Rbt.	Blue	P	M	K	H	ST-26	E&J	Body #350	A
53,400	May 11	Roadster	Blue	P	M	H	H	"Spec. 1911 body" #7089			A
53,500	May 12	Touring	Blue	P	M	K	H	ST-26	E&J	Body #9311	
53,600	May 12	Touring	Blue	AM	M	K	H	ST-26	E&J	Body #8297	
53,700	May 12	Engine only									
53,800	May 12	Touring	Blue	P	M	K	H	ST-26	E&J	Body #9170	
53,890	Invoice missing										
53,900	May 13	Touring	Blue	P	M	K	H	ST-26	E&J	Body #9336	
54,000	May 15	Torpedo	Blue	P	M	K	H	ST-26	E&J	Body #8647	P
54,100	May 15	Touring	Blue	AM	M	K	H	ST-26	E&J	Body #8265	A
54,200	May 16	Torpedo	Blue	P	M	K	H	ST-26	E&J	Body #5431	A
54,202	May 16	Touring	Blue	KH	M	K	H	ST-26	E&J	"All 1911"	
54,300	Invoice missing										
54,301	May 16	Touring	Blue	KH		K	H	ST-26	E&J	Body #8658	A
54,331	May 16	Torpedo	Blue	P	M	K	H	ST-26	E&J	"All 1911"	
54,400	May 16	Touring	Blue	P	M	K	H	ST-26	E&J	Body #9792	A
54,404	May 16	Touring	Blue	P	M	K	H	ST-26	E&J	Body #10005	
54,500	May 17	Touring	Blue	P	M	K	H	ST-26	E&J	Body #9322	A

All ST-26 and E&J unless noted otherwise below.

Ser#	Mfg.	Body Style	Color	Mfgr	W/S	Carb	Coil	Speed-ometer	Gas Lamps	Radiator	
54,600	May 17	Torpedo	Blue	P	M	K	H			"All 1911 motor"	
54,700	May 17	Touring	Blue	AM	M	K	H			"All 1911 motor"	
54,800	May 17	Touring	Blue	AM	M	K	H			"All 1911 motor"	
54,900	May 18	Touring	Blue	AM	M	K	H			"Removable bottom"	
55,000	May 18	Touring	Blue	P	M	K	H			"All 1911 motor"	
55,100	May 19	Roadster	Blue	P	M	K	H			"All 1911 motor"	
		"Special 1911"									
55,200	May 19	Roadster	Blue	P	M	K	H			"All 1911 motor"	
		"Special 1911"									
55,300	May 19	Touring	Blue	KH	M	K	H			"All 1911 motor"	
55,400	May 20	Touring	Blue	KH	M	K	H			"All 1911 motor"	
55,500	May 20	Roadster	Blue	P	M	K	H			"All 1911 motor"	
		"Special 1911"									
55,600	May 22	Touring	Blue	P	M	K	H			"All 1911 motor"	
55,700	May 22	Touring	Blue	AM	VG	K	H			"All 1911 motor"	
55,800	May 22	Touring	Blue	P	VG	H	H			"All 1911 motor"	
55,900	Invoice missing										
55,901	May 23	Roadster	Blue	P	VG	K	H			"All 1911 motor"	
		"Special 1911"									
55,988	May 23	Touring	Blue	KH	VG	K	H	ST-26	E&J		
56,000	May 23	Touring	Blue	AM	M	K	H			"All 1911 motor"	
56,100	May 24	Touring	Blue	AM	M	K	H			"All 1911 motor"	
56,200	May 24	Touring	Blue	AM	VG	K	H			"All 1911 motor"	
56,300	May 24	Touring	Blue	AM	M	K	H	ST-26	E&J	Body #8247	
56,400	May 25	Touring	Blue	KH	M	K	H	ST-26	E&J	Body #9052	P
56,500	May 25	Touring	Blue	P	M	H	H	ST-26	E&J	Body #10662	P
56,600	May 26	Touring	Blue	P	M	K	H	ST-26	E&J	Body #10431	A
56,700	May 26	Torpedo	Blue	P	M	K	H	ST-26	E&J	Body #408	A
		(More likely an Open Runabout, according to the body number)									
56,769	May 26	Touring	Blue	P	M	K	H	ST-26	E&J		
56,800	May 26	Touring	Blue	P	M	K	H	ST-26	E&J	Body #10676	A
56,900	May 27	Touring	Blue	P	M	K	H	ST-26	E&J	Body #10876	A
57,000	May 27	Torpedo	Blue	P	M	K	H	ST-26	E&J	Body #5069	A
57,100	May 31	Touring	Blue	KH	M	K	H	ST-26	E&J	Body #9046	A
57,200	May 31	Touring	Blue	P	M	K	H	ST-26	E&J	Body #10654	A
57,294	Jun 1	Touring	Blue	P	M	K	H	ST-26	E&J	Body #10972	A
57,300	Jun 1	Touring	Blue	AM	M	K	H	ST-26	E&J	Body #10570	A
		"1910 mud shields"									
57,326	Jun 1	Touring	Blue	KH	M	K	H	ST-26	E&J	Body #8952	
57,400	Jun 1	Touring	Blue	KH		K	H				
57,421	Jun 1	Engine only	**"NEW STYLE TRANSMISSION COVER"** (Only a few listed)								
57,500	Jun 2	Roadster	Blue	P	M	K	H	"Special 1911 body" #7754			A

Ser#	Mfg.	Body Style	Color	Mfgr	W/S	Carb	Coil	Speed-ometer	Gas Lamps	Radiator
57,528	Jun 2	Touring	Blue	P	M	H	H		E&J	Body #11109 P
		LAST "Removable bottom" listed. "All 1911 motors" after this date.								
57,600	Jun 2	Torpedo	Blue	P	M	H	H	ST-26	E&J	Body #5904
57,700	Jun 3	Roadster	Blue	P	M	K	H	ST-26	E&J	Body #7695
57,800	Jun 5	Touring	Blue	P	M	H	H	ST-26	E&J	Body #9553
		(RHD, metric, shipped to Hungary)								
57,900	Jun 5	Touring	Blue	KH	M	K	H	ST-26	E&J	Body #9589
58,000	Jun 6	Touring	Blue	AM	M	K	H	ST-26	E&J	Body #10602
58,100	Jun 6	Touring	Blue	P	M	K	H	ST-26	E&J	Body #11133
58,200	Jun 7	Touring	Blue	P	M	K	H	ST-26	E&J	Body #11142
58,300	Jun 8	Engine only (to Canada)								
58,400	Jun 9	Torpedo	Blue			H	H			
58,500	Jun 10	Op. Rbt.	Blue			K	H			
58,600	Jun 12	Touring	Blue	KH	M	K	H	ST-26	E&J	
58,700	Jun 13	Op. Rbt.	Blue	P	M	K	H	ST-26	E&J	
58,800	Jun 14	Touring	Blue	P	M	K	H	ST-26	E&J	
58,900	Jun 15	Touring	Blue	KH	VG	K	H	ST-26	E&J	
59,000	Jun 16	Touring	Blue	P	VG	K	H			
59,100	Jun 12	Engine only (to Canada)								
59,200	Jun 13	Engine only (to Canada)								
59,300	Jun 17	Engine only (to Canada)								
59,321	Jun 16	Torpedo	Blue	P	M	K	H			
59,400	Jun 17	Touring	Blue	KH	V	K	H			"1910 runningboards"
		"1910 runningboards" used on a number of cars.								
59,500	Jun 19	Touring	Blue		V	K	H			"1910 runningboards"
59,600	Jun 20	Touring	Blue		V	K	H			
59,700	Jun 21	Touring	Blue		V	K	H			
59,800	Jun 23	Touring	Blue		V	K	H			
59,900	Jun 23	Torpedo	Blue			K	H			
60,000	Jun 26	Touring	Blue		V	K	H			
60,100	Jun 26	Roadster	Blue		V	K	H			
60,200	Jun 27	Touring	Blue		V	K	H			
60,283	Jun 27	Engine only (to Canada)								
60,300	Jun 28	Torpedo	Blue			K	H			
60,400		Invoice missing								
60,401	Jun 29	Touring	Blue	KH	V	K	H	ST-26	E&J	Body #9565
60,500	Jun 29	Torpedo	Blue	P	M	K	H	ST-26	E&J	
60,600	Jun 30	Touring	Blue	P	M	H	K*	ST-26	E&J	
		* Kingston "Latest type"								
		Beginning in July many invoices were marked "New style cushions."								
60,620	Jul 5	Touring	Blue	P	M	K	H	ST-26	E&J	
60,700	Jul 5	Torpedo	Blue	P	M	K	H	ST-26	E&J	Body #5389
60,765	Jul 7	Touring	Blue	H	R	K	H	ST-26	E&J	Body #10309
60,800	Jul 7	Touring	Blue	P	R	K	K	ST-26	E&J	Body #11300
60,834	Jul 7	Touring	Blue	H	R	K	H	ST-26	E&J	Body #10307
		"No heel door on Hayes bodies"								
60,900	Jul 11	Torpedo	Blue	W	M	K	H	ST-26	E&J	Body #6634
61,000	Jul 11	Touring	Blue	H	R	K	H	ST-26	E&J	Body #10462
61,100	Jul 13	Touring	Blue	H	R	K	H	ST-26	E&J	Body #10396
61,147	Jul 14	Touring	Blue	H	R	K	JB	ST-26	E&J	
		"1912 axle" (12-rivet?)								
61,177	Jul 14	Torpedo	Blue	P		K	JB			Body #7303
61,200	Jul 15	Touring	Blue	H	R	K	JB	ST-26	E&J	Body #10228
61,300	Jul 17	Touring	Blue	H		K	JB	ST-26	BRN	Body #10624
61,400	Jul 20	Touring	Blue	H	R	K	K	ST-26	BRN	Body #10217
61,500	Jul 22	Torpedo	Blue	W	M	K	K	ST-26	BRN	Body #6905
61,600	Jul 25	Touring	Blue	H	R	H	H	ST-26	BRN	Body #12959
61,700	Jul 26	Touring	Blue	H	R	K	JB	ST-26	BRN	Body #10831
61,800	Jul 27	Touring	Blue	H	R	K	JB	ST-26	BRN	Body #10477
61,900	Jul 27	Torpedo	Blue	W	M	K	H	ST-26	BRN	
62,000	Jul 28	Touring	Blue	H	R	K	H	ST-26	BRN	Body #10714
62,100	Jul 29	Touring	Blue	P	R	K	JB	ST-26	BRN	Body #13187
62,200	Jul 23	"Stock Car Racer" built for Kulick								

Shipping Invoices

1911

Ser#	Mfg.	Body Style	Color	Mfgr	W/S	Carb	Coil	Speed-ometer	Gas Lamps	Radiator

Beginning in August many invoices marked "No stripes on gear and fenders."

Ser#	Mfg.	Body Style	Color	Mfgr	W/S	Carb	Coil	Speed-ometer	Gas Lamps	Radiator
62,239	Aug 1	Touring	Blue	P	R	K	JB	ST-26	BRN	Body #13399
62,263	Aug 1	Touring	Blue	H	R	K	JB	ST-26	BRN	"1912 axle"
62,300	Aug 1	Touring	Blue	H	R	K	JB	ST-26	BRN	Body #10420
62,400	Aug 2	Town Car	Blue	P		K	JB			E&J side, BRN tail lamps, No headlmaps, to England. Body #125
62,500	Aug 2	Touring	Blue	P	R	K	JB			Body #13168

BRN side & tail, E&J generator, but no headlamps.

Ser#	Mfg.	Body Style	Color	Mfgr	W/S	Carb	Coil	Speed-ometer	Gas Lamps	Radiator
62,600	Aug 2	Touring	Blue	H		K	JB	ST-26	BRN	Body #11171
62,700	Aug 3	Touring	Blue	H	R	K	JB	R**	BRN	

Any combination of E&J and Brown side and tail lamps and generator might be used in production. ** R=Regular, presumably Stewart Model 26.

Ser#	Mfg.	Body Style	Color	Mfgr	W/S	Carb	Coil	Speed-ometer	Gas Lamps	Radiator
62,800	Aug 5	Town Car	Blue	P	R	K	JB	R	BRN	
62,900	Aug 5	Touring	Blue	P	R	K	JB	R	BRN	
63,000	Aug 7	Touring	Blue	H	R	K	JB	R	BRN	
63,100	Aug 7	Touring	Blue	H	R	K	JB	R	BRN	
63,150	Aug 8	Touring	Blue	P	R	K	JB	—	BRN	1912 axle, 1911 motor
63,200	Aug 8	Touring	Blue	H	R	K	JB	R	BRN	Body #11371
63,300	Aug 11	Touring	Blue	H	R	K	JB	R	BRN	Body #11529
63,400	Aug 9	Touring	Blue	P	R	K	JB	R	BRN	Body #12646
63,500	Aug 10	Touring	Blue	P	R	K	JB	R	BRN	Body #12934
63,600	Aug 11	Touring	Blue	P	R	K	JB	R	BRN	Body #13134
63,700	Aug 12	Touring	Blue	P	R	K	H	R	BRN	
63,762	Aug 16	Touring	Blue	P	R	K	H	R	BRN	
63,800	Aug 12	Touring	Blue	H	R	K	K	R	BRN	Body #11485
63,900	Aug 12	Touring	Blue	P	R	K	K	R	BRN	Body #12836
64,000	Aug 14	Touring	Blue	P	R	K	K	R	BRN	Body #13385
64,100	Invoice missing									
64,101	Aug 15	Touring	Blue	P	R	K	K	R	BRN	Body #13950
64,108	Aug 15	Touring	Blue	P	R	K	K	R	BRN	

"No striping on gear and fenders"

Ser#	Mfg.	Body Style	Color	Mfgr	W/S	Carb	Coil	Speed-ometer	Gas Lamps	Radiator
64,200	Aug 15	Touring	Blue	H	R	K	K	R	BRN	
64,300	Aug 16	Touring	Blue	P	R	K	H	R	BRN	Body #13904
64,400	Aug 16	Touring	Blue	H(KA)	R	K	H	R	BRN	Body #11602
64,500	Aug 17	Touring	Blue	P	R	K	H	R	BRN	
64,550	Aug 17	Touring	Blue	P	R	K	H	R	BRN	
64,600	Aug 17	Touring	Blue	H	R	K	H	R	BRN	
64,627	Aug 17	Touring	Blue	P	R	K	H	R	BRN	Body #13974
64,700	Aug 18	Touring	Blue	P	R	K	H	R	BRN	
64,800	Aug 19	Touring	Blue	P	R	K	H	R	BRN	Body #13571
64,900	Aug 19	Touring	Blue	P	R	K	H	R	BRN	Body #13210

NOTE: Apparently striping on the running gear and fenders was common until August 1911. Many invoices note its discontinuance.

Ser#	Mfg.	Body Style	Color	Mfgr	W/S	Carb	Coil	Speed-ometer	Gas Lamps	Radiator
64,966	Aug 19	Touring	Blue	P	R	K	H	R	BRN	
65,000	Aug 21	Touring	Blue	H(KA)	R	K	H	R	BRN	
65,100	Aug 21	Touring	Blue	H(KA)	R	K	H	R	BRN	Body #12173
65,200	Aug 21	Touring	Blue	H(KA)	R	K	H	R	BRN	Body #12005
65,300	Aug 22	Touring	Blue	P	R	K	H	R	BRN	Body #13253
65,390	Aug 22	Touring	Blue	P/AM	R	K	H	R	BRN	
65,400	Aug 22	Touring	Blue	P	R	K	H	R	BRN	
65,500	Aug 23	Torpedo	Blue	W	M	K	H	R	BRN	Body #6968
65,600	Invoice missing									
65,601	Aug 23	Touring	Blue	HA#		K	JB	R	BRN	Body #14639

HA=Hayes-American. HB=Hayes-Briggs.

Ser#	Mfg.	Body Style	Color	Mfgr	W/S	Carb	Coil	Speed-ometer	Gas Lamps	Radiator
65,700	Aug 24	Touring	Blue	P	R	K	H	R	BRN	Body #14378
65,800	Aug 25	Touring	Blue	P	R	K	H	R	BRN	Body #12451
65,900	Invoice missing									
65,901	Aug 25	Touring	Blue	HA	R	K	H	R	BRN	Body #11483
66,000	Aug 26	Touring	Blue	P	R	K	H	R	BRN	Body #15212
66,002	Aug 25	Touring	Blue	P	R	K	H	R	BRN	"1912 axle"
66,100	Aug 28	Touring	Blue	P	R	K	H	R	BRN	Body #14010
66,200	Aug 28	Touring	Blue	HB	R	K	H	R	BRN	Body #12485
66,300	Aug 29	Touring	Blue	HA	R	H	H	R	BRN	Body #12409
66,399	Aug 29	Touring	Blue	P	R	H	H	R	BRN	Body #14944

66,400 to 66,499 invoices missing

Ser#	Mfg.	Body Style	Color	Mfgr	W/S	Carb	Coil	Speed-ometer	Gas Lamps	Radiator
66,500	Aug 30	Touring	Blue	P	R	H	H	R	BRN	
66,600	Aug 30	Touring	Blue	HA	R	K	H	R	BRN	Body #12595
66,620	Aug 30	Roadster	Blue	P	R	K	H	R	BRN	Body #15763

"1909 rear fenders," Brown side, E&J tail lamps.

Ser#	Mfg.	Body Style	Color	Mfgr	W/S	Carb	Coil	Speed-ometer	Gas Lamps	Radiator
66,700	Aug 31	Touring	Blue	H	R	K	H	R	BRN	Body #12630
66,800	Aug 31	Touring	Blue	P	R	K	H	R	BRN	Body #15775

E&J tail, Brown side and head lamps.

Ser#	Mfg.	Body Style	Color	Mfgr	W/S	Carb	Coil	Speed-ometer	Gas Lamps	Radiator
66,900	Aug 31	Touring	Blue	P	R	K	H	R	BRN	Body #14662

NOTE: The new "1912" speedometer steering arm began in late August 1911.

Ser#	Mfg.	Body Style	Color	Mfgr	W/S	Carb	Coil	Speed-ometer	Gas Lamps	Radiator
66,921	Sep 1	Touring	Blue	H	R	K	H	R	E&J tail, BRN H & S	
67,000	Sep 1	Touring	Blue	P	R	K	H	R	E&J tail, BRN H & S	
67,100	Sep 1	Touring	Blue	P	R	K	H	R	E&J tail, BRN H & S	
67,200	Sep 8	Engine only (RHD, to Canada)								
67,201	Sep 8	Touring	Blue	P	R	K	H	R	All BRN lamps	
67,300	Invoice missing									
67,301	Sep 5	Touring	Blue	HB	R	K	H		All BRN lamps	
67,400	Sep 5	Touring	Blue	HB	R	K	K**		All BRN lamps	

** "1912 Kingston"

Ser#	Mfg.	Body Style	Color	Mfgr	W/S	Carb	Coil	Speed-ometer	Gas Lamps	Radiator
67,500	Sep 6	Op. Rbt.	Blue	P	M	K	H		All BRN lamps	
67,600	Sep 7	Touring	Blue	HB	R	K	H		All BRN lamps	
67,700	Sep 7	Op. Rbt.	Blue	P	–	K	H		All BRN lamps	
67,800	Sep 7	Roadster	Blue	P	R	K	H			"Special 1911"
67,900	Sep 8	Touring	Blue	HB	R	K	H		All BRN lamps	
67,919	Sep 8	Engine only (LHD) to Canada								
68,000	Sep 8	Touring	Blue	P	R	K	H		All BRN lamps	
68,100	Sep 9	Touring	Blue	P	R	K	K		All BRN lamps	
68,150	Sep 11	Runabout	Blue	P	R	K	H		Brown generator	
68,200	Sep 9	Touring	Blue	P	R	K	H		All BRN lamps	
68,300	Sep 11	Touring	Blue	P	R	K	H		All BRN lamps	
68,400	Sep 13*	Op. Rbt.	**Red**	P	–	H	H		All E&J lamps	

* Scratched out, October 26, 1911 added. "Special for KFD (or AFD, or HFD)"

Ser#	Mfg.	Body Style	Color	Mfgr	W/S	Carb	Coil	Speed-ometer	Gas Lamps	Radiator
68,500	Sep 12	Touring	Blue	H/KAR	R	H	H		All BRN lamps	
68,600	Sep 13	Touring	Blue	P	R	H	H		All BRN lamps	
68,700	Sep 14	Roadster	Blue	P	R	K	H		"1912 rear fenders"	
68,800	Sep 15	Touring	Blue	H/KAR	K	H			All BRN lamps	
68,900	Sep 15	Del. Wag.	R/B	P	R	K	H			

(Perhaps the first of the 1912 Delivery Wagons. Apparently red body with standard blue fenders.)

Ser#	Mfg.	Body Style	Color	Mfgr	W/S	Carb	Coil	Speed-ometer	Gas Lamps	Radiator
69,000	Sep 28	Engine only (RHD, to Canada)								
69,100	Sep 15	Touring	Blue	P	R	K	H		All BRN lamps	
69,200	Sep 20	Touring	Blue	P	R	K	K		All BRN lamps	
69,300	Sep 19	Op. Rbt.	Blue	P	M	K	K		All BRN lamps	
69,350	Sep 19	Op. Rbt.	Blue	P	M	K	K		All BRN lamps.	

"1912 axle. No stripes"

Ser#	Mfg.	Body Style	Color	Mfgr	W/S	Carb	Coil	Speed-ometer	Gas Lamps	Radiator
69,400	Invoice missing. Engine used in car 80917, October 18, 1911, according to a note in the file.									
69,401	Sep 20	Touring	Blue	P	R	H	K		All BRN lamps	

NOTE: Records are incomplete beginning mid-September.

Ser#	Mfg.	Body Style	Color	Mfgr	W/S	Carb	Coil	Speed-ometer	Gas Lamps	Radiator
69,506	Sep 25	Del. Wg.	R/B	P	R	K	K		All BRN lamps (R/B = Red/Blue)	
69,600	Oct 9	"Placed in car 80461 October 9, 1911"								
69,700	Oct 10	"Placed in car 80635 October 10, 1911"								
69,806	Sep 24	Touring	Blue	P	R	K	K		All BRN lamps	
69,900	Sep 30	Touring	Blue	P	R	K	K		All BRN lamps	
70,003	Sep 28	Engine only								
70,100	Oct 7	"Placed in car 80321 October 7, 1911"								
70,241	Sep 27	Touring	Blue	H/KAR	K	H			All BRN lamps	
70,499	Sep 28	Touring	Blue	P	R	H	K		All BRN lamps	
70,702	Sep 29	Touring	Blue	P/AMR	H	K			All BRN lamps	
70,750	Oct 5	Engine only		"1912 commutator" (First such note found)						
70,915		Engine only (to Canada)								

Beyond this number, hand-written notes "# xxx placed in car xxx" are all that are in the microfilms. These were apparently written about 1951 when the microfilms were made. The original documents were apparently destroyed. No later invoices are known to exist.

Shipping Invoices

ENGINE SERIAL NUMBERS

The serial (engine) numbers listed here are taken directly from the daily log books of the engine assembly department of the Ford Motor Company. These original books are complete from 1915 until the end of Model T engine production in 1941. (Records prior to 1914 have apparently been lost.) These books are on file at the Ford Archives in Dearborn, Michigan.

While factory engine production records from October 1908 (the beginning of Model T production) until January 1915 are no longer extant, daily production figures (the number of units built) for 1913 and 1914 do exist, and the serial numbers for these two years have been derived from those figures. They appear to be accurate, agreeing with known numbers of that period. The engine (serial) number dates prior to 1913 are from Ford's published records and are not necessarily absolutely accurate. Those numbers noted under "Comments" are believed to be accurate.

Car shipping invoices from about 1,119 to about 70,000 (early 1909 to late 1911) have been found and CAR production dates are noted here with a pound sign (#). Engine and car numbers were the same during this period, but cars (chassis) were assembled after the engines were built; sometimes the same day but sometimes days or weeks later.

During the Model T era, great numbers of engines were assembled at the Ford branches. Apparently Ford printed engine number job sheets which were numbered in advance, and these were attached to engines being assembled These job sheet numbers were stamped into the cylinder block when the job was completed. Groups of these engine number records (not engines) were also shipped out, and these numbers were then stamped on the engines when they were completed at some Ford branch. Some of these record number shipments were noted, but most were not. As a result, while the Highland Park (or, later, the Rouge Plant) assembled engines on the days indicated, other blocks of engines might have been assembled days or weeks later. Where blocks of numbers are noted "omitted," these number records went to other assembly plants; quite often to Manchester, England.

The author cannot stress too strongly that care must be used when attempting to accurately date a car by its engine number. Remember that the dates shown are those when the engine assembly was completed, *not the car*, or the date a block of engine number records were shipped to another assembly plant. Furthermore, Ford only stamped a serial number on a completed engine (engine, transmission, pan, head, etc.) during the Model T era, not on a bare block or a "short block" which was destined for the replacement market. It was common practice to stamp a replacement (unnumbered) engine with the serial number of the original engine. This, of course, accounts for the many engines found today which were, judging from the serial number, built before the casting date. In addition, engines were changed when the original was found to be defective, thereby putting a later engine in an earlier car. To say nothing of the engine swaps made outside the Ford organization over the past eighty years!

501

OCTOBER 1908

Day	First Number	Last Number	Production
	1	11	11

NOVEMBER 1908

Day	First Number	Last Number	Production
	12	101	90

DECEMBER 1908

Day	First Number	Last Number	Production
	102	309	219

JANUARY 1909 (First 500 engines used 3/8" head bolts)

Day	First Number	Last Number	Production
	310	646	337

FEBRUARY 1909

Day	First Number	Last Number	Production
	647	1,052	406

MARCH 1909

Day	First Number	Last Number	Production
	1,053	2,025	973 ** (Ford's published data)
			# Car assembly date
3	1,119 #		
16	1,500 #		
18	1,600 #		
23	1,700 #		
25	1,800 #		
29	1,900 #		
31	2,000 #		

APRIL 1909

Day	First Number	Last Number	Production
	2,026	2,691	666 **
1	2,035 #		First car in April.
2	2,100 #		
7	2,200 #		
13	2,300 #		
17	2,400 #		
22	2,448 #		First thermo-syphon engine.

MAY 1909

Day	First Number	Last Number	Production
	2,692	4,036	1345 **
1	2,455 #		First car in May.
4	2,500 #		
13	2,600 #		Engines were apparently held aside during this period, hence the differences in assembly dates.
27(Apr.)	2,700 #		
7	2,800 # (Engine only)		
11	2,900 #		
12	3,000 #		
14	3,100 #		
17	3,200 #		
19	3,300 #		
20	3,400 #		
22	3,500 #		
24	3,600 #		
25	3,700 #		
27	3,800 #		
27	3,900 #		
29	4,000 #		

JUNE 1909

Day	First Number	Last Number	Production
	4,037	5,980	1944 **
1	4,041 #		First car in June.
1	4,100 #		
2	4,200 # ***		*** Engine only.
5	4,300 # ***		
8	4,400 #		
9	4,500 #		
10	4,600 #		
12	4,700 #		
14	4,800 #		
15	4,900 #		
16	5,000 #		Engine built same date.
17	5,100 #		
18	5,200 #		
21	5,300 #		
22	5,400 #		
23	5,500 #		
24	5,600 #		
25	5,700 #		
28	5,800 #		
29	6,000 #		

JULY 1909

Day	First Number	Last Number	Production
	5,981	8,107	2127 **
1	6,006 #		First car in July.
2	6,100 #		
2	6,200 # ***		*** Engine only.
6	6,300 #		
7	6,400 #		
8	6,500 #		
9	6,600 #		
11	6,700 #		
13	6,800 #		
14	6,900 #		
15	7,000 #		
16	7,100 #		
19	7,200 #		
20	7,300 #		
21	7,400 #		
23	7,500 #		# Car assembly date
24	7,600 #		
26	7,700 #		
28	7,800 #		
28	7,900 #		
30	8,000 #		
31	8,100 #		

AUGUST 1909

Day	First Number	Last Number	Production
	8,108	9,840	1733 **
2	8,109 #		First car in August.
2	8,200 # ***		*** Engine only.
4	8,300 #		
4	8,400 #		
5	8,500 #		
6	8,600 #		
9	8,700 #		
10	8,800 #		
11	8,900 #		
12	9,000 #		
13	9,100 #		
16	9,200 #		
17	9,300 #		
19	9,400 #		
19	9,500 #		
23	9,600 #		
25	9,700 #		
30	9,800 #		
31	9,900 #		

SEPTEMBER 1909

Day	First Number	Last Number	Production
	9,841	11,148	1308 **
2	9,926 #		First car in September.
9	10,000 #		
10	10,100 #		
11	10,200 #		
13	10,300 #		
14	10,400 #		
16	10,500 #		
20	10,600 #		
21	10,700 #		
25	10,800 #		
25	10,900 #		
29	11,000 #		
30	11,100 #		

OCTOBER 1909

Day	First Number	Last Number	Production
	11,149	12,405	1257 **
1	11,146	First number in October	
4	11,200 #		
6	11,300 #		
7	11,400 #		
7	11,500 #		
12	11,600 #		
14	11,700 # ***		*** Engine only.
16	11,800 #		
18	11,900 #		
21	12,000 #		
23	12,100 #		
26	12,200 #		
28	12,300 #		
29	12,400 #		

NOVEMBER 1909

Day	First Number	Last Number	Production
	12,406	13,132	727 **
1	12,438 #		First car in November
2	12,500 #		
4	12,600 #		
9	12,700 #		
12	12,800 #		
17	12,900 #		"Roller bearing rear axle"
22	13,000 #		
29	13,100 #		
30	13,200 # ***		*** Engine only

DECEMBER 1909

Day	First Number	Last Number	Production
	13,133	14,161	1029 **
1	13,240 #		First car in December.
3	13,300 #		
7	13,400 #		
9	13,500 # ***		*** Engine only.
11	13,600 #		
15	13,700 #		
17	13,800 #		
23	13,900 #		
29	14,000 #		
31	14,100 #		

Note: Other records show 1909 fiscal production (October 1, 1908 to September 30, 1909) running from 1 to 11,100.

JANUARY 1910

Day	First Number	Last Number	Production
	14,162	15,500 **	1339 **
3	14,165 # ****		** These even numbers are not believed to be accurate (they are Ford's published figures)
3	14,200 #		
5	14,300 #		
6	14,400 #		
6	14,500 # ***		*** First car in 1910.
7	14,600 #		
10	14,700 #		*** Engine only.

First Number	Last Number	Production		First Number	Last Number	Production

JANUARY 1910

Day	First Number	Last Number	Production
12	14,800 #		
14	14,900 #		
15	15,000 #		# Car assembly date
19	15,100 #		
21	15,200 #		
24	15,300 # ***		
26	15,400 #		
31	15,500 #		
31	15,600 # ***		

FEBRUARY 1910

Day	First Number	Last Number	Production
	15,501	16,600 **	1100 **
1	15,517 #		First car in February
1	15,675 #		First "reinforced housing"
2	15,700 #		
4	15,800 #		
7	15,900 #		
9	16,000 #		
10	16,100 #		
15	16,200 #		
15	16,278 #		First "Special flywheel"
18	16,300 #		
23	16,400 #		
25	16,500 #		

MARCH 1910

Day	First Number	Last Number	Production
	16,601	19,700 **	3100 **
1	16,591 #		First car in March
1	16,600 #		
1	16,700 #		
1	16,800 # ***		*** Engine only.
2	16,900 #		
4	17,000 #		
5	17,100 #		
7	17,200 #		
9	17,300 #		
9	17,400 #		
10	17,500 #		
11	17,600 #		
14	17,700 #		
15	17,800 #		
16	17,900 #		
17	17,985 #		First marked "new magneto"
17	18,000 #		
18	18,100 #		
19	18,200 #		
21	18,300 #		
22	18,400 #		
23	18,500 #		
24	18,600 # ***		
24	18,700 # ***		
23	18,800 #		
24	18,900 #		
25	19,000 #		
26	19,100 #		
28	19,200 #		
29	19,300 #		
30	19,400 #		
31	19,500 #		
31	19,600 #		

APRIL 1910

Day	First Number	Last Number	Production
	19,701	23,100 **	3400 **
1	19,647 #		First car in April
1	19,700 #		
2	19,800 #		
4	19,900 #		
5	20,000 #		
6	20,100 #		
6	20,200 #		
4	20,002 #		"New style crankcase"
7	20,300 #		
8	20,400 #		
8	20,500 #		Note: The first 20,500 cars used 9/16" magnets, then 5/8" according to Ford records, but other records indicate the change was made about 17,985 (March 1910).
11	20,600 #		
11	20,700 #		
12	20,800 #		
13	20,900 #		
15	21,000 #		
15	21,100 #		
16	21,200 #		
18	21,300 #		
19	21,400 #		
19	21,500 #		
20	21,600 #		
20	21,700 #		
21	21,800 #		# Car assembly date
21	21,900 #		
22	22,000 #		
22	22,100 #		
23	22,200 #		
25	22,300 #		
25	22,400 #		

(continued, right column)

Day	First Number	Last Number	Production
26	22,500 #		
26	22,600 #		
26	22,700 #		
27	22,800 #		
28	22,900 #		
28	23,000 #		
29	23,100 #		
29	23,200 #		
30	23,300 #		

MAY 1910

Day	First Number	Last Number	Production
	23,101	26,500 **	3400 **
2	23,348 #		First car in May
2	23,400 #		
3	23,500 #		
3	23,600 #		
4	23,700 #		
6	23,800 #		
6	23,900 #		
7	24,000 #		
7	24,100 #		
9	24,200 #		
9	24,300 #		
10	24,400 #		
11	24,500 #		
11	24,600 #		
12	24,700 #		
12	24,800 #		
13	24,900 #		
13	25,000 #		
16	25,100 #		
16	25,200 #		
17	25,300 #		
18	25,400 #		
18	25,500 #		
19	25,600 #		
19	25,700 #		
20	25,800 #		
21	25,900 #		
23	26,000 #		
23	26,100 #		
24	26,200 #		
25	26,300 #		
25	26,400 #		
26	26,500 #		
27	26,600 #		
27	26,700 #		
28	26,800 #		
31	26,900 #		

JUNE 1910

Day	First Number	Last Number	Production
	26,501	29,500 *	3000 **
1	26,933 #		First car in June
1	27,000 #		
2	27,100 #		
2	27,200 #		
3	27,300 #		
3	27,400 #		
4	27,500 #		
6	27,600 #		
6	27,700 #		
7	27,800 #		
8	27,900 #		
8	28,000 #		
9	28,100 #		
10	28,200 #		
11	28,300 #		
13	28,400 #		
14	28,500 #		
16	28,600 #		
16	28,700 #		
17	28,800 #		
20	28,900 #		
21	29,000 #		
22	29,100 #		
23	29,200 #		
23	29,300 #		
29	29,400 #		
29	29,500 # ***		*** Engine only.

JULY 1910

Day	First Number	Last Number	Production
	29,501	30,200 **	700 **
1	29,565 #		First car in July
6	29,600 #		
8	29,700 #		# Car assembly date
12	29,800 #		
13	29,900 #		
20	30,000 #		
22	30,100 #		
26	30,200 #		
28	30,300 #		

Serial Numbers

AUGUST 1910

	30,201	31,000 ** 800 **
1	30,357 #	First car in August
2	30,400 #	
12	30,500 #	
17	30,600 #	
19	30,700 #	
23	30,800 #	
25	30,900 #	
29	31,000 #	
31	31,100 #	

SEPTEMBER 1910

	31,001	31,900 ** 900 **
1	31,132 #	First car in September
7	31,200 #	
9	31,300 #	Dates are mixed in production
13	31,400 #	
20	31,500 #	
11	31,600 #	
7	31,700 #	
*	31,800 #	(January 26, 1911)

OCTOBER 1910

	31,901	32,500 ** 600 **
3	31,533 #	First car in October
15	31,900 #	
16	32,000 # ***	*** Engine only
21	32,100 #	("1911 rear axle" appeared on many
26	32,200 #	invoices beginning approximately
27	32,300 #	October first.)
31	32,400 #	

NOVEMBER 1910

	32,501	33,700 ** 1200 **
1	32,404 #	First car in November
2	32,500 #	
4	32,600 #	
7	32,700 #	
9	32,800 #	
11	32,900 #	
15	33,000 #	
17	33,100 #	
17	33,200 #	
19	33,300 #	
21	33,400 # ***	*** Engine only
23	33,500 #	
25	33,600 # ***	
28	33,700 #	
28	33,800 # ***	
30	33,900 #	

DECEMBER 1910

	33,701	34,900 ** 1200 **
1	33,933 #	First car in December
1	34,000 # ***	
2	34,100 #	
6	34,200 #	
8	34,300 #	
15	34,400 #	
13	34,500 # ***	
19	34,600 #	
28	34,700 #	
21	34,800 # ***	

Note: Other records show fiscal 1910 (October 1, 1909 to September 30, 1910) as having produced cars from 11,101 to 31,900. Another record shows production for the fiscal year as 19,057 engines. The difference in serial numbers is 20,799.

JANUARY 1911

	34,901	37,000 ** 2100 **
3	34,900 #	First car in January
*	35,000 #	(December 29, 1910)
6	35,100 #	(Dates and numbers mixed in
4	35,200 #	production)
6	35,300 #	
9	35,400 #	
11	35,500 #	
14	35,600 #	
14	35,700 #	
17	35,800 #	
18	35,900 #	
19	36,000 #	
20	36,100 #	
23	36,200 #	# Car assembly date
24	36,300 #	
24	36,400 #	
25	36,500 #	
26	36,600 #	
27	36,700 #	
30	36,800 #	
31	36,900 #	
31	37,000 #	

FEBRUARY 1911

	37,001	40,000 ** 3000 **
1	36,989 #	First car in February
2	37,100 #	
2	37,200 #	
3	37,300 #	
7	37,378 #	First "1911 front axle and
6	37,400 #	wide pan transmission
7	37,500 #	cover"
7	37,600 #	
8	37,700 #	
9	37,800 #	
10	37,900 #	
10	38,000 #	
13	38,100 #	
14	38,200 #	
14	38,263 #	First "babbitt bearing engine"
14	38,300 #	
15	38,400 #	
16	38,500 #	
17	38,600 #	
18	38,700 #	
20	38,800 #	
21	38,900 #	
21	39,000 #	
22	39,100 #	
22	39,200 #	
23	39,300 #	
23	39,400 #	
24	39,500 #	
24	39,600 #	
24	39,700 #	
25	39,800 #	
27	39,900 #	
28	40,000 #	
28	40,100 #	
28	40,200 #	
29	40,300 #	

MARCH 1911

	40,001	45,000 ** 5000 **
1	40,232 #	First car in March
1	40,400 #	
2	40,500 #	
2	40,600 #	
3	40,700 #	
3	40,800 # ***	*** Engine only
4	40,900 #	
6	41,000 #	
6	41,100 #	
7	41,200 #	
8	41,300 #	
8	41,400 #	
9	41,500 #	
9	41,600 #	
9	41,700 # ***	
10	41,800 #	
11	41,900 #	
11	42,000 #	
13	42,100 #	
13	42,200 #	
15	42,300 #	
14	42,400 # ***	
15	42,500 #	
15	42,600 #	
17	42,700 #	
17	42,800 #	
17	42,900 #	
20	43,000 #	
20	43,100 #	
20	43,200 #	
21	43,300 #	
21	43,400 #	
22	43,500 #	
22	43,600 #	
22	43,700 #	
24	43,800 #	
24	43,900 #	
24	44,000 #	
25	44,100 #	
27	44,200 #	
27	44,300 #	
28	44,400 #	
28	44,420 #	First "removable bottom"
28	44,500 #	
29	44,600 #	
29	44,700 #	# Car assembly date
30	44,800 #	
30	44,900 #	
31	45,000 #	
31	45,100 #	
31	45,200 #	

	First Number	Last Number	Production
APRIL 1911			
	45,001		50,800 ** 5800 **
1	45,204 #		First car in April
1	45,300 #		
3	45,400 #		
3	45,500 # ***		*** Engine only
3	45,600 #		
4	45,700 #		
4	45,800 #		
5	45,900 #		
5	46,000 #		
6	46,100 #		
6	46,200 #		
6	46,300 #		
7	46,400 #		
7	46,500 #		
8	46,600 #		
10	46,700 #		
11	46,800 #		
10	46,900 #		
11	47,000 #		
11	47,100 #		
12	47,200 #		
12	47,300 #		
13	47,400 #		
14	47,500 #		
13	47,600 #		
14	47,700 #		
14	47,800 #		
14	47,900 #		
15	48,000 #		
17	48,100 #		
17	48,200 #		
18	48,300 #		
18	48,400 #		
19	48,500 #		
19	48,600 #		
19	48,700 #		
20	48,800 #		
20	48,900 #		
21	49,000 #		
21	49,100 #		
22	49,200 #		
22	49,300 #		
24	49,400 #		
24	49,500 #		
25	49,600 #		
26	49,700 # ***		*** Engine only
25	49,800 #		
26	49,900 #		
26	50,000 #		
26	50,100 #		
27	50,200 #		
27	50,300 #		
*	50,400 #		(May 16, 1911) Special 1911 Roadster
28	50,500 #		
28	50,600 #		
29	50,700 #		
29	50,800 # ***		
MAY 1911			
	50,801		57,200 ** 6400 **
1	50,881 #		First car in May
1	50,900 #		
1	51,000 #		
1	51,100 #		
2	51,200 #		
2	51,300 #		
3	51,400 #		
3	51,500 # ***		*** Engine only
3	51,600 #		
3	51,700 #		
4	51,800 #		
4	51,900 #		
5	52,000 #		
5	52,100 #		
5	52,200 #		
6	52,300 #		
6	52,400 #		
10	52,500 #		
8	52,600 #		
9	52,700 #		
9	52,800 #		
9	52,900 #		
10	53,000 #		
10	53,100 #		
10	53,200 #		
11	53,300 #		
11	53,400 #		#Car assembly date
12	53,500 #		
12	53,600 #		
12	53,700 # ***		
12	53,800 #		

	First Number	Last Number	Production
13	53,900 #		
15	54,000 #		
15	54,100 #		
16	54,200 #		
16	54,300 #		
16	54,400 #		
17	54,500 #		
17	54,600 #		
17	54,700 #		
17	54,800 #		
18	54,900 #		
18	55,000 #		
19	55,100 #		
19	55,200 #		
19	55,300 #		
20	55,400 #		
20	55,500 #		
22	55,600 #		
22	55,700 #		
22	55,800 #		
23	55,900 #		
23	56,000 #		
24	56,100 #		
24	56,200 #		
24	56,300 #		
25	56,400 #		
25	56,500 #		
26	56,600 #		
26	56,700 #		
26	56,800 #		
27	56,900 #		
27	57,000 #		
31	57,100 #		
31	57,200 #		
JUNE 1911			
	57,201		60,500 ** 3300 **
1	57,294 #		First car in June
1	57,300 #		
1	57,400 #		
1	57,421 #		First "new style transmission cover"
2	57,500 #		
2	57,528 #		Last "removable bottom"
3	57,700 #		
5	57,800 #		
5	57,900 #		
6	58,000 #		
6	58,100 #		
7	58,200 #		
8	58,300 #		
9	58,400 #		
10	58,500 #		
12	58,600 #		
13	58,700 #		
14	58,800 #		
15	58,900 #		
16	59,000 #		
12	59,100 # ***		*** Engine only.
13	59,200 # ***		
17	59,300 # ***		
17	59,400 #		
19	59,500 #		
20	59,600 #		
21	59,700 #		
23	59,800 #		
23	59,900 #		
26	60,000 #		
26	60,100 #		
27	60,200 #		
28	60,300 #		
29	60,400 #		
29	60,500 #		
30	60,600 #		
JULY 1911			
	60,501		62,100 ** 1600 **
5	60,620 #		First car in July
5	60,700 #		
7	60,800 #		"1912 rear axles" began in July at about 61,000
11	60,900 #		
11	61,000 #		
13	61,100 #		
13	61,187 #		First "1912 rear axle"
15	61,200 #		
17	61,300 #		
20	61,400 #		
22	61,500 #		
25	61,600 #		
26	61,700 #		
27	61,800 #		# Car assembly date
27	61,900 #		
28	62,000 #		
29	62,100 #		
23	62,200 #		"Stock Car Racer built for Kulick"

Serial Numbers

AUGUST 1911

	First Number	Last Number	Production
	62,101	66,700 **	4600 **
1	62,239 #		First car in August
1	62,300 #		
2	62,400 #		
2	62,500 #		
2	62,600 #		
3	62,700 #		
5	62,800 #		
5	62,900 #		
7	63,000 #		
7	63,100 #		
8	63,200 #		
11	63,300 #		
9	63,400 #		
10	63,500 #		
11	63,600 #		
12	63,700 #		
12	63,800 #		
12	63,900 #		
14	64,000 #		
15	64,100 #		
15	64,200 #		
16	64,300 #		
16	64,400 #		
17	64,500 #		
17	64,600 #		
18	64,700 #		
19	64,800 #		
19	64,900 #		
21	65,000 #		
21	65,100 #		
21	65,200 #		
22	65,300 #		
22	65,400 #		
23	65,500 #		
23	65,600 #		
24	65,700 #		
25	65,800 #		
25	65,900 #		
26	66,000 #		
28	66,100 #		
28	66,200 #		
29	66,300 #		
29	66,400 #		
30	66,500 #		
30	66,600 #		
31	66,700 #		
31	66,800 #		
31	66,900 #		

SEPTEMBER 1911

	First Number	Last Number	Production
	66,701	69,876 **	3176 **
1	66,921 #		First car in September
1	67,000 #		
1	67,100 #		
8	67,200 # ***		*** Engine only
5	67,300 #		
5	67,400 #		
6	67,500 #		
7	67,600 #		
7	67,700 #		
7	67,800 #		
8	67,900 #		
8	68,000 #		
9	68,100 #		
9	68,200 #		
11	68,300 #		
13	68,400 #		
12	68,500 #		
13	68,600 #		
14	68,700 #		
15	68,800 #		
15	68,900 #		
28	69,000 # ***		
15	69,100 #		
20	69,200 #		
19	69,300 #		
20	69,400 #		
24	69,500 # ****		**** Estimate (Records lost)
24	69,600 # ****		
24	69,700 # ****		
24	69,800 # ****		
24	69,806 #		
30	69,900 #		
27	70,000 # ****		
27	70,100 # ****		
27	70,241 #		
28	70,499 #		
29	70,702 #		

OCTOBER 1911

	First Number	Last Number	Production
	69,877 *	83,100 **	13224

** Other records show this as the first number for fiscal 1912, but they are apparently in error.

	First Number		
5	70,750 # (Engine only)		

There are apparently no records extant for late 1911 through 1912. The figures given are those published by Ford.

NOVEMBER 1911

	First Number	Last Number	Production
	83,101	86,300	3200

DECEMBER 1911

	86,301	88,900	2600

JANUARY 1912

	88,901	92,000	3100

FEBRUARY 1912

	92,001	95,900	3900

MARCH 1912

	95,901	103,800	7900
12	100,552		Known to be accurate

APRIL 1912

	103,801	112,900	9100

MAY 1912

	112,901	123,800	10900

JUNE 1912

	123,801	132,000	8200

JULY 1912

	132,001	139,700	7700

AUGUST 1912

	139,701	144,500	4800

SEPTEMBER 1912

	144,501	157,424	12924

OCTOBER 1912

	157,425 *	—	

* This number is shown as the first number of fiscal 1913 production

NOVEMBER 1912

	—	—	

DECEMBER 1912

	—	183,563	26139 (October - December)

Note: Records indicate that "B" numbered engines were built at the Detroit plant on Piquette Avenue during fiscal 1913 (October 1, 1912 to September 30, 1913). These engines were numbered B1 through B12,247. No production figures have been found on these engines, and they are NOT included in the figures listed here.

Factory records show that 157,425 was the first number of fiscal 1913 production, and that 348,735 was the last of fiscal 1913. Records also indicate that number 300,000 was built on July 16, 1913, at 1:25 P.M. There are no serial number lists available for 1913 but the daily production figures do exist, beginning with January 1913. The serial numbers here are derived from the first and last numbers, working backwards from 1914. Using this method, the figures come out within one (1) for the 1913 fiscal year, which might indicate all is in order.

There is a problem. Using the above method, number 300,000 should have been built on June 26. There were about 12,500 engines built between June 26 and July 16; a figure mightly close to the 12,247 "B" engines.

One might presume the "B" engines were built in the first part of fiscal 1913 (October 1912 to January 1913) instead of the regular numbers, with the regular number sequence following. This would move the 300,000 number to the proper date, but then the ending number would be off.

Other possibilities exist for the error, including the one that the July 16 date is wrong, but the true answer is anyone's guess at this time. In any event, the 1913 numbers are tentative until such a time as other records might be found.

JANUARY 1913

	First Number	Last Number	Production
2	183,564	184,233	670
3	184,234	184,952	719
4	184,953	185,480	528
6	185,481	186,276	796
7	186,277	186,895	619
8	186,896	187,730	835
9	187,731	188,589	859
10	188,590	189,289	700
11	189,290	189,863	574
13	189,864	190,779	916
14	190,780	191,560	781
15	191,561	192,361	801
16	192,362	193,103	742
17	193,104	193,868	765
18	193,869	194,291	423
20	194,292	194,857	566
21	194,858	195,386	529
22	195,387	195,917	531
23	195,918	196,412	495
24	196,413	196,960	548

JANUARY 1913

Day	First Number	Last Number	Production
25	196,961	197,495	535
27	197,496	198,100	605
28	198,101	198,691	591
29	198,692	199,439	748
30	199,440	200,210	771
31	200,211	200,993	783

FEBRUARY 1913

Day	First Number	Last Number	Production
1	200,994	201,568	575
3	201,569	202,642	1074
4	202,643	203,392	750
5	203,393	204,152	760
6	204,153	205,019	867
7	205,020	205,792	773
8	205,793	206,292	500
10	206,293	207,007	715
11	207,008	207,769	762
12	207,770	208,392	623
13	208,393	209,082	690
14	209,083	209,707	625
15	209,708	210,061	354
17	210,062	210,719	658
18	210,720	211,427	708
19	211,428	212,038	611
20	212,039	212,752	714
21	212,753	213,487	735
22	213,488	214,162	675
24	214,163	214,855	693
25	214,856	215,552	697
26	215,553	216,428	876
27	216,429	217,348	920
28	217,349	218,239	891

MARCH 1913

Day	First Number	Last Number	Production
1	218,240	218,709	470
3	218,710	219,564	855
4	219,565	220,402	838
5	220,403	221,162	760
6	221,163	221,879	717
7	221,880	222,634	755
8	222,635	223,191	557
10	223,192	223,924	733
11	223,925	224,594	670
12	224,595	225,370	776
13	225,371	226,229	859
14	226,230	227,085	856
15	227,086	227,825	740
17	227,826	228,730	905
18	228,731	229,568	838
19	229,569	230,470	902
20	230,471	231,330	860
21	231,331	232,185	855
22	232,186	232,950	765
24	232,951	233,683	733
25	233,684	234,490	807
26	234,491	235,397	907
27	235,398	236,421	1024
28	236,422	237,331	910
29	237,332	238,150	819
31	238,151	239,151	1001

APRIL 1913

Day	First Number	Last Number	Production
1	239,152	240,091	940
2	240,092	241,041	950
3	241,042	242,052	1011
4	242,053	242,966	914
5	242,967	243,330	364
7	243,331	244,056	726
8	244,057	244,959	903
9	244,960	245,905	946
10	245,906	246,705	800
11	246,706	247,680	975
12	247,681	248,352	672
14	248,353	249,200	848
15	249,201	250,101	901
16	250,102	251,111	1010
17	251,112	251,991	880
18	251,992	252,758	767
19	252,759	253,243	485
21	253,244	254,149	906
22	254,150	254,985	836
23	254,986	255,799	814
24	255,800	256,595	796
25	256,596	257,515	920
26	257,516	257,924	409
28	257,925	258,610	686
29	258,611	259,511	901
30	259,512	260,201	690

MAY 1913

Day	First Number	Last Number	Production
1	260,202	261,023	822
2	261,024	261,856	833
3	261,857	262,420	564
5	262,421	263,163	743
6	263,164	263,814	651
7	263,815	264,715	901
8	264,716	265,619	904
9	265,620	266,536	917
10	266,537	267,320	784
12	267,321	267,980	660
13	267,981	268,999	1019
14	269,000	269,999	1000
15	270,000	270,799	800
16	270,800	271,799	1000
17	271,800	272,549	750
19	272,550	273,319	770
20	273,320	273,970	651
21	273,971	274,592	622
22	274,593	275,592	1000
23	275,593	276,592	1000
24	276,593	277,449	857
26	277,450	278,349	900
27	278,350	279,184	835
28	279,185	279,854	670
29	279,855	280,611	757
31	280,612	281,651	1040

JUNE 1913

Day	First Number	Last Number	Production
2	281,652	282,551	900
3	282,552	283,454	903
4	283,455	284,414	960
5	284,415	285,414	1000
6	285,415	286,416	1002
7	286,417	287,081	665
9	287,082	288,081	1000
10	288,082	289,081	1000
11	289,082	290,081	1000
12	290,082	291,081	1000
13	291,082	292,081	1000
14	292,082	292,581	500
16	292,582	293,431	850
17	293,432	294,381	950
18	294,382	295,306	925
19	295,307	296,256	950
20	296,257	297,206	950
21	297,207	297,681	475
23	297,682	298,481	800
24	298,482	299,185	704
25	299,186	299,812	627
26	299,813	300,782	970
27	300,783	301,515	733
28	301,516	301,995	480
30	301,996	302,915	920

Note: Even numbers are from Ford's production records and may not be accurate.

Records show that 300,000 was built on July 16, at 1:25 P.M.

JULY 1913

Day	First Number	Last Number	Production
1	302,916	303,820	905
2	303,821	304,760	940
3	304,761	305,635	875
4	Closed		
5	Closed		
7	305,636	306,374	739
8	306,375	307,274	900
9	307,275	308,185	911
10	308,186	308,910	725
11	308,911	309,700	790
12	309,701	310,150	450
14	310,151	311,000	850
15	311,001	311,716	716
16	311,717	312,386	670
17	312,387	312,942	556
18	312,943	313,708	766
19	313,709	314,130	422
21	314,131	314,705	575
22	314,706	315,470	765
23	315,471	316,325	855
24	316,326	317,088	763
25	317,089	317,838	750
26	317,839	318,145	307
28	318,146	318,545	400
29	318,546	319,305	760
30	319,306	319,955	650
31	319,956	320,615	660

AUGUST 1913

Day	First Number	Last Number	Production
1	320,616	321,355	740
2	321,356	321,815	460
4	321,816	322,465	650
5	322,466	323,315	850
6	323,316	324,140	825
7	324,141	324,880	740
8	324,881	325,680	800
9	325,681	326,130	450
11	326,131	326,900	770
12	326,901	327,710	810
13	327,711	328,410	700
14	328,411	329,070	660
15	329,071	329,400	330

	First Number	Last Number	LH	RH	LHM	RHM

AUGUST 1913

	First Number	Last Number	LH	RH	LHM	RHM
16	329,401	329,650	250			
18	329,651	330,350	700			
19	330,351	330,720	370			
20	330,721	331,075	355			
21	331,076	331,435	360			
22	331,436	331,995	560			
23	331,996	332,350	355			
25	332,351	333,050	700			
26	333,051	333,800	750			
27	333,801	334,500	700			
28	334,501	335,200	700			
29	335,201	335,985	785			
30	335,986	336,400	415			

SEPTEMBER 1913

	First Number	Last Number	LH	RH	LHM	RHM
2	336,401	337,135	735			
3	337,136	337,690	555			
4	337,691	337,840	150			
5	337,841	338,025	185			
6	338,026	338,130	105			
8	338,131	338,370	240			
9	338,371	338,710	340			
10	338,711	339,180	470			
11	339,181	339,800	620			
12	339,801	340,550	750			
13	340,551	340,795	245			
15	340,796	341,396	601			
16	341,397	342,171	775			
17	342,172	342,906	735			
18	342,907	343,646	740			
19	343,647	344,406	760			
20	344,407	344,845	439			
22	344,846	345,405	560			
23	345,406	346,030	625			
24	346,031	346,735	705			
25	346,736	347,510	775			
26	347,511	348,310	800			
27	348,311	348,735	425			

(Factory records show the ending number of fiscal 1913 as 348,735, and a production of 424; one number off of the production figures.)

OCTOBER 1913

	First Number	Last Number	LH	RH	LHM	RHM
1	348,736	349,235	500			
2	349,236	349,447	212			
3	349,448	349,448	1			
4	349,449	349,542	94			
6	349,543	349,992	450			
7	349,993	350,607	615			
8	350,608	351,132	525			
9	351,133	351,482	350			
10	351,483	352,172	690			
11	352,173	352,572	400			
13	352,573	353,297	725			
14	353,298	353,912	615			
15	353,913	354,662	750			
16	354,663	355,497	835			
17	355,498	356,267	770			
18	356,268	356,682	415			
20	356,683	357,357	675			
21	357,358	358,107	750			
22	358,108	358,912	805			
23	358,913	359,722	810			
24	359,723	360,537	815			
25	360,538	360,992	455			
27	360,993	361,692	700			
28	361,693	362,532	840			
29	362,533	363,332	800			
30	363,333	364,187	855			
31	364,188	364,897	710			

NOVEMBER 1913

	First Number	Last Number	LH	RH	LHM	RHM
1	364,898	365,292	395			
3	365,293	365,852	560			
4	365,853	366,652	800			
5	366,653	367,402	750			
6	367,403	368,182	780			
7	368,183	369,002	820			
8	369,003	369,472	470			
10	369,473	370,132	660			
11	370,133	370,932	800			
12	370,933	371,787	855			
13	371,788	372,637	850			
14	372,638	373,502	865			
15	373,503	374,002	500			
17	374,003	374,832	830			
18	374,833	375,637	805			
19	375,638	376,577	940			
20	376,578	377,437	860			
21	377,438	378,367	930			
22	378,368	378,882	515			
24	378,883	379,707	825			
25	379,708	380,657	950			
26	380,658	381,337	680			
27		Closed				
28	381,338	382,277	940			
29	382,278	382,797	520			

DECEMBER 1913

	First Number	Last Number	LH	RH	LHM	RHM
1	382,798	383,767	970			
2	383,768	384,807	1040			
3	384,808	385,817	1010			
4	385,818	386,872	1055			
5	386,873	387,922	1050			
6	387,923	388,497	575			
8	388,498	389,397	900			
9	389,398	390,437	1040			
10	390,438	391,447	1010			
11	391,448	392,452	1005			
12	392,453	393,537	1085			
13	393,538	394,147	610			
15	394,148	395,167	1020			
16	395,168	396,227	1060			
17	396,228	397,352	1125			
18	397,353	398,477	1125			
19	398,478	399,557	1080			
20	399,558	400,177	620			
22	400,178	401,237	1060			
23	401,238	402,462	1225			
24	402,463	403,512	1050			
25		Closed				
26	403,513	404,512	1000			
27	404,513	405,092	580			
29	405,093	406,147	1055			
30	406,148	407,232	1085			
31	407,233	408,347	1115			

JANUARY 1914

	First Number	Last Number	LH	RH	LHM	RHM
2	408,348	409,347	1000			
3	409,348	409,957	610			
5	409,958	411,012	1055			
6	411,013	412,122	1110			
7	412,123	413,222	1100			
8	413,223	414,342	1120			
9	414,343	415,467	1125			
10	415,468	416,082	615			
12	416,083	416,827	745			
13	416,828	417,892	1065			
14	417,893	418,992	1100			
15	418,993	420,067	1075			
16	420,068	421,177	1110			
17	421,178	422,302	1125			
19	422,303	423,482	1180			
20	423,483	424,672	1190			
21	424,673	425,792	1120			
22	425,793	426,947	1155			
23	426,948	428,097	1150			
24	428,098	429,367	1270			
26	429,368	430,567	1200			
27	430,568	431,769	1202			
28	431,770	432,984	1215			
29	432,985	434,184	1200			
30	434,185	435,384	1200			
31	435,385	436,567	1183			

FEBRUARY 1914

	First Number	Last Number	LH	RH	LHM	RHM
2	436,568	437,667	1100			
3	437,668	438,487	820			
4	438,488	439,337	850			
5	439,338	440,297	960			
6	440,298	441,262	965			
7	441,263	442,167	905			
9	442,168	443,077	910			
10	443,078	444,127	1050			
11	444,128	445,112	985			
12	445,113	446,092	980			
13	446,093	446,962	870			
14	446,963	448,017	1055			
16	448,018	449,077	1060			
17	449,078	450,112	1035			
18	450,113	451,227	1115			
19	451,228	452,327	1100			
20	452,328	453,372	1045			
21	453,373	454,517	1145			
23	454,518	455,557	1040			
24	455,558	456,662	1105			
25	456,663	457,745	1083			
26	457,746	458,870	1125			
27	458,871	459,905	1035			
28	459,906	461,017	1112			

MARCH 1914

	First Number	Last Number	LH	RH	LHM	RHM
2	461,018	462,087	1070			
3	462,088	463,157	1070			
4	463,158	464,177	1020			
5	464,178	465,277	1100			
6	465,278	466,397	1120			
7	466,398	467,547	1150			
9	467,548	468,647	1100			

508

MARCH 1914

	First Number	Last Number	LH	Notes
10	468,648	469,777	1130	
11	469,778	470,877	1100	
12	470,878	471,967	1090	
13	471,968	473,077	1110	
14	473,078	474,197	1120	
16	474,198	475,317	1120	
17	475,318	476,452	1135	
18	476,453	477,537	1085	"New Commutator" at 477,165
19	477,538	478,467	930	
20	478,468	479,292	825	
21	479,293	480,197	905	
23	480,198	481,112	915	
24	481,113	482,027	915	
25	482,028	482,892	865	
26	482,893	483,707	815	
27	483,708	484,607	900	
28	484,608	485,507	900	
30	485,508	486,412	905	
31	486,413	487,282	870	

APRIL 1914

	First Number	Last Number	LH	Notes
1	487,283	488,182	900	
2	488,183	489,084	902	
3	489,085	489,999	915	
4	490,000	490,900	901	
6	490,901	491,800	900	
7	491,801	492,726	926	
8	492,727	493,644	918	
9	493,645	494,544	900	
10	494,545	495,309	765	
11	495,310	496,060	751	
13	Closed			
14	496,061	496,780	720	
15	496,781	497,400	620	
16	497,401	497,965	565	
17	497,966	498,365	400	
18	498,366	498,955	590	
20	498,956	499,790	835	
21	499,791	500,720	930	500,000 at 10 A.M.
22	500,721	501,535	815	
23	501,536	502,145	610	
24	502,146	502,895	750	
25	502,896	503,765	870	
27	503,766	504,335	570	
28	504,336	504,905	570	
29	504,906	505,808	903	
30	505,809	506,822	1014	

MAY 1914

	First Number	Last Number	LH
1	506,823	507,822	1000
2	507,823	508,822	1000
4	508,823	509,825	1003
5	509,826	510,725	900
6	510,726	511,750	1025
7	511,751	512,750	1000
8	512,751	513,750	1000
9	513,751	514,822	1072
11	514,823	515,847	1025
12	515,848	516,325	478
13	Closed "Flood"		
14	Closed "Flood"		
15	516,326	517,160	835
16	517,161	518,010	850
18	518,011	518,865	855
19	518,866	519,720	855
20	519,721	520,535	815
21	520,536	521,005	470
22	521,006	521,825	820
23	521,826	522,210	385
25	522,211	523,000	790
26	523,001	523,720	720
27	523,721	524,520	800
28	524,521	525,240	720
29	525,241	526,040	800
30	Closed		

JUNE 1914

	First Number	Last Number	LH
1	526,041	526,790	750
2	526,791	527,520	730
3	527,521	528,295	775
4	528,296	528,945	650
5	528,946	529,610	665
6	Closed		
8	529,611	530,260	650
9	530,261	530,810	550
10	530,811	531,462	652
11	531,463	532,113	651
12	532,114	532,768	655
13	Closed		
15	532,769	533,419	651
16	533,420	534,072	653
17	534,073	534,729	657
18	534,730	535,400	671
19	535,401	536,060	660
20	Closed		
22	536,061	536,661	601
23	536,662	537,196	535
24	537,197	537,711	515
25	537,712	538,415	704
26	538,416	539,165	750
27	539,166	539,540	375
29	539,541	540,190	650
30	540,191	540,850	660

JULY 1914

	First Number	Last Number	LH
1	540,851	541,505	655
2	541,506	542,180	675
3	542,181	542,865	685
4	Closed		
6	542,866	543,485	620
7	543,486	544,130	645
8	544,131	544,685	555
9	544,686	545,385	700
10	545,386	546,125	740
11	546,126	546,460	335
13	546,461	547,120	660
14	547,121	547,720	600
15	547,721	548,270	550
16	548,271	548,735	465
17	548,736	549,275	540
18	Closed		
20	549,276	549,825	550
21	549,826	550,378	553
22	550,379	550,938	560
23	Closed July 23 to August 3 for inventory.		

AUGUST 1914

	First Number	Last Number	LH
3	550,939	551,418	480
4	551,419	552,033	615
5	552,034	552,653	620
6	552,654	553,338	685
7	553,339	553,939	601
8	Closed		
10	553,940	554,609	670
11	554,610	555,186	577
12	555,187	555,947	761
13	555,948	556,672	725
14	556,673	557,429	757
15	557,430	558,189	760
17	558,190	558,962	773
18	558,963	559,772	810
19	559,773	560,612	840
20	560,613	561,472	860
21	561,473	562,347	875
22	562,348	563,222	875
24	563,223	564,052	830
25	564,053	564,982	930
26	564,983	565,768	786
27	565,769	566,638	870
28	566,639	567,508	870
29	567,509	568,392	884
31	568,393	569,238	846

SEPTEMBER 1914

	First Number	Last Number	LH	Notes
1	569,239	570,063	825	
2	570,064	570,835	772	
3	570,836	571,595	760	
4	571,596	572,450	855	Beginning with 572,437, "new style coils" began to be used in some engines.
5	572,451	573,270	820	
7	Closed			
8	573,271	574,130	860	
9	574,131	574,970	840	
10	574,971	575,915	945	
11	575,916	576,840	925	
12	576,841	577,700	860	
14	577,701	578,560	860	Start 3/4" magnets with 578,042
15	578,561	579,388	828	
16	579,389	580,278	890	
17	580,279	581,128	850	
18	581,129	582,033	905	
19	582,034	582,972	939	
21	582,973	583,799	827	
22	583,800	584,721	922	
23	584,722	585,711	990	
24	585,712	586,711	1000	
25	586,712	587,714	1003	
26	587,715	588,732	1018	
28	588,733	589,585	853	
29	589,586	590,718	1133	
30	590,719	591,735	1017	

OCTOBER 1914

	First Number	Last Number	LH
1	591,736	592,675	940
2	592,676	593,387	712
3	593,388	594,210	823
5	594,211	595,210	1000
6	595,211	596,160	950

OCTOBER 1914

Day	First Number	Last Number	LH	RH	LHM	RHM
7	596,161	596,995	835			
8	596,996	597,995	1000			
9	597,996	598,995	1000			
10	598,996	599,825	830			
12	599,826	600,583	758			
13	600,584	601,583	1000			
14	601,584	602,585	1002			
15	602,586	603,590	1005			
16	603,591	604,600	1010			
17	604,601	605,625	1025			
19	605,626	606,625	1000			
20	606,626	607,628	1003			
21	607,629	608,633	1005			
22	608,634	609,633	1000			
23	609,634	610,635	1002			
24	610,636	611,650	1015			
26	611,651	612,665	1015			
27	612,666	613,690	1025			
28	613,691	614,695	1005			
29	614,696	615,710	1015			
30	615,711	616,625	915			
31	616,626	617,535	910			

"New style coils in all production"

NOVEMBER 1914

Day	First Number	Last Number	LH	RH	LHM	RHM
2	617,536	618,365	830			
3	618,366	619,065	700			
4	619,066	619,670	605			
5	619,671	620,455	785			
6	620,456	621,245	790			
7	621,246	622,085	840			
9	622,086	622,915	830			
10	622,916	623,645	730			
11	623,646	624,345	700			
12	624,346	625,180	835			
13	625,181	625,905	725			
14	625,906	626,605	700			
16	626,606	627,440	835			
17	627,441	628,290	850			
18	628,291	629,155	865			
19	629,156	630,005	850			
20	630,006	630,755	750			
21	630,756	631,630	875			
23	631,631	632,580	950			
24	632,581	633,465	885			
25	633,466	634,315	850			
26	Closed					
27	634,316	635,140	825			
28	635,141	635,990	850			
30	635,991	636,735	745			

DECEMBER 1914

Day	First Number	Last Number	LH	RH	LHM	RHM
1	636,736	637,620	885			
2	637,621	638,520	900			
3	638,521	639,380	860			
4	639,381	640,130	750			
5	640,131	640,735	605			
7	640,736	641,420	685			
8	641,421	642,170	750			
9	642,171	643,055	885			
10	643,056	643,955	900			
11	643,956	644,855	900			
12	644,856	645,735	880			
14	645,736	646,636	901			
15	646,637	647,461	825			
16	647,462	648,326	865			
17	648,327	649,141	815			
18	649,142	649,691	550			
19	649,692	649,915	224			
21	649,916	650,385	470			
22	650,386	650,960	575			
23	650,961	651,735	775			
24	651,736	652,610	875			
25	Closed					
26	Closed					
28	652,611	653,410	800			
29	653,411	654,285	875			
30	654,286	655,135	850			
31	655,136	656,063 *	928			

* Production figures make this 656,063 but 656,074 is given as the first number for 1915. The 656,074 number is no doubt a factory error since the first day's production was listed as 875, which would make the beginning number 656,064.

NOTE: In the records which follow: LH = Left hand; RH = Right hand; LHM = Left hand metric; and RHM = Right hand metric. "Metric" means the spark plug holes were metric thread, for overseas shipment.

JANUARY 1915

Day	First Number	Last Number	LH	RH	LHM	RHM	
4	656,064 *	656,938	875				* *Records show this as
5	656,939	657,840	902				656,074. See note for
6	657,841	658,805	965				December 1914.
7	658,806	659,805	992			8	

Day	First Number	Last Number	LH	RH	LHM	RHM
8	659,806	660,806	1001			
9	660,807	661,813	1007			
11	661,814	662,813	925	1		74
12	662,814	663,817	1004			
13	663,818	664,817	1000			
14	664,818	665,867	1030	20		
15	665,868	666,887	1020			
16	666,888	667,938	1051			
18	667,939	668,913	975			
19	668,914	669,915	1002			
20	669,916	670,915	800	200		
21	670,916	671,940	835	190		
22	671,941	672,970	790	240		
23	672,971	674,038	868	200		
25	674,039	675,153	950	165		
26	675,154	676,185	830	202		
27	676,186	677,160	860	115		
28	677,161	678,215	931	86	38	
29	678,216	679,250	740	295		
30	679,251	680,348	942	156		

FEBRUARY 1915

Day	First Number	Last Number	LH	RH	LHM	RHM
1	680,349	681,373	905	115	5	
2	681,374	682,423	990	60		
3	682,424	683,523	1100			
4	683,524	684,583	1060			
5	684,584	685,683	1100			
6	685,684	686,798	1115			
8	686,799	687,838	993	10		37
9	687,839	688,898	1059		1	
10	688,899	689,962	1060		4	
11	689,963	691,092	1127	3		
12	691,093	692,177	1078			7
13	692,178	693,273	1096			
15	693,274	694,323	1041			9
16	694,324	695,403	1068		2	10
17	695,404	696,513	1092	10		8
18	696,514	697,638	1103	3	9	10
19	697,639	698,764	1107		19	
20	698,765	699,873	1109			
22	699,874	700,998	1115			10
23	700,999	702,118	1085	25		10
24	702,119	703,243	865	250		10
25	703,244	704,378	769	350	6	10
26	704,379	705,578	776	300	24	
27	705,579	706,623	884	250	11	

MARCH 1915

Day	First Number	Last Number	LH	RH	LHM	RHM
1	706,624	707,738	873	204	2	36
2	707,739	708,888	896	245	9	
3	788,889	710,038	950	200		
4	710,039	711,179	941	200		
5	711,180	712,329	1025	125		
6	712,330	713,483	929	225		
8	713,484	714,598	961	154		
9	714,599	715,723	861	264		
10	715,724	716,863	890	250		
11	716,864	718,005	992	150		
12	718,006	719,170	965	200		
13	719,171	720,345	963	209		3
15	720,346	721,470	1010	115		
16	721,471	722,590	916	190	14	
17	722,591	723,770	990	175	14	1
18	723,771	724,955	1104	75	3	3
19	724,956	726,145	810	380		
20	726,146	727,345	895	300		5
22	727,346	728,510	1030	135		
23	728,511	729,695	855	330		
24	729,696	730,860	911	247	7	
25	730,861	731,935	1075			
26	731,936	733,100	1160		1	4
27	733,101	734,300	1190	1	8	1
29	734,301	735,505	1205			
30	735,506	736,712	1080		1	100	25
31	736,713	737,938	1220	5		2

APRIL 1915

Day	First Number	Last Number	LH	RH	LHM	RHM
1	737,939	739,178	1240			
2	739,179	740,408	1225	5		

(Ford records show the last number as 774,408)

Day	First Number	Last Number	LH	RH	LHM	RHM
3	740,409	741,650	1205	10	27	
5	741,651	742,920	1265		5	
6	742,921	744,220	1288		12	
7	744,221	745,560	1340			
8	745,561	746,935	1362	2		11
9	746,936	748,265	1330			
10	748,266	749,650	1385			
12	749,651	751,010	1353		5	2
13	751,011	752,410	1400			
14	752,411	753,860	1449		1	
15	753,861	755,260	1381		4	15
16	755,261	756,610	1324		15	11
17	756,611	757,950	1334	6		
19	757,951	759,400	1448		2	

	First Number	Last Number	LH	RH	LHM	RHM

APRIL 1915

Day	First Number	Last Number	LH	RH	LHM	RHM
20	759,401	760,850	1450			
21	760,851	762,325	1475			
22	762,326	763,700	1375			
23	763,701	764,750	1039	10	1	
24	764,751	766,475	1725			
26	766,476	767,900	1380	25		20
27	767,901	769,315	1415			
28	769,316	770,565	1237			13
29	770,566	771,990	1411	14		
30	771,991	773,490	1485	4	6	6

MAY 1915

Day	First Number	Last Number	LH	RH	LHM	RHM
1	773,491	775,950	1460			
3	775,951	776,460	1494		2	14
4	776,461	777,991	1525			5
5	777,992	779,490	1488	3		9
6	779,491	780,990	1500			
7	780,991	782,190	1196	2	2	
8	782,191	783,550	1343			17
10	783,551	784,900	1350			
11	784,901	786,125	1218		2	5
12	786,126	787,675	1549			1
13	787,676	788,715	1040			
14	788,716	790,015	1285	8		7
15	790,016	791,440	1415	5		5
17	791,441	792,740	1284		16	
18	792,741	794,240	1480		20	
19	794,241	795,715	1461		2	12
20	795,716	797,150	1415	10		10
21	797,151	797,885	723	6	6	
22	797,886	799,140	1247	7	1	
24	799,141	800,440	1295			5
25	800,441	801,630	1185			5
26	801,631	802,540	910			
27	802,541	802,975	435			
28	802,976	804,310	1335			
29	804,311	805,840	1499		25	6

JUNE 1915

Day	First Number	Last Number	LH	RH	LHM	RHM
1	805,841	807,270	1404		25	
2	807,271	808,770	1500			
3	808,771	810,295	1517	6		2
4	810,296	811,795	1483		3	14
5	811,796	813,120	1316	3	6	
7	813,121	814,445	1293			32
8	814,446	815,725	1265			15
9	815,726	816,880	1154			1
10	816,881	817,770	876			14
11	817,771	818,500	728			2
12	818,501	819,450	944	6		
14	819,451	820,260	810			
15	820,261	821,710	1450			
16	821,711	823,510	1766		26	8
17	823,511	825,015	1493		1	11

Began installing transmission tail shaft oil seal disk.

Day	First Number	Last Number	LH	RH	LHM	RHM
18	825,016	826,565	1537	5	8	
19	826,566	828,150	1584			1
21	828,151	829,650	1500			
22	829,651	831,155	1475	15		15
23	831,156	832,235	1046	10	24	
24	832,236	833,026	791			
25	833,027	834,476	1422	25	3	
26	834,477	836,100	1594			30
28	836,101	837,525	1395			30
29	837,526	838,825	1278	2	20	
30	838,826	839,925	1089	10	1	

JULY 1915

Day	First Number	Last Number	LH	RH	LHM	RHM
1	839,926	840,670	737	8		
2	840,671	841,735	1047		3	15
3	841,736	842,775	1025			15
6	842,776	843,500	708		1	16
7	843,501	844,465	957			8
8	844,466	845,365	889		11	
9	845,366	846,238	782	61		30
10	846,239	846,703	442			23
12	846,704	847,643	730	210		
13	847,644	848,478	632	200		3
14	848,479	849,313	772	50	13	
15	849,314	850,283	899	70	1	
16	850,284	851,123	759	79	2	
17	851,124	851,488	265*	100	*255 in records.	
19	851,489	852,123	535	100		
20	852,124	853,098	771	200		4
21	853,099	854,023	924	1		
22	854,024	854,943	845			75
23	854,944	855,758	735		2	78
24	855,759	856,513	755			

Closed July 25 to August 9

AUGUST 1915

Day	First Number	Last Number	LH	RH	LHM	RHM
9	856,514	857,248	725		10	
10	857,249	858,458	1200	7	3	
11	858,459	859,598	1115	25		
12	859,599	860,838	1103	137		
13	860,839	861,978	1128		12	
14	861,979	863,243	1258			7
16	863,244	864,508	1245		20	
17	864,509	865,753	1047	173		25
18	865,754	867,093	1324		10	6
19	867,094	868,343	1209	4		37
20	868,344	869,258	777	119	14	5
21	869,259	870,383	792	306		27
23	870,384	871,658	1050	195		30
24	871,659	873,003	1258	85		2
25	873,004	874,303	1157	108		35
26	874,304	875,638	1115	177	13	30
27	875,639	876,988	1198	110	42	
28	876,989	878,383	1304	91		
30	878,384	879,708	1165	160		
31	879,709	881,063	1300			55

SEPTEMBER 1915

Day	First Number	Last Number	LH	RH	LHM	RHM
1	881,064	882,463	1287	53		60
2	882,464	883,763	1132	165		3
3	883,764	885,113	1155	195		
4	885,114	886,413	1244	56		
7	886,414	887,838	1250	175		
8	887,839	889,223	1194	150		41
9	889,224	890,633	1262	148		
10	890,634	892,063	1322	107		1
11	892,064	893,513	1242	175	2	31
13	893,514	894,988	1370	105		
14	894,989	896,373	1297	88		
15	896,374	897,739	1162	190	14	
16	897,740	898,764	853	114		58
17	898,765	900,264	1394	100	4	2
18	900,265	901,713	1322	105		22
20	901,714	903,113	1211	170		19
21	903,114	904,513	1248	152		
22	904,514	905,593	901	177	2	
23	905,594	906,953	1144	170		46
24	906,954	907,745	704	83		5
25	907,746	908,615	839	1	30	
27	908,616	909,600	752	217		16
28	909,601	910,970	1111	198		61
29	910,971	912,420	1190	250		10
30	912,421	914,026	1431	138		37

OCTOBER 1915

Day	First Number	Last Number	LH	RH	LHM	RHM
1	914,027	915,506	1253	255	2	
2	915,507	917,076	1489	77	4	
4	917,077	918,501	1337	84	3	1
5	918,502	919,420	765	154		
6	919,421	920,820	1214	156	30	
7	920,821	921,785	605	360		
8	921,786	922,945	995	165		
9	922,946	924,370	1225	200		
11	924,371	925,900	1385	125	16	4
12	925,901	927,235	1185	148		2
13	927,236	928,605	1158	160	52	
14	928,606	930,030	1215	210		
15	930,031	931,260	1114	100		16
16	931,261	932,530	1040	230		
18	932,531	933,900	1237	130	3	
19	933,901	935,300	1323	75	2	
20	935,301	936,780	1480			
21	936,781	938,170	1365	9	3	3
22	938,171	939,570	1320	80		
23	939,571	941,170	1564	22	7	7
25	941,171	942,570	1299	95	1	5
26	942,571	943,920	1080	270		
27	943,921	945,320	1076	276	2	26
28	945,321	946,370	715	290		45
29	946,371	947,625	1115	130	10	
30	947,626	949,225	1379	214	7	

NOVEMBER 1915

Day	First Number	Last Number	LH	RH	LHM	RHM
1	949,226	950,725	1391	106		3
2	950,726	951,990	1239	11	15	
3	951,991	953,300	1149	150		11
4	953,301	954,915	1580	35		
5	954,916	956,325	1347	55	7	1
6	956,326	956,905	530	50		
8	956,906	958,375	1452	18		
9	958,376	959,875	1098	387		15
10	959,876	961,450	1498	67	5	5
11	961,451	963,000	1450	88		12
12	963,001	964,460	1258	190		12
13	964,461	965,860	914	475	7	4
15	965,861	967,360	1312	139		49
16	967,361	968,930	1155	385	5	25
17	968,931	970,530	1275	179		146
18	970,531	972,080	1525	8		17
19	972,081	973,520	1413		2	25
20	973,521	975,060	1454		14	72
22	975,061	976,640	1580			
23	976,641	978,240	1438	40		122

Serial Numbers

NOVEMBER 1915

	First Number	Last Number	LH	RH	LHM	RHM
24	978,241	979,620	812	304		264
25	Closed					
26	979,621	981,185	1505	3	10	47
27	981,186	982,835	1646		4	
29	982,836	984,360	1464		15	46
30	984,361	986,060	1693		1	6

DECEMBER 1915

	First Number	Last Number	LH	RH	LHM	RHM
1	986,061	987,645	1583			2
2	987,646	989,335	1690			
3	989,336	990,645	1270		40	
4	990,646	992,185	1517		22	1
6	992,186	993,835	1641		6	3
7	993,836	995,550	1504		181	30
8	995,551	997,315	1703		50	12
9	997,316	999,040	1719		6	
10	999,041	1,000,640	1599		1	

1,000,000 at 1:53-1/2 P.M.

	First Number	Last Number	LH	RH	LHM	RHM
11	1,000,641	1,002,185	1545			
13	1,002,186	1,003,735	1550			
14	1,003,736	1,005,310	1575			
15	1,005,311	1,006,910	1600			
16	1,006,911	1,008,350	1440			
17	1,008,351	1,009,635	1283		1	1
18	1,009,636	1,011,460	1825			
20	1,011,461	1,013,095	1635			
21	1,013,096	1,014,635	1540			
22	1,014,636	1,016,335	1700			
23	1,016,336	1,018,035	1698		2	
24	1,018,036	1,019,760	1725			
25	Closed					
27	1,019,761	1,021,210	1450			
28	1,021,211	1,022,835	1625			
29	1,022,836	1,024,735	1900			
30	1,024,736	1,026,510	1774			1
31	1,026,511	1,028,313	1802		1	

JANUARY 1916

	First Number	Last Number	LH	RH	LHM	RHM
3	1,028,314	1,030,123	1803		7	
4	1,030,124	1,031,798	1648			27
5	1,031,799	1,033,473	1634	18	10	10
6	1,033,474	1,035,248	1752	21	2	
7	1,035,249	1,037,123	1860			15
8	1,037,124	1,038,948	1801	10	5	9
10	1,038,949	1,040,788	1828	2		10
11	1,040,789	1,042,418	1476	65		89
12	1,042,419	1,044,068	1632			18
13	1,044,069	1,045,778	1710			
14	1,045,779	1,047,678	1900			
15	1,047,679	1,049,348	1670			
17	1,049,349	1,051,148	1800			
18	1,051,149	1,052,498	1166	181	3	
19	1,052,499	1,054,233	1605	130		
20	1,054,234	1,055,818	1245	340		
21	1,055,819	1,057,493	1432	243		
22	1,057,494	1,059,309	1614	200	1	
24	1,059,310	1,061,108	1687	113		
25	1,061,109	1,063,098	1864	76		
26	1,063,099	1,064,958	1857	2	1	
27	1,064,959	1,066,788	1815	15		
28	1,066,789	1,068,618	1815	15		
29	1,068,619	1,070,568	2000			
31	1,070,569	1,071,928	1345	15		

FEBRUARY 1916

	First Number	Last Number	LH	RH	LHM	RHM
1	1,071,929	1,073,938	2010			
2	1,073,939	1,075,778	1832			8
3	1,075,779	1,077,788	2010			
4	1,077,789	1,079,888	2100			
5	1,079,889	1,081,988	2084		6	10
7	1,081,989	1,083,813	1825			
8	1,083,814	1,085,743	1910			20
9	1,085,744	1,087,508	1727	12	21	5
10	1,087,509	1,089,418	1871	5	15	19
11	1,089,419	1,091,268	1835			15
12	1,091,269	1,093,068	1619	151	25	5
14	1,093,069	1,095,068	1895	85	10	10
15	1,095,069	1,096,858	1603	165	10	12
16	1,096,859	1,098,783	1759	150		16
17	1,098,784	1,100,443	1533	100		27
18	1,100,444	1,102,393	1810	124		16
19	1,102,394	1,104,023	1611	4		15
21	1,104,024	1,105,948	1901		24	
22	1,105,949	1,107,863	1904		5	6
23	1,107,864	1,109,463	1467	100		33
24	1,109,464	1,111,343	1848		12	20
25	1,111,344	1,113,233	1738	122		30
26	1,113,234	1,115,203	1839	100		31
28	1,115,204	1,117,138	1784	139		12
29	1,117,139	1,119,003	1765	100		

MARCH 1916

	First Number	Last Number	LH	RH	LHM	RHM
1	1,119,004	1,120,833	1802	20	8	
2	1,120,834	1,122,933	1980	120		
3	1,122,934	1,124,933	1875	115	10	
4	1,124,934	1,126,933	1770	220	10	
6	1,126,934	1,128,733	1615	140	15	30
7	1,128,734	1,130,733	1848	95		57
8	1,130,734	1,132,733	1905	45		50
9	1,132,734	1,134,493	1693	62		5
10	1,134,494	1,136,493	1746	203	2	49
11	1,136,494	1,138,633	1907	200	28	5
13	1,138,634	1,140,683	1850	200		
14	1,140,684	1,142,783	1894	202	3	1
15	1,142,784	1,144,783	1750	250		
16	1,144,784	1,146,713	1668	256	6	
17	1,146,714	1,148,313	1370	230		
18	1,148,314	1,149,583	1020	250		
20	1,149,584	1,151,398	1574	240		1
21	1,151,399	1,153,423	1760	255		10
22	1,153,424	1,155,573	1890	250		10
23	1,155,574	1,157,648	1910	155		10
24	1,157,649	1,159,648	1525	460	15	
25	1,159,649	1,161,408	1220	540		
27	1,161,409	1,161,898	490			
28	1,161,899	1,163,583	1661	3	20	1
29	1,163,584	1,165,023	1440			
30	1,165,024	1,167,023	2000			
31	1,167,024	1,169,023	2000			

APRIL 1916

	First Number	Last Number	LH	RH	LHM	RHM
1	1,169,024	1,170,873	1850			
3	1,170,874	1,172,573	1690		9	1
4	1,172,574	1,174,523	1938			12
5	1,174,524	1,176,473	1940		10	
6	1,176,474	1,178,473	1890		6	104
7	1,178,474	1,180,523	1984			66
8	1,180,524	1,182,273	1659			91
10	1,182,274	1,184,248	1924			51
11	1,184,249	1,186,252 *	1974 *			30

* Factory shows 1,186,248, with a production of 2000 total, but the figures add up to the numbers shown here.

	First Number	Last Number	LH	RH	LHM	RHM
12	1,186,253	1,188,352	2082	2	16	
13	1,188,353	1,190,458	2051			55
14	1,190,459	1,192,558	2080	20		
15	1,192,559	1,194,673	2095	20		
17	1,194,674	1,196,773	2063	37		
18	1,196,774	1,198,774	2000			
19	1,198,775	1,200,873	2088			12
20	1,200,874	1,202,973	2100			
21	1,202,974	1,205,078	2086	18		1
22	1,205,079	1,207,183	2105			
24	1,207,184	1,208,608	1417			8
25	1,208,609	1,211,018	2294	6		110
26	1,211,019	1,213,268	2168		3	79
27	1,213,269	1,215,368	2009			91
28	1,215,369	1,217,468	2040	55		5
29	1,217,469	1,219,573	2015	5		85

MAY 1916

	First Number	Last Number	LH	RH	LHM	RHM
1	1,219,574	1,221,673	1955	70		75
2	1,221,674	1,223,823	2015	31	100	4
3	1,223,824	1,225,923	1900	50	150	
4	1,225,924	1,228,073	1858	47	245	
5	1,228,074	1,230,223	2125			25
6	1,230,224	1,232,383	1894	266		
8	1,232,384	1,234,518	2012	6		117
9	1,234,519	1,236,618	2100			
10	1,236,619	1,238,748	2130			
11	1,238,748	1,240,648	1900			
12	1,240,649	1,242,248	1600			
13	1,242,249	1,243,948	1700			
15	1,243,949	1,245,958	2010			
16	1,245,959	1,247,963	1996			9
17	1,247,964	1,250,088	2125			
18	1,250,089	1,252,243	2146	9		
19	1,252,244	1,254,403	2160			
20	1,254,404	1,256,573	2170			
22	1,256,574	1,258,728	2155			
23	1,258,729	1,260,883	2155			
24	1,260,884	1,262,883	2000			
25	1,262,884	1,265,039	2136			20
26	1,265,040	1,267,064	2025			
27	1,267,065	1,269,073	2009			
29	1,269,074	1,271,233	2160			
30	Closed					
31	1,271,234	1,273,413	2180			

JUNE 1916

	First Number	Last Number	LH	RH	LHM	RHM
1	1,273,414	1,275,573	2160			
2	1,275,574	1,277,733	2160			
3	1,277,734	1,279,893	2160			
5	1,279,894	1,281,903	2010			
6	1,281,904	1,284,113	2210			
7	1,284,114	1,286,273	2160			
8	1,286,274	1,288,373	2100			
9	1,288,374	1,290,473	2100			
10	1,290,474	1,292,637	2165			

	First Number	Last Number	LH	RH	LHM	RHM

JUNE 1916

	First Number	Last Number	LH	RH	LHM	RHM
12	1,292,638	1,294,693	2055			
13	1,294,694	1,296,343	1650			
14	1,296,344	1,298,368	2025			
15	1,298,369	1,300,688	2309	11		
16	1,300,689	1,302,938	2238	12		
17	1,302,939	1,304,998	2058	2		
19	1,304,999	1,307,180	2182			
20	1,307,181	1,309,398	2218			
21	1,309,399	1,311,448	2050			
22	1,311,449	1,313,633	2110			75
23	1,313,634	1,315,817	2094			90
24	1,315,818	1,317,648	1826			5
26	1,317,649	1,319,848	2160			40
27	1,319,849	1,321,888	1975			65
28	1,321,889	1,324,053	2100			65
29	1,324,054	1,326,023	1895			75
30	1,326,024	1,328,148	1900	225		

JULY 1916

	First Number	Last Number	LH	RH	LHM	RHM
1	1,328,149	1,330,373	2165	60		
4	Closed					
5	1,330,374	1,331,573	1118	82		
6	1,331,574	1,333,648	1955	120		
7	1,333,649	1,335,998	2269	81		
8	1,335,999	1,338,178	2113	67		
10	1,338,179	1,340,103	1770	155		
11	1,340,104	1,342,353	2138	112		
12	1,342,354	1,344,593	2106	134		
13	1,344,594	1,346,093	1310	1		189
14	1,346,094	1,348,293	1925			275
15	1,348,294	1,350,308	1865			150
17	1,350,309	1,352,368	1989			71
18	1,352,369	1,353,408	900	140		
19	1,353,409	1,355,173	1590	175		
20	1,355,174	1,356,773	1560			40
21	1,356,774	1,359,108*	2025			310
22	1,359,109	1,361,258	2050			100

* Records show 1,357,500

	First Number	Last Number	LH	RH	LHM	RHM
24	1,361,259	1,362,813	1360			195
25	1,362,814	1,362,989	176 **			

** The factory changed the records to begin fiscal 1917 with 1,362,814, but the 176 engines were actually built on July 25. The August 7 production figures include these 176 engines.

AUGUST 1916

	First Number	Last Number	LH	RH	LHM	RHM
7	1,362,990	1,364,013	1125 **			75
8	1,364,014	1,365,338	1245			80
9	1,365,339	1,367,013	1617	35		23
10	1,367,014	1,368,813	1800			
11	1,368,814	1,370,623	1804	6		
12	1,370,624	1,372,623	2000			
14	1,372,624	1,373,748	1125			
15	1,373,749	1,374,848	1100			
16	1,374,849	1,376,848	2000			
17	1,376,849	1,378,773	1925			
18	1,378,774	1,380,773	2000			
19	1,380,774	1,382,698	1925			
21	1,382,699	1,384,398	1676	24		
22	1,384,399	1,386,208	1810			
23	1,386,209	1,388,233	2025			
24	1,388,234	1,390,033	1800			
25	1,390,034	1,392,033	2000			
26	1,392,034	1,393,998	1865			100
28	1,393,999	1,395,898	1900			
29	1,395,899	1,397,398	1400			100
30	1,397,399	1,399,288	1780			120
31	1,399,289	1,400,913	1515			100

SEPTEMBER 1916

	First Number	Last Number	LH	RH	LHM	RHM
1	1,400,914	1,402,413	1385			115
2	1,402,414	1,404,413	1935			65
4	Closed					
5	1,404,414	1,406,423	2010			
6	1,406,424	1,408,323	1900			
7	1,408,324	1,410,338	2015			
8	1,410,339	1,412,348	2010			
9	1,412,349	1,414,348	2000			
11	1,414,349	1,416,348	2000			
12	1,416,349	1,418,098	1750			
13	1,418,099	1,419,913	1815			
14	1,419,914	1,421,913	2000			
15	1,421,914	1,424,023	2110			
16	1,424,024	1,426,198	2175			
18	1,426,199	1,428,398	2200			
19	1,428,399	1,430,598	2175	25		
20	1,430,599	1,432,608	2010			
21	1,432,609	1,434,758	2143	7		
22	1,434,759	1,436,873	2110	4		
23	1,436,874	1,438,998	2125			
25	1,438,999	1,441,223	2225			
26	1,441,224	1,443,423	2200			
27	1,443,424	1,445,623	2200			
28	1,445,624	1,447,723	2084	16		

	First Number	Last Number	LH	RH	LHM	RHM
29	1,447,724	1,449,973	2250			
30	1,449,974	1,452,213	2240			

OCTOBER 1916

	First Number	Last Number	LH	RH	LHM	RHM
2	1,452,214	1,454,238	2025			
3	1,454,239	1,456,538 *	2300			
4	1,456,539	1,458,763	2225			
5	1,458,764	1,460,763	1999	1		
6	1,460,764	1,463,113	2350			
7	1,463,114	1,465,438	2325			
9	1,465,439	1,467,738	2200			100
10	1,467,739	1,470,053	2205			110
11	1,470,054	1,472,353	2200			100
12	1,472,354	1,474,663	2220			90
13	1,474,664	1,476,973	2310			
14	1,476,974	1,479,338	2365			
16	1,479,339	1,481,653	2315			
17	1,481,654	1,483,963	2310			
18	1,483,964	1,486,263	2300			
19	1,486,264	1,488,163	1891	9		
20	1,488,164	1,490,463	2285	15		
21	1,490,464	1,492,763	2300			
23	1,492,764	1,495,063	2300			
24	1,495,064	1,497,363	2300			
25	1,497,364	1,499,663	2300			
26	1,499,664	1,501,963	2300			
27	1,501,964	1,503,938	1865			110
28	1,503,939	1,506,238	2100			200
30	1,506,239	1,508,248	1930			80
31	1,508,249	1,510,398	2050			100

* Records show 1,454,538 but 1,456,539 is listed as 1st # of 10-4

NOVEMBER 1916

	First Number	Last Number	LH	RH	LHM	RHM
1	1,510,399	1,512,623	2110			115
2	1,512,624	1,514,488	1767			98
3	1,514,489	1,516,898	2410			
4	1,516,899	1,519,238	2340			
6	1,519,239	1,521,638	2400			
7	1,521,639	1,523,888	2250			
8	1,523,889	1,526,188	2300			
9	1,526,189	1,528,238	2050			
10	1,528,239	1,530,588	2350			
11	1,530,589	1,533,038	2450			
13	1,533,039	1,535,538	2300	200		
14	1,535,539	1,537,938	2240	160		
15	1,537,939	1,540,463	2375	150		
16	1,540,464	1,542,963	2350	150		
17	1,542,964	1,545,388	2268	157		
18	1,545,389	1,547,798	2265	145		
20	1,547,799	1,550,088	2105	185		
21	1,550,089	1,552,433	2137	208		
22	1,552,434	1,554,873	2152	288		
23	1,554,874	1,557,238	2089	168		108
24	1,557,239	1,559,703	2199	175		92
25	1,559,704	1,562,303	2493	107		
27	1,562,304	1,564,646	2242	101		
28	1,564,647	1,567,176	2310	220		
29	1,567,177	1,569,776	2444	156		
30	Closed					

DECEMBER 1916

	First Number	Last Number	LH	RH	LHM	RHM
1	1,569,777	1,572,276	2328	172		
2	1,572,277	1,574,626	2158	192		
4	1,574,627	1,576,891	2170	95		
5	1,576,892	1,579,411	2142	378		
6	1,579,412	1,582,061	2455	195		
7	1,582,062	1,584,666	2390	215		
8	1,584,667	1,587,221	2350	205		
9	1,587,222	1,589,881	2555	105		
11	1,589,882	1,592,446	2290	275		
12	1,592,447	1,595,046	2425	175		
13	1,595,047	1,597,346	2165	135		
14	1,597,347	1,600,076	2630		100	
15	1,600,077	1,602,501	2250		175	
16	1,602,502	1,604,951	2225		225	
18	1,604,952	1,607,551	2450	150		
19	1,607,552	1,610,016	2281	184		
20	1,610,017	1,612,316	2216	9		75
21	1,612,317	1,614,516	2125			75

Closed December 22 until January 3, 1917

JANUARY 1917

	First Number	Last Number	LH	RH	LHM	RHM
3	1,614,517	1,616,216	1695	5		
4	1,616,217	1,618,691	2321	24		130
5	1,618,692	1,621,491	2675			125
6	1,621,492	1,624,491	2895			105
8	1,624,492	1,627,336	2686	24		135
9	1,627,337	1,630,136	2748			52
10	1,630,137	1,633,041	2890	12		3
11	1,633,042	1,635,881	2840			
12	1,635,882	1,638,771	2890			
13	1,638,772	1,641,681	2910			
15	1,641,682	1,644,536	2831	24		
16	1,644,537	1,647,441	2815	90		
17	1,647,442	1,650,001	2548			12
18	1,650,002	1,651,801	1800			

First Number	Last Number	LH	RH	LHM	RHM

JANUARY 1917

Day	First Number	Last Number	LH	RH	LHM	RHM
19	1,651,802	1,654,081	2074		100	106
20	1,654,082	1,656,836	2659		96	
22	1,656,837	1,659,641	2690		140	
23	1,659,642	1,661,921	2231	4	20	
24	1,661,922	1,664,601	2680			
25	1,664,602	1,667,401	2564		143	93
26	1,667,402	1,670,076	2675			
27	1,670,077	1,672,686	2596	14		
29	1,672,687	1,675,211	2400	125		
30	1,675,212	1,677,071	1860			
31	1,677,072	1,679,591	2290	130		100

FEBRUARY 1917

Day	First Number	Last Number	LH	RH	LHM	RHM
1	1,679,592	1,682,341	2623	122		5
2	1,682,342	1,685,031	2502	128	35	25
3	1,685,032	1,685,791	760			
5	1,685,792	1,688,306	2355	160		
6	1,688,307	1,690,951	2495	150		
7	1,690,952	1,693,876	2923			2
8	1,693,877	1,696,686	2610	200		
9	1,696,687	1,699,531	2837	8		
10	1,699,532	1,702,256	2600			125
12	1,702,257	1,704,931	2555			120
13	1,704,932	1,707,721	2785			5
14	1,707,722	1,710,331	2457			153
15	1,710,332	1,712,646	2081	222		12
16	1,712,647	1,715,446	2680			120
17	1,715,447	1,717,956	2381	4		125
19	1,717,957	1,720,086	2068			62
20	1,720,087	1,722,766	2679			1
21	1,722,767	1,725,216	2286			164
22	1,725,217	1,727,496	2280			
23	1,727,497	1,730,166	2504			166
24	1,730,167	1,733,066	2866			34
26	1,733,067	1,734,531	1465			
27	1,734,532	1,737,251	2708	12		
28	1,737,252	1,739,906	2455			200

MARCH 1917

Day	First Number	Last Number	LH	RH	LHM	RHM
1	1,739,907	1,742,371	2370			95
2	1,742,372	1,744,256	1885			
3	1,744,257	1,746,911	2655			
5	1,746,912	1,749,511	2600			
6	1,749,512	1,752,296	2785			
7	1,752,297	1,754,996	2700			
8	1,754,997	1,757,666	2669		1	
9	1,757,667	1,760,016	2350			
10	1,760,017	1,762,246	2206	24		
12	1,762,247	1,764,796	2550			
13	1,764,797	1,767,216	2420			
14	1,767,217	1,769,786	2570			
15	1,769,787	1,772,406	2567			53
16	1,772,407	1,775,156	2553	196		1
17	1,775,157	1,777,886	2279	410		41
19	1,777,887	1,780,616	2728	1		1
20	1,780,617	1,783,116	2260	130		110
21	1,783,117	1,785,886	2770			
22	1,785,887	1,788,686	2800			
23	1,788,687	1,791,686	2918		11	71
24	1,791,687	1,794,286	2598			2
26	1,794,287	1,796,886	2600			
27	1,796,887	1,799,886	2708	292		
28	1,799,887	1,802,986	3075	25		
29	1,802,987	1,805,986	2898			102
30	1,805,987	1,808,986	2770		100	130
31	1,808,987	1,812,013	2985	15		27

APRIL 1917

Day	First Number	Last Number	LH	RH	LHM	RHM
2	1,812,014	1,815,013	2900			100
3	1,815,014	1,818,013	2899		90	11
4	1,818,014	1,821,013	2812			188
5	1,821,014	1,824,013	2672	35		293
6	1,824,014	1,827,013	2745			255
7	1,827,014	1,830,013	2850		142	8
9	1,830,014	1,832,913	2743	157		
10	1,832,914	1,835,913	3000			
11	1,835,914	1,838,913	2983	17		
12	1,838,914	1,841,963	2935		115	
13	1,841,964	1,844,978	3013			2
14	1,844,979	1,848,038	3060			
16	1,848,039	1,851,038	2975		25	
17	1,851,039	1,854,038	2930		70	
18	1,854,039	1,857,038	2990		10	
19	1,857,039	1,860,113	3075			
20	1,860,114	1,863,128	2964			51
21	1,863,129	1,866,238	2990	35		85
23	1,866,239	1,869,273	3035			
24	1,869,274	1,872,353	3080			
25	1,872,354	1,875,554	3200			
26	1,875,555	1,878,758	3205			
27	1,878,759	1,881,858	3100			
28	1,881,859	1,884,913	3055			
30	1,884,914	1,888,043	2997			133

MAY 1917

Day	First Number	Last Number	LH	RH	LHM	RHM
1	1,888,044	1,891,253	3210			
2	1,891,254	1,894,413	3160			
3	1,894,414	1,897,573	3160			
4	1,897,574	1,900,728	3155			
5	1,900,729	1,903,878	3150			
7	1,903,879	1,907,133	3219	36		
8	1,907,134	1,910,293	3160			
9	1,910,294	1,913,493	3107			93
10	1,913,494	1,916,703	3160	3		47
11	1,916,704	1,919,883	2967	23		190
12	1,919,884	1,923,093	3090			120
14	1,923,094	1,926,163	2970			100
15	1,926,164	1,928,433	2270			
16	1,928,434	1,931,703	3270			
17	1,931,704	1,935,228	3325			200
18	1,935,229	1,938,228	2747			253
19	1,938,229	1,941,103	2875			
21	1,941,104	1,944,248	3145			
22	1,944,249	1,947,413	2930	224		11
23	1,947,414	1,949,039	1550			75
24	1,949,040	1,952,398	3360			
25	1,952,399	1,955,763	3365			
26	1,955,764	1,959,104	3331			10
28	1,959,105	1,962,239	3035			100
29	1,962,240	1,965,484	2842	63		350
30	Closed					
31	1,965,485	1,968,619	3006	97	20	12

JUNE 1917

Day	First Number	Last Number	LH	RH	LHM	RHM
1	1,968,620	1,971,629	2918		87	5
2	1,971,630	1,974,644	2990	20		5
4	1,974,645	1,977,659	3001			4
5	Closed					
6	1,977,660	1,980,534	2875			
7	1,980,535	1,983,659	3089	36		
8	1,983,660	1,986,809	3150			
9	1,986,810	1,989,810	2995			5
11	1,989,811	1,992,835	3025			
12	1,992,836	1,995,834	3000			
13	1,995,835	1,998,839	3005			
14	1,998,840	2,001,849	3010			
		2,000,000 at 1:02 P.M.				
15	2,001,850	2,004,854	2992	13		
16	2,004,855	2,007,854	3000			
18	2,007,855	2,010,884	2955	75		
19	2,010,885	2,013,889	2841	164		
20	2,013,890	2,016,915	2837	189		
21	2,016,916	2,019,920	2788	217		
22	2,019,921	2,022,922	2783	219		
23	2,022,923	2,025,954	2984	138		
25	2,025,955	2,028,954	2923	77		
26	2,028,955	2,031,957	2788	215		
27	2,031,958	2,034,547	2385	203	2	
28	2,034,548	2,038,101	3254	293	7	
29	2,038,102	2,041,101	2890	97	13	
30	2,041,102	2,044,131	3006			24

JULY 1917

Day	First Number	Last Number	LH	RH	LHM	RHM
2	2,044,132	2,047,136	2877		128	
3	2,047,137	2,050,146	3009		1	
4	Closed					
5	2,050,147	2,053,161	3015			
6	2,053,162	2,056,187	3026			
7	2,056,188	2,059,231	3044			
9	2,059,232	2,062,231	2923		77	
10	2,062,232	2,065,241	3010			
11	2,065,242	2,068,256	3015			
12	2,068,257	2,071,271	2970		45	
13	2,071,272	2,074,291	2986		34	
14	2,074,292	2,077,331	3008		32	
16	2,077,332	2,080,351	2963		57	
17	2,080,352	2,083,371	2923		97	
18	2,083,372	2,086,371	2922		78	
19	2,086,372	2,089,396	2946		79	
20	2,089,397	2,092,422	2904		122	
21	2,092,423	2,095,423	2777		224	
23	2,095,424	2,098,427	2894		110	
24	2,098,428	2,101,427	2887		113	
25	2,101,428	2,104,427	2881		119	
26	2,104,428	2,107,427	3000			
27	2,107,428	2,110,427	2996		4	
28	2,110,428	2,113,501	1702		1372	
	Closed July 29 to August 12.					

AUGUST 1917

Day	First Number	Last Number	LH	RH	LHM	RHM
13	2,113,502	2,115,766	2134		131	
14	2,115,767	2,118,766	2834	15	151	
15	2,118,767	2,121,766	2937		63	
16	2,121,767	2,124,879	3113			
17	2,124,880	2,127,884	2804	201		
18	2,127,885	2,130,906	2824	198		
20	2,130,907	2,133,916	2787	223		
21	2,133,917	2,136,777	2781	80		

AUGUST 1917

Date	First Number	Last Number	LH	RH	LHM	RHM
22	2,136,778	2,139,792	2692	323		
23	2,139,793	2,142,502	2676	34		
24	2,143,503	2,145,322	2524			296
25	2,145,323	2,148,247	2744			181
27	2,148,248	2,151,197	2752	50		148
28	2,151,198	2,154,153	2889			67
29	2,154,154	2,157,068	2794			121
30	2,157,069	2,159,988	2822			98
31	2,159,989	2,162,888	2734	100		66

SEPTEMBER 1917

Date	First Number	Last Number	LH	RH	LHM	RHM
1	2,162,889	2,165,793	2793	12		100
3	Closed					
4	2,165,794	2,168,749	2956			
5	2,168,750	2,171,817	2976	10		82
6	2,171,818	2,174,843	2968	58		
7	2,174,844	2,177,873	3028	2		
8	2,177,874	2,180,905	2878			154
10	2,180,906	2,183,940	3031			4
11	2,183,941	2,186,946	2974	32		
12	2,186,947	2,189,959	3012			
13	2,189,960	2,192,968	3010			
14	2,192,969	2,195,968	3000			
15	2,195,969	2,198,988	3020			
17	2,198,989	2,201,266	2112		166	
18	2,201,267	2,202,008	602	6	134	
19	2,202,009	2,204,859	2696		155	
20	2,204,860	2,207,864	2849		156	
21	2,207,865	2,211,000	2643		493	
22	2,211,001	2,213,405	2405			
24	2,213,406	2,216,310	2662	243		
25	2,216,311	2,219,222	2566	300	46	
26	2,219,223	2,222,130	2683	225		
27	2,222,131	2,225,050	2620	300		
28	2,225,051	2,228,105	2943	11	101	
29	2,228,106	2,231,009	2649	8	247	

OCTOBER 1917

Date	First Number	Last Number	LH	RH	LHM	RHM
1	2,231,010	2,233,909	2670	21		209
2	2,233,910	2,236,814	2705			200
3	2,236,815	2,239,714	2700			200
4	2,239,715	2,242,622	2608			300
5	2,242,623	2,245,529	2907			
6	2,245,530	2,248,449	2808			112
8	2,248,450	2,251,452	2791			212
9	2,251,453	2,254,462	2597	6	200	207
10	2,254,463	2,257,487	2825		100	100
11	2,257,488	2,260,537	2850		100	100
12	2,260,538	2,263,612	2825		250	
13	2,263,613	2,266,569	2888	69		
15	2,266,570	2,269,479	2650	200		60
16	2,269,480	2,272,439	2809	151		
17	2,272,440	2,275,449	2800	210		
18	2,275,450	2,278,454	2858	147		
19	2,278,455	2,281,464	2759	251		
20	2,281,465	2,283,919	2402	53		
22	2,283,920	2,286,674	2643	12		100
23	2,286,675	2,289,427	2548			205
24	2,289,428	2,292,432	2855			150
25	2,292,433	2,295,452	2867			153
26	2,295,453	2,298,457	2854			151
27	2,298,458	2,301,469	2912			100
29	2,301,470	2,304,479	2707			103
30	2,304,480	2,307,594	2915			
31	2,307,595	2,310,409	2455	30	270	60

NOVEMBER 1917

Date	First Number	Last Number	LH	RH	LHM	RHM
1	2,310,410	2,313,519	2710		200	
2	2,313,520	2,316,424	2560	45	100	
3	2,316,425	2,319,234	2610		200	
5	2,319,235	2,322,249	2615		200	
6	2,322,250	2,325,059	2785		25	
7	2,325,060	2,328,059	2600	200		
8	2,328,060	2,330,884	2525	100		200
9	2,330,885	2,333,889	2605	200		
10	2,333,890	2,336,699	2517	200		93
12	2,336,700	2,339,502	2801	2		
13	2,339,503	2,342,714	2463	298		
14	2,342,715	2,345,726	2767	45		
15	2,345,727	2,348,939	2613			200
16	2,348,940	2,351,949	2662	48		100
17	2,351,950	2,354,949	2700			100
19	2,354,950	2,357,650	2301			200
20	2,357,651	2,360,452	2402			200
21	2,360,453	2,363,555	2803			100
22	2,363,556	2,366,462	2607			100
23	2,366,463	2,369,387	2538			187
24	2,369,388	2,372,316	2616			113
26	2,372,317	2,375,166	2450			200
27	2,375,167	2,378,096	2530			200
28	2,378,097	2,381,031	2535			200
29	Closed					
30	2,381,032	2,383,951	2620			40

DECEMBER 1917

Date	First Number	Last Number	LH	RH	LHM	RHM
1	2,383,952	2,386,826	2575			100
3	2,386,827	2,389,636	2410	200		
4	2,389,637	2,392,464	2428	200		
5	2,392,465	2,395,139	2375	100		
6	2,395,140	2,397,189	1850			
7	2,397,190	2,399,219	1530	300		
8	2,399,220	2,401,719	2150	150		
10	2,401,720	2,404,369	2325	125		
11	2,404,370	2,407,084	2510	5		
12	2,407,085	2,409,534	2050		200	
13	2,409,535	2,412,034	2300			
14	2,412,035	2,415,037	2903		100	
15	2,415,038	2,417,854	2717		100	
17	2,417,855	2,420,254	2400			
18	2,420,255	2,423,254	2600			
19	2,423,255	2,426,254	2400		200	
20	2,426,255	2,429,049	2395		200	
21	2,429,050	2,431,849	2500	34	66	
22	2,431,850	2,434,654	2405		200	
24	2,434,655	2,436,704	1811			39
25	Closed					
26	2,436,705	2,438,914	2010			
27	2,438,915	2,441,626	2512			
28	2,441,627	2,444,339	2421			92
29	2,444,340	2,447,054	2315			200
31	2,447,055	2,449,179	1479			246

JANUARY 1918

Date	First Number	Last Number	LH	RH	LHM	RHM
2	2,449,180	2,451,994	2615			
3	2,451,995	2,454,812	2219			400
4	2,454,813	2,457,524	2412	100		
5	2,457,525	2,460,239	2481			34
7	2,460,240	2,461,200				
	(2,461,201	2,461,400		(200 shipped to Long Island, NY)		
	2,461,401	2,462,950	2511	(See 1-16-18 production)		
8	2,462,951	2,464,570	1620			
9	2,464,571	2,468,196	3626			
10	2,468,197	2,470,806	2610			
11	2,470,807	2,473,431	2594			31
12	2,473,432	2,475,789	2358			
14	2,475,790	2,477,389	1600			
15	2,477,390	2,479,691	2302			
16	2,479,692	2,481,941	2250			
	2,461,201	2,461,400	200	(Returned from L.I., NY)		
17	2,481,942	2,484,449	2430		78	
18	Closed from January 18 to 22 ("Shut down to save coal")					
23	2,484,450	2,487,199	2550	**		

** Note: Production figures are off by 200. The figure should be 2750 to make the serial numbers agree. Probably due to the Long Island returns.

Date	First Number	Last Number	LH	RH	LHM	RHM
24	2,487,200	2,490,025	2626			
25	2,490,026	2,492,640	2465		150	
26	2,492,641	2,495,254	2540		74	
29	2,495,255	2,497,874	2520		100	
30	2,497,875	2,500,499	2525		100	
31	2,500,500	2,503,204	2658		47	

Note: Engine record numbers, not engines, were shipped to Long Island, New York. Unnumbered "knocked down" (unassembled) engine blocks were also shipped; the numbers to be stamped in upon completion. Actual dates of assembly of these engines is unknown.

FEBRUARY 1918

Date	First Number	Last Number	LH	RH	LHM	RHM
1	2,503,205	2,505,819	2610	5		
2	2,505,820	2,508,439	2565		55	
5	2,508,440	2,509,744	1305			
6	2,509,745	2,512,419	2675			
7	2,512,420	2,515,099	2618	62		
8	2,515,100	2,517,799	2700			
9	2,517,800	2,520,524	2673		52	
12	2,520,525	2,523,174	2450		200	
13	2,523,175	2,525,889	2615			100
14	2,525,890	2,528,614	2525			200
15	2,528,615	2,531,314	2400			300
16	2,531,315	2,534,024	2510	15		185
18	2,534,025	2,536,139	2015			100
19	2,536,140	2,538,744	2405			200
20	2,538,745	2,541,419	2658			17
21	2,541,420	2,543,722	2203		100	
22	2,543,723	2,545,647	1725		200	
23	2,545,648	2,548,074	2365		62	
25	2,548,075	2,550,574	2500			
26	2,550,575	2,553,214	2640			
27	2,553,215	2,555,814	2400	200		
28	2,555,815	2,558,189	2275	100		

MARCH 1918

Date	First Number	Last Number	LH	RH	LHM	RHM
1	2,558,190	2,560,804	2415	200		
2	2,560,805	2,563,489	2485	200		
4	2,563,490	2,566,144	2455	200		
5	2,566,145	2,568,404	2095	130	35	
6	2,568,405	2,570,629	2225			
7	2,570,630	2,572,729	1920		180	
8	2,572,730	2,574,929	2000		200	

	First Number	Last Number	LH	RH	LHM	RHM
MARCH 1918						
9	2,574,930	2,577,129	2200			
11	2,577,130	2,579,334	2205			
12	2,579,335	2,581,334	2000			
13	2,581,335	2,583,336	1802	200		
14	2,583,337	2,585,346	1810	200		
15	2,585,347	2,586,900				
	(2,586,901	2,587,500)		(600 to L.I.)		
	2,587,501	2,587,556	1610			
16	2,587,557	2,588,800				
	(2,588,801	2,589,200)		(400 to L.I.)		
	2,589,201	2,589,629	1373	100		

Note: Production figures do not include the numbers to Long Island.

	First Number	Last Number	LH	RH	LHM	RHM
18	2,589,630	2,591,279	1450	200		
19	2,591,280	2,593,079	1700	100		
20	2,593,080	2,595,079	1731	269		
21	2,595,080	2,597,024	1745		200	
22	2,597,025	2,599,029	1976		29	
23	2,599,030	2,601,054	1800		225	
25	2,601,055	2,602,879	1679		146	
26	2,602,880	2,603,600				
	(2,603,601	2,604,000)		(400 to L.I.)		
	2,604,001	2,604,679	1400			
27	2,604,680	2,605,700				
	(2,605,701	2,606,300)		(600 to L.I.)		
	2,606,301	2,606,689	1410			
28	2,606,690	2,608,239	1550			
29	2,608,240	2,609,839	1600			
30	2,609,840	2,611,439	1600			
APRIL 1918						
1	2,611,440	2,612,864	1425			
2	2,612,865	2,614,474	1610			
3	2,614,475	2,616,184	1710			
4	2,616,185	2,617,000				
	(2,617,001	2,617,600)		(600 to L.I.)		
	2,617,601	2,618,064	1280			
5	2,618,065	2,618,700				
	(2,618,701	2,619,100)		(400 to L.I.)		
	2,619,101	2,619,614	1150			
6	2,619,615	2,620,800				
	(2,620,801	2,621,000)		(200 to L.I.)		
	2,621,001	2,621,194	1380			
8	2,621,195	2,622,000				
	(2,622,001	2,622,200)		(200 to L.I.)		
	2,622,201	2,622,894	1500			
9	2,622,895	2,623,800				
	(2,623,801	2,624,000)		(200 to L.I.)		
	2,624,001	2,624,744	1650			
10	2,624,745	2,625,400				
	(2,625,401	2,625,600)		(200 to L.I.)		
	2,625,601	2,626,584	1640			
11	2,626,585	2,627,400				
	(2,627,401	2,627,600)		(200 to L.I.)		
	2,627,601	2,628,254	1470			
12	2,628,255	2,629,954	1700			
13	2,629,955	2,630,800				
	(2,630,801	2,631,000)		(200 to L.I.)		
	2,631,001	2,631,834	1680			
15	2,631,835	2,632,600				
	(2,632,601	2,632,800)		(200 to L.I.)		
	2,632,801	2,633,539	1505			
16	2,633,540	2,634,100				
	(2,634,101	2,634,300)		(200 to L.I.)		
	2,634,301	2,635,369	1630			
17	2,635,370	2,636,400				
	(2,636,401	2,636,600)		(200 to L.I.)		
	2,636,601	2,637,319	1750			
18	2,637,320	2,638,000				
	(2,638,001	2,638,200)		(200 to L.I.)		
	2,638,201	2,638,994	1475			
19	2,638,995	2,640,894	1748	152		
20	2,640,895	2,641,500				
	(2,641,501	2,641,700)		(200 to L.I.)		
	2,641,701	2,642,994	1900			
22	2,642,995	2,643,800				
	(2,643,801	2,644,000)		(200 to L.I.)		
	2,644,001	2,645,004	1810			
23	2,645,005	2,645,600				
	(2,645,601	2,645,800)		(200 to L.I.)		
	2,645,801	2,646,979	1704			
24	2,646,980	2,647,600				
	(2,647,601	2,647,800)		(200 to L.I.)		
	2,647,801	2,648,204	825	200		
25	2,648,205	2,648,800				
	(2,648,801	2,649,000)		(200 to L.I.)		
	2,649,001	2,650,009	1605			
26	2,650,010	2,651,809	1700	100		
27	2,651,810	2,652,800				
	(2,652,801	2,653,000)		(200 to L.I.)		
	2,653,001	2,653,694	1385	300		
29	2,653,695	2,654,300				
	(2,654,301	2,654,500)		(200 to L.I.)		
	2,654,501	2,655,614	1620	100		
30	2,655,615	2,657,000				
	(2,657,001	2,657,200)		(200 to L.I.)		
	2,657,201	2,657,479	1465	200		
MAY 1918						
1	2,657,480	2,658,000				
	(2,658,001	2,658,200)		(200 to L.I.)		
	2,658,201	2,659,059	1324	56		
2	2,659,060	2,659,800				
	(2,659,801	2,660,000)		(200 to L.I.)		
	2,660,001	2,660,644	1385			
3	2,660,645	2,662,544	1900			
4	2,662,545	2,663,300				
	(2,663,301	2,663,500)		(200 to L.I.)		
	2,663,501	2,664,624	1880			
6	2,664,625	2,665,200				
	(2,665,201	2,665,400)		(200 to L.I.)		
	2,665,401	2,666,189	1365			
7	2,666,190	2,666,800				
	(2,666,801	2,667,000)		(200 to L.I.)		
	2,667,001	2,667,914	1525			
8	2,667,915	2,668,800				
	(2,668,801	2,669,000)		(200 to L.I.)		
	2,669,001	2,669,824	1710			
9	2,669,825	2,670,300				
	(2,670,301	2,670,500)		(200 to L.I.)		
	2,670,501	2,671,524	1500			
10	2,671,525	2,673,374	1850			
11	2,673,375	2,674,000				
	(2,764,001	2,674,200)		(200 to L.I.)		
	2,674,201	2,675,224	1650			
13	2,675,225	2,675,800				
	(2,675,801	2,676,000)		(200 to L.I.)		
	2,676,001	2,677,224	1800			
14	2,677,225	2,677,800				
	(2,677,801	2,678,000)		(200 to L.I.)		
	2,678,001	2,679,089	1665			
15	2,679,090	2,679,800				
	(2,679,801	2,680,000)		(200 to L.I.)		
	2,680,001	2,681,069	1780			
16	2,681,070	2,681,600				
	(2,681,601	2,681,800)		(200 to L.I.)		
	2,681,801	2,682,994	1725			
17	2,682,995	2,684,694	1500	200		
18	2,684,695	2,685,100				
	(2,685,101	2,685,300)		(200 to L.I.)		
	2,685,301	2,686,544	1450	200		
20	2,686,545	2,686,679	135			
21	2,686,680	2,687,200				
	(2,687,201	2,687,400)		(200 to L.I.)		
	2,687,401	2,688,400				
	(2,688,401	2,688,600)		(200 to L.I.)		
	2,688,601	2,688,654	1075	500		
22	2,688,655	2,689,300				
	(2,689,301	2,689,500)		(200 to L.I.)		
	2,689,501	2,690,229	1375			
23	2,690,230	2,691,000				
	(2,691,001	2,691,200)		(200 to L.I.)		
	2,691,201	2,691,454	825	200		
24	2,691,455	2,692,864	1360	50		
25	2,692,865	2,693,400				
	(2,693,401	2,693,600)		(200 to L.I.)		
	2,693,601	2,694,364	1200	100		
27	2,694,365	2,694,700				
	(2,694,701	2,694,900)		(200 to L.I.)		
	2,694,901	2,695,649	1085			
28	2,695,650	2,696,100				
	(2,696,101	2,696,300)		(200 to L.I.)		
	2,696,301	2,697,374	1325		200	
29	2,697,375	2,697,500				
	(2,697,501	2,697,700)		(200 to L.I.)		
	2,697,701	2,699,054	1280		200	
30	Closed					
31	2,699,055	2,700,100				
	(2,700,101	2,700,700)		(600 to L.I.)		
	2,700,701	2,700,789	1235		300	
JUNE 1918						
1	2,700,790	2,701,500				
	(2,701,501	2,701,700)		(200 to L.I.)		
	2,701,701	2,702,314	1325			
3	2,702,315	2,702,700				
	(2,702,701	2,702,900)		(200 to L.I.)		
	2,702,901	2,703,894	1380			
4	2,703,895	2,704,500				
	(2,704,501	2,704,700)		(200 to L.I.)		
	2,704,701	2,705,494	1194		206	
5	2,705,495	2,706,000				
	(2,706,001	2,706,200)		(200 to L.I.)		
	2,706,201	2,707,079	1385			
6	2,707,080	2,707,600				
	(2,707,601	2,707,800)		(200 to L.I.)		
	2,707,801	2,708,579	1300			

	First Number	Last Number	LH	RH	LHM	RHM

JUNE 1918

	First Number	Last Number	LH	RH	LHM	RHM
7	2,708,580	2,709,879	1300			
8	2,709,880	2,711,319	1440			
10	2,711,320	2,711,700				
	(2,711,701	2,711,900)			(200 to L.I.)	
	2,711,901	2,712,899	1380			
11	2,712,900	2,713,300				
	(2,713,301	2,713,500)			(200 to L.I.)	
	2,713,501	2,714,519	1420			
12	2,714,520	2,714,700				
	(2,714,701	2,714,900)			(200 to L.I.)	
	2,714,901	2,716,134	1415			
13	2,716,135	2,716,400				
	(2,716,401	2,716,600)			(200 to L.I.)	
	2,716,601	2,717,719	1385			
14	2,717,720	2,719,129	1410			
15	2,719,130	2,720,329	1200			
17	2,720,330	2,721,000				
	(2,721,001	2,721,200)			(200 to L.I.)	
	2,721,201	2,721,269	740			
18	2,721,270	2,721,500				
	(2,721,501	2,721,700)			(200 to L.I.)	
	2,721,701	2,722,809	1240			100
19	2,722,810	2,723,100				
	(2,723,101	2,723,300)			(200 to L.I.)	
	2,723,301	2,724,434	1291			134
20	2,724,435	2,725,939	1039			366
21	2,725,940					
	(#	)			(200 to L.I.)	
		2,727,214	736		25	314
22	2,727,215					
	(#	)			200 to L.I.)	
		2,728,629	1168			247

\# Records show 2,727,101 to 2,727,300 being shipped to Long Island, but they also show 2,727,214 as the last number of June 21, which would have been a part of the L.I. shipment. Another group of 200 went to L.I. on the 22nd, and the numbers were not noted.

	First Number	Last Number	LH	RH	LHM	RHM
24	2,728,630	2,729,000				
	(2,729,001	2,729,200)			(200 to L.I.)	
	2,729,201	2,730,234	1405			
25	2,730,235	2,730,400				
	(2,730,401	2,730,600)			(200 to L.I.)	
	2,730,601	2,731,844	1371			39
26	2,731,845	2,732,300				
	(2,732,301	2,732,500)			(200 to L.I.)	
	2,732,501	2,733,409	1340			25
27	2,733,410	2,734,474	1030			35
28	2,734,475	2,735,679	1145			60
29	Closed					

JULY 1918

	First Number	Last Number	LH	RH	LHM	RHM
1	2,735,680	2,736,600				
	(2,736,601	2,736,800)			(200 to L.I.)	
	2,736,801	2,737,284	1365			40
2	2,737,285	2,738,964	1480			
3	2,738,965	2,739,800				
	(2,739,801	2,740,000)			(200 to L.I.)	
	2,740,001	2,740,614	1450			
4	Closed					
5	2,740,615	2,742,039	1425			
6	2,742,040	2,743,379	1340			
8	2,743,380	2,744,559	1180			
9	2,744,560	2,745,664	1105			
10	2,745,665	2,746,619	955			
11	2,746,620	2,747,584	965			
12	2,747,585	2,748,324	740			
13	2,748,325	2,748,544	220			
15	2,748,545	2,749,012	468			
16	2,749,013	2,749,712	672	28		
17	2,749,713	2,750,272	560			
18	2,750,273	2,750,514	242			
19	2,750,515	2,751,114	600			
20	2,751,115	2,751,719	605			
22	2,751,720	2,752,469	750			
23	2,752,470	2,753,179	710			
24	2,753,180	2,753,959	780			
25	2,753,960	2,754,739	780			
26	2,754,740	2,755,499	760			
27	2,755,500	2,756,251	752			

Closed July 28 to August 1

AUGUST 1918

	First Number	Last Number	LH	RH	LHM	RHM
1	2,756,252	2,757,051	800			
2	2,757,052	2,757,881	830			
3	2,757,882	2,758,761	880			
5	2,758,762	2,759,596	835			
6	2,759,597	2,760,456	860			
7	2,760,457	2,761,356	900			
8	2,761,357	2,762,256	900			
9	2,762,257	2,763,156	900			
10	2,763,157	2,763,981	825			
12	2,763,982	2,764,521	540			
13	2,764,522	2,765,021	500			

	First Number	Last Number	LH	RH	LHM	RHM
14	2,765,022	2,765,526	505			
15	2,765,527	2,766,036	510			
16	2,766,037	2,766,541	505			
17	2,766,542	2,767,091	550			
19	2,767,092	2,767,651	560			
20	2,767,652	2,768,236	585			
21	2,768,237	2,768,811	575			
22	2,768,812	2,769,411	600			
23	2,769,412	2,770,016	605			
24	2,770,017	2,770,636	626			
26	2,770,637	2,771,261	625			
27	2,771,262	2,771,901	640			
28	2,771,902	2,772,406	505			
29	2,772,407	2,773,156	750			
30	2,773,157	2,773,871	715			
31	2,773,872	2,774,621	750			

SEPTEMBER 1918

	First Number	Last Number	LH	RH	LHM	RHM
2	2,774,622	2,775,221	600			
3	2,775,222	2,775,926	705			
4	2,775,927	2,776,626	700			
5	2,776,627	2,777,336	710			
6	2,777,337	2,778,086	750			
7	2,778,087	2,778,821	735			
9	2,778,822	2,779,471	650			
10	2,779,472	2,780,021	550			
11	2,780,022	2,780,421	400			
12	2,780,422	2,780,886	465			
13	2,780,887	2,781,411	525			
14	2,781,412	2,781,931	495	25		
16	2,781,932	2,782,451	495	25		
17	2,782,452	2,783,001	525	25		
18	2,783,002	2,783,531	505	25		
19	2,783,532	2,784,011	455	25		
20	2,784,012	2,784,416	380	25		
21	2,784,417	2,784,886	445	25		
23	2,784,887	2,785,391	480	25		
24	2,785,392	2,785,936	495	50		
25	2,785,937	2,786,451	490	25		
26	2,786,452	2,786,851	249	151		
27	2,786,852	2,787,256	151	254		
28	2,787,257	2,787,536	159	121		
30	2,787,537	2,787,821	285			

OCTOBER 1918

	First Number	Last Number	LH	RH	LHM	RHM
1	2,787,822	2,788,331	183	327		
2	2,788,332	2,788,671	234	106		
3	2,788,672	2,788,946	121	154		
4	2,788,947	2,788,966		20		
5	Closed					
7	2,788,967	2,789,341	355	20		
8	2,789,342	2,789,666	20	305		
9	2,789,667	2,789,966	283	17		
10	2,789,967	2,790,266	45	255		
	Closed October 11 to October 19					
19	2,790,267	2,790,671	405			
21	2,790,672	2,790,951	280			
22	2,790,952	2,791,156	205			
23	2,791,157	2,791,356	138	62		
24	2,791,357	2,791,561	155	50		
25	2,791,562	2,791,771	139	71		
26	2,791,772	2,791,976	186	19		
28	2,791,977	2,792,076	100			
29	Closed					
30	Closed					
31	2,792,077	2,792,306	230			

NOVEMBER 1918

	First Number	Last Number	LH	RH	LHM	RHM
1	2,792,307	2,792,541	235			
2	2,792,542	2,792,791	250			
4	2,792,792	2,792,981	190			
5	2,792,982	2,793,111	130			
6	2,793,112	2,793,271	160			
7	2,793,272	2,793,451	180			
8	2,793,452	2,793,651	200			
9	2,793,652	2,793,856	205			
11	Closed. (End of World War I.)					
12	2,793,857	2,794,081	225			
13	2,794,082	2,794,316	235			
14	2,794,317	2,794,781	465			
15	2,794,782	2,795,286	505			
16	2,795,287	2,795,821	535			
18	2,795,822	2,796,431	610			
19	2,796,432	2,797,031	600			
20	2,797,032	2,797,631	600			
21	2,797,632	2,798,366	717			18
22	2,798,367	2,799,281	915			
23	2,799,282	2,800,111	830			
25	2,800,112	2,801,112	750	250		
26	2,801,113	2,802,057	745	200		
27	2,802,058	2,803,062	817	188		
28	Closed					
29	2,803,063	2,804,077	852	163		
30	2,804,078	2,805,097	773	247		

Serial Numbers

DECEMBER 1918

Day	First Number	Last Number	LH	RH	LHM	RHM
2	2,805,098	2,806,102	602	403		
3	2,806,103	2,807,252	1130	20		
4	2,807,253	2,808,502	1048	202		
5	2,808,503	2,809,852	1152	198		
6	2,809,853	2,811,127	1048	227		
7	2,811,128	2,812,487	887	473		
9	2,812,488	2,813,802	996	319		
10	2,813,803	2,815,178	1228	147		
11	2,815,179	2,816,683	1505	(First starter engine made, 2,815,891.)		
12	2,816,684	2,818,288	1605			
13	2,818,289	2,819,648	1360			
14	2,819,649	2,821,148	1500			
16	2,821,149	2,821,688	540			
17	2,821,689	2,823,088	1400			
18	2,823,089	2,824,628	1540			
19	2,824,629	2,826,028	1400			
20	2,826,029	2,827,101	1075			
21	2,827,102	2,828,576	1475			
23	2,828,577	2,830,176	1600			
24	2,830,177	2,831,426	1250			

Closed December 25 to January 2, 1919

JANUARY 1919

Day	First Number	Last Number	LH	RH	LHM	RHM
2	2,831,427	2,833,001	1575	Begin starter production.		
3	2,833,002	2,834,626	1625			
4	2,834,627	2,836,226	1600			
6	2,836,227	2,836,700				
	(2,836,701	2,836,900)		200 to L.I.		
	2,836,901	2,838,076	1550			100
7	2,838,077	2,838,600				
	(2,838,601	2,838,800)		200 to L.I.		
	2,838,801	2,839,986	1524			186
8	2,839,987	2,840,800				
	(2,840,801	2,841,000)		200 to L.I.		
	2,841,001	2,841,936	1636			114
9	2,841,937	2,842,700				
	(2,842,701	2,842,900)		200 to L.I.		
	2,842,901	2,843,761	1613			12
10	2,843,762	2,844,600				
	(2,844,601	2,844,800)		200 to L.I.		
	2,844,801	2,845,536	1575			
11	2,845,537	2,847,411	1875			
13	2,847,412	2,848,600				
	(2,848,601	2,848,800)		200 to L.I.		
	2,848,801	2,849,216	1605			
14	2,849,217	2,850,300				
	(2,850,301	2,850,500)		200 to L.I.		
	2,850,501	2,851,256	1840			
15	2,851,257	2,853,231	1676			99
16	2,853,232	2,854,500				
	(2,854,501	2,854,700)		200 to L.I.		
	2,854,701	2,855,341	1810			100
17	2,855,342	2,856,600				
	(2,856,601	2,856,800)		200 to L.I.		
	2,856,801	2,857,471	1875			55
18	2,857,472	2,859,446	1920			55
20	2,859,447	2,861,756	2110			
21	2,861,757	2,862,800				
	(2,862,801	2,863,000)		200 to L.I.		
	2,863,001	2,863,691	1726	9		
22	2,863,692	2,864,300				
	(2,864,301	2,864,500)		200 to L.I.		
	2,864,501	2,865,421	1530			
23	2,865,422	2,866,000				
	(2,866,001	2,866,200)		200 to L.I.		
	2,866,201	2,867,171	1550			
24	2,867,172	2,867,700				
	(2,867,701	2,867,900)		200 to L.I.		
	2,867,901	2,869,336	1964	1		
25	2,869,337	2,870,991	1655			
27	2,870,992	2,871,400				
	(2,871,401	2,871,600)		200 to L.I.		
	2,871,601	2,873,236	2045			
28	2,873,237	2,874,000				
	(2,874,001	2,874,200)		200 to L.I.		
	2,874,201	2,875,291	1855			
29	2,875,292	2,875,600				
	(2,875,601	2,875,800)		200 to L.I.		
	2,875,801	2,875,976	485			
30	2,875,977	2,976,000				
	(2,876,001	2,876,200)		200 to L.I.		
	2,876,201	2,878,081	1905			
31	2,878,082	2,878,500				
	(2,878,501	2,878,700)		200 to L.I.		
	2,878,701	2,880,166	1846			39

FEBRUARY 1919

Day	First Number	Last Number	LH	RH	LHM	RHM
1	2,880,167	2,880,600				
	(2,880,601	2,880,800)		200 to L.I.		
	2,880,801	2,882,011	1642			3
3	2,882,012	2,882,600				
	(2,882,601	2,882,800)		200 to L.I.		
4	2,882,801	2,884,276	2065			
4	2,884,277	2,885,200				
	(2,885,201	2,885,400)		200 to L.I.		
	2,885,401	2,886,406	1930			
5	2,886,407	2,888,686	2280			
6	2,888,687	2,890,811	2125			
7	2,890,812	2,892,666	1855			
8	2,892,667	2,894,206	1540			
10	2,894,207	2,896,441	2235			
11	2,896,442	2,898,491	2050			
12	2,898,492	2,900,596	2105			
13	2,900,597	2,902,956	2360			
14	2,902,957	2,904,851	1895			
15	2,904,852	2,906,901	2050			
17	2,906,902	2,907,700				
	(2,907,701	2,907,900)		200 to L.I.		
	2,907,901	2,909,196	2095			
18	2,909,197	2,911,526	2330			
19	2,911,527	2,913,736	2210			
20	2,913,737	2,916,156	2420			
21	2,916,157	2,918,246	2090			
22	2,918,247	2,920,746	2500			
24	2,920,747	2,923,246	2500			
25	2,923,247	2,924,500				
	(2,924,501	2,924,700)		200 to L.I.		
	2,924,701	2,925,761	2315			
26	2,925,762	2,927,991	2230			
27	2,927,992	2,930,496	2505			
28	2,930,497	2,933,046	2550			

MARCH 1919

Day	First Number	Last Number	LH	RH	LHM	RHM
1	2,933,047	2,935,156	2110			
3	2,935,157	2,937,311	2155			
4	2,937,312	2,939,391	2080			
5	2,939,392	2,941,986	2595			
6	2,941,987	2,944,406	2420			
7	2,944,407	2,946,856	2450			
8	2,946,857	2,949,281	2425			
10	2,949,282	2,951,836	2555			
11	2,951,837	2,954,361	2525			
12	2,954,362	2,956,991	2630			
13	2,956,992	2,959,446	2449	6		
14	2,959,447	2,961,000				
	(2,961,001	2,961,400)		400 to L.I.		
	2,961,401	2,962,496	2650			
15	2,962,497	2,965,056	2560			
17	2,965,057	2,966,700				
	(2,966,701	2,966,900)		200 to L.I.		
	2,966,901	2,967,771	2515			
18	2,967,772	2,969,000				
	(2,969,001	2,969,200)		200 to L.I.		
	2,969,201	2,970,471	2500			
19	2,970,472	2,971,200				
	(2,971,201	2,971,400)		200 to L.I.		
	2,971,401	2,972,931	2260			
20	2,972,932	2,974,000				
	(2,974,001	2,974,200)		200 to L.I.		
	2,974,201	2,975,561	2430			
21	2,975,562	2,976,500				
	(2,976,501	2,976,700)		200 to L.I.		
	2,976,701	2,978,311	2550			
22	2,978,312	2,980,586	2275			
24	2,980,587	2,981,600				
	(2,981,601	2,981,800)		200 to L.I.		
	2,981,801	2,983,051	2265			
25	2,983,052	2,983,900				
	(2,983,901	2,984,100)		200 to L.I.		
	2,984,101	2,985,096	1845			
26	2,985,097	2,986,000				
	(2,986,001	2,986,200)		200 to L.I.		
	2,986,201	2,987,296	2000			
27	2,987,297	2,988,200				
	(2,988,201	2,988,400)		200 to L.I.		
	2,988,401	2,989,866	2370			
28	2,989,867	2,990,800				
	(2,990,801	2,991,000)		200 to L.I.		
	2,991,001	2,992,346	2280			
29	2,992,347	2,994,646	2300			
31	2,994,647	2,995,800				
	(2,995,801	2,996,000)		200 to L.I.		
	2,996,001	2,997,146	2300			

APRIL 1919

Day	First Number	Last Number	LH	RH	LHM	RHM
1	2,997,147	2,998,200				
	(2,998,201	2,998,400)		200 to L.I.		
	2,998,401	2,999,761	2415			
2	2,999,762	3,001,000	(3,000,000 at 8:15 A.M.)			
	(3,001,001	3,001,200)		200 to L.I.		
	3,001,201	3,002,571	2610			
3	3,002,572	3,003,800				
	(3,003,801	3,004,000)		200 to L.I.		
	3,004,001	3,005,406	2635			

Date	First Number	Last Number	LH	RH	LHM	RHM
APRIL 1919						
	3,005,407	3,006,500				
	(3,006,501	3,006,700)		200 to L.I.		
	3,006,701	3,008,176	2570			
5	3,008,177	3,010,601	2425			
7	3,010,602	3,011,800				
	(3,011,801	3,012,000)		200 to L.I.		
	3,012,001	3,013,331	2530			
8	3,013,332	3,014,500				
	(3,014,501	3,014,700)		200 to L.I.		
	3,014,701	3,016,126	2595			
9	3,016,127	3,017,400				
	(3,017,401	3,017,600)		200 to L.I.		
	3,017,601	3,018,966	2640			
10	3,018,967	3,020,200				
	(3,020,201	3,020,400)		200 to L.I.		
	3,020,401	3,021,816	2650			
11	3,021,817	3,023,100				
	(3,023,101	3,023,300)		200 to L.I.		
	3,023,301	3,024,666	2650			
12	3,024,667	3,027,166	2500			
14	3,027,167	3,028,000				
	(3,028,001	3,028,200)		200 to L.I.		
	3,028,201	3,029,811	2445			
15	3,029,812	3,030,900				
	(3,030,901	3,031,100)		200 to L.I.		
	3,031,101	3,032,511	2500			
16	3,032,512	3,033,400				
	(3,033,401	3,033,600)		200 to L.I.		
	3,033,601	3,035,261	2550			
17	3,035,262	3,036,200				
	(3,036,201	3,036,400)		200 to L.I.		
	3,036,401	3,038,041	2580			
18	3,038,042	3,039,100				
	(3,039,101	3,039,300)		200 to L.I.		
	3,039,301	3,039,916	1675			
19	3,039,917	3,042,486	2570			
21	3,042,487	3,043,400				
	(3,043,401	3,043,600)		200 to L.I.		
	3,043,601	3,044,951	2265			
22	3,044,952	3,046,000				
	(3,046,001	3,046,200)		200 to L.I.		
	3,046,201	3,047,761	2610			
23	3,047,762	3,048,800				
	(3,048,801	3,049,000)		200 to L.I.		
	3,049,001	3,050,626	2665			
24	3,050,627	3,051,700				
	(3,051,701	3,051,900)		200 to L.I.		
	3,051,901	3,053,576	2750			
25	3,053,577	3,054,900				
	(3,054,901	3,055,100)		200 to L.I.		
	3,055,101	3,056,621	2845			
26	3,056,622	3,059,356	2735			
28	3,059,357	3,062,136	2780			
29	3,062,137	3,064,906	2770			
30	3,064,907	3,067,736	2830			
MAY 1919						
1	3,067,737	3,069,100				
	(3,069,101	3,069,300)		200 to L.I.		
	3,069,301	3,070,641	2705			
2	3,070,642	3,072,100				
	(3,072,101	3,072,300)		200 to L.I.		
	3,072,301	3,073,781	2940			
3	3,073,782	3,076,681	2900			
5	3,076,682	3,078,100				
	(3,078,101	3,078,300)		200 to L.I.		
	3,078,301	3,079,721	2840			
6	3,079,722	3,081,200				
	(3,081,201	3,081,400)		200 to L.I.		
	3,081,401	3,082,771	2850			
7	3,082,772	3,084,200				
	(3,084,201	3,084,400)		200 to L.I.		
	3,084,401	3,085,776	2805			
8	3,085,777	3,087,200				
	(3,087,201	3,087,400)		200 to L.I.		
	3,087,401	3,088,836	2860			
9	3,088,837	3,090,300				
	(3,090,301	3,090,500)		200 to L.I.		
	3,090,501	3,091,986	2950			
10	3,091,987	3,094,886	2900			
12	3,094,887	3,096,000				
	(3,096,001	3,096,200)		200 to L.I.		
	3,096,201	3,097,846	2760			
13	3,097,847	3,099,000				
	(3,099,001	3,099,200)		200 to L.I.		
	3,099,201	3,100,786	2740			
14	3,100,787	3,101,700				
	(3,101,701	3,101,900)		200 to L.I.		
	3,101,901	3,103,966	2980			
15	3,103,967	3,105,000				
	(3,105,001	3,105,200)		200 to L.I.		
	3,105,201	3,107,046	2880			
16	3,107,047	3,108,100				
	(3,108,101	3,108,300)		200 to L.I.		
	3,108,301	3,110,056	2810			
17	3,110,057	3,112,861	2805			
19	Closed					
20	3,112,862	3,114,000				
	(3,114,001	3,114,200)		200 to L.I.		
	3,114,201	3,115,861	2800			
21	3,115,862	3,116,900				
	(3,116,901	3,117,100)		200 to L.I.		
	3,117,101	3,118,861	2800			
22	3,118,862	3,119,900				
	(3,119,901	3,120,100)		200 to L.I.		
	3,120,101	3,121,861	2800			
23	3,121,862	3,123,000				
	(3,123,001	3,123,200)		200 to L.I.		
	3,123,201	3,124,671	2610			
24	3,124,672	3,125,800				
	(3,125,801	3,126,000)		200 to L.I.		
	3,126,001	3,127,606	2735			
26	3,127,607	3,128,800				
	(3,128,801	3,129,000)		200 to L.I.		
	3,129,001	3,130,811	3005			
27	3,130,812	3,132,100				
	(3,132,101	3,132,300)		200 to L.I.		
	3,132,301	3,134,021	3010			
28	3,134,022	3,135,300				
	(3,135,301	3,135,600)		300 to L.I.		
	3,135,601	3,137,061	2740	(Last non-starter block made)		
29	3,137,062	3,138,400				
	(3,138,401	3,138,700)		300 to L.I.		
	3,138,701	3,139,951	2590			
30	Closed May 30 and 31					
JUNE 1919						
2	3,139,952	3,141,200				
	(3,141,201	3,141,400)		200 to L.I.		
	3,141,401	3,142,906	2755			
3	3,142,907	3,144,200				
	(3,144,201	3,144,400)		200 to L.I.		
	3,144,401	3,145,716	2610			
4	3,145,717	3,147,100				
	(3,147,101	3,147,300)		200 to L.I.		
	3,147,301	3,148,916	3000			
5	3,148,917	3,150,200				
	(3,150,201	3,150,400)		200 to L.I.		
	3,150,401	3,151,801	2685			
6	3,151,802	3,153,200				
	(3,153,201	3,153,400)		200 to L.I.		
	3,153,401	3,154,851	2850			
7	3,154,852	3,157,456	2605			
9	3,157,457	3,158,700				
	(3,158,701	3,158,900)		200 to L.I.		100
	3,158,901	3,160,356	2600			
10	3,160,357	3,161,500				
	(3,161,501	3,161,700)		200 to L.I.		100
	3,161,701	3,163,306	2650			
11	3,163,307	3,164,400				
	(3,164,401	3,164,600)		200 to L.I.		200
	3,164,601	3,166,356	2650			
12	3,166,357	3,167,400				
	(3,167,401	3,167,600)		200 to L.I.		300
	3,167,601	3,169,706	2850			
13	3,169,707	3,171,000				
	(3,171,001	3,171,200)		200 to L.I.		12
	3,171,201	3,172,931	3013			
14	3,172,932	3,175,931	3000			
16	3,175,932	3,177,000				
	(3,177,001	3,177,200)		200 to L.I.		
	3,177,201	3,178,700				
	(3,178,701	3,178,780)		80 to L.I.		
	3,178,781	3,179,041	2830			
17	3,179,042	3,180,100				
	(3,180,101	3,180,160)		60 to L.I.		
	3,180,161	3,180,200				
	(3,180,201	3,180,320)		120 to L.I.		
	3,180,321	3,182,041	2820			
18	3,182,042	3,183,400				
	(3,183,401	3,183,700)		300 to L.I.		
	3,183,701	3,185,100				
	(3,185,101	3,185,180)		80 to L.I.		
	3,185,181	3,185,301	2880			
19	3,185,302	3,186,400				
	(3,186,401	3,186,680)		280 to L.I.		
	3,186,681	3,188,000				
	(3,188,001	3,188,280)		280 to L.I.		
	3,188,281	3,188,281	2420			
20	3,188,282	3,190,551	2270			
21	Closed					
23	3,190,552	3,192,000				
	(3,192,001	3,192,280)		280 to L.I.		
	3,192,281	3,193,961	3130			

JUNE 1919

Day	First Number	Last Number	LH	RH	LHM	RHM
24	3,193,962	3,195,400				
	(3,195,401	3,195,680)		280 to L.I.		
	3,195,681	3,197,461	3220			
25	3,197,462	3,199,000				
	(3,199,001	3,199,280)		280 to L.I.		
	3,199,281	3,200,646	2905			
26	3,200,647	3,202,300				
	(3,202,301	3,202,580)		280 to L.I.		
	3,202,581	3,203,486	2560			
27	3,203,487	3,205,100				
	(3,205,101	3,205,380)		280 to L.I.		
	3,205,381	3,206,501	2735			
28	3,206,502	3,209,001	2500			
30	3,209,002	3,210,100				
	(3,210,101	3,210,500)		400 to L.I.		
	3,210,501	3,210,700				
	(3,210,701	3,210,780)		80 to L.I.		
	3,210,781	3,210,841	1360			

JULY 1919

Day	First Number	Last Number	LH	RH	LHM	RHM
1	3,210,842	3,212,400				
	(3,212,401	3,213,200)		800 to L.I.		
	3,213,201	3,213,576	1935			
2	3,213,577	3,215,700				
	(3,215,701	3,215,820)		120 to L.I.		
	3,215,821	3,216,200				
	(3,216,201	3,216,400)		200 to L.I.		
	3,216,401	3,216,581	2685			
3	3,216,582	3,219,300				
	(3,219,301	3,219,550)		250 to L.I.		
	3,219,551	3,219,681	2850			
4	Closed July 4 to July 7					
7	3,219,682	3,222,481	2350	300		
	(3,222,501	3,222,650)		150 to L.I.		
8	3,222,482	3,222,500				
	3,222,651	3,225,066	2185	400		
9	3,225,067	3,227,621	2255	300		
10	3,227,622	3,229,800				
	(3,229,801	3,230,320)		520 TO L.I.		
	3,230,321	3,230,526	2377	8		
11	3,230,527	3,232,000				
	(3,232,001	3,232,280)		280 to L.I.		
	3,232,281	3,233,671	2919	36		
12	3,233,672	3,236,611	2850			
14	3,236,612	3,239,100				
	(3,239,101	3,239,500)		400 to L.I.		
	3,239,501	3,239,501	2390	100		
15	3,239,502	3,241,300				
	(3,241,301	3,241,500)		200 to L.I.		
	3,241,501	3,241,641	1734	206		
16	3,241,642	3,243,700				
	(3,243,701	3,244,030)		330 to L.I.		
	3,244,031	3,244,400				
	(3,244,401	3,244,500)		100 to L.I.		
	3,244,501	3,244,501	2295	135		
17	3,244,502	3,247,106	2605			
18	3,247,107	3,249,200				
	(3,249,201	3,249,570)		370 to L.I.		
	3,249,571	3,250,431	2955			
19	3,250,432	3,251,996	1565			
21	3,251,997	3,253,000				
	(3,253,001	3,253,200)		200 to L.I.		
	3,253,201	3,254,951	2755			
22	3,254,952	3,257,500				
	(3,257,501	3,257,750)		250 to L.I.		
	3,257,751	3,257,971	2770			
23	3,257,972	3,260,000				
	(3,260,001	3,260,200)		200 to L.I.		
	3,260,201	3,260,700				
	(3,260,701	3,260,850)		150 to L.I.		
	3,260,851	3,260,971	2650			
24	3,260,972	3,263,520				
	(3,263,521	3,263,920)		400 to L.I.		
	3,263,921	3,263,921	2550			
25	3,263,922	3,266,000				
	(3,266,001	3,266,200)		200 to L.I.		
	3,266,201	3,267,071	2950			
26	3,267,072	3,269,711	2640			
	("A-4-24 motor 3,293,121")?					
28	3,269,712	3,272,000				
	(3,272,001	3,272,400)		400 to L.I.		
	3,272,401	3,272,661	2550			
29	3,272,662	3,274,300				
	(3,274,301	3,274,500)		200 to L.I.		
	3,274,501	3,275,386	2525			
30	3,275,387	3,277,851	2465			
	Closed July 31 to August 4.					

AUGUST 1919

Day	First Number	Last Number	LH	RH	LHM	RHM
4	3,277,852	3,280,200				
	(3,280,201	3,280,500)		300 to L.I.		
	3,280,501	3,280,561	2410			

(August continued)

Day	First Number	Last Number	LH	RH	LHM	RHM
5	3,280,562	3,282,900				
	(3,282,901	3,283,200)		300 to L.I.		
	3,283,201	3,283,203				
	(3,283,204	3,283,253)		50 to L.I.		
	3,283,254	3,283,431	2520			
6	3,283,432	3,285,800				
	(3,285,801	3,286,100)		300 to L.I.		
	3,286,101	3,286,331	2600			
7	3,286,332	3,288,000				
	(3,288,001	3,288,150)		150 to L.I.		
	3,288,151	3,289,100				
	(3,289,101	3,289,200)		100 to L.I.		
	3,289,201	3,289,281	2700			
8	3,289,282	3,291,700				
	(3,291,701	3,291,900)		200 to L.I.		
	3,291,901	3,292,050				
	(3,292,051	3,292,200)		150 to L.I.		
	3,292,201	3,292,381	2750			
9	3,292,382	3,295,150				
	(3,295,151	3,295,200)		50 to L.I.		
	3,295,201	3,295,381	2950			
11	3,295,382	3,296,900				
	(3,296,901	3,297,150)		250 to L.I.		
	3,297,151	3,298,526	2895			
12	3,298,527	3,300,800				
	(3,300,801	3,301,000)		200 to L.I.		
	3,301,001	3,301,726	3000			
13	3,301,727	3,304,000				
	(3,304,001	3,304,400)		400 to L.I.		
	3,304,401	3,304,926	2800			
14	3,304,927	3,307,000				
	(3,307,001	3,307,300)		300 to L.I.		
	3,307,301	3,308,000				
	(3,308,001	3,308,050)		50 to L.I.		
	3,308,051	3,308,126	2850			
15	3,308,127	3,310,000				
	(3,310,001	3,310,200)		200 to L.I.		
	3,310,201	3,311,326	3000			
16	Closed					
18	3,311,327	3,313,500				
	(3,313,501	3,313,700)		200 to L.I.		
	3,313,701	3,314,661	3135			
19	3,314,662	3,316,100				
	(3,316,101	3,316,150)		50 to L.I.		
	3,316,151	3,317,871	3160			50
20	3,317,872	3,319,000				
	3,319,001	3,319,056				56
	3,319,057	3,321,076	2949			
21	3,321,077	3,323,200				
	(3,323,201	3,323,500)		300 to L.I.		
	3,323,501	3,324,316	2939			1 (3,322,501)
22	3,324,317	3,325,600				
	3,325,601	3,325,643				43
	3,325,644	3,326,500				
	(3,326,501	3,326,800)		300 to L.I.		
	3,326,801	3,327,526	2867			
23	3,327,527	3,328,900				
	3,328,901	3,329,050				150
	3,329,051	3,330,726	3050			
25	3,330,727	3,332,500				
	3,332,501	3,332,609				109
	3,332,610	3,335,800				
	(3,335,801	3,336,000)		200 to L.I.		
	3,336,001	3,333,926	2871			
26	3,333,927	3,335,000				
	3,335,001	3,335,125				125
	3,335,126	3,335,800				
	(3,335,801	3,336,000)		200 to L.I.		
	3,336,001	3,337,126	2875			
27	3,337,127	3,338,200				
	3,338,201	3,338,400				200
	3,338,401	3,340,331	3005			
28	3,340,332	3,341,900				
	3,341,901	3,342,075				175
	3,342,076	3,343,546	3040			
29	3,343,547	3,345,600				
	3,345,601	3,345,800				200
	3,345,801	3,346,876	3130			
30	Closed					

SEPTEMBER 1919

Day	First Number	Last Number	LH	RH	LHM	RHM
1	Closed					
2	3,346,877	3,349,200				
	3,349,201	3,349,400				200
	3,349,401	3,349,876	2800			
3	3,349,877	3,352,000				
	(3,352,001	3,352,200)		200 to L.I.		
	3,352,201	3,353,326	3250			
4	3,353,327	3,355,000				1351
	(3,355,001	3,355,200)		200 to L.I.		
	3,355,201	3,356,551	1674			

	First Number	Last Number	LH	RH	LHM	RHM

SEPTEMBER 1919

	First Number	Last Number	LH	RH	LHM	RHM
5	3,356,552	3,358,600				
	(3,358,601	3,358,800)		200 to L.I.		
	3,358,801	3,359,600				
	(3,359,601	3,359,800)		200 to L.I.		
	3,359,801	3,359,801	2850			
6	3,359,802	3,361,800				
	(3,361,801	3,362,000)		200 to L.I.		
	3,362,001	3,362,170				170
	3,362,171	3,363,051	2880			
8	3,363,052	3,365,000				
	(3,365,001	3,365,200)		200 to L.I.		
	3,365,201	3,366,276	3025			
9	3,366,277	3,368,000				
	(3,368,001	3,368,400)		400 to L.I.		
	3,368,401	3,369,581	2905			
10	3,369,582	3,371,800				
	(3,371,801	3,372,000)		200 to L.I.		
	3,372,001	3,372,881	3100			
11	3,372,882	3,374,500				
	(3,374,501	3,374,900)		400 to L.I.		
	3,374,901	3,376,191	2910			
12	3,376,192	3,377,800				
	(3,377,801	3,378,000)		200 to L.I.		
	3,378,001	3,379,511	3120			
13	3,379,512	3,382,836	3325			
15	3,382,837	3,384,400				
	(3,384,401	3,384,600)		200 to L.I.		
	3,384,601	3,386,161	3125			
16	3,386,162	3,387,500				
	(3,387,501	3,387,700)		200 to L.I.		
	3,387,701	3,389,200				
	(3,389,201	3,389,400)		200 to L.I.		
	3,389,401	3,389,511	2950			
17	3,389,512	3,391,000				
	(3,391,001	3,391,200)		200 to L.I.		
	3,391,201	3,392,836	3125			
18	3,392,837	3,394,400				
	(3,394,401	3,394,600)		200 to L.I.		
	3,394,601	3,396,186	3150			
19	3,396,187	3,397,600				
	(3,397,601	3,397,800)		200 to L.I.		
	3,397,801	3,398,000				
	3,398,001	3,398,200				200
	3,398,201	3,399,496	2910			
20	3,399,497	3,401,000				
	3,401,001	3,401,100				100
	3,401,101	3,401,300		200 to L.I.		
	3,401,301	3,402,600	2804			
	3,402,601	3,402,696				96
22	3,402,697	3,402,700				104
	3,402,701	3,404,000				
	(3,404,001	3,404,100)		100 to L.I.		
	3,404,101	3,406,001	3001			
23	3,406,002	3,407,200				
	3,407,201	3,407,400				200
	(3,407,401	3,407,600)		200 to L.I.		
	3,407,601	3,408,500				
	3,408,501	3,408,600				100
	3,408,601	3,409,301	2800			
24	3,409,302	3,410,200				
	3,410,201	3,410,500				300
	(3,410,501	3,410,700)		200 to L.I.		
	3,410,701	3,411,876	2075			
25	3,411,877	3,412,800				
	(3,412,801	3,413,000)		200 to L.I.		
	3,413,001	3,413,100				100
	3,413,101	3,414,000				
	(3,414,001	3,414,200)		200 to L.I.		
	3,414,201	3,415,676	3300			
26	3,415,677	3,417,000				
	(3,417,001	3,417,200)		200 to L.I.		
	3,417,201	3,419,216	3340			
27	3,419,217	3,420,400				
	3,420,401	3,420,500				100
	(3,420,501	3,420,700)		200 to L.I.		
	3,420,701	3,422,521	3005			
29	3,422,522	3,424,000				
	3,424,001	3,424,300				300
	3,424,301	3,425,200				
	(3,425,201	3,425,400)		200 to L.I.		
	3,425,401	3,425,600				
	(3,425,601	3,425,700)		100 to L.I.		
	3,425,701	3,425,961	2840			
30	3,425,962	3,428,000				
	(3,428,001	3,428,300)		300 to L.I.		
	3,428,301	3,428,900				
	3,428,901	3,429,100				200
	3,429,101	3,429,401	2940			

OCTOBER 1919

	First Number	Last Number	LH	RH	LHM	RHM
1	3,429,402	3,430,900				
	3,430,901	3,431,000				100
	(3,431,001	3,431,200)		200 to L.I.		
	3,431,201	3,432,200				
	(3,432,201	3,432,400)		200 to L.I.		
	3,432,401	3,432,841	2940			
2	3,432,842	3,434,200				
	3,434,201	3,434,400				200
	(3,434,401	3,434,500)		100 to L.I.		
	3,434,501	3,435,800				
	(3,435,801	3,435,900)		100 to L.I.		
	3,435,901	3,436,061	2830			
3	3,436,062	3,437,500				
	(3,437,501	3,437,700)		200 to L.I.		
	3,437,701	3,437,800				100
	3,437,801	3,439,571	3200			
4	3,439,572	3,440,800				
	(3,440,801	3,441,000)		200 to L.I.		
	3,441,001	3,441,100				100
	3,441,101	3,442,000				
	3,442,001	3,442,100				100
	3,442,101	3,442,776	2805			
6	3,442,777	3,444,800				
	(3,444,801	3,445,000)		200 to L.I.		
	3,445,001	3,445,200				200
	3,445,201	3,446,091	2915			
7	3,446,092	3,447,600				
	(3,447,601	3,448,000)		400 to L.I.		
	3,448,001	3,449,000				
	3,449,001	3,449,100				100
	3,449,101	3,449,396	2805			
8	3,449,397	3,450,800				
	(3,450,801	3,451,000)		200 to L.I.		
	3,451,001	3,452,696	3100			
9	3,452,697	3,453,800				
	(3,453,801	3,454,000)		200 to L.I.		
	3,454,001	3,456,001	3105			
10	3,456,002	3,457,200				
	(3,457,201	3,457,400)		200 to L.I.		
	3,457,401	3,459,306	3105			
11	3,459,307	3,460,400				
	(3,460,401	3,460,600)		200 to L.I.		
	3,460,601	3,462,466	2960			
13	3,462,467	3,464,000				
	(3,464,001	3,464,200)		200 to L.I.		
	3,464,201	3,465,441	2775			
14	3,465,442	3,466,800				
	(3,466,801	3,467,200)		400 to L.I.		
	3,467,201	3,468,741	2900			
15	3,468,742	3,470,100				
	(3,470,101	3,470,500)		400 to L.I.		
	3,470,501	3,471,911	2770			
16	3,471,912	3,473,400				
	3,473,401	3,473,700				300
	(3,473,701	3,473,900)		200 to L.I.		
	3,473,901	3,474,911	2500			
17	3,474,912	3,476,500				
	(3,476,501	3,476,700)		200 to L.I.		
	3,476,701	3,477,921	2810			
18	3,477,922	3,479,500				
	3,479,501	3,479,700				200
	(3,479,701	3,479,900)		200 to L.I.		
	3,479,901	3,480,941	2620			
20	3,480,942	3,482,600				
	3,482,601	3,482,800				200
	(3,482,801	3,483,000)		200 to L.I.		
	3,483,001	3,483,966	2625			
21	3,483,967	3,485,700				
	3,485,701	3,485,900				200
	(3,485,901	3,486,300)		400 to L.I.		
	3,486,301	3,487,181	2615			
22	3,487,182	3,488,700				
	3,488,701	3,488,800				100
	(3,488,801	3,489,000)		200 to L.I.		
	3,489,001	3,490,281	2800			
23	3,490,282	3,491,800				
	3,491,801	3,492,000				200
	(3,492,001	3,492,200)		200 to L.I.		
	3,492,201	3,493,381	2700			
24	3,493,382	3,494,900				
	3,494,901	3,495,100				200
	(3,495,101	3,495,300)		200 to L.I.		
	3,495,301	3,496,481	2700			
25	3,496,482	3,497,900				
	3,497,901	3,498,100				200
	(3,498,101	3,498,300)		200 to L.I.		
	3,498,301	3,499,581	2700			
27	3,499,582	3,501,200				
	(3,501,201	3,501,400)		200 to L.I.		
	3,501,401	3,502,686	2905			

Serial Numbers

OCTOBER 1919

Date	First Number	Last Number	LH	RH	LHM	RHM
28	3,502,687	3,504,100				
	3,504,101	3,504,200		100		
	(3,504,201	3,504,600)		400 to L.I.		
	3,504,601	3,505,986	2800			
29	3,505,987	3,507,500				
	3,507,501	3,507,700		200		
	(3,507,701	3,507,900)		200 to L.I.		
	3,507,901	3,509,141	2755			
30	3,509,142	3,510,600				
	3,510,601	3,510,800		200		
	(3,510,801	3,511,200)		400 to L.I.		
	3,511,201	3,512,291	2550			
31	3,512,292	3,513,700				
	(3,513,701	3,513,900)		200 to L.I.		
	3,513,901	3,515,431	2940			

NOVEMBER 1919

Date	First Number	Last Number	LH	RH	LHM	RHM
1	3,515,432	3,516,800				
	3,516,801	3,517,000		200		
	(3,517,001	3,517,200)		200 to L.I.		
	3,517,201	3,518,531	2700			
3	3,518,532	3,520,000				
	3,520,001	3,520,200		200		
	(3,520,201	3,520,400)		200 to L.I.		
	3,520,401	3,521,371	2440			
4	3,521,372	3,523,200				
	(3,523,201	3,523,600)		400 to L.I.		
	3,523,601	3,524,631	2860			
5	3,524,632	3,526,100				
	(3,526,101	3,526,300)		200 to L.I.		
	3,526,301	3,527,591	2760			
6	3,527,592	3,529,200				
	(3,529,201	3,529,400)		200 to L.I.		
	3,529,401	3,530,641	2850			
7	3,530,642	3,532,100				
	(3,532,101	3,532,300)		200 to L.I.		
	3,532,301	3,533,741	2900			
8	3,533,742	3,535,200				
	(3,535,201	3,535,400)		200 to L.I.		
	3,535,401	3,536,841	2900			
10	3,536,842	3,538,300				
	(3,538,301	3,538,500)		200 to L.I.		
	3,538,501	3,539,896	2855			
11	3,539,897	3,541,400				
	(3,541,401	3,541,800)		400 to L.I.		
	3,541,801	3,542,921	2625			
12	3,542,922	3,544,500				
	(3,544,501	3,544,700)		200 to L.I.		
	3,544,701	3,545,926	2805			
13	3,545,927	3,547,400				
	(3,547,401	3,547,800)		400 to L.I.		
	3,547,801	3,549,236	2910			
14	3,549,237	3,550,800				
	3,550,801	3,551,000		200		
	(3,551,001	3,551,200)		200 to L.I.		
	3,551,201	3,552,336	2700			
15	3,552,337	3,553,800				
	3,553,801	3,554,000		200		
	(3,554,001	3,554,200)		200 to L.I.		
	3,554,201	3,555,336	2600			
17	3,555,337	3,556,776	1440			
18	3,556,777	3,557,100				
	3,557,101	3,557,300		200		
	(3,557,301	3,557,500)		200 to L.I.		
	3,557,501	3,559,861	2686			
19	3,559,862	3,560,200				
	3,560,201	3,560,400		200 to Manchester		
	(3,560,401	3,560,800)		400 to L.I.		
	3,560,801	3,562,700				
	(3,562,701	3,562,900)		200 to L.I.		
	3,562,901	3,563,000				
	3,563,001	3,563,200		200		
	3,563,201	3,563,461	2600			
20	3,563,462	3,564,100				
	(3,564,101	3,564,300)		200 to L.I		
	3,564,301	3,564,900				
	3,564,901	3,565,100		200		
	3,565,101	3,566,516	2655			
21	3,566,517	3,568,400				
	(3,568,401	3,568,600)		200 to L.I.		
	3,568,601	3,569,691	2975			
22	3,569,692	3,570,000				
	3,570,001	3,570,200		200		
	3,570,201	3,571,400				
	(3,571,401	3,571,600)		200 to L.I.		
	3,571,601	3,572,800	2709			
	3,572,801	3,572,831		31		
24	3,572,832	3,573,000		169		
	3,573,001	3,574,500				
	3,574,501	3,574,600		100		
	3,574,601	3,575,581	2481			
25	3,575,582	3,577,400				
	3,577,401	3,577,600		200		
	3,577,601	3,578,000		400 to L.I.		
	3,578,001	3,578,816	2635			
26	3,578,817	3,580,200				
	3,580,201	3,580,400		200		
	(3,580,401	3,580,600)		200 to L.I.		
	3,580,601	3,581,951	2735			
27	Closed					
28	3,581,952	3,583,200				
	3,583,201	3,583,400		200		
	(3,583,401	3,583,600)		200 to L.I.		
	3,583,601	3,584,966	2615			
29	3,584,967	3,586,400				
	3,586,401	3,586,600		200		
	(3,586,601	3,586,800)		200 to L.I.		
	3,586,801	3,587,996	2630			

DECEMBER 1919

Date	First Number	Last Number	LH	RH	LHM	RHM
1	3,587,997	3,589,400				
	3,589,401	3,589,600		200		
	(3,589,601	3,589,800)		200 to L.I.		
	3,589,801	3,590,831	2435			
2	3,590,832	3,592,400				
	3,592,401	3,592,600		200		
	(3,592,601	3,593,000)		400 to L.I.		
	3,593,001	3,594,056	2625			
3	3,594,057	3,595,500				
	3,595,501	3,595,700		200		
	(3,595,701	3,595,900)		200 to L.I.		
	3,595,901	3,596,696	2240			
4	3,596,697	3,598,300				
	3,598,301	3,598,400		100		
	(3,598,401	3,598,800)		400 to L.I.		
	3,598,801	3,599,431	2235			
5	3,599,432	3,600,700				
	(3,600,701	3,600,900)		200 to L.I.		
	3,600,901	3,602,881	3250			
6	3,602,882	3,603,800				
	3,603,801	3,603,900		100		
	3,603,901	3,604,600				
	(3,604,601	3,604,800)		200 to L.I.		
	3,604,801	3,606,746	3565			
8	3,606,747	3,606,900				
	3,606,901	3,607,000		100		
	(3,607,001	3,607,200)		200 to L.I.		
	(3,607,201	3,607,400)		200 to Manchester		
	3,607,401	3,608,200				
	(3,608,201	3,608,300)		100 to Manchester		
	3,608,301	3,610,046	2700			
9	3,610,047	3,610,900				
	3,610,901	3,611,100		200		
	(3,611,101	3,611,500)		400 to L.I.		
	3,611,501	3,613,471	2825			
10	3,613,471	3,614,500				
	(3,614,501	3,614,700)		200 to L.I.		
	3,614,701	3,616,000				
	3,616,001	3,616,500		500		
	3,616,501	3,616,596	2425			
11	3,616,597	3,618,000				
	(3,618,001	3,618,200)		200 to L.I.		
	3,618,201	3,619,336	2540			
12	3,619,337	3,620,800				
	(3,620,801	3,621,000)		200 to L.I.		
	3,621,001	3,621,346	1810			
13	3,621,347	3,622,000				
	(3,622,001	3,622,200)		200 to L.I.		
	3,622,201	3,624,396	2850			
15	3,624,397	3,624,500				
	(3,624,501	3,624,700)		200 to L.I.		
	3,624,701	3,627,951	2955			
16	3,627,952	3,628,200				
	(3,628,201	3,628,600)		400 to L.I.		
	3,628,601	3,631,221	2470			
17	3,631,222	3,632,700				
	(3,632,701	3,632,900)		200 to L.I.		
	3,632,901	3,634,681	2660			
18	3,634,682	3,635,000				
	(3,635,001	3,635,800)		800 to Manchester		
	3,635,801	3,637,881	2400			
19	3,637,882	3,638,300				
	(3,638,301	3,638,700)		400 to L.I.		
	3,638,701	3,640,916	2635			
20	3,640,917	3,641,600				
	(3,641,601	3,641,800)		200 to L.I.		
	3,641,801	3,643,916	2800			
22	3,643,917	3,644,200				
	(3,644,201	3,644,400)		200 to L.I.		
	3,644,401	3,646,000				
	3,646,001	3,646,200		200		
	3,646,201	3,646,721	2405			

	First Number	Last Number	Production	

DECEMBER 1919

	First Number	Last Number	Production	
23	3,646,722	3,647,400		
	(3,647,401	3,647,800)		400 to L.I.
	3,647,801	3,648,000		200
	3,648,001	3,649,101	1780	
24	3,649,102	3,650,000		
	(3,650,001	3,650,200)		200 to L.I.
	3,650,201	3,650,846	1545	
25	Closed December 25 to 29			
29	3,650,847	3,651,500		
	3,651,501	3,651,600		100
	3,651,601	3,651,800		
	(3,651,801	3,652,000)		200 to L.I.
	3,652,001	3,652,700		
	3,652,701	3,653,100		400
	3,653,101	3,653,631	2085	
30	3,653,632	3,654,000		
	(3,654,001	3,654,400)		400 TO L.I.
	3,654,401	3,655,200		
	3,655,201	3,655,400		200
	3,655,401	3,656,000		
	3,656,001	3,656,400		400
	3,656,401	3,656,901	2270	
31	3,656,902	3,657,300		
	(3,657,301	3,657,700)		400 to L.I.
	3,657,701	3,659,971	2670	

Blocks of engine numbers and "knocked down" engines continued to be shipped to Long Island and to other assembly plants. The serial numbers are listed in the records but are not shown here after December, for they serve little purpose other than being of some interest. The production figures shown from here on are for Highland Park only. The differences between the serial numbers and the production numbers are due to the shipments to the branches.

	First Number	Last Number	Production	
2	3,659,972	3,663,186	2815	200
3	3,663,187	3,666,386	2900	100
5	3,666,387	3,669,821	2835	200
6	3,669,822	3,673,321	2900	200
7	3,673,322	3,676,581	2860	200
8	3,676,582	3,680,151	2970	200
9	3,680,152	3,683,581	3030	200
10	3,683,582	3,687,086	3185	120
12	3,687,087	3,690,636	2950	
13	3,690,637	3,693,651	2215	
14	3,693,652	3,696,771	2420	
15	3,696,772	3,700,321	2750	
16	3,700,322	3,703,701	2780	
17	3,703,702	3,706,876	2575	
19	3,706,877	3,710,146	2670	200
20	3,710,147	3,713,591	2845	200
21	3,713,592	3,716,601	2810	
22	3,716,602	3,719,761	2760	200
23	3,719,762	3,722,801	2640	
24	3,722,802	3,725,411	2310	100
26	3,725,412	3,728,191	1980	400
27	3,728,192	3,731,011	2620	
28	3,731,012	3,734,051	2440	200
29	3,734,052	3,737,086	2449	386
30	3,737,087	3,739,936	2077	73
31	3,739,937	3,743,076	2440	

FEBRUARY 1920

	First Number	Last Number	Production	
2	3,743,077	3,746,211	2235	
3	3,746,212	3,749,511	2400	
4	3,749,512	3,752,386	2175	
5	3,752,387	3,755,186	2600	
6	3,755,187	3,758,441	2655	400
7	3,758,442	3,761,541	2500	400
9	3,761,542	3,764,641	2600	500
10	3,764,642	3,767,926	3085	200
11	3,767,927	3,771,086	2860	300
12	3,771,087	3,774,121	2735	300
13	3,774,122	3,777,221	2800	300
14	3,777,222	3,780,241	2620	400
16	3,780,242	3,783,251	2410	400
17	3,783,252	3,786,266	2415	400
18	3,786,267	3,789,316	2650	
19	3,789,317	3,792,361	2633	12
20	3,792,362	3,795,386	2624	
21	3,795,387	3,798,396	2610	
23	3,798,397	3,801,786	2790	
24	3,801,787	3,804,821	2435	
25	3,804,822	3,808,026	2765	
26	3,808,027	3,811,166	2580	300
27	3,811,167	3,814,051	2585	300
28	3,814,052	3,817,076	2925	100

MARCH 1920

	First Number	Last Number	Production	
1	3,817,077	3,820,296	2570	400
2	3,820,297	3,823,526	2380	400
3	3,823,527	3,826,526	2500	200
4	3,826,527	3,830,026	3100	
5	3,830,027	3,833,491	3065	

	First Number	Last Number	Production	
6	3,833,492	3,837,041	3150	
8	3,837,042	3,840,566	3075	
9	3,840,567	3,844,131	3115	
10	3,844,132	3,847,701	3070	
11	3,847,702	3,851,271	2970	
12	3,851,272	3,854,846	3075	
13	3,854,847	3,858,416	3070	
15	3,858,417	3,861,816	2900	
16	3,861,817	3,865,226	2910	
17	3,865,227	3,868,641	2915	
18	3,868,642	3,872,041	2900	
19	3,872,042	3,875,446	2905	
20	3,875,447	3,878,846	2900	
22	3,878,847	3,881,951	2305	
23	3,881,952	3,885,351	2500	
24	3,885,352	3,888,801	2550	
25	3,888,802	3,892,301	2600	
26	3,892,302	3,895,801	2600	
27	3,895,802	3,899,311	2610	
29	3,899,312	3,902,851	3090	
30	3,902,852	3,906,401	3150	
31	3,906,402	3,910,001	3300	

APRIL 1920

	First Number	Last Number	Production	
1	3,910,002	3,913,221	3020	
2	3,913,222	3,915,646	2225	
3	3,915,647	3,918,671	2825	
5	3,918,672	3,921,721	2550	300
6	3,921,722	3,924,896	2475	500
7	3,924,897	3,927,906	2403	207
8	3,927,907	3,931,406	2900	
9	3,931,407	3,934,906	3100	
10	3,934,907	3,938,306	3000	
12	3,938,307	3,941,266	2960	"Strike started"
13	3,941,267	3,944,106	2840	
14	3,944,107	3,947,381	2925	
15	3,947,382	3,950,261	2880	
16	3,950,262	3,952,266	2005	
17	3,952,267	3,952,991	725	
19	3,952,992	3,953,616	625	
20	3,953,617	3,954,191	575	
21	Closed April 21 to April 26 because of strike.			
26	3,954,192	3,956,426	1735	
27	3,956,427	3,959,576	2050	
28	3,959,577	3,962,901	2175	
29	3,962,902	3,965,771	2020	
30	3,965,772	3,969,151	2380	

MAY 1920

	First Number	Last Number	Production	
1	3,969,152	3,972,666	2215	"Start large fans and
3	3,972,667	3,976,216	2450	pulleys for truck
4	3,976,217	3,979,751	2535	motors"
5	3,979,752	3,983,256	2955	
6	3,983,257	3,986,756	2700	200
7	3,986,757	3,990,261	3005	100
8	3,990,262	3,993,761	2839	161
10	3,993,762	3,996,891	2191	339
11	3,996,892	4,000,396	2905	200
	(4,000,000 at 10:15 P.M.)			
12	4,000,397	4,003,496	2400	500
13	4,003,497	4,006,546	2550	300
	(Began using 24 disks in transmission)			
14	4,006,547	4,009,896	2800	200
15	4,009,897	4,013,101	2430	375
17	4,013,102	4,016,631	2715	
18	4,016,632	4,020,231	2765	
19	4,020,232	4,023,751	2695	
20	4,023,752	4,027,276	2650	- Began using 25 disks
21	4,027,277	4,030,851	2750	in transmission.
22	4,030,852	4,034,351	2650	
24	4,034,352	4,037,976	2800	
25	4,037,977	4,041,651	2850	- New coil shims
26	4,041,652	4,045,201	3150	beginning at 2 P.M.
27	4,045,202	4,048,731	3130	
28	4,048,732	4,052,281	3350	
29	4,052,282	4,055,281	2800	

JUNE 1920

	First Number	Last Number	Production	
1	4,055,282	4,058,606	2825	
2	4,058,607	4,062,116	3010	
3	4,062,117	4,065,686	3070	
4	4,065,687	4,069,251	3065	
5	4,069,252	4,072,581	2830	
7	4,072,582	4,075,811	2730	300
8	4,075,812	4,079,011	2700	300
9	4,079,012	4,082,421	2910	300
10	4,082,422	4,085,621	2883	117
11	4,085,622	4,086,546	2840	
12	4,086,662	4,091,661	2800	
14	4,091,662	4,094,736	2875	
15	4,094,737	4,098,241	3055	
16	4,098,242	4,101,616	2925	
17	4,101,617	4,104,966	2900	
18	4,104,067	4,108,341	2925	
19	4,108,342	4,111,501	2710	

Serial Numbers

JUNE 1920

Day	First Number	Last Number	Production	
21	4,111,502	4,114,816	2865	
22	4,114,817	4,118,276	3010	
23	4,118,277	4,121,801	2775	
24	4,121,802	4,124,981	2680	
25	4,124,982	4,128,306	2725	400
26	4,128,307	4,131,981	2050	400
28	4,131,982	4,134,981	2550	300
29	4,134,982	4,138,146	2659	306
30	4,138,147	4,141,451	3025	

JULY 1920

Day	First Number	Last Number	Production	
1	4,141,452	4,144,551	2800	200
2	4,144,552	4,147,921	2970	200
3	4,147,922	4,151,041	2620	300
5	Closed			
6	4,151,042	4,154,071	2630	200
7	4,154,072	4,157,586	3223	92
8	4,157,587	4,161,136	3050	
9	4,161,137	4,164,686	3050	
10	4,164,687	4,168,186	3000	
12	4,168,187	4,171,696	2810	
13	4,171,697	4,175,196	2800	
14	4,175,197	4,178,721	2825	
15	4,178,722	4,182,246	2825	
16	4,182,247	4,185,756	2810	
17	4,185,757	4,189,256	2800	
19	4,189,257	4,192,956	2600	
20	4,192,957	4,196,676	2620	
21	4,196,677	4,200,376	2600	
22	4,200,377	4,203,951	2475	
23	4,203,952	4,207,531	2480	
24	4,207,532	4,211,191	2560	
26	4,211,192	4,214,876	2485	200
27	4,214,877	4,218,546	2570	100
28	4,218,547	4,222,216	2470	200
29	4,222,217	4,225,916	2488	212
30	4,225,917	4,229,621	2705	
31	4,229,622	4,233,351	2730	

AUGUST 1920

Day	First Number	Last Number	Production
2	4,233,352	4,236,886	2335
3	4,236,887	4,239,436	2550
4	4,239,437	4,242,236	2800
5	4,242,237	4,245,246	2560
6	4,245,247	4,250,351	2555
7	4,250,352	4,253,386	2560
9	4,253,387	4,256,836	2550
10	4,256,837	4,260,071	2560
11	4,260,072	4,263,156	2585
12	4,263,157	4,266,226	1270
13	4,266,227	4,270,021	1945
14	4,270,022	4,273,486	2265
16	4,273,487	4,276,936	2250
17	4,276,937	4,280,736	2200
18	4,280,737	4,284,646	2110
19	4,284,647	4,288,441	2195
20	4,288,442	4,292,681	2240
21	4,292,682	4,295,911	2230
23	4,295,912	4,299,951	2240
24	4,299,952	4,303,801	2650
25	4,303,802	4,307,931	2730
26	4,307,932	4,311,831	2700
27	4,311,832	4,315,781	2750
28	4,315,782	4,320,206	2825
30	4,320,207	4,324,256	2850
31	4,324,257	4,329,901	2245

SEPTEMBER 1920

Day	First Number	Last Number	Production
1	4,329,902	4,333,751	2650
2	4,333,752	4,337,611	2660
3	4,337,612	4,341,476	2665
4	4,341,477	4,345,326	2650
6	Closed		
7	4,345,327	4,349,176	2650
8	4,349,177	4,353,041	2665
9	4,353,042	4,356,901	2660
10	4,356,902	4,360,771	2670
11	4,360,772	4,364,621	2650
13	4,364,622	4,368,511	2265
14	4,368,512	4,372,411	2275
15	4,372,412	4,376,261	2225
16	4,376,262	4,380,116	2230
17	4,380,117	4,383,966	2225
18	4,383,967	4,387,816	2225
20	4,387,817	4,391,671	2430
21	4,391,672	4,395,526	2430
22	4,395,527	4,399,376	2425
23	4,399,377	4,403,231	2430
24	4,403,232	4,407,081	2425
25	4,407,082	4,410,931	2425
27	4,410,932	4,414,781	2850
28	4,414,782	4,418,631	2850
29	4,418,632	4,422,486	2855
30	4,422,487	4,426,386	2900

OCTOBER 1920

Day	First Number	Last Number	Production
1	4,426,387	4,430,261	2875
2	4,430,262	4,434,161	2900
4	4,434,162	4,438,061	2500
5	4,438,062	4,442,061	2800
6	4,442,062	4,447,061	3600
7	4,447,062	4,452,061	3600
8	4,452,062	4,456,586	3125
9	4,456,587	4,460,886	2900
11	4,460,887	4,465,086	3000
12	4,465,087	4,469,286	3000
13	4,469,287	4,473,496	3010
14	4,473,497	4,477,945	3249
15	4,477,946	4,482,306	3161
16	4,482,307	4,483,781	875
18	4,483,782	4,487,661	2440
19	4,487,662	4,492,526	3415
20	4,492,527	4,497,446	3480
21	4,497,447	4,502,329	3433
22	4,502,330	4,504,629	1800
25	4,504,630	4,509,281	3352
26	4,509,282	4,513,932	3451
27	4,513,933	4,518,942	3110
28	4,518,943	4,524,031	2689
29	4,524,032	4,526,541	1210

Start of sand-cast piston rings in 2 and 3 grooves. Centrifugal cast in the top groove.

NOVEMBER 1920

Day	First Number	Last Number	Production
1	4,526,542	4,531,466	2925
2	Closed		
3	4,531,467	4,536,450	2984
4	4,536,451	4,541,476	3026
5	4,541,477	4,544,092	1616
6	Closed		
8	4,544,093	4,549,113	3421
9	4,549,114	4,553,998	3285
10	4,553,999	4,558,903	3305
11	4,558,904	4,563,909	3006
12	4,563,910	4,566,431	1672
13	Closed		
15	4,566,432	4,571,408	2977
16	4,571,409	4,576,326	3118
17	4,576,327	4,580,946	3570
18	4,580,947	4,586,208	3562
19	4,586,209	4,589,193	1785
20	Closed		
22	4,589,194	4,595,257	3614
23	4,595,258	4,600,647	3740
24	4,600,648	4,606,320	3723
25	Closed November 25 to 29		
29	4,606,321	4,612,126	3806
30	4,612,127	4,617,928	3902

DECEMBER 1920

Day	First Number	Last Number	Production
1	4,617,929	4,623,272	3902
2	4,623,273	4,628,609	3737
3	4,628,610	4,631,335	1876
4	Closed		
6	4,631,336	4,636,668	3733
7	4,636,669	4,641,835	3567
8	4,641,836	4,647,005	3570
9	4,647,006	4,652,297	3442
10	4,652,298	4,654,922	1725
11	Closed		
13	4,654,923	4,660,282	3460
14	4,660,283	4,665,667	3485
15	4,665,668	4,670,928	3561
16	4,670,929	4,676,178	3750
17	4,676,179	4,678,954	1876
18	Closed		
20	4,678,955	4,684,204	3730
21	4,684,205	4,689,504	3800
22	4,689,505	4,695,169	3765
23	4,695,170	4,698,419	3250
24	Closed until February 1, 1921.		

Start using all sand-cast piston rings.

JANUARY 1921

Factory closed all of January. Daily production figures no longer listed in the records. The production figures shown hereafter are the differences between the serial numbers, NOT necessarily the actual number produced.

FEBRUARY 1921

Day	First Number	Last Number	Production
1	4,698,420	4,699,337	918
2	4,699,338	4,700,266	929
3	4,700,267	4,701,367	1101
4	4,701,368	4,702,580	1213
7	4,702,581	4,704,033	1453
8	4,704,034	4,705,729	1696
9	4,705,730	4,707,529	1800
10	4,707,530	4,709,408	1879
11	4,709,409	4,711,376	1968
14	4,711,377	4,713,300	1924
15	4,713,301	4,715,445	2145

FEBRUARY 1921

Day	First Number	Last Number	Production	Note
16	4,715,446	4,717,651	2206	
17	4,717,652	4,719,902	2251	
18	4,719,903	4,721,934	2032	
21	4,721,935	4,724,149	2215	
22	4,724,150	4,726,651	2502	
23	4,726,652	4,729,192	2541	– No longer use balanced
24	4,729,193	4,731,527	2335	magnets.
25	4,731,528	4,734,001	2474	
28	4,734,002	4,736,431	2430	

MARCH 1921

Day	First Number	Last Number	Production	Note
1	4,736,432	4,739,104	2673	
2	4,739,105	4,741,662	2558	
3	4,741,663	4,744,142	2480	
4	4,744,143	4,746,853	2711	
7	4,746,854	4,749,527	2674	
8	4,749,528	4,751,967	2440	
9	4,751,968	4,754,520	2553	
10	4,754,521	4,757,196	2676	
11	4,757,197	4,759,956	2760	
14	4,759,957	4,762,677	2721	
15	4,762,678	4,765,457	2780	
16	4,765,458	4,768,308	2851	
17	4,768,309	4,771,226	2918	
18	4,771,227	4,774,245	3019	
21	4,774,246	4,777,517	3272	Outside make pistons
22	4,777,518	4,780,992	3475	this week.
23	4,780,993	4,784,557	3565	
24	4,784,558	4,788,192	3635	
25	4,788,193	4,791,825	3633	
26	4,791,826	4,795,429	3604	
28	4,795,430	4,799,080	3651	
29	4,799,081	4,802,747	3667	
30	4,802,748	4,806,410	3663	
31	4,806,411	4,810,014	3604	

APRIL 1921

Day	First Number	Last Number	Production	Note
1	4,810,015	4,813,644	3630	"50 men sent home.
2	4,813,645	4,817,196	3552	Building too many."
4	4,817,197	4,820,766	3570	
5	4,820,767	4,824,317	3551	
6	4,824,318	4,827,870	3553	
7	4,827,871	4,831,426	3556	
8	4,831,427	4,834,983	3557	
9	4,834,984	4,838,536	3553	
11	4,838,537	4,842,092	1756	
12	4,842,093	4,845,653	3561	
13	4,845,654	4,849,220	3567	
14	4,849,221	4,852,795	3575	
15	4,852,796	4,856,357	3562	
16	4,856,358	4,859,921	3564	
18	4,859,922	4,863,540	3619	
19	4,863,541	4,867,441	3901	
20	4,867,442	4,871,351	3910	
21	4,871,352	4,875,366	4015	
22	4,875,367	4,879,369	4003	
23	4,879,370	4,883,384	4015	
25	4,883,385	4,887,405	4021	
26	4,887,406	4,891,406	4001	
27	4,891,407	4,895,448	4042	
28	4,895,449	4,899,466	4018	
29	4,899,467	4,903,480	4014	
30	4,903,481	4,907,505	4025	

MAY 1921

Day	First Number	Last Number	Production	Note
2	4,907,506	4,911,526	4021	
3	4,911,527	4,915,556	4030	
4	4,915,557	4,919,585	4029	
5	4,919,586	4,923,599	4014	
6	4,923,600	4,927,614	4015	
7	4,927,615	4,931,636	4022	
9	4,931,637	4,935,674	4038	
10	4,935,675	4,939,694	4020	
11	4,939,695	4,943,708	4014	
12	4,943,709	4,947,720	4012	"Started using Heinze
13	4,947,721	4,951,731	4011	commutators."
14	4,951,732	4,955,741	4010	
16	4,955,742	4,959,752	4011	
17	4,959,753	4,963,769	4017	
18	4,963,770	4,967,798	4029	
19	4,967,799	4,971,848	4050	
20	4,971,849	4,975,870	4022	
21	4,975,871	4,979,894	4024	
23	4,979,895	4,983,931	4037	
24	4,983,932	4,987,951	4020	
25	4,987,952	4,991,961	4011	
26	4,991,962	4,995,962	4001	
27	4,995,963	4,999,964	4002	
28	4,999,965	5,003,968	4004	
	5,000,000 at 7:05 A.M. "To Edsel Ford."			
31	5,003,969	5,008,005	4037	

JUNE 1921

Day	First Number	Last Number	Production
1	5,008,006	5,012,030	4025
2	5,012,031	5,016,052	4023
3	5,016,053	5,020,070	4018
4	5,020,071	5,024,085	4015
6	5,024,086	5,028,091	4006
7	5,028,092	5,032,094	4003
8	5,032,095	5,036,106	4012
9	5,036,107	5,040,126	4020
10	5,040,127	5,044,144	4018
11	5,044,145	5,048,148	4004
13	5,048,149	5,052,155	4007
14	5,052,156	5,056,178	4023
15	5,056,179	5,060,205	4027
16	5,060,206	5,064,222	4017
17	5,064,223	5,068,233	4011
18	5,068,234	5,072,237	4004
20	5,072,238	5,076,258	4021
21	5,076,259	5,080,268	4010
22	5,080,269	5,084,271	4003
23	5,084,272	5,088,321	4050
24	5,088,322	5,092,550	4229
25	5,092,551	5,096,825	4275
27	5,096,826	5,101,046	4221
28	5,101,047	5,105,372	4326
29	5,105,373	5,109,963	4591
30	5,109,964	5,114,533	4570

JULY 1921

Day	First Number	Last Number	Production
1	5,114,534	5,119,078	4545
2	5,119,079	5,123,480	4402
4	Closed		
5	5,123,481	5,127,640	4160
6	5,127,641	5,131,790	4150

"Began to center commutator counterbore with camshaft."

Day	First Number	Last Number	Production
7	5,131,791	5,136,227	4437
8	5,136,228	5,140,805	4578
9	5,140,806	5,145,213	4408
11	5,145,214	5,149,633	4420
12	5,149,634	5,154,147	4514
13	5,154,148	5,158,568	4421
14	5,158,569	5,162,984	4416
15	5,162,985	5,167,397	4413
16	5,167,398	5,171,816	4419
18	5,171,817	5,176,401	4585
19	5,176,402	5,180,821	4420
20	5,180,822	5,185,240	4419
21	5,185,241	5,189,656	4416
22	5,189,657	5,193,896	4240
23	5,193,897	5,198,125	4229
25	5,198,126	5,202,300	4175
26	5,202,301	5,206,476	4176
27	5,206,477	5,210,678	4202
28	5,210,679	5,214,800	4121
29	5,214,801	5,219,000	4200
30	5,219,001	5,223,135	4135

AUGUST 1921

Day	First Number	Last Number	Production
1	5,223,136	5,227,266	4131
2	5,227,267	5,231,494	4228
3	5,231,495	5,235,720	4226
4	5,235,721	5,239,942	4222
5	5,239,943	5,244,143	4201
6	5,244,144	5,248,367	4224
8	5,248,368	5,252,585	4218
9	5,252,586	5,256,800	4215

"New style crankcase on all production"

Day	First Number	Last Number	Production
10	5,256,801	5,261,012	4212
11	5,261,013	5,265,237	4225
12	5,265,238	5,269,452	4215
13	5,269,453	5,273,672	4220
15	5,273,673	5,277,882	4210
16	5,277,883	5,282,100	4218
17	5,282,101	5,286,314	4214
18	5,286,315	5,290,522	4208
19	5,290,523	5,294,726	4204
20	5,294,727	5,298,931	4205
22	5,298,932	5,303,216	4285
23	5,303,217	5,307,502	4286
24	5,307,503	5,311,794	4292
25	5,311,795	5,316,088	4294
26	5,316,089	5,320,382	4294
27	5,320,383	5,324,669	4287
29	5,324,670	5,328,966	4297
30	5,328,967	5,333,252	4286
31	5,333,253	5,337,545	4293

SEPTEMBER 1921

Day	First Number	Last Number	Production
1	5,337,546	5,341,831	4286
2	5,341,832	5,346,126	4295
3	5,346,127	5,350,415	4289
5	Closed		
6	5,350,416	5,354,706	4291
7	5,354,707	5,358,995	4289

Serial Numbers

	First Number	Last Number	Production

SEPTEMBER 1921

Day	First Number	Last Number	Production	
8	5,358,996	5,363,288	4293	
9	5,363,289	5,367,575	4287	
10	5,367,576	5,371,860	4285	
12	5,371,861	5,376,150	4290	
13	5,376,151	5,380,451	4301	
14	5,380,452	5,384,757	4306	
15	5,384,758	5,389,064	4307	
16	5,389,065	5,393,358	4294	
19	5,393,359	5,397,645	4287	
20	5,397,646	5,400,000	2355	
	(5,400,001	5,415,000)		15,000 to Cork, Ireland
	5,415,001	5,416,548	1548	
21	5,416,549	5,420,448	3900	
22	5,420,449	5,424,354	3906	
23	5,424,355	5,428,263	3909	
26	5,428,264	5,432,180	3917	
27	5,432,181	5,436,100	3920	
28	5,436,101	5,440,014	3914	
29	5,440,015	5,443,916	3902	
30	5,443,917	5,447,816	3900	

OCTOBER 1921

Day	First Number	Last Number	Production	
3	5,447,817	5,451,720	3904	
4	5,451,721	5,455,627	3907	
5	5,455,628	5,459,537	3910	
6	5,459,538	5,463,441	3904	
7	5,463,442	5,467,344	3903	
10	5,467,345	5,471,248	3904	"Began brass rollers"
11	5,471,249	5,475,155	3907	
12	5,475,156	5,479,058	3903	
13	5,479,059	5,482,962	3904	"All brass rollers"
14	5,482,963	5,486,872	3910	
17	5,486,873	5,490,779	3907	
18	5,490,780	5,494,683	3904	
19	5,494,684	5,498,592	3909	
20	5,498,593	5,502,482	3890	
21	5,502,483	5,506,347	3865	
24	5,506,348	5,510,141	3794	
25	5,510,142	5,514,039	3898	

"New commutator shield begun" (Center hole now has lip)

Day	First Number	Last Number	Production
26	5,514,040	5,517,908	3869
27	5,517,909	5,521,773	3865
28	5,521,774	5,525,643	3870
31	5,525,644	5,529,519	3876

NOVEMBER 1921

Beginning of production of one-piece valve door engines, along with older two-door engines.

Day	First Number	Last Number	Production	1-pc door engines	
1	5,529,520	5,533,389	3870	1032	
2	5,533,390	5,537,252	3863	264	(Now all brass
3	5,537,253	5,541,119	3867	373	rollers)
4	5,541,120	5,544,988	3869	265	
7	5,544,989	5,548,852	3864	180	
8	5,548,853	5,552,717	3865	182	"Start copper
9	5,552,718	5,556,578	3861	191	plate rollers"
10	5,556,579	5,560,445	3867	249	
14	5,560,446	5,564,308	3863	159	
15	5,564,309	5,568,173	3865	159	

Beginning of rolled-thread head bolts

Day	First Number	Last Number	Production	1-pc
16	5,568,174	5,572,037	3864	110
17	5,572,038	5,575,903	3866	187
18	5,575,904	5,579,766	3863	150
21	5,579,767	5,583,520	3754	131

New commutator spring (T689) beginning with 5,580,021.

Day	First Number	Last Number	Production	1-pc
22	5,583,521	5,587,271	3751	160
23	5,587,272	5,591,026	3755	146
24	Closed November 24 to 28.			
28	5,591,027	5,594,780	3754	397
29	5,594,781	5,598,946	4166	155
30	5,598,947	5,602,301	3355	191

DECEMBER 1921

Day	First Number	Last Number	Production	1-pc
1	5,602,302	5,606,054	3753	185
5	5,606,055	5,609,807	3753	188
6	5,609,808	5,613,563	3756	247
7	5,613,564	5,617,317	3744	212
8	5,617,318	5,621,071	3754	212
9	Closed			
12	5,621,072	5,624,826	3755	273
13	5,624,827	5,628,314	3488	245
14	5,628,315	5,631,540	3226	246
15	5,631,541	5,635,571	4031	393
16	Closed			
19	5,635,572	5,638,071	2500	378
20	Closed December 20 to January 9, 1922			

JANUARY 1922

Day	First Number	Last Number	Production	
9	5,638,072	5,641,577	3506	544
10	5,641,578	5,645,081	3504	407
11	5,645,082	5,648,588	3507	383
12	5,648,589	5,652,093	3505	628
13	Closed			
16	Closed			
17	5,652,094	5,655,877	3784	1128
18	5,655,878	5,659,658	3781	1033
19	5,659,659	5,663,161	3503	962
20	Closed			
23	5,663,162	5,666,670	3509	986
24	5,666,671	5,670,182	3512	822
25	5,670,183	5,673,690	3508	1016
26	5,673,691	5,677,199	3509	895
27	Closed			
30	5,677,200	5,680,505	3306	846
31	5,680,506	5,683,808	3303	967

FEBRUARY 1922

Day	First Number	Last Number	Production	
1	5,683,809	5,687,110	3302	1096
2	5,687,111	5,690,410	3300	950
3	Closed			
6	5,690,411	5,693,712	3302	969
7	5,693,713	5,697,016	3304	1112
8	5,697,017	5,700,325	3309	1028
9	5,700,326	5,703,632	3307	511
10	Closed			
13	5,703,633	5,706,932	3300	1026
14	5,706,933	5,710,241	3309	1219
15	5,710,242	5,713,545	3304	1296
16	5,713,546	5,716,849	3304	1233
17	Closed			
20	5,716,850	5,720,251	3402	1273
21	5,720,252	5,723,660	3409	1395
22	5,723,661	5,727,064	3404	1774
23	5,727,065	5,730,470	3406	1836
24	Closed			
27	5,730,471	5,733,872	3402	1995
28	5,733,873	5,737,278	3406	2212

MARCH 1922

Day	First Number	Last Number	Production	
1	5,737,279	5,740,685	3407	2119
2	5,740,686	5,744,089	3404	2453
3	Closed			
6	5,744,090	5,747,492	3403	2268
7	5,747,493	5,750,897	3405	2341
8	5,750,898	5,754,304	3407	2470
9	5,754,305	5,757,713	3409	2407
10	Closed			
13	5,757,714	5,761,119	3406	2523
14	Closed			
15	5,761,120	5,764,524	3405	2927
16	5,764,525	5,767,928	3404	3014
17	5,767,929	5,771,334	3406	3075
20	5,771,335	5,775,287	3953	3363
21	5,775,288	5,779,362	4075	3520
22	5,779,363	5,783,506	4144	3690
23	5,783,507	5,787,652	4146	3685
24	5,787,653	5,791,814	4162	3840
27	5,791,815	5,795,998	4184	3890
28	5,795,999	5,800,150	4152	3995
29	5,800,151	5,804,305	4155	4057
30	5,804,306	5,808,458	4153	4110
31	5,808,459	5,812,608	4150	4115

APRIL 1922   All one-piece doors beginning April 3.

Day	First Number	Last Number	Production	
3	5,812,609	5,816,752	4144	
4	5,816,753	5,819,000	2248	
	(5,819,001	5,834,000)		15,000 to Manchester
	5,834,001	5,835,928	1928	
5	5,835,929	5,840,143	4215	
6	5,840,144	5,844,284	4141	
7	5,844,285	5,848,484	3900	
8	5,848,485	5,850,724	2240	
10	5,850,725	5,855,016	4292	
11	5,855,017	5,859,287	4271	
12	5,859,288	5,863,496	4209	
13	5,863,497	5,867,628	4132	
14	5,867,629	5,871,840	4212	
15	5,871,841	5,876,074	4234	
17	5,876,075	5,880,175	4101	
18	5,880,176	5,884,346	4171	
19	5,884,347	5,887,884	3538	
20	5,887,885	5,891,831	3947	
21	5,891,832	5,896,234	4403	
22	5,896,235	5,898,074	1840	
24	5,898,075	5,901,256	3182	
25	5,901,257	5,905,250	3994	
26	5,905,251	5,909,756	4506	
27	5,909,757	5,913,966	4210	
28	5,913,967	5,918,466	4500	
29	5,918,467	5,922,968	4502	

MAY 1922

Day	First Number	Last Number	Production
1	5,922,969	5,927,483	4515
2	5,927,484	5,932,116	4633
3	5,932,117	5,936,922	4806
4	5,936,923	5,941,845	4923
5	5,941,846	5,946,969	5124
6	5,946,970	5,952,109	5140
8	5,952,110	5,957,265	5156

	First Number	Last Number	Production

MAY 1922

Day	First Number	Last Number	Production
9	5,957,266	5,962,471	5206
10	5,962,472	5,967,674	5203
11	5,967,675	5,972,874	5200
12	5,972,875	5,978,107	5233
13	5,978,108	5,983,357	5250
15	5,983,358	5,988,701	5344
16	5,988,702	5,994,105	5404
17	5,994,106	5,999,315	5210
18	5,999,316	6,004,617	5302
		6,000,000 at 9:14 A.M., to Edsel Ford	
19	6,004,618	6,010,026	5409
20	6,010,027	6,015,439	5413
22	6,015,440	6,020,846	5407
23	6,020,847	6,026,251	5405
24	6,026,252	6,031,653	5402
25	6,031,654	6,037,053	5400
26	6,037,054	6,042,458	5405
27	6,042,459	6,047,864	5406
29	6,047,865	6,053,264	5400
30	Closed		
31	6,053,265	6,058,671	5407

JUNE 1922

Day	First Number	Last Number	Production
1	6,058,672	6,063,644	4973
2	6,063,645	6,069,193	5549
3	6,069,194	6,074,815	5622
5	6,074,816	6,080,352	5537
6	6,080,353	6,085,752	5400
7	6,085,753	6,091,162	5410
8	6,091,163	6,096,570	5408
9	6,096,571	6,101,977	5407
10	6,101,978	6,107,383	5406
12	6,107,384	6,112,783	5400
13	6,112,784	6,118,190	5407
14	6,118,191	6,123,595	5405
15	6,123,596	6,128,996	5401
16	6,128,997	6,134,398	5402
17	6,134,399	6,139,809	5411
19	6,139,810	6,145,234	5425
20	6,145,235	6,150,687	5453
21	6,150,688	6,156,146	5459
22	6,156,147	6,161,606	5460
23	6,161,607	6,167,061	5455
24	6,167,062	6,172,514	5453
26	6,172,515	6,177,969	5455
27	6,177,970	6,183,422	5453
28	6,183,423	6,188,886	5464
29	6,188,887	6,194,342	5456
30	6,194,343	6,199,796	5454

JULY 1922

Day	First Number	Last Number	Production
1	6,199,797	6,205,253	5457
3	6,205,254	6,210,713	5450
4	Closed		
5	6,210,714	6,216,166	5453
6	6,216,167	6,221,626	5460
7	6,221,627	6,227,084	5458
8	6,227,085	6,232,540	5456
10	6,232,541	6,237,990	5450
11	6,237,991	6,243,448	5458
12	6,243,449	6,248,900	5452
13	6,248,901	6,254,358	5458
14	6,254,359	6,259,812	5454
15	6,259,813	6,265,266	5454
17	6,265,267	6,270,722	5456
18	6,270,723	6,276,174	5452
19	6,276,175	6,281,626	5452
20	6,281,627	6,286,879	5253
21	6,286,880	6,292,134	5255
22	6,292,135	6,297,384	5250
24	6,297,385	6,302,641	5257
25	6,302,642	6,307,897	5256
26	6,307,898	6,313,158	5261
27	6,313,159	6,318,410	5252
28	6,318,411	6,323,668	5258
29	6,323,669	6,328,934	5266
31	6,328,935	6,334,196	5262

AUGUST 1922

Day	First Number	Last Number	Production
1	6,334,197	6,339,446	5250
2	6,339,447	6,344,702	5256
3	6,344,703	6,349,958	5256
4	6,349,959	6,355,213	5255
5	6,355,214	6,360,463	5250
7	6,360,464	6,365,279	4816
8	6,365,280	6,370,966	5687
9	6,370,967	6,376,222	5256
10	6,376,223	6,381,476	5254
11	6,381,477	6,386,728	5252
12	6,386,729	6,391,981	5253
14	6,391,982	6,397,235	5254
15	6,397,236	6,402,491	5256
16	6,402,492	6,407,744	5253

Day	First Number	Last Number	Production
17	6,407,745	6,412,994	5250
18	6,412,995	6,418,249	5255
19	6,418,250	6,421,299	3050
21	6,421,300	6,426,556	5257
22	6,426,557	6,431,431	4875
23	6,431,432	6,436,282	4851
24	6,436,283	6,441,536	5254
25	6,441,537	6,446,808	5272
26	6,446,809	6,452,092	5284
28	6,452,093	6,457,348	5256
29	6,457,349	6,462,632	5284
30	6,462,633	6,467,914	5282
31	6,467,915	6,473,196	5282

SEPTEMBER 1922

Day	First Number	Last Number	Production	
1	6,473,197	6,478,462	5266	
2	6,478,463	6,483,714	5252	
5	6,483,715	6,485,000	1286	
	(6,485,001	6,500,000)		15,000 to Manchester
	6,500,001	6,503,968	3968	(Shipped 8-30-22)
6	6,503,969	6,509,223	5255	
7	6,509,224	6,514,474	5251	
8	6,514,475	6,519,726	5252	
9	6,519,727	6,524,976	5250	
	(6,521,696 to 6,521,751 built with "special camshafts")			
11	6,524,977	6,530,232	5256	
12	6,530,233	6,535,489	5257	
13	6,535,490	6,540,741	5252	
14	6,540,742	6,543,606	2865	
15	No production September 15 to 22			
22	6,543,607	6,546,500	2894	
23	6,546,501	6,551,006	4506	
25	6,551,007	6,556,258	5252	
26	6,556,259	6,561,513	5255	
27	6,561,514	6,566,816	5303	
28	6,566,817	6,572,122	5306	
29	6,572,123	6,577,424	5302	
30	6,577,425	6,582,724	5300	

OCTOBER 1922

Day	First Number	Last Number	Production
2	6,582,725	6,588,025	5301
3	6,588,026	6,593,336	5311
4	6,593,337	6,598,646	5310
5	6,598,647	6,603,949	5303
6	6,603,950	6,609,261	5312
7	6,609,262	6,614,568	5307
9	6,614,569	6,619,873	5305
10	6,619,874	6,625,175	5302
11	6,625,176	6,630,482	5307
12	6,630,483	6,635,787	5305
13	6,635,788	6,641,089	5302
14	6,641,090	6,646,089	5000
16	6,646,090	6,651,204	5115
17	6,651,205	6,655,671	4467
18	6,655,672	6,658,333	2662
	"Production down due to shortage of crankcases"		
19	6,658,334	6,659,858	1525
20	6,659,859	6,665,259	5401
21	6,665,260	6,670,665	5396
23	6,670,666	6,676,065	5410
24	6,676,066	6,681,465	5400
25	6,681,466	6,686,865	5400
26	6,686,866	6,692,265	5440
27	6,692,266	6,697,669	5404
28	6,697,670	6,703,074	5405
30	6,703,075	6,708,474	5400
31	6,708,475	6,713,881	5407

NOVEMBER 1922

Day	First Number	Last Number	Production
1	6,713,882	6,719,282	5401
2	6,719,283	6,724,684	5402
3	6,724,685	6,730,084	5400
4	6,730,085	6,735,165	5081
6	6,735,166	6,740,892	5727
7	6,740,893	6,746,292	5400
8	6,746,293	6,751,696	5404
9	6,751,697	6,757,103	5407
10	6,757,104	6,762,510	5407
11	6,762,511	6,767,910	5400
13	6,767,911	6,773,321	5411
14	6,773,322	6,778,731	5410
15	6,778,732	6,784,142	5411
16	6,784,143	6,789,561	5419
17	6,789,562	6,794,964	5403
18	6,794,965	6,800,374	5410
20	6,800,375	6,805,300	4926
21	6,805,301	6,810,216	4916
22	6,810,217	6,815,137	4921
23	6,815,138	6,820,057	4920
24	6,820,058	6,824,979	4928
25	6,824,980	6,829,898	4919
27	6,829,899	6,834,820	4922
28	6,834,821	6,839,744	4924
29	6,839,745	6,844,681	4937

Serial Numbers

	First Number	Last Number	Production

DECEMBER 1922

Day	First Number	Last Number	Production
1	6,844,682	6,849,601	4920
2	6,849,602	6,854,524	4923
4	6,854,525	6,859,445	4921
5	6,859,446	6,864,368	4923
6	6,864,369	6,869,288	4920
7	6,869,289	6,874,213	4925
8	6,874,214	6,879,137	4924
9	6,879,138	6,884,057	4920
11	6,884,058	6,888,979	4922
12	6,888,980	6,893,905	4926
13	6,893,906	6,898,829	4924
14	6,898,830	6,903,750	4921
15	6,903,751	6,908,302	4552
16	6,908,303	6,913,242	4940
18	6,913,243	6,917,651	4409
19	6,917,652	6,923,012	5361
20	6,923,013	6,928,354	5342

"Started to use 3/8" washer at #4 stud on exhaust manifold to keep from bending hot air pipe."

Day	First Number	Last Number	Production
21	6,928,355	6,933,374	5020
22	6,933,375	6,938,299	4925
23	6,938,300	6,943,223	4924
26	6,943,224	6,948,147	4924
27	6,948,148	6,953,071	4924
28	Closed December 28 to January 2 for inventory.		

JANUARY 1923

Day	First Number	Last Number	Production
2	6,953,072	6,957,771	4700
3	6,957,772	6,962,677	4906
4	6,962,678	6,967,780	5103
5	6,967,781	6,972,690	4910
6	6,972,691	6,977,590	4900
8	6,977,591	6,982,502	4912
9	6,982,503	6,987,417	4915
10	6,987,418	6,992,321	4904
11	6,992,322	6,997,227	4906
12	6,997,228	7,001,759	4532

7,000,000 at 6:48 P.M.

Day	First Number	Last Number	Production
13	7,001,760	7,006,670	4911
15	7,006,671	7,011,580	4910
16	7,011,581	7,016,492	4912
17	7,016,493	7,021,396	4904
18	7,021,397	7,026,304	4908
19	7,026,305	7,031,213	4909
20	7,031,214	7,036,294	5081
22	7,036,295	7,041,448	5154
23	7,041,449	7,046,650	5202
24	7,046,651	7,051,900	5250
25	7,051,901	7,057,301	5401
26	7,057,302	7,062,701	5400
27	7,062,702	7,067,991	5290
29	7,067,992	7,073,398	5407
30	7,073,399	7,078,823	5425
31	7,078,824	7,084,225	5402

FEBRUARY 1923

Day	First Number	Last Number	Production
1	7,084,226	7,089,670	5445
2	7,089,671	7,095,108	5438
3	7,095,109	7,100,568	5460
5	7,100,569	7,106,033	5465
6	7,106,034	7,111,190	5157
7	7,111,191	7,116,672	5482
8	7,116,673	7,122,172	5500
9	7,122,173	7,127,674	5502
10	7,127,675	7,133,176	5502
12	7,133,177	7,138,362	5186
13	7,138,363	7,144,005	5643
14	7,144,006	7,149,716	5711
15	7,149,717	7,155,355	5639
16	7,155,356	7,160,965	5610
17	7,160,966	7,166,060	5095
19	7,166,061	7,171,361	5301
20	7,171,362	7,177,164	5803
21	7,177,165	7,182,965	5801
22	7,182,966	7,188,770	5805
23	7,188,771	7,194,591	5821
24	7,194,592	7,200,392	5801
26	7,200,393	7,206,200	5808
27	7,206,201	7,212,007	5807
28	7,212,008	7,217,971	5964

MARCH 1923

Day	First Number	Last Number	Production
1	7,217,972	7,223,974	6003
2	7,223,975	7,229,915	5941
3	7,229,916	7,235,915	6000
5	7,235,916	7,241,917	6002
6	7,241,918	7,247,966	6049
7	7,247,967	7,253,981	6015
8	7,253,982	7,260,037	6056
9	7,260,038	7,266,123	6086
10	7,266,124	7,272,225	6102
12	7,272,226	7,278,045	5820
13	7,278,046	7,284,180	6135
14	7,284,181	7,290,300	6120
15	7,290,301	7,296,404	6104
16	7,296,405	7,302,461	6057
17	7,302,462	7,308,625	6164
19	7,308,626	7,314,844	6219
20	7,314,845	7,321,144	6300
21	7,321,145	7,327,545	6401
22	7,327,546	7,334,046	6501
23	7,334,047	7,340,548	6502
24	7,340,549	7,347,055	6507
26	7,347,056	7,353,559	6504
27	7,353,560	7,360,061	6502
28	7,360,062	7,366,582	6521
29	7,366,583	7,373,093	6511
30	7,373,094	7,379,603	6510
31	7,379,604	7,386,111	6508

APRIL 1923

Day	First Number	Last Number	Production	
2	7,386,112	7,392,451	6340	
3	7,392,452	7,395,000	2549	
	(7,395,001	7,410,000)		15,000 to Manchester (Shipped 2-1-23)
	7,410,001	7,413,951	3951	
4	7,413,952	7,420,017	6066	
5	7,420,018	7,426,517	6500	
6	7,426,518	7,433,017	6500	
7	7,433,018	7,439,517	6500	
9	7,439,518	7,446,019	6502	
10	7,446,020	7,452,519	6500	
11	7,452,520	7,459,021	6502	
12	7,459,022	7,465,531	6510	
13	7,465,532	7,472,171	6640	
14	7,472,172	7,478,806	6635	
16	7,478,807	7,485,441	6635	
17	7,485,442	7,492,076	6635	
18	7,492,077	7,498,714	6638	
19	7,498,715	7,505,349	6635	
20	7,505,350	7,511,856	6507	
21	7,511,857	7,518,356	6500	
23	7,518,357	7,524,658	6302	
24	7,524,659	7,531,261	6603	
25	7,531,262	7,537,863	6602	
26	7,537,864	7,544,428	6565	
27	7,544,429	7,550,990	6562	
28	7,550,991	7,557,590	6600	
30	7,557,591	7,564,111	6521	

MAY 1923

Day	First Number	Last Number	Production
1	7,564,112	7,570,613	6502
2	7,570,614	7,577,128	6515
3	7,577,129	7,583,658	6530
4	7,583,659	7,590,186	6528
5	7,590,187	7,596,718	6532
7	7,596,719	7,603,322	6604
8	7,603,323	7,609,822	6500
9	7,609,823	7,616,361	6539
10	7,616,362	7,623,013	6652
11	7,623,014	7,629,666	6653
12	7,629,667	7,636,318	6652
14	7,636,319	7,642,985	6666
15	7,642,986	7,649,651	6666
16	7,649,652	7,656,403	6752
17	7,656,404	7,663,153	6750
18	7,663,154	7,669,908	6755
19	7,669,909	7,676,668	6760
21	7,676,669	7,683,521	6853
22	7,683,522	7,690,371	6850
23	7,690,372	7,697,225	6854
24	7,697,226	7,704,075	6850
25	7,704,076	7,710,931	6856
26	7,710,932	7,717,794	6863
28	7,717,795	7,724,654	6860
29	7,724,655	7,731,513	6859
30	Closed		
31	7,731,514	7,738,372	6859

JUNE 1923

Day	First Number	Last Number	Production
1	7,738,373	7,745,221	6849
2	7,745,222	7,752,072	6851
4	7,752,073	7,758,135	6063
5	7,758,136	7,765,143	7008
6	7,765,144	7,772,243	7100
7	7,772,244	7,779,093	6850
8	7,779,094	7,786,293	7200
9	7,786,294	7,793,201	6908
11	7,793,202	7,800,051	6850
12	7,800,052	7,806,905	6854
13	7,806,906	7,813,774	6869
14	7,813,775	7,820,637	6863
15	7,820,638	7,827,491	6854
16	7,827,492	7,834,376	6885
18	7,834,377	7,841,233	6857
19	7,841,234	7,848,088	6855
20	7,848,089	7,854,897	6809
21	7,854,898	7,861,451	6554

	First Number	Last Number	Production	

JUNE 1923

Day	First Number	Last Number	Production	Notes
22	7,861,452	7,867,838	6387	
23	7,867,839	7,873,699	5861	
25	7,873,700	7,879,106	5407	
26	7,879,107	7,885,206	6100	
27	7,885,207	7,891,626	6420	
28	7,891,627	7,895,000	3374	
	(7,895,001	7,910,000)		15,000 to Manchester
	7,910,001	7,913,072	3072	
29	7,913,073	7,919,974	6902	
30	7,919,975	7,927,374	7400	

JULY 1923

Day	First Number	Last Number	Production	Notes
2	7,927,375	7,934,780	7406	
3	7,934,781	7,940,000	5220	
	(7,940,001	7,955,000)		15,000 to Manchester
	7,955,001	7,957,339	2339	
4	Closed			
5	7,957,340	7,964,512	7173	
6	7,964,513	7,971,687	7175	
7	7,971,688	7,979,264	7577	
9	7,979,265	7,986,765	7501	
10	7,986,766	7,993,965	7200	
11	7,993,966	8,001,043	7078	
				8,000,000 at 10:19 P.M.
12	8,001,044	8,008,545	7502	
13	8,008,546	8,016,090	7545	
14	8,016,091	8,023,264	7174	
16	8,023,265	8,030,294	7030	"All motors now
17	8,030,295	8,037,526	7232	rolled thread"
18	8,037,527	8,044,535	7009	
19	8,044,536	8,045,000	465	
	(8,045,001	8,046,000)		1000 to Cork, Ireland
	8,046,001	8,052,540	6540	
20	8,052,541	8,059,546	7006	
21	8,059,547	8,066,449	6903	
23	8,066,450	8,073,507	7058	
24	8,073,508	8,080,575	7068	
25	8,080,576	8,087,590	7015	
26	8,087,591	8,094,605	7015	
27	8,094,606	8,101,607	7002	
28	8,101,608	8,108,637	7130	
30	8,108,638	8,115,665	7028	
31	8,115,666	8,122,674	7009	

AUGUST 1923

Day	First Number	Last Number	Production	Notes
1	8,122,675	8,129,686	7012	
2	8,129,687	8,136,689	7003	
3	8,136,690	8,143,691	7002	
4	8,143,692	8,150,694	7003	
6	8,150,695	8,157,702	7008	
7	8,157,703	8,164,702	7000	
8	8,164,703	8,171,707	7005	
9	8,171,708	8,178,707	7000	
10	8,178,708	8,184,753	6046	
11	8,184,754	8,191,753	7000	
13	8,191,754	8,198,756	7003	
14	8,198,757	8,205,763	7007	
15	8,205,764	8,213,065	7302	
16	8,213,066	8,220,365	7300	
17	8,220,366	8,227,451	7086	
18	8,227,452	8,234,647	7196	
20	8,234,648	8,241,653	7006	
21	8,241,654	8,248,680	7027	
22	8,248,681	8,255,748	7068	
23	8,255,749	8,262,776	7028	
24	8,262,777	8,269,800	7024	
25	8,269,801	8,276,816	7016	
27	8,276,817	8,283,826	7010	
28	8,283,827	8,290,770	6944	
29	8,290,771	8,297,698	6928	
30	8,297,699	8,304,639	6941	
31	8,304,640	8,311,581	6942	

SEPTEMBER 1923

Day	First Number	Last Number	Production	Notes
1	8,311,582	8,318,511	6930	
3	Closed			
4	8,318,512	8,325,432	6921	
5	8,325,433	8,332,362	6930	
6	8,332,363	8,339,273	6911	
7	8,339,274	8,346,218	6945	
8	8,346,219	8,353,130	6912	
10	8,353,131	8,360,054	6924	
11	8,360,055	8,366,982	6928	
12	8,366,983	8,373,912	6930	
13	8,373,913	8,380,833	6921	
14	8,380,834	8,387,751	6918	
15	8,387,752	8,394,668	6917	
17	8,394,669	8,401,584	6916	
18	8,401,585	8,408,512	6928	
19	8,408,513	8,415,442	6930	
20	8,415,443	8,422,345	6903	
21	8,422,346	8,429,247	6902	
22	8,429,248	8,436,165	6918	
24	8,436,166	8,443,075	6910	
25	8,443,076	8,449,996	6921	
26	8,449,997	8,456,912	6916	
27	8,456,913	8,463,825	6913	
28	8,463,826	8,470,743	6918	
29	8,470,744	8,477,681	6938	

OCTOBER 1923

Day	First Number	Last Number	Production	Notes
1	8,477,682	8,484,151	6470	
2	8,484,152	8,489,644	5493	
3	8,489,645	8,497,269	7625	
4	8,497,270	8,504,896	7627	
5	8,504,897	8,512,204	7308	
6	8,512,205	8,519,113	6909	
8	8,519,114	8,526,016	6903	
9	8,526,017	8,532,622	6606	
10	8,532,623	8,538,986	6364	
11	8,538,987	8,545,687	6701	
12	8,545,688	8,552,587	6900	
13	8,552,588	8,559,787	7200	
15	8,559,788	8,567,287	7500	
16	8,567,288	8,574,337	7050	
17	8,574,338	8,581,240	6903	
18	8,581,241	8,588,142	6902	
19	8,588,143	8,595,047	6905	
20	8,595,048	8,601,949	6902	
22	8,601,950	8,608,869	6920	
23	8,608,870	8,615,792	6923	
24	8,615,793	8,622,736	6944	
25	8,622,737	8,629,647	6911	
26	8,629,648	8,636,576	6929	
27	8,636,577	8,643,502	6926	
29	8,643,503	8,650,428	6926	
30	8,650,429	8,657,357	6929	
31	8,657,358	8,664,281	6924	

NOVEMBER 1923

Day	First Number	Last Number	Production	Notes
1	8,664,282	8,671,201	6920	
2	8,671,202	8,678,127	6926	
3	8,678,128	8,685,029	6902	
5	8,685,030	8,691,953	6924	
6	8,691,954	8,698,880	6927	
7	8,698,881	8,705,802	6922	
8	8,705,803	8,712,720	6918	
9	8,712,721	8,719,642	6922	
10	8,719,643	8,726,558	6916	
12	8,726,559	8,733,476	6918	
13	8,733,477	8,740,589	7113	
14	8,740,590	8,747,705	7116	
15	8,747,706	8,754,834	7129	
16	8,754,835	8,761,000	6166	
	(8,761,001	8,763,000)		2000 to Cork
	8,763,001	8,763,961	961	
17	8,763,962	8,771,076	7115	
19	8,771,077	8,778,196	7120	
20	8,778,197	8,785,310	7114	
21	8,785,311	8,792,431	7121	
22	8,792,432	8,799,556	7125	
23	8,799,557	8,806,704	7148	
24	8,806,705	8,813,874	7170	
26	8,813,875	8,821,085	7211	
27	8,821,086	8,828,363	7278	
28	8,828,364	8,835,665	7302	
29	Closed			
30	8,835,666	8,843,065	7400	

DECEMBER 1923

Day	First Number	Last Number	Production	Notes
1	8,843,066	8,850,615	7550	
3	8,850,616	8,858,218	7603	
4	8,858,219	8,865,870	7652	
5	8,865,871	8,873,520	7650	
6	8,873,521	8,881,175	7655	
7	8,881,176	8,888,829	7654	
8	8,888,830	8,896,483	7654	
10	8,896,484	8,904,140	7657	
11	8,904,141	8,911,796	7656	
12	8,911,797	8,919,454	7658	
13	8,919,455	8,927,181	7727	
14	8,927,182	8,934,921	7740	
15	8,934,922	8,942,743	7822	
17	8,942,744	8,950,518	7775	
18	8,950,519	8,958,578	8060	
19	8,958,579	8,966,755	8177	
20	8,966,756	8,974,831	8076	
21	8,974,832	8,982,896	8065	
22	8,982,897	8,990,899	8003	
24	8,990,900	8,997,402	6503	
25	Closed			
26	8,997,403	9,004,547	7145	
				9,000,000 at 1:05 P.M.
27	9,004,548	9,008,371	3824	"2,000,000 this year!"
	Closed December 28 to January 2			

Serial Numbers

	First Number	Last Number	Production	

JANUARY 1924

Day	First Number	Last Number	Production	Notes
2	9,008,372	9,015,596	7224	
3	9,015,597	9,023,597	8001	
4	9,023,598	9,031,831	8234	
5	9,031,832	9,040,062	8231	
7	9,040,063	9,048,293	8231	
8	9,048,294	9,056,530	8237	
9	9,056,531	9,064,760	8230	
10	9,064,761	9,072,990	8230	
11	9,072,991	9,081,227	8237	
12	9,081,228	9,089,466	8239	
14	9,089,467	9,097,718	8252	
15	9,097,719	9,105,972	8254	
16	9,105,973	9,114,247	8275	
17	9,114,248	9,122,548	8301	
18	9,122,549	9,125,000	2452	
	(9,125,001	9,140,000)		15,000 to Manchester
	9,140,001	9,145,788	5788	
19	9,145,789	9,154,020	8232	
21	9,154,021	9,161,835	7815	
22	9,161,836	9,169,836	8001	
23	9,169,837	9,177,840	8004	
24	9,177,841	9,185,840	8000	
25	9,185,841	9,193,641	7801	
26	9,193,642	9,201,441	7800	
28	9,201,442	9,209,247	7806	
29	9,209,248	9,217,055	7808	
30	9,217,056	9,224,859	7804	
31	9,224,860	9,232,671	7812	

FEBRUARY 1924

Day	First Number	Last Number	Production
1	9,232,672	9,240,475	7804
2	9,240,476	9,248,276	7801
4	9,248,277	9,256,079	7803
5	9,256,080	9,263,879	7810
6	9,263,880	9,271,681	7802
7	9,271,682	9,279,486	7805
8	9,279,487	9,287,293	7807
9	9,287,294	9,295,094	7801
11	9,295,095	9,302,901	7807
12	9,302,902	9,310,711	7810
13	9,310,712	9,318,518	7807
14	9,318,519	9,326,326	7808
15	9,326,327	9,334,131	7805
16	9,334,132	9,341,941	7810
18	9,341,942	9,349,745	7804
19	9,349,746	9,357,549	7804
20	9,357,550	9,365,357	7808
21	9,365,358	9,373,160	7803
22	9,373,161	9,380,961	7801
23	9,380,962	9,388,763	7802
25	9,388,764	9,396,570	7807
26	9,396,571	9,404,296	7726
27	9,404,297	9,412,101	7805
28	9,412,102	9,419,913	7812
29	9,419,914	9,427,721	7808

MARCH 1924

Day	First Number	Last Number	Production	Notes
1	9,427,722	9,435,521	7800	
3	9,435,522	9,443,328	7807	
4	9,443,329	9,451,129	7801	
5	9,451,130	9,458,905	7776	
6	9,458,906	9,466,716	7811	
7	9,466,717	9,474,525	7809	
8	9,474,526	9,482,331	7806	
10	9,482,332	9,490,138	7807	
11	9,490,139	9,497,938	7800	
12	9,497,939	9,505,740	7802	Began lightweight pistons.
13	9,505,741	9,513,543	7803	
14	No production.			
15	9,513,544	9,521,245	7702	
17	9,521,246	9,528,877	7632	
18	9,528,878	9,536,680	7803	
19	9,536,681	9,544,481	7801	
20	9,544,482	9,552,287	7806	
21	9,552,288	9,560,091	7804	
22	9,560,092	9,567,894	7803	
24	9,567,895	9,575,694	7800	
25	9,575,695	9,583,497	7803	
26	9,583,498	9,591,302	7805	
27	9,591,303	9,599,104	7802	
28	9,599,105	9,606,904	7800	
29	9,606,905	9,614,711	7807	
31	9,614,712	9,622,521	7810	

APRIL 1924

Day	First Number	Last Number	Production	Notes
1	9,622,522	9,630,321	7800	
2	9,630,322	9,638,121	7800	"Started using ground pistons on some production"
3	9,638,122	9,645,925	7804	
4	9,645,926	9,653,729	7804	
5	9,653,730	9,661,531	7802	
7	9,661,532	9,669,335	7804	
8	9,669,336	9,677,135	7800	
9	9,677,136	9,684,787	7652	
10	9,684,788	9,692,618	7831	
11	9,692,619	9,700,559	7941	
12	9,700,560	9,708,362	7803	
14	9,708,363	9,716,166	7804	
15	9,716,167	9,723,970	7804	
16	9,723,971	9,731,771	7801	
17	9,731,772	9,739,575	7804	
18	9,739,576	9,747,377	7802	
19	9,747,378	9,755,180	7803	

"Started using new T410 and T411 (camshaft and front bearing) on some production"

Day	First Number	Last Number	Production	Notes
21	9,755,181	9,762,407	7227	
22	9,762,408	9,769,624	7217	
23	9,769,625	9,776,844	7220	
24	9,776,845	9,778,203	1359	

"Closed at 9:31 A.M., No gas."

Day	First Number	Last Number	Production	Notes
25	9,778,204	9,785,422	7219	98% production
26	9,785,423	9,792,642	7220	with new cam.
28	9,792,643	9,799,893	7251	
29	9,799,894	9,807,208	7315	"All use new T410
30	9,807,209	9,814,521	7313	and T411."

MAY 1924

Day	First Number	Last Number	Production
1	9,814,522	9,821,739	7218
2	9,821,740	9,828,960	7221
3	9,828,961	9,836,178	7218
5	9,836,179	9,843,398	7220

"New piston pins, starting with 9,836,501 on some production."

Day	First Number	Last Number	Production	Notes
6	9,843,399	9,850,621	7223	
7	9,850,622	9,857,840	7219	
8	9,857,841	9,865,061	7221	
9	9,865,062	9,872,286	7225	
10	9,872,287	9,879,512	7226	
12	9,879,513	9,886,733	7221	
13	9,886,734	9,893,955	7222	
14	9,893,956	9,901,175	7220	
15	9,901,176	9,908,401	7226	
16	9,908,402	9,915,620	7219	
17	9,915,621	9,922,838	7218	
19	9,922,839	9,930,062	7224	
20	9,930,063	9,937,283	7221	
21	9,937,284	9,943,783	6500	
22	9,943,784	9,949,586	5803	
23	9,949,587	9,955,642	6056	
24	9,955,643	9,962,879	7237	
26	9,962,880	9,966,000	3121	
	(9,966,001	9,969,000)		3000 to Cork (5-1-24)
	9,969,001	9,973,288	4288	
27	9,973,289	9,980,733	7445	
28	9,980,734	9,984,771	4038	
30	Closed			

JUNE 1924

Day	First Number	Last Number	Production	Notes
1	9,984,772	9,992,048	7277	
3	9,992,049	9,999,350	7302	
4	9,999,351	10,006,660	7310	
		10,000,000 at 7:47 A.M.		
5	10,006,661	10,014,440	7780	
6	10,014,441	10,018,241	3801	
9	10,018,242	10,026,032	7791	
10	10,026,033	10,033,840	7808	
11	10,033,841	10,041,846	8006	
12	10,041,847	10,049,863	8017	
13	10,049,864	10,051,883	2020	
16	10,051,884	10,059,961	8078	
17	10,059,962	10,068,042	8081	
18	10,068,043	10,076,145	8103	
19	10,076,146	10,084,252	8107	
20	10,084,253	10,086,253	2001	
23	10,086,254	10,093,054	6801	
24	10,093,055	10,100,404	7350	
25	10,100,405	10,108,205	7801	
26	10,108,206	10,116,308	8103	
27	10,116,309	10,118,348	2040	
30	10,118,349	10,126,471	8123	

JULY 1924

Day	First Number	Last Number	Production	Notes
1	10,126,472	10,134,577	8106	
2	10,134,578	10,142,684	8107	
3	10,142,685	10,144,730	2046	
4	Closed			
7	10,144,731	10,152,683	7953	
8	10,152,684	10,160,684	8001	
9	10,160,685	10,168,591	7907	
10	10,168,592	10,170,605	2014	
11	Closed July 11 to 14			
14	10,170,606	10,178,240	7635	

"All rolled-thread head bolts after July 14."

Day	First Number	Last Number	Production	Notes
15	10,178,241	10,186,240	8000	
16	10,186,241	10,194,044	7804	
17	10,194,045	10,202,045	8001	"New style transmission
18	10,202,046	10,204,055	2010	covers and large-funnel
19	10,204,056	10,211,569	7514	oil tube begun."

Four-dip pan first used July 18.

JULY 1924

Day	First Number	Last Number	Production	Notes
21	Closed			
22	10,211,570	10,218,770	7201	
23	10,218,771	10,226,333	7563	
24	10,226,334	10,233,862	7529	
25	10,233,863	10,235,769	1907	
28	10,235,770	10,243,331	7562	
29	10,243,332	10,251,101	7770	
30	10,251,102	10,258,792	7691	
31	10,258,793	10,266,471	7679	

AUGUST 1924

Day	First Number	Last Number	Production	Notes
1	10,266,472	10,270,632	4161	
4	10,270,633	10,278,133	7501	
5	10,278,134	10,285,503	7370	
6	10,285,504	10,292,981	7478	
7	10,292,982	10,300,756	7775	
8	10,300,757	10,304,931	4175	
11	10,304,932	10,312,451	7520	
12	10,312,452	10,320,078	7627	"All engines have
13	10,320,079	10,327,580	7502	large oil tube."
14	10,327,581	10,335,190	7610	
15	10,335,191	10,337,091	1901	
18	10,337,092	10,344,542	7451	
19	10,344,543	10,352,072	7530	
20	10,352,073	10,359,230	7158	
21	10,359,231	10,365,873	6643	
22	10,365,874	10,369,691	3818	
25	10,369,692	10,375,721	6030	
26	10,375,722	10,382,721	7000	
27	10,382,722	10,389,997	7276	
28	10,389,998	10,397,397	7400	
29	10,397,398	10,404,821	7424	

SEPTEMBER 1924

Day	First Number	Last Number	Production	Notes
1	Closed			
2	10,404,822	10,411,821	7000	
3	10,411,822	10,418,994	7173	
4	10,418,995	10,426,151	7157	
5	10,426,152	10,433,281	7130	
8	10,433,282	10,440,485	7204	
9	10,440,486	10,447,536	7051	
10	10,447,537	10,454,584	7048	
11	10,454,585	10,461,610	7076	
12	10,461,611	10,468,671	7061	
15	10,468,672	10,475,725	7054	
16	10,475,726	10,482,729	7004	
17	10,482,730	10,489,802	7073	
18	10,489,803	10,496,860	7058	
19	10,496,861	10,503,961	7101	
20	10,503,962	10,511,471	7510	
22	10,511,472	10,518,508	7037	
23	10,518,509	10,525,559	7051	
24	10,525,560	10,532,613	7054	

(10,566,001 to 10,566,100 to the River Rouge plant September 24.)

Day	First Number	Last Number	Production	Notes
25	10,532,614	10,539,665	7052	
26	10,539,666	10,546,721	7056	
29	10,546,722	10,553,771	7050	H.P. (Highland Park)
		10,566,001	1	R. (River Rouge Plant)
30	10,553,772	10,560,821	7050	H.P.
	10,566,002	10,566,009	8	R.

OCTOBER 1924

Day	First Number	Last Number	Production	Notes
1	10,560,822	10,566,000	5179	H.P.
	10,566,101	10,567,922	1822	H.P. (7620 total H.P.)
	10,566,010	10,566,021	12	R.
2	10,567,923	10,574,927	7005	H.P.
	10,566,022	10,566,035	14	R.
3	10,574,928	10,581,931	7004	H.P.
	10,566,036	10,566,049	14	R.
6	10,581,932	10,587,000	5069	H.P.
	(10,587,001	10,587,500)		Shipped to Rouge Plant
	10,587,501	10,589,434	1934	H.P. (7003 total H.P.)
	10,566,050	10,566,066	17	R.
7	10,589,435	10,596,435	7001	H.P.
	10,566,067	10,566,086	20	R.
8	10,596,436	10,603,437	7002	H.P.
	10,566,087	10,566,100	14	R.
	10,587,001	10,587,007	7	R. (21 total Rouge)
9	10,603,438	10,610,266	6829	H.P.
	10,587,008	10,587,027	20	R.
10	10,610,267	10,617,220	6954	H.P.
	10,587,028	10,587,046	19	R.
13	10,617,221	10,622,908	5688	H.P.
	10,587,047	10,587,067	21	R.
14	10,622,909	10,625,000	2092	H.P.
	(10,625,001	10,640,000)		15,000 to Manchester
	10,640,001	10,644,573	4573	H.P. (6665 total H.P.)
	10,587,068	10,587,099	32	R.
15	10,644,574	10,651,451	6878	H.P.
	10,587,100	10,587,141	41	R.
16	10,651,452	10,658,653	7202	H.P.
	10,587,142	10,587,145	4	R.
17	10,658,654	10,665,799	7146	H.P.
20	10,587,146	10,587,218	73	R.
	10,665,800	10,672,750	6951	H.P.
	10,587,219	10,587,269	51	R.
21	10,672,751	10,679,565	6815	H.P.
	10,587,270	10,587,471	202	R.
22	10,679,566	10,686,277	6712	H.P.
	10,587,472	10,587,500	29	R.
	10,707,001	10,707,257	257	R. (286 total Rouge)
23	10,686,278	10,692,919	6642	H.P.
	10,707,258	10,707,615	358	R.
24	10,692,920	10,699,431	6512	H.P.
	10,707,616	10,708,105	490	R.
27	10,699,432	10,705,698	6267	H.P.
	10,708,106	10,708,838	733	R.
28	10,705,699	10,707,000	1302	H.P.
	10,713,001	10,716,978	3978	H.P. (5280 total H.P.)
	10,708,839	10,709,798	960	R.
29	10,716,979	10,722,724	5746	H.P.
	10,709,799	10,711,052	1254	R.
30	10,722,725	10,728,809	6085	H.P.
	10,711,053	10,712,371	1319	R.
31	10,728,810	10,734,505	5696	H.P.
	10,712,372	10,713,000	629	R.
	10,764,001	10,764,951	951	R. (1580 total Rouge)

NOVEMBER 1924

Day	First Number	Last Number	Production	Notes
1	10,734,506	10,740,308	5803	H.P.
	10,764,952	10,766,410	1459	R.
3	10,740,309	10,746,067	5759	H.P.
	10,766,411	10,767,887	1477	R.
4	10,746,068	10,751,668	5621	H.P.
	10,767,888	10,769,527	1640	R.
5	10,751,669	10,757,274	5586	H.P.
	10,769,528	10,771,153	1626	R.
6	10,757,275	10,762,883	5609	H.P.
	10,771,154	10,772,795	1642	R.
7	10,762,884	10,764,000	1117	H.P.
	10,774,001	10,778,462	4462	H.P. (5579 total H.P.)
	10,772,796	10,774,000	1205	R.
	10,805,001	10,805,472	472	R. (1677 total Rouge)
8	10,778,463	10,784,101	5639	H.P.
	10,805,473	10,807,107	1635	R.
10	10,784,102	10,789,672	5571	H.P.
	10,807,108	10,808,765	1658	R.
11	10,789,673	10,795,094	5422	H.P.
	10,808,766	10,810,575	1810	R.
12	10,795,095	10,800,357	5263	H.P.
	10,810,576	10,812,550	1975	R.
13	10,800,358	10,805,000	4643	H.P.
	10,825,001	10,825,470	470	H.P. (5113 total H.P.)
	10,812,551	10,814,580	2030	R.
14	10,825,471	10,830,474	5005	H.P.
	10,814,581	10,816,734	2154	R.
17	10,830,475	10,835,323	4849	H.P.
	10,816,735	10,818,964	2230	R.
18	10,835,324	10,840,154	4831	H.P.
	10,818,965	10,821,364	2400	R.
19	10,840,155	10,844,816	4662	H.P.
	10,821,365	10,823,902	2538	R.
20	10,844,817	10,849,177	4361	H.P.
	(10,851,001 to 10,871,000 to Rouge)			
	10,823,903	10,825,000	1098	R.
	10,851,001	10,852,653	1653	R. (2751 total Rouge)
21	10,849,178	10,851,000	1822	H.P.
	10,871,001	10,873,570	2570	H.P. (4392 total H.P.)
	10,852,654	10,855,388	2735	R.
24	10,873,571	10,877,843	4273	H.P.
	10,855,389	10,858,116	2728	R.
25	10,877,844	10,882,055	4212	H.P.
	10,858,117	10,860,916	2800	R.
26	10,882,056	10,886,259	4203	H.P.
	10,860,917	10,863,730	2814	R.
27	Closed November 27 to December 1			

DECEMBER 1924

Day	First Number	Last Number	Production	Notes
1	10,886,260	10,890,417	4158	H.P.
	10,863,731	10,866,622	2892	R.
2	10,890,418	10,894,628	4211	H.P.
	10,866,623	10,869,412	2790	R.
3	10,894,629	10,899,022	4394	H.P.
	10,869,413	10,871,000	1588	R.
	10,914,001	10,915,037	1037	R. (2625 total Rouge)
4	10,899,023	10,903,315	4293	H.P.
	10,915,038	10,917,798	2761	R.
5	10,903,316	10,907,635	4320	H.P.
	10,917,799	10,920,503	2705	R.
8	10,907,636	10,911,295	3660	H.P.
	10,920,504	10,923,267	2764	R.
9	10,911,296	10,914,000	2704	H.P.
	(10,914,001	10,934,000)		To Rouge
	10,934,001	10,934,758	758	H.P. (3462 total H.P.)
	10,923,268	10,926,278	3011	R.
10	10,934,759	10,938,076	3318	H.P.
	10,926,279	10,929,750	3472	R.

DECEMBER 1924

Day	First Number	Last Number	Production	Note
11	10,938,077	10,941,435	3359	H.P.
	10,929,751	10,933,350	3600	R.
12	Closed			
13	10,941,436	10,945,136	3701	H.P.
	10,933,351	10,934,000	650	R.
	10,959,001	10,961,806	2806	R. (3456 total Rouge)
15	10,945,137	10,948,906	3770	H.P.
	10,961,807	10,966,206	4400	R.
16	10,948,907	10,950,951	2045	H.P.
	10,966,207	10,970,856	4650	R.
17	10,950,952	10,953,001	2050	H.P.
	10,970,857	10,975,691	4825	R.
18	10,953,002	10,955,471	2470	H.P.
	10,975,692	10,980,191	4500	R.
19	10,955,472	10,957,707	2236	H.P.
	10,980,192	10,984,845	4654	R.
22	10,957,708	10,959,000	1293	H.P.
	(10,959,001	10,998,000)		To Rouge
	10,998,001	10,998,812	812	H.P. (2105 total H.P.)
	10,984,846	10,989,510	5446	R.
23	No production			
24	10,998,813	10,999,000	188	H.P.
	10,996,801	10,997,941	1141	H.P. (From Rouge)
	10,989,511	10,994,033	4523*	R.

Closed December 25 to January 5, 1925

* 4495 is shown in the records but the actual difference in numbers is 4523. This difference was discovered in 1926, and the records were then adjusted to cover this error.

Beginning in January 1925 the River Rouge plant became the major engine assembly facility. The Highland Park plant continued manufacturing engines but the engine numbers were supplied by the Rouge. This shift in operations began in September of 1924 and was completed over the Christmas holidays of 1924.

JANUARY 1925

Day	First Number	Last Number		Production	Note
5	10,994,034	10,996,800		2767	
	10,997,942	10,998,000		58	
	10,998,001	10,999,900		900	H.P.
	10,999,001	11,000,001		1001	
	(11,000,002	11,000,031)			To Highland Park
	11,000,032	11,002,129		2098	
6	11,002,130	11,007,984		5855	
7	11,007,985	11,011,900		3916	
	(11,011,901	11,012,000)			To H.P.
	11,012,001	11,013,829		1829	(5448 total)
8	11,013,830	11,020,034		6205	
9	11,020,035	11,027,036		7002	
10	11,000,002	11,000,031	**	30	H.P. (** Out of
	11,011,901	11,011,916	**	16	H.P. sequence)
	11,027,037	11,030,172		3136	
12	11,030,173	11,036,752		6580	
13	11,036,753	11,043,254		6502	
14	11,011,917	11,011,946	**	30	H.P.
	11,043,255	11,048,724		5470	
15	11,011,947	11,011,956	**	10	H.P.
	11,048,725	11,055,089		6365	
16	11,055,090	11,061,071		5982	
17	11,061,072	11,062,965		1894	
19	11,011,957	11,011,966	**	10	H.P.
	11,062,966	11,066,900		3935	
	(11,066,901	11,067,000)			To H.P.
	11,067,001	11,069,044		2044	(5989 total Rouge)
20	11,069,045	11,075,494		6450	
21	11,075,495	11,081,794		6300	
22	11,011,967	11,011,986	**	20	H.P.
	11,081,795	11,088,277		6483	
23	11,011,987	11,011,996	**	10	H.P.
	11,088,278	11,094,669		6392	
24	11,094,670	11,100,919		6250	
26	11,100,920	11,107,204		6285	
27	11,107,205	11,113,604		6400	
28	11,113,605	11,119,484		5880	(** Out of Sequence)
29	11,119,485	11,125,894		6410	
30	11,011,997	11,012,000	**	3	H.P.
	11,066,901	11,066,938	**	38	H.P.
	11,125,895	11,132,254		6360	
31	11,132,255	11,135,308		3054	

FEBRUARY 1925

Day	First Number	Last Number		Production	Note
2	11,135,309	11,141,712		6404	
3	11,141,713	11,148,123		6411	
4	11,148,124	11,154,533		6410	
5	11,154,534	11,160,989		6456	
6	11,160,990	11,167,414		6425	
7	11,167,415	11,172,959		5545	
9	11,172,960	11,179,169		6210	
10	11,179,170	11,185,344		6175	
11	11,185,345	11,191,969		6625	
12	11,191,970	11,198,371		6402	
13	11,066,939	11,067,000	**	62	H.P.
	11,198,372	11,204,715		6344	

Day	First Number	Last Number	Production	Note
14	11,204,716	11,210,818	6103	
16	11,210,819	11,217,268	6450	
17	11,217,269	11,223,668	6400	
18	11,223,669	11,230,078	6410	
19	11,230,079	11,236,490	6412	
20	11,236,491	11,242,893	6403	
21	11,242,894	11,249,293	6400	
23	11,249,294	11,255,695	6402	
24	11,255,696	11,262,095	6400	
25	11,262,096	11,268,498	6403	
26	11,268,499	11,272,000	3502	
	(11,272,001	11,287,000)		(15,000 to Manchester)
	11,287,001	11,289,615	2615	(6117 total)
27	11,289,616	11,296,019	6404	
28	11,296,020	11,302,019	6000	

MARCH 1925

Day	First Number	Last Number	Production	Note
2	11,302,020	11,308,221	6202	
3	11,308,222	11,314,621	6400	
4	11,314,622	11,321,024	6403	
5	11,321,025	11,327,526	6502	
6	11,327,527	11,333,106	5580	
7	11,333,107	11,339,982	6876	
9	11,339,983	11,346,607	6625	
10	11,346,608	11,353,610	7003	
11	11,353,611	11,360,610	7000	"n/s (new style?) pan doors on crankcases."
12	11,360,611	11,363,693	3083	
13	11,363,694	11,371,378	7685	
14	11,371,379	11,378,381	7003	
16	11,378,382	11,385,491	7110	
17	11,385,492	11,392,927	7436	

Began using only one bushing in transmission brake drum.

Day	First Number	Last Number	Production	Note
18	11,392,928	11,399,563	6636	
19	11,399,564	11,407,013	7450	
20	11,407,014	11,414,313	7300	
21	11,414,314	11,421,414	7101	
23	11,421,415	11,427,869	6455	
24	11,427,870	11,434,871	7002	
25	11,434,872	11,442,178	7307	
26	11,442,179	11,449,218	7040	
27	11,442,219	11,456,320	7102	
28	11,456,321	11,463,428	7108	
30	11,463,429	11,470,548	7120	
31	11,470,549	11,477,655	7107	

APRIL 1925

Day	First Number	Last Number	Production
1	11,477,656	11,484,757	7102
2	11,484,758	11,491,869	7112
3	11,491,870	11,499,071	7202
4	11,499,072	11,506,273	7202
6	11,506,274	11,513,274	7001
7	11,513,275	11,520,214	6940
8	11,520,215	11,527,489	7275
9	11,527,490	11,534,779	7290
10	11,534,780	11,542,034	7255
11	11,542,035	11,549,035	7001
13	11,549,036	11,555,635	6600
14	11,555,636	11,562,842	7207
15	11,562,843	11,570,064	7222
16	11,570,065	11,577,295	7231
17	11,577,296	11,584,596	7301
18	11,584,597	11,591,946	7350
20	11,591,947	11,599,366	7420
21	11,599,367	11,606,711	7345
22	11,606,712	11,614,436	7725
23	11,614,437	11,622,048	7612
24	11,622,049	11,629,849	7801
25	11,629,850	11,637,026	7177
27	11,637,027	11,644,886	7860
28	11,644,887	11,652,488	7602
29	11,652,489	11,660,513	8025
30	11,660,514	11,668,647	8134

MAY 1925

Day	First Number	Last Number	Production
1	11,668,648	11,676,777	8130
2	11,676,778	11,684,938	8161
4	11,684,939	11,693,058	8120
5	11,693,059	11,701,233	8175
6	11,701,234	11,709,388	8155
7	11,709,389	11,717,625	8237
8	11,717,626	11,725,872	8247
9	11,725,873	11,733,974	8102
11	11,733,975	11,742,100	8126
12	11,742,101	11,750,102	8002
13	11,750,103	11,758,453	8351
14	11,758,454	11,766,454	8001
15	11,766,455	11,774,558	8104
16	11,774,559	11,782,659	8101
18	11,782,660	11,790,689	8030
19	11,790,690	11,798,789	8100
20	11,798,790	11,806,791	8002
21	11,806,792	11,814,551	7760
22	11,814,552	11,822,206	7655
23	11,822,207	11,829,732	7526

MAY 1925

	First Number	Last Number	Production
25	11,829,733	11,837,574	7842
26	11,837,575	11,845,580	8006
27	11,845,581	11,853,587	8007
28	11,853,588	11,861,602	8015
29	11,861,603	11,869,207	7605

JUNE 1925

	First Number	Last Number	Production
1	11,869,208	11,876,608	7401
2	11,876,609	11,884,429	7821
3	11,884,430	11,891,839	7410
4	11,891,840	11,899,270	7431
5	11,899,271	11,906,471	7201
6	11,906,472	11,912,911	6440
8	11,912,912	11,919,942	7031
9	11,919,943	11,927,512	7570
10	11,927,513	11,935,157	7645
11	11,935,158	11,942,792	7635
12	11,942,793	11,950,431	7639
13	11,950,432	11,958,031	7600
15	11,958,032	11,965,534	7503
16	11,965,535	11,973,171	7637
17	11,973,172	11,980,811	7640
18	11,980,812	11,988,413	7602
19	11,988,414	11,996,021	7608
20	11,996,022	12,003,321	7300
22	12,003,322	12,005,000	1679
	(12,005,001	12,006,000)	"Omitted"(Shipped elsewhere)
	12,006,001	12,011,573	5573 (7252 total)
23	12,011,574	12,018,853	7280
24	12,018,854	12,026,124	7271
25	12,026,125	12,033,410	7286
26	12,033,411	12,040,700	7290
27	12,040,701	12,047,980	7280
29	12,047,981	12,055,232	7252
30	12,055,233	12,062,486	7254

JULY 1925

	First Number	Last Number	Production
1	12,062,487	12,069,758	7272
2	12,069,759	12,077,039	7281
3	12,077,040	12,084,291	7252
6	12,084,292	12,091,192	6901
7	12,091,193	12,098,313	7121
8	12,098,314	12,105,629	7316
9	12,105,630	12,112,949	7320
10	12,112,950	12,120,266	7317
11	12,120,267	12,127,567	7301
13	12,127,568	12,134,868	7301
14	12,134,869	12,141,603	6735
15	12,141,604	12,149,007	7404
16	12,149,008	12,156,345	7338
17	12,156,346	12,163,657	7312
18	12,163,658	12,170,958	7301
20	12,170,959	12,178,262	7304
21	12,178,263	12,185,572	7310
22	12,185,573	12,192,893	7321
23	12,192,894	12,200,204	7311

Started to dip oil tube in solder 1/2" from end.

	First Number	Last Number	Production
24	12,200,205	12,207,508	7304
25	12,207,509	12,214,216	6708
27	12,214,217	12,220,166	5950

Last old style engine 12,218,728 at 5:51 P.M. "Began new style on 3rd shift."

	First Number	Last Number	Production
28	12,220,167	12,222,528	2362
29	Closed July 29 to August 3.		

AUGUST 1925 (Beginning of "1926" production)

	First Number	Last Number	Production
3	12,222,529	12,225,878	3350
4	12,225,879	12,229,458	3580
5	12,229,459	12,233,043	3585
6	12,233,044	12,236,603	3560
7	12,236,604	12,240,175	3572

All production now with one bushing in brake drum.

	First Number	Last Number	Production
8	12,240,176	12,243,727	3552
10	12,243,728	12,247,282	3555
11	12,247,283	12,250,854	3572
12	12,250,855	12,254,419	3565
13	12,254,420	12,257,980	3561
14	12,257,981	12,261,556	3576
17	12,261,557	12,265,093	3536
18	12,265,094	12,266,782	1689
19	12,266,783	12,270,334	3552
20	12,270,335	12,273,919	3585
21	12,273,920	12,277,498	3579
24	Closed		
25	12,277,499	12,281,065	3567
26	12,281,066	12,284,567	3502
27	12,284,568	12,287,668	3101
28	12,287,669	12,290,760	3092

SEPTEMBER 1925

	First Number	Last Number	Production	
1	12,290,761	12,293,846	3086	
2	12,293,847	12,297,161	3315	
3	12,297,162	12,300,601	3440	
4	12,300,602	12,304,023	3422	
5	12,304,024	12,307,434	3411	
8	12,307,435	12,310,935	3501	
9	12,310,936	12,314,790	3855	
10	Closed September 10 to 14			
14	12,314,791	12,318,730	3940	
15	12,318,731	12,323,330	4600	
16	12,323,331	12,328,331	5001	
17	12,328,332	12,333,485	5154	
18	12,333,486	12,338,837	5352	
19	12,338,838	12,344,215	5378	
21	12,344,216	12,349,365	5150	
22	12,349,366	12,355,116	5751	
23	12,355,117	12,361,027	5911	
24	12,361,028	12,367,031	6004	
25	12,367,032	12,373,156	6125	
26	12,373,157	12,379,307	6151	
28	12,379,308	12,385,475	6168	
29	12,385,476	12,392,284	6809	
30	12,392,285	12,399,496	7212	

OCTOBER 1925

	First Number	Last Number	Production	
1	12,399,497	12,407,501	8005	
2	12,407,502	12,415,507	8006	
3	12,415,508	12,423,518	8011	
5	12,423,519	12,431,522	8004	
6	12,431,523	12,439,529	8007	
7	12,439,530	12,447,539	8010	
8	12,447,540	12,455,545	8006	
9	12,455,546	12,463,548	8003	
10	12,463,549	12,471,553	8005	
12	12,471,554	12,479,554	8001	
13	12,479,555	12,487,554	8000	
14	12,487,555	12,495,559	8005	
15	12,495,560	12,503,576	8017	
16	12,503,577	12,511,578	8002	
17	12,511,579	12,519,583	8005	
19	12,519,584	12,527,834	8251	
20	12,527,835	12,536,335	8501	
21	12,536,336	12,544,835	8500	
22	12,544,836	12,553,340	8505	
23	12,553,341	12,561,846	8506	
24	12,561,847	12,570,348	8502	
26	12,570,349	12,578,854	8506	Began using bolts in valve doors.
27	12,578,855	12,587,366	8512	
28	12,587,367	12,595,867	8501	
29	12,595,868	12,604,410	8543	
30	12,604,411	12,612,955	8545	
31	12,612,956	12,621,501	8546	

NOVEMBER 1925

	First Number	Last Number	Production	
2	12,621,502	12,630,003	8502	
3	12,630,004	12,638,503	8500	
4	12,638,504	12,647,014	8511	
5	12,647,015	12,655,516	8502	
6	12,655,517	12,664,019	8503	
7	12,664,020	12,672,523	8504	
9	12,672,524	12,681,025	8502	
10	12,681,026	12,689,533	8508	
11	12,689,534	12,698,034	8501	
12	12,698,035	12,706,534	8500	
13	12,706,535	12,715,040	8506	
14	12,715,041	12,723,545	8505	
16	12,723,546	12,732,048	8503	100% production with crankcase support straps.
17	12,732,049	12,740,558	8510	
18	12,740,559	12,749,065	8507	
19	12,749,066	12,757,576	8511	
20	12,757,577	12,765,880	8304	
21	12,765,881	12,774,181	8301	
23	12,774,182	12,782,484	8303	
24	12,782,485	12,790,785	8301	
25	12,790,786	12,799,090	8305	
26	Closed			
27	12,799,091	12,807,093	8003	
28	12,807,094	12,815,108	8015	
30	12,815,109	12,823,126	8018	

DECEMBER 1925

	First Number	Last Number	Production
1	12,823,127	12,831,134	8008
2	12,831,135	12,839,149	8015
3	12,839,150	12,847,156	8007
4	12,847,157	12,855,159	8003
5	12,855,160	12,863,164	8005
7	12,863,165	12,871,171	8007
8	12,871,172	12,879,174	8003
9	12,879,175	12,887,176	8002
10	12,887,177	12,895,178	8002
11	12,895,179	12,903,184	8006
12	12,903,185	12,911,185	8001
14	12,911,186	12,919,201	8016
15	12,919,202	12,927,202	8001
16	12,927,203	12,935,205	8003
17	12,935,206	12,943,217	8012
18	12,943,218	12,951,220	8003
19	12,951,221	12,959,221	8001

Serial Numbers

DECEMBER 1925

	First Number	Last Number	Production	
21	12,959,222	12,965,448	6227	
22	12,965,449	12,970,000	4552	
	(12,970,001	12,980,000)		(10,000 to Manchester)
	12,980,001	12,981,450	1450	(6002 total)
23	12,981,451	12,987,456	6006	
24	12,987,457	12,990,076	2620	
25	Closed December 25 to January 5, 1926.			

An error in the records was discovered which indicated that twenty-two less engines had been built than had been recorded. Twenty of these were in 1924, and two in 1925. To set things straight, the production records were altered to show twenty-two engines which were not actually built. The last number of 1924 was 12,990,076, and the first number of 1926 was actually 12,990,077, but the factory records show 12,990,055 as the first number of 1926.

JANUARY 1926

	First Number	Last Number	Production	
5	12,990,077 *	12,997,713	7658	* See note above.
6	12,997,714	13,005,377	7664	
7	13,005,378	13,013,034	7657	
8	13,013,035	13,020,694	7660	
9	13,020,695	13,024,585	3891	
11	13,024,586	13,028,450	3865	
12	13,028,451	13,036,109	7659	
13	13,036,110	13,043,778	7669	
14	13,043,779	13,051,442	7664	
15	13,051,443	13,059,100	7658	
16	13,059,101	13,062,957	3857	
18	13,062,958	13,066,808	3851	
19	13,066,809	13,074,409	7601	
20	13,074,410	13,082,086	7677	
21	13,082,087	13,089,738	7652	
22	13,089,739	13,097,393	7655	
23	13,097,394	13,101,244	3851	
25	13,101,245	13,105,074	3830	
26	13,105,075	13,112,494	7420	
27	13,112,495	13,119,961	7467	
28	13,119,962	13,127,470	7509	
29	13,127,471	13,134,820	7350	
30	13,134,821	13,138,675	3855	

FEBRUARY 1926

	First Number	Last Number	Production	
1	13,138,676	13,142,445	3770	
2	13,142,446	13,149,961	7516	
3	13,149,962	13,157,482	7521	
4	13,157,483	13,164,993	7511	
5	13,164,994	13,172,508	7515	
6	13,172,509	13,176,243	3735	
8	13,176,244	13,179,998	3755	
9	13,179,999	13,187,502	7504	
10	13,187,503	13,195,004	7502	
11	13,195,005	13,202,504	7500	
12	13,202,505	13,210,005	7501	
13	13,210,006	13,213,455	3450	
15	13,213,456	13,216,874	3419	
16	13,216,875	13,223,798	6924	
17	13,223,799	13,230,525	6727	
18	13,230,526	13,237,638	7113	
19	13,237,639	13,245,139	7501	
20	13,245,140	13,248,890	3751	
22	13,248,891	13,252,000	3110	
	(13,252,001	13,253,200)		(1200 "omitted")
	13,253,201	13,253,775	575	(3685 total)
23	13,253,776	13,260,777	7002	
24	13,260,778	13,268,181	7404	
25	13,268,182	13,275,083	6902	
26	13,275,084	13,282,588	7505	
27	13,282,589	13,286,289	3701	

MARCH 1926

	First Number	Last Number	Production	
1	13,286,290	13,289,959	3670	
2	13,289,960	13,297,461	7502	
3	13,297,462	13,304,965	7504	
4	13,304,966	13,312,468	7503	
5	13,312,469	13,319,970	7502	
6	13,319,971	13,323,723	3753	
8	13,323,724	13,327,475	3752	
9	13,327,476	13,334,993	7518	
10	13,334,994	13,342,502	7509	
11	13,342,503	13,350,014	7512	
12	13,350,015	13,357,523	7509	
13	13,357,524	13,361,279	3756	
15	13,361,280	13,365,030	3751	
16	13,365,031	13,372,535	7505	
17	13,372,536	13,380,037	7502	
18	13,380,038	13,387,537	7500	
19	13,387,538	13,395,040	7503	
20	13,395,041	13,398,645	3605	
22	13,398,646	13,402,397	3752	
23	13,402,398	13,409,904	7507	
24	13,409,905	13,417,409	7505	
25	13,417,410	13,424,913	7504	
26	13,424,914	13,432,416	7503	

	First Number	Last Number	Production	
27	13,432,417	13,436,116	3700	
29	13,436,117	13,439,868	3752	
30	13,439,869	13,447,375	7507	
31	13,447,376	13,454,889	7514	

APRIL 1926

	First Number	Last Number	Production	
1	13,454,890	13,462,391	7502	
2	13,462,392	13,469,714	7323	
5	13,469,715	13,476,715	7001	
6	13,476,716	13,484,300	7585	
7	13,484,301	13,491,873	7573	
8	13,491,874	13,499,483	7610	
9	13,499,484	13,506,985	7502	
12	13,506,986	13,514,487	7502	
13	13,514,488	13,521,990	7503	
14	13,521,991	13,529,491	7501	
15	13,529,492	13,536,994	7503	
16	13,536,995	13,544,520	7526	
19	13,544,521	13,552,026	7506	
20	13,552,027	13,559,528	7502	
21	13,559,529	13,567,074	7546	
22	13,567,075	13,574,606	7532	
23	13,574,607	13,582,166	7560	
26	13,582,167	13,589,681	7515	
27	13,589,682	13,597,185	7504	
28	13,597,186	13,604,692	7507	
29	13,604,693	13,612,198	7506	
30	13,612,199	13,619,705	7507	

MAY 1926

	First Number	Last Number	Production	
3	13,619,706	13,627,208	7503	
4	13,627,209	13,634,714	7506	
5	13,634,715	13,642,225	7511	
6	13,642,226	13,649,734	7509	
7	13,649,735	13,657,239	7505	
10	13,657,240	13,664,743	7504	
11	13,664,744	13,672,258	7515	
12	13,672,259	13,679,767	7509	
13	13,679,768	13,687,279	7512	
14	13,687,280	13,694,789	7510	
17	13,694,790	13,702,194	7405	
18	13,702,195	13,709,701	7507	
19	13,709,702	13,717,203	7502	
20	13,717,204	13,724,703	7500	
21	13,724,704	13,732,293	7590	
24	13,732,294	13,739,796	7443	
25	13,739,797	13,747,298	7502	Began using T4441 bolt
26	13,747,299	13,754,807	7509	in place of T516
27	13,754,808	13,762,312	7505	manifold stud.
28	13,762,313	13,769,814	7502	

JUNE 1926

	First Number	Last Number	Production	
1	13,769,815	13,777,317	7503	
2	13,777,318	13,784,619	7302	
3	13,784,620	13,790,000	5381	
	(13,790,001	13,800,000)		(10,000 to Manchester 4-24-26)
	13,800,001	13,801,574	1574	(6955 total)
4	13,801,575	13,808,009	6435	
7	13,808,010	13,814,710	6701	
8	13,814,711	13,822,128	7418	
9	13,822,129	13,825,356	3228	
10	13,825,357	13,832,638	7282	
11	13,832,639	13,836,043	3405	
14	13,836,044	13,843,247	7204	
15	13,843,248	13,850,450	7203	
16	Closed			
17	13,850,451	13,857,379	6929	
18	13,857,380	13,864,284	6905	
21	13,864,285	13,871,014	6730	
22	13,871,015	13,878,075	7061	
23	13,878,076	13,885,077	7002	
24	13,885,078	13,892,077	7000	
25	Closed			
28	13,892,078	13,898,680	6603	
29	13,898,681	13,905,680	7000	
30	13,905,681	13,912,754	7074	

JULY 1926

	First Number	Last Number	Production	
1	13,912,755	13,919,475	6721	
2	13,919,476	13,924,975	5500	
5	Closed			
6	13,924,976	13,930,892	5917	
7	13,930,893	13,937,392	6500	
8	13,937,393	13,943,893	6501	
9	13,943,894	13,950,393	6500	
12	13,950,394	13,956,663	6270	
13	13,956,664	13,963,166	6503	
14	13,963,167	13,969,668	6502	
15	13,969,669	13,976,169	6501	
16	13,976,170	13,982,669	6500	
19	13,982,670	13,989,172	6503	"Holley Vaporizer
20	13,989,173	13,995,677	6505	on all production."
21	13,995,678	14,002,183	6506	
		14,000,000 at 4:30 P.M.		
22	14,002,184	14,008,836	6653	

JULY 1926

	First Number	Last Number	Production
23	14,008,837	14,015,539	6703
26	14,015,540	14,022,241	6702
27	14,022,242	14,028,948	6707

"Began painting in Pyroxyln on July 27."

	First Number	Last Number	Production
28	14,028,949	14,035,713	6765
29	14,035,714	14,042,473	6760
30	14,042,474	14,049,029	6556

AUGUST 1926

	First Number	Last Number	Production	
2	14,049,030	14,055,580	6551	
3	14,055,581	14,062,154	6574	
4	14,062,155	14,068,907	6753	
5	14,068,908	14,075,469	6562	
6	14,075,470	14,081,975	6506	
9	14,081,976	14,088,628	6653	
10	14,088,629	14,095,278	6650	
11	14,095,279	14,098,800	3522	
	(14,098,801	14,100,000)		(1,200 "omitted")
	14,100,001	14,103,128	3128	(6650 total)
12	14,103,129	14,109,758	6630	
13	14,109,759	14,116,261	6503	
16	14,116,262	14,122,611	6350	
17	14,122,612	14,128,611	6000	
18	14,128,612	14,135,318	6707	
19	14,135,319	14,142,037	6719	
20	14,142,038	14,148,797	6760	
23	14,148,798	14,155,407	6610	
24	14,155,408	14,162,022	6615	
25	14,162,023	14,168,643	6621	
26	14,168,644	14,175,257	6614	
27	14,175,258	14,181,881	6624	
30	14,181,882	14,187,787	5906	
31	14,187,788	14,194,489	6702	

SEPTEMBER 1926

	First Number	Last Number	Production
1	14,194,490	14,201,245	6756
2	14,201,246	14,207,981	6736
3	14,207,982	14,214,753	6802
6	Closed		
7	14,214,754	14,221,355	6602
8	14,221,356	14,227,956	6601
9	14,227,957	14,234,466	6510
10	14,234,467	14,240,968	6502
13	14,240,969	14,247,468	6500
14	14,247,469	14,253,974	6506
15	14,253,975	14,260,485	6511
16	14,260,486	14,266,998	6513
17	14,266,999	14,273,499	6501
20	14,273,500	14,279,909	6410
21	14,279,910	14,286,318	6409
22	14,286,319	14,292,726	6408
23	14,292,727	14,299,133	6407
24	14,299,134	14,305,535	6402
27	14,305,536	14,311,935	6400
28	14,311,936	14,318,342	6407
29	14,318,343	14,324,743	6401
30	14,324,744	14,331,152	6409

OCTOBER 1926

	First Number	Last Number	Production	
1	14,331,153	14,337,564	6412	
4	14,337,565	14,343,971	6407	
5	14,343,972	14,350,384	6413	
6	14,350,385	14,356,719	6335	
7	14,356,720	14,363,035	6316	
8	14,363,036	14,369,352	6317	
11	14,369,353	14,375,658	6306	
12	14,375,659	14,381,958	6300	
13	14,381,959	14,388,260	6302	
14	14,388,261	14,390,000	1740	
	(14,390,001	14,400,000)		(10,000 to Manchester)
	14,400,001	14,404,560	4560	(6,300 total)
15	14,404,561	14,410,763	6203	
18	14,410,764	14,416,963	6200	
19	14,416,964	14,423,165	6202	
20	14,423,166	14,429,366	6201	
21	14,429,367	14,435,567	6201	
22	14,435,568	14,441,770	6203	
25	14,441,771	14,447,974	6204	
26	14,447,975	14,453,899	5925	
27	14,453,900	14,459,849	5950	
28	14,459,850	14,466,049	6200	
29	14,466,050	14,472,253	6204	

NOVEMBER 1926

	First Number	Last Number	Production
1	14,472,254	14,478,084	5831
2	14,478,085	14,483,709	5625
3	14,483,710	14,489,111	5402
4	14,489,112	14,494,612	5501
5	14,494,613	14,500,512	5900
8	14,500,513	14,506,312	5800
9	14,506,313	14,512,115	5803
10	14,512,116	14,517,835	5720
11	14,517,836	14,523,636	5801
12	14,523,637	14,526,538	2902
15	14,526,539	14,532,076	5538
16	14,532,077	14,537,411	5335
17	14,537,412	14,542,946	5535
18	14,542,947	14,548,776	5830
19	14,548,777	14,551,408	2632

Noted in the records on November 18, 1926: "Motor numbers ground off and replacement numbers: 10,000,000 changed to 14,548,000; 12,000,000 changed to 14,546,000; and 13,000,000 changed to 14,549,000."

	First Number	Last Number	Production
22	14,551,409	14,557,017	5609
23	14,557,018	14,562,841	5824
24	14,562,842	14,565,701	2860
25	Closed November 25 to November 29		
29	14,565,702	14,571,421	5720
30	14,571,422	14,577,135	5714

DECEMBER 1926

	First Number	Last Number	Production
1	Closed from December 1 to December 6		
6	14,577,136	14,582,838	5703
7	14,582,839	14,588,545	5707
8	14,588,546	14,594,067	5522
9	14,594,068	14,599,130	5063
10	Closed		
13	14,599,131	14,604,155	5025
14	14,604,156	14,609,179	5024
15	14,609,180	14,614,204	5025
16	14,614,205	14,619,254	5050
17	Closed December 17 to January 3, 1927		

JANUARY 1927

	First Number	Last Number	Production
3	14,619,255	14,624,355	5101
4	14,624,356	14,629,987	5632
5	14,629,988	14,635,754	5767
10	14,635,755	14,641,310	5556
11	14,641,311	14,647,013	5703
12	14,647,014	14,652,728	5715
13	14,652,729	14,658,558	5830
17	14,658,559	14,664,261	5703
18	14,664,262	14,669,981	5720
19	14,669,982	14,675,683	5702
24	14,675,684	14,681,398	5715
25	14,681,399	14,687,098	5700
26	14,687,099	14,692,800	5702
31	14,692,801	14,698,502	5702

FEBRUARY 1927

	First Number	Last Number	Production
1	14,698,503	14,703,959	5457

No production February 2 to 7

	First Number	Last Number	Production
7	14,703,960	14,708,967	5008
8	14,708,968	14,713,967	5000
9	14,713,968	14,718,832	4865
10	14,718,833	14,721,290	2458
14	14,721,291	14,726,241	4951
15	14,726,242	14,731,253	5012
16	14,731,254	14,736,107	4854
17	14,736,108	14,738,438	2331
21	14,738,439	14,743,178	4740
22	14,743,179	14,748,184	5006
23	14,748,185	14,753,199	5015
24	14,753,200	14,758,070	4871
28	14,758,071	14,762,945	4875

MARCH 1927

	First Number	Last Number	Production
1	14,762,946	14,767,951	5006
2	14,767,952	14,772,885	4934
3	14,772,886	14,777,673	4788
7	14,777,674	14,782,433	4760
8	14,782,434	14,787,213	4780
9	14,787,214	14,792,004	4791
10	14,792,005	14,794,434	2430
14	14,794,435	14,799,093	4659
15	14,799,094	14,803,812	4719
16	14,803,813	14,808,524	4712
17	14,808,525	14,813,337	4813
21	14,813,338	14,818,107	4770
22	14,818,108	14,822,881	4774
23	14,822,882	14,827,646	4765
24	14,827,647	14,832,416	4770
28	14,832,417	14,837,164	4748
29	14,837,165	14,841,913	4749
30	14,841,914	14,846,658	4745
31	14,846,659	14,851,445	4787

APRIL 1927

	First Number	Last Number	Production
4	14,851,446	14,856,147	4702
5	14,856,148	14,860,901	4754
6	14,860,902	14,865,603	4702
7	14,865,604	14,870,353	4750
11	14,870,354	14,875,055	4702
12	14,875,056	14,879,756	4701
13	14,879,757	14,884,496	4740
14	14,884,497	14,889,379	4883
18	14,889,380	14,894,152	4773
19	14,894,153	14,898,911	4759
20	14,898,912	14,903,667	4756
21	14,903,668	14,908,455	4788

Serial Numbers

APRIL 1927

Day	First Number	Last Number	Production	Notes
25	14,908,456	14,913,208	4753	
26	14,913,209	14,917,955	4747	
27	14,917,956	14,922,712	4757	
28	14,922,713	14,927,495	4783	

MAY 1927

Day	First Number	Last Number	Production	Notes
2	14,927,496	14,932,252	4757	
3	14,932,253	14,937,016	4764	
4	14,937,017	14,941,767	4751	
5	14,941,768	14,946,518	4751	
9	14,946,519	14,951,228	4710	
10	14,951,229	14,955,963	4735	
11	14,955,964	14,960,684	4721	
12	14,960,685	14,965,417	4733	
16	14,965,418	14,970,122	4705	
17	14,970,123	14,974,823	4701	
18	14,974,824	14,979,545	4722	
19	14,979,546	14,984,263	4718	
23	14,984,264	14,988,964	4701	
24	14,988,965	14,991,000		
	(14,991,901	14,995,900)		(4000 to Manchester)
	14,995,901	14,997,514	2514	(4550 total)
25	14,997,515	14,999,998	2484	
	(14,999,200 used to renumber engine 14,000,000)			
	(14,999,999	15,000,001)	3	held out for next day
	15,000,002	15,002,217	2216	(4700 total)
26	14,999,999	15,000,001	3	
	15,002,218	15,006,625	4408	
31	15,006,626	15,007,032	407	

A car bearing the engine number of 15,007,033 is reputed to be the last Model T Ford produced. Engine production, for the most part listed as "truck" continued through the year. Ford branches apparently continued assembling cars until stocks of parts were depleted. 69,198 engines were built in 1927 between May and December of 1927 (15,007,034 to 15,076,231).

JUNE 1927

Day	First Number	Last Number	Production
1	15,007,033	15,007,446	414
2	15,007,447	15,007,861	415
6	15,007,862	15,008,284	423
7	15,008,285	15,008,701	417
8	15,008,702	15,009,125	424
9	15,009,126	15,009,560	435
10	15,009,561	15,009,996	436
13	15,009,997	15,010,437	441
14	15,010,438	15,010,880	443
15	15,010,881	15,011,325	445
16	15,011,326	15,011,827	502
17	15,011,828	15,012,328	501
20	15,012,329	15,012,831	503
21	15,012,832	15,013,338	507
22	15,013,339	15,013,842	504
23	15,013,843	15,014,348	506
27	15,014,349	15,014,850	502
28	15,014,851	15,015,356	506
29	15,015,357	15,015,864	508
30	15,015,865	15,016,374	510

Daily production figures continue in the factory records but only the monthly production is shown here after June 1927.

JULY

	First Number	Last Number	Production
	15,016,375	15,023,924	7550

AUGUST

	First Number	Last Number	Production
	15,023,925	15,034,669	10745

SEPTEMBER

	First Number	Last Number	Production
	15,034,670	15,047,409	12740

OCTOBER

	First Number	Last Number	Production
	15,047,410	15,059,396	11987

First Model A engine produced on October 20. (Only 1 made)

NOVEMBER

	First Number	Last Number	Production
	15,059,397	15,068,957	9561

DECEMBER

	First Number	Last Number	Production
	15,068,958	15,076,231	7274

1928

Month	First Number	Last Number	Production	Notes
JANUARY	15,076,232	15,081,163	4932	
FEBRUARY	15,081,164	15,086,394	5231	
MARCH	15,086,395	15,091,184	4790	
APRIL	15,091,185	15,097,000	5816	
	(15,097,001	15,098,000)		(1000 "omitted")
	15,098,001	15,098,381	381	(6197 total)
MAY	15,098,382	15,107,771	9390	
JUNE	15,107,772	15,118,348	10577	
JULY				

Month	First Number	Last Number	Production	Notes
	15,118,349	15,127,973	9625	
AUGUST	15,127,974	15,137,550	9577	
SEPTEMBER	15,137,551	15,142,855	5305	
OCTOBER	15,142,856	15,148,053	5198	
NOVEMBER	15,148,054	15,149,646	1593	
DECEMBER	15,149,647	15,150,381	735	

1929

Month	First Number	Last Number	Production	Notes
JANUARY	15,150,382	15,152,127	1746	
FEBRUARY	15,152,128	15,153,662	1535	
MARCH	15,153,663	15,154,200	538	
	(15,154,201	15,154,250)		(50 "omitted")
	15,154,251	15,154,757	507	(1045 total)
APRIL	15,154,758	15,155,000	243	
	(15,155,001	15,155,050)		(50 to Dallas)
	15,155,051	15,155,250	200	
	(15,155,251	15,155,330)		(80 to Somerville)
	15,155,331	15,156,000	670	
	(15,156,001	15,156,020)		(20 to St. Paul)
	15,156,021	15,156,134	114	(1227 total)
MAY	15,156,135	15,157,700	1566	
	(15,157,701	15,157,752)		(52 to Somerville)
	15,157,753	15,158,335	583	(2149 total)
JUNE	15,158,336	15,160,345	2010	
JULY	15,160,346	15,162,100	1755	
	(15,162,101	15,162,116)		(16 to Chester, PA)
	15,162,117	15,162,310	194	(1949 total)
AUGUST	15,162,311	15,163,000	690	
	(15,163,001	15,163,010)		(10 to Chester, PA)
	15,163,011	15,165,673	2663	(3353 total)
SEPTEMBER	15,165,674	15,169,414	3741	
OCTOBER	15,169,415	15,170,468	1054	
NOVEMBER	15,170,469	15,170,784	316	
DECEMBER	15,170,785	15,170,988	204	

1930

Month	First Number	Last Number	Production
JANUARY	15,170,989	15,171,574	586
FEBRUARY	15,171,575	15,172,030	456
MARCH	15,172,031	15,172,363	333
APRIL	15,172,364	15,172,997	634
MAY	15,172,998	15,173,626	629
JUNE	15,173,627	15,174,112	486
JULY	15,174,113	15,174,202	90

First reconditioned engines with "R" preceding the number (July 2).

Month	First Number	Last Number	Production
AUGUST	15,174,203	15,174,518	316
SEPTEMBER	15,174,519	15,174,830	312
OCTOBER	15,174,831	15,175,122	292
NOVEMBER	15,175,123	15,175,498	376
DECEMBER	15,175,499	15,175,690	192

1931

Month	First Number	Last Number	Production
JANUARY	15,175,691	15,175,825	135
FEBRUARY	15,175,826	15,175,966	141
MARCH	15,175,967	15,176,074	108
APRIL	15,176,075	15,176,171	97
MAY	15,176,172	15,176,207	36

1931

Month	First Number	Last Number	Production
JUNE	15,176,208	15,176,314	107
JULY	15,176,315	15,176,432	118
AUGUST	15,176,433	15,176,439	7
SEPTEMBER	15,176,440	15,176,591	152
OCTOBER	15,176,592	15,176,650	58
NOVEMBER	15,176,651	15,176,686	36
DECEMBER	No production		

1932

Month	First Number	Last Number	Production
MARCH	15,176,687	15,176,691	5

1933

Month	First Number	Last Number	Production
OCTOBER	15,176,692	15,176,696	5
NOVEMBER	15,176,697	15,176,702	6
DECEMBER	15,176,703	15,176,712	10

1934

	First Number	Last Number	Production
APRIL	15,176,713	15,176,722	10
MAY	15,176,723	15,176,732	10
JUNE	15,176,733	15,176,739	7
JULY	15,176,740	15,176,742	3
SEPTEMBER	15,176,743	15,176,749	7
OCTOBER	15,176,750	15,176,756	7
NOVEMBER	15,176,757	15,176,761	5
DECEMBER	15,176,762	15,176,763	2

1935

	First Number	Last Number	Production
JANUARY	15,186,764	15,176,777	14
FEBRUARY	15,176,778		1
MARCH	15,176,779	15,176,782	4
APRIL	15,176,783	15,176,787	5
MAY	15,176,788	15,176,792	5
AUGUST	15,176,793	15,176,796	4
SEPTEMBER	15,176,797	15,176,799	3
OCTOBER	15,176,800	15,176,804	5
DECEMBER	15,176,805	15,176,807	3

1936

	First Number	Last Number	Production
JANUARY	15,176,808	15,176,811	4
MARCH	15,176,812		1
APRIL	15,176,813	15,176,816	5
MAY	15,176,817		1
AUGUST	15,176,818	15,176,820	3
SEPTEMBER	15,176,821	15,176,822	2
NOVEMBER	15,176,823		1
DECEMBER	15,176,824		1

	First Number	Last Number	Production
1937	15,176,825	15,176,853	29
1938	15,176,854	15,176,862	9
1939	15,176,863	15,176,877	15
1940	15,176,878	15,176,881	4
1941	15,176,882	15,176,888	7

The last Model T Ford engine was built on August 4, 1941. A total of 169,856 engines were built after the last Model T Ford was produced at the main plant in Dearborn.

CANADIAN SERIAL NUMBERS

Until 1913, Canadian-built Fords used engines supplied by the Highland Park plant, and their serial numbers were a part of the U.S. numbers. Beginning in 1913, however, Ford of Canada began their own engine assembly and assigned unique Canadian engine numbers, beginning with C1. Generally all Canadian engine numbers begin with a "C" but some exceptions seem to appear, with "HC" and "SC" being noted, as well as some without any letter.

Ford of Canada had a unique "deal" with Ford (U.S.) in that they were the sole suppliers of the entire British Empire except for Great Britain (England, Ireland, Wales and Scotland) itself. Consequently, Canadian-built engines and cars are found all over the world, and in particular, Australia and New Zealand (and Canada, of course). A good deal of engine data listed here came from Australia. The location of the particular engine is noted: "A" is for Australia, "NZ" is New Zealand, "C" is Canada, "GB" is Great Britain, and "US" is the United States.

Records of Canadian engine serial numbers are incomplete, and those that do exist would appear to be even less accurate than those supplied by Ford in the U.S. The following compilation is made up of three Canadian sources plus engine number data supplied by many members of the Model T Ford Club of America from all over the world.

Canadian numbers marked with a single asterisk (*) are from a list compiled by the Canadian Ford Archives. Those marked with two asterisks (**) are from *Ford Owner and Dealer* magazine of June 1922, and those marked with a pound sign (#) are from the Canadian Ford Service Bulletins. None of these lists is believed to be accurate except in cases where indicated otherwise. For example, it is also highly unlikely that almost every month would begin and end on even numbers, as they indicate. The Bulletin numbers are out of sequence, which may be correct, but one wonders if they could have been as far out as they indicate.

It is the author's guess that Ford (U.S. and Canada) approximated their serial number dates in an effort to avoid confusion. Since numbered engines could have been shipped to distant assembly plants, cars with adjacent engine numbers could have been assembled weeks or months apart. Had they used accurate engine manufacturing dates, they might have had a lot of explaining to do as to why an earlier number appeared in a later car. Just a theory.

Those numbers shown without a manufacturing date were supplied by members, and list casting dates where available. Even here there is confusion, as in the U.S. engines. Some engines were apparently built before they were cast, and many were apparently built a long time after they were cast. Ford in the U.S. did not "age" its engines as

is commonly believed. Ford often built the engine the same day the block was cast. It would seem strange if Ford of Canada would not do likewise. Where the casting date is later than the serial number date, it is probable that replacement engines were given an earlier number.

Judging from existing Canadian engines, the cylinder block castings were supplied from Highland Park until about December 1919. The "Made in USA" was ground off, and there is no "Made in Canada." Beginning about number C230,000 the Canadian plant began their own casting, and the "Made in Canada" began to appear on the side of the cylinder block. As usual, there is some overlapping, with U.S. and Canadian blocks being used for a time.

Casting dates on Canadian engines followed the same pattern as the U.S. engines, and apparently not all engines were dated. Generally, this date appeared as month-day-year (10-22-19 would be October 22, 1919, for example). Beginning about January 1923, Ford of Canada began to use a letter instead of the year number. 1923 was indicated by an "A," 1924 by a "B," 1925 by a "C," 1926 by a "D," and 1927 by an "E." All these letter dates are believed to be calendar years, not model or fiscal years.

Where "years" are indicated in the following list, they are just approximated. There is a good deal of uncertainty about when Canadian models changed. Some records seem to indicate a fiscal year (August to July the next year) and some a calendar year.

PRODUCTION FIGURES
From the Ford of Canada Archives
Apparently fiscal years until 1921

			Total Can.
1908	458	(None were Model T)	
1909-10	1,280		1,280
1910-11	2,805		4,085
1911-12	6,388		10,473
1912-13	11,584		22,057
1913-14	15,657		37,714
1914-15	18,771		56,485
1915-16	32,646		89,131
1916-17	50,043		139,174
1917-18	46,914		186,088
1918-19	39,112		225,200
1919-20	55,616		280,816
1920	15,626	(August-December)	296,442

Calendar years after 1920

		(U.S figures)		(Total Canada)
1921	42,349	42,348	338,791	42,349
1922	50,266	50,266	389,057	92,615
1923	79,115	79,834	468,172	171,730
1924	71,726	71,371	539,898	243,456
1925	79,244	79,289	619,142	322,700
1926	100,611	100,651	719,753	423,311
1927	37,677	37,313	757,030	460,988

(Canada shows 757,888 which would include the 458 cars built in 1908. These were no doubt Models N and S, not Model T, since Detroit made only 309 Model T's in 1908.)

1913

C		Mfg. Date	Casting date	
C	1	5- 1-13		# **
C	1	5-20-13		*
C	323		3-18-13	A
C	325		6-28-13	A
C	995		3-31-13	A
C	1,237			US
C	1,270		1-15-13	A
C	1,500	7-31-13		# * **
C	1,501	8- 1-13		# **
C	2,617		3-25-13	US
C	2,771			US
C	2,980			A
C	3,249			A
C	3,838		3-28-13	A
C	3,861		8-13-13	A
C	4,474			NZ
C	5,168			A
C	5,190		2-11-13	A
C	5,274			NZ
C	5,736		10-20-13	A
C	6,064		6-15-13	A
C	6,401		10-16-13	A
C	8,401		10-16-13	A
C	9,598			C
C	9,645		12-15-13	C
C	11,650		8-10-13	C
C	11,807			C

1914

C	12,109		1-23-14	A
C	12,115		12-29-13	A
C	12,261		1-22-14	A
C	13,244		12-23-13	C
C	14,982		3-18-14	A
C	15,515		3-16-14	A
C	15,947		2-20-14	A
C	16,411		2-27-14	A
C	16,500	7-31-14		# * **
C	16,501	8- 1-14		# **
C	18,300		1- 2-14	C
C	18,750			US
C	20,977		9-14-14	A
C	21,165		9-23-14	A
C	23,488		11- 4-14	C

1915

C	25,288		1-28-15	A
C	25,696			A
C	26,397		1-13-15	US
C	27,655		2-27-15	C
C	28,717		2-11-15	A
C	29,484			C
C	31,194		4-20-15	A
C	31,654		3- 7-15	A
C	32,734		7- 3-15	NZ
C	33,699		6 - 6-14	A
C	33,727		5-14-14	–
C	35,254			US
C	37,500	7-31-15		# * **
C	37,501	8- 1-15		# **
C	37,746		6-18-15	A
C	38,018		4-10-15	A
C	38,609		12- 6-15	A
C	41,163		8-12-15	A
C	42,077			NZ
C	44,039		4-19-15	A
C	44,516		9-17-15	A
C	45,003			NZ
C	45,106		9- 1-15	A
C	45,776		9-29-15	A
C	46,560		10-22-15	A

1916

C	51,749			
C	53,026		11-23-15	A
C	53,776		9-12-15	A
C	54,968		12-16-15	A
C	55,512		2-17-16	C
C	56,773		2-25-16	C
C	56,981		2-25-16	A
C	57,543		2-24-16	A
C	58,149		3-19-16	A
C	58,687		12-21-15	A

1916

C		Mfg. Date	Casting date	
C	59,872		3- 4-16	A
C	60,210		8- 8-16	A
C	60,370		?-10-16	C
C	60,458			A
C	60,941		3-11-16	A
C	62,053		2-18-16	A
C	62,385		3-21-16	A
C	62,389		8-25-16	A
C	64,158			C
C	65,001		12- 4-15	A
C	65,229		1- 7-16	NZ
C	66,677		1- 8-16	C
C	67,095		11- -15?	A
C	67,148		1-14-16	A
C	68,052		3- 3-16	A
C	70,000	7-31-16		# * **
C	70,001	8- 1-16		# **
C	73,351		6-15-15	C

1917

C	75,375		1- 8-17	C
C	77,138		2- 8-15?	C
C	81,843		?-30-17	C
C	84,515		11-22-16	C
C	91,841		1-18-17	C
C	94,901			C
C	96,598			C
C	96,605		7-19-16	C
C	98,674			A
C	102,809		6-22-?	US
C	104,014		7- 1-15	C
C	107,565			NZ
C	109,169		5- 4-17	C
C	110,602		5-24-17	A
C	112,644		5-17-17	C
C	113,406		5-21-17	A
C	113,622			NZ
C	114,432		6- 5-17	C
C	115,448		6-18-17	C
C	118,233		7-19-17	A
C	118,326		7-19-17	A
C	120,443			C
C	121,000	7-31-17		# * **
C	121,001	8- 1-17		# **
C	129,291		9- 7-17	A
C	129,502		9-24-17	A
C	132,201		10-18-17	C (No "C" on number)
C	135,683		10-25-17	A
C	139,315		10-30-17	C
C	143,000		12-18-A	C
C	143,483?			C
C	143,670		12-14-17	C

1918

C	148,501		1-25-18	C
C	150,532		2- 1-18	C
C	152,422		2-18-18	A
C	152,604		7-22-18	A
C	155,918		3-13-18	C
C	159,736		3-18-18	A
C	159,737		3-13-18	A
C	163,385		4- -18	A
C	170,000	7-31-18		# * **
C	170,001	8- 1-18		# **
C	177,543		4-25-18	A
C	177,573		4-22-18	A
C	179,880		9-27-18	A
C	179,881		11-12-17	A
C	180,134		11-13-17	A
C	180,150		11-15-17	A
C	180,186		11- 3-17	A
C	180,188		11-19-17	A
C	181,985		12-13-17	A
C	183,898		12-10-17	A
C	184,244			NZ
C	186,052		12-31-18	A

(Listed as last of 1918 by Ford of Canada)

Notes: *=Ford Archives (Canada), **=Ford Owner & Dealer (June 1922), #=Ford Service Bulletins (Canada)

1919

	Mfg. Date	Casting date	
C 189,068		3-19-19	A
C 189,147		3-22-19	A
C 194,385		2-11-19	C
C 196,288		4-30-19	A
C 196,303		5- 5-19	A
C 197,394			NZ
C 197,405			NZ
C 198,191			C
C 202,957		6-19-19	C
C 203,992		6-19-19	GB
C 206,015		7-12-19	GB
C 208,500	7-31-19		# * **
C 208,501	8- 1-19		# **
C 212,500	8-31-19		# * **
C 212,501	9- 1-19		# **
C 216,500	9-30-19		# * **
C 216,501	10- 1-19		# **
C 220,204		9-24-19	A
C 222,500	10-31-19		# * **
C 222,501	11- 1-19		# **
C 224,846		12- 1-21	A
(No "C" on number)			
C 227,500	11-30-19		# * **
C 227,501	12- 1-19		# **
C 227,549		10-17-19	A
C 230,069		12-28-19	A "Made in Canada"
C 230,524		12-18-19	A
C 230,658		12-12-19	A
C 230,660		12-24-19	A
C 231,000	12-31-19		# * **

1920

	Mfg. Date	Casting date	
C 231,001	1- 1-20		# **
C 232,757			C
C 232,977		11-15-19	C
C 234,000	1-31-20		# * **
C 234,001	2- 1-20		# **
C 234,508		9-12-19	C
C 234,967		1-12-20	A
C 237,500	2-29-20		# * **
C 237,501	3- 1-20		# **
C 237,794			NZ
C 239,581			NZ
C 239,644		12- 3-20	A
C 241,500	3-31-20		# * **
C 241,501	4- 1-20		# **
C 245,500	4-30-20		# * **
C 245,501	5- 1-20		# **
C 246,632			C
C 247,803		3- 8-20	US
C 251,000	5-31-20		# * **
C 251,001	6- 1-20		# **
C 252,994		5-13-20	C
C 253,487		4- 9-20	C
C 256,874		4-22-20	A
C 257,000	6-30-20		# * **
C 257,001	7- 1-20		# **
C 260,451		6-20-20	A
C 262,500	7-31-20		# * **
C 262,501	8- 1-20		# **
C 262,923		7-16-20	A
C 266,000	8-31-20		# * **
C 266,001	9- 1-20		# **
C 268,021		8-21-20	C
C 269,135			C
C 269,500	9-30-20		# * **
C 269,501	10- 1-20		# **
C 270,217		8-21-20	C
C 271,392		8-13-20	C
C 272,374		6-20-20	A
C 272,456		8-23-20	A
C 274,835			C
C 275,500	10-31-20		# * **
C 275,501	11- 1-20		# **
C 277,237			C
C 277,473			NZ
C 278,500	11-30-20		# * **
C 278,501	12- 1-20		# **

1920

	Mfg. Date	Casting date	
C 281,000	12-28-20		#
	12-31-20		* **
C 281,001	12-28-20		**

1921

	Mfg. Date	Casting date	
C 281,500	1-17-21		# * **
C 282,000	3-21-21		#
	2-16-21		**
C 282,108		7-20-20	A
C 282,125		9-21-20	A
C 282,500	2-16-21		#
	3-21-21		* **
C 283,000	2-15-21		# **
C 283,500	2-25-21		# * **
C 283,501	2-26-21		*
C 284,000	3- 4-21		#
	2-10-21		**
C 284,500	2-10-21		#
	3- 4-21		* **
C 284,501	3- 4-21	1-22-20	A *
C 285,000	2-15-21		# **
C 285,500	3-14-21		# * **
C 285,501	3-14-21		*
C 285,521		10-11-20	C
C 286,000	3-15-21		# **
C 287,000	3-24-21		# * **
C 287,500	4-11-21		#
	3- 1-21		**
C 287,501	3-24-21		*
C 288,000	3- 1-21		#
	4-11-21		* **
C 288,001	4-11-21		*
C 288,001	3- 3-21		# **
C 289,000	3-22-21		# * **
C 289,001	4-22-21		*
C 289,500	4- 8-21		# **
C 290,000	4-20-21		# * **
C 290,001	4-30-21		*
C 290,500	5-17-21		# **
C 291,000	3-28-21		# **
C 291,001	3-31-21		# * **
C 292,000	4-30-21		#
	4-23-21		**
C 293,000	4-23-21		#
C 293,500	4-26-21		#
	4-30-21		* **
C 293,501	5-14-21		*
C 294,000	5- 3-21		**
	5-30-21		#
C 294,500	5- 5-21		#
C 294,787		4- 4-21	C
C 295,000	5- 9-21		#
C 295,500	5-17-21		#
C 296,000	5-14-21		#
C 296,500	5- 3-21		#
C 297,000	5-19-21		#
C 297,500	5-25-21		#
C 298,000	5-27-21		#
C 298,500	5-28-21		#
C 299,000	5-21-21		# **
C 299,500	5-31-21		# * **
C 299,501	6- 1-21		*
C 300,000	6- 3-21		# **
C 300,500	6- 3-21		#
C 301,000	6- 7-21		#
C 301,500	6-11-21		#
C 302,000	6-15-21		#
C 302,500	6-17-21		#
C 303,000	6-15-21		#
C 303,500	6-25-21		#
C 303,904		5- 4-21	C
C 304,000	6-11-21		#
C 304,500	6-23-21		#
C 305,000	7- 9-21		#
C 305,500	6-29-21		#
C 306,000	7-14-21		#
C 306,500	7-12-21		#
C 307,000	7-21-21		#
C 307,100	6-30-21		*
C 307,101	7- 1-21		*
C 307,533			C
C 308,000	8- 9-21		#
C 308,500	7-14-21		#

Notes: *=Ford Archives (Canada), **=Ford Owner & Dealer (June 1922), #=Ford Service Bulletins (Canada)

1921

Serial	Mfg. Date	Casting date	
C 309,000	7-27-21		#
C 309,360			US
C 309,500	8-26-21		#
C 310,000	9-10-21		#
C 310,226		4-14-21	C
C 310,500	9-26-21		#
C 311,000	8-11-21		#
C 311,300	7-31-21		*
C 311,301	8- 1-21		*
C 311,500	8-24-21		#
C 311,800	8-31-21		*
C 311,801	9- 1-21		*
C 312,000	9-16-21		#
C 312,500	8-24-21		#
C 313,000	9- 9-21		#
C 313,500	2- 7-22		#
C 314,000	3- 2-22		
C 314,500	10- 5-21		#
C 315,000	9- 8-21		#
C 315,500	10-11-21		#
C 315,713		4-26-21	A
C 316,000	9-28-21		#
C 316,500	10-12-21		#
C 317,000	None given		#
C 317,300	9-30-21		*
C 317,301	10- 1-21		*
C 317,500	10-27-21		#
C 318,000	11-22-21		#
C 318,500	10-18-21		#
C 319,000	12- 1-21		#

1922

Serial	Mfg. Date	Casting date	
C 319,500	4- 7-22		#
C 319,700	10-31-21		*
C 319,701	11- 1-21		*
C 320,000	1- 9-22		#
C 320,500	10-31-21		#
C 321,000	1-20-22		#
C 321,500	2- 7-22		#
C 322,000	2-21-22		#
C 322,397		10-10-21	A
C 322,500	11-23-21		#
C 322,560		11- 4-21	A
C 322,791		8-29-21	A
C 322,800	11-30-21		*
C 322,801	12- 1-21		*
C 323,000	2-28-22		#
C 323,300	12-31-21		*
C 323,301	1- 1-22		*
C 323,500	2- 6-22		#
C 324,000	2- 8-22		#
C 324,500	12-22-21		#
C 325,000	12-15-21		#
C 325,500	1- 4-22		#
C 326,000	1-18-22		#
C 326,500	1-19-22		#
C 327,000	2- 2-22		#
C 327,500	3-15-22		#
C 327,600	1-31-22		*
C 327,601	2- 1-22		*
C 328,000	3- 8-22		#
C 328,500	4- 4-22		#
C 329,000	3-24-22		#
C 329,500	2-20-22		#
C 330,000	2-22-22		#
C 330,500	3-28-22		#
C 331,000	2-28-22		# *
C 331,001	3- 1-22		*
C 331,500	3- 3-22		#
C 332,000	3-15-22		#
C 332,500	4- 7-22		#
C 333,000	4-29-22		#
C 333,500	4- 9-22		#
C 333,741		2-27-22	A

1922

Serial	Mfg. Date	Casting date	
C 334,000	3-20-22		#
C 334,500	3-22-22		#
C 335,000	4-18-22		#
C 335,500	4-27-22		#
C 336,000	4-27-22		#
C 336,400	3-31-22		*
C 336,401	4- 1-22		*
C 336,500	4- 2-22		#
C 337,000	4- 5-22		#
C 338,000	4- 6-22		#
C 338,302		3-16-21	C
C 338,500	4-11-22		#
C 338,586		1-27-22	A
C 339,000	4-18-22		#
C 339,045		4- 6-22	C
C 339,500	4-22-22		#
C 340,000	4-22-22		#
C 340,039		4-12-22	C
C 340,500	4-25-22		#
C 341,000	4-28-22		#
C 341,100	4-30-22		*
C 341,101	5- 1-22		*
C 341,500	5- 4-22		#
C 342,000	5- 4-22		#
C 342,500	5- 9-22		#
C 343,000	5-12-22		#
C 343,500	5-11-22		#
C 343,522		1- 5-22	A
C 344,000	5-13-22		#
C 344,500	5-20-22		#
C 345,000	5-25-22		#
C 345,500	5-20-22		#
C 346,000	5-22-22		#
C 346,500	5-29-22		#
C 346,600	5-31-22		*
C 346,601	6- 1-22		*
C 347,000	6- 1-22		#
C 347,500	6- 7-22		#
C 348,000	6- 1-22		#
C 348,500	6-10-22		#
C 349,000	6-20-22		#
C 349,500	6-14-22		#
C 350,000	6-19-22		#
C 350,063		6-19-22	A
C 350,500	6-22-22		#
C 351,000	6-26-22		#
C 351,260		5-12-22	A
C 351,500	6-27-22		#
C 352,000	6-29-22		#
C 352,500	6-22-22		#
C 353,000	6-20-22		#
C 353,100	6-30-22		*
C 353,001	7- 1-22		*
C 353,500	7- 5-22		#
C 354,000	7-10-22		#
C 354,500	7-13-22		#
C 355,000	7-19-22		#
C 355,500	7-15-22		#
C 356,000	7-19-22		#
C 356,500	7-20-22		#
C 357,000	7-22-22		#
C 357,200	7-31-22		*
C 357,201	8- 1-22		*
C 357,500	8- 8-22		#
C 358,000	8- 2-22		#
C 358,500	8-15-22		#
C 358,692		7- 5-22	A
C 359,000	8-18-22		#
C 359,500	8-28-22		#
C 360,000	8-18-22		#
C 360,500	9- 3-22		#
C 361,000	2-28-22 !!		#
C 360,176		6- 6-22	A
C 361,200	8-31-22		*
C 361,201	9- 1-22		*
C 361,500	9- 8-22		#

Notes: *=Ford Archives (Canada), **=Ford Owner & Dealer (June 1922), #=Ford Service Bulletins (Canada)

Serial	Mfg. Date	Casting date	
C 362,000	9- 1-22		#
C 362,500	9-12-22		#
C 363,000	9-21-22		#
C 363,500	9-28-22		#
C 364,000	9-23-22		#
C 364,400	9-30-22		*
C 364,401	10- 1-22		*
C 364,500	10- 5-22		#
C 364,882		10-21-22	A
C 365,000	10- 6-22		#
C 365,447		2- 7-22	C
C 365,500	10- 4-22		#
C 366,000	10-11-22		#
C 366,500	10-19-22		#
C 367,000	10-12-22		#
C 367,025		9-27-22	A
C 367,191		8- 8-22	A
C 367,500	10-20-22		#
C 368,000	10-24-22		#
C 368,500	10-31-22		*
	11- 1-22		#
C 368,501	11- 1-22		*
C 369,000	11-10-22		#
C 369,500	11-19-22		#
C 370,000	11- 9-22		#
C 370,144		8-25-22	A
C 370,500	11-16-22		#
C 371,000	11-22-22		#
	11-27-22		#
C 371,500	11-22-22		#
C 371,892		10-16-22	A
C 371,901		10-18-22	A
C 372,000	11-29-22		#
C 372,100	11-30-22		*
C 372,101	12- 1-22		*
C 372,500	12-13-22		#
C 373,000	12-29-22		#
C 373,500	12- 5-22		#
C 374,000	12-13-22		#
C 374,110		12- 6-22	A
C 374,262		12- 6-22	NZ
C 374,500	12-18-22		#
C 374,836		12-13-22	A
C 375,000	12-22-22		#
C 375,048		12-12-22	A
C 375,142		12-13-22	A

1923

Serial	Mfg. Date	Casting date	
C 375,500	1- 3-23		#
C 376,000	12-29-22		#
C 376,100	12-31,22		*
C 376,101	1- 1-23		*
C 376,500	1-10-23		#
C 377,000	1- 5-23		#
C 377,500	1-10-23		#
C 377,656			C
C 378,000	1-15-23		#
C 378,437			US
C 378,500	1-16-23		#
C 379,000	1-16-23		#
C 379,500	1-20-23		#
C 380,000	1-19-23		#
C 380,391		1-16-23	A
C 380,500	1-24-23		#
C 381,000	1-27-23		#
C 381,500	2- 8-23		#
C 382,000	1-30-23		#
C 382,300	1-31-23		*
C 382,301	2- 1-23		*
C 382,500	2- 3-23		#
C 382,613		1-26-23	A
C 383,000	2- 6-23		#
C 383,500	2-10-23		#
C 384,000	2-12-23		#
C 384,500	2-12-23		#
C 385,000	2-13-23		#
C 385,500	2-17-23		#
C 386,000	2-17-23		#
C 386,500	2-21-23		#
C 386,558		2- 9-23	A

1923

Serial	Mfg. Date	Casting date	
C 386,732		2-13-23	A
C 387,000	2-23-23		#
C 387,500	2-28-23		#
C 387,659		2-12-23	A
C 388,000	2-28-23		#
C 388,337		2- 5-23	C
(2-8-23 on transmission cover)			
C 388,500	2-28-23		*
	3- 1-23		#
C 388,501	3- 1-23		*
C 389,000	3-13-23		#
C 389,500	3- 2-23		#
C 390,000	3- 6-23		#
C 390,500	3- 9-23		#
C 391,000	3-26-23		#
C 391,447		3- 3-23	C
C 391,500	3-13-23		#
C 392,000	3-14-23		#
C 392,500	3-15-23		#
C 392,589		1-30-23	A
C 393,000	3-17-23		#
C 393,500	3-21-23		#
C 394,000	3-22-23		#
C 394,307		3- 1-23	C
C 394,500	3-22-23		#
C 394,564			A
C 395,000	4- 6-23		#
C 395,086		3-27-23	A
C 395,157		3-28-23	A
C 395,500	3-24-23		#
C 396,000	3-28-23		#
C 396,500	3-29-23		#
C 396,600	3-31-23		*
C 396,601	4- 1-23		*
C 397,000	4- 2-23		#
C 397,500	4- 3-23		#
C 398,000	4- 5-23		#
C 398,500	4- 6-23		#
C 399,000	4-10-23		#
C 399,467		3-28-23	C
C 399,500	4-12-23		#
C 400,001	4-12-23		#
C 400,089		12-14-22	A
C 401,790		4- 4-23	A
C 404,400	4-30-23		*
C 404,401	5- 1-23		*
C 407,122		4- 2-23	A
C 407,182		5- 4-A	A
C 407,407		5- 5-A	C
C 408,473		11-14-22	A
C 409,906		10-31-22	A
C 409,971		10-27-22	A
C 410,294		11-16-22	A
C 410,982			NZ
C 412,500	5-31-23		*
C 412,501	6- 1-23		*
C 413,387			A
C 414,702			C
C 416,196			NZ
C 417,098		8-13-A	A
C 419,600	6-30-23		*
C 419,601	7- 1-23		*
C 419,964			NZ
C 424,589		7-19-A	C
C 427,002		7-14-A	A
C 427,147		7-10-A	A
C 427,300	7-31-23		*
C 427,301	8- 1-23		*
C 427,879		7-20-A	A
C 428,752		6-28-A	C
C 431,334		8- -23	C
C 432,800	8-30-23		*
C 432,801	9- 1-23		*
C 436,691		8- 7-A	C
C 437,800	9-30-23		*
C 437,801	10- 1-23		*
C 438,843		8-14-A	A
C 438,860		8- 1-A	A
C 439,347		6-11-A	A

Notes: *=Ford Archives (Canada), **=Ford Owner & Dealer (June 1922), #=Ford Service Bulletins (Canada)

1923

Serial	Mfg. Date	Casting date	
C 444,668		10- 8-23	A
C 444,719		10- 8-A	A
C 446,300	10-30-23		*
C 446,301	11- 1-23		*
C 447,722			NZ
C 450,845		10- 1-A	A
C 451,077		10-18-A	A
C 451,183		11-18-A	A
C 451,900	11-30-23		*
C 451,901	12- 1-23		*
C 452,058		10-19-A	A
C 454,500	12-13-23		#
C 455,000	12-21-23		#
C 455,461		12- 6-A	A
C 455,500	12-18-23		#
C 455,665		?- 6-23	NZ

1924

Serial	Mfg. Date	Casting date	
C 456,000	1- 3-24		#
C 456,043		None	C
C 456,500	12-27-23		#
C 457,000	12-19-23		#
C 457,500	12-26-23		#
C 457,784		12-17-A	A
C 457,851		12-15-A	A
C 458,000	12-28-23		#
C 458,500	12-28-23		#
		12-31-23	*
C 458,501	1- 2-24		*
C 459,000	1- 8-24		#
C 459,152		11-30-A	A
C 459,500	1- 8-24		#
C 460,000	1-10-24		#
C 460,500	1-15-24		#
C 460,579		12- 8-A	C
C 461,000	1-14-24		#
C 461,500	1-17-24		#
C 461,838		12-17-B	A
C 462,000	1-29-24		#
C 462,500	1-19-24		#
C 463,000	1-17-24		#
C 463,500	1-29-24		#
C 463,934		12-12-A	A
C 464,000	1-24-24		#
C 464,043		12-13-A	A
C 464,199		3- 1-B	A
C 464,447		1- 9-B	A
C 464,500	1-29-24		#
C 464,642		1-15-B	A
C 465,000	2-12-24		#
C 465,500	2-19-24		#
C 466,000	2-13-24		#
C 466,048	1-31-24		*
C 466,049	2- 1-24		*
C 466,500	2- 4-24		#
C 467,000	2-12-24		#
C 467,500	2-18-24		#
C 468,000	2-23-24		#
C 468,500	2-19-24		#
C 468,679		1-11-B	A
C 469,000	2-20-24		#
C 469,500	2-22-24		#
C 469,520		2-12-B	A
C 470,000	2-23-24		#
C 470,500	2-26-24		#
C 470,977		12-12-A	A
(1-15-B on cylinder head)			
C 471,000	2-25-24		#
C 471,500	2-27-24		#
C 472,000	3- 4-24		#
C 472,051		2- 4-B	A
C 472,500	2-29-24		#
C 472,555	2-29-24		*
C 472,556	3- 1-24		*
C 473,000	3- 7-24		#
C 473,500	3- 7-24		#
C 474,000	3-27-24		#
C 474,115			US
C 474,500	3- 7-24		#
C 474,553		2-29-B	C

1924

Serial	Mfg. Date	Casting date	
C 475,000	3-11-24		#
C 475,500	3-19-24		#
C 476,000	3-14-24		#
C 476,500	3-12-24		#
C 477,000	3-19-24		#
C 477,500	3-19-24		#
C 478,000	4- 1-24		#
C 478,500	3-26-24		#
C 478,518		3-20-B	C
C 479,000	3-21-24		#
C 479,500	3-28-24		#
C 479,908		2-12-B	A
C 479,998		3-12-B	A
C 480,000	3-25-24		#
C 480,017		3-11-B	A
C 480,500	3-29-24		#
C 481,256	3-31-24		*
C 481,257	4- 1-24		*
C 481,738		3-20-B	A
C 482,037			NZ
C 483,244		8-14-A	A
C 484,929		3- 8-A	A
C 485,405		4- 3-B	A
C 485,785		11- 8-A	A
C 485,826		11-21-A	A
C 486,122		4- 8-B	A
C 487,798		12-14-A	C
C 488,211		11-20-A	A
C 488,885	4-30-24		*
C 488,886	5- 1-24		*
C 489,940		18-10-A ?	C
C 491,739		2- 5-B	A
C 494,228		3-21-B	A
C 494,679		4- 7-B	A
C 497,577	5-31-24		*
C 497,578	6- 1-24		*
C 499,832			NZ
C 501,829		8-12-B	C
C 504,060	6-30-24		*
C 504,061	7- 1-24		*
C 505,646		4-13-D	C
C 506,800		11-12-A	C
C 506,976		5- 9-B	A
C 506,987			NZ
C 507,473		None	C
C 509,813	7-31-24		*
C 509,814	8- 1-24		*
C 510,055		10-14-A	C
C 510,320		1-30-B	C
C 513,405	8-31-24		*
C 513,406	9- 1-24		*
C 514,520			C
C 514,544			NZ
C 514,728		5-19-B	A
C 514,967		11- 6-A	A
C 516,008		11- 7-B	A
C 517,614	9-30-24		*
C 517,615	10- 1-24		*
No known records exist after 517,615			
C 520,038		10-25-A	C
C 521,694		11-27-A	C
C 525,286		5-22-B	A
C 526,982			US
C 527,248			NZ
C 527,822		12- 9-B	A
C 528,831		10-22-B	A
C 530,299		12- 9-B	A
C 530,389		12-11-B	A
C 530,770			NZ
C 531,745			C
C 532,687			C
C 533,742		10-14-B	A
C 534,040			NZ
C 535,793		10-20-B	A

1925

Serial	Mfg. Date	Casting date	
C 542,105		2-10-C	A
C 542,216		1-21-C	A
C 544,097		2-23-C	C
C 543,444		2-16-C	A

Notes: *=Ford Archives (Canada), **=Ford Owner & Dealer (June 1922), #=Ford Service Bulletins (Canada)

1925

	Mfg. Date	Casting date	
C 543,604		2-20-C	A
C 547,385			C
C 551,832		3-18-C	A
C 555,366		8-31-C	A
C 558,773		4-14-C	A
C 559,221			C
C 559,371		3-31-C	A
C 561,855		4-27-C	A
C 562,938		11-11-B	C
C 573,464			NZ
C 576,184		6-26-C	A
C 580,659		7-15-C	A
C 581,875			NZ
C 582,062			NZ
C 583,988		7-13-B	A
C 585,662		7-17-C	C
C 586,904		7-15-C	C
C 591,469		1- 2-C	A
C 595,077			NZ
C 596,051			C '26 style engine
C 598,496		1- 7-C	A
C 598,548		1- 8-C	A
C 598,781		10-24-C	A
C 598,798		10-24-C?	A
C 599,170			C
C 600,000	11- 2-25		C

(Known to be an accurate date)

C 601,782			NZ
C 606,219		2-14-C	C '26 style engine
C 612,455			C
C 614,616		6-22-C	A
C 614,749		12-11-C	A
C 615,722			C
C 615,877		12-23-C	A

1926

C 616,008		12-23-D	A
C 616,560		12-23-C	A
C 616,570		1-18-D	A
C 616,645		7-13-D	A
C 622,045			NZ
C 624,264		2- 6-D	C
C 626,578			C
C 626,637		2-10-D	A
C 628,797		2-16-D	A
C 628,896			A
C 629,227		12-16-27	C

(Pre-'26 engine, odd casting date)

C 629,938		2-16-D	C
C 630,985		2-25-D	NZ
C 631,348			C
C 634,634			C
C 634,707			C
C 635,774		3- 3-D	C
C 636,117			A
C 636,615		2-23-D	A
C 637,349		3- 5-D	A
C 638,248		3-20-D	C
C 638,292			C
C 638,531		10-28-C	A
C 642,200		3-12-D	GB
C 643,704		8-24-D	C
C 644,063		3-28-D	C
C 644,860			C
C 645,590		3-30-D	C
C 648,237		3-30-D	A
C 650,632		4- 8-D	C
C 650,640		4- 9-D	C
C 652,170		6- 1-D	C
C 654,801			C
C 656,724		4- 6-D	C
C 658,048			C
C 658,230		10-30-C	C
C 659,004		4-24-D	C
C 660,923		9-20-C	C
C 661,307			C
C 661,812		5- 5-D	C
C 663,021		4-29-D	C
C 663,076		8- -26	US

(Date on transmission cover)

C 663,825		5-17-D	C
C 665,110			C
C 665,438		5- -26	C
C 665,809		5-26-D	C
C 669,548			C
C 669,784		6- 9-D	C

1926

	Mfg. Date	Casting date	
C 670,110			C
C 670,286		6- 7-D	D
C 670,827			US
C 670,843			C
C 673,433		9-14-D	A
C 673,621		8-16-D	A
C 673,849		9-11-D	A
C 673,974		6-17-D	C
C 674,947		6-15-D	

(3-26-D on transmission cover)

C 675,649		6-23-D	C
C 676,237		5-23-D	C
C 676,617		8-28-D	C
C 677,589		6-24-D	C
C 678,106			NZ
C 678,633		6-30-D	C
C 678,640		6- 7-D	A
C 679,926		7- 9-D	US

(6-22-D on transmission cover)

C 680,128			US
C 680,138		6-28-D	C
C 682,111			C
C 682,463			C
C 686,312		7-30-D	C
C 686,929		3-28-D	C
C 687,729		—	C
C 688,092			NZ
C 688,106			C
C 689,621		—	C

(7-15-D on transmission cover)

C 690,079		7-22-D	C
C 691,208		8-17-D	C
C 693,243			C
C 695,944			NZ
C 697,896		6-21-D	A
C 697,930		6-21-D	A
C 698,192			A
C 700,000	10- 5-26		

(Known to be an accurate date)

C 700,805		10-28-D	C
C 701,195		3- 4-D	C
C 702,510		6-30-D	A
C 703,113		10- 4-D	A
C 703,397		8-16-D	A
C 704,711		10-14-D	A
C 705,810			C
C 706,339			C
C 707,598		10-25-D	C
C 709,841		11- 1-D	A
C 709,881		10-21-D	A
C 711,893		11-16-D	A
C 713,099		11-11-D	A
C 713,746			A
C 714,068		12- 8-D	A
C 714,077		12- 8-D	A
C 714,153			C
C 714,264		1- 8-D	A
C 714,917		12- 9-D	A
C 717,448		12-28-D	C

1927

C 718,142		1- 8-E	A
C 718,220			A
C 718,309		8- 6-D	A
C 718,536		11-23-D	C
C 719,778		1- 6-E	A
C 720,040		1-14-E	A
C 720,059		12-16-D	A
C 720,744		1-26-E	A
C 721,012		1-22-E	A

(12-1-D on transmission cover)

C 721,199		12-16-D	A
C 721,380		12-11-D	A

(12-17-D on transmission cover)

C 721,419		1-10-E	A
C 724,451		1-11-27	C
C 727,084			US
C 727,451		1-11-27	C
C 727,866		12- 1-D	A
C 727,881		2-16-E	A
C 728,606		2-21-E	A
C 734,890		8-11-E	C
C 739,264			C
C 740,156			C

Notes: *=Ford Archives (Canada), **=Ford Owner & Dealer (June 1922), #=Ford Service Bulletins (Canada)

Canadian Serial Numbers

1927

	Mfg. Date	Casting date	
C 742,600		1-10-E	A
C 744,813		3- 7-25	C ??
C 747,813		4-25-E	C
C 748,623			NZ
C 787,152			C
No number		3- 1-F	C

Notes: *=Ford Archives (Canada), **=Ford Owner & Dealer (June 1922), #=Ford Service Bulletins (Canada)

DOCUMENTATION

This chapter lists, in chronological order, the sources of some of the information on which this book is based. The sources, where known, are shown just after each date. Ford Archives sources are shown as "Acc. ###." ("Acc." means "Accession," which refers to the location at the Archives.)

These notes by no means cover the author's total resources. Much of the data has been derived from observation of existing original cars, from a general consensus between known "experts" in the field, Ford parts books, service manuals, and anywhere else it could be found.

You will find a good deal of interesting reading in this chapter. Some of the material can be found in no other publications. For instance, did you know that Ford first came out with four-to-one rear axle gears before the ten-tooth pinion? On July 2, 1919, in the records at the Ford Archives, they show a twelve-tooth pinion and a forty-eight tooth ring gear. The ten-tooth pinion is noted on January 24, 1920, superseding the two odd gears. (The ten-tooth pinion was used with the standard ring gear.)

Or did you know that Ford experimented with many timers, various starter Bendix covers, or flywheels with integral gear teeth? You'll find this information, and more, in this chapter.

1908

APR 1 *Ford Times*
Model T mentioned. Letter from dealer said, "....will open some eyes"!

JUN 1 *Ford Times*
Pictures of the Model T Landaulet

JUN 15 *Ford Times*
"Watch the Fords Go By" moving electric sign erected on top of the Temple Theater building on June 8. 35 feet long by 22 feet high, it pictured the Model T Touring in motion.

JUL 1 *Ford Times*
Story comparing the Model A (1903) and the Model T. Picture of the Model T Touring.
"High Price Quality in a Low Price Car" slogan used in an ad for the 6-40 (Model K) Runabout.

SEP 15 *Ford Times*
"To Be Built" sign erected on the site of the Highland Park Plant on September 3.
"Model T Ready for Delivery" notice. "By October 1." "No retail orders until every dealer has a demonstrator." "By the middle of October we will have a Model T Coupe listing at $950. November 1 for the Town Car at $1000. Landaulet at $950."
The top for the Model T Touring is listed at $80 extra.
The last page has an illustration of the Model T Touring, printed in red.

SEP 28 (Ford Archives)
Model T engine number 1 built. (Car shipped October 1.)

OCT 1 *Ford Times*
Coverage of the Model T features. Notes that the Model T engine block sells at $30, the same price as one dual-cylinder casting of the Model N-R-S engine. Article features the new engine. Price of the Touring is $850, without top, windshield and gas lamps.

OCT 15 *Ford Times*
Continuing coverage of the Model T (chassis features). "It's a veritable Pullman for easy riding." A 1357 mile trip is described in which 67 gallons of gas and 11-1/2 gallons of oil were used. "20 mpg gas and 85 mpg oil" noted but figures given indicate 118 mpg oil.

NOV 1 *Ford Times*
Picture of the engine crankcase showing the oil dam at the rear main bearing. Photo of the Highland Park Plant in progress, dated November 10, 1908.

DEC 15 *Ford Times*
Picture of the pressed-steel transmission cover.

DEC 19 (Ford Archives)
Three-pedal cars under production. (Model T) Numerous modifications in design were made. A factory letter indicates that after 500 cars the three-pedal modification was made. At about car number 800 all used the three-pedal system.
According to factory shipping invoices, 1909 cars could have been supplied with Prestolite tanks (in place of carbide generators). Weed chains, robe rails, foot rests, auto chimes, dragon horns, tire carriers and bumper rails were also factory options listed. Touring cars came without tops, or with several styles of tops, some lined. Tops came in gray, but most were black.

1909

JAN 1 *Ford Times*
Windshield for Tourings announced.

JAN 15 *Ford Times*
Model T Runabout pictured.

JAN 19 (Factory Letter, Ford Archives)
Design for thermo-syphon engine finalized. First 500 engines used 3/8" head bolts. 7/16" for the next 2000. (Water pump engines.)

FEB 1 *Ford Times*
Speedometers pictured. The National at $30, the Jones Model 21 at $30, and the Stewart Model 11 at $25. All have odometers that read to a maximum of 9999.9 miles.

MAR 1 *Ford Times*
Ford Roadster at $975 in Canada, $825 U.S. described. No top, windshield, headlamps or speedometer, but with oil lamps and horn.

APR 22 (Shipping invoices)
First thermo-syphon engine, number 2,448, built.

MAY 15 *Ford Times*
Thermo-syphon cooling described as used on all cars.

JUN 1 *Ford Times*
Aluminum transmission cover pictured.
An article titled "A Question of Color" describes how all cars will be Brewster Green with black trimming and a red stripe when the present stock of red Tourings and gray Roadsters have been shipped.
This article has been quoted in many sources as the "proof" that this was the beginning of the "green" era. Actually, green cars had been built much earlier; this article really indicated the discontinuance of the red and gray bodies, and the standardization of the green color on all cars.

JUL 1 *Ford Times*
Tourabout at $850 announced for August 1 delivery. The rear seat was the same shape as the front (scalloped design).

E. G. Liebold Reminisces, Vol. 10, Page 814
(Ford Archives) said:
"I don't know why they changed from red to black but I presume it was because carriages and buggies in the early days were largely black or what was known as a Brewster Green. I think that the Model T's after the red ones WERE a Brewster Green. That was so dark that it could almost be termed black."

JUL 15 (Letter of July 23, 1909, Ford Archives)
T-87B driveshaft used after car 7,000. (July 1909) (Removable pinion instead of riveted type.)

AUG 1 *Ford Times*
1910 cars announced. "Substantially the same as 1909. The Model T Ford cars as now being shipped on all orders is the 1910 car."

SEP 1 *Ford Times*
New Coupe has a larger body. No gas lamps. Announced for October delivery. A rear deck with a metal rail for Roadsters and Tourabouts is shown at $9.00. This is a flat wooden panel with a pipe-like metal railing, open at the front.

1909

OCT (Acc. 509, July 14, 1913, Ford Archives)
Babbitt bearing rear axle used on first 12,000 cars. (October)

OCT 1 *Ford Times*
Gas lamps, top, windshield and speedometer now standard equipment on the Touring, Tourabout and Runabout. Closed cars still supplied less the gas lamps. "Unequipped" open cars available on special order.

NOV 1 *Ford Times*
Coupe dimensions: door opening, 21-7/8". Front of cushion to dash, 24-3/8" Front of cushion to rear, 19". Width of seat, 39-1/2". Height, top of seat cushion to roof, 39-1/2". Floor to roof, 54".

NOV (Shipping invoices)
First listings of "Roller bearing rear axle."

1910

JAN (Factory Letter, Ford Archives)
T-213 front spindle tie rod tubing modified after 15,000. (T-213 is the tubing part of T-2717 (T-268) tie rod.)
T-1410C running boards used after 15,000. (Not listed in any parts books; this must have been the 1910 style with the interrupted rib design.)

FEB 1 *Ford Times*
Prices for bodies only: Coupe, $300. Town Car, $450. Runabout, $75. Touring, $125. Much emphasis on the interchangeability of bodies.
Ads show Coupe and price of an extra body, "Two cars for the price of one."

FEB 1 (Shipping invoices)
First listing of "reinforced housing" (rear axle).

MAR (Acc. 509, July 14, 1913, Ford Archives)
The babbitt driveshaft pinion bearing was used on the first 18,000 cars. (Until March 17, 1910.)

MAR 17
Factory invoices indicate "new magneto" for the first time, beginning with 17,985.

APR (Acc. 509, Letter dated January 13, 1913)
9/16" magnets used on the first 20,500 cars. Invoices indicate the first was 17,985, however.

APR 4 (Shipping invoices)
"New style crankcase" first listed on invoice.

JUN 1 *Ford Times*
List of stolen cars. "S/N 2080, red with black top" and "5644, green" are noted.

JUN 24 (Factory Letter)
New type front axle designed. Also noted that the fan tension spring would be discontinued for 1911. (The spring was replaced with an adjustment screw at the same location as the old spring.)

OCT --- (Shipping invoices)
"1911 rear axle" noted on many invoices. This is the 6-rivet type with the reinforced flanges at the center, NOT the 12-rivet type.

OCT 25 (Shipping invoices)
First Torpedo Runabout, an experimental sample, built on a chassis built Oct. 5, was produced. S/N 31,673.

OCT 26 (Shipping invoices)
First note of "1911 metal body." (S/N 32,200)

DEC --- (Shipping invoices)
"Seamed style radiator" noted on many invoices. Green (1910?) and blue (1911?) Tourings built during December.

1911

JAN 1 *Ford Times*
Torpedo Runabout first advertised. New 1911 Touring at $780. With three oil lamps, horn and tools only, $700.

FEB --- (Shipping invoices)
Many cars marked "1911 front axle" and "1911 transmission cover" (the square-hole cover but wider than the 1910).
The first babbitt-bearing engine blocks appeared at about 38,263.

MAR 28 (Shipping invoices)
First marked "Removable Bottom." (S/N 44,420)

APR 1 *Ford Times*
First appearance of non-Ford ads in the magazine.

APR 7 (Shipping invoices)
First noted "All 1911 motor." (S/N 46,326)

JUN 1 *Ford Times*
List of Ford colors of all models:

Model A	Runabout	Carmine	$850
	Tonneau	Carmine	950
Model B	Touring	Dark Green	2000
Model C	Runabout	Dark Green	900
	Tonneau	or Red	1000
Model F		Dark Green	1000
Model N		Maroon,	600
		Dark Green or Black	
Model R		Brewster Green	750
		or Carmine Red	
Model S	Roadster	Red or Green	750
		with Yellow gear	
	Runabout	Red	
Model K	Touring	Blue	2800
Mod.6-40	Roadster	Red	2800
Model T	All types	Brewster Green *	

* Prior to June, 1909, Model T's came in carmine Red, gray, and Brewster Green in 1909. The same green continued until late 1910 when the extremely dark blue became standard (1911 models?).

JULY (Shipping invoices)
"1912" (12-rivet type) rear axle housings began at about 61,000.

AUG --- (Shipping invoices)
Many invoices marked "No stripes on gear and fenders." Many invoices were so noted, which might indicate that such striping was common up to that time.
The spindle arm with the hole for the speedometer swivel began during August 1911.

OCT 1 (Acc. 509, Letter dated Sept. 15, 1911)
Prices to be effective this date: Touring, $690. Roadster, $590. Town Car, $900. Delivery Wagon, $700. Torpedo, $725. Open Runabout, $680. Coupe, $840.
"Coupe to be discontinued in a few weeks." Dealers were advised that cars shipped until October 1 would be billed at the old price but that they should be sold after that date at the new price. No rebate was to be given.

1911

OCT 2   (Acc. 509)
Old-style commutators no longer avail able. New front plate and a new commutator to be furnished for replacements.

OCT 6   (Acc. 509, Letter)
Motor and body numbers not to agree in the future.

OCT 12   (Acc. 509)
New 1912 Torpedo using the standard height seats was announced at $590.

OCT 13   (Acc. 509, Letter)
All Kingston coil boxes and coils recalled as being unsatisfactory. Heinze coils and boxes were used for replacement at no charge on customer's cars.

OCT 17   (Acc. 509, Letter)
"Some days ago, we wrote you that we would not permit the selecting of any particular car as a demonstrator; that you had to sell the car to the customer you demonstrated it to, as we would not permit the making of second-hand of any cars. Some question has been raised by some of the Branch managers as to the practicality of this plan, and we have written them that it is our opinion cars could be sold without any demonstration whatever; that the guarantee that went with the cars was sufficient to warrant the investment by users. If our organization for taking care of the cars; if our financial standing and reputation is not sufficient to back up an investment of $700, or more, then we are not entitled to the business, and further, a customer is not entitled to more than that.

"We have bought hundreds of thousands of dollars worth of machinery without a demonstration, and bought it simply on the guarantee and reputation of the concern selling us. We knew the concern had the ability to carry out their guarantee and their record proved that they had the disposition. We believe that we have established a reputation of ability to take care of our guarantee and we are confident that we have satisfied the public of our disposition to do so.

"Therefore, from now on we will permit no demonstrations to be made of the delivery wagon. Salesmen will have to sell them off the floor or not at all. Therefore, there will be no excuse for cars becoming second-hand, or being sold at a reduced price, or being on the streets at all. We have long had it in mind that cars could be sold without a demonstration, if the cars were sufficiently reliable and sufficiently backed up by a good guarantee. We are, therefore, going to adopt it in the case of the Delivery Wagons."

(Signed by the Secretary-Treasurer of the Ford Motor Company.)

OCT 20   (Acc. 509, Letter)
"In the writer's haste in getting out the letter of October 17 on this subject (Delivery Wagons), we stated in the last paragraph that there would be no excuse for cars being on the streets at all. We should not have said this, as we intend to grant you the privilege of taking the cars to the prospective purchaser's place of business for exhibition purposes only. We cannot expect the customers to come up to your store, so you may take the cars to their place of business for exhibition purposes, but you will not do any demonstrating or perform any service for them."

OCT 27   (Acc. 509, Letter)
1912 Torpedo announced at $590. "An improvement over the previous design as a result of complaints of low seat."

NOV 1   *Ford Times*
1912 style Touring and a new Torpedo shown. "Fore doors" in which the left side will not open are described. Town Cars now have detachable front doors.

NOV 21   (Acc. 509, Letter)
Discount allowed by Ford dealers to outside shops on parts reduced to 15% (from 20%).

DEC 6   (Acc. 509, Letter)
Discounts allowed on cars to any one customer, in any one year: 10, 2%; 20, 4%; 40, 8%; 50 or more, 10% maximum).

1912

JAN 5   (Factory Letter 261)
T-4322 Hub brake cable. Changed from 12 feet to 14 feet.
T-4335 hub brake cable clamp. Changed number required from 8 to 4.
T-4333 Hub brake cable assembly. Removed the cable clamps from one end and showed the cable to be fastened by being wound with fine brass wire (#20 B&S = .032) and soldered in place.
Apparently Ford used rear brake cables on some cars, possibly for foreign markets.

JAN 9   (Factory Letter 263)
T-520 starting crank handle. "Replaced knurling on handle with ridges and grooves. Changed material from hard rubber to aluminum and specified the handle to be black enamel."

JAN 15   (Factory Letter 265)
T-4334 Hub brake cable pulley. "Change radius at bottom of groove from 1/32 to 1/16"."

JAN 18   (Factory Letter 267)
T-4322 Hub brake cable. Changed diameter from 1/8 to 5/32.
T-4334 Hub brake cable pulley. Changed radius at bottom of groove for cable from 1/16 to 5/64.

JAN 19   (Branch letter #15 to Atlanta)
In response to requests for unpainted Delivery Cars, this letter announced the availability of this style "delivered in the lead," which is just the undercoat. Included in this letter is the following: "You understand, of course, that the chassis will all be black, including the fenders, this lead proposition applying only to the body." This seems to indicate that chassis and fenders on all cars were all black at this date because it hardly seems likely that chassis and fenders would be painted black just for the Delivery Cars.

JAN 24   (Factory Letter 268)
T-4333 Hub brake cable assembly. Changed size of cable from 1/8 to 5/32. Also changed size of cable clamps.

FEB 10   (Factory Letter 274)
T-686 Hot air pipe. "This pipe has been redesigned and material changed from cast iron to cold rolled steel."

1912

FEB 15 (Factory Letter 276)

T-520 starting crank handle. (Aluminum) "Removed ridges from outside of handle and added dimensions specifying the exact shape of same. Called for polish all over."

FEB 20 (Factory Letter 277)

T-5015 Steering gear case (for worm steering gears). New drawing.

T-904 Steering gear case specified to be used with regular steering gear.

T-983, T4128 and T5010 Worm steering gear assemblies.

It would appear that, as with the brake cables, Ford used some sort of a worm steering gear on some production. Reference to such steering parts was also found in the 1920 Factory Parts List.

MAR 8 (Factory Letter 281)

T-91-1/2 "Changed name from rear spring hanger (with wide flanges on stud end) to rear spring hanger. Changed radius for flange on stud end from 5/8 to 1/2. This makes the flanges on both ends the same diameter. Also changed the number required from 2 to 4."

T-91 Rear spring hanger (with narrow flange on stud end) Obsolete and replaced by T91-1/2.

T-246 front spring hanger replaces T229 as described above.

MAR 16 (Factory Letter 284)

T-991 "Changed name from steering worm sector to steering worm wheel. Have also specified this piece to be a complete wheel instead of only a sector, thereby allowing the wheel to be turned around from one side to the other as the teeth become worn out. This will allow one piece to be used twice as long as before."

APR 16 (Factory Letter 295)

T-240B front and rear hub cap. "Have specified the note "Made in U.S.A." to be placed on cap."

T-2530 & 2531 running boards. Specified to have the "Made in U.S.A." added.

T-400C cylinder block also to have the U.S.A. added.

MAY 9 (Factory Letter 304)

T-901B "Steering wheel rim changed from 12-3/8" i.d. to 12-1/2". This changes the outside diameter from 15" to 15-1/8"."

MAY 15 (Factory Letter 305)

T-240B hub cap. Specified that the note "Made in U.S.A." be embossed instead of stamped. "This means that all the letters on this cap will be embossed and the background oxidized."

JUN 11 (Factory Letter 314)

T-410 camshaft. "Redesigned, bringing the shape of the cams up to date with the change in T-533 (drawing of the cams); also changing the angle between the Exhaust and Inlet cams from 111 degrees to 113 25' degrees. This change to take place on the 1913 car. (To be used when present stock of camshafts is used up.)"

T-901B steering wheel. Cross section made larger, from 1-1/4 to 1-3/8". Inside diameter now 12-1/4, O.D. the same."

T-156 1/8" brass pipe plug used on cylinder head (four used). Head drilled and 1/8" drill to combustion chambers. (Drilled with 21/64" later, according to letter #319 of 7-3-12.)

JUN 13 (Factory Letter 315)

T-2852 and 2853. New (1913) rear axle housings specified for use on 1913 cars.

JUN 14 (Factory Letter 316)

T-4476 Cylinder oil tube funnel. "To be a brass casting and only to be used until the brass stamping funnels can again be obtained, after which the brass casting will be obsolete."

Note: During July many references were made to the "1913" touring car bodies.

JUN 14 (Acc. 509, Letter)

Production sold out (except for 1,000 Delivery Wagons) until September 1. No orders accepted except for Delivery Wagons.

JUL 29 (Factory Letter 329)

T-55 Hub brake shoe. "Redesigned and change number required from two to four. The new shoe will require two brake shoe springs."

AUG 10 (Factory Letter 335)

T-410 camshaft. Angle between intake and exhaust cams changed from 113 degrees 25 min. to 115 degrees 21-1/2 min.

AUG 16 (Factory Letter 337)

T-685 Breather pipe cap. " 'Made in U.S.A.' under the name 'Ford'; also specified the name 'Ford' to be embossed, and the 'Made in U.S.A.' to be stamped."

AUG 27 (Acc. 509, Letter)

Orders being accepted for all models except the Roadster.

AUG 30 (Factory Letter 342)

T-428 Exhaust and intake valve stem bushing. "New drawing. This bushing is to be used when, owing to the variation of the cylinder castings, the holes for valve stems do not come concentric with the bosses for same, in which case the bosses are machined off, and a 1/2 inch hole reamed in the casting, allowing for this special bushing to be pressed in place."

SEP 4 (Factory Letter 344)

T-528B Starting Crank Ratchet. "Redesigned changing material from drop forging to pressed steel." (This experimental ratchet was noted earlier in the Factory Letters as being made at the Buffalo plant, which was formerly the Keim company which developed the deep pressings for the crankcase, rear axles, etc.)

SEP 28 (Acc. 509, Letter)

Prices (1913 models?): Touring, $600. Torpedo, $525. Delivery Wagon, $625. Town Car, $800.

OCT 1 (Factory Letter 352)

T-1414-B and 1413-B Front Fenders. Notes the change in the front flange (bill) from the 1912 pattern to the new 1913 pattern (no bill). Further comments that if one fender is replaced on an older car, both fenders would be needed to have a "matched set." Other minor modifications were made in the overall design to better facilitate installation on the 1913 cars.

1912

OCT 5   (Acc. 509, Letter)
"The only equipment permitted to be attached to any Ford cars is a robe rail, a clock, and a tool box on the running board. No exhaust cut-outs, trunk racks, bumpers, batteries or other items mentioned in previous letters should be recommended or permitted to be put on Ford cars either by our branches or by our dealers; and, as previously noted, our guarantee will become void if devices of this sort are attached."

OCT 11   (Factory Letter 355)
T-603. "Changed name from Fan Pulley Driven to Fan. We have made this change in name because the pulley has been re-designed, specifying the fan blades and pulley to be cast in one piece. Change material from bronze to aluminum. We call your attention to the fact that when this drawing was first issued as experimental, the ends of the blades were 2" wide. They have been changed to 2-1/2" wide."
T-1546 Transmission Cover Door. "Redesigned this piece making it a simple flat piece of sheet steel."

OCT 18   (Factory Letter 357)
T-1215. Muffler Asbestos. "Added note specifying this asbestos to be dyed black. Note: If possible we would like to have the muffler asbestos which we have on hand colored black in some way, also that the muffler straps be black enameled."

OCT 28   (Acc. 509, Letter)
Torpedo Runabouts sold out. None to be available until January 1, 1913.

NOV 1   *Ford Times*
1913 Models illustrated.

NOV 5   (Letter, Ford to Chicago branch, Acc. 509)
"Whenever you have the occasion to furnish rear axle housings in pairs, be sure to send out the 1913 design. You are also privileged to replace old housings with the new ones at half the catalog price whenever such an exchange is desired by the customer.
"We will furnish 1913 fenders for both 1912 and 1913 cars and will discontinue altogether any further 1912 type fenders. Where customers object to the absence of visor on the forward end of the front fenders, instruct them to trim off the opposite 1912 fender to correspond."

NOV 6   (Letter, Ford to the Buffalo branch.)
"Under separate cover we are mailing you a small quantity of prints of the new Ford Touring Car for 1913. You will notice that these prints are exceptionally clear ones, and we believe they can be used to good advantage by your salesmen."
Which would seem to indicate they made "1913" cars long before they were actually delivered.

NOV 6   (Acc. 509, Letter)
Kingston Master Vibrator coils discontinued. Replaced with 4-coil Heinze or Kingston boxes at $10 exchange. About 10% of 1913 cars to use K-W coils. (Apparently Ford installed master vibrator coils at the factory or branches.)

NOV 11   (Acc. 509)
Steering rods and balls 2725, 2725B, 2726, 2726B, 2727, 2727B discontinued. Brazed units only available from here on.

DEC 1   *Ford Times*
1913 Runabout shown.

DEC 3   (Acc. 509, Letter)
Delivery Wagons sold out and discontinued.

DEC 3   (Factory Letter 374)
T-902-B Steering Gear Spider. "Changed material from brass to malleable iron, changed note specifying spider to be black enameled instead of polished." (Refers to blueprint; the change probably was made earlier.)

DEC 5   (Acc. 509, Letter)
Model N camshafts recalled because of a possibility of the dowel pin hole being drilled incorrectly.

DEC 13   (Factory Letter 382)
T-512-B Inlet Pipe. "Changed material from pressed aluminum to cast iron."

DEC 19   (Factory Letter 384)
T-619 Fan Assembly. Pressed blades, riveted to pulley, style reinstated. Notes that blades will be made of heavier material than earlier. Drawing to show pressed steel blades riveted to bronze pulley.

DEC 27   (Factory Letter 387)
T-4446 Commutator Head. "Changed material from 'W' brass casting to aluminum, and specified this piece to be a die casting."

DEC 31   (Factory Letter)
26,139 cars produced from October 1, 1912 to this date. (Fiscal 1913 production.)

1913

JAN 3   (Factory Letter 389)
T-518-B Exhaust Pack Nut, T-511-B Exhaust Pipe, etc. specified. This new design replaces the old style where the pipe fit into the manifold. The pipe now has a flange, typical of all later Model T's.

JAN 24   (Factory Letter 394)
T-518-B Exhaust Pack Nut. "This design never used. We have therefore marked drawing obsolete under date 1-20-13." T-518 (old number) revised to conform to new pipe design.
T-5403 Touring Car Body. "Called for reinforcing sills to be fastened to the top of the regular body sills by #14 x 2" F.H.W.S. (4 screws for each sill) the reinforcing sill to reach from the rear of the front heel board to the front of rear heel board, the sill to the 1" thick, and the sides in line with those on the regular body sill. This means of course that the rear sill plates will have to be put on top of the reinforcing sill. We have called for a filler between the reinforcing sill and the inside of circular panel at the rear edge of rear door, the filler to be nailed and glued in place." Note continues regarding the use of more nails to hold the body metal in place.

JAN 28   (Factory Letter 395)
T-5637 Body Reinforcing Bracket (to Frame) Bolt. "Four required, Touring Car, 1913."
T-5453 Body Reinforcing Bracket. New Drawing. "Two required, Touring Car, 1913."
T-5638. Sketch showing location of Body Reinforcing Bracket. "We have made this sketch for the purpose of showing customers who are having trouble with the touring car bodies how the trouble can be overcome. The material has been ordered and we will be able to supply same in the near future. For your information will state that the construction of the body has been improved upon and undoubtedly will not need this reinforcement as soon at the change

1913

can be brought about. We will therefore order only enough material of the above parts as shown on sketch to take care of the bodies which have already been built."

FEB 4   (Acc. 509, Letter)
Runabouts supplied with turtle deck only. "No rumble seats."

FEB 8   (Factory Letter 398)
T-4332 Hub Brake Cable. "We have changed the diameter from 1/4" to 15/64"." Had also changed the size of the wires and the number of wires that made up this cable.

FEB 12   (Letter from Ford to the Chicago branch)
"We have decided to place an extra body bracket just beneath the tonneau door hinge of the Touring Car body, extending from the frame of the body sill as you will observe from blue print enclosed. We have entered order to send you one hundred pair of these brackets and we want you to put them on every car now in stock. It is also our object to supply larger dealers with a quantity of these brackets so that they can install them before the cars are put out on the road next spring. The purpose of this bracket is to stiffen the body sill and prevent too much play in the door when the top is down, also binding in the door when the top straps are drawn up too tightly."

Installation instructions followed with hints on how to add or subtract shim washers in order to align the doors.

MAR 4   (Letter, Ford to the Cincinnati branch)
"In attaching the Touring Car body reinforcing brackets, be sure they are fitted 1/8" to 3/16" from the top of the frame so that when the bolts are put in it will pull the sill down. Unless the sill is sprung down 1/8" or so when the bracket is attached but little benefit will be derived by the reinforcement. All bodies coming through from now on will be fitted with heavier sills so that attachment of extra brackets will be unnecessary."

MAR 5   (Factory Letter 404)
General description of revised muffler, now using tubes which are spot welded together at the seams rather than being riveted as previously. Initially the shells (tubes) would be made to conform to the size of the cast end pieces until the supply of old stock was used up. The old diameter was 5" while the new one was 5-1/4".

MAR 15   (Factory Letter 406)
New frame with longer rear cross-member was described. Old parts to be used for replacement only. Notes that this frame will be used on a number of cars initially but the number was unknown at the time.

MAR 29   (Factory Letter 410)
1914 coil unit noted. No details as to what it was.

APR 5   (Factory Letter 411)
T-5464 Front Fender Peak. "This peak to be added for fitting up the front fenders which we are now using so that they may be used on 1911 and 1912 cars. This peak nearly makes the appearance of the fenders conform to the appearance of the fenders on the 1911 and 1912 cars. If however a customer should call for a set of front fenders to be used for repairs, it would not be necessary to add this peak." This peak was to be riveted in place, using just one rivet.

APR 12   (Factory Letter 413)
Coil box parts (T-5807 through T-5857) listed but no details. This may have been the Ford-made standard coil box. Previously the coil box assemblies were purchased outside.

APR 16   (Factory Letter 415)
T-4099 Sediment Bulb assembly. Parts listed for new pressed-steel sediment bulb which was to be used in production and for repairs. Old brass bulb obsoleted. In letter #419, May 3, the assembly was given part number T-5859.

APR 27   (Acc. 509, Letter)
Windshields manufactured by Rands, Vanguard and Diamond Mfg. Co.

MAY ----   (Acc. 575, Box 19)
Note indicates the longer rear cross-member "after 114,000 1913 cars."
Other records indicate 1913 production began with 157,425 on October 1, 1912, which would make the new cross-member at or about 271,425. (May 16, 1913.)

MAY 1   (Acc. 509, Letter)
Change in valve timing, apparently made in late 1912 or early 1913, is noted in a letter to the branches.)

MAY 29   (Factory Letter 423)
Some 1914 Touring body parts listed.

MAY 29   (Factory Letter 424)
T-5668 and 5669 body reinforcement for 1913 Touring body with 2-1/4" sills. T-5676 and 5677 reinforcements for bodies with 3-1/4" sills.

JUN 4   (Acc. 509)
"218,900 to 242,300 built between April 1 and 30; 242,300 to 260,000 between May 1 and 31."

JUN 6   (Factory Letter 425)
Location of body reinforcement bolt holes changed.

JUN 12   (Letter from Ford to all branches)
"In order that all our branches may clearly understand the handling of complaints on present touring car bodies we submit the following:
"It is expected that you will furnish all Dealers with body sill reinforcements, wood reinforcements for the rear seat frame and also rear corner brackets as shown in the attached blue print. To make a satisfactory and permanent repair all of this material should be put in. We have found that the sills break most frequently within a few inches of the rear end and in such cases the rear corner brackets will serve to bind the sills together. The wood reinforcements in the rear seat will relieve the rear ends of the sills from all strain, consequently there is no necessity of replacing the sills on account of the wood splitting at the end. In applying the steel stamping underneath the tonneau door you will find it necessary to chisel out the wood at the lower rear corner on all Beaudette bodies and perhaps shim up other makes of bodies where the bracket spreads out at the rear.
"As this body trouble is going to be more or less general perhaps you had better employ one or two good body men to do this work. We believe this will be better that to leave the work to the ordinary shop mechanics to handle. As the season advances you will probably have a great deal of this work to do and you might as well prepare for it now."

1913

JUN 14   (Factory Letter 426)

T-1314 Hood handle. "Redesigned, and change material from pressed steel to aluminum casting."

Body brackets (5668, 5669, 5676 and 5677) revised again. Now have two bolt holes at the front end, instead of three. Also specified 5/16 x 2-1/8" carriage bolts to be used instead of 5/16 x 1-1/2 lag screws be used. (Step bolts were specified instead of carriage bolts in later notes regarding these brackets.)

JUN 28   (Factory Letter 430)

Noted changes in the transmission cover door material (not in the design). Stated that the cover door is to be "pickled and annealed." No mention of paint. The finish had been mentioned in previous letters, and was the same as in this letter.

JUL 1   (Factory Letter 431)

Many notes on 1914 Touring body which would seem to indicate that this body was now used in production.

JUL 5   (Acc. 509, Letter)

260,000 to 282,700 built June 1 to 30.

JUL 10   (Factory Letter 433)

T-4099 Pressed-steel sediment bulb and its components apparently never used. Brass bulb and parts were again specified for production, as apparently they had always been. Noted that gasoline tanks which had been built to accommodate the pressed-steel bulb could be repunched and by using a larger reinforcement (T-4097) to cover the holes these tanks could be used with the brass bulb.

JUL 14   (Factory Letter 434)

Noted that 1913 Touring bodies were made by Herbert, Fisher, Wilson, and Beaudette. Apparently the Beaudette bodies differed in construction from the others. Beaudette bodies with a filler block on the rear door hinge posts apparently did not need the steel reinforcing pieces.

JUL 14   (Acc. 509, Letter)

1913 cars used new style exhaust manifold and pipe. (Pipe now has the flanged end.)
"Babbitt driveshaft bearing used in first 18,000 cars."

JUL 16   (Acc. 575)

"Engine 300,000 built at 1:25 P.M." (Engine production records indicate this was built on June 26, 1913.)

JUL 28   (Acc. 509, Letter)

"1914" prices effective August 1, 1913: Touring, $550. Runabout, $500. Town Car, $750

       (Acc. 833, Photo 75)

1914-type Touring body with 1913 windshield and wheels which are striped. (No body striping.)

JUL 30   (Factory Letter 439)

New design of turtle deck on Torpedos (Runabouts) noted for 1914 models. This was probably the change from the "square" corners to the rounded ones.

Also a note under Gas Lamp brackets noted, "and since we are contemplating the use of electric headlamps, we would not use more of these brackets ...."

AUG 4   (Factory Letter 440)

T-528-B Starting Crank Ratchet. "We have redesigned the shape of the notches, and to show the new design we have added special sketch giving the development of the outside surface of notches when bent in place. We ask that you kindly call the attention of the people who are to make these ratchets to the fact that this sketch does not show the correct shape of these notches when in the blank before being drawn, which shape will have to be determined by cutting and trying....."

The note continues but seems to indicate that the pressed steel ratchet was still being used.

AUG 5   (Acc. 509, Letter)

282,700 to 298,200 built July 1 to 31.

AUG 29   (Factory Letter 446)

T-1215 Muffler asbestos. "Removed note specifying this asbestos to be dyed black."

SEP 4   (Acc. 509, Letter)

298,200 to 306,800 built August 1 to 30.

SEP 27   (Factory Letter 450)

T-55 Brake Shoe revised to be made in one piece again.

OCT 18   (Factory Letter 455)

T-800-D Crankcase. Noted changes made earlier in which the separate drain cup had been replaced by just stamping the crankcase instead. (The "drain cup" refers to the "teacup" pan used until sometime in 1913.)

NOV 4   (Acc. 509, Letter to all branches)

306,800 to 314,800 built September 1 to 30. Announced that speedometers will no longer be supplied on cars for a few months, and that a credit of $6 will be allowed on the price of the car. They said that as soon as a satisfactory replacement unit was found, they would supply it at the $6 price for installation on customer's cars. Furthermore, the branches would not be allowed to buy speedometers for customers.

NOV 18   (Acc. 509, Letter)

60" tread to be discontinued. (But wasn't.)

NOV 24   (Letter from Ford to the Denver branch)

"Kindly give us by return mail your present inventory of the following:
T-5668 reinforcement, right
T-5669 reinforcement, left
T-5675 rear seat frame reinforcement
T-5678 rear corner bracket."
These are the 1913 touring body reinforcement parts.

FACTORY LETTER TO BRANCHES

FROM: Ford Motor Company, Detroit Office

December 2, 1913

The following is a revised list of paints and our new numbers for same, kindly order all paints by these numbers:

F-101	1763	First Coat Plastic Black Japan, Fenders and shields
F-102	1001	Second Coat Black Japan, Fenders and shields
F-103	258	First Coat Blue Dipping, Hoods & Rear Axles
F-104	1355	Second Coat Quick Drying Black, Rear Axles
F-105	40	First Coat Brushing Black Japan, Front Axles

Documentation

1913

F-106	459	Second Coat Brushing Black Japan, Front Axles
F-107	450	Blue Black Baking, Coil Box
F-108	1843	First Coat Black Wheel Surfacer, Wheels
F-109	260	Second Coat Blue Color Varnish, Wheels
F-110	417	Second Coat Black Brushing, Frame
F-111	488	First Coat Red Baking Metal Body Primer, Body
F-112	66	Black Glaze Putty ---- Second Operation Body, Body
F-113	948	Second Coat Blue Ground, Body
F-114	619	Solid Rubbing Body Blue, Repairs only
F-115	480	3rd & 4th Coat Body Spraying Blue Color Varnish, Body
F-116	908	5th Coat Black Striping Color, Not used regularly
F-117	1435	Fine French Gray Deep Striping, Wheels
F-118	1761	Oil Proof Steel Blue, Painting Machines
F-119	896	Black Engine Dipping, Finishing Crank Cases
F-120		White Cold Water Paint
F-121		Ivory Drop Black "E"
F-122		Black Radiator Paste

This list supersedes all previous ones that we have mailed you.

Ford Motor Company
Manufacturing Department

DEC 9 (Factory Letter 462)
Noted that the 1/2" pipe plugs used for water jacket seals were no longer used.

DEC 27 (Factory Letter 463)
T-543-B Oil Tube. Now specified as having mounting ear integral with the funnel instead of the separate clamp. The clamps would continue to be made until the supply of old tubes was used up.

1914

JAN 1 *Ford Times*
1914 cars first illustrated (but had appeared earlier).
By January of 1914 Ford was using the one-piece driveshaft. A number of modifications had been made to the rear axle in an effort to cut costs. Most of the bronze bushings had been eliminated. The outer housings continued in the style set in 1912 (12-rivet type).

MAR 18 (Archives)
New commutator shield used beginning with 477,165, this date.

APR 21 (Archives)
Engine 500,000 built at 10 A.M.

AUG 1 (Acc. 509, Letter)
Prices: Touring, $490. Runabout, $440. Town Car, $690. Prices do not include a possible $40 to $60 rebate pending on the sale of 300,000 cars by August 1, 1915. Rebate to be made to the original purchasers of the cars only.

AUG 26 (Archives)
"Start one hole in center main bearing."

SEP 4 (Engine production records)
"New style coils" began with 572,437.

SEP 14 (Engine production records)
"Start 3/4" magnets with 578,042."

SEP 23 (Acc. 509, Letter)
Sedan and Coupelet announced.

(Acc. 833, Photo 1527)
1915 Coupelet. Shows fork-mounted electric headlamps.

(Acc. 833, Photo 1528)
Same Coupelet, rear view, shows 1914 rear axle.

(Acc. 833, Photo 1621)
1915 Sedan. Fork-mounted headlamps and lantern-like side lamp. Curved front and rear fenders.

(Acc. 833, Photo 1546)
1915 Sedan with gas headlamps.

(Acc. 833, Photo 1470)
1915 style Touring with odd post-mounted electric headlamps, no louvers in the hood, brass steering wheel spider and 1914-type steering gear box.

(Acc. 833, Photo 1633)
1915 Touring, now with louvered hood.

OCT 12 (Archives)
All motors used new coils and 3/4" magnets. The new magneto began with #578,042. (Engine production records show 572,437, September 4, which is believed to be the correct number.)

NOV 2 (Acc. 509, Letter)
Prices of Sedan, $565. Coupelet, $340.

DEC 19 (Acc. 509, Letter)
Longer intake manifold announced for Sedans.

DEC 24 (Acc. 509, Letter)
Longer intake manifold announced December 19 to be discontinued in favor of the use of the Kingston carburetor which has better fuel flow (sedans only).

DEC 31 (Factory Letter)
"All sedans equipped with Kingston carburetors because of better fuel flow. 5/16" pipe recommended." The longer intake manifolds were furnished as a field modification.

1915

JAN 7 (Acc. 509, Letter)
Longer intake manifold now standard on sedans.

JAN 12 (Factory Letter)
Gas lamp tube no longer supplied on radiators as all cars now have electric lights. A tube, P/N T-4052X, was supplied for use on the earlier cars when the radiator was replaced.

JAN 23 (Acc. 575, Box 19)
Will use 10,000 electric horns. If satisfactory, these horns will be used to replace bulb horns in manufacturing. A note to reduce the stock of bulb horns.

JAN 25 (Acc. 509, Letter)
"New" Runabouts announced for delivery in a week to ten days.

JAN 30 (Acc. 575, Box 19)
T-7915 horn wire. T-7916 horn switch wire. T-7917 horn switch wire. T-5018 electric horn mounting bolt. All for use in the 10,000 cars referred to in the letter of January 23. (According to another letter dated April 17, 1915, the bulb horns were still being used on some production at that date.)

1915

FEB 6   (Acc. 509, Letter)
New-style Touring and Runabout bodies shipped to branches for use as models, not for use in production.

FEB 8   (Factory Letter)
Branches asked to submit a list of inventory for 1914 parts left over after the change to the 1915-style cars.

FEB 10   (Acc. 509, Letter)
New type (1915 style) Runabouts and Tourings now being shipped from the Highland Park plant.

FEB 13   (Acc. 509, Letter)
Ford advertising halted. Production listed as 40-50,000 behind schedule.

FEB 15   (Factory Letter)
Repeat of letter of Feb. 13. Ford unable to produce enough cars to fill orders, so why advertise. Noted that there were plenty of closed cars still available, however.

FEB 20   (Letter to Houston branch)
Letter concerning poor sales of closed cars; notes lack of salesmanship.

FEB 26   (Letter to Branches)
Carloads of new Tourings and Runabouts to be shipped to the branches and used as samples.

MAR 24   (Acc. 509, Letter)
Letter concerning leaks between the dash and the cowl. Noted that no felt or rubber was being used at the factory but that dealers should install same if customers complained about leaks at this point.

MAR 24   (Acc. 509, Letter)
Letter requesting opinions as to the desirability of discontinuing the left rear door on the Touring.

MAR 31   (Acc. 509, Letter)
Flanged oil rings with felt packing supplied for oil side and tail lamps to prevent their being blown out. The problem was noted in a letter of March 27, at which time the factory noted that they were shipping felts only for in-the-field modifications.

APR 1   *Ford Times*
First pictures of the new 1915 Touring and Roadster.

APR 3   (Acc. 509, Letter)
"300,000 sales assured except for a 'calamity or catastrophe'."

APR 7   (Acc. 509, Letter)
"New (1915) style rear axle housings in short supply. Use 1914 type for repairs."

APR 13   (Acc. 509, Letter)
Early E&J T-6511X electric headlamps with 8-5/8" lenses discontinued as a replacement part. From this date on, the standard lamps would be supplied as replacements. Note: This is believed to be the lamp which mounted on the gas lamp forks. T-6511X was the number for all the magneto-powered lamps until 1917.

APR 29   (Factory Letter)
"On or after May 1, the use of body numbers will be discontinued (by Ford) and no records will be kept of same."

MAY 11   (Acc. 575, Box 19)
T-604. Lug on fan support arm finally eliminated. Note to change the drawing. (This may have occurred earlier.)

JUN 17   (Factory Letter and engine production records)
Welch plug used in tail shaft of the transmission brake drum to prevent oil leaks out through the universal joint.

JUN 19   (Acc. 575, Box 19)
Headlight door. Change from brass to black steel specified.

JUN 26   (Factory Letter)
"Hereafter when ordering body panels for 1915 cars, please give both the car and body numbers. The body number will be found on the right sill just inside the front door. This number will be preceded by a letter which indicates by whom the body was made.
"The above information is necessary as panels for bodies made by our various suppliers vary somewhat."

JUL 17   (Acc. 575, Box 19)
List of chassis parts. Shows change to long rear cross-member was made after 114,000 1913 cars (May 1913).

OCT 7   (Acc. 833, Photo 4847)
Picture of 1916 style Coupelet (port holes) with brass-trimmed lamps.

OCT 16   (Acc. 575, Box 19)
Electric horns specified for all 1916 cars. Notes that 10,000 electric horns were used in 1915 but the wording is such that there may have been more.

NOV 6   (Acc. 575, Box 19)
New gasoline tank specified for 1916 sedans (now under the driver's seat).

NOV 15   (Acc. 78, Box 1, Letter)
All steering assemblies being shipped with horn button and wiring.

NOV 30   (Acc. 575, Box 19)
New rear brake backing plates (with reinforcing ribs) specified.
T-6432 electric horn, made by K-W and others, specified.

DEC 10   (Engine production records)
Engine number 1,000,000 assembled at 1:53-1/2 P.M.

1916

JAN 1   (Acc. 78, Box 1, #91)
30 x 3-1/2 non-skid tires to be supplied by U.S. Tire Co. Branches instructed to use up smooth tires first.

FEB 9   (Acc. 78, Box 1, #100)
Firestone tires being supplied to branches. 30 x 3 at $10.35; 30 x 3-1/2 at $13.10; less 20% discount.

MAR 27   (Acc. 575)
Use of cotter pins on crankcase discontinued. (They were apparently reinstated at a later date because they were used on later cars.)

NOV 28   (Acc. 78)
Decision to discontinue asbestos muffler wrap was announced. Mufflers to be painted with F-140 paint.

1917

---- (Acc. 575, Box 14, #826)
Riveted style windshield frame and brackets were used in 1915 and 1916 and on the first 450,000 1917 cars. (Until about April 1917.)

MAR 1 (Acc. 78)
"New springs (front), hangers and perches, and rear spring hangers eliminate T-218 oilers and require T-2944 oiler." (Oilers now on the perches and springs instead of on hangers.)

MAR 14 (Acc. 78)
Mention of new style windshield mounting brackets as having been used, and of the discontinuance of the 1915-16 style for replacement.

MAR 22 (Acc. 78. Letter to all branches)
"As we expect to paint all bodies black by April 15th, we ask that you kindly give us an inventory of all the F-113 (blue body paint) you now have on hand, and that you do not requisition any more of this material beyond your needs to April 15th."

MAR 28 (Acc. 78, Box 1)
New style perches, hangers, etc. now being supplied to the branches. Warns of non-interchangeability of the new parts.

APR 2 (Acc. 78)
Tire prices increased to $12.75 for the 30 x 3; $16.25 for the 30 x 3-1/2, less 20% discount to branches.

APR 15 (Acc. 78)
April 17 to be the last issue of the *Ford Times*.

APR 19 (Acc. 78)
Windshield hinge (with the unequal length arms) noted.

APR 19 (Acc. 78)
Brass hub caps no longer available.

APR 24 (Acc. 78)
One-bolt muffler now in regular production.

APR 28 (Acc. 78)
"Ford" being cast into many parts to stop bogus parts being sold as genuine.

MAY 10 (Acc. 575, Box 11)
T-751 triple gear changed to one-piece design. A number of modifications were made until November 25, 1918.

JUN 14 (Archives)
Engine number 2,000,000 built at 1:02 P.M.

JUL 27 (Acc. 78)
Model TT (truck) announced at $600 F.O.B., less 15%.

AUG 9 (Acc. 78)
"About August 15, touring bodies will be supplied with rear seat tool box and frame will be made of wood."

AUG 21 (Acc. 78)
Prices: Touring, $360. Runabout, $345. Town Car, $595. Coupelet, $505. Sedan, $645. Chassis, $325. Truck, $600.

AUG 25 (Acc. 78)
New splash aprons (T-7986, 7987) eliminating clearance stamping at rear. "Perfectly plain from front to rear." Steering column shafts milled for one key instead of two at the steering wheel.

SEP 10 (Acc. 78)
Coupelet bodies to have gas tank in rear deck. New design of Touring top sockets and bows.

OCT 1 (Acc. 78)
Transmission cover with blank clutch hole (not drilled through the right side) in production. A new clutch shaft was required with this change.

OCT 6 (Acc. 78)
Prices: Touring, $360. Runabout, $345. Town Car, $645. Sedan, $695. Coupelet, $560. Chassis, $325. Truck, $600.

OCT 30 (Acc. 78)
"Profit sharing" minimum wage reduced to 18 years (from 21).

NOV 1 (Acc. 78)
7-leaf front springs to replace former 6-leaf as stock is used up.

DEC 20 (Acc. 78)
Truck rear frame cross-members were recalled and replaced with stronger design which was identified with an "X".

1918

SEP 21 (Archives)
"Last metric engines produced." (Not true, for metric engines continued at least until 1920, at which time they were no longer noted on the production records ---- but may have still been built.)

DEC 9 (Acc. 575, Box 11)
T-7944 gas tank bottom on sedans (1916-1919) changed.

DEC 11 (Archives)
First starter-type engine made, #2,815,891.

DEC 18 (Acc. 575, Box 11)
T-8731 hood clips. Cotter pin hole enlarged from 9/64" to 5/32".

DEC 21 (Acc. 78)
Announcement of starters for closed cars on or about January 15, 1919, at $75.

DEC 21 (Acc. 575, Box 11)
T-690C. Reinforcing boss added for fan adjusting screw. (This is the timing gear cover plate, T-3009B. The T-690C plate is shown in the Parts Lists as the starter-type cover.)

DEC 24 (Acc. 575, Box 11)
"We have specified the following parts to be used for repairs only: T-7914, T-7923, T-1473, T-7260." (Side lamp brackets, bolts, etc.)

DEC 24 (Acc. 575, Box 11, #718)
Bendix cover flange, T-1767; cap, T-1762; and shell, T-1766, replaced the one-piece design. The assembly part number was T-1763. (The one-piece design was reinstated April 17, 1919, (Acc. 575, Box 11, #727).)

DEC 27 (Acc. 575, Box 11)
Groove added to flywheel pocket for crankshaft flange, and inside edge of magnet shoulder to assure clean corners. (Part T-701B.)

1918

DEC 27 (Acc. 575, Box 11, #718)
T-7426 carburetor adjusting rod fork flattened on one end and punched 5/64" for cotter pin. Hole enlarged to 3/32" February 17, 1919.

DEC 31 (Acc. 575, Box 11, #720)
T-431 valve springs to be zinc plated instead of painted black.

1919

JAN (Acc. 575, Box 11)
T-8793 starter switch plunger for coupe only.
T-8794 starter switch plunger for sedan.

JAN 1 (Acc. 575, #331)
Experimental Holley vapor manifold noted. 25 were purchased for trials.

JAN 4 (Acc. 575, Box 11)
T-4481A timer with roller. T-4481B timer with brush instead of roller (new design).

JAN 7 (Acc. 575, Box 11, #720)
Water outlet hose made 4" long (from 3-1/2") for a better joint. (P/N T-448.)

JAN 13 (Acc. 575, Box 11, #723)
T-5418A & B running boards for coupe and sedan (L & R). T-7987A & B splash shields for same.

JAN 15 (Acc. 575, Box 11, #720)
T-4483 exhaust manifold. Flange added at bottom to hold glands in place during assembly.

JAN 18 (Acc. 575, Box 11)
T-555 float chamber gasket, new, and used on all cars.
T-7660 instrument panel for 1919 coupe.
T-7661 instrument panel for 1919 sedan.
T-7610 right rear axle housing. Oil hole relocated to a point 1-3/4" below the centerline.

JAN 25 (Acc. 575, Box 11, #719)
Bendix cover zinc plated. T-7994 rear fender bracket (to running board) made from scrap of clutch disks instead of 20 ga. steel.

JAN 31 (Acc. 575, Box 11, #720)
T-8793 and T-8794 starter switch plungers obsoleted.

FEB --- (Acc. 575, Box 11, #721)
Choke bell crank arm "raven finished." New spindle arm (T-270B) after the first 56,000 1919 cars. T-270A obsoleted, to be replaced with the new arm.
T-8795 priming rod (long) for sedans; T-8796 rod for coupes.

FEB 5 (Acc. 575, Box 11, #719)
"We have specified the following parts to be used on all models of 1919 cars, including trucks, and changed the symbol numbers as listed below:
T-350 dust cap (was TT-202)
T-351 bearing, R/H (was TT-250)
T-352 bearing, L/H (was TT-251)
T-354 felt retainer (was TT-201)
T-355 spindle cone (was TT-205)
T-356 inner bearing (was TT-252)
T-357 inner bearing cup (was TT-235)
T-358 outer bearing cup (was TT-234)
T-359 cone, right (was TT-207)
T-360 cone, left (was TT-206)"
These are the roller bearing front wheel parts, first used on the truck chassis. According to the Parts Lists, the ball bearings were still used on the open cars without demountables and starters, but this note says "all models."

FEB 10 (Acc. 575, Box 11, #723)
"Ford Motor Company" specified on ammeter face.

FEB 12 (Acc. 575, Box 11, #725)
T-7675A ignition switch on first 200 cars.
T-7675B ignition switch on next 2000 cars.
T-7675C ignition switch on next 3000 cars.
T-7675D ignition switch after first 5200 cars.

FEB 17 (Acc. 575, Box 11, #724)
Choke bell crank made from crankcase scrap.

FORD FACTORY LETTER
FROM: Ford Motor Company, Detroit Office
February 20, 1919
General Letter No. 347
Kindly note general information and changes to date:

CLOSED BODY PAINTING
As closed bodies are now being painted black, instead of green as heretofore, also carmine striped, it becomes imperative that the branches prepare to repair bodies when needed according to the new color. It is necessary that someone in your paint shop, accustomed to the method of striping, be assigned to this work, as this section of body painting is something new for branches to contend with. Striping pencils and carmine paint for striping will be furnished to you for this purpose upon receipt of request for same.

NEW PAINT SPECIFICATIONS
These are being sent you at this time and comprise the change in sedan, coupe, touring car and torpedo body painting, according to the latest information. You will note the change in the Symbol number of paint used in painting closed bodies, as well as that for touring car and torpedo bodies, and wheel paint, as called to your attention in our general letters of the 11th and 12th. F-165 and F-166 will be held for repairs only on closed bodies which were formerly painted green.

CHANGES IN BRUSH LIST
Attached is the new brush list comprising changes to date of February 20th. Have added the number required per thousand cars, and it is decided that branches should order material on this basis. No material should be ordered locally as the main plant can supply your needs at any time.

INSTRUMENT BOARD
One length of board is being furnished for sedans, both Wadsworth and Fisher made, and as the Wadsworth body is somewhat wider between pillars at instrument board section than the Fisher body, it becomes necessary for various reasons that one length be furnished for both jobs and when branch receives same it will be in order to cut off ends of the board to fit Fisher body if Fisher bodies are being received. After cutting the boards to size, see that the imitation leather is again placed over ends of boards in a workmanlike manner. Instruments will be shipped to branch from main plant with instrument boards until the body manufacturers can bring the instrument boards through to fit their respective bodies, after which they will ship bodies with the instruments and wiring fastened thereto so that same can be fastened to dash assembly in accordance with diagrams which you have at this time. Coupe bodies are now going forward with the instrument board in position.

F-196 CARMINE STRIPING PAINT
This material is intended for striping closed bodies when making repairs and can be ordered from main plant upon requisition.

Documentation

1919

FEB 21 (Acc. 575, Box 11, #720, 723)
Following parts are zinc plated: T8793 starter switch plunger.
T-1311 hood clip spring. TT-67 hub brake shoe spring (truck).
T-8734 hood clip sprint. T-841B transmission band spring.
T-935 throttle lever rod spring. T-292 spring (misc. uses).

FEB 21 (Acc. 575, Box 11, #724)
T-701C starter-type flywheel used on all cars.

FEB 26 (Acc. 575, Box 11, #724)
T-8778 spare-tire carrier, sedan and coupe only.

MAR 3 (Acc. 575, Box 1, #357)
Demountable rims not painted, nor are the bolts. Finished in a galvanized (zinc, or ternplate) coating.

MAR 4 (Acc. 575, Box 11, #726)
"Ford" added to the transmission covers. Instrument panel "leather covered" on early production (closed cars). "Ford" script added to many parts in an effort to stop accessory manufacturers from selling bogus parts as genuine Ford.

MAR 15 (Acc. 575, Box 11, #726)
Starter-type transmission cover used on all cars.

MAR 19 (Acc. 575, Box 11, #726)
Hub caps. Steel type discontinued. All to be brass (nickel-plated) in the future.

MAR 21 (Acc. 575, Box 11, #726)
T-1773 timing gear cover plate, T-1761 transmission cover plate, made from two pieces from center of clutch plate stock spot welded together. T-1758 transmission cover front plate made from two pieces 20 ga. fender stock, spot welded together. (These are the cover plates used to blank the holes when there is no starter or generator.)

MAR 25 (Acc. 575, Box 1, #367)
"Sufficient demountables for all closed cars to have them. Price increased $25."

MAR 28 (Acc. 575, Box 11, #726)
T-4491 starter crank pin changed to a rivet rather than the pin which had been riveted in place. (The riveting process caused oil leaks.)

APR 2 (Engine production records)
Engine 3,000,000 built 8:15 A.M.

APR 10 (Acc. 575, Box 11, #727)
T-8837 spare tire carrier redesigned.

APR 14 (Acc. 78, #385)
New radius rod used at first on the TT chassis. Roller bearings at first on the TT and on the closed cars.

APR 17 (Acc. 575, Box 11, #727)
One-piece Bendix cover reinstated, replacing the three-piece assembly of December 24, 1918.

APR 18 (Acc. 575, Box 11, #729)
T-400D (starter type) cylinder specified for all cars.

APR 30 (Acc. 575, Box 11, #732)
T-6604 wood instrument panel for touring and torpedo specified in a letter to the branches.
T-7845, 7846 windshield bracket with integral side lamp bracket used on open cars without starter only.

T-7845B and T-7846B bracket used with starter cars (has no oil lamp bracket).

APR 30 (Acc. 78, #405)
"Coupelet" is coupe with the removable pillars. "Coupe" has solid pillars. First 10,000 has spare tire carriers with forged brackets.

MAY 1 (Acc. 575, Box 11, #732)
T-6606 instrument board (new).

MAY 2 (Acc. 78, #408)
Oil lamps discontinued on truck chassis.

MAY 3 (Acc. 575, Box 11, #733)
Ammeter to now read "Ford" instead of "Ford Motor Company."

MAY 5 (Acc. 575, Box 11, #733)
Throttle levers to be zinc-plated and buffed instead of brass and nickel-plated.
Gear case: regular and worm steering gears indicated.

MAY 7 (Acc. 78, #413)
Demountable rims supplied on some open cars.

MAY 15
Rear axle hub design made to eliminate machining. New grease retainer cups needed. T-7687 generator to cutout wire changed to read "for repairs only" indicating that the cutout was now located on the generator.

MAY 19 (Acc. 78, #420)
Starters on some open cars (appeared prior to this date). New windshield brackets on electric cars; the old type with the integral lamp brackets to be continued on the non-electric cars. (Oil lamps were not supplied on the starter-equipped open or closed cars.)

MAY 28 (Engine production records)
Last non-starter engine block made on this date.

JUN 5 (Acc. 78, #436)
All cars to have starter-type engines; trucks to get whatever non-starter engines are left.
Valve cover plates now to be held in place with a screw instead of a stud and nut.

JUN 7 (Acc. 575, Box 11, #743)
Muffler rear end, T-1201, redesigned with outlet 10 degrees above horizontal centerline to deflect exhaust away from the spare tire. Former design had the outlet at the bottom of the end plate.

JUN 9 (Acc. 78, #441)
Price list shows TT (truck) with starter at $75. extra.

JUN 16 (Acc. 575, Box 11, #745)
T-519B. Changed diameter for the hole for the starting crank spring from 1/16" to #50 drill (.070"). This change was made in order to use up 12,000 #50 drills which were on hand, and was to take effect as soon as the change could be made without holding up production.

JUN 19 (Acc. 575, Box 11, #746)
Differential gasket announced (T-139). .015" original material reduced to .009" in letter of June 20, 1919.

JUN 23 (Acc. 575, Box 11, #748)
Steering gear cover again specified to have nickel plate.

1919

JUL 2 (Acc. 575, Box 11, #749, 750)
4:1 rear axle gears indicated. T-16 12-tooth pinion; T-12 48-tooth ring gear. T-418C piston lighter by 5 oz. (Was 2 lbs, 7 oz.)

JUL 14 (Acc. 575, Box 11, #752)
T-246B (front) and T91-1/2 (rear) spring hangers of butt-welded design noted.

JUL 19 (Acc. 575, Box 11, #751)
Valve cover doors changed from 20 ga. steel to 16 ga. steel. 1920 model cars now specified.

JUL 22 (Acc. 575, Box 11, #754)
New timing gear cover, T-1754, to be replaced by T-1769 when replacing T-400C (non-starter cylinder block) with T-400D (starter type) in repairs.

JUL 30 (Acc. 575, Box 12, #784)
T-1520 universal ball cap shim, two required, new.

AUG --- (Acc. 575, Box 11, #761)
Leather covered instrument panels are indicated on open cars and closed cars in early production. Of wood, they were superseded by metal panels by mid-1919.

AUG 19 (Acc. 575, Box 11, #758)
T-7320 resistor made by Ward Leonard to be used at branches for headlight dimming, enabling the use of old magneto-type headlamps on cars with starters. Used until new design headlamps could be supplied to the branches.
Horns made by K-W, Heinze, Garford, Connecticut.
Upholstery for 1918-1920 seems to be the same. Body parts are the same from 1916 to 1920.

AUG 27 (Acc. 575, Box 11, #758)
Spring type radiator mounting, specified for trucks earlier now used for all cars.

SEP --- (Acc. 575, Box 12, #766)
Tail light and license brackets for Roadster, Touring, with and without demountable rims, redesigned. T-8767, 8768, 8771 are the new part numbers.

OCT 21 (Acc. 575, Box 12, #767)
Holes punched in radiator fins for better cooling. 72 5/16" diameter holes between regular tube holes.

NOV --- (Acc. 575, Box 12, #769)
Side lamps by Brown, E&J and Victor were supplied on open cars without starter (only).

NOV 3 (Acc. 575, Box 12, #769)
Round and elliptical gas tanks mentioned.

NOV 3 Factory Blueprint (Archives)
T246C "U" spring hangers first drawn.

NOV 5 (Acc. 575, Box 12, #769)
Wooden instrument panels reinstated due to shortage of the steel type. These were leather covered as before.

NOV 14 (Acc. 575, Box 12, #770)
Elliptical tank part numbers shown with note that they cannot be used in open cars until the seat frames are changed ---- about four months.

NOV 21 (Acc. 78, #591)
Solid molding used on Runabouts to be replaced with stamped type on deck side panels, eliminating 3/5ths of the solid molding.

DEC 4 (Acc. 575, Box 12, #774)
Brackets which hold the gas tank redesigned to move the tank 7/16" towards the rear for better clearance at heel board. (Tank T-4018 bracket)

DEC 5 (Acc. 575, Box 12, #775)
New fan pulley, T-608, 602, 615. T-608 drive pulley made from crankcase stock.

DEC 8 (Acc. 575, Box 12, #774)
Hole in seat frame cover (bottom) enlarged from 2-3/4" to 4".

DEC 10 (Acc. 575, Box 12, #775)
Commutator brush discontinued. Returned to roller type.

DEC 13 (Acc. 575, Box 12, #776)
T-901B steering wheel rim made of wood, covered with "Fordite" or of solid "Fordite."

DEC 17 (Acc. 575, Box 12, #776)
T-826E transmission cover. Holes for mounting Bendix cover rotated 30 degrees for ease in assembly. (On April 6, 1920, the holes were changed back to the original position.)

1920

JAN 5 (Acc. 575, Box 12, #779)
T-701 flywheel. Experimental design with teeth cast or cut in wheel, was discontinued as unsatisfactory.

JAN 7 (Acc. 575, Box 12, #779)
T-8779 priming knob changed from cold-rolled Bessemer to an aluminum die casting.

JAN 12 (Acc. 575, Box 12, #780)
Pressed-steel running board brackets, T-336B.

JAN 22 (Acc. 575, Box 12, #781)
Lower radiator support thimble, T-1114, drawn from "starfish" rather than solid blank.

JAN 24 (Acc. 575, Box 12, #782)
Ten-tooth pinion to be used with T-12B ring gear. T-12 48-tooth ring gear obsoleted. Old T-16, 12-tooth pinion, obsoleted.

FEB 14 (Acc. 575, Box 12, #785)
T-418C piston machined for lighter weight, using the same piston blank.

APR 6 (Acc. 575, Box 12, #792)
Transmission cover: Bendix cover holes moved back to position prior to change of December 17, 1919. Machining changes in the cover made.

APR 10 (Acc. 575, Box 12, #793)
Bendix cover given slots instead of 17/64" holes to facilitate installation.

APR 23 (Acc. 575, Box 12, #795)
Pressed-steel muffler, experimental design, 500 per day. P/N T-1200C.

MAY 1 (Ford Archives)
"Start large fans and pulleys for truck motors."

MAY 11 (Ford Archives)
Engine #4,000,000 built at 10:15 P.M.

MAY 11 (Acc. 575, Box 12, #797)
Three types of commutators used. T-4481-A1, brass; T-4481-A2, aluminum die casting; T-4481-A3, pressed steel.

1920

MAY 13 (Ford Archives)
Began using 24 disks in transmission.

MAY 20 (Ford Archives)
Began using 25 disks in transmission.

MAY 20 (Acc. 575, Box 12, #798)
More experimental commutators. T-4481-A3, -A4; T-4446-B1, -B2.

MAY 20 (Acc. 575, Box 14, #826)
Timer roller assembly made of bronze (T-672-A1). Roller is of steel.
Aluminum also used (T-672-A2).

JUN 14 (Acc. 575, Box 13, #801)
1921 Touring bodies shown in letter this date.

JUN 22 (Acc. 575, Box 13, #802)
Parts listed for new Touring body of June 14 letter. Now listed for production. (Touring body only.)

JUN 26 (Acc. 575, Box 14, #815)
Thickness of metal in front cross-member increased. Required the moving of several mounting holes in the frame.

JUN 30 (Acc. 575, Box 13, #804)
16" steering wheel OK'd for production. (Removed from "experimental.")

JUL --- (Acc. 575, Box 13, #808)
New license plate brackets, T-491, at front.

JUL 20 (Acc. 575, Box 13, #807)
Hood and hood handle redesigned to eliminate rivets at the handle, for production.

JUL 26 (Acc. 575, Box 13, #807)
1921 Runabout and Touring bodies and parts specified.

AUG 13 (Acc. 575, Box 13, #810)
Pressed-steel muffler ends to be made of two pieces of scrap fender stock instead of one, for use on the 1921 models.

SEP 7 (Acc. 575, Box 14, #813)
Forged brake rods, T-891B, T-1513B obsoleted and replaced with T-804 for 1921 production.

SEP 13 (Acc. 575, Box 14, #814)
Front motor mount T-320B (experimental) indicated. Minor modifications made in construction and dimensions of T-191C driveshaft bearing housing, also experimental.

SEP 20 (Acc. 575, Box 14, #814, 815)
Coupe bodies began to use the elliptical gas tank as the supply permitted. Specified Coupe bodies with leather lining. Coupe bodies with cloth trim use the square tank.

OCT 11 (Acc. 575, Box 14, #819)
T-1201E, T-1202D, T-1200C muffler assembly adopted as standard for 1921 cars.

OCT 12 (Acc. 575, Box 14, #819)
T-1903 pliers for tool kit had handle shaped for use as a screwdriver, eliminating the need for a separate screwdriver in the tool kit supplied with the cars.
T-1303B (oval) gas tank specified for all chassis except for the Coupe and Sedan.

T-690C timing gear cover modified to allow more clearance for the bottom generator mounting bolt.

OCT 18 (Acc. 575, Box 14, #819)
Pressed-steel commutator case adopted as standard, eliminating the cast-iron, aluminum and bronze types they had experimented with. Apparently experiments continued on the cast case (noted in a letter #835, April 19, 1921).

OCT 22 (Acc. 575, Box 14, #820)
New front and rear spring hanger adopted. (This is the forged "L" shaped, one-piece per half, type.)

DEC 30 (Acc. 575, Box 14, #831)
Green-visor headlamp lens adopted, P/N T-6576B. These were discontinued by June of 1921 (replaced with "H" lens).

1921

FEB 15 (Acc. 575, Box 14, #831)
Coupe body had apparently been modified to have the gas tank under the seat in part of 1920 production. Directive advising of change back to the square tank in the rear deck made this date. The height of the coupe seat seemed to be the problem.

APR 1 (Acc. 575, Box 14, #832)
Oil holes in the frame rails for the brake lever shaft discontinued.

APR 26 (Acc. 575, Box 14, #836)
Bendix cover now painted black instead of zinc plated.

MAY 12 (Engine production records)
"Began using Heinze commutators."

MAY 28 (Engine production records)
Engine 5,000,000 built at 7:05 A.M. Given to Edsel Ford.

AUG 6 (Engine production records)
"Began to center commutator counterbore with camshaft."

AUG 9 (Engine production records)
"New style crankcase in all production."

OCT 10 (Engine production records)
"Began brass rollers" (commutator). By October 13 they were using all brass rollers.

OCT 15 (Acc. 78, Box 47-49)
Sample "new style" bodies shipped from Highland Park to branches, to be used as samples.

OCT 25 (Engine production records)
"New commutator shield begun." (The center hole now had a lip.)

NOV 1 (Engine production records)
First engine with one-piece valve door. The older two-door engines continued until April 3, 1922.

NOV 8 (Engine production records)
"Start copper plate rollers." (These are the copper-plated steel rollers.)

NOV 15 (Engine production records)
Began using rolled-thread head bolts.

DEC 29 (Acc. 78, Box 47-49)
Commutator brushes of bronze and steel being supplied. Aluminum type discontinued.

1922

MAR 31 (Engine production records)
Began to use rolled-thread head bolts. Production continued in both these and the older cut-thread bolts until July 14.

APR 3 (Engine production records)
All production is now one-piece valve door engines.

APR 4 (Acc. 78, Box 47-49)
New closed cars described, New door handles and new (walnut brown) upholstery.

MAY 18 (Engine production records)
Engine 6,000,000 built at 9:14 A.M. Given to Edsel Ford.

JUL 14 (Engine production records)
All engines now use rolled-thread head bolts, first used beginning March 31, 1922.

OCT 10 (Letter from Louisville Branch)
New Fordor Sedan described. Price: $725, FOB Detroit. Dealers asked to not advertise it and to sell it only when the standard (centerdoor) sedan could not be sold to a customer.
"A new four-door, five-passenger sedan body has been added to the line of standard Ford body types. This body is an entirely new development in design and construction, and does not in any way displace the present two-door sedan, which will continue to come thru.
"While this new four-door body will go into production within the next several weeks, the output will necessarily be limited for some time to come; therefore your sales effort on the present two-door type should be increased rather than relaxed. This present type still represents one of the best automobile values on the market, and the new type of body will simply broaden the field of sedan prospects, so far as Ford business is concerned.
"The price of the new four-door sedan is ($725.00) Seven hundred and twenty-five dollars, F.O.B. Detroit, and the differential between it and the two-door type is large enough to prevent competition between the two models. There is no reason why you should lose a single sedan order because of inability to deliver the new type, WHICH SHOULD ONLY BE MENTIONED TO PROSPECTS WHO HAVE PREVIOUSLY GIVEN CAREFUL CONSIDERATION TO THE PURCHASE OF A FOUR-DOOR SEDAN, AND WILL NOT BE SATISFIED WITH ANY OTHER TYPE. (sic)
"Continue pushing the sale of the two-door sedan, and only accept orders for the four-door type to prevent actual loss of business.
"VERY LITTLE PUBLICITY ON THE NEW SEDAN IS BEING GIVEN OUT. THEREFORE, FOR THE PRESENT, PREPARE NO ADVERTISING COPY ON IT, AND SEND OUT NO LITERATURE. IN THIS WAY YOUR SELLING PROBLEM WILL BE GREATLY SIMPLIFIED.
"Attached is a description of the features of the new four-door sedan, and a little later it is expected that a descriptive folder with illustrations will be ready for use."

FEATURES OF THE FOUR-DOOR SEDAN

"The body is approximately three inches longer than the two-door type Sedan, the extra length providing additional leg room for the occupants of the rear seat.
"All body panels are of aluminum with embossed molding, the metal extending up around the window sills and runways so that there are no wood parts exposed on the entire body. This feature insures a uniform finish and will largely prevent checking or other paint trouble.

"The body though longer that the present design weighs approximately 80 lbs. less. The saving in weight is gained by the use of aluminum panels in place of steel and also a lighter roof construction.
"The roof is of the soft type with artificial leather reinforced and padded, making it as durable and substantial as the old fiber board type, and eliminating the possibility of vibration noises. The overall height of the body is one inch less that the present design. With the straighter roof line the car has the appearance of greatly increased length.
"A permanent leather visor above the windshield adds greatly to the appearance of the car while protecting the driver from the glare of the sun.
"The tire carrier is of a new and improved design which permits the spare tire to set at an angle that corresponds with the lines of the body.
"The front door openings are 23-4/8 (sic) inches and the rear door openings are the same width as on the present two-door sedan.
"Door handles are of the straight bar type made from hard black rubber with nickel tips and fittings. All doors are equipped with locks. Three of the locks are operated by levers from the interior of the body while the right front door is operated by a key from the outside.
"All doors are equipped with special Ford design double roller dovetail guides at center as well as rubber bumpers top and bottom to prevent rattling.
"The upper sash of the windshield is adjustable either outwardly or inwardly to provide the proper degree of ventilation. An improved design of clamp permits it to be easily adjusted and securely fastened in any position. The lower section of the windshield is stationary which is a factor in preventing rain from leaking into the body.
"The windows in all four doors are operated by means of crank type window regulators, while the rear windows are operated by the present lever type used in the two-door Sedan.
"All interior fittings, including window regulators, door pull handles, door latch levers, etc., are finished in oxidized silver.
"A dome light is operated by a button on the right rear body pillar.
"Upholstery material is of improved design with a fine dark stripe on a brown background of a shade that will not easily show dust and dirt. Silk window curtains to harmonize are provided for the three rear windows.
"The rear seat cushion is 46-1/2 inches by 20 inches, or one inch wider than in the two-door Sedan. The front seat is 42-1/2 inches by 19 inches and will accommodate a third person if necessary. The front seat cushion is divided in the center making it necessary to raise but one-half of the cushion to fill the gasoline tank. Therefore, the driver may have the tank filled without leaving his seat.
"Seat cushions are held in position by means of dowel pins in place of the covered binding strip used on our two-door Sedan.
"The price of the new Sedan is $725.00 F.O.B. Detroit."

NOV 7 (Acc. 78, Box 47-49)
One-man top restyled; now had gentle curve down at the rear bow. This change made "after first 100,000 cars."

NOV 14 (Acc. 78, Box 47-49)
Fordor sedans to be striped across the cowl and completely around the body except over the T molding on doors and molding on back panel. Stripe was not less than 5/16" nor more than 3/8" below the belt molding, and not less than 3/32" nor more than 1/8" wide.

1922

NOV 24   (Acc. 78, Box 47-49)
Nine-leaf rear spring adopted for sedans.

DEC 20   (Engine production records)
"Began using 3/8" washer at #4 manifold stud to keep from bending hot air pipe."

1923

JAN 12   (Engine production records)
Engine 7,000,000 built at 6:48 P.M.

FEB 5   (Engine production records)
Start top piston ring 1/16" lower.

FEB 15   (Engine production records)
Start tapered piston rings.

MAR 29   (Acc. 78, Box 47-49)
Metal sill covers installed at rear doors on touring cars, painted black. Rear floor mat changed from wool to rubber.

APR 7   (Acc. 78, Box 47-49)
Letter indicates that the steel firewall was now standard. This was the "low" steel firewall.

JUL 11   (Engine production records)
Engine 8,000,000 built at 10:19 P.M.

SEP 10   (Engine production records)
"Ford USA" stamped on export motors, below number plate.

SEP 11   (Letter from Louisville Plant)
Prices of bodies for replacement: Fordor sedan, $430. Coupe, $235. Touring, $80. Runabout, $60. FOB Detroit.

SEP 25   (Acc. 78, Box 47-49)
"Ford USA" no longer on engine block.

DEC 26   (Engine production records)
Engine 9,000,000 built at 1:05 P.M.

1924

JAN 9   (Ford Archives)
Announcement of all-steel body and cab for trucks. Express body to which stakes, etc., might be added.

JAN 18   (Letter from Chicago Branch)
The Ford Motor Company enters the new year with a new product, an all-steel combination truck body and cab mounted on the standard Ford One Ton Chassis to be sold as a complete unit.

The new body is of the open express type, so constructed that it may be readily converted into other body combinations by using stakes, side boards, canopy top, screen sides, etc.

"In fact" says the Ford statement, "the purpose in producing the new body was to place a low cost general utility truck, meeting body (sic) agricultural and commercial requirements at the disposal of ton truck users."

The body is built of steel to withstand the most severe usage and presents a new development in construction. The steel sills are reinforced with wood in order to lessen vibration and road shocks, thus making for more durability and longer life.

The loading space is seven feet two inches in length by four feet in width and of convenient and practical depth. The end gate is strongly braced and secured by heavy chains which hold it in position when lowered.

The cab, also of steel construction is extra roomy. The seat is of artificial leather, well-cushioned by four inch springs. Protection from the weather is afforded by close fitting door curtains mounted on uprights and opening and closing with the door. An oblong window in the back of the cab gives ample facilities for rear vision, adding to the safety as well as the convenience of the driver.

The new truck which is already on display in many Ford dealers show rooms throughout the country, sells complete with steel cab and closed body for $490.00 F.O.B. Detroit, being priced in accordance with the standard Ford policy.

In addition to the saving offered truck users in this body, is the convenience of now being able to buy the Ford One Ton truck complete and ready to put into service.

MAR 12   (Engine production records)
Lightweight pistons first used.

MAR 18   (Letter from Chicago Branch)
"We hear stories that some salesmen are telling their customers to be sure and look at the motor number of any car when they buy in order to be sure they get a late motor number. These particular salesmen are just making a lot of trouble for themselves because at the new plant we have hundreds of motors that have been standing there for thirty days or more and will be going into the cars in the course of production. This means that all dealers will receive motor numbers from the Burnham plant that will be considerably lower in number than those motors received from the Chicago plant so just stop your salesmen making any remarks at all about motor numbers because in so doing they are going to make a lot of trouble for you when we start shipping from the new plant."

A.W.L. Gilpin
Branch Manager

P.S. In correspondence the old Ford plant in Chicago is referred to as the Chicago plant and the new plant is referred to as the Burnham plant because it is near the Burnham railroad yards.

MAR 23   (Engine production records)
Start 1/32" babbitt in connecting rods. In all beginning April 23.

MAR 24   (Ford Archives)
Truck prices: Chassis, $370. Chassis and cab, $435. Chassis, cab and body, $490. Chassis, cab, body and canopy roof, $520. Same with side screens, $545. Chassis and body (no cab), $425. Chassis, body and canopy, $455. Chassis, body, canopy and screens, $480.

APR 19   (Engine production records)
New camshaft and front bearing in all production. Start 1/32" babbitt in universal ball cap. In all by April 29.

APR 29   (Engine production records)
New camshaft and bearing in all production.

MAY 7   (Engine production records)
New rear cam bearing begun. In all by May 21.

JUN 4   (Engine production records)
Engine 10,000,000 built at 7:47 A.M.

JUN 6   (Engine production records)
1/32" babbitt in front and center crankshaft bearings. In all production beginning July 16.

1924

JUL 17 (Engine production records)
New style transmission covers began. New oil tube with a larger funnel began this date and was used in all production beginning August 12.

JUL 18 (Engine production records)
New (four-dip) crankcase begun.

SEP 17 (Letter from Chicago plant)
Windshield wiper, dash light and rear vision mirror are three new accessories now being offered by the Ford Motor Company through its extensive dealer and service station organization. In presenting these accessories, the company has followed the policy prevailing in the marketing of all its products, that of giving the highest quality at the lowest possible cost.

The Ford windshield wiper is constructed so that the double ply rubber is always pressed firmly against the glass and all vibration is eliminated, yet the wiper is easily operated. The steel handle has a polished white metal grip which will not rust.

The rear vision mirror is made of polished plate glass manufactured by the Ford Motor Company. The mirror is held firmly by felt clamps and an ingenious arrangement not only permits easy adjustment to any desired position, but also locks the mirror in position, holding it there firmly and thus relieving the driver of the inconvenience of making frequent adjustments in order to maintain clear rear vision.

The Ford dash light is neat and attractively finished in black to harmonize with the instrument board. A feature is the manner in which the base of the light fits into the panel instead of simply being attached to the surface. This eliminates all possibility of it shaking loose.

A Ford emergency kit, consisting of two headlight bulbs, a tail light bulb, a spark plug and a tube repair outfit, also in included in the Ford accessory line.

SEP 29 (Engine production records)
First engine (10,566,001) built at River Rouge Plant. Production continued at Highland Park until February 13, 1925; the last number produced there being 11,067,000. (The Rouge plant's last number the same day was 11,198,371.)

FORD FACTORY LETTER
From Ford Motor Company, Detroit office
September 29, 1924
Change in the upholstery in the Ford Fordor Sedan, which has been effected lately, has given the car a most attractive interior.

This Ford type, which has been highly popular since its introduction into the Ford line, is now upholstered in a soft, durable cloth of blue-slate background relieved by a royal blue stripe. Head lining and floor rugs harmonize nicely in color and blue silk curtains on the three rear windows give an added tone of richness to the interior, equally effective in the day time and under the soft glow of the dome light at night.

Appointments are complete, the Ford dash light, windshield wiper and rear vision mirror now being part of the standard equipment of the Fordor Sedan.

With the change in upholstery, the closed car buyer is given a little more variety in the selection of a car for family use ---- the Fordor with its blue interior and the always attractive Tudor, upholstered in dark brown.

Upholstery in the Ford coupe also remains in brown cloth, affording the most practical and pleasing effect under the wide variety of uses to which this popular Ford closed type is adapted.

DEC 24 (Ford Archives)
Platform stake body added to truck line.

1925

FEB 5 (Letter from the Chicago Branch)
We are rather interested in knowing about what proportion of prospects would be interested in Ford Cars, both open and closed, equipped with balloon tires. Say for instance, if an additional price of $25.00 for the balloon equipment, less of course, the regular discount to the dealer were charged, what proportion of cars do you suppose you would ask us to ship you so equipped if the company decided to furnish balloon tires?

It would probably depend largely on your answer whether or not balloon tire equipment would be used as standard equipment on part of our production.

FEB 23 (Letter from the Chicago Branch)
The following are the recommendations for air pressures to be used in 4.40/21" tires on Ford cars: Roadster, 25 pounds. Touring and Coupe, 30 pounds. Sedan types, 35 pounds. These pressures are for both front and rear.

MAR 4 (Ford Archives)
Pickup bed for Runabout announced.

MAR 6 (Letter from Firestone Tire and Rubber Co.)
The Ford Motor Company have (sic) approved the Balloon tire and furnish it as original equipment. This offers you an opportunity for increased sales and profit. New car sales ---- changeovers from hundreds of present Ford owners, who will want to bring their cars up to date and enjoy the comfort, safety and economy of Balloon tires.
(The letter then recommends the tire pressures listed February 23.)

Firestone Balloons are furnished with combination Dill Dust Caps and, if properly tightened, will help to maintain constant pressure and minimize leakage. (The letter continues with a description of the tires and a suggested price of $64.80 for a set of four with wheels and a spare rim.)

----- (Ford Archives)
Prices: Touring, $290. Runabout, $260. Tudor, $580. Fordor, $660. Coupe, $520. Chassis, $225. Runabout with pickup body, $281; with starter and demountable rims, $366. Starter for Touring and Runabout, $65. Demountables for touring and runabout, $20. (Electric equipment and demountables were standard equipment on the closed cars.)

MAR 17 (Engine production records)
Began using only one bushing in the transmission brake drum.

APR 15 (Letter from the Chicago Branch, with Detroit date line)
As a delivery unit to meet requirements for equipment lighter than that of the ton truck, The Ford Motor Company has just added a pick-up body to its commercial car line.

The new body is designed for use on the Ford Runabout, taking the place of the rear deck, and is well adapted to all kinds of light hauling and quick delivery. The Runabout seat affords comfortable riding for the driver and there is ample room for another passenger. Full protection against inclement weather is provided by the top and side curtains.

The new body is of all steel construction and sturdily built. It is 3 feet, 4-3/4 inches wide and 4 feet,

Documentation

1925

8 inches long. Sides are thirteen inches deep to the flare, so that loading space is sufficient to meet all demands of light delivery. The end gate is the same as that on the express type body of the ton truck and when partially lowered is securely held in place by chains.

APR 9   (Ford Archives)
Closed cab for trucks announced.

APR 17   (Ford Factory letter)
The 250,000th Ford left the final assembly line in Manchester, England. English Fords are about 90% British material. "All cylinder blocks are cast and machined in the plant at Cork, Ireland, which operates under the name of Henry Ford & Son, Ltd."

APR 29   (Ford Factory letter)
A closed cab is the latest equipment offered by the Ford Motor Company for the Ford ton truck. The new cab, which is all-steel, affords protection for the driver and is adaptable for use with standard Ford truck bodies, both the express and the stake types.

Doors of the cab are exceptionally wide and the plate glass windows in the doors may be lowered. The upper portion of the windshield swings either in or out so as to suit ventilation requirements. The seat accommodates three persons comfortably and there are special springs in both the seat and back cushions. Panels in the back of the cab may be easily removed to permit access to the truck body.

A combined priming and carburetor adjusting rod is now standard on all Ford closed cars, and is being furnished without extra cost. Where formerly the driver primed from the instrument board and adjusted the carburetor from the dash beneath, both operations may now be performed from the same accessory on the instrument board.

Ford owners who desire to "dress up" their cars with nickel-plated radiator shells and head lamp doors may now secure these accessories from Ford dealers. This equipment is being supplied by the Ford Motor Company to authorized dealers throughout the country.

APR 30   (Factory Letter)
Windshield wing assemblies announced at $7.50 pair. Nickel plated radiator shell, apron and headlamp rims offered. T-3947D shell at $5.00. T-3977B apron, $.75. T-6575BRX headlamp rim, less lens, $1.00. All at 40% discount to the dealer.

MAY 2   (Letter from the Chicago Branch)
Leather inner axle oil seal announced. Part # T-198AR, it sold for 30 cents a pair. Instructions were given on its installation, and the importance of keeping the bearing well greased is stressed.

MAY 14   (Factory Letter)
Leather "Dope Washers" announced. These were the leather grease seals that go inside the outer rear wheel bearings. P/N T-198AR or cars, TT-198AR for trucks.

NATURAL WOOD WHEELS announced. T-291-1 front wheel, balloon, with hub and less rim, at $5.50 each. T-2815G rear wheel, balloon, with hub and less rim, at $5.50 each. These were sold as a set to the dealer for $13.20. They were to be sold to the customer on an exchange basis (for black balloon wheels) for $15.00. Ford would allow a credit of $6.00 for the returned set.

JUN 1   (Letter from the Chicago Branch)
Transmission bands with the detachable ear on all production was noted. The letter gave instructions on the removal and installation, and notes that it was necessary to cut off approximately 1-1/2" of the clutch pedal shaft, as well as installing a new transmission band adjusting screw extension T-1525-R when these bands were used on earlier (non-detachable bands) transmissions. (2-1/2" to be cut off is specified in a letter of July 28.)

JUL 8   (Letter from the Chicago Branch)
"We have discontinued marking high-speed trucks with white paint on the axle housing cap, and are now marking them by stamping "H.S." with dies on top of the worm housing."

JUL 27   (Engine production records)
Last old style engine (12,218,728) built at 5:51 P.M. and new (1926) type engines began on the third shift.

JUL 28   (Letter from Chicago Branch)
Notes that they have found it necessary to cut 2-1/2" off the clutch pedal shaft (T3427) when installing quick-change bands in earlier cars. (Was 1-1/2")

AUG 22   (Letter from Chicago Branch)
Announcement of the "improved Ford car," stating that it would be first advertised to the public in the afternoon papers August 26, and the morning papers on August 27, with weekly publications the following week. The cars were not to be displayed before the 26th. The letter stressed that the term "New Ford" should not be used; rather "Improved Changes in Body and Chassis," or "Improved Ford Cars."

AUG 26   The official news release on the "Improved Fords."
Changes are Most Pronounced ---- Bodies Longer, Lower and All-Steel.
Goes to Colors in Closed cars. Many Other Refinements Made ---- Brakes are Larger, More Powerful.

Body changes and chassis refinements more pronounced than any made since the adoption of the Model T chassis were announced here today by the Ford Motor Company. There will be no advance in price, it also was stated.

Outstanding features of the improvements in both open and enclosed types are lower, all-steel bodies on a lowered chassis, complete new design in most body types, a change from black in color in closed cars, larger, lower fenders, newly designed seats and larger, more powerful brakes.

Longer lines, effected through higher radiator and redesigned cowl and bodies are apparent in all the improved Ford cars, but are especially pronounced in the open types. Wide crown fenders hung close to the wheels contribute to the general effect of lowness and smartness.

While Runabout and Touring Car remain in black, the closed bodies are finished in harmonic color schemes, enhanced by nickel radiators. The Coupe and Tudor bodies are finished in deep channel green while the Fordor is rich Windsor Maroon.

Greater comfort is provided for driver and passengers in both open and closed cars by larger compartments, more deeply cushioned seats and greater leg room.

Many new conveniences are also incorporated in the improved cars. In the Runabout, Touring Car, Coupe and Tudor, the gasoline tank is under the cowl and filled through an ingeniously located filler cap completely hidden from sight by a cover similar in appearance to a cowl ventilator. One-piece windshield and narrowed

1925

pillars in the Tudor and Coupe offer the driver greatly increased visibility and improved ventilation.

Driving comfort is materially increased by lower seats, scientifically improved back rests and lowered steering wheel. Brake and clutch pedals are wider and more conveniently spaced.

Four doors are now provided on the Touring Car and two on the Runabout permitting the driver to take his place from the left side of the car. Curtains, held secure by rods, open with the doors.

Most important in the mechanical changes are the improved brakes. The transmission brake drum and bands have been considerably increased in size which gives the foot brake softer and more positive action as well as longer life. The rear wheel brake drums are larger and the brake is of self energizing type.

Cord tires are now standard equipment on all Ford cars.

At the main offices of the company it was stated today that production of the new line is under way in all assembly plants of the company throughout the country and the improved cars are being sent to dealers for showing.

AUG 30 (General letter from Detroit)

Edsel B. Ford, president of the Ford Motor Company, in a statement issued yesterday following the announcement of improved Ford bodies and chassis refinements, said:

"We do not want the impression to prevail that we are producing new Ford Cars.

"Bodies for Ford cars have been materially improved but the Model T chassis remains unchanged except for a lowering of the frame and a few other important changes. Bodies, in four types, have been completely redesigned and built lower to contribute to better appearance, driving and riding comfort and roadability of the cars.

"Body improvements and chassis refinements at this time are more pronounced than at any previous time since the adoption of the Model T chassis. They are, however, entirely in accordance with the policy of the Ford Motor Company to give the public the benefit of every improvement which we find practical for Ford cars.

"By preserving the design of the Model T chassis, the company is safeguarding continued good service for owners of approximately 9,000,000 Ford cars and trucks now in use throughout the country as well as for new car purchasers."

SEP 11 (News release from Detroit)

Beauty is Keynote of Longer, lower Bodies ---- Many New Conveniences.

It is no exaggeration to say that Ford dealer show rooms in (name of city) were literally packed with people during the past week, all eager to see the new Ford cars which went on display for the first time (name day).

There were exclamations of surprise from everyone and enthusiastic comments of all kinds were heard everywhere the cars were exhibited whether in show rooms or on the streets.

The cars are most attractive. Graceful lines have been effected through the combination of lower bodies on a lowered chassis frame. Through unnumerable (sic) changes there has been blended into one whole an exceptionally pleasing line of cars. From the higher radiator, rising into the body lines, on back to the improved spare tire carrier at the rear and the tail light and license bracket on the fender, every car is distinctive.

Those desiring a two passenger car will find it hard to choose between the Coupe and the Runabout. Both these types have particularly good lines. The rear deck of each has been considerably enlarged, and is now full width with increased luggage carrying capacity.

The Touring car, most popular of all Ford cars, has a considerably longer appearance and seats are wider.

The Tudor Sedan, likewise has been redesigned not only in lines, but in interior arrangement and seating comfort, while the Fordor has many charms for those who prefer a car of this type.

Examination of the cars reveal many other conveniences and refinements which provide improved braking facilities, permit quicker adjustments and contribute in many ways to easier driving, all of which can be better appreciated by personal examination than by any description.

While they embody features which give them new beauty, riding and driving comfort, the improved Fords are built on the same Model T chassis which is the foundation of the dependable and economical performance of more than 9,000,000 Ford cars now in service all over the world.

COMMERCIAL BODY SPECIFICATIONS
(From Chicago Branch, January 19, 1926)

All dimensions in inches

	Open Cab	Closed Cab	Stake Body	Platform Body	Express Body	Screen Sides	Canopy Roof	Pickup Body
Height	58-13/16	53	26		13-13-16	36-1/8	48-1/4	13
Width	52-3/8	51	60	66	48		48	40-3/4
Length	43-7/8	45-1/2	97-1/2	100-1/2	86	86	86	56
Door Width	16-3/8	28-3/4						
Door Length	20-1/2	52-3/32						
Height of Canopy Roof from ground		90-25/35						
Height of Express body from ground		32						
Height of Platform body from ground		38-21/32						

Documentation

1925

OCT 26   (Engine production records)
Began using bolts on the valve doors. (A letter of June 5, 1919, indicated this change was made in 1919. Apparently both bolts and studs had been used during the early 1920's.)

NOV 16   (Engine production records)
100% of production now used the support straps at the rear of the engine block.

DEC 31   (Letter from the Chicago Branch)
The letter is regarding the importance of adjusting the rear wheel brakes, and gives the following procedure:
"To properly adjust the brakes, set the hand brake lever in the fourth notch (high gear) from the front of the quadrant. Make sure that brake drums are contracted. Then adjust the clevis on end of rod until hole in clevis lines up with hole in controller shaft. Insert the pin through the hole. Then turn the rear wheels to ascertain whether the brakes are dragging on the drum. If both wheels run free, pull the hand brake lever back to the sixth notch of quadrant. Then try wheels again. Brakes should just start holding at this point. Now the brakes are properly adjusted. Insert cotter keys in the end of the clevis pin."

1926

JAN 1   (Engine production records)
Engine 13,000,000 built.

JAN 7   (Letter to dealers from Fargo, ND branch)
"Ford wire wheels as shown in colored folder on Ford National Show Week, retail for $50 per set of five. Bumpers retail at $15 per pair.
"We give you this information to answer inquiries that may arise during Show Week.
"Bumpers and wire wheels will be available THRU SERVICE STOCK ONLY on or about February 1.
"Automatic windshield wipers for open and closed cars will be available within the next week or ten days at the following prices: T-3318R Automatic windshield wiper (open cars), $5.00. T-3320R (closed cars), $5.00. Less 40%."

JAN 8   (Letter to dealers from Chicago branch)
"To all Chicago Branch Dealers:
"We are mailing you under separate cover a personal letter signed by Mr. Edsel B. Ford, requesting you to paint on the roof of your place of business, the name of the City or Town in which you are located, and I wish that you would personally see to it that the letters of the name are carried out in accordance with Mr. Ford's letter.
"I would suggest that in painting these letters, wherever it is possible for you to make these larger than 12 inches high that you do so, owing to the fact that on a dark day it would be a difficult matter for a Pilot to see letters only 12 inches high.
"I sincerely hope that you will comply with Mr. Ford's request, making it possible for the writer to advise Mr. Ford that our dealers have responded 100%."
Very Truly Yours,
Ford Motor Company
O. L. Arnold
Manager
Presumably Edsel hoped that pilots would land to purchase a new Ford, and this marking would make it easier for them to find the dealer.

FEB 4   (Letter to dealers from Fargo branch)
"8-leaf front spring standard on 'Improved Fords.' "

FEB 11   (Letter to dealers from Fargo branch)
Factory prices dropped to: Touring, $310. Runabout, $290. Fordor, $565. Tudor, $520. Coupe, $500.

FEB 15   (Letter from the Chicago branch)
"The following are the suggested labor prices for installing Ford accessories: Bumpers, $2.00 per set. Snubbing units, $1.00 per set. Automatic windshield wiper, .75. Top boot & Gypsy Curtains, no charge. Windshield wings, no charge.
"The cost of installing wire wheels is included in the exchange price of the wire wheels in accordance with Supplement No. 1 to General Letter No. 496."

FEB 23   (Letter #1430 to dealers from Fargo branch)
"The fan eccentric has been redesigned by adding a flange on the outside edge toward the radiator and a lug on the inside edge. The cylinder head outlet connection has also been redesigned to correspond.
"To adjust the fan with this redesigned fan eccentric and outlet connection, it will be necessary to loosen the nut on the fanshaft bolt sufficient so the fan eccentric can be moved with a wrench on the lug.
"To tighten the fan belt, turn the lug up and to loosen the fan belt, turn the lug down.
"After securing the proper adjustment, tighten the nut on the fanshaft, which will draw up on the fan eccentric plate and hold the fan eccentric in place at all times.
"At the time of adopting the redesigned outlet connection and fan eccentric for regular production, it was deemed advisable to hold the above parts for service on all cars having this outlet connection assembled, but due to unsatisfactory results and several complaints, these parts will be considered obsolete as soon as sufficient stocks of redesigned parts are available for regular production. (Ed. note: this seems a bit confusing. I presume they are referring to the original "worm drive" eccentric as the one being unsatisfactory, not the "new" design indicated above.)
"Please instruct all concerned to replace broken old-style outlet connections with the new style connection, fan eccentric, fan eccentric plate and fanshaft, returning all broken parts together with your stock of old style parts, for credit allowance."

MAR 3   (Letter to dealers from Fargo branch)
Dual stop/tail light announced. $2.50 less 40%.

MAR 11   (Letter to dealers from Fargo branch)
"We have just received our first allotment of a limited supply of Ford wire wheels and are pleased to advise you that a set of five wheels complete was forwarded to you on the 10th.
"Production is very limited . . . .
"Extra charge for 5 wheels and 4 tires, $50. 5 wheels and 5 tires, $75."

MAR 15   (General letter 1457 from Fargo branch)
"We expect to be in a position to furnish Genuine Ford Bumpers within the next thirty days.
"You will be pleased with the appearance, the quality and price of this new product. These bumpers have been carefully designed and are made to attach to the frame ---- very rigidly and securely ---- the frame being drilled so that installation is a simple matter. Best quality spring steel is used in construction. The test employed to determine the steel best adapted to this use are very interesting, consisting of actual impact tests against obstacles at predetermined speeds.
"The price is $15.00 per pair list, subject to dealers' usual discount of 40% ----this price, considering the high quality and appearance of the bumpers, should enable you

1926

to obtain a large volume of this class of business, providing the proper sales effort is applied by your organization.....

"Each bumper is packed individually in a carton and clearly marked with the name, T number and models to which bumper can be applied. Following are the T numbers and the cars fitted:

T-3101R ---- Front bumper assy (all model T)
T-3119R ---- Rear bumper assy (Fordor, Tudor, Touring)
T-3120R ---- Rear bumper assy (Coupe, Runabout)

"Since bumpers are now classified as Ford products, we will expect all dealers to sell the Genuine article and are enclosing an order blank for your convenience....."

MAR 22   (Letter 1463 from the Fargo branch))
"We can now furnish khaki or black top boots, khaki gypsy curtains and windshield wings for the open models; automatic windshield wipers, open and closed types; and natural wood wheels in unlimited quantities and expect to be able to furnish bumpers, snubbing units and the combination stop and tail lamp assembly within a very short time, therefore, we ask that you make immediate necessary arrangements to line up your organization to properly merchandise the complete line of Ford accessories."

MAY 25   (Engine production records)
Began using bolt instead of studs for manifolds.

APR 19   (Letter from the Chicago branch)
"The Police Department has called to our attention the fact that our license brackets obscure the license place on all cars equipped with bumpers.

"In order that we may comply with the law, our headlamps are being changed so that when assembled to the car, they are fastened together with a tie rod which will make the lamps and fenders more rigid and will change the position of the license plate so that it will not be covered by the bumpers.

"This change will go into effect in the very near future. We are giving you this information in advance in order that you may take care of your stock order accordingly."

MAY 7   (Letter from the Chicago branch)
"We are now in a position to supply part 2511B-T221 washer, which should be used in conjunction with 2511-T198A rear axle oil retainer, to increase the efficiency and life of the retainer. This is accomplished by the pressure exerted by the lugs of the retainer washer, which hold the leather collar firmly against the axle shaft.

"As all production axles will shortly carry this improvement it will be necessary that this washer be included with all grease retainers supplied through your stock department or installed in your shop.

(The letter continues with the prices (25 cents for the new washer and leather, and 50 cents for the set of two. The leather retainer is 2511, and the washer is 2511B. The set is 2511C.

JUN 1   (Letter from the Chicago branch)
"The Ruckstell Mfg. Company, manufacturers of the Ruckstell Axle advise that a price reduction of about 28% on both the truck and passenger axles has become effective. This reduction is as follows: Truck axle, from $112.00 to $79.80. Passenger axle, from $70.00 to $49.80."

JUN 19   (Letter to dealers from Fargo branch)
Prices: Chassis with starter, $300. Runabout with starter and balloon tires, $360. Touring with starter and balloon tires, $380. Coupe with balloon tires, $485. Tudor with balloon tires, $495. Fordor with balloon tires, $545. Truck with balloon front tires, no starter, $325. With starter, $375.

JUN 28   (Letter to dealers from Fargo branch)
Set of 5 wire wheels reduced to $40.

JUL 9   (Letter from the Chicago branch)
Announced that only balloon wheels could be taken in exchange for wire wheels since the high pressure (30x3-1/2) were no longer used in production. The factory allowed $11.50 for a set of the wood wheels, and apparently they were used in new production of cars.

JUL 19   (Engine production records)
Holley Vaporizer on all production.

JUL 21   (Engine production records)
Engine 14,000,000 built at 4:30 P.M.

JUL 24   (Letter to dealers from Fargo branch)
"After extensive tests we have adopted the Holley Vaporizer for Ford cars and trucks.

"This Vaporizer can be installed on any new motor without fear of trouble if the car is driven carefully for the first few hundred miles the same as is necessary for any new car. This is due to the fact that the piston rings in all engines since May 15, 1926 have been fitted with wider gaps, which permits better lubrication.

"Some dealers may have the impression that the Vaporizer is beneficial only in cold weather. As a matter of fact, test show that the intake temperature with the Vaporizer is no higher than with the standard carburetor."

JUL 27   (Engine production records)
Started to paint motors with Pyroxylin. (Drake Green indicated in one note.)

AUG 21   (Letter to dealers from Fargo branch)
"The use of felt packing for the front end of the crankshaft has been discontinued on cars and trucks and we are now using a braided asbestos packing with a rubber core. This packing is much more durable since the heat of the engine will not break down or soften it."

SEP 8   (Letter to dealers from Fargo branch)
"The Vaporizer now used on the Ford car is so designed that efficient operation is secured from the engine even though low grade fuels are used. Some of these low grade fuels have a tendency, however, to carbonize the hot plate, which condition is indicated by a lower warming up of the engine and the need for a richer mixture. When this is noticed, the hot plate should be taken out and the carbon removed.

"The formation of carbon on the hot plate depends entirely upon the grade of fuel used and where a good fuel is burned, it should seldom be necessary to clean the plate. Some low grade fuels result in a carbon formation within 2500 to 3000 miles and we suggest that the plate be cleaned after this period of service providing there is any indication of carbon.

"To remove the hot plate it is merely necessary to run out the four screws in the plate casting and back off the knurled nut at the top. This permits the plate casting to be moved back so that the thin plate can be drawn out. After scraping off the carbon, the plate should be placed in the same position as before removal, that is, with the raised corrugation extending inward, since the Vaporizer

1926

will not function properly if the plate is reversed.

"We also wish to direct your attention to the necessity for exercising care in adjusting the needle valve. Our experience has shown that practically every complaint of excessive gas consumption has resulted from the needle valve having been screwed too tightly against the seat. The groove thus cut in the needle renders it impossible to secure a good adjustment and there is no alternative but to install a new needle valve."

SEP 9   (Letter from the Chicago branch)

"It is necessary that our dealers properly instruct new owners regarding the adjustment of the Holley Vaporizer, which is standard equipment on all Ford cars. Perfect satisfaction results from proper adjustment.

"Turn vaporizer adjusting rod clockwise to shut off fuel, and open from 5/8 to 7/8 of a turn for running. To start, pull out rod to choke vaporizer. If cold, open 1/2 turn more, but close down to regular running position within five minutes."

SEP 25   United States District Court, Eastern Judicial District of Missouri.

A judgment against the Ford Motor Company, in favor of Parks and Bohne, Inc., holders of original patents of transmission bands with removable ears, was made on this date. Just how Ford made restitution is not specified in the document.

OCT 27   (Letter from the Chicago branch)

"For your information, we are listing below the new colors which will be furnished on all types of cars and trucks, as well as the change in the standard equipment of the Fordor, all of which are effective immediately:

OPEN CARS: Phoenix Brown (M604), or Gun Metal Blue (M601), both with Orange Stripe (M641).

CLOSED CARS: Highland Green (M603), or Fawn Gray (M605), both with Cream Stripe (M643), or Royal Maroon (M606) with Vermillion Stripe (M646).

RUNABOUT WITH PICK-UP BODY: Commercial Green (M608) with Cream Stripe (M643).

PICK-UP BODY AND ROADSTER DECK (Sold through service): Black Pyroxylin, no stripe.

ALL TRUCK BODY EQUIPMENT: Commercial Green (M608).

COMMERCIAL CHASSIS: Black enamel hood and shell.

TT CHASSIS: Commercial green hood, black enamel shell.

FORDORS: Wire wheels standard equipment.

OCT 28   (Letter from the Chicago branch)

"FORDORS: Black wire wheels are now standard equipment at no extra cost. Should your customer desire colored wire wheels instead of black, we recommend an extra charge of $10.00 be made for the change-over."

OCT 29   (Ford letter to all dealers)

"For your information and guidance we are listing below the standard colors for both open and closed cars:

OPEN CARS

Gun Metal Blue Pyroxylin (no stripe)

Phoenix Brown (no stripe)

CLOSED CARS

Highland Green Pyroxylin with cream stripe

Fawn Gray Pyroxylin with cream stripe

Royal Maroon Pyroxylin with vermillion stripe

"The Roadster will come through in Gun Metal Blue and Phoenix Brown Pyroxylin, however, when pick-up box is required on the Roadster the entire outfit will come through in Commercial Green Pyroxylin just the same as the truck with cab and body. Pick-up boxes sold through

service will come through in black.

"Effective immediately black wire wheels are standard equipment on Fordor Sedans with no additional charge to the customer. However, should the customer desire colored wire wheels on the Fordor, we suggest an extra charge of $10.00 per car. This applies to the Fordor only."

NOV 1   (Letter from the Chicago branch)

A number of price and part number changes, plus the following:

"NOTE----All colored hoods will hereafter be carried under catalog number 4050E, and dealers should specify Channel Green, Drake Green, Highland Green, Windsor Maroon, Royal Maroon, Moleskin, Gunmetal Blue, Phoenix Brown, or Fawn Gray, when ordering. The list price of any of these colored hoods is $8.00 each.

NOV 12   (Letter from the Chicago branch)

The following is a list of paints sold through the Ford factory:

M-109	Emerald Green Pyroxylin striping (New No. M-642)
M-111	Black touch-up
M-118	Champagne Striping (New No. M-644)
M-123	Drake Green satin finish Pyroxylin New No. M-637)
M-125	Moleskin satin finish Pyroxylin (New No. M-630)
M-127	Black satin finish Pyroxylin (New No. M-632)
M-134	Straw enamel, to be replaced by M-627
M-136	Casino Red enamel, to be replaced with M-628
M-140	Emerald Green enamel, to be replaced with M-629
M-145	Pyroxylin thinner, to be replaced with M-647-S
M-165	Black enamel
M-193	Drake Green Pyroxylin touch-up, to be replaced with M-637
M-194	Moleskin Pyroxylin touch-up, to be replaced with M-630
M-210	Tractor gray
M-212	Tractor red
M-213	Tractor black
M-392	Channel green enamel
M-393	Windsor maroon enamel
M-401	Tack rag varnish
M-430	Spar varnish
M-626	Royal maroon Pyroxylin ground
M-627	Straw Pyroxylin for wire wheels
M-628	Casino red Pyroxylin for wire wheels
M-629	Emerald green Pyroxylin for wire wheels
M-630	Moleskin Pyroxylin (Old No. M-125)
M-631	Gunmetal blue Pyroxylin
M-632	Black Pyroxylin (Old No. M-127)
M-633	Highland green Pyroxylin
M-634	Phoenix brown Pyroxylin
M-635	Fawn gray Pyroxylin
M-636	Royal maroon Pyroxylin
M-637	Drake green Pyroxylin (Old No. M-123)
M-638	Pyroxylin Primer (Old No. M-701)
M-639	Pyroxylin Glaze (Old No. M-702)
M-640	Pyroxylin surfacer (Old No. M-703)
M-641	Orange Pyroxylin striping
M-642	Emerald Green Pyroxylin striping (Old No. M-109)
M-643	Cream Pyroxylin striping
M-644	Champagne Pyroxylin striping
M-646	Vermillion Pyroxylin striping
M-647-S	Pyroxylin thinner (Replaces M-145 for service)
M-701	Pyroxylin Primer (New No. M-638)
M-702	Pyroxylin glaze (New No. M-639)
M-703	Pyroxylin surfacer (New No. M-640)

No other paints (except for use on Lincoln cars) are to

1926

be sold by branches without first obtaining permission from the Detroit office.

Dealers desiring to obtain a glossy finish on refinished cars, may desire to purchase M-623, Clear Pyroxylin. When receiving requests for M-623, you should advise the dealers that they may obtain the desired gloss finish by spraying with a double coat of Pyroxylin finish thinner which they can make up as follows:

M-647-S Pyroxylin thinner, 80%. Pyroxylin (desired color M-631, M-632, etc.), 20%.

NOV 16 (Letter from the Chicago branch)
"For the past two months all carburetors furnished, both the NH and Holley vaporizers, have been constructed with a heavier and more buoyant float, T-6333-B, in order to compensate for the pressure exerted by a full tank of fuel in Ford cars equipped with gasoline tanks under the cowl. The more buoyant float eliminates the tendency for the pressure exerted by the fuel tank, to cause the carburetor to leak when traveling over rough and heavily graveled roads.

"Leakage under these conditions naturally increases the gasoline consumption and reflects unfavorably on our product.

"It is therefore our intention to furnish, gratis to dealer, the new type float T-6333-B, as replacement of previous type float in cases where owners complain of unsatisfactory mileage. The old type float should be returned to this Branch, accompanied by our form 340 parts return sheet properly filled out, listing the motor number, etc., and reference should be made to this letter on same. We will then make return shipment to you of the new type float.

"It is understood that there is no necessity for replacing a float in any old style cars or in trucks or present type fordors which carry the gasoline tank under the driver's seat."

NOV 16 (Letter from the Chicago branch)
"Radiator carcass (3 tube type) T-8736-G and flat tube type T-8736-F are now obsolete and will no longer be furnished through production or service stock.

"The new type radiator (4 tube type) T-8736-H, is now being used entirely. This item is carried under the old service number, namely, 3925-E."

NOV 18 (Engine production records)
"Motor numbers ground off and replacement numbers: 10,000,000 to 14,548,000; 12,000,000 to 14,546,000; and 13,000,000 to 14,549,000."

NOV 29 (Letter from the Chicago branch)
32x6 eight-ply tires offered as optional equipment on the trucks, at an extra charge of $35 per set of two tires. These tires used the same wheel and rim as the standard 30x5 tires.

DEC 15 (Letter from the Chicago branch)
"In case you or your salesmen feel hesitant about forcefully denying all rumors of a "new car" caused by unauthorized and unfounded newspaper, magazine and trade paper articles as well as through any kind of propaganda, we call your attention to the emphatic statement recently made my Mr. Edsel Ford, as follows:

"There will be no new model and no new Ford car is going to be introduced. Nor are we planning on any six or eight cylinder car."

"What stronger denial can be made? What further statement is needed? What better answer can you give the prospect who calls your attention to such propaganda or rumors?

"Don't let such unfounded information interfere with your placing the best Ford car ever built in the hands of prospective buyers in your community.

"And we say "best Ford car" because of the complimentary letters received and appreciative comments made on all sides by individual owners as well as commercial users as to the more efficient and more flexible motor with its greatly improved operation resulting in more power, quicker getaway and increased gasoline mileage. And who are very much impressed with the improved appearance of our car generally ---- durability of the new Pyroxylin finish in various colors ---- high quality of upholstering ---- and the increased riding comfort of our all-steel bodies and balloon tires.

"The Ford Car today stands supreme in offering the greatest automobile value and its popularity is ever increasing as indicated by sales totaling over A MILLION AND A HALF so far this year."

DEC 15 (Letter from the Chicago branch)
This letter noted that there were a number of complaints about the poor quality of the carbon brushes supplied for use in the Model T generator. The letter explained that the so-called defective brushes which were returned to the factory were all checked and met the manufacturer's specifications.

In this letter they say: "Ford generators were designed to charge 12 amperes when cold and 9 amperes when hot. Therefore, when this charging rate is exceeded the bond of the brush is being dried out and deposited on the commutator causing the coating or blackened condition."

DEC 31 (Letter from the Chicago branch)
"Effective January 3rd, 1927, the Tudor Sedan will be equipped with black wire wheels as standard equipment at no extra cost."

1927

JAN 3 (Letter from Ford to all dealers)
"Effective January 3rd, the Tudor Sedan will be equipped with black wire wheels as standard equipment at no extra cost."

JAN 14 (Letter to dealers from Fargo branch)
"With the resumption of assembling operations, Tudor Sedans are being regularly equipped with black wire wheels as standard equipment at no extra cost."

FEB 11 (Ford letter to branches and dealers)
"Commencing Monday fourteenth (sic) all Ford Coupes delivered or shipped should be equipped with black wire wheels at no charge in billing price to dealer and effective Monday February twenty-first black wheels of this type will be considered standard equipment at no extra cost to customer, same as Tudor and Fordor."

FEB 14 (Letter to dealers from Fargo branch)
"Effective Feb. 14 all Ford Coupes delivered or shipped to dealers will be equipped with black wire wheels at no change in price. Beginning Monday, Feb. 21, black wire wheels of this type will be considered standard AT NO EXTRA COST TO CUSTOMER, same as the Tudor and Fordor."

MAR 2 (Letter GL1600 from the Fargo branch)
"For your information, the following is a comparative analysis of the babbitt in a connecting rod rebabbitted by an outside concern, and standard Ford babbitt:

	Outside	Standard Ford
Tin	82.96%	85-86%
Lead	5.00%	.10(max.)%
Copper	5.15%	7.00-7.5%
Antimony	6.89%	7.00-7.50% "

1927

The letter continues, stating that the increased copper in the Ford babbitt gives greater wear, and stresses that the dealers should use the Ford babbitt instead of any outside material.

MAR 21   (Factory letter to branches)
"Since the standardizing on blue and brown colors for our open cars, requests have been made by various fleet owners to have the Runabout with Pickup Body painted in black to match other Ford Pickup Cars operated by such fleet.

"Such requests have been approved and it has been decided that any of our regular colors, in addition to black finish, should be optional on the Runabout with Pickup Body upon specific request of the Fleet owners as well as individual buyers.

"The above also applies to Foreign Branches and European Companies."

MAR 30   (Letter from Ford to all dealers)
Announced the approval of the Kingston vaporizer for the Model T with a note that some may be used as standard equipment "on a small percentage of our production."

The Kingston unit listed at $9.00 and they made a special introductory price of $4.50, shipping one to each dealer.

MAY 26   (Engine production records)
Engine 15,000,000 built this date. 14,999,999 to 15,000,001 were held out of May 25 production. The last number built May 25 was 15,002,217.

MAY 31   (Engine production records)
All-steel valves now used in all engines except those for export.

JUL 29   (Letter 1668 from the Fargo branch)
"A special all-steel valve for Model T cars and trucks is now available through service stock, and in order to effect a complete initial distribution of this product to all dealers, we will include a small quantity with your next parts order.

"This all-steel valve is very much superior to the present type valve and we therefore recommend its use in your repair and service work.

"The price is 25 cents each, subject to dealers' regular discount, and your future requirements may be ordered in the usual manner with your next monthly stock order."

1941

AUG 4   (Engine production records)
The last Model T Ford engine was built at the River Rouge plant. It was S/N 15,176,888. (Seven T engines were built in 1941.)

169,856 Model T engines were built after the end of car production at the Detroit plant.

The Model T Ford Rear Axle

With the exception of body styles, and details of a few minor components, no single part of the Model T Ford underwent as many modifications as did the rear axle assembly. The internal parts of the rear axle assembly evolved somewhat but the basic design, after the first 18,000 cars, remained fairly stable. Not so with the external appearance; the design of the rear axle housings.

Ford cars built prior to the introduction of the Model T used a rear axle housing with a cast center section and steel axle tubes. The new Model T featured a new and less costly all-steel, drawn housing. Of one piece, each half of the rear axle housing was a masterful design in simplicity and cost-cutting. This axle housing, along with the engine base (oil pan) were major engineering feats at the time. Never before had steel been drawn to such an extent. [1]

The basic idea was a good one but the resulting product was not. Pressed (or drawn) steel has more tensile strength than cast iron but is not as rigid. Steel will bend and flex a good deal before it breaks, while cast iron remains relatively inflexible, up to its breaking point. It didn't take much service in the field before the flexing weakness of the Model T rear axle became apparent. Any number of accessory braces were offered by outside manufacturers to shore up the sagging center section but none did much more than just help.

Ford, of course, became aware of the problems, and considerable effort was made to find solutions. After about six years of Model T production, and after three major revisions in design, a final design had evolved which was satisfactory. Externally, this "ultimate" rear axle housing resembled the rear axle of the N-R-S Fords of 1906-1908 ---- a cast center section with steel axle tubes.

The internal construction of the assembly also underwent a number of changes; some major and some minor. The first axles used babbitt pinion and inner axle bearings, a flaw discovered very early in production. After the first 7,500 cars the pinion bearing was enlarged, but was still babbitt. At about car 12,000 the inner axle bearings were changed to the roller type, the same as had been used at the outer ends of the axle. This change required a modification of the axle housings; the addition of bearing supports at the inner ends of the housings. Now six rivets could be seen around the bell housing; the rivets which secured these bearing supports. After about 18,000 cars, the driveshaft pinion bearing was also changed to a roller, requiring another modification; the addition of a heavy reinforcement at the area where the driveshaft and rear axle housings were joined.[2]

The first Model T rear axles continued the radition of the earlier Fords ---- the axle shafts were of straight design, not having a taper at the outer ends to fit the wheel hubs. The hubs were a tight fit on the axle, though, and were driven (prevented from turning) by a woodruff key. A hole was drilled through the hub and axle into which a pin was fit to prevent the hub from coming off. This pin, in turn, was held in place by the hub cap which covered the holes. While initially secure, it didn't take long for the hub and axle to wear, resulting in ultimate failure. During early 1911, the tapered rear axle was adopted.

There were many relatively minor modifications made in the internal construction of the differential, and these will be covered in the text to follow.

Any attempt to clearly define the date of any change ends in frustration. The numbers and dates we have selected for this study are approximate. There are gaps in our information on part numbers, factory numbers, and details of some of the modifications. Ford, for the most part, kept the same part number for similar parts. The *factory number* often changed with a new design but did not *always* change. Examples: the axle housings; same part number but changing factory numbers. Rear radius rods, however, went through a number of modifications with no changes in either the part number or the factory number.

To add to the confusion, numbers were repeated for different parts. The early differential case bolt nut (2504) was discontinued (supplied with the bolt, actually) and later this number was that of the gasket used between the two halves, a modification made in 1919.

A number of design modifications must have been made but never implemented, or saw very short periods of production. This is especially true of the first few years of the Model T. Gaps in the factory number sequence cannot be explained with the information we have available at this time.

Keep in mind, too, that the dates listed are approximate and that cars on either side of the date may have used either the earlier design or the later. For example, we list 1915 as the year of the final housing design but we know that "1915" Fords

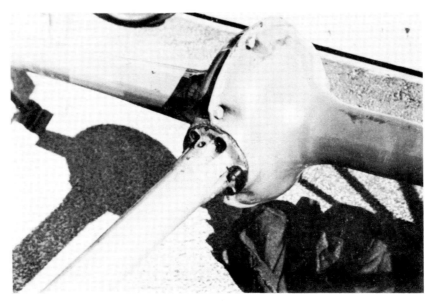

The early 1909 rear axle assembly. Note the lack of the pinion bearing spool and that there are no rivets around the center section. This design was used on the first 12,000 cars, after which the inner axle bearings were changed to roller and the six rivets per side appeared. The babbitt pinion bearing was used on the first 18,000 cars.

were built with the "1914" rear axle, and later, with the "1916" brake backing plates.

In the text that follows, both the part number and the factory number are shown. (The *part number* is the number shown in the Parts Lists ; the "factory number" is the one found on the part itself, if there is one.) For example:2542(87); 2542 is the part number, and 87 is the factory number of the driveshaft used in the early cars. The first *Parts Lists* used only factory numbers, incidentally.

THE INITIAL DESIGN
Early 1909

AXLE HOUSINGS
Part number 2501, factory number 1, right
Part number 2502, factory number 2, left
(Used on the first 12,000 cars)%2

The axle housings were of drawn steel and with the exception of the brake backing plates, were of one-piece design. There were no rivets around the center section. The inner axle bearings were babbitt bushings [2507(51)]. The brake backing plates, initially, were pressed steel, then cast iron, and were smooth surfaced inside and out, with no reinforcing ribs. The oil filler screw plug had a screwdriver slot for removal.

AXLE SHAFTS
Part number 2505, factory number 48

These axle were straight, having no taper at the wheel hub. The wheel was held in place by means of a woodruff key and a pin. Part number of the key was 2816(26) and the pin was 2817(27). The axle gear [2520(13)] was secured by a woodruff key [2521(21)] and a pin [2522(36)] in a manner similar

to the hub except that this pin was peened to keep it in place.

The outer axle (wheel) bearings were Timken roller [2508(97)] as in all Model T Fords. The bearing sleeves, 2509(170) right, and 2509(161) left, were similar to the later design (after around 1911) except that the locating "dimple" was located about 3/4 inch from the end instead of the usual 1/2 inch. The part and factory numbers of these bearing sleeves did not change when the dimple was moved.

DIFFERENTIAL GEAR ASSEMBLY

The left section (10) carried the ring gear (12) and the two were held together with ten rivets (38). The center spider [2526(15)] had a bronze bushing [2527(18)] in the center where the axles rode. The

TOP: The first production rear axle assembly. The universal joint housing is missing in this photo. Note the unusual brake rod supports, typical of the early Fords

CENTER LEFT: The non-tapered rear axle showing the keyway and the hole for the retaining pin. The pin was held in place by the hub cap. Note the smooth surface of the brake backing plate.

CENTER RIGHT: The rear hub, showing the hole for the above-mentioned retaining pin. Note the shape of the hub; almost the same as that of the front wheel hub, and typical of the hubs used until early 1911 when the tapered axle appeared. Few early Fords survived with the original axles and hubs.

LEFT: Another view of the axle and hub. The key is not installed in this photo, and the keyway does not line up with that in the hub. The design, poor as it was, continued until early 1911.

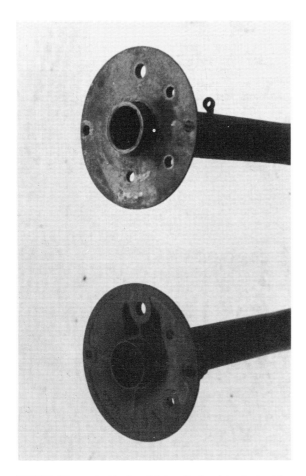

2539

ABOVE: The early (top) and later (bottom) brake backing plates. Note the deeper construction of the later type.

BELOW: For comparison, on the outside, the early backing plate (upper) looks similar to the later.

TOP: Catalog illustration of the babbitt driveshaft pinion bearing, used on the first 18,000 cars

CENTER: Outside surface of the early brake backing plate.

BELOW: Outside surface of the later backing plates, showing the recessed center and the reinforcing ribs. (the brake shoes here are of the later type; the original shoes of this era used only one spring.

three differential gears [2524(14)] also had bronze bushings [2525(93)].

The right half of the differential case [2513(11)], and the left half mentioned above, both had bronze bushings [2517(19)] where they fit over the axle gears. A bronze thrust washer [2528(30)] and two steel washers [2529(31)] were used on each side to locate the differential assembly in the axle housings. The two differential gear cases (above) were held together with studs [2514(52)] and nuts [2515(53)]. The original nuts were slotted through their circumference (through the side) and were peened down to lock them in place. Castellated nuts and locking wires came later.

BRAKE SHOES

Early production brake shoes, factory number 55, were bronze, as in the N-R-S models. These were replaced with the cast iron type [2566(55)] early in production. These iron shoes differed from the later type (after about 1913) in that they used only one retracting spring [2570(67)] across the open (cam) end and a clip [2560(63)] across the anchor end (if one can say that the brake shoe really has an "end").

DRIVESHAFT

Part number 2542(87) for the shaft; 2541(154) for the shaft and pinion assembly. The pinion gear [2543(16)] was held with a woodruff key, and the end of the driveshaft was peened to hold it in place.

After car 7,500 a new driveshaft [still 2542(87)] was used. Similar to the earlier type, it came in a number of pinion bearing area diameters. Accompanying the new shaft were new pinion bearings, still babbitt, part numbers 2539(24B) and 2539(24C). Driveshaft diameter now had to be specified when replacements were needed.

DRIVESHAFT HOUSING
Part number 2533, factory number 153

The housing was of two-piece design. The universal joint housing was a separate part [2577(70)] and was bolted to the rear tube [2533(153)]. The pinion gear bearing (24) was a babbitt bushing. The pinion thrust washer was factory number 22. The bearing behind the universal joint [2540(69), later 2581(69)] was also babbitt.

UNIVERSAL JOINT

Consisted of a male yoke (45) and a female yoke (46) which were joined by a pair of bronze rings (49) which were riveted together in the same manner as in the later all-steel universal joints.

LATER 1909, 1910, & early 1911

AXLE HOUSINGS
2501(1A) right, 2502(2A) left

After the first 12,000 cars (October 1909), the housing were modified to accept roller bearings at

The early differential gear spider [2526(150)] had a bronze bushing for the axle ends, and smaller arms for the differential gears, which also had bronze bushings. Provision for lubrication was poor in the early rear axles. Note the wear on the arms.

the inner ends of the axles. It was at this time that the six rivets appeared on each side of the center section (hence the "six rivet" rear end). These rivets secured the roller bearing sleeve supports, replacing the previous babbitt inner bearings. The roller bearings and their sleeves were the same as those used at the wheels.

This design apparently continued for about another 6,000 cars and was again modified to accept the new roller bearing driveshaft assembly. The part numbers for the new design were 2501(1B) right, and 2502(2B) left. The new modification consisted primarily of the addition of a forged reinforcing plate around the driveshaft mounting area, to offer support for the new roller bearing sleeve. The axle housings were drilled for 3/8 inch diameter studs to tie the driveshaft and axle housings together.

A minor modification made about this time was the addition of brazed-in-place washers around the

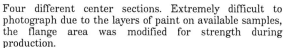

Four different center sections. Extremely difficult to photograph due to the layers of paint on available samples, the flange area was modified for strength during production.

UPPER LEFT: The initial design, which ran into 1910. The flange on the left half has a rim which overlaps the flat flange on the right housing. The two are bolted together with no reinforcement.

UPPER RIGHT: The first modification was the use of small washers brazed in place around the bolt holes on the right housing. The photo shows the relative thickness of the flange around the bolt holes (the flanges themselves are alike). Both of the above housings in the photo use the roller bearing driveshaft.

LOWER LEFT: The third change was to replace the washers with a metal ring, again brazed in place around the circumference of the right housing flange. Note how the seam is relatively smooth on the right side; the thickness of the ring filling in the overlap of the left housing's flange.

LOWER RIGHT: The fourth modification was to add another ring around the flange on the left housing. Now the center seam appeared considerably thicker.

The dates of these modifications are unknown but it is believed that the washers were added in early 1910, the right-hand ring by mid-1910, and the left-hand ring in late 1910.

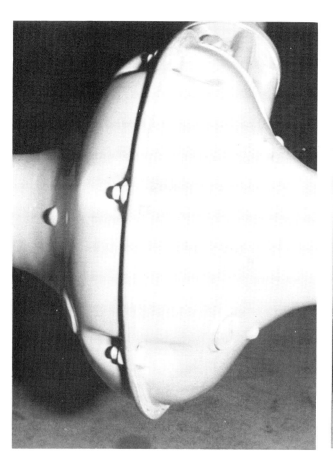

Rear Axles   578

bolt holes on the right-hand housing, in an effort to beef up this area. Later in 1910, these washers were dropped in favor of a heavy ring which was brazed around the outside circumference of the right-hand housing. Still later, a similar ring was added to the left housing, making the appearance of the "seam" much thicker. It is believed that all six-rivet housings used in 1911 used this final design.

The brake backing plate was modified during 1909 production (date unknown). Of more rugged design, the plate was deeper and had a number of reinforcing ribs (or webs) on its outer (wheel side) surface (see illustration).

AXLE SHAFTS

After the initial production, the axle shaft was modified to use two woodruff keys at the axle gear end, the gear still being pinned in place. This new axle was 2505(48). During 1910 (apparently) the axles were again modified. Similar to the earlier shaft, the axle gear was now held with a larger woodruff key and two "C" clips, as in all later axles. This axle was 2505-1/2(48B); the key was 2521(21B), and the clips were 2519A(118). Both these shafts were of the non-tapered type.

The tapered axle appeared in early 1911 and the non-tapered type was discontinued, even for the replacement market. The factory offered the new type with a new wheel hub as part number 2505C. It is believed that the tapered axle appeared in the six-rivet housings, before the introduction of the "1912" twelve-rivet rear axle.

DIFFERENTIAL GEAR ASSEMBLY
Part number 2511

The left differential housing [2512(10)] was modified to accept screws [2519(103)] to hold the ring gear, greatly simplifying repairs. The new housing was 2512(10B). The ring gear [2518(12B)] was drilled and tapped to accept the screws. Otherwise, the gear was identical to the previous (riveted) type.

The arms of the differential spider [2526(15)] were 9/16 inch in diameter. Bronze bushings were retained in all gears, housings and the spider. The spider evolved through factory number changes (15B and 15C).

DRIVESHAFT

Part number 2542(87) was used in the early cars in which the pinion bearing was a babbitt bushing. Around 18,000 the driveshaft was again changed, this time to accept the removable pinion, the roller bearing, and the new thrust bearing assembly. This shaft was 2595B(87D).[3]

An annular ball bearing was now used as a thrust bearing, replacing the washers previously employed. It consisted of an assembly of two races, fifteen balls, a ball retainer, and a clip to hold it all together. This bearing was placed ahead of the

In early 1910 the pinion bearing was changed to the roller type. This required a new driveshaft housing and modifications to the rear axle housings. A heavy reinforcement plate was added to the front of the housings to support the new pinion bearing spool. The spool was held with 3/8 inch studs and nuts. This assembly continued until summer of 1911.

pinion roller bearing. The thrust bearing was available as an assembly [2589B(185)], or the individual parts could be had.

DRIVESHAFT HOUSING
Part number 2582, factory number 74C

With the change to the roller bearing on the driveshaft, the driveshaft housing was modified to accept the new bearing spool [2583(191)]. The housing and pinion spool was secured by 3/8 by 4-7/16 inch studs [2584(183)]. The bearing spool used a steel bearing sleeve [2593(107)] and was constructed so that the studs were enclosed. The design was typical of the spools used until mid-1920, with minor variations.

BRAKE SHOES
2566 (55)

Now of cast iron, they used the one spring [2570(67)] and the clip [2560(63)] as described earlier. The spring was only 1-1/4 inch long.

UNIVERSAL JOINT
2571 (151)

The bronze ring universal joint was changed to the all-iron type in early 1909. The new assembly was made up of 2672(45B) male, 2573(46B) female, and two 575(49) forged rings, riveted together with four 2576(50) rivets. This design continued unchanged through 1927.

1911 - 1912

AXLE HOUSINGS
2501B (1E) right, 2502B (2E) left

In the summer of 1911 the axle housings were redesigned. The new style had a cast center section, with the axle tubes of steel, flared and riveted in place ith twelve rivets on each side. Ford referred to this design as the "1912" axle, and it is commonly referred to today as the "12-rivet" or "clamshell" rear end. The design was an improvement but not a solution to the general weakness of the housing design. This axle housing would be replaced in later 1912 with another type.

Two axle housings from early 1910. Both have the reinforcing plate for the roller bearing driveshaft. The one on the right has the plain flange (no reinforcing washers) and the smooth-surfaced brake backing plates; and indication that most, if not all, 1909 cars had such brake plates. The housing on the left has the reinforcing washers and the recessed backing plate.

During 1911 the wheel bearing sleeves were modified slightly, as mentioned earlier. The locating dimple was moved out a quarter-inch closer to the outside edge (now 1/2 inch instead of 3/4 inch from the end). This change was made during production and no part number change was made to indicate the change. These sleeves came in rights and lefts but it wasn't until 1914 that such was indicated in the *Parts Lists*. Until 1914 the books indicated 2509(170) as the number for both; then 2509(170) became the right, and 2509B(161) was the left.

AXLES

Early in 1911, and not coincidental with the changes in the six-rivet housing, the tapered-end axles superseded the straight type. The new axle was 2505D(2818) and this type continued without change through 1927. The new axle was supplied as a replacement for the earlier cars, and such replacement also required new wheel hubs. A

The brake backing plate. Although there were minor design variations, this style continued until late 1915.

View of the brake backing plate assembly showing the forged-end radius rods (used until about 1914) and the forged-end brake rods (used until about 1921 with minor variations in style).

The mid-1911-12 axle housing. The center section is now a casting with the flared axle tubes riveted in place. The support rod shown here is an accessory, such items were never supplied by Ford.

replacement "kit" (hub, axle, and gear) was offered as P/N 2505C.

DRIVESHAFT AND HOUSING

The shaft with the tapered end and removable gear was by this time standard, and was P/N 2595B(87D)[4] . This shaft had evolved through a number of changes in the first year and there seems to be no way of knowing just when one type superseded the other. 2595B, like the axle shafts, continued unchanged through 1927.

The driveshaft housing continued to be of the two-piece design with the separate universal joint housing. The pinion spool and the flange on the driveshaft housing were now drilled to accept larger (13/32 inch) studs [2584B(183B)]. The spool was 2583(191B).

DIFFERENTIAL GEAR ASSEMBLY

A new differential spider [2526B(15C)] was introduced around 1911. It differed from the earlier in that the three arms for the differential gears were increased to 5/8 inch diameter at the gear bearing surfaces. The bronze bushing for the axles was continued.

The three differential gears [2524B(14C)] were modified to accept bronze bushings that would fit the larger bearings on the spider. The differential case 2512B(10C) left, and 2513B(11C) right was also modified to suit the larger spider. Other internal and external parts continued without significant change.

LATE 1912 TO EARLY 1915

2501D (2835B) right
2502D (2836B) left

The center section was again altered in late 1912.[5] Still of cast iron as in the "1912" axle, the new design was more rounded and somewhat stronger. The axle tubes were still flared and riveted with twelve rivets to the center section. The brake backing plates continued unchanged. Somewhere during this era the oil filler plug was changed to the hex-headed screw type.

DIFFERENTIAL GEAR ASSEMBLY

Early production continued using the same components as were used in the "1912" axle. During 1913, apparently, the bronze bushings in the differential case for the axle gears were discontinued, and the gear hubs were enlarged to fit. The new case was 2512C(10D) left, and 2513C(11D) right. The axle gears were now 2520(13B).

Rear Axles

With the change to the tapered axle in early 1911, a new wheel hub appeared. These hubs had evolved over the years but the two types shown here are typical. The straight-bore type is on the left, and the tapered-bore is on the right.

RADIUS RODS

Sometime during this period, probably during 1914, the radius rods were modified to cut costs. The forged fork at the rear was eliminated and the rod tubing was now pressed flat and then split to form an integral fork. The two rods were still interchangeable from side to side.

BRAKE SHOES
2655 (55)

While similar to the cast iron shoes used earlier, the shoes were modified and now used two retracting springs; the second one across the anchor side. Although the brake shoes were supplied in

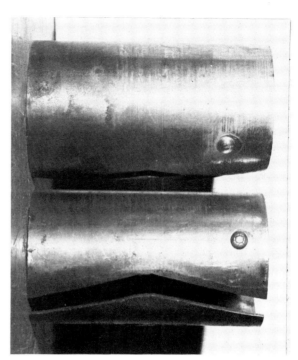

Two axle bearing sleeves. The upper one is the earlier, used until about 1912. Note that the "dimple" is about 3/4 inch from the end, while on the later type (lower) it is only about 1/2 inch from the end.

one piece, they would break at the anchor pin, and this new spring held them in place (replacing the clip used earlier). The springs were new and longer (3-3/8 inch), P/N 2570(2862). This brake shoe continued until the 1926 models in August 1925.

During the early years (perhaps until 1912) a different type of rear axle bearing sleeve was used. The early style had the locating dimple 3/4 inch from the end. The axle housing in which it was used is on the left. Later production saw the dimple moved out about 1/4 inch and its housing is shown on the right. Aside from the location of the dimple, the sleeves are alike, but they are not interchangeable.

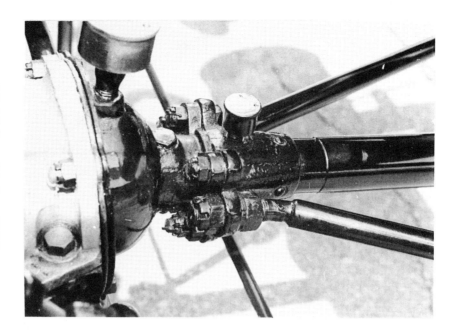

While the initial 1911 production continued the use of the 1910 rear axle, a new type was introduced about July 1911. Called the "1912 axle," the center section was now cast iron. The axles were of the tapered type.

The driveshaft housing was of the two-piece design; the "two-piece" referring to the separate universal joint housing.

The rear radius rods had forged forks and no seams on the inner side. They were interchangeable from side to side. The brake rods also had forged forks.

Rear Axles

Late 1912 to early 1915

DRIVESHAFT HOUSING

Late in 1913 or perhaps early 1914 production, the one-piece driveshaft housing appeared. The universal joint housing was now integral with the torque tube. In spite of this change, the part number [2582(153D)] remained the same.

1915

AXLE HOUSINGS
2501E (2835C) right
2502E (2836C) left

After six years of experimenting, Ford finally developed an axle housing which was satisfactory ---- one that looked surprisingly like the one used on the earlier N-R-S cars of 1906-1908. The center section casting was now extended to receive straight axle tubes, which were retained by six rivets. This was the final design and except for some relatively minor changes it continued through 1927. The brake backing plates, used in previous axles, continued with little change.

DIFFERENTIAL GEAR ASSEMBLY

A new differential spider, 2526B(15D), appeared in late 1914. Similar to the earlier spider, the new design eliminated the bronze bushings in the three differential gears. This was done by making the three arms larger (see photo). New gears [2524C(14D)] were also used but these were about the same as the earlier gears except they did not have the bronze bushings. The older gears could be used here if the bronze bushings were removed.

According to the *Parts Lists* the side thrust bearings were changed from bronze to babbitt about this time as well. Thus ended the use of bronze in the Ford rear axle assembly. There were no other significant changes.

Prior to about 1914 the differential gear housings had bronze bushings for the axle gears, and the gears had smaller hubs. With the elimination of the bushings, the gears were made with larger hubs and these remained standard through 1927.

The new one-piece driveshaft front universal joint housing. The ball joint is now an integral part of the joint housing, and is typical of the 1914 to 1927 construction. (The break light switch shown is a modern addition.)

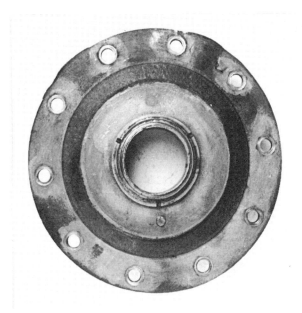

The early (before 1914) differential gear case is shown above. Note the bronze bushings in the center, and the complete lack of any provision for internal lubrication. Whatever grease was packed in during assembly was supposed to do the job for life. Unfortunately, grease got out faster than it got in, and wear was quite a problem.

LEFT: The final design of the right differential gear case included cast-in notches which would allow lubrication to seep inside. Note the relocation of the webs and of the pin used to hold the thrust washer.

Rear Axles

The 1915-1918 rear axle housing

1916

Late in 1915 the brake backing plates were modified and now included a series of ribs on the inside surfaces. This backing plate continued until the redesign in mid-1925 when Ford went to the eleven-inch brake drums in the 1926 models.

1917

Major changes! The pins [2531B(7640)] that held the steel thrust washers were made a bit shorter and were of a stepped, dual diameter, design. This modification was made to prevent these pins from scoring the babbitt thrust washer bearings.

1919

In a series of production modifications the rear axle was modified in detail during the late 1918 to 1920 period. The first change made, perhaps in 1918, was to move the oil filler hole in the right housing 1-3/4 inch below the centerline of the

housing, about an inch lower than it had been. This was done to prevent overfilling and subsequent leakage at the axle ends. A help, but not a cure.

During 1919 the axle housing ends were modified to eliminate a machining operation. This change required a new oil seal retaining cup [2510-1/2(56B)] which was slightly larger in diameter (2-7/16 inch instead of 2-13/32 inch). Also during this period, perhaps at the time of the filler hole change, the center sections were machined to take a paper gasket [2504(139)] between the two halves. After this series of alterations the axle housings were given new part numbers: 2501(7635C) left, and 2502(7636C) right.

During 1919 Ford announced the availability of new rear end gears with a four-to-one ratio. The ring gear had forty-eight teeth, and the pinion had twelve. This option saw little use, though, because in late 1919 Ford developed the ten-tooth pinion which would work with the standard forty-tooth ring gear.[6]

The final design of the differential gear spider. The arms on the new type were larger. The gears themselves were similar; the bronze bushings were just eliminated in the later type. The old type [2526B(15C)] and its gear [2524B(14C)] is on the left; the new spider [2526B(15D)] and its gear [2524C(14D)] is on the right.

Rear Axles

586

Typical 1919 through 1927 rear axle center section. Note that the filler hole is now 1-3/4 inch below the centerline, about an inch lower that the earlier types. The pinion bearing spool show here is typical 1920-1927 with the exposed bolts.

1920

During 1920 production (the date is uncertain) the pinion bearing spool was changed from the iron casting to a steel forging. The new design eliminated the need for the separate bearing sleeve [2593(107)]. The new spool [2583B(191C)] no longer enclosed the mounting studs, and cap screws replaced the studs and nuts used in the earlier models. This new spool is easily identified by its exposed screws, and it was the final design, continuing without change through 1927.

With the new bearing spool, a new thrust bearing was introduced. The design was simplified and the new bearing consisted of just three parts: two identical earing plates [2591(188)] and a ball bearing assembly [2591B(162)]. The three parts could be ordered together as 2589C(185B).

The new bearing assembly was not directly interchangeable with the old. The previous driveshaft flange was recessed to fit over the cast spool, and the rim around this recess had to be ground off to fit the new spool. Of course ,the new driveshaft housing did not have this rim, and it could be used with the earlier spool as a replacement. The new driveshaft housing was 2582(153B).

In a letter to its branches, dated September 7, 1920, Ford announced the discontinuance of the forged-end brake rods for "1921 production." These were identified at factory number 804 (no part number) but no such change is indicated in the *Parts Lists*. (F/N 804 does not appear in the *Parts Lists* but is listed in the 1920 factory parts catalog. The standard brake rod is 3468(891B). Factory number 891B is listed in the 1920 factory catalog as "brake rod (R.H.) assembly.") In any event, the brake rods were now of the less costly stamped yoke design.

Brake backing plate, typical of the later 1915 to 1925 production. Note the reinforcing ribs below the axle, added in late 1915.

Rear Axles

The exposed bolt, forged steel pinion bearing spool which was introduced during 1920.

1921-1922

During 1921 the rear radius rods were redesigned, again for production economy. Similar to the previous rods, these were still of pressed steel but now had a seam along the under side. Since it was now possible for water to get inside and cause rust, the new rods were made in pairs: 2547(152) right, and 2547B(158) left. The rods are installed with the seam down, but being otherwise identical, they can be reversed (seam up). This final modification ended all but minor production changes until the "Improved Ford" of 1926 was introduced in August 1925.

1926-1927

AXLE HOUSINGS
2501B (7635B) right
2502B (7636B) left

While the basic design of the rear axle assembly was unchanged, the brake backing plates were all new for the 1926 models introduced in August of 1925. The "Improved Ford" now had rear hub brakes that were eleven inches in diameter and the backing plates were altered to match. Other than the brake parts, radius and brake rods, all parts were interchangeable with the earlier design.

The part numbers for the older housings (pre-1926) were changed to 2501(7635AR) right, and 2502(7636AR) left. The addition of an "R" to a factory number generally indicated a replacement for an obsolete part in the *Price List of Parts*.

A minor improvement in the 1926 rear axle was the addition of an oil seal inside the outer wheel bearings. It fit between the bearing sleeve and the end of the axle housing tube, sealing the axle

bearing from the differential lubricant, and thus helped to reduce the typical Ford rear wheel oil leak. This seal was part number 2511(198A) and its retaining washer was 2511B(221).

Near the end of production, the oil filler plug was changed to a half-inch pipe plug, replacing the hex-head screw used since 1913. Apparently this change was made in some, but not all, production beginning in late 1926.

BRAKES

The brake shoes were now of pressed steel and were asbestos lined. The brake actuating cam was considerably larger and pivoted off-center so that when operated the brakes tended to be self-energizing. There was no rear anchor as in the previous design, the operating cam taking the entire load.

For some strange reason, Ford retained the transmission brake as the normal service brake, using these new rear brakes as before, just for "emergency." The larger brakes could have made excellent service brakes had they been connected to the foot pedal.

The brake backing plates were of sheet metal, riveted to the new cast support. The brake shoes were held in place by clips that were a part of the backing plate. These clips were riveted in place on the early production, then stamped as an integral part of the backing plate later on. There were a number of variations in the design of the backing plates, and we have not been able to determine which was used at any particular time. Evidence seems to indicate that the backing plates came in different configurations at the same time periods.

RADIUS AND BRAKE RODS

The radius rods were modified to have a larger fork at the rear end to clear the relocated brake operating cam and lever. Their basic design continued; seamed construction with pressed fork ends. Part numbers were 2547C(152B) right, and 2547D(158B) left.

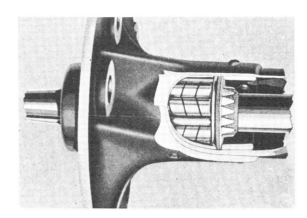

New in the 1926-1927 rear axles, but applicable to all earlier ones (and shown here in the pre-1926 axle), were the inner oil seals. They were a help but not a cure for the ever-present rear axle oil leaks.

The brake rods were also new, being a bit shorter and with a different "bend" to clear the radius rods. They were numbers 3468C(891C) right, and 3469C(1513C) left.

Of course, different hubs and brake drums were used during this period. The hubs used with the wooden wheels were the same as in earlier years but they were bolted to eleven inch, pressed steel, brake drums. The hubs and drums for the wire wheels were of all-new design and were supplied as a unit; the drums being of pressed steel and pressed on a forged hub.

A minor modification needed for the new axle assembly was a new spring perch. The modified brake backing plate assembly relocated the perch mounting area, and the new perch was of a shorter, simpler, and stronger design to fit the new location.

The new (1926-27) brake drum and backing plate, shown here in the wooden wheel application. Note that even though a new oil seal was used to prevent any possibility of leakage, provision was made for such leakage to escape at the bottom rather than just collect in the drum. In use, the oil did leak, it did leak out the bottom, and it did collect in the drum.

SYNOPSIS

If you have studied the foregoing and compared it with previous similar articles, you will note some variations; particularly in the 1909 to 1912 period. Most noticeable is our belief that in spite of the great number of 1909 Fords around today which have the roller driveshaft bearing, this feature did not appear until about January 1910. Ford literature leaves little doubt, particularly among the invoices we studied at the Ford Archives. There, the first note of a "reinforced housing" was on February 1, 1910, car number 15,667. This could have referred to the added washers around the bolt holes on the housings, or even the added

reinforcing ring around the flange, but it is doubtful that these relatively minor modifications would have been noted. Based on the fact that letters on file at the Ford Archives give 15,000 as the number at which the roller bearing was added, and that that number was assembled on January 15, 1910, it seems unlikely that any 1909 cars had the roller pinion bearing.

"Roller bearing rear axle" appeared on an invoice for car 13,100, November 29, 1909. While other literature gives 12,000 as the starting number, there is little doubt that the roller bearings at the inner axle ends came before the roller bearing driveshaft.

During December 1910, cars were built with "1911 rear axle" written on the invoice. This may have referred to the housing with the two reinforcing rings, or it may have meant the tapered-end axles. Our belief is that the note refers to the housing, and that the axles came later.

Car number 61,197 (July 13, 1911) was the first on which the invoice was marked "1912 rear axle." Here we believe this to refer to the new design housing, which we now call the "twelve-rivet" or "clamshell" rear end.

REAR END SPOTTER'S GUIDE

To simplify the task of identifying the "correct" rear axle for a given period, the following is our present belief:

1909
Pressed steel axle housing with no rivets until about car number 12,000, then pressed steel with six rivets. Smooth brake backing plates (visible only with the wheel off). Babbitt pinion bearing (no bearing spool).

1910
Six-rivet pressed steel housings with reinforcing washers in early 1910, then the reinforcing ring instead of the washers later, and two reinforcing rings in late 1910 and early 1911. Roller bearing driveshaft with 3/8 inch retaining studs. Brake backing plates with reinforcing ribs on the wheel side (visible only with the wheel off).

1911
Continues the late 1910 design. Tapered axles added early in the year.

LATE 1911-1912
Twelve-rivet "clamshell" rear axle with the relatively narrow cast center section. Driveshaft bearing spool held with 13/32 inch studs.

LATE 1912-EARLY 1915
Larger "1913-14" axle housing with the flared and riveted axle tubes. 1914 and later cars used the pressed-end radius rods, replacing the forged-end type used earlier. The one-piece driveshaft became standard about 1914.

1915

New design center section with the straight axle tubes inserted into the cast center section. The first of the "standard" Ford rear axles. Brake backing plates were the same as in the earlier cars (no reinforcing ribs visible). One-piece driveshaft housing.

LATE 1915-1918

Same as 1915 except the brake backing plates now have reinforcing ribs on the external (outside) surface.

1919-1925

Similar to the previous type. The oil filler hole is now 1-3/4 inch below the centerline. The center sections are machined to accept a paper gasket. In late 1920 the pinion bearing spool was changed to the forged type with the exposed bolts. Radius rods were of the seamed type (with the seams on the underside) beginning in 1921. 1920 was the last year in which the forged-end brake rods were used.

1926-1927

Generally the same as the 1925 style except for the larger rear brakes, with matching brake and radius rods. 1927 axles used the 1/2 inch pipe plug at the filler hole. A half-inch pipe plug, with a square hole for a wrench, replaced the hex-head screw used earlier, appeared in later production.

As in all Model T lore, dates are approximate. Typically, Ford made changes during production, with considerable overlapping of the old and the new designs. Therefore, let this only be a guide; not the word of God.

Reader comments and additional information or corrections are always welcome. If you have something to add, please let us know.

A new 1915 Runabout showing the 1914 style rear axle housings.

NOTES

1. The art of drawing steel into complex and deep forms was new at the beginning of the century. One of the pioneers in this field was the John R. Keim Mills, Inc., of Buffalo, New York. Keim manufactured bicycles and associated parts. One of its employees was William S. Knudsen. Knudsen had been credited with the concept of drawing rear axle housings, and since Keim was one of the major developers of the process, they were the suppliers for the original Model T rear axle housings and crankcases. Ford purchased the Keim company in 1911 and as a part of the deal, Knudsen joined Ford and acted as production manager until his parting in April of 1921.

Knudsen moved to Chevrolet, spearheading that firm's rise to first place in sales. In 1921, Ford sold fourteen cars to every Chevrolet. The sales gap closed rapidly, and Chevrolet became first in sales in 1927 (when Ford closed down for six months). William Knudsen ultimately became president of General Motors. The Keim plant was converted to become the Buffalo Ford assembly plant.

2. There is conflicting information as the dates of the changes to the roller bearings. The *Parts Lists* say "1910" in some places and "1911" in others. A Factory letter in the files at the Ford Archives indicates the pinion bearing was changed to the roller type at car number 18,000. The same letter indicates the inner axle bearings were changed to roller at 12,000.

3. A letter in the files at the Ford Archives, dated July 23, 1909, indicates that the driveshaft with the removable gear was used after number 7,000. This modification may have made the change in the babbitt bearing and thrust washer necessary. Again, different sources give different and conflicting dates for these modifications.

4. We are not certain if the earlier (pressed steel) housing was drilled for the larger studs, or if this change occurred with the change to the cast center section in late 1911.

5. A letter, dated November 5, 1912, in the files at the Ford Archives indicates that the 1913-style cars were then in production with the new axle.

6. A Factory Letter, dated January 20, 1920, announced the new ten-tooth pinion and the discontinuance of the previous four-to-one gear set.

Model T Ford Tools

The tools used on or supplied with the Model T Ford seem to be of an almost univeral interest. It is almost a certainty that one or more such tools will be found at any swap meet or flea market, car oriented or not. The identification of these tools presents an interesting problem. Some time ago (1982) the author made a "stab" at the subject, listing every tool we could find from all the material at hand. Since that time, th author has found a few more, and these are included in the following pages.

This coverage deals only with those tools supplied by Ford, not the many that were manufactured by others for use on the Model T, such as K. R. Wilson, Western Auto, etc. This compilation lists every Ford-supplied tool listed in over sixty-five *Parts Lists of Parts*, Ford *Service Bulletins*, and other pieces of literature. The listings show each tool's "history." "History" means its price, description, factory number changes, etc.

Under each tool number is a list of dates, factory numbers and prices. The first date shown is that of the first publication in which the tool was listed, and its price. Subsequent dates are those of catalogs in which a price, factory or part number, or description was changed. For example, the first tool listed, the 1349 Hub Cap Wrench, appeared for the first time in the January 1911 *Parts List*. In May 1915 the price dropped to ten cents. In October 1917 the price rose to fifteen cents and in November 1918 to twenty cents, etc. The last date listed under each tool was either the date of the last catalog in which the tool was shown, or the date of the last catalog used in this compilation (October 1927).

A brief description of each tool is given. Where the tool was supplied as a part of the tool kit which came with each car, it is listed as "Regular Equipment."

Copies of the *Parts Lists* illustrations are included as an aid in identification. These illustrations were used, unchanged, year after year; reproductions herein are of those in which some change was made. Unfortunately, not all tools are illustrated. In addition, there were many years in which there were no tool illustrations in the parts books.

It is important to remember that the catalog illustrations are not necessarily an accurate picture of any given tool. Ford, for the most part, did not manufacture these tools, and most were supplied by more than one outside vendor. Consequently, a particular tool supplied by one company could differ in some manner with that supplied by another. In addition, tools were modified from time to time, with no change being indicated in the parts books. A typical example of such a change might be in the 1903 pliers. Early in the 1920's one handle of the pliers was formed so that it could be used as a screwdriver (making the 1902 screwdriver unnecessary and saving a few cents on each car). There is no change in the description or factory number to indicate this modification.

Initially, tools had part numbers similar to those used on other parts of the Model T. For example, part number 4000 Socket Wrench was factory number 1926 from June 1909 until January 1911. In the January 1911 catalog just the factory number (1926) was listed. Beginning about 1917, tools were given "3Z" numbers, some of which superseded the earlier factory numbers. About 1920 the "5Z" numbers appeared and these in many cases replaced the 3Z series.

This compilation lists the tools under the latest part number. This does not mean that, for example, the 2333 Wrench, superseded by 3Z-655, and later by 5Z-162 were all exactly the same tool. The design may or may not have changed with the change in the number. Tools are just grouped in this manner to make comparison easier.

There are also cases where a tool was shown as superseded by another number, but the new number was never listed. Example: 2319 "T" screwdriver was shown as being changed to 3Z-642 in the February 1917 catalog but the 3Z-642 was never listed (nor was the 2319 later).

Furthermore, the quality of most of these tools pales in comparison with modern tools that might do the same job. In most cases, the modern socket set is heads and shoulders above the original tool, not only in quality but in ease of use. Yet there are a number of Ford tools for which there is no satisfactory modern equivalent. This is particularly true of some of the pullers, and special wrenches for the transmission, exhaust manifold, and other areas.

So, here it is! If any reader knows of a missing tool, or can offer more information, please drop the author a note. The author can come up with all manner of real or imagined "facts" on the Model T itself, but on the tools his imagination fails him.....

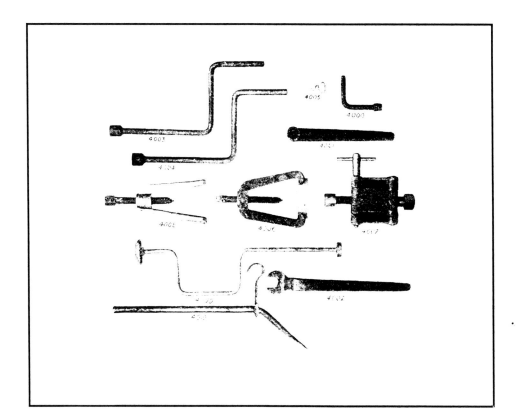

Tool Illustrations used in 1909-1910

Part #	Catalog Date	Factory #	Price	Notes

1349 HUB CAP WRENCH — REGULAR EQUIPMENT

Part #	Catalog Date	Factory #	Price	Notes
	Jan 11	1349	.25	Pressed-steel combination wrench
	May 15	1349	.10	for hub, front wheel bearing
	Oct 17	1349	.15	cone, crankcase drain plug, etc.
	Nov 18	1349	.20	While retaining the same factory
	Jun 22	1349	.15	number, there were many variations
	Oct 27	1349	.15	in the design over the years.

1370 CLAMPING SCREW (For clutch disk drum puller)

| | Jan 11 | 1370 | .10 | |
| | Jul 11 | 1370 | .10 | |

1387 ADJUSTABLE WRENCH (Monkey wrench)

	Jan 11	1387	.60	REGULAR EQUIPMENT
	Dec 11	1387	.40	
	May 15	1387	.25	
	Feb 17	1387	.40	
	Oct 17	1387	.50	
	Aug 20	1387	.60	
	Jul 21	1387	.50	
	Jun 22	1387	.40	
	Oct 27	1387	.40	

1902 SCREWDRIVER — REGULAR EQUIPMENT

	Jan 11	1902	.30	
	Dec 11	1902	.25	
	May 15	1902	.15	
	Jul 18	1902	.20	
	Nov 18	1902	.25	
	Mar 20	1902	.35	About 1920 the pliers
	Aug 20	1902	.50	handle was modified for use
	Sep 21	1902	.50	as screwdriver.

1903 PLIERS — REGULAR EQUIPMENT

	Jan 11	1903	.50	
	Dec 11	1903	.30	
	May 15	1903	.20	
	Oct 17	1903	.25	
	Nov 18	1903	.30	
	May 20	1903	.35	About 1920 the handle was
	Aug 20	1903	.50	ground to form a screwdriver
	Jul 21	1903	.40	blade about eliminating the
	Nov 21	1903	.25	need for the 1902
	Oct 27	1903	.25	screwdriver.

1904 SPARK PLUG WRENCH

	Jan 11	1904	.30	REGULAR EQUIPMENT
	Dec 11	1904	.25	
	May 12	2178	.25	
	Jan 13	2178	.25	2335 later

1917 DOUBLE END WRENCH

	Jan 11	1917	.30	REGULAR EQUIPMENT
	Dec 11	1917	.20	
	May 15	1917	.10	
	Jun 18	1917	.15	
	Nov 18	1917	.25	
	Apr 19	1917	.20	
	Jul 19	1917	.15	
	Nov 19	1917	.20	
	May 20	1917	.25	
	Jul 21	1917	.20	
	Aug 23	1917	.15	
	Oct 27	1917	.15	

1924 See 3Z-598

1925 SOCKET WRENCH (For 5/8" cylinder head cap screws)

4004				
	Jun 09	1925	.50	(Crank Type)
1925				
	Jan 11	1925	.50	
	Jul 11	1925	.50	

1926 SOCKET WRENCH (Piston pin bolt, cars 1 to 2500)

4000				
	Jun 09	1926	.40	
1926				
	Jan 11	1926	.40	
	Dec 11	1926	.25	
	Sep 12	1926	.25	

1927 SCREWDRIVER (For commutator screws)

4005				
	Jun 09	1927	.05	
1927				
	Jan 11	1927	.05	
	Jul 11	1927	.05	

1928 SOCKET WRENCH (Crankshaft bearing nut)

4001				
	Jun 09	1928	.30	
1928				
	Jan 11	1928	.40	
	Jul 11	1928	.40	

1929 See 5Z-210
1930X See 5Z-319
1933X See 5Z-287

1934 CAP SCREW (Clamp screw for 1933X puller)

| | Jan 11 | 1934 | .15 | |
| | Jul 11 | 1934 | .15 | |

1935 SCREW (For 1933X puller)

| | Jan 11 | 1935 | .35 | |
| | Jul 11 | 1935 | .35 | |

1936X See 5Z-326

1937 SCREW (For 1936X gear puller)

| | Jan 11 | 1937 | .35 | |
| | Jul 11 | 1937 | .35 | |

1938 VALVE SPRING LIFTER HOOK

| | Jan 11 | 1938 | .30 | |
| | Jul 11 | 1938 | .30 | |

1953X See 5Z-314
1957 See 5Z-280

1974 "L" SOCKET WRENCH (Driveshaft and rear axle stud nut)

| | Jan 11 | 1974 | .40 | (For 3/8" nuts) |
| | Oct 13 | 1974 | .40 | |

1974B See 5Z-158
1975 See 5Z-152
1978 See 20Z-340

2318 "T" SOCKET WRENCH (Short, 3/4")

| | Jan 11 | 2318 | .50 | |
| | Jul 11 | 2318 | .50 | |

2319 "T" SCREWDRIVER (For camshaft set screw)

	Jan 11	2319	.50	6-1/2" long
	May 15	2319	.30	
	Feb 16	2319	.40	
	Feb 17	3Z-642	.40	(3Z-642 never listed)

2320 See 5Z-160
2321 See 5Z-153
2322 See 5Z-155
2323 See 5Z-195
2324 See 5Z-209

2327 BRACE WRENCH (Short, 9/16")

| | Jan 11 | 2327 | .60 | |
| | Jul 11 | 2327 | .60 | |

2328 See 5Z-289
2331 See 5Z-290

Part #	Catalog Date	Factory #	Price	Notes
2332				**BRACE SCREWDRIVER** (Magnet screws, 13-3/4" long)
	Jan 11	2332	.50	
	May 15	2332	.25	
	Feb 16	2332	.50	
	Feb 17	3Z-653	.35	
2333	See 5Z-162			
2335				**"L" SOCKET WRENCH** (5/8" cylinder head bolts)
	Jan 11	2335	.50	(Combination open end and
	Jan 13	2335	.50	socket wrench)
2335				**WRENCH** (Spark plug and cylinder head)
	Oct 13	5893	.50	**REGULAR EQUIPMENT**
	May 15	5893	.30	
	Oct 17	5893	.35	
	Nov 18	5893	.60	
	Dec 18	5893	.50	
	Aug 23	5893	.40	
	Apr 27	5893	.35	
	Oct 27	5893	.35	
2336				**TOOL ROLL** **REGULAR EQUIPMENT**
	Jan 11	—	.35	
	May 12	1979	.35	
	May 15	1979	.25	
	Nov 16	1979	.30	
	May 17	1979	.35	
	Apr 19	1979	.30	
	Aug 23	1979	.25	
	Jun 24	1979	.20	
	Aug 26	1979A	.20	
	Oct 27	1979A	.20	
2337				**OIL CAN** **REGULAR EQUIPMENT**
	Jan 11	—	.20	
	May 12	1384	.20	
	Jan 13	3425/342	.20	
	May 15	3425/342	.15	
	Jun 18	1384	.15	
	Nov 19	1384	.25	
	Aug 20	1384	.40	
	Jul 21	1384	.30	
	Jun 22	1384	.25	
	Aug 23	1384	.20	
	Oct 27	1384	.20	
2338				**TIRE PUMP** **REGULAR EQUIPMENT**
	Dec 11	—	4.50	
	May 12	1368	4.50	
	May 15	1368	2.00	
	Feb 17	1368	1.30	
	Oct 17	1368	1.50	
	Aug 20	1368	2.00	
	Nov 21	1368	1.75	
	Jun 22	1368	1.50	
	Aug 23	1368	1.40	
	Nov 23	1368	1.30	
	May 25	1368	1.10	
	Dec 25	1368	1.00	
	Oct 27	1368	1.00	
2339				**SPEEDOMETER WRENCH**
	Dec 11	—	.20	
2340				**TIRE IRON** **REGULAR EQUIPMENT**
	Dec 11	—	.15	
	May 12	2340	.15	
	Jan 13	4069	.15	
	May 15	4069	.10	
	Feb 17	3Z-703	.10	
	Nov 18	4069	.15	
	Oct 27	4069	.15	
2341	See 3Z-619			
2341B	See 5Z-156			
2342	See 5Z-324			

Part #	Catalog Date	Factory #	Price	Notes
2342				**METAL TOOL BOX** (21 x 9 x 9")
	Jan 13	3409	4.00	
	Jan 14	3409	2.50	
2343			**JACK**	**REGULAR EQUIPMENT**
	May 17	3389	.95	
	Oct 17	3389	1.20	
	Dec 17	3389	1.00	
	Mar 20	3389	1.50	
	Dec 20	3389	2.00	
	Nov 21	3389	1.50	
	Mar 24	3389	1.40	
	May 25	3389	1.25	
	Oct 26	3389	1.00	
	Oct 27	3389	1.00	
2344				**JACK HANDLE**
	Dec 25	3391	.15	
	Oct 27	3391	.15	
2891				**"T" SOCKET WRENCH** (Wire wheels, 10" bar)
	Aug 26	Use 5Z161		
	Jan 27	2839	.45	(8-1/4" high)
	Oct 27	2839	.45	
TT3389X			**JACK** (Truck)	
	Jun 18	3389	2.25	
	Nov 19	3389	2.50	
	Mar 20	3389	3.00	
	Dec 22	3389	2.50	
	Mar 24	3389	2.40	
	Dec 25	3389	2.25	
	Oct 26	3389	1.75	
TT3389BX				
	Jan 27	3389B	1.75	
	Oct 27	3389B	1.75	
TT3391X			**JACK HANDLE** (Truck jack)	
	Dec 25	—	.20	
	Oct 27	—	.20	
4000	See 1926			
4001	See 1928			
4002	See 5Z-210			
4003	See 3Z-598			
4004	See 1925			
4005	See 1927			
4006	See 5Z-326			
4007	See 5Z-287			
4008	See 5Z-280			
4010	See 5Z-319			
4011	See 20Z-340			
TT4069				**LARGE TIRE IRON** (Old 5Z-322)
	Dec 22	—	.45	
	Jun 24	—	.40	
	Oct 27	—	.40	
TT5893X				**WRENCH** (Spark plug, cylinder head, rim nut — Truck)
	Dec 25	—	.40	
	Oct 26	—	.35	
	Oct 27	—	.35	
3Z-79A				**CAMSHAFT PULLER** (Service Bulletin, Sept. 15, 1919)
3Z-598				**BRACE SOCKET WRENCH** (9/16" for 3/8" cap screws)
4003				
	Jun 09	1924	.30	(12" long)
	Apr 10	1924	.50	
1924				
	Jan 11	1924	.50	
	May 15	1924	.30	
	Feb 17	3Z-598	.20	
3Z-598				
	Oct 17	3Z-598	.20	
	Dec 17	3Z-598	.35	

Part #	Catalog Date	Factory #	Price	Notes

3Z-601 See 5Z-210
3Z-602 See 5Z-319
3Z-604 See 5Z-280
3Z-211 See 5Z-326
3Z-612 See 5Z-287
3Z-614 See 5Z-314

3Z-615 "L" SOCKET WRENCH (Differential case stud nut)

	Oct 17	3Z-615	.40	
	Nov 18	3Z-615	.60	
	Dec 18	3Z-615	.60	

3Z-616 See 5Z-152
3Z-617 See 5Z-457
3Z-617-1 See 20Z-340
3Z-617-2 See 20Z-340-1
3Z-617-3 See 21Z-356

3Z-619 "L" WRENCH (Main bearing bolt)
2341

	May 12	2069	.50	
	May 15	2069	.25	
	Feb 17	3Z-619	.25	

3Z-619

	Oct 17	3Z-619	.40	
	Jun 18	3Z-619	.45	
	Nov 18	3Z-619	.75	
	Dec 18	3Z-619	.60	
	Nov 21	3Z-619	.45	
	Apr 22	3Z-619	.50	
	Jun 22	3Z-619	.50	

3Z-620 See 5Z-158
3Z-624 See 5Z-204
3Z-627 See 5Z-196

3Z-628 MOTOR LIFTING TONGS

| | Jul 20 | 3Z628 | 3.00 | (Listed in Service Bulletins) |

3Z-629 OPEN END WRENCH (Rear spring perch nut)

	Oct 17	3Z-629	.90	
	Dec 17	3Z-629	1.00	
	Jul 18	3Z-629	1.00	

3Z-631 COMMUTATOR ROD BENDING IRON
(Service Bulletins May 15, 1919)

3Z-643 See 5Z-160
3Z-644 See 5Z-153
3Z-645 See 5Z-155
3Z-646 See 5Z-195
3Z-647 See 5Z-209
3Z-652 See 5Z-290
3Z-655 See 5Z-162

3Z-657 BODY LIFTING HOOK
(Booklet, "Service Equipment for Ford Agents")

3Z-670 BRACE WRENCH (Fan bracket bolt nut)

	Oct 17	3Z-670	.80	
	Dec 17	3Z-670	1.00	
	Dec 18	3Z-670	.75	
	Apr 19	3Z-670	.75	

3Z-671 WRENCH (Dash to body bracket bolt nut)

| | Oct 17 | 3Z-671 | .80 | |
| | Dec 17 | 3Z-671 | 1.00 | |

3Z-672 PEDAL BENDING IRON
(Service Bulletin, Feb. 1, 1920)

3Z-673 See 5Z-161
3Z-675 See 5Z-206

3Z-684 BRACE WRENCH (Running board bolt nuts, 19/32" square)

	Oct 17	3Z-684	.80	
	Dec 17	3Z-684	.90	
	Jun 18	3Z-684	1.00	
	Jul 18	3Z-684	1.00	

3Z-686 See 5Z-212

3Z-698 BRACE WRENCH (5/8")

	Oct 17	3Z-698	.70	
	Dec 17	3Z-698	.90	
	Nov 18	3Z-698	1.25	
	Dec 18	3Z-698	1.00	
	Apr 19	3Z-698	.80	
	Jul 21	Use 5Z-285		
	Nov 21	3Z-698	.40	
	Apr 23	3Z-698	.40	

3Z-699 See 5Z-193

3Z-701 HUB CAP WRENCH
(Booklet, "Service Equipment for Ford Agents")

3Z-702 BRACE WRENCH (Radiator stud nut)

| | Oct 17 | 3Z-702 | .80 | |
| | Dec 17 | 3Z-702 | 1.00 | |

3Z-703 See 5Z-322

3Z-711 "L" SOCKET WRENCH (Cylinder head bolt, truck)

	Oct 17	3Z-711	.40	(Also for rear axle housing)
	Dec 17	3Z-711	.50	
	Apr 18	3Z-711	.50	
	Jun 18	3Z-711	.50	Now listed for truck axle
	Aug 20	3Z-711	.50	

3Z-719 See 5Z-154

3Z-738 RIVETING BAR (For starting crank ratchet pin)

	Oct 17	3Z-738	.50	
	Jun 18	3Z-738	.60	
	Aug 20	3Z-738	.60	

3Z-744 PEDAL ADJUSTING IRON
(Service bulletin, Feb. 1, 1920)

3Z-751 See 5Z-286

3Z-755 "L" SOCKET WRENCH (3/8")

3Z-765 BRACE WRENCH (Coil box to dash bolt nut)

	Oct 17	3Z-765	.75	
	Dec 17	3Z-765	.90	
	Dec 18	3Z-765	.50	
	Jul 19	3Z-765	.75	
	Mar 20	3Z-765	.75	

3Z-775 SOCKET WRENCH (9/16" for cap screws. 8-7/16" long)

	Apr 18	3Z-775	.40	
	Nov 18	3Z-775	.50	
	Apr 19	3Z-775	.40	
	Jul 19	3Z-775	.50	
	Nov 19	3Z-775	.60	
	Jul 21	Use 5Z-155		
	Jun 22	3Z-775	.30	
	Apr 23	3Z-775	.30	

3Z-783 See 5Z-156
3Z-783 See 5Z-159
3Z-786 See 5Z-285

3Z-788 SPARK PLUG BRACE WRENCH
(Service Bulletin, Apr. 1, 1920)

3Z-790 See 5Z-165

Tools

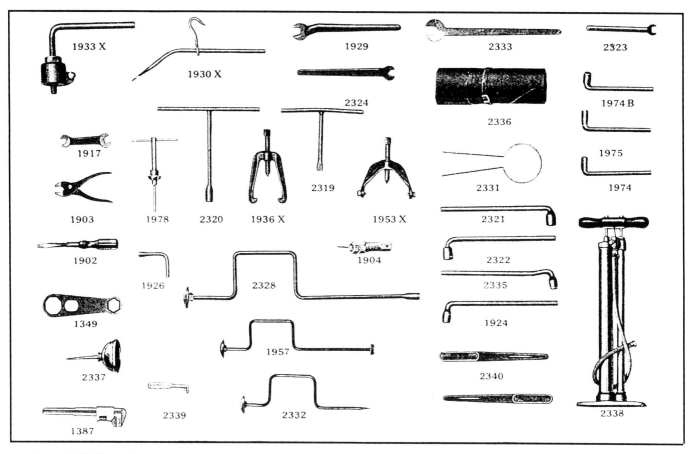

Above: Tool Illustrations used 1912-1914

Below: Tool Illustrations used 1915-1917

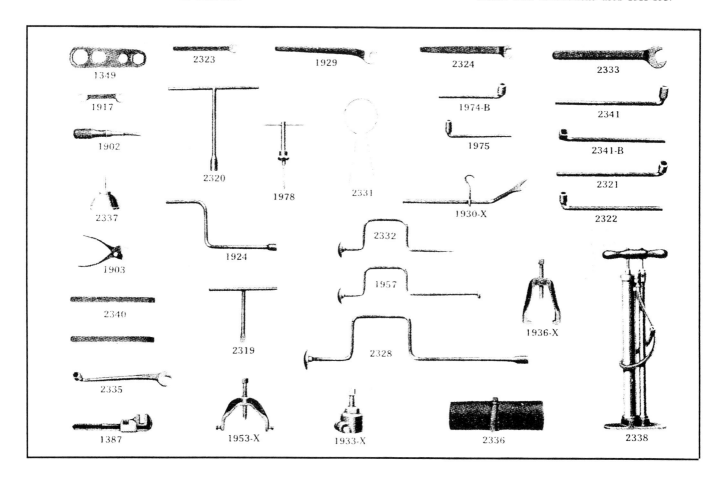

MODEL T FORD TOOLS

Part #	Catalog Date	Factory #	Price	Notes

3Z-794 PULLER (Cam shaft)

	Oct 17	3Z-794	1.70	
	Jun 18	3Z-794	2.00	
	Nov 18	3Z-794	3.00	
	Dec 18	3Z-794	3.00	

3Z-1173 See 5Z-289
3Z-1179 See 5Z-210
3Z-1223B See 5Z-289

3Z-1325 DRIVER (Front spindle inner bearing cone)

	Oct 17	3Z-1325	.60	
	Dec 17	3Z-1325	.75	
	Jul 18	3Z-1325	.75	

3Z-1327 "L" WRENCH (Steering post nut, 49/64")

	Oct 17	3Z-1327	.60	

3Z-1955 DRIFT (Front wheel ball race)

	Oct 17	3Z-1955	.30	
	Jul 18	3Z-1955	.40	
	May 20	3Z-1955	.50	

3Z-1956 See 5Z-232
3Z-2010 See 5Z-157
3Z-2034 See 5Z-324

3Z-2231 VALVE SEAT WRENCH (Kingston carburetor)

3Z-2232 VALVE SEAT TOOLS (Kingston carburetor)
3Z-2233

3Z-2234 FLOAT GAUGE (Kingston carburetor)

3Z-2235 FLOAT ADJUSTER (Kingston carburetor)
(These Kingston tools listed in Service Bulletin, July 1, 1919)

3Z-2256 REAR WHEEL PULLER (Truck)

3Z-2257 See 5Z-288
3Z-2304 See 5Z-325
3Z-2316 See 5Z-313

3Z-2336 SET OF KINGSTON CARBURETOR TOOLS
(Service Bulletin, July 1, 1919)

3Z-2393 GAUGE (Service Bulletin, January 1, 1920)

3Z-3217 SPRAY NOZZEL WRENCH (Holley carburetor, Service Bulletin, July 1, 1919)

3Z-3217-1 SPRAY NOZZEL WRENCH (Holley carburetor, Service Bulletin, Dec. 15, 1919)

3Z-3218 FLOAT VALVE SEAT WRENCH (Holley carburetor, Service Bulletin, July 1, 1919)

3Z-3219 FLOAT VALVE SEATING TOOL
(*Ford Owner*, June 1924)

3Z-3220 OVERFLOW TUBE WRENCH (Holley carburetor, Service Bulletin, July 1, 1919)

3Z-3221 LOW SPEED TUBE TOOL (Holley carburetor, *Ford Owner*, June 1924)

3Z-3222 INLET NEEDLE SEATING TOOL (Holley carburetor, Service Bulletin, July 1, 1919)

3Z-3222-2 INLET NEEDLE SEATING TOOL (Holley carburetor, Service Bulletin, Nov. 15, 1919)

3Z-3223 FLOAT SEATING TOOL (Holley carburetor, Service Beuletin, Nov. 15, 1919)

3Z-4114 INLET NEEDLE SEATING TOOL (Holley and Kingston, Service Bulletin, 11-1-19)

3Z-4120 FLOAT VALVE SEATING TOOL (Holley and Kingston, Service Bulletin, 11-1-19)

3Z-4137 See 5Z-163

3Z-4675 SPRAY NOZZEL WRENCH (Holley carburetor, Service Bulletin, Nov. 1, 1919)

3Z-4712 See 5Z-323
3Z-4730 See 5Z-319

5Z-152 "L" WRENCH (Rear axle housing bolt nut, for 3/8" nuts)

1975				
	Jan 11	1975	.50	(7-25/64" long)
	May 15	1975	.25	
	Feb 17	3Z-616	.20	
3Z-616				
	Oct 17	3Z-616	.25	
	Dec 17	3Z-616	.30	
	Nov 18	3Z-616	.60	
	Apr 19	3Z-616	.50	
5Z-152				
	Dec 20	5Z-152	.50	
	Jul 21	5Z-152	.40	
	Oct 26	5Z-152	.30	
	Oct 27	5Z-152	.30	

5Z-153 "L" SOCKET WRENCH (For crankshaft bearing bolt)

2321				
	Jan 11	2321	.50	(12-1/32" long)
	May 15	2321	.30	
	Feb 17	3Z-644	.30	
3Z-644				
	Oct 17	3Z-644	.30	
	Apr 18	3Z-644	.40	
	Nov 18	3Z-644	.70	
	Apr 19	3Z-644	.50	
	Nov 19	3Z-644	.60	
	May 20	3Z-644	.70	
5Z-153				
	Dec 20	5Z-153	.70	
	Jul 21	5Z-153	.60	
	Jun 24	5Z-153	.50	
	Oct 26	5Z-153	.40	
	Oct 27	5Z-153	.40	

5Z-154 "L" SOCKET WRENCH (Body bracket bolt)

3Z-719				
	Oct 17	3Z-719	.45	
	Jul 18	3Z-719	.60	
	Nov 18	3Z-719	.90	
	Apr 19	3Z-719	.65	
5Z-154				
	Dec 20	5Z-154	.65	
	Jul 21	5Z-154	.50	
	Nov 21	5Z-154	.40	
	Apr 22	5Z-154	.30	
	Oct 27	5Z-154	.30	

5Z-155 "L" SOCKET WRENCH (9/16" 12" long)

2322				
	Jan 11	2322	.50	
	May 15	2322	.30	
	Feb 17	3Z-645	.30	
3Z-645				
	Oct 17	3Z-645	.30	
	Nov 18	3Z-645	.60	
	Apr 19	3Z-645	.50	
	Nov 19	3Z-645	.60	5Z-155 later
5Z-155				
	Dec 20	5Z-155	.60	
	Jul 21	5Z-155	.50	
	Nov 21	5Z-155	.40	
	Apr 22	5Z-155	.45	
	Oct 26	5Z-155	.35	
	Oct 27	5Z-155	.35	

Tools

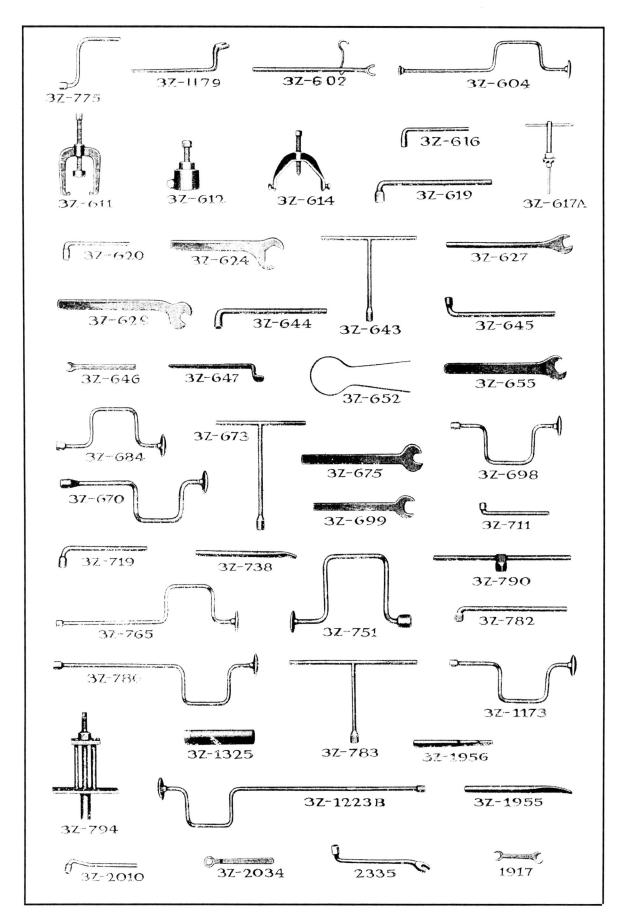

Tool Illustrations used 1917-1920

MODEL T FORD TOOLS

Part #	Catalog Date	Factory #	Price	Notes
5Z-156	**"L" SOCKET WRENCH** (Main bearing bolt, square head)			
2341B				
	Oct 14	7427	.50	
	May 15	7427	.25	
	Feb 17	3Z-782	.25	
3Z-782				
	Oct 17	3Z-782	.40	
	Nov 18	3Z-782	.75	
	Dec 18	3Z-782	.60	
	Apr 19	3Z-782	.50	
5Z-156				
	Dec 20	5Z-156	.50	
	Jun 24	5Z-156	.45	
	Oct 26	5Z-156	.35	
	Oct 27	5Z-156	.35	
5Z-157	**"L" SOCKET WRENCH** (#4 connecting rod)			
3Z-2010				
	Oct 17	3Z-2010	.30	
	Jul 18	3Z-2010	.40	
	Nov 18	3Z-2010	.75	
	Apr 19	3Z-2010	.50	
	Jul 19	3Z-2010	.40	
	Nov 19	3Z-2010	.50	
5Z-157				
	Dec 20	5Z-157	.50	
	Nov 21	5Z-157	.40	
	Oct 26	5Z-157	.30	
	Oct 27	5Z-157	.30	
5Z-158	**"L" SOCKET WRENCH** (Driveshaft and rear axle stud nut)			
1974B				
	Dec 11	—	.40	For 13/32" nuts
	May 12	2073	.40	
	May 15	2073	.25	
	Feb 17	3Z-620	.20	
3Z-620				
	Oct 17	3Z-620	.35	
	Nov 18	3Z-620	.60	
	Apr 19	3Z-620	.50	
5Z-158				
	Dec 20	5Z-158	.50	
	Jun 24	5Z-158	.45	
	Oct 26	5Z-158	.30	
	Oct 27	5Z-158	.30	
5Z-159	**"T" SOCKET WRENCH** (Connecting rods)			
3Z-783				
	Oct 17	3Z-783	1.25	
	Apr 18	3Z-783	1.00	
	Nov 18	3Z-783	1.50	
	Apr 19	3Z-783	1.00	
	Jul 19	3Z-783	.90	
5Z-159				
	Dec 20	5Z-159	.90	
	Jul 21	5Z-159	.75	
	Apr 22	5Z-159	.55	
	Oct 26	5Z-159	.45	
	Oct 27	5Z-159	.45	
5Z-160	**"T" SOCKET WRENCH** (9/16", 9-1/4" long)			
2320				
	Jan 11	2320	.50	
	Feb 17	3Z-643	.30	
	May 17	3Z-643	.35	
3Z-643				
	Oct 17	3Z-643	.35	
	Dec 17	3Z-643	.30	
	Jun 18	3Z-643	.45	
	Nov 18	3Z-643	.60	
	Nov 19	3Z-643	.75	
5Z-160				
	Dec 20	5Z-160	.75	
	Jun 24	5Z-160	.60	
	May 25	5Z-160	.50	
	Oct 26	5Z-160	.45	
	Oct 27	5Z-160	.45	
5Z-161	**"T" SOCKET WRENCH** (Front and center body bracket bolt nut)			
3Z-673				
	Oct 17	3Z-673	.80	
	Nov 18	3Z-673	1.00	
	Apr 19	3Z-673	.75	
	May 20	3Z-673	1.00	
5Z-161				
	Dec 20	5Z-161	1.00	
	Jul 21	5Z-161	.80	
	Nov 21	5Z-161	.65	
	Apr 22	5Z-161	.55	
	Jun 24	5Z-161	.50	
	May 25	5Z-161	.45	
	Oct 26	5Z-161	.40	Also wire wheel lug wrench in August 1926 parts book.
	Oct 27	5Z-161	.40	
5Z-162	**OFFSET END WRENCH** (Large cam gear lock nut, 14" long)			
2333				
	Jan 11	2333	.40	
	May 15	2333	.30	
	Feb 17	3Z-655	.30	
3Z-655				
	Oct 17	3Z-655	.45	
	Dec 17	3Z-655	.50	
	Apr 18	3Z-655	.60	
	Nov 18	3Z-655	.80	
	Apr 19	3Z-655	.70	
5Z-162				
	Dec 20	5Z-162	.70	
	Jul 21	5Z-162	.60	
	Nov 21	5Z-162	.55	
	Jun 24	5Z-162	.75	
	May 25	5Z-162	.75	5Z-821 later
5Z-163	**WRENCH** (Generator third brush)			
3Z-4137				
	Aug 20	3Z-4137	.30	
5Z-163				
	Jul 21	5Z-163	.30	
	Nov 21	5Z-163	.25	
	Apr 22	5Z-163	.20	
	Jul 24	5Z-163	.20	5Z-249 later
5Z-165	**"T" WRENCH** (Driveshaft pinion)			
3Z-790				
	Oct 17	3Z-790	1.50	
	Dec 18	3Z-790	1.20	
	Apr 19	3Z-790	1.00	
5Z-165				
	Dec 20	5Z-165	1.00	
	Jul 21	5Z-165	.80	
	Nov 21	5Z-165	.70	
	Apr 22	5Z-165	.65	
	Jun 24	5Z-165	.60	
	Oct 26	5Z-165	.55	
	Oct 27	5Z-165	.55	
5Z-193	**OPEN END WRENCH** (Spindle cone adjusting)			
3Z-699				
	Oct 17	3Z-699	.50	
	Dec 18	3Z-699	.75	
	Apr 19	3Z-699	.60	
	Jul 19	3Z-699	.50	
5Z-193				
	Dec 20	5Z-193	.50	
	Jul 21	5Z-193	.40	
	Nov 21	5Z-193	.30	
	Apr 22	5Z-193	.25	
	Jun 24	5Z-193	.35	
	Oct 27	5Z-193	.35	

Tools

MODEL T FORD TOOLS

Part #	Catalog Date	Factory #	Price	Notes

5Z-195 OPEN END WRENCH (9/16", 7-1/2" long)
2323

	Jan 11	2323	.35	
	May 15	2323	.20	
	Feb 17	3Z-646	.15	

3Z-646

	Oct 17	3Z-646	.25	
	Dec 17	3Z-646	.30	
	Nov 18	3Z-646	.50	
	Dec 18	3Z-646	.30	

5Z-195

	Dec 20	5Z-195	.30	
	Apr 22	5Z-195	.25	
	Oct 26	5Z-195	.20	
	Oct 27	5Z-195	.20	

5Z-196 OPEN END WRENCH (Rear axle entering)
3Z-627

	Oct 17	3Z-627	.40	
	Dec 17	3Z-627	.90	
	Jun 18	3Z-627	1.00	
	Nov 18	3Z-627	1.50	
	Dec 18	3Z-627	1.25	
	Apr 19	3Z-627	1.00	
	Jul 19	3Z-627	.75	

5Z-196

	Dec 20	5Z-196	.75	
	Jul 21	5Z-196	.50	
	Nov 21	5Z-196	.40	
	Apr 22	5Z-196	.30	
	Oct 26	5Z-196	.35	
	Oct 27	5Z-196	.35	

5Z-197 OPEN END WRENCH (Rear spring perch)

	Dec 25	5Z-197	1.25	
	Oct 26	5Z-197	1.00	
	Apr 27	5Z-197	.65	
	Oct 27	5Z-197	.65	

5Z-204 OPEN END WRENCH (Exhaust pack nut)
3Z-624

	Oct 17	3Z-624	1.20	
	Dec 17	3Z-624	1.00	
	Nov 18	3Z-624	1.50	
	Dec 18	3Z-624	1.25	

5Z-204

	Dec 20	5Z-204	1.25	
	Jul 21	5Z-204	1.25	
	Nov 21	5Z-204	1.00	
	Jun 24	5Z-204	.90	
	Oct 26	5Z-204	.80	
	Oct 27	5Z-204	.80	

5Z-206 OPEN END WRENCH (Rear axle)
3Z-675

	Oct 17	3Z-675	.90	
	Dec 17	3Z-675	1.00	
	Dec 18	3Z-675	1.15	
	Apr 19	3Z-675	1.00	

5Z-206

	Dec 20	5Z-206	1.00	
	Jul 21	5Z-206	.80	
	Nov 21	5Z-206	.70	
	Apr 22	5Z-206	.65	
	Jun 24	5Z-206	.55	

5Z-206R

	May 25	5Z-206R	.55	

5Z-206 DOUBLE OPEN END WRENCH
(Rear axle and rear spring perch)

	May 25	—	.80	

5Z-209 OFFSET END WRENCH (Connecting rod clamp screw)
2324

	Jan 11	2324	.40	10-1/4" long
	May 15	2324	.35	
	Feb 17	3Z-647	.35	

3Z-647

	Oct 17	3Z-647	.35	
	Jul 18	3Z-647	.40	
	Nov 18	3Z-647	.75	
	Dec 18	3z-647	.50	
	Nov 19	3Z-647	.75	

5Z-209

	Dec 20	5Z-209	.75	
	Jul 21	5Z-209	.60	
	Nov 21	5Z-209	.45	
	Oct 26	5Z-209	.40	
	Oct 27	5Z-209	.40	

5Z-210 WRENCH (Flywheel cap screw, 11-3/8" long)
4002

	Jun 09	1929	.30	

1929

	Jan 11	1929	.30	
	Feb 17	1929	.20	

3Z-601

	Oct 17	3Z-601	.25	
	Dec 17	3Z-601	.35	
	Apr 18	3Z-601	.35	

3Z-1179 (13-1/2" long)

	Jun 18	3Z-1179	.60	
	Nov 18	3Z-1179	.75	
	Apr 19	3Z-1179	.60	
	Nov 19	3Z-1179	.90	
	May 20	3Z-1179	1.25	

5Z-210

	Dec 20	5Z-210	1.25	
	Jul 21	5Z-210	1.00	
	Nov 21	5Z-210	.75	
	Jun 24	5Z-210	.65	
	May 25	5Z-210	.60	
	Oct 26	5Z-210	.55	
	Oct 27	5Z-210	.55	

5Z-212 OPEN END WRENCH (23/32" for body bracket bolt)
3Z-686

	Oct 17	3Z-686	.30	
	Nov 18	3Z-686	.50	
	Jul 19	3Z-686	.40	

5Z-212

	Dec 20	5Z-212	.40	
	Jul 21	5Z-212	.30	
	Apr 22	5Z-212	.25	

5Z-212-1

	May 25	5Z-212-1	.25	
	Oct 27	5Z-212-1	.25	

5Z-212-2 OPEN END WRENCH (21/32" for body bracket bolt)

	May 25	5Z-212-2	.25	
	Oct 27	5Z-212-2	.25	

5Z-232 DRIVER (Spindle arm bushing)
3Z-1956

	Oct 17	3Z-1956	.90	

5Z-232

	Dec 20	5Z-232	.90	
	Jul 21	5Z-232	.60	
	Nov 21	5Z-232	.40	
	Apr 22	5Z-232	.30	
	Aug 23	5Z-232	.40	
	Oct 26	5Z-232	.35	
	Oct 27	5Z-232	.35	

5Z-233 SPINDLE ARM BUSHING DRIVER
(Also 5Z-1956)

5Z-248 WRENCH (Rear axle nut)

	Dec 25	5Z-248	1.25	
	Apr 27	5Z-248	.90	
	Oct 27	5Z-248	.90	

MODEL T FORD TOOLS

Part #	Catalog Date	Factory #	Price	Notes

5Z-249 WRENCH (Generator third brush, new style)
5Z-249

	Catalog Date	Factory #	Price	Notes
	Dec 20	5Z-249	.30	
	Nov 21	5Z-249	.25	
	Apr 22	5Z-249	.20	
	May 25	5Z-249	.10	5Z-806 later

5Z-280 VALVE GRINDER (Speed wrench type)
4009

	Catalog Date	Factory #	Price	Notes
	Jun 09	1957	1.00	
1957				
	Jan 11	1957	1.00	
	May 15	1957	.75	
	Feb 17	3Z-604	.75	
3Z-604				
	Oct 17	3Z-604	.90	
	Nov 18	3Z-604	1.25	
	Apr 19	3Z-604	1.00	
	Jul 21	3Z-604	.75	
5Z-280				
	Sep 21	5Z-280	.75	
	May 25	5Z-280	.60	
	Oct 26	5Z-280	.50	
	Oct 27	5Z-280	.50	

5Z-285 BRACE WRENCH (Cylinder head cap screws)
3Z-786

	Catalog Date	Factory #	Price	Notes
	Oct 17	3Z-786	.75	
	Dec 17	3Z-786	.90	
	Nov 18	3Z-786	1.20	
	Apr 19	3Z-786	1.00	
5Z-285				
	Jul 21	5Z-285	.80	
	Sep 21	5Z-285	.75	
	Jun 24	5Z-285	.65	
	May 25	5Z-285	.60	
	Oct 26	5Z-285	.50	
	Oct 27	5Z-285	.50	

5Z-286 BRACE WRENCH (Rear axle housing plug)
3Z-751

	Catalog Date	Factory #	Price	Notes
	Oct 17	3Z-751	1.00	
	Dec 17	3Z-751	1.20	
	Apr 19	3Z-751	1.00	
	May 20	3Z-751	1.25	
5Z-286				
	Jul 21	5Z-286	1.00	
	Sep 21	5Z-286	.80	
	Jun 24	5Z-286	.65	
	Jul 24	5Z-286	.65	

5Z-287 REAR WHEEL PULLER
4007

	Catalog Date	Factory #	Price	Notes
	Jun 09	1940	2.00	
1933X				
	Jan 11	1933	1.50	
	May 12	1933/1945	1.50	
	Oct 14	1933/1945	1.00	
	May 15	1933/1945	.75	
	Feb 17	3Z-605/-607	.75	
3Z-612				
	Oct 17	3Z-612	1.00	
	Dec 17	3Z-612	.90	
	Apr 18	3Z-612	1.00	
	Nov 18	3Z-612	1.25	
	Jul 19	3Z-612	1.00	
	Nov 19	3Z-612	1.50	
5Z-287				
	Jul 21	5Z-287	1.50	
	Nov 21	5Z-287	1.25	
	Dec 22	5Z-287	1.00	
	Jun 24	5Z-287	.80	
	Oct 26	5Z-287	.65	
	Apr 27	5Z-287	.65	5Z-1170 later

5Z-288 REAR WHEEL PULLER ASSEMBLY
3Z-2257

	Catalog Date	Factory #	Price	Notes
	Apr 18	3Z-2257	1.00	(Truck)
	Nov 19	3Z-2257	1.25	
	May 20	3Z-2257	1.50	
5Z-288				
	Jul 21	5Z-288	1.50	
	Dec 22	5Z-288	1.20	
	Jun 24	5Z-288	1.00	
	Oct 26	5Z-288	.80	5Z-1171 later

5Z-289 BRACE WRENCH (Front radius rod ball cap screw)
3Z-1173

	Catalog Date	Factory #	Price	Notes
	Oct 17	3Z-1173	.60	
	Dec 17	3Z-1173	.90	
	Nov 18	3Z-1173	1.20	
	Apr 19	3Z-1173	1.00	
	Jul 21	Use 5Z-289		
2328	(9/16", 24-3/8" long)			
	Jan 11	2328	.60	
	May 15	2328	.40	
	Feb 16	2328	.75	
	Feb 17	Use 3Z-1223B		
3Z-1223B				
	Oct 17	3Z-1223B	.90	
	Apr 18	3Z-1223B	1.00	
	Nov 18	3Z-1223B	1.50	
	Dec 18	3Z-1223B	1.30	
	Apr 19	3Z-1223B	1.00	5Z-289 later
5Z-289				
	Jul 21	5Z-289	1.00	
	Nov 21	5Z-289	.85	
	Apr 22	5Z-289	.75	
	Jun 24	5Z-289	.65	
	May 25	5Z-289	.65	

5Z-289-1 BRACE WRENCH (Transmission cover bolt and nut)

	Catalog Date	Factory #	Price	Notes
	Apr 26	5Z-289-1	.55	
	Oct 26	5Z-289-1	.50	
	Oct 27	5Z-289-1	.50	

5Z-289-2 SOCKET WRENCH
(Radiator stud, and crankcase to cylinder nut)

	Catalog Date	Factory #	Price	Notes
	Dec 25	5Z-289-2	.65	
	Oct 26	5Z-289-2	.55	
	Oct 27	5Z-289-2	.55	

5Z-289-3 BRACE WRENCH (Universal ball cap)

	Catalog Date	Factory #	Price	Notes
	Apr 26	5Z-289-3	.70	
	Oct 26	5Z-289-3	.60	
	Oct 27	5Z-289-3	.60	

5Z-290 PISTON RING SQUEEZER
2331

	Catalog Date	Factory #	Price	Notes
	Jan 11	2331	.25	
	May 15	2331	.20	
	Feb 17	3Z-652	.20	
3Z-652				
	Oct 17	3Z-652	.60	
	Apr 18	3Z-652	.35	
	Jul 19	3Z-652	.25	
	May 20	3Z-652	.30	
5Z-290				
	Jul 21	5Z-290	.30	
	Oct 27	5Z-290	.30	

5Z-313 FIXTURE For Assembling Roller Bearing Cups
3Z-2316

	Catalog Date	Factory #	Price	Notes
	Jul 21	3Z-2316	8.00	
5Z-313				
	Sep 21	5Z-313	8.00	
	Jun 22	5Z-313	8.00	

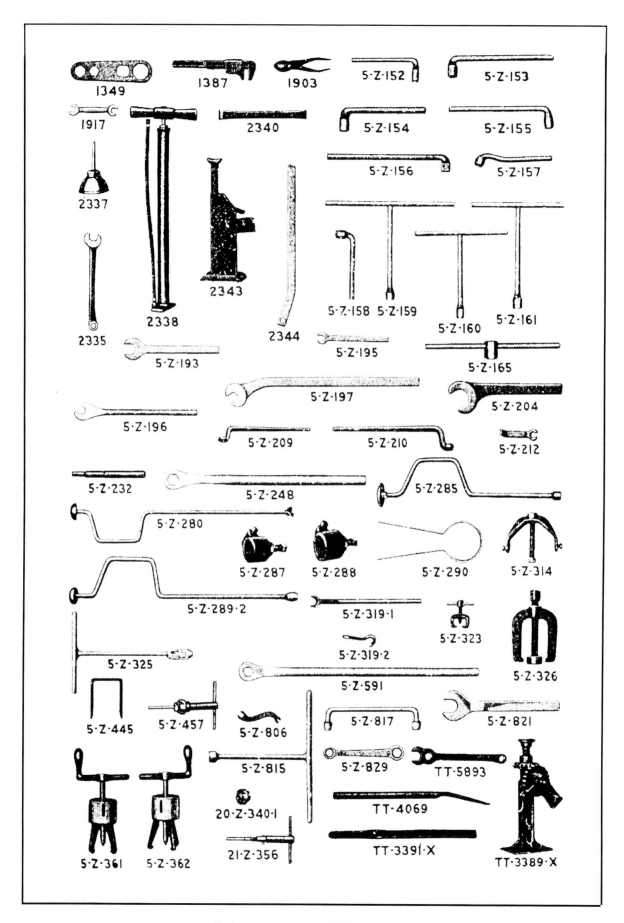

Tool Illustrations used 1925 and later.

Part #	Catalog Date	Factory #	Price	Notes

5Z-314 TRANSMISSION CLUTCH DRUM PULLER

4008

	Jun 09	1954	1.50	

1953X

	Jan 11	1953	1.50	
	May 12	1370/1953/1955	1.50	
	May 15	1370/1953/1955	1.25	
	Feb 17	3Z-613/3Z-609	1.25	

3Z-614

	Oct 17	3Z-614	.75	
	Apr 18	3Z-614	.60	
	Jun 18	3Z-614	1.00	
	Nov 18	3Z-614	1.50	
	Apr 19	3Z-614	1.50	

5Z-314

	Sep 21	5Z-314	1.25	
	Nov 21	5Z-314	1.00	
	Dec 22	5Z-314	.75	
	Jun 24	5Z-314	.65	
	Oct 26	5Z-314	.55	
	Oct 27	5Z-314	.55	

5Z-319 VALVE SPRING LIFTER (15" long)

4010

	Jun 09	1930	.50	

1930X

	Jan 11	1930	.75	
	May 12	1930/1938	.75	
	May 15	1930/1938	.40	
	Feb 17	3Z-602	.25	
	May 17	3Z-602	.35	

3Z-602

	Oct 17	3Z-602	.35	
	Apr 18	3Z-602	.60	
	Nov 18	3Z-602	.80	
	Apr 19	3Z-602	.50	
	Jul 19	3Z-602	.40	

3Z-4730

	May 20	3Z-4730	.50	

5Z-319

	Sep 21	5Z-319	.50	
	Nov 21	5Z-319	.40	
	Apr 22	5Z-319	.30	(5Z-319-1 lever)
	Oct 27	5Z-319	.30	(5Z-319-2 hook)

5Z-320 PULLER (Small timing gear)

	Aug 26	5Z-320	.80	
	Oct 26	5Z-320	.75	
	Apr 27	5Z-320	.65	
	Oct 27	5Z-320	.65	

5Z-322 TIRE IRON

3Z-703

	Apr 19	3Z-703	.50	
	May 20	3Z-703	.60	
	Jul 21	3Z-703	.60	

5Z-322

	Sep 21	5Z-322	.60	
	Nov 21	5Z-322	.50	
	Apr 22	5Z-322	.45	
	Jun 22	5Z-322	.45	
	Dec 22	Use TT-4069		

5Z-323 PULLER (Bendix shaft head)

3Z-4712

	Aug 20	3Z-4712	1.50	

5Z-323

	Sep 21	5Z-323	1.50	
	Nov 21	5Z-323	1.25	
	Dec 22	5Z-323	1.00	
	Jun 24	5Z-323	.80	
	May 25	5Z-323	.60	
	Oct 26	5Z-323	.50	
	Oct 27	5Z-323	.50	

5Z-324 RATCHET WRENCH (Transmission band adjustment)

2342

	Jun 16	7472	.75	
	Feb 17	16Z-1411	.75	

3Z-2034

	Oct 17	3Z-2034	.50	
	Nov 18	3Z-2034	.60	
	Apr 19	3Z-2034	.50	
	Nov 19	3Z-2034	.60	
	Jul 21	3Z-2034	.50	

5Z-324

	Sep 21	5Z-324	.50	
	May 25	5Z-324	.30	

5Z-325 BRACE WRENCH WITH UNIVERSAL JOINT

3Z-2304

	Mar 20	3Z-2304	2.50	#4 connecting rod

5Z-325

	Sep 21	5Z-325	2.50	
	Jun 24	5Z-325	2.00	
	May 25	5Z-325	1.80	
	Dec 25	5Z-325	1.60	
	Oct 26	5Z-325	1.50	
	Oct 27	5Z-325	1.50	

5Z-326 TRANSMISSION GEAR PULLER

4006

	Jun 09	1939	1.50	Listed as "Cam gear puller until 1921, then shown as the puller for both gears.

1936X

	Jan 11	1936	1.50	
	May 12	1936/1937	1.50	
	May 15	1936/1937	1.00	
	Feb 17	3Z-608/-609	1.00	
	May 17	3Z-608/-609	.60	

3Z-611

	Oct 17	3Z-611	.60	
	Apr 18	3Z-611	1.00	
	Jun 18	3Z-611	2.00	
	Nov 19	3Z-611	2.25	
	Jul 21	3Z-611	2.00	

5Z-326

	Sep 21	5Z-326	2.00	
	Nov 21	5Z-326	1.50	
	Jun 24	5Z-326	1.70	
	Dec 25	5Z-326	1.50	
	Oct 27	5Z-326	1.50	

5Z-361 PULLER (Large timing gear) 16Z-4992

	Aug 20	16Z-4992	11.00	
	Feb 22	16Z-4992	11.00	

5Z-361

	Apr 22	5Z-361	11.00	
	Dec 22	5Z-361	9.00	
	Jun 24	5Z-361	7.00	
	May 25	5Z-361	6.50	
	Oct 26	5Z-361	6.00	
	Oct 27	5Z-361	6.00	

5Z-362 CAM GEAR PULLER (Three spoke design)

	Dec 22	5Z-362	6.50	
	May 25	5Z-362	6.00	
	Oct 27	5Z-362	6.00	

5Z-445 TRANSMISSION BAND CLAMP

	May 25	5Z-445	.15	
	Oct 27	5Z-445	.15	

MODEL T Ford TOOLS

Part #	Catalog Date	Factory #	Price	Notes

5Z-457 VALVE SEAT REAMER
4011
| | Jun 09 | — | 3.00 | |
1978
	Jan 11	1978	2.50	
	May 15	1978	1.50	
	Feb 17	3Z-617	1.50	
3Z-617
	Oct 17	3Z-617	1.50	
3Z-617-1
	Jun 18	3Z-617-1	2.10	
	Jul 18	3Z-617-1	2.50	
	Nov 18	3Z-617-1	3.00	
	Apr 19	3Z-617-1	2.50	
	Aug 19	3Z-617-1	2.75	
20Z-340
	Jul 21	20Z-340	2.75	
	Dec 21	20Z-340	2.00	
	Jun 22	20Z-340	2.00	
	Dec 22	5Z-457	2.50	
	May 25	5Z-457	3.00	
	Dec 25	5Z-457	2.90	
	Oct 27	5Z-457	2.90	

5Z-591 WRENCH (Rear axle nut, truck)
	Dec 25	5Z-591	1.50	
	Apr 27	5Z-591	1.10	
	Oct 27	5Z-591	1.10	

5Z-806 DOUBLE END WRENCH (Generator third brush adjusting)
	May 25	5Z-806	.20	
	Dec 25	5Z-806	.15	
	Oct 26	5Z-806	.10	
	Oct 27	5Z-806	.10	

5Z-815 "T" SOCKET WRENCH (Crankshaft center main bearing)
	May 25	5Z-815	.55	
	Oct 26	5Z-815	.50	
	Oct 27	5Z-815	.50	

5Z-817 DOUBLE END WRENCH (9/16" and 5/8" for carburetor and generator bolts)
	May 25	5Z-817	.50	
	Oct 26	5Z-817	.45	
	Oct 27	5Z-817	.45	

5Z-821 OPEN END WRENCH (Large timing gear nut)
| | May 25 | 5Z-821 | .50 | |
| | Oct 27 | 5Z-821 | .50 | |

5Z-829 RATCHET WRENCH (Double end, transmission band and oil drain)
	May 25	5Z-829	.50	
	Oct 26	5Z-829	.40	
	Oct 27	5Z-829	.40	

5Z-1080 "L" SOCKET WRENCH (Front spring perch nut)
| | Apr 26 | 5Z-1080 | .65 | |
| | Oct 27 | 5Z-1080 | .65 | |

5Z-1156 BENDING IRON (Headlight bracket)
| | Aug 26 | 5Z-1156 | 1.25 | For adjusting headlights |
| | Oct 27 | 5Z-1156 | 1.25 | |

5Z-1157 PRY BAR (For rear brake spring)
| | Aug 26 | 5Z-1157 | .40 | |
| | Oct 27 | 5Z-1157 | .40 | |

5Z-1170 REAR WHEEL PULLER ASSEMBLY
| | Oct 26 | 5Z-1170 | 2.25 | 5Z-1497 later |

5Z-1171 REAR WHEEL PULLER ASSEMBLY (Truck)
| | Oct 26 | 5Z-1171 | 2.25 | 5Z-1498 later |

5Z-1172 REAR WHEEL PULLER ASSEMBLY (For wire wheels)
| | Oct 26 | 5Z-1172 | 1.75 | |
| | Oct 27 | 5Z-1172 | 1.75 | |

5Z-1497 REAR WHEEL PULLER ASSEMBLY (Replaces 5Z-1170)
| | Jan 27 | 5Z-1497 | 2.25 | |
| | Oct 27 | 5Z-1497 | 2.25 | |

5Z-1498 REAR WHEEL PULLER ASSEMBLY (Truck)
| | Jan 27 | 5Z-1498 | 2.25 | (Replaces 5Z1171) |
| | Oct 27 | 5Z-1498 | 2.25 | |

12Z-37 PISTON PIN REAMER (Service Bulletin, May 1924)

16Z-1411 See 5Z-324

16Z-2040 STEERING WHEEL PULLER
("Service Equipment for Ford Agents")

16Z-2053 CLAMP PLATE
(To hold cylinder block while scraping bearings) ("Service Equipment for Ford Agents")

16Z-2114 LINE REAMER
(Camshaft bearings, "Service Equipment for Ford Agents")

16Z-2809 ENGINE SUPPORT FIXTURE
(For servicing engine, "Service Equipment.....")

16Z-4349 PISTON HOLDING FIXTURE
("Service Equipment for Ford Agents")

16Z-4992 See 5Z-361

18Z-245 COIL AND MAGNETO TESTING DEVICE
(Service Bulletin, July 1, 1919)

18Z-2040 STEERING WHEEL HUB PULLER
(Service Bulletin, July 1, 1919)

20Z-9-1 FACING TOOL (Service bulletin, September 15, 1919)

20Z-340 VALVE SEAT REAMER See 5Z-457

20Z-340-1 VALVE SEAT REAMER CUTTER
3Z-617-2
| | Mar 20 | 3Z-617-2 | 1.85 | |
20Z-340
| | Dec 20 | 20Z-340 | 1.85 | |
20Z-340-1
	Jul 21	20Z-340-1	1.65	
	Dec 21	20Z-340-1	1.25	
	Dec 22	20Z-340-1	1.50	
	Dec 25	20Z-340-1	1.40	
	Oct 27	20Z-340-1	1.40	

21Z-356 VALVE SEAT REAMER HANDLE
3Z-617-3
| | Aug 20 | 3Z-617-3 | 1.50 | |
21Z-356
	Jul 21	21Z-356	1.10	
	Dec 22	21Z-356	1.00	
	May 25	21Z-356	1.50	
	Oct 27	21Z-356	1.50	

24Z-643 CONNECTING ROD ALIGNMENT JIG
("Service Equipment for Ford Agents")

24Z-1192 COMMUTATOR GAUGE
(Service Bulletin, July 1, 1919)

24Z-2036 CHOKE TUBE GAUGE (Holley carburetor)
(Ford Owner, June 1924)

24Z-2337 SPRAY NEEDLE GAUGE (Holley carburetor)
(Ford Owner, June 1924)

MODEL T FORD TOOLS

24Z-2390 LOW SPEED TUBE CLEARANCE GAUGE (Holley)
(Service Bulletin 7-1-1919)

24Z-2391 THROTTLE ROD GAUGE (Holley carburetor)
(Ford Owner, June 1924)

24Z-2392 NOZZEL GAUGE (Holley carburetor)
(Ford Owner, June 1924)

24Z-2393 FLOAT LEVEL GAUGE (Holley carburetor)
(Service Bulletin, July 1, 1919)

24Z-3990 FLOAT GAUGE & ADJUSTING TOOL
(Service Bulletin, Nov. 1, 1919)

24Z-6576 CYLINDER FRONT COVER GAUGE
(Service Bulletin, Jan. 2, 1925)

28Z-20 PISTON BUSHING REAMER
(Service Bulletin, July 1, 1919)

28Z-67 CAMSHAFT BEARING REAMER
(Service Bulletin, July 1, 1919)

28Z-97 SLOW SPEED GEAR BUSHING REAMER
(Service Bulletin, July 1, 1919)

28Z-109 SPINDLE BUSHING REAMER
(Service Bulletin, July 1, 1919)

28Z-132 HIGH SPEED DRIVER GEAR BUSHING REAMER
(Service Bulletin, 7-1-1919)

28Z-186 SPINDLE ARM & SPRING PERCH BUSHING EXPANSION REAMER (Service Bulletin, 7-1-1919)

28Z-253 REVERSE GEAR BUSHING REAMER
(Service Bulletin, July 1, 1919)

28Z-457 CAMSHAFT BEARING LINE REAMER
(Service Bulletin, July 1, 1919)

56Z-168 FORD GASKET DISPLAY BOARD
(Service Bulletin, January 1, 1925)

Tools

It is next to impossible to index every part of a Model T Ford. An attempt has been made to list the major pieces, many of which are in the same photo as some other assembly. If you are seeking some item which is not listed, check the listing for some part which is in the same area. (Speedometer gears, for example, can be seen under "front axle" in many cases.)

PHOTO INDEX

PHOTO INDEX

PHOTO INDEX

ESSENTIAL OLD CAR BOOKS FROM KRAUSE PUBLICATIONS
700 E. State St., Iola, WI 54990-0001

STANDARD CATALOG OF AMERICAN MOTORS
* All the facts and figures for AMC models from 1902-1987
* Hundreds of photos help you find your favorites fast
* I-to-6 pricing by condition
* All data, codes and specifications for restoration accuracy
        $19.95 plus shipping

STANDARD CATALOG OF FORD
* Profiles every Ford automobile built from 1903-1990
* More than 500 photographs aid in vehicle identification
* Internationally-acclaimed I-to-6 pricing by condition
* All data, codes, & specifications
        $19.95 plus shipping

STANDARD CATALOG OF CHEVROLET
* Details every Chevrolet built between 1912-1990
* Includes chassis specs, body types, and shipping weights
* 500 photographs from the factory
* I-to-6 pricing by condition
* Historical profiles & stories
        $19.95 plus shipping

STANDARD CATALOG OF CHRYSLER
* Presents every Chrysler car manufactured from 1924-1990
* 1990 values are listed through the 1983 model year
* 500 photos for visual identification
* Internationally-acclaimed I-to-6 pricing by vehicle condition
        $19.95 plus shipping

STANDARD CATALOG OF BUICK
* Profiles every Cadillac built from 1903-1990
* Historical details and technical specifications
* I-to-6 pricing by condition
* All data, codes, and specs
* 500 photos from the factory
        $18.95 plus shipping

STANDARD CATALOG OF CADILLAC
* Details each Cadillac model built from 1903-1990
* 500 photographs present visual identification of selected models
* 1-6 conditional pricing through the 1984 model year
* All data, codes, & specifications
        $18.95 plus shipping

STANDARD CATALOG OF AMERICAN CARS 1805-1942
* 5,000 auto manufacturers detailed from 1805-1942
* 6,000 makes listed alphabetically
* 4,500 photos for identification
* Original selling prices and current values by condition
* ID data, numbers, codes & specs
        $45.00 plus shipping

STANDARD CATALOG OF AMERICAN CARS 1946-1975
* Profiles of American cars from 1946 through 1975
* More than 1,000 vehicle listings
* 1,500 photos for identification
* Original selling prices and current values by condition
* ID data, numbers, codes & specs
        $27.95 plus shipping

STANDARD CATALOG OF AMERICAN CARS, 1976-1986
* Contains thousands of cars manufactured in America
* Helps you pinpoint tomorrow's collector cars today
* Extensive lists of options, accessories, and prices
* ID data, numbers, codes & specs
        $19.95 plus shipping

1994 STANDARD GUIDE TO CARS & PRICES
* Today's prices for vehicles built from 1901 through 1986
* Original factory prices from year of manufacture
* I-to-6 prices by condition
* Hundreds of photos for ease of identification
        $15.95 plus shipping

STANDARD CATALOG OF AMERICAN LIGHT-DUTY TRUCKS, 1896-1986, 2nd Edition
* More than 500 truck listings from 1896 through 1986
* Over 2,000 photographs for ease of identification
* Original selling price and 1987 values by condition
* ID data, numbers, codes & specs
        $29.95 plus shipping

100 YEARS OF AMERICAN CARS
* Over 500 photos of America's greatest automobiles – a chronicle of change
* Includes descriptive information and special articles – a history on wheels
* The industry pioneers, the greatest classics, plus roadsters, racers and road rockets
* Cars that shaped a century of promise and progress, from 1893-1993
        $18.95 plus shipping

COLLECTOR CAR DIGEST
* You get the "Best of OLD CARS WEEKLY" from 1987 through 1988
* All your favorite feature stories and columns in one handy edition
* Includes "Doc Boneyard," "Speaking of Chevys," "Watching the Fords Go By"
* Plus "Collecting Chryslers," Wreck of the Week," & more
        $24.95 plus shipping

OLD CARS QUESTIONS & ANSWERS
* Hundreds of collector car questions...and their accompanying answers for you
* Subjects include auto history, how-to, engines, paint, body work
* Plus collecting tips, restoration expertise, investment advice, and much, much more
* Auto facts and trivia will help you become an expert on old cars
        $6.95 plus shipping

MASTERCARD / VISA ORDERS, CALL TOLL-FREE

(800) 258-0929
Dept. 712

**Mon.-Fri. 6:30 am - 8 pm
Saturday 8 am - 2 pm
Central Standard Time**